Writing
from Sources

Writing
from Sources

EIGHTH EDITION

Brenda Spatt

The City University of New York

BEDFORD/ST. MARTIN'S   Boston ◆ New York

For Bedford/St. Martin's

Developmental Editor: Joelle Hann
Production Supervisor: Andrew Ensor
Senior Marketing Manager: Molly Parke
Project Management: Books By Design, Inc.
Cover Design: Billy Boardman
Cover Art: *Laminated Paper* © David Arky/Corbis.
Composition: Books By Design, Inc.
Printing and Binding: RR Donnelley & Sons Company

President: Joan E. Feinberg
Editorial Director: Denise B. Wydra
Editor in Chief: Karen S. Henry
Director of Development: Erica T. Appel
Director of Marketing: Karen R. Soeltz
Director of Production: Susan W. Brown
Assistant Director of Editorial Production: Elise S. Kaiser
Manager, Publishing Services: Emily Berleth

Library of Congress Control Number: 2010921022

5 4 3
f e

For information, write: Bedford/St. Martin's, 75 Arlington Street, Boston, MA 02116
(617-399-4000)

ISBN-10: 0-312-60290-1
ISBN-13: 978-0-312-60290-1

To the Instructor

I like to think of *Writing from Sources* as the college textbook that explains everything that first-year students need to know about writing a research essay. According to one instructor, "There is nothing that is not in the text" of *Writing from Sources*. Its comprehensive, step-by-step approach, building gradually in complexity, reinforced with a wealth of examples and opportunities for practice, provides the solid foundation in reading and writing skills that many of your students may lack or only partially may have acquired.

What would you like your students to achieve in your course? You want them to read critically, alertly, and analytically so that they can evaluate research materials; to convey their understanding of what they read through the skills of summary, quotation, and paraphrase; to understand appropriate and inappropriate ways of developing a thesis and an argument; to synthesize and write from sources—print and electronic—responsibly, using sufficient and correct documentation; to understand what plagiarism means; and to resist the temptation to "borrow," paste, or otherwise engage in academic theft.

Writing from Sources takes an incremental approach to these skills—starting with reading and ending with writing the research essay—that requires some commitment of time and effort on the part of students and instructors. But if you follow the sequence of readings, exercises, and assignments, choosing those that best suit your class's needs, you will give your students their best opportunity to become proficient writers of research essays at the beginning of their journey through an academic education.

In preparing the eighth edition, I have been well aware that the typical first-year student has greatly changed in interests, in reading habits and preferences, in reliance on technology, and in degree of comfort with long and complex printed materials. However sound and comprehensive its approach, if a textbook like *Writing from Sources* is going to fulfill its purpose, it must work for students at a variety of levels. Some may have basic deficiencies in reading and analysis and may need slow and careful instruction using less-demanding texts; others with more advanced skills may be more adept at the multitasking typical of Web activity than at reading and interpreting books and journal articles. For a generation of students that have grown up with the Internet and its quickly changing focus, I have tried to choose readings that will be interesting without being overly complex, that are long enough to demonstrate the presentation and development of a thesis but are not so long as to discourage the novice reader.

As you can tell from the table of contents, many exercises and assignments in the eighth edition offer only one reading on the principle that a single well-targeted choice is better than a plethora of options. That is not to say that readings are few and far between: *Writing from Sources* provides more than sixty—many of them new to the book—to be used as models, as practice material for the thirty-nine exercises, and as sources for the nine essay assignments. In key slots, two or three alternatives enable instructors to mix and match their choices to suit classes of varying degrees of preparedness.

For this edition, instead of including a separate casebook in an appendix, I've provided two clusters of readings, interspersed throughout, focusing on topics that your students are likely to be familiar with and interested in:

- *The college experience.* Nine readings explore a variety of issues that can serve as an orientation for students new to college: What is the purpose of higher education? Who should attend college? What's a fair way to award grades? How does plagiarism affect students and instructors?

- *The Web experience.* Seven readings discuss the ways in which our reliance on the Internet for work and entertainment has affected our popular culture, our thought processes, and our relationships.

In addition, authors like Ursula K. Le Guin, Steven Pinker, and Roger Scruton offer compelling answers to a variety of other questions, such as whether altruism is an inborn quality, why America became a hygienic nation, whether U.S. immigration laws are humane, if and when torture is permissible, why good manners are still necessary, and whether Wikipedia is a milestone or a roadblock on the information highway.

The eighth edition retains the previous edition's emphasis on familiarizing students with academic sources from the first exercise. As well as research-based, documented excerpts from scholarly books and articles, there are also readings taken from general-interest periodicals ranging from the *New York Times* and *Chronicle of Higher Education* to the *American Scholar*, *Harper's*, and the *Atlantic*. Electronic sources are well-represented in the readings (many of which have appeared both in print and online) and in the coverage of documentation, which has been updated in accordance with new MLA and APA guidelines.

We have also made the appearance of *Writing from Sources* more engaging and student-friendly—within the text itself, revised to make sentences clearer and more straightforward (without sacrificing content), and in the design of text on the page, through the inclusion of signals that enable students more easily to follow a sequence of topics. These signals include headings and boxes that target and summarize information; fonts that clearly distinguish between text, student writing, and professional writing; a range of visuals, including pictures, graphics, and cartoons; and more marginal annotations (a popular feature of the seventh edition).

Two helpful supplements provide extra resources for instructors and students using *Writing from Sources*:

- The Instructor's Edition of *Writing from Sources* offers answers to the book's exercises, suggests essay topics for many of the assignments, provides discussion points for all of the readings, and contains suggestions for organizing the course as a whole—all within a bound-in Instructor's Manual. The stand-alone manual is also downloadable from the book's companion Web site at bedfordstmartins.com/writingfromsources or the catalog page at bedfordstmartins.com. To order the Instructor's Edition use ISBN-13: 978-0-312-60291-8.

- The book's companion Web site at bedfordstmartins.com/writingfromsources contains additional exercises developed to accompany this edition, help for writing essay examinations, as well as access to Bedford/St. Martin's free tutorials and resources on research and writing. This valuable adjunct to the book will give you much greater flexibility in your choice of assignments while allowing your students the opportunity to practice important skills on their own.

Finally, here's a summary of the major changes and additions to the eighth edition of *Writing from Sources*:

- The text has been streamlined and the navigation improved without any loss of coverage.

- New readings—60 percent of the total—targeted to your students and drawn from scholarly and general-interest, as well as online, sources.

- Two new reading clusters for multiple-source assignments: one on the college experience and one on the Web experience.

- More annotated passages to give students more precise and immediate guidance.

- More examples of research-based writing with source citations throughout the book that demonstrate correct methods currently in use.

- Updated coverage of electronic sources, such as academic and popular databases and search engines.

- A new easier-to-follow layout that clearly distinguishes between the text, professional writing, and student examples.

- A new companion Web site with new exercise sets developed for this edition, a full-length annotated research essay in MLA style, help for writing essay examinations, and much more.

Acknowledgments

As always, I am greatly obliged to all the instructors who reviewed the seventh edition. Their experience teaching this course and their insightful suggestions for using *Writing from Sources* in the classroom informed the entire process of revision. I made so many changes, reconceived so many sequences, with the following instructors in mind: Michael Aceto, East Carolina University; Mary Paniccia Carden, Edinboro University of Pennsylvania; Larnell Dunkley, Harold Washington College; Robin Gallaher, Northwestern Missouri State University; Laura Halliday, Southern Illinois University; Kevin Hayes, Essex County College; Elizabeth Imafuji, Anderson University; Noel Kinnamon, Mars Hill College; Larry LaFond, Southern Illinois University; Leticia Lopez, Bellevue Community College; Meghan McGuire, Mars Hill College; Lyle W. Morgan, Pittsburg State University; Jonathan Randle, Mississippi College; Thomas B. Smith, Northwest Missouri State University; Cliff Toliver, Missouri Southern State University; Steffanie E. Triller, Harry S. Truman College/ City Colleges of Chicago.

I am particularly grateful to three instructors, veteran users and fans of the book, who were especially generous with their time and interest. The eighth edition owes a special debt to Laurie Leach, Hawaii Pacific University; Gail Levy, Leeward Community College; and Cliff Toliver, Missouri Southern State University. My editors, Joelle Hann, Erica Appel, Nancy Perry, and Emily Berleth, afforded me the kind of experienced and knowledgeable guidance that has put this book into your hands in record time. Editorial assistant Andrew Flynn was always at my service, offering help in matters great and small. Terina Martin-Ang and Alice Morgan illuminated the crucial distinctions between inference and implication for Exercise 5. Finally, as ever, *Writing from Sources* is dedicated to all the students who have benefited from it over the last 30 years.

To the Student

Every day, as you talk, write, and work, you use sources. Much of the knowledge and many of the ideas that you communicate to others originate outside yourself. You have learned from your school classes and from observing the world around you, from reading, from watching television and movies, from the Internet, and from a multitude of other experiences. Most of the time, you don't consciously think about where you got the information; you simply go about your activities—talking, writing, and making decisions—based on what you know.

Sources in College

In college, your contact with sources intensifies. Each class, each book, bombards you with new facts and ideas. Your academic success depends on how well you can understand what you read and hear in your courses, distinguish between the more important and the less important, relate new facts and ideas to what you already have learned, and, especially, communicate your findings to others.

Most college writing contains material that you take from sources as well as ideas that are your own. Depending on the individual course and assignment, a college paper may emphasize your own conclusions, supported by your research, or it may emphasize the research itself, showing that you have assembled and mastered a certain body of information. Either way, the paper will contain something of others and something of you. If 20 students in your class are all assigned the same topic, the other 19 papers will all be somewhat different from yours.

Sources in the Professional World

College writing assignments help you to consolidate what you have learned in your classes and expand your capacity for constructive thinking and clear communication. These are not merely academic skills; in most careers, success depends on these abilities. You will listen to the *opinions* of your boss, your colleagues, and your customers; read the *case histories* of your clients or patients; study the marketing *reports* of your salespeople or the product *specifications* of your suppliers; or perhaps even grade the *papers* of your students! Whatever your job, the decisions that you make and the actions that you take will depend on your ability to understand and evaluate what your sources are saying (whether orally or in writing), to recognize any important pattern or theme, and to form conclusions. As you build on other people's ideas, you will be expected to remember which facts and opinions came from which sources and give appropriate credit. Chances are that you will also be expected to draft a memo, a letter, a report, or a case history that will summarize your information and present and support your conclusions.

To help you see the connection between college and professional writing, here are some typical essay topics for various college courses, each followed by a parallel writing assignment that you might have to do on the job. Notice that all of the pairs of assignments call for many of the same skills: the writer must consult a variety of sources, present what he or she has learned from those sources, and interpret that knowledge in the light of experience.

ACADEMIC ASSIGNMENT	PROFESSIONAL ASSIGNMENT	SOURCES
For a *political science* course, you choose a law now being debated in Congress or the state legislature and argue for its passage.	As a *lobbyist, consumer advocate,* or *public relations expert*, you prepare a pamphlet to arouse public interest in your agency's after-school program.	debates *Congressional Record* editorials periodical articles your opinions
For a *health sciences* course, you summarize present knowledge about the appropriate circumstances for prescribing tranquilizers and suggest some safeguards for their use.	As a *member of a medical research team*, you draft a report summarizing present knowledge about a new medication for diabetes and suggesting likely directions for your team's research.	books journal articles government and pharmaceutical industry reports online abstracts
For a *psychology* course, you analyze the positive and negative effects of peer-group pressure.	As a *social worker* attached to a halfway house for adolescents, you write a case history of three boys, determining whether they are to be sent to separate homes or kept in the same facility.	textbooks journal articles case studies interviews Web sites personal experience photographs

ACADEMIC ASSIGNMENT	PROFESSIONAL ASSIGNMENT	SOURCES
For a *business management* course, you decide which department or service of your college should be eliminated if the budget were cut by 3 percent next year; you defend your choice.	As an *assistant to a management consultant*, you draft a memo recommending measures to save a manufacturing company that is in severe financial trouble.	ledgers interviews newspaper articles journal articles financial reports Dow Jones news charts

For a *sociology* or *history* course, you compare reactions to unemployment in the 1990s with reactions to unemployment in the 1930s.	As a *staff member in the social-services agency* of a small city, you prepare a report on the consequences that would result from closing a major factory.	newspaper
		   articles
		magazine
		   articles
		books
		interviews
		statistics
		Web sites
		charts

For a *physical education* course, you classify the ways in which a team can react to a losing streak and recommend some ways in which coaches can maintain team morale.	As a *member of a special committee of physical-education teachers*, you help plan an action paper that will improve your district's performance in interscholastic sports.	textbooks
		articles
		observation and
		   personal
		   experience
		Web sites

For an *anthropology* course, you contrast the system of punishment used by a tribe that you have studied with the penal code used in your hometown or college town.	As *assistant to the head of the local correction agency*, you prepare a report comparing the success of eight minimum-security prisons around the country.	textbooks
		lectures
		articles
		statistics and
		   other data
		observation
		   and personal
		   experience
		charts and graphs

For a *physics* course, you write a definition of "black holes" and explain why theories about them were fully developed in the second half of the twentieth century—not earlier, not later.	As a *physicist* working for a university research team, you write a grant application based on an imminent breakthrough in your field.	books journal articles online abstracts e-mail Web sites

(continued)

ACADEMIC ASSIGNMENT	PROFESSIONAL ASSIGNMENT	SOURCES
For a *nutrition* course, you explain why adolescents prefer junk food.	As a *dietician* at the cafeteria of a local high school, you write a memo that accounts for the increasing waste of food and recommends changes in the menus.	textbooks articles interviews observation Web sites e-mail
For an *engineering* course, you describe changes and improvements in techniques of American coal mining over the last hundred years.	As a *mining engineer*, you write a report determining whether it is cost-effective for your company to take over the derelict mine that you were sent to survey.	books articles observation and experience e-mail Web sites photographs

Writing from Sources will help you learn the basic procedures that are common to all kinds of academic and professional writing and will provide enough practice in these skills to enable you to write from sources confidently and successfully. Here are the basic skills.

1. *Choosing a topic:*
   - deciding what you are actually writing about
   - interpreting the requests of your instructor, boss, or client, and determining the scope and limits of the assignment
   - making the project manageable
2. *Finding sources and acquiring information:*
   - deciding how much supporting information you are going to need (if any) and locating it
   - evaluating sources and determining which are most suitable and trustworthy for your purpose
   - taking notes on your sources and on your own reactions
   - judging when you have sufficient information
3. *Determining your main idea:*
   - determining your intention in writing this assignment and your probable conclusions
   - redefining the scope and objective in the light of what you have learned from your sources
   - establishing a thesis

4. *Presenting your sources:*
   - using summary, paraphrase, and quotation
   - deciding when to use each skill

5. *Organizing your material:*
   - determining what must be included and what may be eliminated
   - arranging your evidence in the most efficient and convincing way so that your reader will reach the same conclusions as you
   - calling attention to common patterns and ideas that will reinforce your thesis
   - making sure that your presentation has a beginning, a middle, and an end, and that the stages are in logical order

6. *Writing your assignment:*
   - breaking down the mass of information into easily understood units or paragraphs
   - constructing each paragraph so that it will advance your main idea
   - providing examples and details that will support your argument
   - writing an introduction and, as needed, a conclusion
   - if appropriate, choosing visuals to supplement your essay

7. *Giving credit to your sources:*
   - ensuring that your reader knows who is responsible for which idea
   - distinguishing between the evidence of your sources and your own interpretation and evaluation
   - judging the relative reliability and usefulness of each source so that the reader can appreciate why you chose to use it

This list of skills may seem overwhelming right now. But remember: you will be learning these procedures *gradually*. In Parts I and II, you will learn how to get the most out of what you read and how to use the skills of summary, quotation, and paraphrase to present accurate accounts of your sources. In Part III, you will begin to apply these skills as you prepare an essay based on a single reading and then a synthesis essay drawing on a group of sources. Finally, in Part IV, you will begin the complex process of research.

The best way to gain confidence and facility in writing from sources is to master each skill so that it becomes automatic, like riding a bicycle or driving a car. To help you break down the task into workable units, each procedure will first be illustrated with a variety of models and then followed by exercises to give you as much practice as you need before going on to the next step. As you begin to write essays for other courses, you can concentrate more and more on *what* you are writing rather than on *how* to write from sources, for these methods will have become natural and automatic.

A Note about Documentation and Academic Writing

Colleges are academic institutions that expect you to understand and adhere to generally accepted standards of scholarship. Simply put, this means that you don't cheat when you take examinations and you don't plagiarize when you prepare your written assignments. By academic standards, plagiarism violates the very principles and the body of knowledge that you've come to college to learn. Plagiarism means presenting the words or ideas of someone else as your own.

To make sure that you don't inadvertently abuse the rules that define academic integrity, *Writing from Sources* asks you to devote a great deal of time and attention to learning how to *document your sources*, giving appropriate credit to each of the authors whose ideas or words you use when you write your essay. As you learn how to use summary, quotation, and paraphrase to present your sources, you'll learn how to ensure that your reader knows who these sources are and where and when they were published, as well as which material in your essay is theirs and which material is yours. This is called attribution—giving a person or an organization credit for being the author of a text or the source of an idea.

There are complex systems of documentation that make the attribution of sources absolutely clear, and you will probably be asked to use two or three of them during your time at college.

- The **MLA** (Modern Language Association) and **APA** (American Psychological Association) systems both use names and page numbers in parentheses at the end of material obtained from sources.
- The **footnote/endnote** system, as outlined in *The Chicago Manual of Style*, places information about sources at the bottom of the page or at the end of the essay, keyed by a set of numbers.

In Chapter 11, you can see two research papers, one using the MLA system and the other using the APA system. Every system of documentation requires the inclusion of a bibliography, which usually comprises all the works mentioned (or "cited") in the essay, article, or book. Different disciplines require different forms of documentation, and your instructor will generally tell you which one to use.

As you look through the readings in *Writing from Sources*, you will notice that some of the authors use documentation—most often endnotes—to cite their sources, and some do not. That's because some of the authors were writing for an academic audience and some were not. Most nonfiction books, as well as articles in newspapers and popular magazines, are intended to provide information and commentary for a general audience. The authors are expected to include the names of their sources (and, as appropriate, the name of the specific book or article being cited), but they aren't required to include formal documentation. Not so for the authors you'll find in this book whose work was published in scholarly journals or by academic presses. When you prepare research papers for your courses, you may use popular sources, academic sources, or a combination of both that will depend on your assignment. But as a student in an academic institution, you'll always be expected to provide full documentation for all your sources.

Contents

PART II
PRESENTING SOURCES TO OTHERS

2 Summarizing Sources 75

PART III
WRITING FROM SOURCES

PART IV
WRITING THE RESEARCH ESSAY

Appendix A: Writing Essay Examinations

Available online at www.bedfordstmartins.com/writingfromsources

Writing
from Sources

Part I

MAKING SOURCES YOUR OWN

Academic writers continually study and use the ideas of others. However good and original their own ideas may be, they must explore the work of authorities in their field, determine its value and relevance to their own work, and then integrate the ideas and words of others with their own. We call this process research.

To make use of another person's ideas in developing your own work, you first need to appreciate (and even temporarily share) that person's point of view. In this chapter, you will learn to better understand what you read by asking basic questions about the author's words and meaning, and by writing down (or typing out) what interests and puzzles you alongside the text. This skill is called annotation. Then, as your questions become more complex, you focus on identifying the text's main idea or thesis and the strategies the author uses to present and support that thesis. By asking these questions, you can eventually understand *what* the author wants to say, and *how* and *why* he or she is trying to say it. This chapter ends by examining some argumentation techniques, including an analysis of *inference* as a logical tool and a review of some methods of presenting *evidence*. Throughout, as you work with texts by a range of authors, you will learn how these concepts apply to your own writing.

·1·

Reading for Understanding

Before class began, I happened to walk around the room and I glanced at some of the books lying open on the desks. Not one book had a mark in it! Not one underlining! Every page was absolutely clean! These twenty-five students all owned the book, and they'd all read it. They all knew that there'd be an exam at the end of the week; and yet not one of them had had the sense to make a marginal note!

Teacher of an English honors class

Why was this teacher so horrified? The students had fulfilled their part of the college contract by reading the book and coming to class. Why write anything down, they might argue, when the ideas are already printed on the page. All you have to do is read the assignment and, later on, review by skimming it again. Sometimes it pays to underline an important point, but only in very long chapters, so that you don't have to read every word all over again.

Not true! Reading is hard work. Responding to what you are reading and thinking about an author's ideas requires concentration.

As with any job, active reading becomes more rewarding if you have a product to show for your efforts. In active reading, this product is *notes*: the result of a mental dialogue between your mind and the author's.

Underlining

Underlining is used for selection and emphasis. When you underline, you are distinguishing between what is important (and worth rereading) and what you can skip on later readings. Underlining text on a first reading is usually hard, since you don't yet know which material is crucial to the work's main ideas.

3

Guidelines for Effective Reading

■ As you read and reread, note which ideas make you react.

■ Pause frequently—not to take a break but to think about and respond to what you have read. If the reading has been difficult, these pauses will provide time for you to ask questions.

■ **Working with sources on paper:** Have a pen or pencil in your hand so that you can make lines, checks, and comments in and around what you are reading. You may even want to use several colors to help you distinguish between different ideas or themes as they recur. Of course, if you don't own the book or periodical, make a copy of key pages or take notes on separate paper. If you underline or write in a library copy, you are committing an act of vandalism, like writing graffiti on a wall.

■ **Working with sources on the computer:** If the material comes from a computer screen, print out key pages and work with a hard copy. Or if the material is downloaded into a file, type comments and questions into the text [using brackets to indicate your own work].

Pointless underlining: Too often, underlining just indicates that the eyes have run over the lines. Pages are underlined or highlighted so completely that there is hardly anything left over. Everything has been chosen for emphasis.

Productive underlining: Underlining requires selection. Some points are worth reviewing, and some are not. You probably would want to underline:

- important generalizations and topic sentences
- examples that have helped you understand a difficult idea
- transitional points, where the argument changes

You can also *circle* and *bracket* words and phrases that seem worth rereading and remembering. Or put *checks in the margin*. However you choose to mark the text, deciding what to mark is an important tool.

Annotating

Annotation refers to the comments you write in the margins when you interpret, evaluate, or question the author's meaning, define a word or phrase, or clarify a point.

You are annotating when you jot down short explanations, summaries, or definitions in the margin. You are also annotating when you note down an idea of your own: a question or counterargument, perhaps, or a point for comparison. Not every reading deserves to be annotated. Since the process takes time and concentration, save your marginal notes for material that is especially difficult or stimulating.

Annotating: *Land of Desire*

Here is an example of a passage that has been annotated on the second reading. Difficult words have been defined; a few ideas have been summarized; and some problems and questions have been raised. As you can see, the author uses footnotes to document his sources. Later, you will learn how to use several systems of documentation. It's rarely necessary to annotate the notes.

Documentation means providing evidence to prove that a statement is true.

from LAND OF DESIRE: MERCHANTS, POWER, AND THE RISE OF A NEW AMERICAN CULTURE

William Leach

A finalist in 1993 for the National Book Award for nonfiction, Land of Desire *is concerned with America's development as a consumer culture. In this part of the book, William Leach, a professor of history at Columbia University, is demonstrating some of the ways in which stores and restaurants encouraged people to patronize them.*

Topic: *When and why did we start to tip waiters in restaurants?*

To make customers feel welcome, merchants trained workers to treat them as "special people" and as "guests." The numbers of service workers, including those entrusted with the care of customers, rose fivefold between 1870 and 1910, at two and a half times the rate of increase of industrial workers. Among them were the restaurant and hotel employees hired to wait on tables in exchange for wages and "tips," nearly all recent immigrants, mostly poor Germans and Austrians, but also Italians, Greeks, and Swiss, who suffered nerve-wracking seven-day weeks, eleven-hour days, low wages, and the sometimes terrible heat of the kitchens. Neglected by major unions until just before World War I, they endured sweated conditions equal in their misery only to those of the garment and textile workers of the day.[83]

Tipping was supposed to encourage waiters and waitresses to tolerate these conditions in exchange for possible windfalls from customers. Tipping

Annotations:
why quotes?
entrust: customers are precious possessions
all European
depends on luck, not good service

service grew faster than industry (same in recent years)
Did they speak English? Who trained them?
sweatshops = long hours/low wages
barely endure

tastes and manners of the upper classes

was an unusual practice in the United States before 1890 (although common in the luxurious and (aristocratic) European hotels), when the prevailing "American Plan" entailed serving meals at fixed times, no frills, no tipping, and little or no follow-up service. After 1900 the European system of culinary service expanded very quickly in the United States, introduced first to the (fancy) establishments and then, year by year, to the more popularly priced places. By 1913 some European tourists were even expressing "outrage" at the extent of tipping in the United States.[84] Its effect on workers was (extremely) mixed. On the one hand, it helped keep wages low, increased the frenzy and tension of waiting, and lengthened the hours. "The tipping business is a great evil," wrote an old, retired waiter in the 1940s. "It gives the waiter an inferiority complex — makes him feel he is at the mercy of the customers all the time."[85] On the other hand, some waiters were stirred by the "speculative excitement" of tipping, the risk and chance. *chance = luck, not opportunity*

For customers, however, tipping was intended to have only one effect — to make them feel at home and in the (lap of luxury). On the backs of an ever-growing sweated workforce, it aristocratized consumption, integrating upper-class patterns of comfort into the middle-class lifestyle. Tips rewarded waiters and waitresses for making the customer "feel like 'somebody,'" as one restaurant owner put it. Such a "feeling," he wrote, "depends" on the "service of the waiter," who ushers us to "our table" and "anticipates our every want or whim." "Courteous service is a valuable asset to the restaurateur. There is a curious little twist to most of us: We enjoy the luxurious feeling of affluence, of being 'somebody,' of having our wishes catered to."[86]

meals at any time; more choice in return for higher prices

waiter portrayed as victim

cliché

statement of theme expressed in parag. 2

all these quotation marks are distracting

all an illusion

— margin notes (right) —

"American Plan" — based on middle-class culture

middle class attracted by upper-class style

Hours were longer because of tipping or because of greater service?

3

tipping as a marketing device

it's the customer who has the inferiority complex

83. Matthew Josephson, *The History of the Hotel and Restaurant Employees and Bartenders International Union, AFL-CIO* (New York, 1955), pp. 4–5, 84–95.

84. Barger, *Distribution's Place*, pp. 4, 92–93. Also, on the earlier "American plan," see Josephson, pp. 4–5.

85. Quoted in Josephson, p. 90.

86. W. L. Dodd, "Service, Sanitation, and Quality," *The American Restaurant* (August 1920): 37.

As this passage demonstrates, annotation works by reminding you of ideas that you have thought about and understood. Some marginal notes provide a shorter version of the major ideas of the passage. Others remind you of places where you disagreed with the author, looked at the ideas in a new way, or thought of fresh evidence. Your marginal notes can even suggest the topic for an essay of your own—for example, *Is tipping a fair way to pay for service? Is a good restaurant meal or a night out based on an illusion of luxury?*

You can also make marginal comments about pictures or other graphics that accompany a text. In "The Weight of the World," published in the *Atlantic Monthly* in 2003, Don Peck uses maps to support his analysis of the increase in obesity worldwide. In fact, the maps are more thought-provoking—and therefore worth annotating—than is Peck's text. Here's what an annotated excerpt from the text and some of the maps might look like:

17% rise in 23 years

What determines ideal weight? Does it vary according to environment or only by sex and age?

Probably depends on health factors if it's a scientific definition of obese

The United States contains more fat people—by a large margin—than any other nation. Sixty-four percent of American adults are overweight, versus 47 percent in 1980. Some nine million Americans are now "morbidly obese," meaning roughly a hundred pounds or more overweight, and weight-related conditions cause about 300,000 premature deaths a year in this country—more than anything else except smoking.

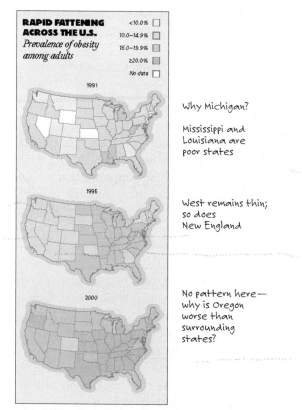

Why Michigan?

Mississippi and Louisiana are poor states

West remains thin; so does New England

No pattern here— why is Oregon worse than surrounding states?

Annotated Visual from Don Peck's "The Weight of the World"

Important! When you write marginal notes, *try always to use your own words* instead of copying or abbreviating a phrase from the text. Expressing it yourself will help you to understand and remember the point.

EXERCISE 1: Annotating a Passage

A. As your instructor indicates, read either the passage from Katherine Ashenburg's *The Dirt on Clean: An Unsanitized History* or the passage from Steven Pinker's *The Blank Slate: The Modern Denial of Human Nature.*

B. Then reread the passage carefully, underlining and circling key ideas and inserting annotations in the margins. Remember to include the photograph and its caption in your marginal comments.

from THE DIRT ON CLEAN: AN UNSANITIZED HISTORY
Katherine Ashenburg

A Canadian journalist, Katherine Ashenburg has edited the arts section of the Toronto Globe and Mail *and produced programs for the Canadian Broadcasting Company. She is also the author of* The Mourner's Dance: What We Do When People Die.

> Topic: *Why did Americans become the most super-clean people in the world?*

Before the Civil War, Americans were as dirty as Europeans. As in Europe, the odd wealthy maverick nourished a craving for cleanliness, but at the beginning of the century, most Americans, like their British cousins, regarded unwashed bodies as inevitable and unworrying if not positively healthful. By the 1880s, however, something happened that no one could have predicted. The United States — rising, pushing and still raw in many ways — had become the Western country that most embraced the gospel of hygiene. And by the end of the century, urban Americans, at least, routinely distinguished between filthy Europeans and their own "clean" ways.

Why did Americans take the lead? One answer is, because they could. Water mains and sewers were installed in new cities more easily than in ancient ones. With abundant, cheap land, houses with ample space for bathrooms became the domestic norm, in contrast to Europe's old, crowded apartments. Because servants were always in short supply in democratic America, labor-saving devices were prized. High on the list was plumbing, and from the 1870s American plumbing outstripped that of every other country.

But to say "because they could" only pushes the question further back. America's physical and technological advances were important but not definitive. More widespread cleanliness, although difficult, would have been possible in Europe sooner if people had wanted it more, since plumbing technology existed long before there was a popular demand for it. Why did Americans, apparently more than Germans, Spaniards, French and English people, want to be clean? They feared disease, and had repeated outbreaks of typhoid and cholera,

[marginal annotations]

1

gospel = law, new expert

was this to further prove that America is better than Europe? Inferiority complex?

2

People are more expensive than plumbing

3

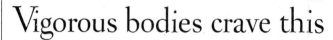
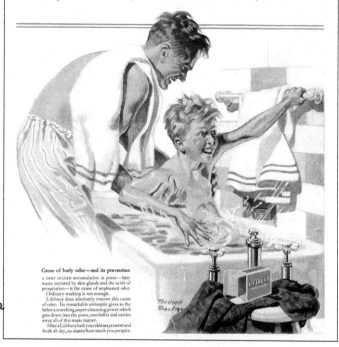

Cause of body odor—and its prevention:

A DEEP SEATED accumulation in pores—fatty waste secreted by skin glands and the acids of perspiration—is the cause of unpleasant odor.

Ordinary washing is not enough.

Lifebuoy does absolutely remove this cause of odor. Its remarkable antiseptic gives to the lather a searching, super-cleansing power which gets down into the pores, emulsifies and carries away all of this waste matter.

After a Lifebuoy bath your skin stays sweet and fresh all day, no matter how much you perspire.

Lifebuoy soap made bathing fun, while its "searching, super-cleansing power" emulsified odor-causing waste matter and carried it away

Ever since Black Plague wouldn't Europe want to be as clean as possible?

but no more so than the Europeans. They were influenced by the same scientific theories — from the mistaken belief in the dangers of miasma to Pasteur's germ theory, which became widely accepted only at the beginning of the twentieth century.

There was no one overriding reason why America became the standard-bearer of personal cleanliness, but rather a confluence of several reasons. Americans prided themselves on their penchant for innovation, from the remarkable invention of New World democracy to the Yankee ingenuity that produced a better apple-corer. Scrupulous personal cleanliness and the means to achieve it — piped-in hot water, toilet soap, even the advertising that alerted people to the benefits of hygiene — were new. Without an inherited caste system, Americans were looking for more egalitarian ways to define civility and mark status,

Another thing to prove themselves to Europe

creating their own royal system

4

and cleanliness, which was increasingly within the grasp of most Americans, turned out to be a good way to do that. Their success during the Civil War in controlling disease through hygiene led them to see it as progressive and civic-minded. They loved what was religious and patriotic, and by the last decades of the century, cleanliness had become firmly linked not only to godliness but also to the American way. . . .

from THE BLANK SLATE:
THE MODERN DENIAL OF HUMAN NATURE
Steven Pinker   *Handout*

Holder of a named chair at Harvard, Steven Pinker is an experimental psychologist specializing in issues of language development in children and visual cognition. His books — such as How the Mind Works *and* The Stuff of Thought — *are intended for a general as well as an academic audience.*

Topic: *In a ruthless world, what motivates us to help each other?*

It's no mystery why organisms sometimes harm one another. Evolution has no conscience, and if one creature hurts another to benefit itself, such as by eating, parasitizing, intimidating, or cuckolding it, its descendants will come to predominate, complete with those nasty habits. All this is familiar from the vernacular sense of "Darwinian" as a synonym for "ruthless" and from Tennyson's depiction of nature as red in tooth and claw. If that were all there was to the evolution of the human condition, we would have to agree with the rock song: Life sucks, then you die.

But of course life doesn't always suck. Many creatures cooperate, nurture, and make peace, and humans in particular find comfort and joy in their families, friends, and communities. . . . There are several reasons why organisms may evolve a willingness to do good deeds. They may help other creatures while pursuing their own interests, say, when they form a herd that confuses predators or live off each other's by-products. This is called mutualism, symbiosis, or cooperation. Among humans, friends who have common tastes, hobbies, or enemies are a kind of symbiont pair. The two parents of a brood of children are an even better example. Their genes are tied up in the same package, their children, so what is good for one is good for the other, and each has an interest in keeping the other alive and healthy. These shared interests set the stage for companionate love and marital love to evolve.

And in some cases organisms may benefit other organisms at a *cost* to themselves, which biologists call altruism. Altruism in this technical sense can evolve in two main ways. First, since relatives share genes, any gene that

1

2

3

inclines an organism toward helping a relative will increase the chance of survival of a copy of itself that sits inside that relative, even if the helper sacrifices its own fitness in the generous act. Such genes will, on average, come to predominate, as long as the cost to the helper is less than the benefit to the recipient discounted by their degree of relatedness. Family love — the cherishing of children, siblings, parents, grandparents, uncles and aunts, nieces and nephews, and cousins — can evolve. This is called nepotistic altruism.

Altruism can also evolve when organisms trade favors. One helps another by grooming, feeding, protecting, or backing him, and is helped in turn when the needs reverse. This is called reciprocal altruism, and it can evolve when the parties recognize each other, interact repeatedly, can confer a large benefit on others at small cost to themselves, keep a memory for favors offered or denied, and are impelled to reciprocate accordingly. Reciprocal altruism can evolve because cooperators do better than hermits or misanthropes. They enjoy the gains of trading their surpluses, pulling ticks out of one another's hair, saving each other from drowning or starvation, and babysitting each other's children. Reciprocators can also do better over the long run than the cheaters who take favors without returning them, because the reciprocators will come to recognize the cheaters and shun or punish them.

The demands of reciprocal altruism can explain why the social and moralistic emotions evolved. Sympathy and trust prompt people to extend the first favor. Gratitude and loyalty prompt them to repay favors. Guilt and shame deter them from hurting or failing to repay others. Anger and contempt prompt them to avoid or punish cheaters. And among humans, any tendency of an individual to reciprocate or cheat does not have to be witnessed firsthand but can be recounted by language. This leads to an interest in the reputation of others, transmitted by gossip and public approval or condemnation, and a concern with one's own reputation. Partnerships, friendships, alliances, and communities can emerge, cemented by these emotions and concerns.

Annotating: "A Question of Degree"

The next step is to apply annotating skills to a full-length essay. Written by Blanche Blank, who was a professor of education at Hunter College of the City University of New York, "A Question of Degree" is 17 paragraphs long. Here is what the first two paragraphs look like with basic annotations about the meaning of words and phrases:

everyone believes it

Perhaps we should rethink an idea fast becoming an <u>undisputed</u> <u>premise</u> of American life: that a college degree is a (necessary) (and perhaps even a (sufficient)) precondition for success. I do not wish to quarrel with the

necessary vs. sufficient?

assumptions made about the benefits of orthodox education. I want only to expose its false god: the four-year, all-purpose, degree-granting college, aimed at the so-called college-age population and by now almost universally accepted as the stepping-stone to "meaningful" and "better" jobs.

= false idol

quotes mean B.B. doesn't agree

What is wrong with the current college/work cycle can be seen in the following anomalies: we are selling college to the youth of America as a take-off pad for the material good life. College is literally advertised and packaged as a means for getting more money through "better" jobs at the same time that Harvard graduates are taking jobs as taxi drivers. This situation is a perversion of the true spirit of a university, a perversion of a humane social ethic and, at bottom, a patent fraud. To take the last point first, the economy simply is not geared to guaranteeing these presumptive "better" jobs; the colleges are not geared to training for such jobs; and the ethical propriety of the entire enterprise is very questionable. We are by definition (rather than by analysis) establishing two kinds of work: work labeled "better" because it has a degree requirement tagged to it and non-degree work, which, through this logic, becomes automatically "low level."

inconsistencies

high salary + expensive possessions

2
college leads to work

presented to the public

= corruption

= obvious

colleges can't deliver what they promise

morality definition = by saying so

analysis = by observing what's right and real

Asking Questions

As you read actively and try to understand what you read, you will start asking questions about the text. Sometimes you will want to write your answers down; sometimes answering your questions in your head is enough.

As the questions in the following box suggest, to understand what you read, your mind has to sweep back and forth between each sentence on the page and the larger context of the whole paragraph or essay. You can misunderstand the author's meaning if you interpret ideas out of context, ignoring the way in which they fit into the work as a whole.

Context means the overall framework in which a word, passage, or idea occurs.

Understanding takes time and careful reading. Being a fast reader is not necessarily an advantage. In fact, it is usually on the second reading, when you begin to grasp the overall meaning and structure of the work, that questions begin to pop into your head and you begin to read more effectively.

Asking Questions: "A Question of Degree"

Now, read "A Question of Degree," and answer the questions asked in the margins. These questions go beyond the simple definitions of the previous annotation, asking *why* and *how*. Your answers can be brief, but *use your own words.*

Questions to Aid Understanding

- What is the meaning of this word?
- How should I understand that phrase?
- Where do I have difficulty understanding the text? Why? Which passages are easy for me? Why?
- What does this passage remind me of?
- What is the topic sentence of the paragraph?
- What is the connection between these two points?
- What is the transitional word telling me?
- This concept is difficult: how would I express it in my own words?
- Is this point a digression from the main idea, or does it fit in with what I've already read?
- Can the whole page be summarized briefly?
- What point is the writer trying to make?

Some of the sample questions may seem very subtle to you, and you may wonder whether you would have thought of all of them yourself. But they are model questions, to show you what you *could* ask if you wanted to gain an especially thorough understanding of the essay.

When you're sure of the answers to these questions, you're sure of the author's meaning. Then, compare your answers with those on pages 17–21.

A QUESTION OF DEGREE

Blanche D. Blank

Topic: *Are college degrees really necessary and important?*

Perhaps we should rethink an idea fast becoming an undisputed premise of American life: that a college degree is a necessary (and perhaps even a sufficient) precondition for success. I do not wish to quarrel with the assumptions made about the benefits of orthodox education. I want only to expose its false god: the four-year, all-purpose, degree-granting college, aimed at the so-called college-age population and by now almost universally accepted as the stepping-stone to "meaningful" and "better" jobs.

What is wrong with the current college/work cycle can be seen in the following anomalies: we are selling college to the youth of America as a take-off pad for the material good life. College is literally advertised and packaged as a means for getting more money through "better" jobs at the same time that Harvard graduates are taking jobs as taxi drivers. This situation is a perversion of

A. In what context can a college degree be a false god?

B. Why does Blank put "meaningful" and "better" in quotation marks?

C. What conclusion can be drawn from the "Harvard graduates" sentence?

2. I saying the spirit of university is being manipulated
I saying it's manipulative of humans in general

the true spirit of a university, a perversion of a humane social ethic and, at bottom, a patent fraud. To take the last point first, the economy simply is not geared to guaranteeing these presumptive "better" jobs; the colleges are not geared to training for such jobs; and the ethical propriety of the entire enterprise is very questionable. We are by definition (rather than by analysis) establishing two kinds of work: work labeled "better" because it has a degree requirement tagged to it and nondegree work, which, through this logic, becomes automatically "low level."

1. colleges cannot provide better jobs
2. what makes one job better than another?

D. How many perversions does Blank mention? Can you distinguish between them?

E. In the last two sentences, what are the two types of "fraud" that are described?

F. What is the "practical curriculum"?

G. What is the danger to the universities?

This process is also destroying our universities. The "practical curriculum" must become paramount; the students must become prisoners; the colleges must become servants of big business and big government. Under these conditions the university can no longer be an independent source of scientific and philosophic truth-seeking and moral criticism.

what universities say you must learn

3 Universities can't just teach. They are now controlled by government, not people, ideas it what is must

Finally, and most important, we are destroying the spirit of youth by making college compulsory at adolescence when it may be least congruent with emotional and physical needs; and we are denying college as an optional and continuing experience later in life, when it might be most congruent with intellectual and recreational needs.

4

H. What groups have suffered as a result of "compulsory" college?

The young forced to choose their life at a young age and the "old" who can't change their life after youth

Let me propose an important step to reverse these trends and thus help restore freedom and dignity to both our colleges and our workplaces. We should outlaw employment discrimination based on college degrees. This would simply be another facet of our "equal opportunity" policy and would add college degrees to sex, age, race, religion and ethnic group as inherently unfair bases for employment selection.

5

I. What is Blank's contribution to "our 'equal opportunity' policy"?

The college degree

People would, wherever possible, demonstrate their capacities on the job. Where that proved impractical, outside tests could still serve. The medical boards, bar exams, mechanical, mathematical and verbal aptitude tests might still be used by various enterprises. The burden of proof of their legitimacy, however, would remain with the using agencies. So too would the costs. Where the colleges were best equipped to impart a necessary skill they would do so, but only where it would be natural to the main thrust of a university endeavor.

6

J. What does "legitimacy" mean in this context?

whether or not those passing the test are actually qualified

The need for this rethinking and for this type of legislation may best be illustrated by a case study. Joe V. is a typical liberal-arts graduate, fired by imaginative art and literature. He took a job with a large New York City bank, where he had the opportunity to enter the "assistant manager training program." The trainees rotated among different bank departments to gain technical know-how and experience and also received classroom instruction, including some sessions on "how to write a business letter." The program was virtually restricted to college graduates. At the end of the line, the trainees became assistant bank managers: a position consisting largely of giving simple advice to bank customers and a modest amount of supervision of employees.

7

College can't prepare you for everything

Joe searched for some connection <u>between his job and the training program,</u> <u>on the one hand, and his college-whetted appetites and skills on the other.</u> <u>He found none.</u>

In giving Joe preference for the training program, the bank had bypassed a few enthusiastic aspirants already dedicated to a banking career and daily demonstrating their competence in closely related jobs. After questioning his superiors about the system, Joe could only conclude that the "top brass" had some very diffuse and not-too-well-researched or even well-thought-out conceptions about college men. <u>The executives admitted that a college degree</u> <u>did not of itself ensure the motivation or the verbal or social skills needed.</u> <u>Nor</u> were they clear about what skills were most desirable for their increasingly diverse branches. Yet, they clung to the college prerequisite.

8

K. What point(s) does the example of Joe help to prove?

A college educated man and a non-college educated man were equals, yet college man was taken simply because he had a degree

Business allows the colleges to act as recruiting, screening and training agencies for them because it saves money and time. Why colleges allow themselves to act as servicing agents may not be as apparent. One reason may be that colleges are increasingly becoming <u>conventional bureaucracies.</u> It is inevitable, therefore, that they should respond to the first and unchallenged law of bureaucracy: Expand! <u>The more that colleges can persuade outside institu-</u> <u>tions to restrict employment in favor of their clientele, the stronger is the</u> <u>college's hold and attraction.</u> This rationale becomes even clearer when we understand that the budgets of public universities hang on the number of students "serviced." Seen from this perspective, then, it is perhaps easier to understand why such matters as "university independence," or "the propriety" of using the public bankroll to support <u>enterprises</u> that are expected to make private profits, can be dismissed. (Conflict of interest) is difficult to discern when the interests involved are your own. . . .

9

L. What are the colleges' reasons for cooperating with business?

In short, more money!

M. What is the conflict of interest?

Are you educating me or are you torturing me so I can get a job I should've got before but now you make money

<u>What is equally questionable</u> is whether a college degree, as such, <u>is proper</u> <u>evidence that those new skills that are truly needed will be delivered.</u> A friend who works for the Manpower Training Program feels that there is a clear divide between actual job needs and college-degree requirements. One of her chief frustrations is the knowledge that many persons with the ability to do paraprofessional mental-health work are lost to jobs they could hold with pleasure and profit because the training program also requires a two-year associate arts degree.

10

Obviously, society can and does manipulate job status. I hope that we can manipulate it in favor of the greatest number of people. (More energy should be spent in trying to upgrade the dignity of all socially useful work and to eliminate the use of human beings for any work that proves to be truly destructive of the human spirit.) Outlawing the use of degrees as prerequisites for virtually every job that our media portray as "better" should carry us a long step toward a healthier society. Among other things, there is far more evidence that work can make college meaningful than that college can make work meaningful.

Education is to better ourselves not to create a gap that separates people and allows others to put down "uneducated" people

N. What does this sentence mean?

O. Is Blank recommending that everyone go to work before attending college?

what you do with a college degree is more important than the degree alone

must be in debt in order to have opportunity for money

P. What does "prisoners of economic necessity" mean?

My concern about this degree/work cycle might be far less acute, however, if everyone caught up in the system were having a good time. But we seem to be generating a college population that oscillates between apathy and hostility. One of the major reasons for this joylessness in our university life is that the students see themselves as prisoners of economic necessity. They have bought the media messages about better jobs, and so they do their time. But the promised land of "better" jobs is, on the one hand, not materializing; and on the other hand the student is by now socialized to find such "better" jobs distasteful even if they were to materialize.

Q. What are the "compulsory schools" and how would their role change if Blank's proposal were adopted?

Teach us how to live, not just how to think

One of the major improvements that could result from the proposed legislation against degree requirements for employment would be a new stocktaking on the part of all our educational agencies. Compulsory schools, for example, would understand that the basic skills for work and family life in our society would have to be compressed into those years of schooling.

Colleges and universities, on the other hand, might be encouraged to be as unrestricted, as continuous and as open as possible. They would be released from the pressures of ensuring economic survival through a practical curriculum. They might best be modeled after museums. Hours would be extensive, fees minimal, and services available to anyone ready to comply with course-by-course demands. Colleges under these circumstances would have a clearly understood focus, which might well be the traditional one of serving as a gathering place for those persons who want to search for philosophic and scientific

R. What role does Blank envisage for the university in a healthier society?

— "truths." *to be a museum or like a museum*

S. What are the "strange and gratuitous practices" of the universities? What purpose do they serve?

Requiring more money for the right to say you're a Ph.D. or have a Masters

This proposal should help our universities rid themselves of some strange and gratuitous practices. For example, the university would no longer have to organize itself into hierarchical levels: B.A., M.A., Ph.D. There would simply be courses of greater and lesser complexity in each of the disciplines. In this way graduate education might be more rationally understood and accepted for what it is — more education.

The new freedom might also relieve colleges of the growing practice of instituting extensive "work programs," "internships" and "independent study" programs. The very names of these enterprises are tacit admissions that the campus itself is not necessary for many genuinely educational experiences. But, along with "external degree" programs, they seem to pronounce that whatever one has learned in life by whatever diverse and interesting routes cannot be recognized as increasing one's dignity, worth, usefulness or self-enjoyment until it is converted into degree credits.

T. What, according to Blank, would be a "rational order of priorities"?

Again, learn to be a well-rounded person and worker before being a well rounded student

The legislation I propose would offer a more rational order of priorities. It would help recapture the genuine and variegated dignity of the workplace along with the genuine and more specialized dignity of the university. It should help restore to people of all ages and inclinations a sense of their own basic worth and offer them as many roads as possible to reach Rome.

12

13

14

15

16

17

Answering Questions: "A Question of Degree"

Paragraph One

A. In what context can a college degree be a false god?

A. Colleges are worshiped by students who believe that the degree will magically ensure a good career and a better life. Blank suggests that college degrees no longer have magic powers.

B. Why does Blank put "meaningful" and "better" in quotation marks?

B. Blank doesn't believe the adjectives are applicable; she is using quotation marks to show her disagreement with the idea that some jobs should be seen as better or more meaningful than others.

Paragraph Two

C. What conclusion can be drawn from the "Harvard graduates" sentence?

C. If Harvard graduates are driving taxis, a degree does not ensure a high-level job.

D. How many perversions does Blank mention? Can you distinguish between them?

D. When degrees are regarded as vocational qualifications, the university's proper purpose is perverted; society's conception of proper qualifications for employment and advancement is perverted; and, by implication, young people's belief in the reliability of rewards promised by society is perverted.

E. In the last two sentences, what are the two types of "fraud" that are described?

E. One kind of fraud is the deception practiced on young college students who won't get the good jobs they expect. A second type of fraud is practiced on workers without degrees whose efforts and successes are undervalued because of the division into "better" and "worse" jobs.

Paragraph Three

F. What is the "practical curriculum"?

F. "Practical curriculum" refers to courses that will train college students for specific jobs; the term is probably being contrasted with "liberal arts."

G. What is the danger to the universities?

G. The emphasis on vocational training perverts the universities' traditional pursuit of knowledge for its own sake, as it makes financing and curriculum very closely connected with the economic needs of the businesses and professions for which students will be trained.

Paragraph Four

H. What groups have suffered as a result of "compulsory" college?

H. Blank has so far referred to four groups: students in college; workers who have never been to college; members of universities, both staff and students, interested in a liberal-arts curriculum; and older people who might want to return to college after a working career.

Paragraph Five

I. What is Blank's contribution to "our 'equal opportunity' policy"?

I. Blank suggests that a college degree does not indicate suitability for employment and therefore that requiring it should be classed as discriminatory, along with sex, age, etc.

Paragraph Six

J. What does "legitimacy" mean in this context?

J. If certain professions choose to test the qualifications of aspirants, professional organizations should prove that examinations are necessary and that the results will measure the applicant's suitability for the job.

These organizations should be responsible for the arrangements and the financing; at present, colleges serve as a "free" testing service.

Paragraphs Seven and Eight

K. What point(s) does the example of Joe help to prove?

K. Joe's experience supports Blank's argument that college training is not often needed in order to perform most kinds of work. Joe's expectations that his college education would prepare him for work were also pitched too high, as Blank has suggested, while the experience of other bank employees who were passed over in favor of Joe exemplifies the plight of those workers without college degrees <u>whose experience is not sufficiently valued.</u>

Paragraph Nine

L. What are the colleges' reasons for cooperating with business?

L. Colleges are competing for students in order to increase their enrollment; they therefore want to be able to assure applicants that many companies prefer to hire their graduates. Having become overorganized, with many levels of authority, the bureaucratic universities regard enrollment as an end in itself.

M. What is the conflict of interest?

M. The interests of an institution funded by the public might be said to be in conflict with the interests of a private, profit-making company.

Paragraph Eleven

N. What does this sentence mean?

N. Instead of discriminating between kinds of workers and kinds of work, we should distinguish between work that benefits everyone and should therefore be considered admirable, and work that is degrading and should, if possible, not be performed by people.

O. Is Blank recommending that everyone go to work before attending college?

O. Although Blank is not insisting that working is preferable to or should have priority over a college education, she implies that most people gain more significant knowledge from the work experience than from college.

Paragraph Twelve

P. What does "prisoners of economic necessity" mean?

P. Young people who believe that a degree will get them better jobs have no choice but to spend a four-year term in college, whether or not they are intellectually and temperamentally suited to the experience.

Paragraph Thirteen

Q. What are the "compulsory schools" and how would their role change if Blank's proposal were adopted?

Q. Compulsory schools are grade and high schools, which students must attend up to a set age. If students were not automatically expected to go on to college, the lower schools would have to offer a more comprehensive and complete education than they do now.

Paragraph Fourteen

R. What role does Blank envisage for the university in a healthier society?

R. Blank sees the colleges in a role quite apart from the mainstream of life. Colleges would be easily accessible centers of learning, to which people could go for intellectual inquiry and stimulation in their spare time.

Paragraph Fifteen

S. What are the "strange and gratuitous practices" of the universities? What purpose do they serve?

S. The universities divide the process of education into a series of clearly defined levels of attainment. Blank finds these divisions "gratuitous" or un-necessary, perhaps because they are "hierarchical" and distin-guish between those of greater or lesser achievement and status.

Paragraph Seventeen

T. What, according to Blank, would be a "rational order of priorities"?

T. Blank's first priority is the self-respect of the average member of society who currently may be disappointed and frustrated at not being valued for his or her work. Another priority is restoration of the university to its purely intellectual role.

EXERCISE 2: Understanding What You Read

A. Read "Cuss Time," by Jill McCorkle, twice.

B. On the second reading, answer the comprehension questions in the margins. You will notice that some of the "questions" resemble instructions, very much like examination questions, directing you to explain, define, or in other ways analyze the reading. *Answer in complete sentences*, and use your own words as much as you can.

CUSS TIME

Jill McCorkle

A fiction writer and teacher of creative writing at North Carolina State University, Jill McCorkle has won several awards for her novels and short stories, including the Dos Passos Prize for Excellence in Literature. This essay appeared in The American Scholar.

> Topic: *How do we deal with rage and disgust and all the undesirable emotions that society would prefer us to suppress?*

A. Why does McCorkle begin with her father's story?

My dad often told a story from his days as a mail carrier where he con-fronted a little boy no more than five perched up in a tree in a yard severely marked by poverty and neglect. The kid looked down with dirty face and clothes and said, "Whatcha want, you old son of a bitch?" We laughed at his

1

B. Use your own words to describe the family's feelings expressed in the last sentence.

aggressive assertion, but there was something sad and tender in it, too. There was the recognition of his own reality and the hope that his anger and toughness might in time lead him to a better place.

One day when my son was eight, he came into the kitchen while I was cooking and said: "You put bad words in your books, don't you?" No doubt he had overheard my mother, who often tells people who ask about my work: "Well you'll never find her books in the Christian bookstore." 2

I said that sometimes — when character and situation called for it — I did use *strong* language, that I couldn't imagine a realistic portrait of human nature, particularly in our contemporary society, without it. 3

C. Why is it all right for her son to express himself freely when he writes fiction?

"So can I do that?" he asked, and of course I told him absolutely — that when he writes a short story or novel, he will have all the freedom in the world to do so. 4

He pulled a ripped sheet of notebook paper from behind his back. "Would you like to hear the first of my book?" 5

This was when I stopped what I was doing and gave him my full attention, boy in Red Sox shirt and baggy jeans — his uniform of many years. "Now," he said. "Keep in mind that this is a 14-year-old girl who is being made to marry a guy she's never even met and she's mad." I could only assume he had read or heard something in school to inspire this — stories of another culture used to enlighten and remind us of our basic rights and freedoms and how important they are. He paused, giving a very serious look before clearing his throat, shaking the paper, and beginning. 6

D. What's the impact of the boy's statement?

E. Explain the significance of the verb "captured," vs. "expressed" or "conveyed."

F. Why does she put the story among her treasures?

"Goddamnit why would I want to marry that piece of shit boy? I'm damn mad as hell." 7

He stopped and looked at me, waiting for my response. It was one of those important parental moments, recognized as it is happening, so I took a few seconds. "Well," I said. "You certainly have captured her anger and frustration." He nodded, a look of great satisfaction on his face, and wandered back to where he was playing video games. Needless to say I confiscated that piece of paper and carefully placed it in the box of treasured writings I have saved. It is right in there with a letter he wrote his sister claiming he had "Shitey conselars" at a camp he was unhappily attending. 8

G. Why doesn't McCorkle simply tell the story in sequence?

H. How does the idea of embarrassment add to our understanding of freedom?

A year or so before this took place, I had given him permission to have what we called "cuss time." It began when I realized that he was silently mouthing a lot of new vocabulary while riding in the car or drawing. He saw me see him one day and he was embarrassed, so I told him I knew that urge to test a word and how important it is to do so. Thus the origin of cuss time. Every day for five minutes, usually right after school, he could say anything he wanted. He liked to bounce on the already beaten up leather sofa while saying the words, sounds emitted as his feet left the cushion. It was a kind of Trampoline Tourette's — *hell, bitch, doo-doo* — and I'll confess I was always happy that we 9

I. What is "endearing" about the fact that the boy doesn't distinguish between degrees of profanity?

J. How does McCorkle contrast the three generations that appear in this essay?

K. Put the first sentence of this paragraph in your own words.

L. In some ways, this essay is as much about choice as about freedom to choose. How is that point expressed in paragraph 11?

M. How does the discussion of "potential" develop the points McCorkle has previously emphasized? How does the cartoon comment on this discussion?

were never interrupted by UPS or a friend stopping by. What I found particularly endearing is that in his world, all words that were considered inappropriate for public voice weighed exactly the same. *Fart* and *fuck* and *fanny* were equals. *Shit* and *ass*. When the kitchen timer rang, all cussing ended until the next day.

I found it liberating to watch his liberation. I was a kid who had gotten my mouth washed out with soap regularly, and all that ever did — other than leave me foaming and gagging — was to make me furious and determined to say everything even more. It's one of the basic laws of human nature, isn't it? The more we are denied something, the more we want it? The more silence given to this or that topic, the more power. All you need to do is look to the binge-drinking or eating-disorder cases that surround us, the multitudes of church sex scandals, to show that the demand for abstinence or any kind of total denial of thought or expression or action can often lead to dangerous consequences. When we know we *can* choose to do this or that, we don't feel as frantic to do so, to make a sudden move or decision that might be the worst thing for us. 10

When our words and actions are filled with possibilities and potential, we are more likely to weigh out the options. I am convinced that the anticipation of cuss time — the *freedom* of cuss time — kept my son from being overheard by some person in authority who might have had no choice but to reprimand him and assign punishment. 11

Potential is a powerful word. I remember feeling so sad when my children turned a year old and I knew, from reading about human development, that they had forever lost the potential they were born with to emulate the 12

"*He's swearing in full sentences now.*"

N. Why does McCorkle include so many references to language, reading, and fiction?

languages of other cultures, clicks and hums and throat sounds foreign to me. For that short period of time, a mere 12 months, they could have been dropped anywhere in the world and fully adapted accordingly. But beyond this linguistic loss, we are at risk of losing something far greater each and every time we're confronted with censorship and denial. Perfectly good words are taken from our vocabulary, limiting the expression of a thought or an opinion. I recently read about high schoolers who are not allowed to use the word *vagina*. And what should they say instead? When you read about something like this (just one recent example of many), you really have to stop and wonder. Is this restriction because someone in charge thinks vaginas are *bad*? I once had a story editor ask me not to use the word *placenta*. I wanted to say: "Now tell me again how you got here?" *Oh, right, an angel of God placed you into the bill of the stork.*

O. Describe the interplay between the individual and society in this paragraph.

Word by single word, our history will be rewritten if we don't guard and protect it, truth lost to some individual's idea about what is right or wrong. These speech monitors—the Word Gestapo (speaking of words some would have us deny and forget)—attempt to define and dictate what is acceptable and what is not.   13

P. Who or what is the "Word Gestapo"?

Q. How does McCorkle move from Lenny Bruce to issues of "power and control"?

Lenny Bruce,[1] while pushing the First Amendment as far as it can go, famously said, "Take away the right to say *fuck* and you take away the right to say *fuck the government*." And maybe that's *really* what all the rules are about—power and control—someone else's over you. Though I felt the impulse to tell my son cuss time was a secret of sorts, "our own little game," I stifled the urge, knowing what a dangerous and manipulative thing the use of a "secret" can be. Besides, any suggestion of denial of the act would have worked against everything I was trying to give him. Of course, it wasn't any time at all before several little boys started asking to ride the bus home with him. "Can I do cuss time?" they pleaded. I sadly had to tell them the truth: they were not of legal age and so cuss time was something only their own parents could give them.   14

R. How does cussing make one a "better, more confident person"?

I have often thought what a better, more confident person I would have been if only I had grown up with cuss time instead of soap licking.   15

S. What's the significance of the anecdote about the elderly woman?

My first public reading from my work was when I was 25 years old. At the end, as I stood at the podium speaking to people, I noticed an elderly woman slowly making her way down the aisle. I waited for her to reach me only to have her shake a finger in my face and say, "And you look like such a nice girl!" Unfortunately, I was still conditioned to want her to believe that I *was* a nice girl,   16

[1]Lenny Bruce was a stand-up comedian in the early 1960s who tested the limits of freedom of speech by expressing much of his act in obscenities; he was arrested several times and was ultimately tried and convicted for using obscene language in a public setting.

conditioned to care more about what other people thought of me than what I thought of myself. It was only after the fact that I felt angry, that I wanted to go back and ask if she was even paying attention to what I was reading about — a situation of hurt humans expressing their feelings. I wanted to say, you have every right to your opinions and thoughts but that doesn't make you *right*. I wanted to say *fuck you*, and even knowing it would have been completely out of character for me to do so, I like knowing that I *could* have.

By limiting or denying freedom of speech and expression, we take away a lot of potential. We take away thoughts and ideas before they even have the opportunity to hatch. We build a world around negatives — you can't say, think, or do this or that. We teach that if you are safely camouflaged in what is acceptable and walk that narrow road — benign or neutral words, membership in institutions where we are told what to think and believe — then you can get away with a lot of things. You can deny who you are and all that came before you and still be thought of as a *good* person. And what can be positive in that? In fact, what is more positive than a child with an individual mind full of thoughts and sounds and the need to express them who has the freedom to discover under safe and accommodating conditions the best way to communicate something? In other words, you old son of a bitch, I say *Let freedom ring!*

17

T. Is cursing the only way to express one's individuality?

U. What's the effect of all the negative words in the first part of this paragraph?

V. Contrast society's idea of a "good person" and McCorkle's.

W. What balance, if any, does McCorkle find between freedom and necessary restraint?

Questioning the Author

Asking questions about a text helps you to understand the meaning of words, sentences, and paragraphs. Still, having done so, you may not yet fully understand the meaning of the text itself: the author's *reason* for writing it, the *validity* and *persuasiveness* of the ideas. Has the author's point been made? Was it worth making?

To analyze these issues of *intention*, you need to use some standard vocabulary: thesis, bias, and tone.

Thesis vs. Topic

A topic means a **subject***: what is being discussed or written about. It is often a question to answer.*

A thesis means a statement of intention and purpose, expressing the central idea of an essay.

Once committed to a thesis, the author undertakes to support and validate this central idea thoroughly and convincingly. The thesis should be a substantial generalization that can stand by itself. It should not be confused with a *topic*.

What Is a Thesis?

A thesis will be a broad statement, worth defending, that defines the scope and limits of the essay.

1. The thesis will be a substantial generalization that can stand by itself. It should answer, not ask, a question.
2. The thesis will be *broad* enough and *arguable* enough to be worth defending. It will not be an obvious truth.
3. The thesis will define the *scope* and *limits* of the essay. The author should stay within the boundaries of the thesis and not digress into other topics.

■ The thesis should be a *statement*, not a question. The author is not just raising a question for exploration but attempting to *answer that question*.

These are topics, not theses. | **Topic:** Who should go to college?
Topic: How can students succeed in college?

Thesis: Only students who will make the fullest use of their education should go to college.

■ The thesis should be *broad* enough and *arguable* enough to be worth defending. It should not be an obvious truth.

Who would disagree? It's hardly worth arguing. | **Too obvious:** Poorly prepared students can find college work difficult.

Too specific to sustain an essay. | **Too narrow:** Some of the students in my history course found the second assignment too difficult.

Solves the problem of how can students succeed in college. | **Thesis:** To help unprepared students succeed, colleges should provide a full range of support services.

Answers the question— who should go to college?—by *defining* that group. | **Thesis:** Since college can be difficult for poorly prepared students, admission should depend on the applicant's meeting certain standards of achievement.

■ The thesis should define the *scope* and *limits* of the essay. The author should stay within the boundaries of the thesis and not digress into other topics. Which of the following statements correctly corresponds to the scope of "A Question of Degree"?

Too narrow: Employment discrimination arises from an overemphasis on college degrees.

Too broad: College is wasted on the young.

A good thesis, which is often complex, cannot always be expressed in a short sentence.

Thesis: Regarding the college degree as a prerequisite for a good job and a better life can only discourage a fair and efficient system of employment and subvert the true purpose of higher education.

Intention

The author's general purpose in writing is to present a thesis clearly and support it convincingly. The thesis will vary according to the nature of the topic and what the author intends to do with it.

If thesis denotes *what* the essay is about, intention suggests *how* it will be developed. Take, for example, **the topic of** *college drinking*. In this group of four theses, notice how the author's intention changes with each one.

1. Students have ample opportunity to drink to excess on our campus.

   The author's intention is to **explain** why it's easy to get drunk at her college—probably by citing *facts* and *statistics* such as the number of bars near campus and the rules on liquor in dormitories, as well as *anecdotes* and *examples*. With a thesis like this one, the reader can't easily tell whether the author approves of, disapproves of, or is indifferent toward the drinking.

2. The behavior of students who drink to excess can represent a cry for help.

   Here, the author has made an interesting observation and undertakes to **analyze** or **interpret** it. Developing a theory about the habits of college drinkers and what they signify requires a more complex level of inquiry and speculation than does exploring how easy it is to get access to alcoholic beverages. Such a theory might also be supported by *anecdotes* and *examples*, as well as by the "hard" evidence of *facts* and *statistics*, but that evidence will have to be correctly interpreted if the reader is to be convinced. While the thesis might be controversial—you can disagree with it—the author intends to do something other than merely defend one side of the issue.

3. Students who drink to excess should be expelled.

   No question here that the author will be engaged in **persuasion**, defending a thesis that represents a particular point of view. Doing so may or may not include the explanation and analysis mentioned above, but it will certainly require presenting a *line of reasoning* for the reader to follow.

4. Because the deficiencies of their colleges cause many students to drink to excess, colleges ought to provide a better environment for learning.

This thesis combines elements from all three of the previous examples. Do many students drink to excess? **Explain and demonstrate.** Why do they drink to excess? **Analyze and interpret.** What should be done about this problem? ("Deficiencies" indicates that this writer isn't going to be neutral about this issue.) **Argue and persuade.**

Developing a Thesis

Authors can develop a thesis in several ways, depending on their intention. A complex thesis involves several methods of approach, usually including:

- explanation
- analysis and interpretation
- argument and persuasion

Recognizing Intention

You can often determine an author's intention just by reading the first few paragraphs of an essay and asking some questions. Look at the following examples:

Botstein's thesis is clear and upfront: his intention is to persuade his readers that high schools should be abolished. He starts by alluding to the worthless values prevalent in schools.

A. The national outpouring after the Littleton shootings has forced us to confront something we have suspected for a long time: the American high school is obsolete and should be abolished. In the last month, high school students present and past have come forward with stories about cliques and the artificial intensity of a world defined by insiders and outsiders, in which the insiders hold sway because of superficial definitions of good looks and attractiveness, popularity and sports prowess.

LEON BOTSTEIN, from "Let Teenagers Try Adulthood"

Jekanowski is citing statistics to explain and demonstrate one aspect of his thesis about the need for time-saving products.

B. With today's hectic lifestyles, time-saving products are increasingly in demand. Perhaps one of the most obvious examples is fast food. The rate of growth in consumer expenditures on fast food has led most other segments of the food-away-from-home market for much of the last two decades. Since 1982, the amount consumers spent at fast food outlets grew at an annual rate of 6.8 percent (through 1997) compared with a 4.7 percent growth in table service restaurant expenditures. The proportion of away-from-home food expenditures on fast food increased from 29.3 to 34.2 percent between 1982 and 1997, while the restaurant proportion decreased from 41 to 35.7 percent.

MARK D. JEKANOWSKI, from "Causes and
Consequences of Fast Food Sales Growth"

Bok's likely intention is to *analyze* and *interpret* this aspect of Roman behavior. We can't tell yet what her *thesis* will be.

C. No people before or since have so revelled in displays of mortal combat as did the Romans during the last two centuries BC and the first three centuries thereafter, nor derived such pleasure from spectacles in which slaves and convicts were exposed to wild beasts and killed in front of cheering spectators. According to Nicolaus of Damascus, writing in the first decade AD, Romans even regaled themselves with lethal violence at private banquets; he describes dinner guests relishing the spectacles of gladiators fighting to the death:

> Hosts would invite their friends to dinner not merely for other entertainment, but that they might witness two or three pairs of contestants in a gladiatorial combat; on these occasions, when sated with dining and drink, they called in the gladiators. No sooner did one have his throat cut than the masters applauded with delight at this feat.

SISSELA BOK, from *Mayhem: Violence as Public Entertainment*

Bias

Because authors often have strong feelings about proving their point, they may, unintentionally, be less than objective in their choice of methods, evidence, and words. For example, a work can lose credibility if the author's bias leads him or her to omit or distort evidence.

Bias means a preconceived preference or prejudice.

If you think you detect bias at a specific point in a text, consider the entire presentation. Determine whether the presentation is *balanced* and all relevant points are given a fair hearing, or whether the author consistently gives unreasonable weight to one side of the issue.

Knowing something about the author's background may help you to determine whether he or she has an ax to grind. In a previous example, we can't be sure whether Mark D. Jekanowski is extolling fast food or merely recording its growth in popularity. Knowing that, at the time of writing, he was an agricultural economist with the U.S. Department of Agriculture might reassure you about his objectivity. Does that impression change when you learn from a Google search that he subsequently became a senior consultant, with responsibilities including research on consumer demand, for a consulting firm specializing in agribusiness? (See pp. 342–343 and 349–350 for more information about detecting bias in sources.)

Tone

Most academic authors write in a measured, straightforward style; serious subjects call for a serious tone. But, outside of academia, there are many exceptions. Some writers use *humor* to win over their readers. Others will try *irony* to make a point, so that readers, unsure whether the author means what she says, have to question apparently obvious assumptions.

In describing how snobbery works, Joseph Epstein establishes a light, almost flippant tone, poking fun at himself as well as others:

> Nearly every human being deserves respect, but the question is, how much? And who does the calculations? By one's own reckoning, it is safe to say that a great deal of respect is owed. By the world's reckoning, the estimate is, somehow, almost inevitably likely to be lower. Journals kept by the young tend to give off a strong whiff of depression, chiefly because the world doesn't yet recognize the youthful journal keeper's genius, however unproven it may be. Sometimes one feels one isn't getting the consideration (another euphemism for deference) one deserves as a veteran, senior man or woman, someone whose mettle has been established. Awaiting a decision from an editor that takes longer than I think it ought, I find myself mumbling about the ignorance of people who don't understand that I am much too important to be kept waiting so long.
>
> JOSEPH EPSTEIN, from *Snobbery: The American Version*

Sometimes the tone of a work is *strident and overbearing*, which can be a clue to the possibility of bias: the author is so eager to make his case that he may be willing to cut corners to do so. Such a work may be a *polemic*—an argument that aggressively courts controversy. Here, for example, is a passage filled with sweeping generalizations in which the author is rejecting what he says is a common form of American patriotism:

> Many of our superpatriots love this country because it is considered a land of opportunity, a place where people can succeed if they have the right stuff. But individual success usually comes by prevailing over others. And when it comes to the really big prizes in a competitive, money-driven society, almost all of us are losers or simply noncontestants. Room at the top is limited to a select few, mostly those who have been supremely advantaged in family income and social standing from early in life. Even if the U.S. economy does reward the go-getters who sally forth with exceptional capacity and energy, is the quality of life to be measured by the ability of tireless careerists to excel over others? Even if it were easy to become a multimillionaire in America, what is so great about that? Why should one's ability to make large sums of money

be reason to love one's country? What is admirable about a patriotism based on the cash nexus?

MICHAEL PARENTI, from *Superpatriotism*

In another example of immoderate tone, Waller Newell's anger at the misappropriation of the song "Imagine" spills over into his prose:

I am rarely at a loss for words, and like most political junkies I enjoy a good rant, especially after a dose of the television and newspaper opinion makers who can be counted on to make my blood boil — and stir my appetite for more reasoned polemics. But I must confess my stupefaction at how, in the painful months after 9/11, in schools, church basements, and community centers across the land, children's sweet voices swelled in repeated performances of John Lennon's 1970s ballad. That decent people truly believe this song is an appropriate tribute to the victims, that it contains some profound lesson for these trying times, sums up more completely than any other single example how much we desperately need some better guides for manly reflection.

WALLER NEWELL, from *The Code of Man*

Audience

The author's perception of the likely audience for the work may affect the tone. Writing for a general audience reading a popular magazine will be different from writing for an audience of specialists reading a scholarly journal, and writing for an audience inclined to agree with a thesis will probably be less challenging than writing for its opponents. The author has to make assumptions about the readers, and the style of the essay changes accordingly. (For more information on audience, see pp. 343–345.) Identifying an essay's characteristic tone and probable audience can help you to understand how well the author succeeds in supporting the thesis.

Questioning the Author: "The Kindness of Strangers"

Read through "The Kindness of Strangers" by Rubén Martínez, looking at the marginal annotations as you read. Some of the comments are concerned with basic points about the author's meaning; others are more general comments about thesis, method, intention, and tone. Notice how some of them try to sum up what the author has said so far. Others point to a transitional place where the author is turning from one idea to another. Familiarize yourself with this advanced process of annotation, which resembles carrying on a dialogue with the author. What other questions could you ask?

THE KINDNESS OF STRANGERS
Rubén Martínez

Rubén Martínez teaches creative writing at the University of Houston and has written essays and opinion pieces on political issues for a range of newspapers and magazines. His books include Crossing Over: A Mexican Family on the Migrant Trail *(2002) and* The New Americans *(2004), the text that accompanied a PBS series. "The Kindness of Strangers" appeared as an op-ed article in the* New York Times *at a time when the George W. Bush administration was proposing legislation that would allow some immigrants a limited contract to work in the United States.*

Topic: *Is it possible for Americans to accept illegal immigrants into their communities?*

anecdote

The young couple knocks on the heavy wooden door. They are weary and the hour is late; it is bitterly cold.   1

The husband says: "En nombre del cielo, os pido posada," in the name of heaven, I ask thee for lodging.   2

simple style, like a fairy tale

From behind the door comes the answer: "Este no es mesón, sigan adelante, yo no debo abrir, sea algún tunante," this is not an inn, move along, I shouldn't open up, it may be a thief.   3

story has universal relevance—part of the Mexican-American experience

The centuries-old tradition of las posadas is celebrated throughout Mexico and in practically every Mexican neighborhood in America in the days before Christmas. José and María trudge from door to door, turned away again and again until they are finally allowed to bed down in the humble manger where the Christ child is born. Everyone in the neighborhood gets a part in the play.   4

RM turns to interpretation of the story

parable = story with a moral
to grasp the moral, we should play both roles: identify with innkeepers (native-born) and immigrants

Like many traditions, this one can resonate with different tones according to the political tenor of the times. And with the immigration debate on the national agenda — President Bush is once again promoting "guest worker" legislation — this Christmas parable asks us to step inside the shoes of both the protagonists and antagonists, the migrant couple seeking shelter and the innkeepers who, momentarily, hold such power over the couple's fate.   5

Las posadas is a story about hospitality, certainly a "moral value," but not one pollsters ask about. Based on the notion of pilgrimage, a spiritual journey undertaken through the flesh, it is present in practically all the world's religions. Without the hospitality of those who live along the roads of one's pilgrimage — be it the hajj of Islam or a Catholic penitent's journey   6

hospitality = kindness to guests (do guests = strangers?)

to a shrine — one would never arrive at one's destination. Hospitality implies reciprocity: the pilgrim received with generosity will one day have the occasion to return the favor. To shut the door on the wayfaring stranger would be to negate the possibility of one's own journey.

Of course, we shut the door all the time. We conclude, as the innkeepers do in the posada play, that José and María aren't pilgrims at all; they are "thieves" intent on taking from us and giving nothing in return. That is precisely what a strong majority of voters in Arizona apparently believed in November when they passed Proposition 200, which denies most public benefits to illegal migrants; on Wednesday, a federal judge cleared the way for the proposition to become law. "They" have come here merely to feed off America's welfare state — to take something for nothing. We do not extend hospitality to thieves.

Philosophers have long debated the ethics of hospitality, which raises a series of existential, legal and moral questions. Is pure hospitality practicable in a world of human unpredictability? Or is hospitality an indispensable practice precisely because of human unpredictability? In the post-9/11 world, we ponder the question more in terms of national security. How does one discern between the stranger to whom hospitality should be extended, and the stranger who poses a threat? Does war automatically exempt us from showing hospitality? Does a "war without end" permanently suspend such values?

Americans have long had a troubled, contradictory relationship with immigrants. We famously say that we are immigrants, indeed a "land of immigrants," and just as famously render them "them." While Liberty opens her arms to the tired, poor and huddled masses, we also greet the immigrant with ethnic slurs and sweatshop wages, with savage and simplistic representations on our movie and TV screens. We are immigrants who despise immigrants. To enact hospitality in this context is a radical act: it automatically erases the border between us and them. To open one's door to the stranger is to recognize that he no longer is one.

The nativist reacts against the immigrant with prosaic notions of "law and order." José has broken the law by crossing the river without the proper documents. María breaks the law by baby-sitting for money under the table. (The nativist has little to say about the natives who also break the law by hiring illegal aliens; he gains nothing politically by implicating himself in the crime.) But immigration codes are very human laws, born of economic and political realities — laws that blind us from perceiving the migrants for who they really are.

This notion of the foreigner as an economic mercenary has no relation whatsoever to the way migrants regard themselves. Ask Mexicans why they

---

Margin annotations (left):

moral = we are interdependent

we misinterpret the migrants' motives; we can't imagine ourselves in their situation

more abstract tone

RM moves beyond simple parable

"thief" becomes "terrorist"

parallels the double role of innkeeper and migrant

RM is repeating the parable in terms of the nation

Why should one open the door to a stranger? act of faith?

"thieves"

Here, RM is completely identifying with the migrants. Does his sympathy become bias?

shift in point of view from nativist to migrant

Margin annotations (right):

giving and receiving hospitality are essential to achieving a state of grace

7

political parallel

8

asking questions = a way of raising issues without committing to answers

RM moves from the spiritual ("pilgrimage") to the political (protecting borders)

9

returns to the theme of reciprocity

10

laws are good (realistic) and bad (disguise reality)

11

cross the Rio Grande and they will invariably say, "to seek a better life." They do not mean only material gain. Migrants travel through space and time, and are transformed by their encounter with the newness of the landscape, beginning with language. They are changed by their encounter with their other, with us.

like a spiritual pilgrimage

Anyone who has grown up with more than one culture knows that to switch between languages is more than a matter of grammar and accent; meaning itself shifts, sometimes subtly, sometimes profoundly. To travel from one country to another, one language to another, is a journey of both spirit and flesh. The migrants sense this. In America, they are among our most fervently religious communities. In the barrio storefront church, they meditate on and give meaning to their passage—their sacrifice, their yearning for the transcendent, their crossing of the river.

RM's identification with migrants deepens

We're asked to take this view of migrants on faith—RM's language has become spiritual, not analytical as before

12

Biblical image

And so now it is time again to face our contradictions head-on. The Bush administration is pushing an immigration agenda that is questioned from both the right and the left. The proposal offers documentation to immigrants who can prove gainful employment in the form of "contracts" of up to three years. President Bush on Monday repeated that the program would not be an amnesty (like that granted several million illegal immigrants in 1986). Nevertheless, conservatives argue that the program would reward criminals and pose a threat to national security. Liberals complain about institutionalizing the exploitation of foreign labor and the impact on native workers. Both sides reduce the immigrant to caricature. And both still imagine—in their rhetoric, at least—that the broken border between the United States and Mexico can be fixed.

13

i.e., both sides ignore the urgent need for hospitality

borders are artificial and porous

But there was never enough of a border between us for it to have come undone. Immigration laws have always been enforced selectively, largely according to the needs of the labor economy. To a great extent, there is no functioning border, but we insist on believing there is one: imagining a borderless world is a leap into unfamiliar territory, a place where, in a sense, we would all be strangers.

14

summarizing sentence

Yet perhaps it is only in such a place where we might begin to offer genuine hospitality. At the very moment one opens the door to the stranger, one also crosses a border and sees not an immigrant, not an illegal alien, not a Mexican, but a face—a human face.

15

return to "story"

Tonight, in the final representation of the posada, José and María will wearily walk from door to door seeking shelter in the barrios, even as thousands of Josés and Marías arrive at the shore of the Rio Grande, the river they dream of as Jordan. They look to the other side, imagining la vida

16

RM switches point of view again

mejor. The Border Patrol stops some of them. Other migrants, in distress, find doors shut to them when they seek help. But most find a bed to sleep in. With family, with friends, even with strangers — that is the story of immigration in America these days. Perhaps we are a hospitable land, after all. How else could we have become this "land of immigrants"?

We are all pilgrims, but nativists deny the pilgrimage

In New Mexico, one of the most lyrical metaphors in the posada tradition is that of the farolitos, votive candles that glow inside paper sacks weighed down by sand. These light the path toward that place where José and María will finally be recognized for who they are: pilgrims seeking shelter on the road, faces that serve as mirrors to our own.

17

Thesis: For Rubén Martínez, the problem of immigration would be solved by each of us finding enough faith to extend hospitality to strangers.

Method: Broadly interpreting a parable to support the thesis.

Questioning the Author: Points to Consider

- What is the thesis?
- What method is the author using to support this thesis?
- For which audience is the author writing? the general public? peers?
- Is the presentation serious or flippant or ironic?
- Does the author have any special interest in the topic that might amount to bias?
- Does the author try to manipulate the reader in any way?
- Are you inclined to believe everything that you read?
- How well does the author support the thesis? Is the reader convinced?

EXERCISE 3: Examining Intention

A.   Read "When Altruism Isn't Moral," by Sally Satel, twice.

B.   On the second reading, use the margins to ask questions and make comments about the meaning of the author's words and phrases and her thesis and intention.

WHEN ALTRUISM ISN'T MORAL

Sally Satel

A practicing psychiatrist who has taught at Yale University, Sally Satel has written articles about issues in medicine and medical ethics for academic journals and popular periodicals. Her books include How Political Correctness Is Corrupting Medicine. *This essay appeared online in the* Journal of the American Enterprise Institute.

Topic: *What is the best way to save lives by ensuring a sufficient supply of organ donations?*

In early 2006, Matt Thompson of San Jose, California, decided to give a kidney to Sonny Davis, a 65-year-old physicist living in nearby Menlo Park. Thompson was moved to donate after reading an impassioned plea from Davis's wife, who had sent 140 letters to friends and relatives asking them to consider helping her husband. One of the recipients happened to be a colleague of Thompson's, who passed it along, thinking Thompson just might heed the call. Sure enough, Thompson, a devout young Christian and former missionary, contacted the transplant program to volunteer.

But the transplant program at Kaiser Permanente of Northern California turned him down. Had Davis been a family member or a good friend, he would have been acceptable to the program. Thompson was frustrated and surprised, but he and Davis were determined to do the transplant. According to the *San Jose Mercury News*, they "knew they had to forge a bond that would assure Davis's surgeons that Thompson was donating his kidney for the right reasons." This meant, among other things, that Thompson would not profit financially. So the two developed a relationship and convinced the transplant program that no money was secretly being exchanged. On November 14, 2006, the transplant finally took place.

Far more than a human interest tale of a stranger opening his heart to a suffering soul, the story of Sonny Davis and Matt Thompson draws back the curtain on the culture of the organ transplant establishment. It shows that transplant professionals would have allowed a 65-year-old man to languish on dialysis for years or die — a strong probability given his age — while waiting for a kidney, out of fear that he might be remunerating someone for an act that would save his life.

There are about 78,000 people in queue for a kidney from a deceased donor. In places like California, the wait can be up to eight years. And unless a friend or relative gives a kidney to a loved one, he will weaken on dialysis. Four thousand people die each year because they cannot survive the wait. This explains Mrs. Davis's frantic plea to anyone who might volunteer a kidney to her husband.

The woeful inadequacy of our nation's transplant policy is due to its re-   5
liance on "altruism." According to the guiding narrative of the transplant establishment, organs should be a "gift of life," an act of selfless generosity. It's a
beautiful sentiment, no question. In fact, I, myself, am a poster girl for altruism.
In 2006, I received a kidney from a (formerly) casual friend who heard secondhand about my need for a transplant. In her act, there was everything for me to
gain, and, frankly, not much for her. My glorious donor was moved by empathy
and altruism as purely as anyone could ever be.

Yet, it is lethally obvious that altruism is not a valid basis for transplant pol-   6
icy. If we keep thinking of organs solely as gifts, there will never be enough of
them. We need to encourage more living and posthumous donation through
rewards, say, tax credits or lifetime health insurance.

But what about the Matt Thompson–Sonny Davis problem: anxiety sur-   7
rounding the very notion that an organ donor should receive anything of material value for his sacrifice. It is important to understand the nature of this anxiety
because it is a formidable obstacle to devising a rational transplant system.

Arguments against creating incentives to donate fall into two general cate-   8
gories: arguments from corruption and arguments from consequence. These
designations were coined by political philosopher Michael Sandel.

Arguments from consequence go like this: there is nothing intrinsically   9
wrong with compensating donors, but it is not possible to design an incentive-
based system without exploiting them. The worry is that economic straits
could compel reluctant individuals to relinquish a kidney for the sole sake of
enrichment.

This is indeed a troubling situation. Fortunately, it can be addressed with   10
good policy. For example, a state government could provide compensation
such as tax credits, tuition vouchers, a contribution to a tax-free retirement account, or lifelong health coverage. A non-cash reward won't appeal to those in
desperate need of financial help. What they want is quick cash, not delayed in-
kind rewards. A months-long waiting period would dampen impulsivity and
give more than ample time for donor education and careful medical and psychological screening. Finally, donors would receive quality follow-up care,
something the current system does not ensure.

Arguments from corruption proceed from the belief that donors, and per-   11
haps society at large, will be diminished or corrupted if organs are given in return for something of material value. Giving a kidney "for free" is noble but
accepting compensation is illegitimate, a sordid affront to human dignity. Indeed, the debate surrounding incentives for organ donation sometimes resembles a titanic struggle between uplift and greed. "As a rule, the debate is cast as
one in which existing relations of selfless, altruistic exchange are threatened

with replacement by market-based, for-profit alternatives," observes Kieran Healy, a sociologist at Duke University.

Dr. Luc Noel of the World Health Organization subscribes to this false choice. "There are two prevailing concepts of transplantation," he says. "One relies on money and leads to increased inequality, besides putting a price on the integrity of the body and human dignity. The second is based on solidarity and the donor's sole motivation to save a life." The National Kidney Foundation warns against "self-interest on behalf of the donor." The notion also troubles a primary care physician in Columbus, Ohio: "What sort of organ transplant program do we want," he asks, "one that pressures the financially vulnerable with cash incentives, or one that encourages the show of kindness through a loving, voluntary gift of organ donation?"   12

Paradoxically, our current transplant system makes every donation seem like a "loving, voluntary gift of organ donation." Think about it: there is no other legal option. Some altruistic donations come as close to the technical definition: my experience would be one of those. Yet, our current altruism-only system has a dark side: It imposes coercion of its own by putting friends and family members in a bind. They might not want to donate, but they feel obligated, lest their relative die or deteriorate on dialysis. Sociologists have written about familial dynamics that involve guilt, overt pressure, or subtle threats. Consider the "black-sheep donor," a wayward relative who shows up to offer an organ as an act of redemption, hoping to reposition himself in the family's good graces. Some donate as a way to elicit praise and social acceptance. For others, donation is a sullen fulfillment of familial duty, a way to avoid the shame and guilt of allowing a relative to suffer needlessly and perhaps even die.   13

As famed anthropologist Marcel Mauss observed in his classic work, *The Gift*, gifts are never free; they demand reciprocity. "The [given] objects are never completely separated from the men who exchange them," he learned from his work with Polynesian natives in the early 1900s. The same applies to organs. The "tyranny of the gift" is an artful term coined by sociologists Renee Fox and Judith Swazey to capture the way in which immense gratitude at receiving a kidney can morph into a sense of constricting obligation. In their 1992 book, *Spare Parts: Organ Replacement in American Society*, the authors write, "The giver, the receiver, and their families, may find themselves locked in a creditor-debtor vise that binds them one to another in a mutually fettering way." Indeed, the virtue of market-like exchanges is that they are emotionally liberating.   14

An unusual take on altruism comes from the National Kidney Foundation, a vocal opponent of incentivizing organ donation. According to Dolph Chianchiano, its senior vice president for health policy and research, the NKF believes   15 that compensating donors will "cheapen the gift." Such an affront to would-be donors will cause them to hold onto their organs. On one level, this seems absurd. Can you imagine a brother telling his ailing sister, "Gee, sis, I would have given you my kidney but now that I hear that someone across town is accepting a tax credit for his donation, well, forget it."

But if Chianchiano is correct—that some people will withhold voluntary action if remuneration is available to others—then, paradoxically, a regime of donor compensation would be quite the boon to such "altruists." They would have bragging rights: They were the ones who acted out of generosity, not for material gain, a distinction that not only allows them to retain the "warm glow" that comes from performing acts of charity but also intensifies it. Given the importance of "social signaling" through gift-giving ("look at me, so generous, so civic-minded!") the opportunity to accentuate the distinction should be most welcome.   16

No wonder scholars ranging from philosophers to evolutionary biologists to psychologists and economists are skeptical about whether true human altruism even exists. It is more realistic to envision a broad middle ground between the poles of selflessness and greed. It is the arena in which most organ donation already plays out. And it is where compensated donation would likely reside, too.   17

Simply look at our daily lives. Financial and humanitarian motives do not reside in discrete realms. Moreover, it is unclear how their co-mingling is inherently harmful—the goodness of an act is not diminished because someone was paid to perform it. The great teachers who enlighten us and the doctors who heal us inspire no less gratitude because they are paid. A salaried firefighter who risks her life to save a child trapped in a burning building is no less heroic than a volunteer firefighter. Soldiers accept military pay while pursuing a patriotic desire to serve their country. The desire to do well by others while enriching oneself at the same time is as old as humankind. Indeed, the very fact that generosity and remuneration so often intertwine can be leveraged to good ends: to increase the pool of transplantable organs, for instance.   18

The practice of assigning values to body parts has roots in antiquity. The Code of Hammurabi provides an elaborate schedule of compensation for them; for example, it specifies that if an individual should "knock out the teeth of a freed man, he shall pay one-third of a gold mina." Today we routinely assign valuation to the body. Human blood plasma is collected primarily through paid donation. Personal injury lawyers seek damages for bodily harm to their clients. The Veterans Administration puts a price on physical disabilities. We pay for justice in the context of personal injury litigation in the form of legal costs, and for our very lives in the form of medical fees. There is little reason to believe—nor   19 tangible evidence to suggest — that these practices depreciate human worth or undermine human dignity in any way.

It is all too easy to romanticize altruism. Sociologist Amitai Etzioni urges   20
the postponement of paying for organs in favor of what he calls a "communitarian" approach "so that members of society will recognize that donating one's organs . . . is the moral (right) thing to do . . . it entails a moral dialogue, in which the public is engaged, leading to a change in what people expect from one another." Thomas A. Shannon, a professor of religion and social ethics, writes, "I would think it a tragedy if . . . we tried to solve the problem of the organ shortage by commodification rather than by the kindness of strangers who meet in the community and recognize and meet the needs of others in generosity."

To be sure, these skeptics have a right to their moral commitments, but   21
their views must not determine binding policy in a morally pluralistic society. A donor compensation system operating in parallel with our established mechanism of altruistic procurement is the only way to accommodate us all. Moreover, it represents a promising middle ground between the status quo — a procurement system based on the partial myth of selfless altruism — and the dark, corrupt netherworld of organ trafficking. The current regime permits no room for individuals who would welcome an opportunity to be rewarded for rescuing their fellow human beings; and for those who wait for organs in vain, the only dignity left is that with which they must face death.

Using Evidence and Reasoning

The author asserts a thesis and attempts to prove it; the reader decides whether the thesis is convincing. Whether the author is writing an explanatory, analytical, or persuasive essay, *the credibility of the thesis depends upon the strength of the evidence and reasoning.* Why should you believe this thesis? Because the author offers solid evidence as proof and uses a process of logical reasoning to persuade you.

Evidence

Evidence refers to any kind of *concrete information* that can support a thesis. Just as evidence is necessary for a criminal to be convicted in court — there, the thesis to be proved is that John Doe robbed Richard Roe — so authors are expected to cite evidence in supporting a thesis.

Evidence can take several forms. Most authors use more than one.

Facts and Statistics

Authors usually offer *facts* and *statistics* to back up their thesis, especially when they are working in the social sciences. When Mark D. Jekanowski (see pp. 28–29) assures the reader that "the proportion of away-from-home food expenditures on fast food increased from 29.3 to 34.2 percent between 1982 and 1997 . . ." he is using statistics to support his thesis about the growing popularity of fast food.

To prove a thesis about **excessive drinking on a college campus,** an author might cite:

- the college's policy governing drinking in the dormitories (*facts*)
- the number of bars near the campus (*statistics*)
- the number of students who frequent those bars (*statistics*)
- the number of students who have sought help from college counselors for drinking problems (*statistics*)

and so on. Some of this evidence might be obtained from surveys that the author has carried out. Or to provide a broader context for the argument, the author might consult government Web sites or publications such as the *Chronicle of Higher Education* to find additional data about practices on campuses nationwide.

Surveys

Whatever the source, the data must be reliable. Surveys and polls, for example, depend upon *generalizing from a representative sample,* based on an appropriate "population." In other words, they use limited evidence (the opinions of, say, 1,000 respondents) to predict the opinions of a much larger group—possibly the entire nation—by assuming that the opinions of the smaller group reflect proportionately the opinions of the larger. So, a 1989 poll surveying almost 4,000 people from three countries about the state of their national health care was able to conclude that 89 percent of all Americans regarded their health-care system as "fundamentally flawed." The author is using the responses of the 4,000 people surveyed to make larger claims about whole national groups. As you will see in Chapter 4, David Leonhardt cites similar surveys in his article about the link between money and happiness.

The same rules of samples and populations would apply to a survey cited as evidence in an essay on **college drinking**. How many people took part in the survey? If percentages are cited, what was the base population? If an author says that 60 percent of those students surveyed drank excessively, does that mean five, or fifteen, or fifty people? How many drinks were defined as "excessive," and was drinking measured by the day, by the week, or by the month?

Examples

An example is a *single representative instance* that serves to support a thesis. Blanche Blank (see pp. 14–15) uses the example of Joe V. to show her readers that college graduates are overqualified for many kinds of work. In the following passage from *Mapping Human History*, Steve Olson provides a series of examples to demonstrate the absurdity of ethnic enmities:

> Many of the harshest conflicts in the world today are between people who are indistinguishable. If someone took a roomful of Palestinians and Israelis from the Middle East, or of Serbs and Albanians from the Balkans, or of Catholics and Protestants from Ireland, or of Muslims and Hindus from northern India, or of Dayaks and Madurese from Indonesia, gave them all identical outfits and haircuts, and forbade them to speak or gesture, no one could distinguish the members of the other group—at least not to the point of being willing to shoot them. The antagonists in these conflicts have different ethnicities, but they have been so closely linked biologically throughout history that they have not developed marked physical differences.
>
> Yet one of the most perverse dimensions of ethnic thinking is the "racialization" of culture—the tendency to think of another people as not just culturally but genetically distinct. In the Yugoslavian war, the Croats caricatured their Serbian opponents as tall and blond, while the Serbs disparaged the darker hair and skin of the Croats—even though these traits are thoroughly intermixed between the two groups. During World War II the countries of Europe fiercely stereotyped the physical attributes of their enemies, despite a history of intermarriage and migration that has scrambled physical characteristics throughout the continent. In Africa, the warring Tutsis and Hutus often call attention to the physical differences of their antagonists, but most observers have trouble distinguishing individual members of the two groups solely on the basis of appearance.

Keep in mind, though, that because examples are only single instances of a broad and complex situation, they may provide only limited support for the thesis. Specific examples of students whose **drinking** resulted in academic, social, or emotional difficulties may catch your attention, but shouldn't by themselves persuade you that the problem is widespread or serious enough to require action. Rather, they should serve as supplements to more broad-based evidence.

Anecdotes

Anecdotes are stories—extended examples with a beginning, middle, and end—that illustrate the point an author wants to make. Here's the way Stephen L. Carter starts an essay on the topic of civility:

> Let us begin with a common and irritating occurrence. As you sit down to dinner with your family, the telephone rings. When you answer, you find that you are being offered a subscription to the local paper or invited to donate to the volunteer fire department. And although you may enjoy reading your local paper and admire the volunteers who keep the city from burning to the ground,

if you are like me, a wave of frustration passes through you, and you face the serious temptation to say something rude. . . .

And Carter continues to describe how his family deals with this dinner-time interruption. He has used an anecdote as a vivid way of introducing his point about the disappearance of common courtesy in daily life.

Like examples, anecdotes attract and interest the reader (and, for that reason, they are often placed at the beginning of essays). But they can take up a great deal of space. "Anecdotal evidence" is never enough to prove a thesis.

Appeal to Authority

Authors often support their theses by citing their own research or the work of acknowledged authorities. Data and examples have considerably more credibility when they are endorsed by sources with a reputation as *experts in the field*. An author needs to cite the evidence of such sources in reasonable detail and, if possible, convey the strength of their credentials. A thesis should not depend on nameless sources such as "1,000 doctors" or "authorities in the field." (Chapter 8 discusses how you can determine which sources are authoritative and which are not.) Notice the way David Leonhardt cites sources by name in "Maybe Money Does Buy Happiness After All" (pp. 164–167). He identifies the scholar's field ("economist," "psychologist") and university ("University of Pennsylvania," "University of Southern California"); the reputation of the institutions help to validate the research that Leonhardt is presenting.

An author writing about **college drinking** is likely to find evidence in *published sources*—books, magazines, scholarly journals—and *reliable* Web sites. The source of that evidence must be acknowledged in the text, with documentation containing the author's name, the work, and the place and date of its publication. In this way, when you read the essay, you can determine whether the author is citing a reputable and appropriate source and, if you wish, locate that source and find out more about the topic.

Looking for Evidence

- Does the author use facts and/or statistics to support the thesis? If so, do they seem reliable?
- Does the author use examples and anecdotes? If so, are they the main or only evidence for the thesis?
- Are the sources for the evidence acknowledged?
- Do these sources seem credible?
- Are there some points that are not supported by evidence?
- Does the author seem biased?
- Based on the evidence provided, do you accept the author's thesis?

EXERCISE 4: Citing Evidence

A. Read "In Romania, Children Left Behind Suffer the Strains of Migration," by Dan Bilefsky, twice.

B. On your second reading, identify the kinds of evidence cited in the article.

C. Distinguish between *information* supported by evidence, *information* that isn't supported by evidence, and *opinions* offered by the author that derive from the evidence he cites.

D. Consider what additional information Bilefsky could provide to make his evidence more convincing.

IN ROMANIA, CHILDREN LEFT BEHIND
SUFFER THE STRAINS OF MIGRATION
Dan Bilefsky

Dan Bilefsky is a European correspondent and former Brussels bureau chief for the New York Times. *His recent stories have focused on eastern Europe, particularly the Balkan countries.*

> **Topic:** *How are Romanian families affected by the need for parents to seek work in other countries?*

For millions of Romanians, migration has been an economic lifeline. But for 12-year-old Stefan Ciurea, the thought of his mother leaving to work as a maid in Italy was worse than death: he hanged himself with a leather horsewhip from the branch of a cherry tree.   1

After taking one last photograph of himself with his cellphone, Stefan, a quiet, diminutive boy who collected foreign coins and made toy swords out of scrap metal, posted a note to his chest. "I'm sorry we are parting upset," the note said, referring to his pained efforts to stop his mother, Alexandrina, from migrating to Rome, part of an exodus of one-third of Romania's active work force. "You don't have to worry about my funeral because a man owes us money for timber. My sister, you should study hard. Mom, you should take care of yourself because the world is harsh. Please take care of my puppy."   2

Two years later, Ms. Ciurea, a 38-year-old single mother, is a cleaner in Rome, one of an estimated three million Romanians who have migrated westward over the past five years. She said Stefan's suicide had given her a stomach ulcer. After his death, she waited a year before deciding to leave her two other children, who were teenagers, behind.   3

Note: The number of paragraphs has been reduced without any alteration of the text.

But in the end, economics prevailed: she could earn about $770 a month cleaning houses in Italy, more than three times her wage as a seamstress in Romania. "Stefan's death is the tragedy of my life," she said in a telephone interview from Rome. "But I left because I was poor and couldn't feed my children. If I could, I would come back to Romania tomorrow." 4

Many in this poor Balkan country of 22 million dreamed of escaping during decades of dictatorship. The exodus of poor, rural Romanians began after the fall of Communism in 1989 and intensified two years ago when Romania joined the European Union. Spain, Italy and a handful of other countries softened immigration rules to attract less expensive workers from the East. Diligent Romanians became the strawberry pickers, construction workers and housecleaners of choice, doing jobs that workers in richer neighboring countries no longer wanted. 5

But while migration has brought economic gains — migrants sent home nearly $10.3 billion in remittances last year — it has also exacted a heavy toll on the country left behind. The migration ripped apart the social fabric, creating a generation of what some sociologists call the "strawberry orphans." An estimated 170,000 children have one or both parents working abroad, according to a recent study by the Soros Foundation. 6

The same study found that children with parents abroad were more likely to abuse alcohol and cigarettes, have problems with the police and underperform in school. Conversely, some children who blame themselves for their parents' departure become straight-A students in the hope of luring them back. Denisa Ionescu, a psychologist who works with the children of migrants, said they were at higher risk for depression, especially if it was the mother who left, while some of the children suffer from feelings of abandonment. "In Romania, it 7 is the mother who cares for the children," Ms. Ionescu said. "So when the mother leaves, the child's world falls apart." Of the children left behind, 14 have committed suicide over the past three years, according to researchers with the Soros Foundation. It is unclear what role their parents' leaving played in the children's decisions to take their lives, except in the case of Stefan.

But psychologists say the effects of migration have been especially acute because Romania is a largely rural country where close family ties underpin all aspects of life. In some cases, migration causes already dysfunctional families to implode.   8

Gheorghe Ciurea, Stefan's 16-year-old half brother, said Stefan was a quiet, affable boy. But when he learned that his mother was leaving and he would be in the care of Stefan's hard-drinking father, who never married Stefan's mother, he locked himself in his room and refused to come out for days.   9

After the suicide, Stefan's father moved out. Now Gheorghe, whose own father is dead, lives alone in their cramped, messy house in this village about 105 miles northwest of Bucharest. He said he dropped out of high school because he could not afford the tuition. He does odd construction jobs to scrape by. The house is freezing, and he wears a wool coat inside. To pass the time, he plays backgammon. His sister, Alina, 17, lives with her boyfriend. Being alone has forced him to learn to cook. He calls his mother every day. "I miss my mother," he said from Stefan's room. "At some point, she says, she will bring me to Italy so I can work in construction, but I am still waiting. I am still waiting."   10

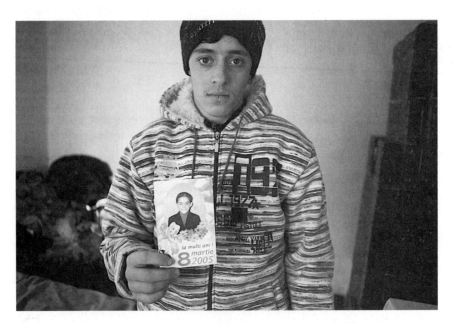

Sixteen-year-old Gheorghe holds a Mother's Day card with a photo of Stefan.

Outside, down a dirt road, dozens of new homes have sprouted, the product of toil abroad. Vasile Dina, the vice mayor of Valea Danului, said he could barely meet the demand for new housing permits. But the wealth came at a price. "We have more tax revenues, nice cars on the road, people send their children to university in Bucharest," Mr. Dina said. "But the sad truth is that if we were still living under Communism, Gheorghe would be going to school—not sitting at home by himself." 11

Mihaela Stefanescu, who coordinated the study for the Soros Foundation, said the billions in remittances had helped eradicate extreme poverty and had empowered working mothers like Alexandrina Ciurea. But she said the migration was also redefining the notion of the traditional Romanian family. Many children of migrants live with grandparents, some of whom are not able to deal with the demands of rearing young children. Divorce among migrants is rising, with sets of parents sometimes migrating to different countries. In extreme cases, children are abandoned or sent to orphanages, child advocates say. Some work as prostitutes or get involved with criminals. 12

An Emmy Award–winning documentary series, "Any Idea What Your Kid Is Doing Right Now?" shown on national television here, featured a family of six children left with their blind father after the mother went to work as a maid in Germany. She met another man and never returned. Soon, some of the children were forced to stop going to school and find work to survive. 13

Ms. Stefanescu said migrating parents were spoiling their children to allay guilt. "People are going on spending sprees in order to overcompensate for their humiliation and guilt at having had to leave the country to support the family," she said. "Migrant kids have new bikes and the latest mobile phones." 14

Economists warn that the benefits of working abroad may prove short-lived, especially if the global economic downturn forces workers to return home to an economy that can no longer absorb them. Some companies dealt with worker shortages caused by the migration by importing workers from Turkey, China and India to fill jobs in construction, agriculture and textiles. Tens of thousands of Romanians are already out of jobs in Spain and Italy, and alarm is growing that a mass return could overstretch an already teetering Romanian economy. "The short-term economic gains of migration will not justify the long-term costs," said Radu Soviani, a leading economist. "It is a national tragedy." 15

Interpreting Evidence

There are three major ways to describe how an author uses evidence and how you form conclusions from that evidence: *stating*, *implying*, and *inferring*. To illustrate these terms, here is an excerpt from "The Other Gender

Gap," a 2004 *New York Times* article. Marshall Poe is asserting that, in recent years, various initiatives have encouraged girls to earn college, graduate, and professional degrees in ever greater numbers. In contrast, far fewer boys achieve comparable academic success: only 70 percent complete high school, 40 percent enter college, and 8 percent go to graduate school. According to Poe, the difference between boys' and girls' characteristic behavior in the classroom, as early as elementary school, might account for this disparity of achievement.

Statement: Girls' ability to focus on a task is one reason why they do well in school.

Statement: Three times as many boys as girls are considered learning disabled.

Statement: Many young men prefer to earn money rather than to remain in the classroom.

From kindergarten on, the education system rewards self-control, obedience, and concentration—qualities that, any teacher can tell you, are much more common among girls than boys, particularly at young ages. Boys fidget, fool around, fight, and worse. Thirty years ago teachers may have accommodated and managed this behavior, in part by devoting more attention to boys than to girls. But as girls have come to attract equal attention, as an inability to sit still has been medicalized, and as the options for curbing student misbehavior have been ever more curtailed, boys may have suffered. Boys make up three quarters of all children categorized as learning disabled today, and they are put in special education at a much higher rate (special education is often misused as a place to stick "problem kids," and children seldom switch from there to the college track). Shorter recess times, less physical education, and more time spent on rote learning (in order to meet testing standards) may have exacerbated the problems that boys tend to experience in the classroom. It is no wonder, then, that many boys disengage academically. Boys are also subject to a range of extrinsic factors that hinder their academic performance and pull them out of school at greater rates than girls. First among these is the labor market. Young men, with or without high school diplomas, earn more than young women, so they are more likely to see work as an *alternative* to school. Employment gives many men immediate monetary gratification along with relief from the drudgery of the classroom.

1

But boys' educational stagnation has long-term economic implications. Not even half the boys in the country are taking advantage of the opportunity to go to college, which has become almost a prerequisite for a middle-class lifestyle. And languishing academic attainment among a large portion of our population spells trouble for the prospects of continued economic growth. Unless more boys begin attending college, the nation may face a shortage of highly skilled workers in the coming decade.

2

Statements

The three sentences in the margins of this excerpt are restatements of information presented in the article. The words are different; the point is the same.

Although the author does not provide data to prove the validity of these three statements, it would be reasonable for you to include this information in an essay, provided that you cite the author—Marshall Poe—and, if possible, document the source: the name of the article, the publication in which it appeared, and the date of its first appearance.

Implications

So far, we have been examining only what the article *explicitly* states. But, in addition, most sources inform you indirectly, by implying obvious conclusions that are not stated in so many words. (To *imply* means to suggest an idea not directly expressed in a statement.) The implications of a statement can be easily found within the statement itself; they just are not directly expressed.

Here, for example, is one of Poe's statements side by side with an implication derived from that statement that Poe himself does not make:

Poe's Statement	**Implication**
Shorter recess times, less physical education, and more time spent on rote learning (in order to meet testing standards) may have *exacerbated the problems* that boys tend to experience in the classroom.	Boys' poor educational *performance might be improved* if they had more outlets for their energy during the school day.

In effect, the emphasis is reversed: Poe stresses the *problem* (an excess of energy); the implication uses the information to suggest a *solution* (more opportunities to work off that energy).

Here is another implication that can be found in the second paragraph of the excerpt:

Poe's Statement	**Implication**
Unless more boys begin attending college, the nation may face a shortage of highly skilled workers in the coming decade.	The increased number of women with college degrees may not be able to compensate for the smaller number of men without advanced skills entering the labor market.

Poe emphasizes the shortage of skilled male workers. The implication considers whether the abundance of women graduates—information found elsewhere in the article—might remedy that shortage. Pessimistically, Poe suggests that it might not do so.

If included in an essay, implications like these would be presented just as you would present a source's statement: by citing the author and documenting the work in which the information can be found. Here's what the *citation* in your text might look like:

> In Marshall Poe's view, the fact that relatively few young men attend and graduate from college is likely to have serious economic consequences. He suggests that the increased number of women with college degrees may not be able to compensate for the diminished number of men without advanced skills entering the labor market.

More on methods of *documentation* can be found in later chapters, particularly Chapter 10.

Inferences

It is also acceptable to draw a conclusion that is *not* implicit in the source, as long as you reach that conclusion through reasoning based on sound evidence. To *infer* means to form a probable conclusion from a statement by reasoning. Unlike implication, inference requires the analysis of information—putting 2 and 2 together—for the hidden idea to be observed. When you express an implication, everything you need is in the text. When you form an inference, you may apply your own knowledge of the subject or experience of life. **The text implies; the reader infers.**

Throughout the first paragraph of this excerpt, Poe focuses on the discomfort that boys feel in the classroom (contrasted, by implication, with the ease with which girls are able to learn). One can, therefore, safely infer, from everything that Poe describes, that *most boys don't like school*. Poe does not explicitly or even implicitly make this point; it can't be found in the text. But it is there for readers to infer if they care to do so.

Inferences tend to push the author's point a little further than anything that can be found in the text. Poe, for example, alludes to the possibility that, in the past, boys' energies might have been "accommodated and managed" by teachers who, previously, had had enough time to focus on their pupils' individual needs. One can extend this point—infer from it—by suggesting that *more teachers and smaller classes might enable boys to have the individual attention they need to do well in school*. Again, this point isn't in the text; it can only be derived from the text, through inference, by the reader. And, like many inferences, this one uses "might" to convey a degree of doubt. An inference is usually a possibility or probability, not a certainty.

As with statements and implications, inferences require that the source be cited and documented. But, for inferences, it becomes important to distinguish in your essay between what the author says and what you infer:

> Marshall Poe reminds us that, in the past, boys' energies might have been "accommodated and managed" by teachers who, previously, had had

enough time to focus on their pupils' individual needs. This supports my point that more teachers and smaller classrooms would give boys the individual attention they need to succeed academically.

Unsupported Inferences

Finally, it's always possible to push inference too far and end up with an assertion for which there is no basis in the source. Here are a few examples of statements that are unsupported by Poe's article:

Boisterous and inattentive behavior was considered natural for boys 30 years ago.

> **Unsupported:** We're given no information about how society regarded boys' behavior 30 years ago; we're only told that teachers dealt with it differently.

Women are likely to earn less than men, so girls have to perform better in school to get ahead.

> **Unsupported:** We're given no information that links academic performance with higher salaries for women.

The same qualities that enable girls to do well at school—self-control, obedience, concentration—also enable workers to succeed at their jobs. Therefore, women could replace men as highly skilled workers and ensure continued economic growth.

> **Unsupported:** This pushes the point so far that it ends up directly contradicting Poe's final statement.

Differentiating among Statement, Implication, and Inference

Statement: The information is provided in the text even though the wording may be different.

Implication: The text suggests an idea that is not directly stated in the source.

Inference: Through reasoning, the reader can form a probable conclusion that is not implicit in the text.

EXERCISE 5: Drawing Inferences

A. Read "For College Athletes, Recruiting Is a Fair (but Flawed) Game," by Libby Sander, twice.

B. On your second reading, decide, according to the information in the article and its accompanying data, which of the following sentences are *stated*, are *implied*, can be *inferred*, or are *unsupported*.

Imp 1. Most potential recruits are satisfied with the frequency of contact with college coaches.

Imp 2. Most potential recruits who visit college campuses experience little or nothing of the institution's classes and academic activities.

Imp 3. Some potential recruits who visit college campuses are satisfied with their experiences; some are not.

Inf 4. High school athletes should be provided with more guidance as they choose their colleges.

Inf but Uns. 5. The need for high school athletes to make campus visits may cause financial problems for some families.

stated 6. According to some college athletes, coaches provide potential recruits with an idealized description of their programs.

Inf 7. Coaches should be prevented from signing up recruits before the end of their senior year.

stated 8. Most high school recruits are given at least a week to accept a college's offer.

uns. *stated* 9. Most recruits do not feel rushed or pressured to make up their minds.

stated 10. The degree of support for a sport shown by the students at a particular campus is important to most potential recruits in making their decisions.

uns. 11. However difficult the recruiting process might be, most athletes adjust to college life.

Inf 12. In the recruiting process, the best interests of the coaches and the best interests of the high school students may be far from identical.

FOR COLLEGE ATHLETES, RECRUITING IS A FAIR (BUT FLAWED) GAME
Libby Sander

Libby Sander has worked as a journalist for six years, specializing in the newspaper industry. She currently is a staff reporter with the Chronicle of Higher Education, *and is a member of the Association for Women in Sports Media. This article appeared in the* Chronicle of Higher Education.

Topic: *How good a job are colleges doing when they recruit athletes?*

Despite all the alarm that recruiting in college sports has spun out of control, for many athletes the process was neither as intrusive, nor as lavish, as its critics have warned, according to a *Chronicle* survey of hundreds of current Division I athletes.   1

But the accelerated pace of recruiting, and the demands it placed on athletes during their sophomore and junior years of high school, left many of them feeling overwhelmed.   2

Some said they were uncomfortable with having to make hasty decisions during their senior year, sometimes in a matter of days, about whether to accept scholarships. And the majority of athletes said they had little exposure to the academic side of campus life, such as meeting with professors or sitting in on classes, during their campus visits.   3

Most of the nearly 300 athletes who responded to the survey, representing 17 men's and women's teams (but not football) at seven universities in the Mid-American Conference, said the institutions they now attend were fairly portrayed to them during the recruiting process. But a few had harsh words for the coaches who recruited them.   4

"Coaches can tell you whatever they want, pretty much what you want to hear," one athlete wrote in response to the online survey, which was conducted in October and November. "But once you sign your name on the dotted line, they can do whatever they want, and you're stuck there."   5

Although a few athletes had no qualms about the process, many found the experience unsettling.   6

"It was very overwhelming and stressful at times," one athlete wrote. "It was a big decision, and not always having a clear idea of what I wanted made it more difficult, especially when I had to tell coaches 'No.'"   7

NCAA [National Collegiate Athletic Association] rules governing athletics recruiting have grown ever more intricate, restricting how and when coaches may communicate with prospective athletes. The rules are intended to protect recruits from overeager coaches who might otherwise push the limits with intrusive telephone calls and visits. Coaches and athletes have found the rules to be helpful and maddening to equal degrees, and the survey results reflected the paradox: For every complaint of having received too many phone calls or too many e-mail messages, there was a wish for more unfettered communication with coaches.   8

The survey also showed that as recruiting spreads to ever-younger athletes, the recruits are making greater numbers of unofficial visits to campuses before their senior year, trips that the students or their families must pay for. More than four-fifths of the surveyed athletes made at least one such   9

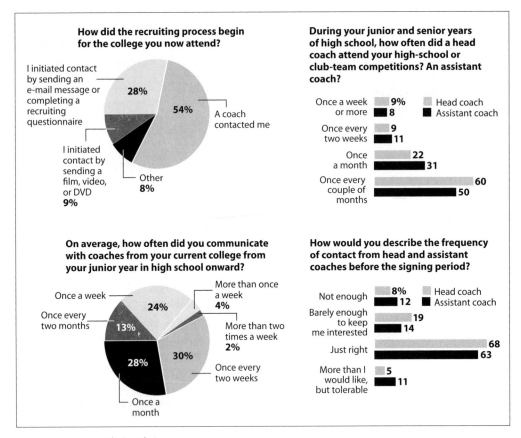

Communicating with Coaches

visit, and nearly one in five players went on five or more unofficial recruiting trips.

The frequent visits also affect current athletes. Coaches call on them to entertain prospective athletes, show them around the campus, and escort them to team gatherings. More than half of the athletes surveyed, in fact, said that on their own official recruiting trips (those the colleges paid for), they had spent 12 or more hours with prospective teammates, attending games or going out for meals. After the visits, 62 percent of the respondents said they had stayed in touch with members of the team they met on their official visits.   10

The athletes urged coaches to offer recruits a practical view of their program both during campus visits and at other times, instead of an unrealistically polished version just for the sake of making a good impression.   11

"It's not terrible to show flaws," one athlete wrote. A program doesn't have to be "perfect" — it just has to be "the right fit."   12

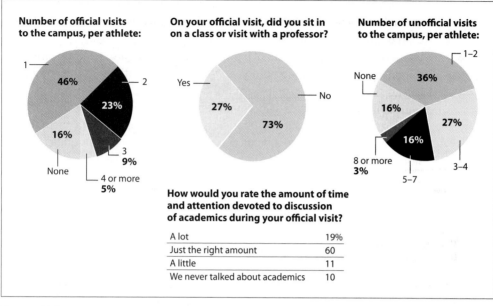

How would you rate the amount of time and attention devoted to discussion of academics during your official visit?

A lot	19%
Just the right amount	60
A little	11
We never talked about academics	10

Campus Visits

How important was it that the institution, the athletics department, and the student body show interest in your sport?

	Institution	Athletics department	Student body
Extremely important	36%	50%	19%
Moderately important	59	47	64
Not at all important	5	3	16

How much time were you given to decide whether to accept a scholarship offer at your current college?

One week or more	85%
Three to six days	9
Two days	3
One day	2
Less than one day	2

How important was the head coach's reputation in deciding whether to join a certain program?

Extremely important	42%
Moderately important	46
Not very important	10
Not at all important	2

How important was the reputation/success of the overall athletics program, and your sport in particular, in making your decision?

	Reputation of the athletics program	Success of my sport
The most important thing	9%	10%
Extremely important, but not the most significant factor	46	49
Moderately important	39	35
Not at all important	6	6

Making the Decision

In a trend that is trickling down from the high-profile sports of football and   13
men's and women's basketball to almost all other sports at the Division I level, a
third of the athletes surveyed said they had committed verbally to their college
teams during their junior year of high school. Except for just 2 percent who committed during their sophomore year, the rest of the athletes who committed
early did so during their senior year but before the sports' official signing dates.

While some athletes said committing early gave them a sense of relief   14
and allowed them to put the recruiting process largely behind them, others
said it placed them in the difficult position of having to make significant decisions far earlier than they would have liked, and often with little time to think
the terms over.

"It's hard to know what you're going to want in a school and make such a   15
huge life choice when you're 16," said one athlete.

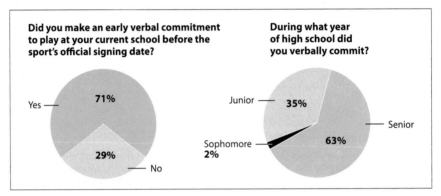

Early Commitments

Using Logical Reasoning

The structure of most texts used in research consists of a *logical progression
of general points that lead to an overall thesis or conclusion*; each point may be followed by more concrete statements of supporting evidence. The sequence of
general points is determined by logical reasoning. For instance, if you look out
a window and observe that the street and sidewalk are wet and the sky is overcast, you would most likely conclude that it had rained recently. You didn't directly observe the rain, but you can infer from past experiences with the same
evidence and apply this inference to a specific experience in the present. Although this may seem like a simpleminded illustration, it is typical of the reasoning we all engage in every day.

Or, to build on the preceding discussion of implication and inference (see
pp. 49–51):

1. Observers typically note that young boys display more physical energy in the classroom than girls do. (*statement*)
2. They are restless and find it difficult to settle down to a task. (*statement*)
3. As a result, many perform poorly in the classroom. (*inference*)
4. To make it easier for boys to learn, we propose that short periods of physical activity be included in the daily schedule. (*conclusion*)

There are two types of reasoning in formal logic—*deductive reasoning* and *inductive reasoning*, each a distinct process for arriving at defensible conclusions based on evidence.

Deductive Reasoning

Deduction means reasoning from general statements to form a logical conclusion.

The classic format for deductive reasoning is the *syllogism*, which consists of a series of carefully limited statements, or premises, pursued to a circumscribed conclusion:

All reptiles are cold-blooded. (premise)
Iguanas are reptiles. (premise)
Therefore, iguanas are cold-blooded. (conclusion)

This is a line of reasoning based on classification, that is, the creation of a generalized category based on shared traits. Members of the group we call "reptiles" have cold-bloodedness in common—in fact, cold-bloodedness is a defining trait of reptiles. Iguanas are members of the group "reptiles," which means that they must also have that shared trait.

Notice that the opening premise of a syllogism is usually a statement that the reader will be willing to grant as true without explicit proof. For example, each of the first two paragraphs of Steven Pinker's *The Blank Slate* (p. 10) begins with a (presumably) shared premise:

1. Evolution has no conscience.
2. Many creatures cooperate, nurture, and make peace.

In each case, Pinker follows his major premise with a secondary premise and a conclusion:

1. Evolution has no conscience, and (major premise)
2. If one creature hurts another to benefit itself . . . (minor premise)
3. Its descendants will come to predominate. (conclusion)

1. Many creatures cooperate, nurture, and make peace. (major premise)
2. [Human] genes are tied up in the same package, their children, so what is good for one is good for the other. (minor premise)
3. Humans in particular find comfort and joy in their families, friends, and communities. (conclusion)

Deductive reasoning follows an almost mathematical rigor; provided the premises are accepted as true and the line of reasoning valid, the conclusion must necessarily be true.

Inductive Reasoning

Induction means reasoning from specific evidence to form a general conclusion.

The conclusions reached through inductive reasoning are always conditional to some extent—that is, there's always the possibility that some new evidence may be introduced to suggest a different conclusion. Given the available evidence, you may be perfectly justified in concluding that a wet street and an overcast sky always mean that it has rained; but suppose one day, observing these conditions, you turn on the radio and learn that a water main in the area has broken overnight. That overcast sky may be coincidental, and you should be prepared to revise your original conclusion based on the new information.

Inductive reasoning uses the available evidence to construct the most likely conclusion.

Using Logic to Establish Common Ground with the Reader

Whether authors support their theses by explanation, interpretation, or persuasion—or all three—most of them use elements of inductive and deductive reasoning to prove their claims. The reader is encouraged to re-create the author's logic and view an issue as the author does. The core of the reasoning is usually *deductive*, consisting of a series of *premises* or *assumptions* that the reader shares—or can be persuaded to share—with the author. These premises often depend on *common cultural values*. That is why a thesis can lose its force over time as values change. One hundred years ago, authors could safely reason from the premise that heroism is defined by slaying the enemy in battle, or that engaging in sex before marriage warrants a girl's expulsion from polite society, or that whipping young children is an effective and acceptable punishment. Today, those statements would not have such wide credibility. In the same way, those readers who reject the concept of evolution will be indifferent to Pinker's premise that "evolution has a conscience" as well as the subsequent statements that follow from that initial assumption.

To establish common ground with the reader, the author usually needs to spell out his or her assumptions and define them so precisely that they seem not only true but inevitable. For instance, few people would challenge a claim that cruelty to animals is wrong, but there is a wide range of opinion regarding exactly what constitutes cruelty, or whether certain specific activities (the use of animals in scientific research, for instance) are or are not cruel. If inflicting pain serves some larger purpose, is it still cruel, or does "cruelty" refer only to *unnecessary* or *unjustifiable* pain? Before contesting the ethics of medical research practices, the author would have to begin by establishing a premise—in this case, a definition of "cruelty"—that the reader will also find acceptable.

Using Logic for Persuasion

To be fully convincing, the reasoning that follows from your premises must be inductive as well as deductive. It must be supported by a range of evidence, which you present, analyze, and interpret for your reader.

Logical Flaws and Fallacies

Sometimes we find it difficult to accept an author's logic:

- The reasoning may be based on an initial premise that is unconvincing or that we don't share.
- The line of reasoning that connects one premise to the next may be flawed.
- The evidence itself may be misrepresented in some way.

Logical fallacies are breakdowns in reasoning; they occur when an author draws unjustifiable conclusions from the available evidence.

Begging the Question

Initial premises are generally expressed with confidence in the reader's agreement—remember, the author assumes that the reader will accept the opening premises without explicit proof. As you read, you should be careful to identify the assumptions an author uses in constructing a line of reasoning. For example, look at the following opening premise, from the second paragraph of an unsigned editorial attacking a proposed ban on tobacco products. The editorial appeared in the magazine *National Review* in 1994.

Even though nine-tenths of smokers don't die of lung cancer, there are clearly health dangers in cigarettes, dangers so constantly warned about that smokers

are clearly aware that these dangers are the price they pay for the enjoyment
and relaxation they get from smoking.

The author claims here that because the health risks connected with smoking
have been widely publicized, the decision to smoke is rational—that is, based
on smokers' weighing their desire for "enjoyment and relaxation" against the
potential health risks. You might grant that the dangers of smoking have been
well documented and publicized, but does it necessarily follow that knowing
the risks involved ensures a rational decision? If, as has also been widely demonstrated, cigarettes are addictive, then the decision to keep smoking may *not*
be entirely rational.

The author here is committing a common logical lapse known as **begging
the question**. The assumption here—that smokers are making a rational decision—is false; yet we are expected to accept the point without question. The key
word here is "clearly"—"smokers are clearly aware"—which may persuade
the careless reader that the point has already been proven. When an author is
begging the question, you often find language that preempts the issue and discourages scrutiny: "obviously," "everyone knows," or "it goes without saying."

Sometimes, the process of begging the question is more subtle. Here, an
author arguing against euthanasia begins with a strong statement:

> Every human being has a natural inclination to continue living. Our reflexes
> and responses fit us to fight attackers, flee wild animals, and dodge out of the
> way of trucks. In our daily lives we exercise the caution and care necessary to
> protect ourselves. Our bodies are similarly structured for survival right down to
> the molecular level. . . . Euthanasia does violence to this natural goal of survival.
> It is literally acting against nature because all the processes of nature are bent
> towards the end of bodily survival.

By limiting his view of existence to purely bodily functions, J. Gay-Williams
simplifies the complex issue of euthanasia. What he omits are the key functions
of the mind, will, and emotions, which, some would say, can override the force
of the instinct toward "bodily survival" and make the choice to die. The key
here is the first sentence: "Every human being has a natural inclination to continue living." This broad assumption allows for no exceptions. *It begs the question by telling only part of the story.*

Post hoc ergo propter hoc

Post hoc ergo propter hoc means after this, therefore because of this. This
logical fallacy assumes that because one event precedes another, it must somehow cause the second event.

It is often true that one event causes a second, later event, as in the case of
rain causing the wet street you observe the next morning. But if you make that
reasoning a universal rule, you might, for instance, conclude that because
swimsuits habitually appear in your local clothing stores in May, and summer

follows in June, swimsuits somehow cause summer. It may be perfectly true that swimsuits appear in stores in May and that summer usually begins in June, but this argument fails to consider alternative explanations—in this case, that the approach of summer actually causes manufacturers to ship and retailers to display swimsuits in May, rather than the other way around; the swimsuits *anticipate*, rather than cause, summer.

False Dilemma

Most fallacies result from a tendency to oversimplify issues, to take short-cuts in dealing with complex and diverse ideas. With the **false dilemma**, an author limits the ground for disagreement by proceeding as if there are only two alternatives; everything else is ignored. Here is part of the argument presented by an author who supports euthanasia:

> Reality dictates the necessity of such laws because, for some dying patients experiencing extreme suffering, a lethal prescription is the only way to end an extended and agonizing death. Consider the terrible dilemma created when so-called passive measures fail to bring about the hoped-for death. Are we to stand helplessly by while a patient whose suicide we legally agreed to assist continues to suffer and deteriorate—perhaps even more so than before? Or do we have a moral imperative, perhaps even a legal responsibility, to not only alleviate the further suffering we have brought about but to take action to fulfill our original agreement [to withdraw life support]?

Barbara Dority has reduced the situation to a simple choice: passive doctor and patient in agony versus active doctor who brings an end to suffering, abides by morality, and keeps her promise. There are many possibilities for intervention between these two extremes, but at least at this point in her argument, the author does not acknowledge them. Through her language, she also loads the dice: does one identify with the ineffectual doctor "stand[ing] helplessly by" or with the heroic doctor with a "moral imperative" who knows how to "take action" to "alleviate . . . suffering"?

Hasty Generalization

The tendency to oversimplify, to base claims on insufficient evidence, can result in the **hasty generalization**. A convincing generalization will be supported by strong evidence, not one or two examples. And when an author does cite examples, consider whether they clearly support the claim. Gertrude Himmelfarb, for example, builds her argument about the decline of morality in our society by criticizing what she claims is an increasing tendency to be nonjudgmental. She offers the following generalization:

> Most of us are uncomfortable with the idea of making moral judgments even in our private lives, let alone with the "intrusion," as we say, of moral judgments into public affairs.

To support her generalization, she observes that public officials, such as the president's cabinet and the Surgeon General, tend to avoid using the word "immoral." In one of her two examples, the Secretary of Health and Human Services is quoted as saying:

> I don't like to put this in moral terms, but I do believe that having children out of wedlock is just wrong.

This last quotation, in itself, hardly strengthens Himmelfarb's initial point since many would consider "wrong" a judgment equivalent to "immoral." Then, on the basis of two examples, she reiterates her original claim:

> It is not only our political and cultural leaders who are prone to this failure of moral nerve. Everyone has been infected by it, to one degree or another.

The argument has moved around in a circle, from one hasty generalization to another.

Ad Hominem

An especially unpleasant kind of logical fallacy is the **ad hominem** [about the man] argument, a personal attack in which an author criticizes a prominent person who holds opposing views without considering whether the criticism is relevant to the issue. The ad hominem argument is often used in political campaigns and other well-publicized controversies.

Paul McHugh, for example, spends the first half of an argument against euthanasia demonstrating why he regards Dr. Jack Kevorkian, who facilitated a number of mercy killings, as "'certifiably' insane." McHugh compares him with other zealots who would do anything to advance their cause and finally cites "the potential for horror in an overvalued idea held by a person in high authority" such as Adolf Hitler. Certainly, the comparison is strained — Dr. Kevorkian is not "in high authority." Yet, even though McHugh now moves to a completely different basis for argument, the infamy generated by the association between Kevorkian and Hitler reverberates throughout the rest of the essay.

False Analogy

Analogy means the idea that if two things are alike in some ways they will be alike in most or all ways.

Authors often support their points by reasoning through analogies. They may compare a disputed idea or situation to some other, less controversial idea in order to reveal a parallel or an inconsistency. For instance, some might claim that the wide availability of *foreign-made consumer products* is analogous to an *infection* that threatens to destroy the health of the nation's economy. What similarities in the two situations are being exploited? What parallels can be drawn between them? In both cases, some entity (in the first case a nation, and in the second a human being) is "invaded" by something potentially harmful (such as a Japanese-made VCR or German-built car in the case of the nation, and a virus or bacterial infection in the case of the person). Analogies can provide vivid and persuasive images, but they are easily distorted when pushed too far.

In a **false analogy**, the two ideas or circumstances being compared are not actually comparable. To illustrate the pitfalls of false analogy, let's return to the editorial from the *National Review* on the proposed tobacco ban. Here's the entire paragraph:

> Even though nine-tenths of smokers don't die of lung cancer, there are clearly health dangers in cigarettes, dangers so constantly warned about that smokers are clearly aware that these dangers are the price they pay for the enjoyment and relaxation they get from smoking. As mortals we make all kinds of trade-offs between health and living. We drive automobiles knowing that forty thousand people die in them in the U.S. each year; we cross busy streets, tolerate potentially explosive gas in our homes, swim in fast-moving rivers, use electricity though it kills thousands, and eat meat and other foods that may clog our arteries and give us heart attacks and strokes. All the . . . demagoguery about the tobacco industry killing people could be applied with similar validity to the automobile industry, the electric utilities, aircraft manufacturers, the meat business, and more.

Here, the reader is asked to compare the health risks associated with smoking with those of parallel but comparatively uncontroversial activities, such as crossing a busy street. According to the author, the situations are comparable because both involve voluntarily engaging in activities known to be health risks. That similarity is used to suggest that laws *prohibiting* smoking would be logically inconsistent because we don't prohibit other risky activities like crossing streets. If potential health risks justify regulation or even prohibition, then many modern activities should, by analogy, be regulated. Yet, in spite of the risks in crossing busy streets, no one ever suggests preventing people from doing so for their own good; smoking, however, is singled out for regulation and possible prohibition. The reader can further *infer* from this line of reasoning that, since we daily engage in all kinds of risky activities, individuals in all cases should be allowed to decide without government interference which risks to take.

To determine whether an analogy is false, one need only decide whether the differences in the two situations are more significant than the similarities. In this case, we need to consider:

- if the decision to smoke and the decision to cross a busy street are *genuinely* comparable; and
- if there may be sound reasons for regulating smoking, and equally sound reasons for *not* regulating crossing the street.

Most people could not live a normal life without crossing a busy street, but the same cannot be said of smoking. In addition, if a minimal amount of caution is exercised in crossing busy streets, most people will not be injured; when injuries do occur, they're the result of accidents or some other unexpected or unusual set of events. The same is true of the other "hazards" described in the editorial (driving automobiles, using gas appliances, and so on): injuries result from their *misuse*. By contrast, cigarettes pose a serious health threat when used exactly as intended by their manufacturers; no amount of caution will protect you from the risks associated with cigarettes.

Misrepresenting Evidence

You might also object to this rejection of the smoking ban on grounds that go beyond the logic of the reasoning to the ways the evidence is presented. The author states, for instance, that 9 in 10 smokers don't die of lung cancer, implying not only that a 10 percent death rate is insignificant but that death or lung cancer is the only potential health risk connected to smoking worth mentioning. The author then tells us that "forty thousand people die" in automobiles each year in the United States. But since that number isn't presented as a percentage of all drivers on the road over the course of the year, it doesn't really address the *comparable* level of risk—those 40,000 may represent fewer than 1 percent of all drivers, which would make driving considerably less risky than smoking. Misrepresenting the evidence in this way prods the careful reader to question the author's trustworthiness and credibility.

Analyzing an Author's Logic

1. What assumptions is the author making as the basis for the thesis? Is it reasonable to assume that the reader shares these assumptions?

2. Does the text provide a logical sequence of assertions that can be easily followed and that leads to a persuasive conclusion? Are there any convincing alternatives to the author's conclusion?

3. Is the reasoning primarily inductive (deriving generalizations from probabilities established by the author) or is it deductive (deriving specific conclusions from broad assertions that are tested and proved)?

4. Are appropriate and sufficient data and examples provided?

5. Are the sources of the evidence clearly indicated?

6. Has the author lapsed into any fallacies that distort the logic and support a false conclusion?

7. What inferences does the author make from the evidence provided? Are they reasonable, or does the author attempt to manipulate the reader's perception of the evidence to suit the purposes of the thesis?

EXERCISE 6: Analyzing an Author's Logic

A. As your instructor indicates, read either the passage from *Democracy's Good Name,* by Michael Mandelbaum, or the passage from *The Death of the Grown-Up: How America's Arrested Development Is Bringing Down Western Civilization,* by Diana West. Read the passage twice.

B. On your second reading of the passage, make marginal comments about the logical processes used by the author (including deduction and induction), the presence of logical fallacies (if any), and the appropriateness and sufficiency of the evidence provided.

C. Consider these questions:

- Which sentences support the author's thesis?
- Which sentences introduce a new premise or a turn in the argument?
- Which sentences contain evidence that supports the thesis? What kind of evidence?
- Are there any flaws in the reasoning?
- How would you sum up the thesis in your own words?
- Are you convinced?

from DEMOCRACY'S GOOD NAME
Michael Mandelbaum

Michael Mandelbaum holds a named chair at the Johns Hopkins School of Advanced International Studies. He has been the author, editor, and coeditor of almost 20 books dealing with the relationship between Russia and the West and with issues of national security. He is also the author of The Meaning of Sports: Why Americans Watch Baseball, Football, and Basketball and What They See When They Do.

Topic: *Why has democracy become the dominant form of government all over the world?*

Democracy's dominant position in the world of the late twentieth and early twenty-first centuries made possible its spread by a snowballing, or "bandwagon" effect: more countries became democratic because so many other countries were already democratic. It became increasingly popular because it was already popular. This, however, begs the important question, how did democracy attain its initial popularity? Here the comparison with popular consumer brands is instructive. Leading brands achieve dominance in their particular markets in two closely related ways: by effective performance and by a good reputation. Democracy rose to a position of global dominance by the same methods.

Consumer products perform effectively when they fulfill the requirements   2
for which they are produced. Often, more than one purpose is involved, and the
relevant purposes can change over time. Some car owners value automobiles
for their price, for example, others for their appearance, still others for the
power of their engines. And in the last three decades of the twentieth century
more and more motorists came to evaluate cars on the basis of how many miles
they could be driven for each gallon of gasoline they used. Similarly, democracy's signal achievement, the tasks it performed effectively and the basis of its
appeal, has varied over the course of modern history. In the twentieth century,
the great global conflicts — World Wars I and II and the Cold War — imposed
stiff military, political, and economic tests on all forms of government. Democracy passed these tests, emerging strengthened from each conflict. Other, rival
forms of government did not. The cumulative effect of the three conflicts was to
help to elevate democratic government to the dominant position it held at the
outset of the twenty-first century.

By their performances, consumer products earn reputations, and the com-   3
panies that make them seek to publicize and enhance these reputations by having well-known and highly regarded persons testify, in paid advertisements, to
their merits. Democracy's reputation rose steadily because the most powerful,
affluent, and generally successful countries of the modern era, Great Britain in
the nineteenth century and the United States in the twentieth, were also the
two countries with the oldest and most deeply rooted traditions of democratic
governance. British and American history served as an advertising campaign for
democracy. It was as if the President of the United States, the Queen of England,
the Pope, and all Nobel laureates endorsed the same brand of automobile.

Products also become popular when they have reputations that are rele-   4
vant to potential customers, reputations that often come not from paid advertising but from observation, informal encounters, and private conversations,
known collectively as "word of mouth." A car will be attractive to a would-be
purchaser if his or her neighbor, or relative, or co-worker, or someone whose
driving habits are similar or who has roughly the same income, drives it with
satisfaction.

Students of American voting behavior have discovered that people's polit-   5
ical choices are influenced by the preferences of those they know. This is called
the "friends and neighbors" effect. Sovereign states are subject to a similar influence. They are disposed to adopt democracy at least in part to the extent that
neighboring and culturally similar political communities have already done so.
Because they seem relevant, the experiences, examples, and reputations of
friends and neighbors have particularly powerful effects.

A fool learns from experience, the saying goes, while a wise person learns   6
from other people's experiences. Both kinds of experience contributed to democracy's remarkable rise. Undemocratic political systems performed badly,

turning the people living under their rule against them; and what helped to make them unacceptable was the superior performance of democratic governments that they observed, which also made democracy attractive. Democracy attained its dominant status, therefore, principally through the example of effective performance. It spread by what is sometimes called the "demonstration effect," with the success of the democracies demonstrating their political system's virtues to others.

By the beginning of the twenty-first century, many countries, in all parts of the world, governed themselves in democratic fashion. Their number helped to make the democratic example an impressive one, and the variety of democracies meant that almost every country could find an example of democracy relevant to its own circumstances. Before there were many democracies, however, there were just a few. Before there were few, there were none. Then there was one.   7

The initial stage in democracy's ascent, the appearance of the first democratic government, was the hardest. Innovation is far more difficult than imitation. The first example of anything by definition lacks a model to copy. Indeed, before the first example of anything appears there is no guarantee that it can actually be produced and perhaps no demand for it. Innovations occur, therefore, as much by accident as by design.   8

By the twenty-first century, the spread of democracy had come to resemble a landslide, which gains momentum as it goes along and at the peak of its power sweeps everything before it.   9

from THE DEATH OF THE GROWN-UP:
HOW AMERICA'S ARRESTED DEVELOPMENT IS
BRINGING DOWN WESTERN CIVILIZATION
Diana West

Diana West is a journalist, columnist, and broadcaster (appearing on CNN). Her work has appeared in the Washington Times, *the* Washington Post, *the* Wall Street Journal, *and the* Weekly Standard. The Death of the Grown-Up *is her first book.*

> Topic: *What are the pernicious effects of increased sexual permissiveness in the twenty-first century?*

By the twenty-first century, shame and embarrassment have zero association with sexuality — or so we are endlessly, numbingly instructed — and, correspondingly, an infantile lack of behavioral restraint may be observed in everything from freak dancing, to "super-size" eating, to McMansion-building. Without the concept of obscenity, without reason for shame, the "self" in self-control sees no greater, larger, socially significant point in holding back.   1

This helps explain a lot of things, from the exponential rise in crime over 2 the past half century, to the ever-rising flood of obscenity, to the breakdown of the family. But shamelessness also sheds light on why it is that American matrons are more likely to host sex-toy parties than Tupperware parties; why the Major Leagues showcase Viagra ads at home plate; why a presidential fundraiser for GOP candidates includes a well-endowing — that is, *contributing* — porn star and pornographer; and why at grocery store checkouts shoppers can check out "hot sex tips" along with a loaf of bread. We have all learned — or, at least we have all been taught — that the mental blush is superseded by the genital tingle.

The paradox is that less restraint doesn't necessarily deliver greater free- 3 dom. That is, our sexual freedom — licentiousness — is greater, but other freedoms may actually be at risk. That's because while personal restraint once curtailed public displays of sexuality, it also made democratic society workable in the first place. Already, we recognize and accommodate a more sexually unruly populace every time we don't let our kids play in the woods behind the park, or walk home from school alone. And already, we recognize and accommodate a more sexually unruly populace every time we sanction and enable the sexual promiscuity of these same kids with the line about how "they're going to do it anyway." Meanwhile, in a Dada-esque, if governmentally official, expression of this same mind-set, state Medicaid programs were buying Viagra for convicted rapists and other high-risk sex offenders in New York, Florida, Texas, and eleven other states until the federal government intervened in 2005. But there is more to it than that.

Possible "2d Thesis"

In a shameless culture — one that speaks trippingly of condoms, semen, 4 and more — self-restraint is continually undermined, and in its absence there is political peril. As Walter Berns wrote,

> To speak in a manner that is more obviously political, there is a connection between self-restraint and shame, and therefore a connection between shame and self-government or democracy. There is, therefore, a political danger in promoting shamelessness and the fullest self-expression or indulgence. To live together requires rules and a governing of the passions, and those who are without shame will be unruly and unrulable; having lost the ability to restrain themselves by observing the rules they collectively give themselves, they will have to be ruled by others.[25]

Berns made his case against pornography in 1971, a time when it was 5 still new to the public square. A quarter century later, Harvard Law School Professor Mary Ann Glendon could comment on its now-familiar presence. In a short essay for *First Things* magazine, Glendon was addressing, with

Tocquevillian echoes, "the decline of the democratic elements in our republican experiment" — namely, judicial usurpation of powers belonging to the political process; and the ceding of powers belonging to individuals to the government. In the process, she reintroduced the subject of pornography and democracy in a newly chilling light. The sexual shamelessness and unconstrained passions that Berns said would make democracy unworkable had become what Glendon called "the democratization of vice," and she saw it as a way of pacifying the charges of the nanny state.

> When regime-threatening questions might come to mind, the oligarchs have authorized a modern form of bread and circuses, an array of new sexual freedoms to compensate for the loss of the most basic civil right of all — the right of self-government. With the democratization of vice, the man in the street can enjoy exotic pastimes once reserved to Roman emperors.[26]

This isn't to suggest that individuals don't still recognize obscenity, or that individuals don't still feel shame. But culturally speaking, obscenity is all but legally obsolete, and shame is a kind of secular sin — a symptom of "hang-ups," of repression, of inhibition, of liberty lost. This point of view, by now consensus, also sees little division between public life and private life. After all, any definition of obscenity depends on an understanding that some things belong in public and some things belong in private. "Activities that were once confined to the private scene — the 'ob-scene,' to make an etymological assumption — are now presented for our delectation and emulation on center stage," Berns wrote, three decades before the voyeuristic mania for so-called reality shows. "Nothing that is appropriate to one place is inappropriate to any other place. No act, we are to infer, no human possibility, no possible physical combination or connection, is shameful."[27]

And so, the question that defines our age becomes: When anything goes, why shouldn't anything go? There is a compelling reason why not. "Repeated exposure to indecency," Rochelle Gurstein writes, "ultimately inures people and threatens to make all of society shameless, in the precise sense that it considers nothing sacred."[28]

Nothing sacred. This condition sounds unnervingly like the one in which the average twenty-first-century youngster is raised. Nothing is sacred when preteen pop concerts feature gyrating, crotch-thrusting boy bands who, as the *New York Times* reported, "tantalized the small girls who shimmied alongside their amused mothers, some of whom could see the attraction in the beefcake."[29]

Nothing is sacred when a media executive packs off his eight-year-old to a midnight premiere of R-rated *Matrix Reloaded*. Nothing is sacred, when, in the comfort of their parents' homes, teens turn into the raunchiest voyeurs this side of a raincoat by watching MTV. Nothing is sacred when, also in the comfort of their parents' homes, teens can start a syphilis epidemic, as in an upscale Georgia suburb where public health officials treated no fewer than two hundred teenagers as young as thirteen who had been leading orgiastic lives after school (thanks to the Playboy cable TV channel, paid for by Mom and Dad) before their parents came home. The public health investigation revealed that a number of the children had upward of fifty partners.[30]

And what about cell phones and the Internet? These hyperconnecting, yet depersonalizing modes of communication give "users"—the term itself is devoid of humanity—an effectively brazen anonymity, again, courtesy parental bill-payers. Teenagers "hang out online, asking questions they might not dare to in real life," says *The New York Times Magazine* in its report on the "underage sexual revolution," a revolution noted as much for its promiscuity as for its detachment. As one sixteen-year-old from New England put it, "Being in a relationship just complicates everything. When you're a friend with benefits"—that smarmy term for sexual favors—"you go over, hook up, then play video games or something. It rocks."   9

And if it doesn't, as another teenaged boy put it to reporter Benoit Denizet-Lewis, "Who needs the hassle of dating when I've got online porn?" In a world without obscenity, in a world without shame, in a world without self-restraint, that's a good question. But is it really "sophisticated"?[31]   10

In Montgomery County, Maryland, a teenage girl came to some measure of local prominence in 2005 as the anonymous "star" of a sex education video. It was for tenth-graders and it was produced by the county school board. The video, along with a new sex-ed curriculum, was ultimately scrapped in the controversy that ensued after it came to parental attention via the Internet. I watched the sex-ed girl online, as well, with her casual attire, her long hair and long fingernails, her too-many-ringed fingers, as she chirpily instructed viewers, in modified Val-gal speak, on the proper way to don a condom. "Oral, anal, and vaginal sex," she said, grasping her demo cucumber, looking straight into the camera—quite shamelessly—all require a condom, she explained. But what else do they require? Deviant behavior? Promiscuity? A superstash of sulfa drugs in case of "breakage"? An appalling lack of self-respect? Equal parts self-deception? Sadomasochistic tendencies? Stupidity? A pattern of duplicity? A scalding hot bath?   11

But what else besides condoms *could* they require? replies the education establishment that, of course, has charge of most children. A modicum of humanity would be welcome, although that doesn't come with the systematic demystification of human intimacy to which we purposefully subject the young of the species. "When sex is a public spectacle, a human relationship has been de-   12 based into a mere animal connection," Irving Kristol wrote in 1971.[32] And when sex education is a public spectacle, the human relationship has been debased into a mere mechanical connection. Stripped of the privacy it needs to flourish, human intimacy loses not just the intimacy but also the humanness, becoming a subhuman, degrading exercise.

25. Berns, "Pornography vs. Democracy," 13.

26. Mary Ann Glendon, "The End of Democracy? A Discussion Continued," *First Things* (January 1997), 23.

27. Berns, "Pornography vs. Democracy," 10–11.

28. Gurstein, *The Repeal of Reticence*, 289.

29. Ann Powers, "Kiddie Pop: Raffi It's Not, But Just What Is It?" *New York Times*, August 21, 1999.

30. *Frontline*, "The Lost Children of Rockdale County." First broadcast 19 October 1999 by PBS. Produced by Rachel Dretzin Goodman and Barak Goodman.

31. Denizet-Lewis, "Friends, Friends with Benefits and the Benefits of the Local Mall."

32. Kristol, *On the Democratic Idea in America*, 37.

West is argumentative and persuasive
Audience is probably an older generation since she seems to a look down on most teens because of their "lack of self-control"
She feels so strongly, she disregards some of the important aspects of sex-ed, or cell phones and internet in today's world. She says it affects government but doesn't give examples. Instead she focuses on what younger people and their parents are doing ~~to~~ wrong.

Part II

PRESENTING SOURCES TO OTHERS

Now, you are making the transition from reader to writer. To use what you have learned from your reading and to write about your sources in an essay, you must next learn about basic methods of *presenting sources* fairly and accurately.

- Chapter 2 shows you how to present a source through summary: the technique of expressing a group of related ideas briefly yet completely.
- Chapter 3 describes the rules to follow when you use quotation: the acknowledgment that a source, not yourself, is responsible for the precise language, as well as the ideas, contained in quoted text.
- Chapter 4 gives you practice in paraphrase: the method of expressing the ideas of others in your own words.

Summary, quotation, and paraphrase are the building blocks of writing from sources. They enable you to demonstrate your understanding of the source while integrating these ideas into your own work. They also help you to avoid the dishonest "borrowings," called *plagiarism*, that occur when the reader cannot tell who wrote what and so gives you credit for work that you did not do.

When you write, you must make it clear to your reader whether a specific idea, phrase, sentence, or group of sentences is the product of your own work or that of another. Whether you summarize, quote, or paraphrase, you must always *acknowledge*, or *document*, your source with a clear *citation* of the author's name.

·2·
Summarizing Sources

When you annotate a text, when you ask yourself questions about its contents, you are helping yourself to understand what you are reading. When you write a summary, you are *recording* your understanding for your own information. When you include the summary in an essay of your own, you are *reporting* your understanding to your reader. In fact, you have already been using summary in your marginal notes when you express an author's idea in a phrase or sentence.

Summarizing a source usually means *condensing ideas or information*. You are not expected to include every repetition and detail. Rather, you extract only those points that seem important—the main ideas, which in the original text may have been interwoven with less important material. A summary of several pages can sometimes be as brief as one sentence.

When writing a brief summary, you should add nothing new to the material in the source, nor should you change the emphasis or provide any new interpretation or evaluation. For the sake of clarity and coherence, you may rearrange the order of the ideas; however, as summarizer, you should strive to remain in the background.

The writer of a research essay depends on the brief summary as a means of referring to source materials. When you discuss another piece of writing, you generally have to summarize the contents briefly to establish for your reader the ideas that you intend to analyze. Summary also enables you to present and explain the relevance of a number of sources all dealing with the same subject.

Summarizing a Paragraph

Before you can begin to summarize a short text—a paragraph, for example—you must read the passage carefully and understand the significance of each idea and how it is linked to the other ideas. Sometimes, the paragraph will contain a series of examples that can be summarized inductively.

The following paragraph can be summarized adequately by one of its own sentences. Which one?

It is often remarked that science has increasingly removed man from a position at the center of the universe. Once upon a time the earth was thought to be the center and the gods were thought to be in close touch with the daily actions of humans. It was not stupid to imagine the earth was at the center, because, one might think, if the earth were moving around the sun, and if you threw a ball vertically upward, it would seem the ball should come down a few feet away from you. Nevertheless, slowly, over many centuries, through the work of Copernicus, Galileo, and many others, we have mostly come to believe that we live on a typical planet orbiting a typical star in a typical galaxy, and indeed that no place in the universe is special.

summarizing sentence?

summarizing sentence?

GORDON KANE, from "Are We the Center of the Universe?"

The first sentence is a broader generalization and a more comprehensive summary than the last sentence. Even when you find a strong sentence that suggests the main idea of the paragraph, you often need to tinker with that sentence, expanding its meaning by giving the language a more general focus. Here is a paragraph in which no one sentence is broad enough to sum up the main idea, but which contains a scattering of useful phrases:

In a discussion [with] a class of teachers, I once said that I liked some of the kids in my class much more than others and that, without saying which ones I liked best, I had told them so. After all, this is something that children know, whatever we tell them; it is futile to lie about it. Naturally, these teachers were horrified. "What a terrible thing to say!" one said. "I love all the children in my class exactly the same." Nonsense; a teacher who says this is lying, to herself or to others, and probably doesn't like any of the children very much. Not that there is anything wrong with that; plenty of adults don't like children, and there is no reason why they should. But the trouble is that they feel they should, which makes them feel guilty, which makes them feel resentful, which in turn makes them try to work off their guilt with indulgence and their resentment with subtle cruelties — cruelties of a kind that can be seen in many classrooms. Above all, it makes them put on the phony, syrupy, sickening voice and manner, and the fake smiles and forced, bright laughter that children see so much of in school, and rightly resent and hate.

JOHN HOLT, from *How Children Fail*

Here, you might begin by combining key phrases: "a teacher who says" that she "love[s] all the children" "is lying, to herself or to others," and makes herself and the children "feel resentful." However, this kind of summarizing sentence resembles a patchwork, with the words and phrasing pulled straight out of the original. Even if you acknowledged the borrowings, by using quotation marks, as above, you would still be left with a weak sentence that is neither yours nor the author's. It is far better to construct an entirely new sentence of your own, such as this one:

> In John Holt's view, although it is only natural for teachers to prefer some students to others, many teachers cannot accept their failure to like all equally well and express their inadequacy and dissatisfaction in ways that are harmful to the children.

Finally, some paragraphs give you no starting point at all for the summary and force you to write an entirely new generalization. How would you summarize this paragraph?

> When we pick up our newspaper at breakfast, we expect — we even demand — that it bring us momentous events since the night before. We turn on the car radio as we drive to work and expect "news" to have occurred since the morning newspaper went to press. Returning in the evening, we expect our house not only to shelter us, to keep us warm in winter and cool in summer, but to relax us, to dignify us, to encompass us with soft music and interesting hobbies, to be a playground, a theater, and a bar. We expect our two-week vacation to be romantic, exotic, cheap, and effortless. We expect a faraway atmosphere if we go to a nearby place; and we expect everything to be relaxing, sanitary, and Americanized if we go to a faraway place. We expect new heroes every season, a literary masterpiece every month, a dramatic spectacular every week, a rare sensation every night. We expect everybody to feel free to disagree, yet we expect everybody to be loyal, not to rock the boat or to take the Fifth Amendment. We expect everybody to believe deeply in his religion, yet not to think less of others for not believing. We expect our nation to be strong and great and vast and varied and prepared for every challenge; yet we expect our "national purpose" to be clear and simple, something to give direction to the lives of nearly two hundred million people and yet can be bought in a paperback at the corner drugstore for a dollar.

DANIEL BOORSTIN, from *The Americans: The National Experience*

What holds this paragraph together? Boorstin's set of examples begins by taking us through the passage of time—a day, the seasons of the year (with holidays)—and expands from events to entertainment to civil liberties. The word *expect* ties them together. Are we expecting everyone to be exactly like us? Do we exist simply to consume? Are we insisting on perfection? We expect more than we can possibly get, Boorstin tells us, more through his barbed tone than through any explicit statement. A summary will convey the futility of those expectations:

> Daniel Boorstin points out that Americans expect to have an entertaining, safe, comfortable, and ethical life in a rich and complex country guided by clear-sighted political leadership; but Boorstin's tone makes it clear that such expectations are unrealistic and can never be fulfilled.

Notice that this summarizing sentence includes Boorstin's name—twice. Mentioning the author's name emphasizes that what you are summarizing is not your own work. By making it clear who is responsible for what, you are avoiding any possibility of *plagiarizing*—borrowing from your source without acknowledgment.

Summarizing a Brief Passage

1. Find a summarizing sentence within the passage (and, if you are using it in your own essay, put it in quotation marks); *or*
2. Combine elements within the passage into a new summarizing sentence; *or*
3. Write your own summarizing sentence.
4. Cite the author's name somewhere in the summary, and use quotation marks around any borrowed phrases.

EXERCISE 7: Summarizing a Paragraph

As your instructor indicates, summarize one or more of the following paragraphs by doing *one* of three things:

1. Underline a sentence that will serve as a comprehensive summary; *or*
2. Combine existing phrases; then rewrite the sentence, based on these phrases, to create a comprehensive summary; *or*
3. Invent a new generalization to provide a comprehensive summary.

Be prepared to explain your summary in class discussion.

A. The neurotic individual may have had some special vulnerability as an infant. Perhaps he was ill a great deal and was given care that singled him out from other children. Perhaps he walked or talked much later — or earlier — than children were expected to, and this evoked unusual treatment. The child whose misshapen feet must be put in casts or the sickly little boy who never can play ball may get out of step with his age mates and with the expectations parents and other adults have about children. Or a child may be very unusually placed in his family. He may be the only boy with six sisters, or a tiny child born between two lusty sets of twins. Or the source of the child's difficulties may be a series of events that deeply affected his relations to people — the death of his mother at the birth of the next child or the prolonged illness or absence of his father. Or a series of coincidences — an accident to a parent, moving to a new town and a severe fright — taken together may alter the child's relationship to the world.

MARGARET MEAD, from *Some Personal Views*

B. We humans have been eating animals as long as we have lived on this earth. Humans may not need to eat meat in order to survive, yet doing so is part of our evolutionary heritage, reflected in the design of our teeth and the structure of our digestion. Eating meat helped make us what we are, in a social and biological sense. Under the pressure of the hunt, the human brain grew in size and complexity, and around the fire where the meat was cooked, human culture first flourished. Granting rights to animals may lift us up from the brutal world of predation, but it will entail the sacrifice of part of our identity — our own animality.

MICHAEL POLLAN, from *An Animal's Place*

C. Are we saving enough? The standard economic view is that at any given time a person has well-defined preferences that stipulate whether he or she will choose to save some portion of a monthly paycheck or spend it all. In other words, people know exactly what they want and what they do not want. In that sense, the savings of any given household is a direct outcome of its members' personal preferences. Economists see these preferences as the sacrosanct realm of the individual. If someone is in debt up to the eyeballs, it is because that person prefers to discount future consumption very heavily relative to current consumption. One may believe that, for whatever reason, it is much better to buy the new car and new clothes now than to worry about the future, if it ever shows up. Many economists believe, then, that savings is a matter of individual choice, and questions about "too much" or "too little" have a moral punch that is not relevant to the decision making of rational people. Who are we to question what this or that person wants out of life?

RONALD T. WILCOX, from *Whatever Happened to Thrift?*
Why Americans Don't Save and What to Do about It

D. There is a lively debate among social scientists about whether increased virtual communication — stretching across space and making distance seem almost arbitrary — has actually brought families closer, especially those with festering emotional wounds or ongoing feuds. Relatives who might not be speaking to or seeing members of their family regularly can be more willing to send them e-mail or text messages and may, therefore, be in more frequent contact. Children today might have regular conversations with their grandparents on the phone or via e-mail, whereas a generation ago the phone call would have been a formal and infrequent event. Still, about 80 percent of communication is nonverbal, some psychologists say, and face-to-face interactions are crucial to forming and sustaining intimate relationships. Body language, facial expressions, tears, giggles, smiles, raised eyebrows, winks; these are all important cues to the many layers of communication. (Sometimes, of course, it's better not to see a frown of disapproval, a furrowed brow or rolling eyes.) "I have the greatest concerns as a therapist that, as the culture continues to advance, we're not attending to the social ties," said Teresa B. Rose, a psychologist in Kansas City. "If most things are mechanical or one step removed from the actual person, then all of those things that are so important for human attachment — like touch and closeness and being able to see the other person — I think that something very important is lost."

SARAH KERSHAW, from "Enough of the Hills and Woods,
Can I Send Grandma an E-Card?" *New York Times*

E. Family love indeed subverts the ideal of what we should feel for every soul in the world. Moral philosophers play with a hypothetical dilemma in which people can run through the left door of a burning building to save some number of children or through the right door to save their own child. If you are a parent, ponder this question: is there *any* number of children that would lead you to pick the left door? Indeed, all of us reveal our preference with our pocketbooks when we spend money on trifles for our own children (a bicycle, orthodontics, an education at a private school or university) instead of saving the lives of unrelated children in the developing world by donating the money to charity. Similarly, the practice of parents bequeathing their wealth to their children is one of the steepest impediments to an economically egalitarian society. Yet few people would allow the government to confiscate 100 percent of their estate, because most people see

their children as an extension of themselves and thus as the proper benefi-
ciaries of their lifelong striving.

STEVEN PINKER, from *The Blank Slate:
The Modern Denial of Human Nature*

F. Three concepts in particular explain the resistance of Arab culture to
Western-style reform. First, by contrast to the West, in the Arab world the
self is never seen as divided. Whereas in the West we imagine ourselves able
to take on multiple, even contradictory roles — as when an official gives
support to a law with which he personally disagrees — to Arabs this self-
segmentation runs contrary to the idea of a person as a unified whole. Second, doubt about fundamental beliefs has always been equated with
unbelief and the threat of chaos. Arabs are, therefore, deeply afraid that un-
certainty over religious fundamentals will lead to that most dreaded of
ends, the breakdown of the community of believers. Third, political institutions have never been separated from the individuals connected with them.
Indeed, personal attachments, whether to a political leader, spiritual guide,
or close relative — focus not on the settled expectations of position but on
the constantly shifting networks of obligation through which each actor
seeks to negotiate an advantageous connection. Taken together, these factors form a cultural fabric of enormous resilience and durability, but one
whose very success also accounts for its resistance to Western ways of viewing the world.

LAWRENCE ROSEN, from "What We Got Wrong," *The American Scholar*

Summarizing an Article

When you want to summarize a longer text in a few sentences, how do you
judge which points are important and which are not? Some texts, especially
newspaper articles, have rambling structures and short paragraphs, so you
don't even have fully developed paragraphs in which to search for summarizing topic sentences. Are there any standard procedures to help you decide
which points to summarize?

Summarizing an Article

1. Read the entire article more than once and note down key points.
2. Ask yourself why the article was written and published.
3. Look for repetitions of and variations on the same idea.

Read "Holdup Man Tells Detectives How to Do It," by Selwyn Raab, a former crime reporter for the *New York Times,* where this article appeared. Some of the main points are indicated in the margins. Would you add any? How would you turn these notes into a summary?

HOLDUP MAN TELLS DETECTIVES HOW TO DO IT

Selwyn Raab

conceals face
peers out

His face hidden by a shabby tan coat, the career holdup man peeked out at his audience of detectives and then proceeded to lecture them on how easy it was to succeed at his trade in New York.   1

nothing the cops can do

"I don't think there's much any individual police officer can do," the guest lecturer told 50 detectives yesterday at an unusual crime seminar sponsored by the Police Department. "Once I knew what the police officer on the beat was up to I wasn't much concerned about the cops."   2

won't give full name

police couldn't catch him

The holdup man, who identified himself only as "Nick," is serving a prison term of 6 to 13 years. He said his most serious arrest occurred after he was shot three times by a supermarket manager — not in any encounter with the police.   3

strengthen deterrent

When asked by a detective taking a course in robbery investigations what the best deterrent would be against gunmen like himself, Nick replied crisply: "Stiffer sentences."   4

After being seriously wounded in his last robbery attempt, Nick said he decided it was time to retire.   5

"I'm close to 40 and not getting any younger," he explained. "I just don't want to spend any more time in jail."   6

Nick also offered the detectives some tips on how robbers pick their targets and make their getaways in the city.   7

no disguise
tries to be anonymous

Except for wearing a hat, Nick said he affected no disguise. "I usually picked a store in a different neighborhood or in another borough where I was unknown."   8

casual preparation

Leads on places to hold up usually came from other criminals or from employees. There were no elaborate plannings or "casings," he said, adding: 9

fear of getting shot

"I liked supermarkets because there's always a lot of cash around. Uniformed guards didn't deter me because they're not armed, they usually just have sticks. It's better to pick a busy area rather than the suburbs. The chances of someone noticing you are greater in residential or suburban areas."   10

don't stand out

The detectives, sitting at desks with notepaper in front of them, were rookies as well as veterans. Besides city detectives, the audience included policemen from the Transit Authority, the Housing Authority, the Yonkers Police Department and from Seattle.   11 *avoid the cops*

They listened carefully as Nick outlined how he or a confederate would inspect the area for signs of uniformed or plainclothes police officers.

12

stay concealed

The retired robber said he had preferred supermarkets or stores with large window advertisements or displays because these materials prevented him from being seen by passers-by on the street.

13

"I was always a little nervous or apprehensive before a job," he continued. "But once you're inside and aware of the reaction of the people and you know the possibilities then your confidence comes back."

14

disappear into the crowd

Nick said he always made his escape in a car and he preferred heavily trafficked roads because it made the getaway vehicle less conspicuous than on little used side streets.

15

guns easy to get

In New York, cheap handguns were selling from $15 to $70, he told the detectives. Such weapons as shotguns or automatic rifles, Nick said, could be rented for about $100 an hour.

16

Nick said he had been a holdup man since the age of 20 and had committed about 30 "jobs," but was uncertain of the exact number. The biggest robbery he had participated in netted a total of $8,000, and overall he got about $30,000 in his criminal activities.

17

motive = self-aggrandizement

Asked why he went back to robbing after his first arrest, Nick said: "I wanted whisky, women and big autos. Like most who rob I was not socially accepted. Big money elevates you above the people you think are looking down on you."

18

short sentence = poor deterrent

Short prison sentences, for first arrests, Nick asserted, probably do little to discourage holdup men. "I see them laying up in jail and it doesn't make any difference," he said. "They just go ahead planning the next one in a different way."

19

not violent

During his "on-and-off" criminal career, Nick said he had never fired any of the guns he carried.

20

stays concealed

After his one-hour appearance as guest lecturer, Nick, his face still covered by his coat, was escorted out of the classroom back to his cell at an undisclosed prison.

21

1. Read the entire article more than once and note down key points.

Pay attention to *minor facts and interesting details*. Notice that most of the marginal notes in this article support and illuminate the central ideas. For example, the fact that Nick chose to hide his face during and after his "lecture" hardly seems worth considering and would never by itself be regarded as crucial. But taken together with some of Nick's remarks, that minor fact helps you to recognize a key point of the article: The robber's reliance on *anonymity* enables him to commit a successful crime; Nick may at some point wish to resume his profession despite his "retirement."

2. Ask yourself why the article was written and published.

What does the newspaper want its readers to learn? A news article's purpose is frequently twofold—to describe an event and to suggest the event's significance—and so it is easy to confuse the *facts* being recorded with the underlying *reasons* for recording them. Here are two one-sentence summaries of the article that are both off the mark because they concentrate too heavily on the event:

> Nick, a convicted retired criminal, was guest speaker at a police seminar
> and told detectives how robbers pick their targets and make their getaways
> in New York.

> Nick, after committing thirty robberies, suggested to detectives some
> possible methods of thwarting future robberies.

Both writers seem too concerned with Nick's colorful history and the peculiarity of his helping the police at all. They ignore the significance of what Nick was actually saying. The second summary—by emphasizing the phrase "thwarting future robberies"—is misleading and almost contradicts the point of the article; in fact, Nick is really suggesting that the police will continue to be ineffectual.

A news article can also mislead you into thinking that a headline is a summary: the headline "Holdup Man Tells Detectives How to Do It" does not summarize the material in the article, but, because it is broad and vague, it "sounds" good. What, for example, is meant by the "it" of the headline—robbery or detection?

3. Look for repetitions of and variations on the same idea.

There is one concrete point that Selwyn Raab and his readers and the police and Nick himself are all interested in: *ways of preventing criminals from committing crimes.* Not only are we told again and again about Nick's contempt for the police, but we are also given his flat statement that only fear of imprisonment ("stiffer sentences") will deter a hardened criminal.

A brief summary of this article, then, would mention *tougher sentencing as a way of preventing crime.* But, in addition, the theme of *the criminal's need for anonymity* ought, if possible, to be incorporated into a complete summary. In Nick's opinion, his career has been relatively successful because he has managed to appear normal and blend into the crowd. The primary and secondary ideas can be joined in a summary like this one:

> An article in the *New York Times* describes Nick, the successful robber, who
> observes with contempt that the police have rarely been able to penetrate

his "anonymous" disguise. Nick argues that the presence of police will not deter most experienced criminals and that only "stiffer sentences" will prevent crime.

EXERCISE 8: Summarizing an Article

A.   Carefully read "How Dumb Do They Think We Are?" by Jonathan Malesic, twice.

B.   Determine the article's purpose and make notes of the points that the author emphasizes.

C.   Then write a comprehensive summary in two or three sentences.

HOW DUMB DO THEY THINK WE ARE?
Jonathan Malesic

Jonathan Malesic presently teaches theology at Kings College in Wilkes-Barre, Pennsylvania, and was formerly in the philosophy department at James Madison University in Virginia. His first book, Secret Faith in the Public Square: An Argument for the Concealment of Christian Identity, *was published in 2009. The three student evaluators whose comments appear on the Web gave him high marks for "helpfulness" and "clarity" and average marks for "easiness." This article appeared in the* Chronicle of Higher Education.

It happened more times last year than I can even recall, but I clearly re-mem-ber the first time. I was grading a paper and came across a sentence that surprised me. It just didn't fit in with what I had read up to that point. I was surprised partly because the sentence made proper use of the word "implacable," whereas in the paragraph before, the student had used an abstract noun ending in "-ship" as a verb. Twice. 1

I read more and found more seismic shifts in the writing style. Magisterial paragraphs were followed by inane ones; syllogisms gave way to circular logic, and back again. I picked one suspect sentence, entered it into an Internet search engine, and in milliseconds, I found it — word for word, punctuation mark for punctuation mark. It turned out much of the rest of the paper had been plagia-rized from the same document. 2

I deduced that the student had also performed a "find-and-replace" function on one key word in the document to make paragraphs that were on a different topic seem as if they were on the topic I had assigned. 3

Did this cheeky twerp think I wouldn't notice? For an hour after I found the   4
paper's origin, I could only sit in my office and stew, comparing the paper to the
Internet version again and again and determining that, at most, one paragraph
was entirely original to the student.

My anger then turned into self-questioning. What did I do to this student   5
to deserve such an insult? How had I failed as a teacher, to make the student
think that stealing someone else's words was acceptable?

Since I was a new assistant professor, I sought my colleagues' advice about   6
the paper. They sympathized, they shared my indignation, but as I calmed
down, they also told me that I shouldn't take it personally. Apparently I would be
seeing cases like this again. Senior colleagues gave matter-of-fact appraisals of
just how many plagiarized papers I could expect in a given class of 25 students.

They were right. Throughout the year, I saw plagiarized papers in nearly   7
every stack I read. At times, I started to think that maybe every paper was
plagiarized.

My extreme and irrational reaction to that first plagiarized paper was partly   8
the result of my having been unprepared for it. I had seen a case or two of cheating when I was a teaching assistant, but it didn't seem like a personal affront. After all, it wasn't my class. Cheating was the professor's problem, so I felt no need
to look for explanations.

There are probably dozens of reasons why some students plagiarize.   9
They're lazy. They're afraid. They perceive plagiarism to be standard practice at
their college. They believe that any means to a good grade are legitimate.

What's most astounding, though — and most insulting — is that students   10
plagiarize in ways that are so easy to catch. They cut and paste without thinking
to cover their tracks. They copy from the most obvious sources possible. They
find and replace words and then do not proofread to ensure clarity.

Do they think we're stupid? If they're going to plagiarize, why can't they at   11
least do it in a way that acknowledges that their audience is intelligent? Don't
they know what the big framed diplomas on our walls mean?

I think that student plagiarists are often poor plagiarists because they don't   12
realize that it's even possible to be a savvy reader, that it's possible to read a text
that has been cobbled together from multiple sources and determine where
one source's contribution ends and another's begins. Those students don't pay
attention to diction, syntax, or tone when they read, so they can't possibly imagine that someone else might.

If that is, in fact, what goes on (or, rather, doesn't go on) in our students'   13
minds when they are copying material from the Internet, then we may have run
into an example of a broad human tendency to take our individual selves as the
standard by which we judge everyone else.

The philosopher Ludwig Feuerbach noticed that tendency, explaining   14
the difference between two bad poets like this: "He who, having written a
bad poem, knows it to be bad, is in his intelligence, and therefore in his nature,
not so limited as he who, having written a bad poem, admires it and thinks
it good."

If Feuerbach is right, then by showing our students what good work is,   15
helping them discover what makes it good work, and explaining how we can
very clearly tell the difference between good and bad work, or the relative
differences between two authors, we are not only improving their minds,
but improving their "natures." That is a lofty word, one that even humanities
professors (maybe especially humanities professors) hesitate to utter. But
maybe we can agree at least that we can try to broaden students' perspectives and raise their standards, so that they can be better critics — and better
self-critics.

Students can't entirely be blamed for the narrow-mindedness they come   16
to college with, but they absolutely can be blamed for persisting in it in the face
of their colleges' best efforts to expand their horizons.

Plagiarism is, therefore, not only dishonest; it is also a sign of students'   17
shamefully entrenched satisfaction with their limitations.

I no longer see cases of blatant plagiarism as personal insults. They are, in-   18
stead, the pathetic bleats of students who think they know enough — maybe all
there really is to know — about how to read and think and write.

The paradox of plagiarism is that in order to be really good at it, you need   19
precisely the reading and writing skills that ought to render plagiarism unnecessary. If my students could recognize what differentiates their own writing
styles from those of authors whose work they find online, then they should also
be able to perform with ease all the tasks I require for their essay assignments:
to read texts carefully, to determine the relative importance of textual evidence,
to formulate a clear thesis, and to defend it convincingly.

I'll grant that my hypothesis that students plagiarize so obviously be-   20
cause they are unable to imagine someone noticing does not cover all cases.
I have caught even students whose other work and class participation ex-
hibit exactly the skills that ought to obviate the perceived need to plagiarize.
Maybe I should be insulted by those students: They know better and still try to
fool me.

I believe in relentlessly exercising my students' critical abilities, but I also   21
believe in punishing plagiarism. A student who plagiarizes refuses to be educated. There shouldn't be room in my classroom for that kind of student. Indeed,
that person is not really a student at all.

Summarizing a Complex Essay

Sometimes, you need to summarize a reading containing a number of complex and abstract ideas, a reading that may be disorganized and therefore difficult to understand and condense. The best way to prepare for such a summary is to *make marginal notes* and then write a list with each key point expressed in a sentence.

Here is an essay by Bertrand Russell, a distinguished British mathematician and philosopher of the early twentieth century. The essay is annotated with marginal notes and followed by a preliminary list of key ideas, a statement of Russell's thesis, and the final summary.

Russell's essay is difficult, so be sure to read it slowly, and more than once. If you get confused at any point, try referring to the list of notes that follows; but be sure to *go back to the essay* after you have identified and understood each numbered point.

First Stage: Marginal Notes

THE SOCIAL RESPONSIBILITY OF SCIENTISTS
Bertrand Russell

Bertrand Russell was a British philosopher, logician, and social critic whose interests ranged from mathematics to education. Winner of the Nobel Prize for literature in 1950, Russell was regarded as a controversial figure, in part because of his activities as an anti-war protester.

responsibility for how discoveries are used?

some scientists: no

scientists as public-spirited citizens

some scientists work in the public interest; others work for the government

Science, ever since it first existed, has had important effects in matters that lie outside the purview of pure science. Men of science have differed as to their responsibility for such effects. Some have said that the function of the scientist in society is to supply knowledge, and that he need not concern himself with the use to which this knowledge is put. I do not think that this view is tenable, especially in our age. The scientist is also a citizen; and citizens who have any special skill have a public duty to see, as far as they can, that their skill is utilized in accordance with the public interest. Historically, the functions of the scientist in public life have generally been recognized. The Royal Society was founded by Charles II as an antidote to "fanaticism" which had plunged England into a long period of civil strife. The scientists of that time did not hesitate to speak out on public issues, such as religious toleration and the folly of prosecutions for witchcraft. But although science has, in various ways at various times, favored what may be called a humanitarian outlook, it has from the first had an intimate and sinister connection with war. Archimedes sold his skill to the

1
2

3

4

Tyrant of Syracuse for use against the Romans; Leonardo secured a salary from the Duke of Milan for his skill in the art of fortification; and Galileo got employment under the Grand Duke of Tuscany because he could calculate the trajectories of projectiles. In the French Revolution the scientists who were not guillotined were set to making new explosives, but Lavoisier was not spared, because he was only discovering hydrogen which, in those days, was not a weapon of war. There have been some honorable exceptions to the subservience of scientists to warmongers. During the Crimean War the British government consulted Faraday as to the feasibility of attack by poisonous gases. Faraday replied that it was entirely feasible, but that it was inhuman and he would have nothing to do with it.

influence of the media

Modern democracy and modern methods of publicity have made the problem of affecting public opinion quite different from what it used to be. The knowledge that the public possesses on any important issue is derived from vast and powerful organizations: the press, radio, and, above all, television. The 5

governments lack information

knowledge that governments possess is more limited. They are too busy to search out the facts for themselves, and consequently they know only what their underlings think good for them unless there is such a powerful movement in a different sense that politicians cannot ignore it. Facts which ought to 6 guide the decisions of statesmen — for instance, as to the possible lethal qualities of fallout — do not acquire their due importance if they remain buried in scientific journals. They acquire their due importance only when they become known to so many voters that they affect the course of the elections. In

special interests suppress information

general, there is an opposition to widespread publicity for such facts. This opposition springs from various sources, some sinister, some comparatively respectable. At the bottom of the moral scale there is the financial interest of the 7 various industries connected with armaments. Then there are various effects of a somewhat thoughtless patriotism, which believes in secrecy and in what is called "toughness." But perhaps more important than either of these is the un-

public is squeamish

pleasantness of the facts, which makes the general public turn aside to pleasanter topics such as divorces and murders. The consequence is that what 8 ought to be known widely throughout the general public will not be known unless great efforts are made by disinterested persons to see that the information reaches the minds and hearts of vast numbers of people. I do not think this work can be successfully accomplished except by the help of men of sci-

scientists have a public duty to speak

ence. They, alone, can speak with the authority that is necessary to combat the misleading statements of those scientists who have permitted themselves to 9 become merchants of death. If disinterested scientists do not speak out, the others will succeed in conveying a distorted impression, not only to the public but also to the politicians.

scientific research depends on funding

It must be admitted that there are obstacles to individual action in our age which did not exist at earlier times. Galileo could make his own telescope. But once when I was talking with a very famous astronomer he explained that the telescope upon which his work depended owed its existence to the benefaction of enormously rich men, and, if he had not stood well with them, his astronomical discoveries would have been impossible. More frequently, a scientist only acquires access to enormously expensive equipment if he stands well with the government of his country. He knows that if he adopts a rebellious attitude he and his family are likely to perish along with the rest of civilized mankind. It is a tragic dilemma, and I do not think that one should censure a man whatever his decision; but I do think — and I think men of science should realize — that unless something rather drastic is done under the leadership or through the inspiration of some part of the scientific world, the human race, like the Gadarene swine, will rush down a steep place to destruction in blind ignorance of the fate that scientific skill has prepared for it.

10

It is impossible in the modern world for a man of science to say with any honesty, "My business is to provide knowledge, and what use is made of the knowledge is not my responsibility." The knowledge that a man of science provides may fall into the hands of men or institutions devoted to utterly unworthy objects. I do not suggest that a man of science, or even a large body of men of science, can altogether prevent this, but they can diminish the magnitude of the evil.

support more benign research

There is another direction in which men of science can attempt to provide leadership. They can suggest and urge in many ways the value of those branches of science of which the important and practical uses are beneficial and not harmful. Consider what might be done if the money at present spent on armaments were spent on increasing and distributing the food supply of the world and diminishing the population pressure. In a few decades, poverty and malnutrition, which now afflict more than half the population of the globe, could be ended. But at present almost all the governments of great states consider that it is better to spend money on killing foreigners than on keeping their own subjects alive. Possibilities of a hopeful sort in whatever field can best be worked out and stated authoritatively by men of science; and, since they can do this work better than others, it is part of their duty to do it.

11

As the world becomes more technically unified, life in an ivory tower becomes increasingly impossible. Not only so; the man who stands out against the powerful organizations which control most of human activity is apt to find himself no longer in the ivory tower, with a wide outlook over a sunny landscape, but in the dark and subterranean dungeon upon which the ivory tower was erected. To risk such a habitation demands courage. It will not be necessary to inhabit the dungeon if there are many who are willing to risk it, for everybody

SUMMARIZING A COMPLEX ESSAY

Speaking out together lessens the risk

knows that the modern world depends upon scientists, and, if they are insistent, they must be listened to. We have it in our power to make a good world; and, therefore, with whatever labor and risk, we must make it.   12

Second Stage: List of Notes

1. Should scientists try to influence the way their discoveries are used?

2. One point of view: the scientist's role is to make the discovery; what happens afterward is not his concern.

3. Russell's point of view: scientists are like any other knowledgeable and public-spirited people; they must make sure that the products of their knowledge work for, not against, society.

4. In the past, some scientists have made public their views on controversial issues like freedom of religion; others have been servants of the war machine.

5. The power to inform and influence the public is now controlled by the news media.

6. Government officials are too busy to be well informed; subordinates feed them only enough information to get them reelected.

7. It is in the interests of various groups, ranging from weapons makers to patriots, to limit the amount of scientific information that the public receives.

8. The public is reluctant to listen to distasteful news.

9. Since the public deserves to hear the truth, scientists, who are respected for their knowledge and who belong to no party or faction, ought to do more to provide the public with information about the potentially lethal consequences of their discoveries. By doing so, they will correct the distortions of those scientists who have allied themselves with warmongers.

10. It is very difficult for scientists to speak out since they depend on government and business interests to finance their work.

11. While scientists cannot entirely stop others from using some of their discoveries for antisocial purposes, they can support other, more constructive kinds of research.

12. Speaking out is worth the risk of incurring the displeasure of powerful people; since the work of scientists is so vital, the risk isn't too great, especially if they act together.

Third Stage: Establish a Thesis

> Russell's thesis: Contrary to the self-interested arguments of many scientists and other groups, scientists have a social responsibility to make sure that their work is used for, not against, the benefit of humanity.

Fourth Stage: Summary

two views of the scientists' responsibility = framework

obstacles to scientific freedom of speech

the need to act despite obstacles = thesis

(1) Some scientists, as well as other groups, consider that they need not influence the way in which their discoveries are used. (2) However, Bertrand Russell, in "The Social Responsibility of Scientists," believes that scientists have a responsibility to make sure that their work is used for, not against, the benefit of humanity. (3) In modern times, he argues, it has been especially difficult for concerned scientists to speak out because (a) many powerful groups prefer to limit and distort what the public is told, (b) because government officials are too busy to be thoroughly informed, (c) because scientists depend on the financial support of business and government, and (d) because the public itself is reluctant to hear distasteful news. (4) Nevertheless, Russell maintains that scientists have the knowledge and the prestige to command public attention, and their work is too vital for their voices to be suppressed. (5) If they act together, they can warn us if their work is likely to be used for an antisocial purpose and, at least, they can propose less destructive alternatives.

This summary of Russell's essay is not a simple compilation of phrases taken from the text, nor a collection of topic sentences, one from each paragraph. Rather, it is a clear, coherent, and unified summary of Russell's ideas, expressed in the writer's own voice and words.

A *framework* is immediately established in the first two sentences of the summary, which contrast the two alternative views of the scientist's responsibility. The third sentence, which describes the four obstacles to scientific freedom of speech, illustrates the *rearrangement of ideas* that is characteristic of summary. While reviewing the list of notes, the summarizer has noticed that points 6, 7, 8, and 10 each refer to a reason why scientific truth may be suppressed; she has therefore brought them together and lined them up in a parallel construction based on the repeated word "because." Finally, the last two sentences contain a *restatement of Russell's thesis* and point out that the obstacles to action are not as formidable as they seem.

Notice that the Russell summary excludes points 1, 4, and 5 on the list of notes: point 1 is included in the presentation of points 2 and 3; point 4 is an example, one that is not essential to an understanding of the essay; and point 5 is not directly related to Russell's argument. In summarizing Russell's essay, you should not include side issues, such as the dangers of making scientific secrets public, for that would be arguing with Russell. Such ideas should be reserved for a full-length essay in which you develop an argument of your own.

> ## Summarizing a Complex Essay
>
> 1. *The summary must be comprehensive.* You should review all your notes and include in your summary all those ideas that are essential to the author's development of the thesis.
> 2. *The summary must be concise.* Eliminate repetitions in your list, even if the author restates the same points. Your summary should be considerably shorter than the source.
> 3. *The summary must be coherent.* It should make sense as a paragraph in its own right; it should not be taken directly from your list of notes and sound like a list of sentences that happen to be strung together in a paragraph format.
> 4. *The summary must be independent.* You are not being asked to imitate or identify yourself with the author whose work you are summarizing. On the contrary, you are expected to maintain your own voice throughout the summary. Even as you are jotting down your list of notes, you should try to *use your own words*. But also avoid introducing comments or criticisms of your own. (That is most likely to occur if you strongly disagree with the material that you are summarizing.) Make it clear to your reader when you are summarizing directly from the text and when you are inferring from or explaining what is being summarized. *Cite the author's name* somewhere in the summary, and use quotation marks around any borrowed phrases.

ASSIGNMENT 1: Summarizing an Essay

Summarize one of the following two essays. Before you begin your summary (on your second reading):

A. Underline and annotate key ideas and arguments.

B. Make a preliminary list of points.

C. Identify the thesis.

Use your own words as much as possible.

from IS GOOGLE MAKING US STUPID?

Nicholas Carr

A journalist specializing in business and technology, Nicholas Carr has written about the future of information technology as it applies to business, and the role of the Internet — and especially Wikipedia — in

the dissemination of knowledge. He is the author of The Big Switch:
Rewiring the World, from Edison to Google *and* Does IT Matter?
Information Technology and the Corrosion of Competitive
Advantage. *This article appeared in* Atlantic Monthly.

[handwritten: Movie reference to start topic]

"Dave, stop. Stop, will you? Stop, Dave. Will you stop, Dave?" So the super-   1
computer HAL pleads with the implacable astronaut Dave Bowman in a famous
and weirdly poignant scene toward the end of Stanley Kubrick's *2001: A Space
Odyssey*. Bowman, having nearly been sent to a deep-space death by the
malfunctioning machine, is calmly, coldly disconnecting the memory circuits
that control its artificial brain. "Dave, my mind is going," HAL says, forlornly. "I can
feel it. I can feel it."

[handwritten: I relate to this →]

I can feel it, too. Over the past few years I've had an uncomfortable sense   2
that someone, or something, has been tinkering with my brain, remapping the
neural circuitry, reprogramming the memory. My mind isn't going — so far as I
can tell — but it's changing. I'm not thinking the way I used to think. I can feel it
most strongly when I'm reading. Immersing myself in a book or a lengthy article
used to be easy. My mind would get caught up in the narrative or the turns of
the argument, and I'd spend hours strolling through long stretches of prose.
That's rarely the case anymore. Now my concentration often starts to drift after
two or three pages. I get fidgety, lose the thread, begin looking for something
else to do. I feel as if I'm always dragging my wayward brain back to the text. The
deep reading that used to come naturally has become a struggle.

[handwritten: Perfect ex. of what tech does to us today]

I think I know what's going on. For more than a decade now, I've been   3
spending a lot of time online, searching and surfing and sometimes adding
to the great databases of the Internet. The Web has been a godsend to me as
a writer. Research that once required days in the stacks or periodical rooms of
libraries can now be done in minutes. A few Google searches, some quick
clicks on hyperlinks, and I've got the telltale fact or pithy quote I was after.
Even when I'm not working, I'm as likely as not to be foraging in the Web's info-
thickets — reading and writing e-mails, scanning headlines and blog posts,
watching videos and listening to podcasts, or just tripping from link to link to
link. (Unlike footnotes, to which they're sometimes likened, hyperlinks don't
merely point to related works; they propel you toward them.)

[handwritten: Ads]

For me, as for others, the Net is becoming a universal medium, the conduit   4
for most of the information that flows through my eyes and ears and into my
mind. The advantages of having immediate access to such an incredibly rich
store of information are many, and they've been widely described and duly ap-
plauded. "The perfect recall of silicon memory," *Wired's* Clive Thompson has
written, "can be an enormous boon to thinking." But that boon comes at a price.
As the media theorist Marshall McLuhan pointed out in the 1960s, media are

Illustration by Guy Billout.

Deep read vs. skim read!

not just passive channels of information. They supply the stuff of thought, but they also shape the process of thought. And what the Net seems to be doing is chipping away my capacity for concentration and contemplation. My mind now expects to take in information the way the Net distributes it: in a swiftly moving stream of particles. Once I was a scuba diver in the sea of words. Now I zip along the surface like a guy on a Jet Ski.

Shows change in gathering info. No more depth

5

I'm not the only one. When I mention my troubles with reading to friends and acquaintances — literary types, most of them — many say they're having similar experiences. The more they use the Web, the more they have to fight to stay focused on long pieces of writing. Some of the bloggers I follow have also begun mentioning the phenomenon. Scott Karp, who writes a blog about on-line media, recently confessed that he has stopped reading books altogether. "I was a lit major in college, and used to be [a] voracious book reader," he wrote. "What happened?" He speculates on the answer: "What if I do all my reading on the web not so much because the way I read has changed, i.e. I'm just seeking convenience, but because the way I THINK has changed?"

imp to specify types of friends

Reading web causes change in thinking? possibly.

uses bloggers as sources. credible?

6

Bruce Friedman, who blogs regularly about the use of computers in medi-cine, also has described how the Internet has altered his mental habits. "I now have almost totally lost the ability to read and absorb a longish article on the web or in print," he wrote earlier this year. A pathologist who has long been on the faculty of the University of Michigan Medical School, Friedman elaborated on his comment in a telephone conversation with me. His thinking, he said, has taken on a "staccato" quality, reflecting the way he quickly scans short passages of text from many sources online. "I can't read *War and Peace* anymore," he admitted. "I've lost the ability to do that. Even a blog post of more than three or four paragraphs is too much to absorb. I skim it."

Anecdotes alone don't prove much. And we still await the long-term neurological and psychological experiments that will provide a definitive picture of how Internet use affects cognition. But a recently published study of online research habits, conducted by scholars from University College London, suggests that we may well be in the midst of a sea change in the way we read and think. As part of the five-year research program, the scholars examined computer logs documenting the behavior of visitors to two popular research sites, one operated by the British Library and one by a U.K. educational consortium, that provide access to journal articles, e-books, and other sources of written information. They found that people using the sites exhibited "a form of skimming activity," hopping from one source to another and rarely returning to any source they'd already visited. They typically read no more than one or two pages of an article or book before they would "bounce" out to another site. Sometimes they'd save a long article, but there's no evidence that they ever went back and actually read it. The authors of the study report:

> It is clear that users are not reading online in the traditional sense; indeed there are signs that new forms of "reading" are emerging as users "power browse" horizontally through titles, contents pages and abstracts going for quick wins. It almost seems that they go online to avoid reading in the traditional sense.

Thanks to the ubiquity of text on the Internet, not to mention the popularity of text-messaging on cell phones, we may well be reading more today than we did in the 1970s or 1980s, when television was our medium of choice. But it's a different kind of reading, and behind it lies a different kind of thinking — perhaps even a new sense of the self. "We are not only *what* we read," says Maryanne Wolf, a developmental psychologist at Tufts University and the author of *Proust and the Squid: The Story and Science of the Reading Brain*. "We are *how* we read." Wolf worries that the style of reading promoted by the Net, a style that puts "efficiency" and "immediacy" above all else, may be weakening our capacity for the kind of deep reading that emerged when an earlier technology, the printing press, made long and complex works of prose commonplace. When we read online, she says, we tend to become "mere decoders of information." Our ability to interpret text, to make the rich mental connections that form when we read deeply and without distraction, remains largely disengaged.

Reading, explains Wolf, is not an instinctive skill for human beings. It's not etched into our genes the way speech is. We have to teach our minds how to translate the symbolic characters we see into the language we understand. And the media or other technologies we use in learning and practicing the craft of reading play an important part in shaping the neural circuits inside our brains. Experiments demonstrate that readers of ideograms, such as the Chinese, develop a mental circuitry for reading that is very different from the circuitry found in those of us whose written language employs an alphabet. The variations extend across many regions of the brain, including those that govern such essential cognitive functions as memory and the interpretation of visual and auditory stimuli. We can expect as well that the circuits woven by our use of the Net will be different from those woven by our reading of books and other printed works. . . .

As we use what the sociologist Daniel Bell has called our "intellectual technologies" — the tools that extend our mental rather than our physical capacities — we inevitably begin to take on the qualities of those technologies. The mechanical clock, which came into common use in the fourteenth century, provides a compelling example. In *Technics and Civilization*, the historian and cultural critic Lewis Mumford described how the clock "disassociated time from human events and helped create the belief in an independent world of mathematically measurable sequences." The "abstract framework of divided time" became "the point of reference for both action and thought."   10

The clock's methodical ticking helped bring into being the scientific mind and the scientific man. But it also took something away. As the late MIT computer scientist Joseph Weizenbaum observed in his 1976 book, *Computer Power and Human Reason: From Judgment to Calculation*, the conception of the world that emerged from the widespread use of timekeeping instruments "remains an impoverished version of the older one, for it rests on a rejection of those direct experiences that formed the basis for, and indeed constituted, the old reality." In deciding when to eat, to work, to sleep, to rise, we stopped listening to our senses and started obeying the clock.   11

The process of adapting to new intellectual technologies is reflected in the changing metaphors we use to explain ourselves to ourselves. When the mechanical clock arrived, people began thinking of their brains as operating "like clockwork." Today, in the age of software, we have come to think of them as operating "like computers." But the changes, neuroscience tells us, go much deeper than metaphor. Thanks to our brain's plasticity, the adaptation occurs also at a biological level.   12

The Internet promises to have particularly far-reaching effects on cognition. In a paper published in 1936, the British mathematician Alan Turing   13 proved that a digital computer, which at the time existed only as a theoretical machine, could be programmed to perform the function of any other information-processing device. And that's what we're seeing today. The Internet, an immeasurably powerful computing system, is subsuming most of our other intellectual technologies. It's becoming our map and our clock, our printing press and our typewriter, our calculator and our telephone, and our radio and TV.

When the Net absorbs a medium, that medium is recreated in the Net's image. It injects the medium's content with hyperlinks, blinking ads, and other digital gewgaws, and it surrounds the content with the content of all the other media it has absorbed. A new e-mail message, for instance, may announce its arrival as we're glancing over the latest headlines at a newspaper's site. The result is to scatter our attention and diffuse our concentration.   14

The Net's influence doesn't end at the edges of a computer screen, either. As people's minds become attuned to the crazy quilt of Internet media, traditional media have to adapt to the audience's new expectations. Television programs add text crawls and pop-up ads, and magazines and newspapers shorten their articles, introduce capsule summaries, and crowd their pages with easy-to-browse info-snippets. When, in March of this year, the *New York Times* decided to devote the second and third pages of every edition to article abstracts, its design director, Tom Bodkin, explained that the "shortcuts" would give harried readers a quick "taste" of the day's news, sparing them the "less efficient" method of actually turning the pages and reading the articles. Old media have little choice but to play by the new-media rules. . . .   15

[Google] has declared that its mission is "to organize the world's information and make it universally accessible and useful." It seeks to develop "the perfect search engine," which it defines as something that "understands exactly what you mean and gives you back exactly what you want." In Google's view, information is a kind of commodity, a utilitarian resource that can be mined and processed with industrial efficiency. The more pieces of information we can "access" and the faster we can extract their gist, the more productive we become as thinkers.   16

Where does it end? Sergey Brin and Larry Page, the gifted young men who founded Google while pursuing doctoral degrees in computer science at Stanford, speak frequently of their desire to turn their search engine into an artificial intelligence, a HAL-like machine that might be connected directly to our brains. "The ultimate search engine is something as smart as people — or smarter," Page said in a speech a few years back. "For us, working on search is a way to work on artificial intelligence." In a 2004 interview with *Newsweek*, Brin said, "Certainly if you had all the world's information directly attached to your brain,   17 or an artificial brain that was smarter than your brain, you'd be better off." Last year, Page told a convention of scientists that Google is "really trying to build artificial intelligence and to do it on a large scale."

Such an ambition is a natural one, even an admirable one, for a pair of math whizzes with vast quantities of cash at their disposal and a small army   18
of computer scientists in their employ. A fundamentally scientific enterprise, Google is motivated by a desire to use technology, in Eric Schmidt's words, "to solve problems that have never been solved before," and artificial intelligence is the hardest problem out there. Why wouldn't Brin and Page want to be the ones to crack it?

Still, their easy assumption that we'd all "be better off" if our brains were supplemented, or even replaced, by an artificial intelligence is unsettling. It sug-   19
gests a belief that intelligence is the output of a mechanical process, a series of discrete steps that can be isolated, measured, and optimized. In Google's world, the world we enter when we go online, there's little place for the fuzziness of contemplation. Ambiguity is not an opening for insight but a bug to be fixed. The human brain is just an outdated computer that needs a faster processor and a bigger hard drive.

The idea that our minds should operate as high-speed data-processing machines is not only built into the workings of the Internet, it is the network's   20
reigning business model as well. The faster we surf across the Web—the more links we click and pages we view—the more opportunities Google and other companies gain to collect information about us and to feed us advertisements. Most of the proprietors of the commercial Internet have a financial stake in collecting the crumbs of data we leave behind as we flit from link to link—the more crumbs, the better. The last thing these companies want is to encourage leisurely reading or slow, concentrated thought. It's in their economic interest to drive us to distraction.

Maybe I'm just a worrywart. Just as there's a tendency to glorify technological progress, there's a countertendency to expect the worst of every new   21
tool or machine. In Plato's *Phaedrus*, Socrates bemoaned the development of writing. He feared that, as people came to rely on the written word as a substitute for the knowledge they used to carry inside their heads, they would, in the words of one of the dialogue's characters, "cease to exercise their memory and become forgetful." And because they would be able to "receive a quantity of information without proper instruction," they would "be thought very knowledgeable when they are for the most part quite ignorant." They would be "filled with the conceit of wisdom instead of real wisdom." Socrates wasn't wrong—the new technology did often have the effects he feared— but he was shortsighted. He couldn't foresee the many ways that writing and

reading would serve to spread information, spur fresh ideas, and expand human knowledge (if not wisdom).

The arrival of Gutenberg's printing press, in the fifteenth century, set off another round of teeth gnashing. The Italian humanist Hieronimo Squarciafico worried that the easy availability of books would lead to intellectual laziness, making men "less studious" and weakening their minds. Others argued that cheaply printed books and broadsheets would undermine religious authority, demean the work of scholars and scribes, and spread sedition and debauchery. As New York University professor Clay Shirky notes, "Most of the arguments made against the printing press were correct, even prescient." But, again, the doomsayers were unable to imagine the myriad blessings that the printed word would deliver.

So, yes, you should be skeptical of my skepticism. Perhaps those who dismiss critics of the Internet as Luddites or nostalgists will be proved correct, and from our hyperactive, data-stoked minds will spring a golden age of intellectual discovery and universal wisdom. Then again, the Net isn't the alphabet, and although it may replace the printing press, it produces something altogether different. The kind of deep reading that a sequence of printed pages promotes is valuable not just for the knowledge we acquire from the author's words but for the intellectual vibrations those words set off within our own minds. In the quiet spaces opened up by the sustained, undistracted reading of a book, or by any other act of contemplation, for that matter, we make our own associations, draw our own inferences and analogies, foster our own ideas. Deep reading, as Maryanne Wolf argues, is indistinguishable from deep thinking.

If we lose those quiet spaces, or fill them up with "content," we will sacrifice something important not only in our selves but in our culture. In a recent essay, the playwright Richard Foreman eloquently described what's at stake:

> I come from a tradition of Western culture, in which the ideal (my ideal) was the complex, dense and "cathedral-like" structure of the highly educated and articulate personality—a man or woman who carried inside themselves a personally constructed and unique version of the entire heritage of the West. [But now] I see within us all (myself included) the replacement of complex inner density with a new kind of self—evolving under the pressure of information overload and the technology of the "instantly available."

As we are drained of our "inner repertory of dense cultural inheritance," Foreman concluded, we risk turning into " 'pancake people' — spread wide and thin as we connect with that vast network of information accessed by the mere touch of a button."

I'm haunted by that scene in *2001*. What makes it so poignant, and so weird, is the computer's emotional response to the disassembly of its mind: its despair as one circuit after another goes dark, its childlike pleading with the astronaut — "I can feel it. I can feel it. I'm afraid" — and its final reversion to what can only be called a state of innocence. HAL's outpouring of feeling contrasts with the emotionlessness that characterizes the human figures in the film, who go about their business with an almost robotic efficiency. Their thoughts and actions feel scripted, as if they're following the steps of an algorithm. In the world of *2001*, people have become so machinelike that the most human character turns out to be a machine. That's the essence of Kubrick's dark prophecy: as we come to rely on computers to mediate our understanding of the world, it is our own intelligence that flattens into artificial intelligence.

A CARNIVORE'S CREDO

Roger Scruton

A British social and political philosopher, Roger Scruton has had academic affiliations to Cambridge University and Birkbeck College in Great Britain and Boston University and the American Enterprise Institute in the United States. His books include The Meaning of Conservatism, Animal Rights and Wrongs, *and* A Short History of Modern Philosophy. *He has been an activist for various social causes, most notably as a defender of fox hunting with hounds.*

Unlike other animals, we are self-conscious. We do not live, as they do, only in the "world of perception," to use Schopenhauer's phrase. Our thoughts and feelings range over the actual and the possible, the probable and the necessary, what will be and what ought to be. Upon these basic facts — traditionally summarized by saying we are rational animals — other and more remarkable facts depend. We have moral, aesthetic, and religious experiences; we pray to things visible and invisible; we laugh, sing, and grieve; are indignant, approving, and dismayed. And we relate to one another in a special way. Human beings are actual or potential members of a moral community, regulated by concepts of right and duty, in which each member enjoys sovereignty over his own affairs, so long as he accords an equal sovereignty to others. With all this comes an immense burden of guilt. Morality and self-consciousness set us in judgment over ourselves, so that we see our actions constantly from outside, judged by ourselves as we are by others. We become cut off from our instincts, and even the spontaneous joy of fellowship is diminished by the screen of judgment through which it first must pass.

Animals rescue us from this predicament. Their mute lack of self-consciousness neutralizes our own possession of it and makes it possible to pour out on them the pent-up store of fellow feeling, without fear of reproach. At the same time, we are acutely aware of their moral incompetence. Their affection, if it can be won at all, is easily won, and based on nothing. However much a man may be loved by his dog, this love brings warmth and security but no release from guilt. It implies no moral approval and leaves the character of its object unassessed and unendorsed. For that very reason, a dog is a far easier companion than a person, and the temptation arises to believe that all animals are really like our pets, with the same moral claims and the same need for consideration that characterizes the animals on whom we depend for companionship. That which distinguishes us from animals — our predicament as self-conscious and judging creatures — leads us constantly to discount the difference, to act as though it were a marginal consideration on which nothing hangs when it comes to the real ethical questions.

But the difference comes immediately to life when we consider the question of eating. Whether or not we think eating people is wrong, we do not think it is on a par with eating other animals. We recoil from the idea that human beings might be on the daily menu along with cabbage, chicken, squirrel, and lentils. This brings to the fore the distinction between our attitude toward the human body, even when dead, and our attitude toward the bodies of other animals. Although elephants and dolphins engage in behavior that shows a partial resemblance to our feelings in the presence of the dead, the emotions with which we approach a corpse are emotions that only a self-conscious being can experience and must be characterized in terms such as "awe," "reverence," and "anxiety." They belong to the philosophically neglected realm of the psyche I have called piety. The corpse is not to be carelessly touched, not to be defiled, not to be abused. Its former occupant surrounds it like an aura, demanding to be mourned. . . .   3

So far as I know, people do not eat their pets, even when the pets belong to species that are commonly eaten. Pets are honorary members of the human community and enjoy some imagined version of the nimbus that surrounds the human body — the nimbus Michelangelo presented in his versions of the Pietà. People bury their dogs and cats, often erecting tombstones over their bodies. And even when this seems absurd, some kind of piety is bestowed on an animal whose companionship has been enjoyed when it is a companion no longer.   4

Pious feelings survive also in the religious prohibitions that attach to the eating of meat. If God takes an interest in what we eat, it can only be because eating and ingesting are acts not only of the body but also of the soul. Yet dietary codes do not prohibit us from defiling the corpses of other animals. They instruct us not to defile *ourselves* by eating what is forbidden. This is further confirmation of the dramatic way in which animals and people are distinguished in our feelings.   5

The fact that eating, for us, is not what it is for other animals is related to the fact that we are moral beings. Eating has in every traditional society been   6 regarded as a social, often religious, act, embellished by ritual and enjoyed as a primary celebration of membership. Rational beings are nourished on conversation, taste, manners, and hospitality, and to divorce food from these practices is to deprive it of its true significance. Rational beings rejoice less in filling themselves than in the sight of food, table, and guests dressed for a ceremonial offering. Their meals are also sacrifices; some anthropologists have argued that the origin of our carnivorous ways lies in the burnt offerings of ancient ritual. At any rate, the giving of food is the core of hospitality.

In the fast-food culture, on the other hand, food is not given but taken. The solitary stuffing of burgers, pizzas, and "TV dinners"; the disappearance of family meals and domestic cooking; the loss of table manners — all these tend to obscure the distinction between eating and feeding. For many people, vegetarianism is a roundabout way of restoring that distinction. Vegetables are gifts of the earth: by eating them we reestablish contact with our roots. They offer a way of reincorporating food into the moral life, hedging it in with moral scruples and revitalizing the precious sense of shame. Meat eating cannot be vindicated without confronting the deep feelings that prompt our dietary habits. The onus lies on the carnivore to show that there is a way of incorporating meat into a life that does not shame the human race, as it is shamed by the solitary "caveman" gluttony of the burger stuffer.

I have hinted that there might be a distinction between virtuous and vicious eating. Virtuous eating involves behavior that is considerate of others and that permits and facilitates the easy continuation of dialogue. Good manners prevent that sudden and disturbing eclipse of the person by the animal, as the fangs sink themselves into the mess on the plate.

It is also a part of virtue to consider what benefits and harms are promoted by your actions — not, I hasten to add, in the manner of the utilitarian, seeking a comprehensive balance sheet of pleasure and pain, but in the manner of the humane person, who wishes to promote kindness and to oppose cruelty — in other words, to promote virtue over vice. The virtue of kindness cannot be understood without also invoking ideas of responsibility, duty, and right. Kindness means treating with gentleness and consideration all those with whom you have dealings, while also fulfilling your obligations toward them. To speak of it brings us to the fundamental question of deontology: What are our obligations, and do they permit us to eat animals?

Animals bred or kept for our uses are not honorary members of the moral community, as pets are. Nevertheless the use we make of them imposes a reciprocal duty to look after them, which spreads forward from the farmer to the slaughterer and from the slaughterer to the consumer, all of whom benefit from these animals and must therefore assume some part of the duty of care. To criticize battery pig farming as violating a duty of care is surely right and proper. But consider the traditional beef farmer, who fattens his calves for thirty

7

8

9

10

months, keeping them on open pasture in the summer and in warm roomy barns in the winter, feeding them on grass, silage, beans, and maize, attending to their ailments, and sending them for slaughter, when the time comes, to the nearby slaughterhouse, where they are instantly dispatched by a humane killer. Such a farmer treats his cattle as well as cattle can be treated, and such animals are as happy as their nature allows. Anybody who cares for animals ought to see this kind of husbandry as a complex moral good, to be defended, on the one hand, against those who would forbid the eating of meat altogether and, on the other hand, against those carnivores who prefer the unseen suffering of the battery farm and the factory abattoir. . . .

The real force of the vegetarian argument stems, I believe, from a revulsion   11
at the vicious carnivore: the meat eater as he has evolved in the solipsistic fast-food culture, with the removal of food from its central place in domestic life and the winning of friends. From Homer to Zola, meat has been seen as the primordial gift to the stranger, the eruption into the world of human conflict of the divine spirit of peace. Reduce meat to an object of solitary greed like chocolate and the question naturally arises: Why should *life* be sacrificed just for this?

The question presents a challenge. It is asking the burger stuffer to *come*   12
clean: to show why it is that his greed should be indulged in this way, why he can presume to kill again and again for the sake of a solitary pleasure that neither creates nor sustains any moral ties. To such a question it is always possible to respond with a shrug of the shoulders. But it is a real question, one of many that people now ask, as the old forms of piety dwindle. Piety is the remedy for religious guilt, and to this emotion we are all witting and unwitting heirs. And I suspect people become vegetarians for precisely that reason: by doing so they overcome the residue of guilt that attaches to every form of hubris, and in particular to the hubris of human freedom.

There is, however, a remedy more in keeping with the Judeo-Christian   13
tradition. We should not abandon our meat-eating habits but *remoralize* them, by reincorporating them into affectionate human relations and using them as instruments of hospitality, conviviality, and peace. That was the remedy practiced by our parents, with their traditional "Sunday roast" coming always at midday, after they had given thanks. Those brought up on fast food are not used to making sacrifices: mealtimes, manners, dinner-table conversation, and the art of cookery itself have all but disappeared from their worldview. But all those things form part of a complex human good, and I cannot help thinking that, when added to the ecological benefits of small-scale livestock farming, they secure for us an honorable place in the scheme of things, and neutralize more effectively than the vegetarian alternative our inherited burden of guilt.

I would suggest that it is not only permissible for those who care about an-   14
imals to eat meat; they have a duty to do so. If meat eating should ever become

confined to those who do not care about animal suffering, then compassionate farming would cease. Where there are conscientious carnivores, there is a motive to raise animals kindly. Moreover, conscientious carnivores show their depraved contemporaries that there is a right and a wrong way to eat. Duty requires us, therefore, to eat our friends.

·3·
Quoting Sources

I hate quotations. Tell me what you know.

Ralph Waldo Emerson (1849)

By necessity, by proclivity, and by delight, we all quote.

Ralph Waldo Emerson (1876)

Like Emerson in 1849, most writers hope to rely entirely on what they know and to express their knowledge in their own words. But, as Emerson realized later, we rarely write about ideas that no one has ever explored. Someone has usually gone part of the way before, so why not build on that person's discoveries—and, perhaps, use their actual words?

In academic writing, presenting the words of another writer through quotation is the most basic way to support your own ideas. Quotation enables you to give credit to your sources for both borrowed ideas and borrowed words.

1. *Appropriate quotation* tells your reader that you know when to quote and when not to quote; you never allow your sources' words to dominate your writing.

2. *Correct quotation* tells your reader that you respect your sources, that you know how to distinguish between your own work and theirs, and that you will not *plagiarize*—make unacknowledged use of another writer's words and ideas.

Reasons for Quoting

1. Quoting for Support

You will most often refer to another writer's work as evidence to support one of your own points. To ensure that the evidence retains its full meaning and impact, you may retain the author's original language, instead of putting the sentences in your own words. Very often, quoted material appears in an essay as an *appeal to authority*; the source being quoted is important enough or familiar enough with the subject (as in an eyewitness account) to make the original words worth quoting. For example, the only quotation in a *New York Times* article describing political and economic chaos in Bolivia presents the opinion of a government official:

> Even the Government acknowledges its shaky position. "The polity is unstable, capricious and chaotic," Adolfo Linares Arraya, Minister of Planning and Co-ordination, said. "The predominance of crisis situations has made the future unforeseeable."

The minister's words in themselves seem vague and glib, and therefore not especially quotable. But his position as representative of the government makes the minister's exact words necessary evidence for the reporter's presentation of the Bolivian crisis.

2. Quoting Vivid or Technical Language

The wording of the source material may be so apt that the point will be lost if you express it in your own words. You will want to quote a sentence that is very compact or that relies on a striking image to make its point. For example, here is a paragraph from a review of a book about Vietnamese history:

> Not many nations have had such a history of scrapping: against Mongols and Chinese seeking to dominate them from the north, and to the south against weaker and more innocent peoples who stood in the way of the Vietnamese march to the rich Mekong Delta and the underpopulated land of Cambodia. Mr. Hodgkin [the author] quotes from a poem by a medieval Vietnamese hero: "By its tradition of defending the country / the army is so powerful it can swallow the evening star."

The quotation adds authentic evidence to the reviewer's discussion and provides a memorable image for the reader.

It is also important to retain the precise terminology of a _technical or legal document._ Changing one word of the text can significantly change its meaning. Here is a sentence from the final paragraph of a Supreme Court decision upholding the civil rights of three tenth-graders who had been suspended by school officials for "spiking" the punch at a meeting of an extracurricular club:

> We hold that a school board member is not immune from liability for damages if he knew or reasonably should have known that the action he took within his sphere of official responsibility would violate the constitutional rights of the student affected, or if he took the action with the malicious intention to cause a deprivation of constitutional rights or other injury to the student.

Virtually every word of the sentence has potential impact on the way this decision will be interpreted in subsequent legal suits. Note, for example, the distinction between "knew" and "reasonably should have known" and the way in which "intention" is qualified by "malicious."

3. Quoting Another Writer to Comment on the Quotation

In your essay, you may want to analyze or comment on the language used by another writer. Your readers should have that writer's exact words in front of them if they are to get the full benefit of your commentary; _you have to quote it in order to talk about it._ Thus, when a writer reviewing Philip Norman's biography of the Beatles wants to criticize the biographer's style, he must supply a sample quotation so that his readers can make up their own minds.

> Worst of all is the overwritten prologue, about John Lennon's death and its impact in Liverpool: "The ruined imperial city, its abandoned river, its tormented suburban plain, knew an anguish greater than the recession and unemployment which have laid Merseyside waste under bombardments more deadly than Hitler's blitz." A moment's thought should have made Norman and his publishers realize that this sort of thing, dashed off in the heat of the moment, would quickly come to seem very embarrassing indeed.

4. Quoting to Gain Distance

Authors generally use quotation to distinguish between themselves and other authors they are citing. Sometimes, however, you want to distance yourself from _your own_ choice of language. For example, you may use quotation marks to indicate that a word or phrase is not in common or standard use. A phrase may be _obsolete,_ no longer in current usage:

Many "flower children" gathered at the rock festivals of the late 1960s.

Or a phrase may be *slang*, not yet having been absorbed into standard English:

> According to some students, the actor Eddie Murphy is "mad" funny.

In effect, you want to use the phrase and at the same time "cover" yourself by signaling your awareness that the phrase is not quite right: you are distancing yourself from your own vocabulary. On the whole, it is better to take full responsibility for your choice of words and to avoid using slang or obsolete vocabulary, with or without quotation marks.

You can achieve a different kind of distance when you use quotation marks to suggest *irony*:

> The actor was joined by his "constant companion."

The quoted phrase is a familiar *euphemism*, a bland expression substituted for a more blunt term. Again, by placing it in quotation marks, the author is both calling attention to and distancing him- or herself from the euphemism.

Quotation marks also serve as a means of *disassociation* for journalists who wish to avoid taking sides on an issue or making editorial comments.

> A fire that roared through a 120-year-old hotel and took at least 11 lives was the work of a "sick arsonist," the county coroner said today. Robert Jennings, the Wayne County coroner, said that he had told county officials that the building was a "fire trap."

The author of this article did not want the responsibility of attributing the fire to a "sick arsonist" or labeling the building a "fire trap" —at any rate, not until the findings of an investigation or a trial make the terminology unquestionably true. Thus, he is careful not only to use quotation marks around certain phrases but also to cite the precise source of the statement.

Reasons to Use Quotation

1. To support a point
2. To preserve vivid or technical language
3. To comment on the quotation
4. To distance yourself from the quotation

Using Quotations

> ## How to Quote
>
> 1. *Insert quotation marks* to indicate that you are borrowing certain words, as well as certain ideas, that appear in your writing.
> 2. *Insert a citation* containing the source's name to give credit for both ideas and words to the author.
>
> **Citation**   **Quotation**
>
> Theodore Roosevelt said,   "Speak softly and carry a big stick; you will go far."

Direct Quotation: Separating Quotations from Your Own Writing

The simplest way to quote is to combine the citation (written by you) with the words you are quoting (exactly as they were said or written by your source). This method of quotation joins together two separate statements, with punctuation—comma or colon—bridging the gap and a capital letter beginning the quoted sentence.

St. Paul declared, "It is better to marry than to burn."

In his first epistle to the Corinthians, St. Paul commented on lust: "It is better to marry than to burn."

In both these forms of direct quotation, the quoted words are not fully integrated into the grammatical structure of your sentence:

- The *quotation marks* separate the citation and the quotation.
- The *comma* or *colon* separates the citation and the quotation.
- The *capital letters* at the beginning of the quotation separate the citation and the quotation.

These separating devices make it clear that two voices appear in the sentence: yours and your source's. In general, you should choose this kind of direct quotation when you want to differentiate between yourself and the quoted words, perhaps because you disagree with them.

The *colon* is used less frequently than the comma. It usually follows a clause that can stand alone as a complete sentence. As such, the colon separates a complete idea of your own from a complementary or supporting idea taken from your source.

Direct Quotation: Integrating Quotations into Your Sentences

In an alternative kind of direct quotation, *only the quotation marks indicate that you are using someone else's words.*

St. Paul declared that "it is better to marry than to burn."

Alvin Toffler defined future shock as "the shattering stress and disorientation that we induce in individuals by subjecting them to too much change in too short a time."

There is no other signal for the reader that separates citation from quotation—no comma or colon, no capital letter. The first word of the quoted material, in this second type of direct quotation, is *not* capitalized, even if it was capitalized in the source.

Source

Beware of all enterprises that require new clothes.

HENRY DAVID THOREAU

Quotation

Thoreau warned his readers to "beware of all enterprises that require new clothes."

The effect is very smooth, and the reader's attention is not distracted from the flow of words.

The Two Kinds of Direct Quotation	
Separated	**Integrated**
■ Comma or colon and quotation marks separate citation and quotation.	■ No punctuation but quotation marks separates citation and quotation.
■ The first letter of the quotation is capitalized.	■ The first letter of the quotation is not capitalized.
■ You are distinguishing between your ideas and those of your source.	■ You are integrating your ideas with those of your source.

Indirect Quotation

You may be tempted to use indirect quotation, in which you report, rather than quote what the source has written. But you would be wise to insert quotation marks whenever you use a source's exact words, whether written or oral.

Direct Quotation

Robert Ingersoll condemned those who deny others their civil liberties: "I am the inferior of any man whose rights I trample underfoot."

Indirect Quotation

Robert Ingersoll proclaimed that he was the inferior of any man whose rights he trampled underfoot.

The indirect quotation does not indicate whose language appears in this sentence. In fact, the lack of quotation marks strongly indicates that the words aren't Ingersoll's—yet they are! Changing "I" to "he" and the present to the past tense has made no real difference: the basic phrasing of the sentence remains Ingersoll's. *To imply, as this indirect quotation could, that the wording is yours, not Ingersoll's, would be plagiarism.*

For this reason, writers use indirect quotation with great care. If one of the two forms of direct quotation does not seem appropriate, you should invent your own wording—called *paraphrase*—to express the source's original statement.

The Historical Present Tense

Certain ideas and statements remain true long after their creators have died. By convention (which means by general agreement), writers often refer to these statements in the present tense. Conventions are agreements, written or unwritten, that a certain practice should be generally used.

Shakespeare <u>states</u>, "This above all: to thine own self be true."

When you are devoting part of your own essay to an exploration of another writer's ideas, you may prefer to present those ideas using a common ground of time through the present tense, called the *historical present*. The historical present is also useful to place a variety of different sources on equal terms, especially when they are from different eras. In the following example, the introductory verbs, all in the present tense, are underlined:

While Shelley <u>acknowledges</u> that poets are creators of language and music and art, he also <u>asserts</u> that they have a civic role: "They are the institutors of laws, and the founders of civil society, and the inventors of the arts of life." Writing one hundred years later, Benedetto Croce <u>affirms</u> Shelley's insistence upon the social and spiritual responsibilities of the poet. According to Croce, Shelley <u>sees</u> poetry "as the eternal source of all intellectual, moral, and civil vitality."

Finally, the historical present is almost always used when you refer to important documents (often written by a group of people, rather than a single author) that remain in force long after they were created. Obvious examples include the Constitution, the Declaration of Independence, the laws of Congress, Supreme Court decisions, the charter of your state government, and the bylaws governing your college or university.

The Constitution <u>guarantees</u> that women—and, indeed, all citizens—shall have the vote in elections; Amendment XIX <u>states</u> that the right to vote "shall not be denied or abridged by the United States or by any State on account of sex."

Punctuating Direct Quotations: Opening the Quotation

You have already learned about punctuating the beginning of the quotation:

1. In a separated direct quotation, the citation is followed by a comma or a colon.
2. In an integrated direct quotation, the citation is followed by no punctuation at all.

Some writers tend to forget this second point and include an unnecessary comma:

Incorrect Quotation

Ernest Hemingway believed that, "what is moral is what you feel good after and what is immoral is what you feel bad after."

Remember that an integrated quotation should have no barriers between citation and quotation:

Correct Quotation

Ernest Hemingway believed that "what is moral is what you feel good after and what is immoral is what you feel bad after."

In the integrated direct quotation, remember that the first letter of the quotation is not capitalized.

Punctuating Direct Quotations: Closing the Quotation

There is no easy way of remembering the proper sequence of punctuation for closing a quotation. The procedure has been determined by conventional and arbitrary agreement, originally for the convenience of printers. Although other countries abide by different conventions, in the United States the following rules apply—and *there are no exceptions.*

1.   All periods and commas are placed inside the terminal quotation marks.

It does not matter whether the period belongs to your sentence or to the quoted sentence: it goes *inside* the marks. This is the most important rule and the one most often ignored. Don't resort to ambiguous devices such as placing the marks directly over the period (.").

> P. T. Barnum is reputed to have said that "there's a sucker born every
> minute."
>   ↑

> P. T. Barnum is reputed to have said that "there's a sucker born every
> minute," and Barnum's circuses undertook to entertain each and every one.
>   ↑

Notice that, in the second example, the comma at the end of the quotation belongs to the framework sentence, not to the quotation itself; nevertheless, it goes *inside* the marks.

2.   Semicolons, colons, and dashes are generally placed outside the terminal quotation marks.

Semicolons, colons, and dashes should be regarded as the punctuation for *your* sentence, and not for the quotation.

> George Santayana wrote that "those who cannot remember the past are
> condemned to repeat it"; today, we are in danger of forgetting the lessons
> of history.   ↑

Occasionally, when a semicolon, colon, or (most likely) a dash appears at the end of the material to be quoted, you will decide to include the punctuation in the quotation; in that case, the punctuation should be placed inside the marks. In the following example, the dash appears in Lucretia Mott's original statement, so it is placed inside the quotation marks.

> Lucretia Mott argued urgently for women's rights: "Let woman then
> go on—not asking favors, but claiming as a right the removal of all
> hindrances to her elevation in the scale of being—" so that, as a result,
>   ↑
> she might "enter profitably into the active business of man."

3. Question marks and exclamation points are sometimes placed inside the quotation marks and sometimes placed outside.

- If the quotation is itself a question or an exclamation, the mark or point goes *inside* the quotation marks.

  > In 1864, General Sherman signaled the arrival of his reinforce-
  > ments: "Hold the fort! I am coming!"
  >   ↑

  The exclamation is General Sherman's; the exclamation point goes inside the quotation.

- If your own sentence is a question or an exclamation, the mark or point goes *outside* a quotation placed at the very end of your sentence.

  > Can anyone today agree with Dumas that "woman inspires us to
  > great things and prevents us from achieving them"?
  >   ↑

  Dumas was *not* asking a question; the question mark goes at the very end of the sentence, after the quotation marks.

  > Sigmund Freud's writings occasionally reveal a remarkable lack of
  > insight: "The great question that has never been answered, and
  > which I have not yet been able to answer despite my thirty years of
  > research into the feminine soul, is: What does a woman want?"
  >   ↑

  Freud himself asked this famous question; the question mark goes inside the quotation.

  > Freud was demonstrating remarkably little insight when he wrote,
  > "What does a woman want?" citing his "thirty years of research into
  > the feminine soul"!   ↑
  >   ↑

  The exclamation is the writer's, not Freud's; the exclamation point goes outside the quotation marks.

- It is possible to construct a sentence that ends logically in two question marks (or exclamation points): one for the quotation and one for your own sentence. In such cases, you need include only one—and, by convention, it should be placed *inside* the quotation marks:

  > What did Freud mean when he asked, "What does a woman want?"
  >   ↑

These rules about punctuation apply only to the quotation of complete sentences or long phrases. Whether it is a quotation or an obsolete, slang, or ironic reference, *a single word or a brief phrase should be fully integrated into your sentence, without being preceded or followed by commas.*

> Winston Churchill's reference to "blood, sweat and tears" rallied the
> English to prepare for war.

Interrupting Quotations

Sometimes you want to break up a long quotation or to vary the way you quote your sources by interrupting a quotation and placing the citation in the middle.

"I do not mind lying," wrote Samuel Butler, "but I hate inaccuracy."

Butler's statement is divided into two separate parts, and therefore you need to use *four* quotation marks: two introductory and two terminal. The citation is joined to the quotation by a comma on either side. There are two danger points:

- If you forget to use the marks at the beginning of the second half of the quotation, you are failing to distinguish your words from Butler's.

- You must also put the first comma *inside* the terminal quotation marks (because commas *always* go inside the terminal quotation marks) and put the comma that concludes the citation *before* the quotation marks (because it is *your* comma, not Butler's).

Quoting inside a Quotation

Sometimes a statement that you want to quote already contains a quotation. In that case, you must use two sets of quotation marks, double and single, to help your reader to distinguish between the two separate sources:

- *Single quotation marks* are used for the words already quoted by your source (and this is the *only* time when it is appropriate to use single quotation marks).
- *Double quotation marks* are used around the entire quotation.

Goethe at times expressed a notable lack of self-confidence: "'Know thyself?' If I knew myself, I'd run away."

At the beginning of World War I, Winston Churchill observed that "the maxim of the British people is 'Business as usual.'"

The same single/double procedure is used even when there is no author's name to be cited.

A Yiddish proverb states that "'for example' is not proof."

Presenting an Extended Quotation

Occasionally, you may have reason to present an extended quotation, a single extract from the same source that runs *more than four printed or typewritten lines.* For extended quotations, you must, by conventional rule, set off the quoted passage by *indenting the entire quotation on the left:*

- Introduce an extended quotation with a colon.

- Start each line of the quotation one inch (or one-half inch) from the left-hand margin; stop each line at your normal right-hand margin.

- Some instructors prefer single-spacing within extended quotations; some prefer double-spacing. If possible, consult your instructor about the style appropriate for your course or discipline. If you are given no guidelines, use double-spacing.

- Omit quotation marks at the beginning and end of the quoted passage; the indented margin (and the introductory citation) will tell your readers that you are quoting.

Here is an example of an extended quotation:

> Although he worked "hard as hell" all winter, Fitzgerald had difficulty finishing *The Great Gatsby.* On April 10, 1924, he wrote to Maxwell Perkins, his editor at Scribner's:
>
>> While I have every hope & plan of finishing my novel in June . . . even [if] it takes me 10 times that long I cannot let it go unless it has the very best I'm capable of in it or even as I feel sometimes better than I'm capable of. It is only in the last four months that I've realized how much I've—well, almost *deteriorated.* . . . What I'm trying to say is just that . . . at last, or at least for the first time in years, I'm doing the best I can.

EXERCISE 9: Quoting Correctly

A. Correct the errors in the following sentences:

1. "The man who views the world at fifty the same as he did at twenty," remarked the boxer Muhammad Ali, has wasted thirty years of his life

2. Do you agree with Jerry Seinfeld that: "A bookstore is one of the only pieces of evidence we have that people are still thinking?"

3. H. L. Mencken cynically remarked that, "Nobody ever went broke underestimating the intelligence of the American public.

4. "It has been my experience, said Abraham Lincoln that "folks who have no vices have very few virtues.

5. The American historian Barbara Tuchman wrote about the ineptitude of generals, arguing that: "The power to command frequently causes failure to think".

6. Obesity is on the rise around the world, says Ann Becker. The Harvard anthropologist reports that the "Sudden increase in eating disorders among teenage girls in Fiji may be linked to the arrival of television in the 1990s and to "Western ideals of beauty."

7. Donald Trump offered this advice—"there's the old story about the boxer after a fight who said: 'that wasn't so tough." What was really tough was my father hitting me on the head with a hammer."

8. Before the Revolutionary War, Patrick Henry made a passionate speech, "is life so dear or peace so sweet, as to be purchased at the price of chains and slavery"? "Forbid it, Almighty God"! I know not what course others may take, but as for me, give me liberty or give me death."!

B.   Use quotations from the following group as directed:

■ Choose one quotation and write a sentence that introduces a direct quotation with separation.

■ Choose a second quotation and write a sentence that introduces a direct quotation with integration.

■ Choose a third quotation and write a sentence that interrupts a quotation with a citation in the middle.

1. I don't know anything about music. In my line you don't have to. (Elvis Presley)

2. All wish to possess knowledge, but few, comparatively speaking, are willing to pay the price. (Juvenal, Roman poet who lived around 100 AD)

3. I don't know what kind of weapons will be used in the third world war, assuming there will be a third world war. But I can tell you what the fourth world war will be fought with—stone clubs. (Albert Einstein)

4. Making predictions is difficult, particularly about the future. (Samuel Goldwyn, Hollywood producer)

5. Stage fright is always waiting outside the door. You either battle or walk away. (Laurence Olivier, British stage and film actor)

6. Money, it turned out, was exactly like sex, you thought of nothing else if you didn't have it and thought of other things if you did. (James Baldwin, American novelist)

7. There is no use whatever trying to help people who do not help themselves. You cannot push anyone up a ladder unless he be willing to climb himself. (Andrew Carnegie, industrialist and philanthropist)

8. You can't say civilization don't advance, however, for in every war they kill you in a new way. (Will Rogers, early twentieth-century comedian)

Quoting Accurately

Quoting is not a collaboration in which you try to improve on your source's words. Don't make minor changes or carelessly leave words out, but faithfully transcribe the exact words, the exact spelling, and the exact punctuation that you find in the original.

Source

Those who corrupt the public mind are just as evil as those who steal from the public purse.

ADLAI STEVENSON

Inexact Quotation

Adlai Stevenson believed that "those who act against the public interest are just as evil as those who steal from the public purse."

Exact Quotation

Adlai Stevenson believed that "those who corrupt the public mind are just as evil as those who steal from the public purse."

Even if you notice an error (or what seems to be an error), you still must copy the original wording. For example, old-fashioned spelling should be retained, as well as regional or national dialect and archaic spelling conventions:

One of Heywood's *Proverbes* tells us that "a new brome swepeth clean."

In one of his humorous stories, Colonel Davy Crockett predicted the reactions to his own death: "It war a great loss to the country and the world, and to ole Kaintuck in particklar. Thar were never known such a member of Congress as Crockett, and never will be agin. The painters and bears will miss him, for he never missed them."

If the material that you are quoting contains errors of syntax, punctuation, or spelling, you can use a conventional way to point out such errors and inform the reader that the mistake was made not by you, but by the source. The Latin word *sic* (meaning "thus") is placed in square brackets and inserted immediately after the error. The [sic] signals that the quotation was "thus" and that you, the writer, were aware of the error, which was not the result of your own carelessness in transcribing the quotation.

In the following example, [sic] calls attention to an error in subject-verb agreement:

Richard Farson points out that "increased understanding and concern has [sic] not been coupled with increased rights."

You may also want to use [sic] to indicate that the source used archaic spelling:

> In describing Elizabeth Billington, an early nineteenth-century singer, W. Clark Russell observed that "her voice was powerful, and resembled the tone of a clarionet [sic]."

It would be tedious, however, to use [sic] to indicate each misspelling in the Davy Crockett quotation; in your essay about Crockett, you could, instead, explain his use of dialect as you discuss his life and writing.

Tailoring Quotations to Fit Your Writing

There are several ways to change quotations to fit the quoted material naturally into your own sentences. Like [sic], these devices are conventions, established by generally accepted agreement: *you cannot improvise; you must follow these rules.* Usually, the conventional rules require you to inform your reader that a change is being made. In other words, they make clear the distinction between your wording and the author's.

Using Ellipses to Delete Words

It is permissible to delete words from a quotation, provided that you indicate to the reader that something has been omitted. Your condensed version is as accurate as the original; it is just shorter. But you must remember to insert the conventional symbol for deletion, *three spaced dots*, called an *ellipsis*. Once made aware by the three dots that your version omits part of the original, any reader who wants to see the omitted portion can consult the original source.

Source

Since the rise of the first neolithic cultures, man has hanged, tortured, burned, and impaled his fellow men. He has done so while devoutly professing religions whose founders enjoined the very opposite upon their followers. It is as though we carried with us, from some dark tree in a vanished forest, an insatiable thirst for cruelty.

LOREN EISELEY

Quotation with Ellipsis

Loren Eiseley tells us that "since the rise of the first neolithic cultures, man has hanged, tortured, burned, and impaled his fellow men. . . . It is as though we carried with us, from some dark tree in a vanished forest, an insatiable thirst for cruelty."

Notice that:

- The three dots are spaced equally, with one space between each dot and the next, and before the first and after the last.
- The dots *must* be three—not two or five.
- The first period is retained, to provide terminal punctuation for the first part of the quotation.

If you wish to delete the end of a quotation, and the ellipsis coincides with the end of your sentence, you must use the three dots, plus a fourth to signify the sentence's end.

Quotation with Terminal Ellipsis

Loren Eiseley provides a harrowing picture of man's darker nature: "Since the rise of the first neolithic cultures, man has hanged, tortured, burned, and impaled his fellow men. He has done so while devoutly professing religions whose founders enjoined the very opposite. . . ."

Here, you'll note:

- There are four dots, three to indicate a deletion and a fourth to indicate the period at the end of the sentence.
- The first dot is placed immediately after the last letter.
- The sentence ends with quotation marks, as usual, with the marks placed *after* the dots, not before.

Three dots can also link two separate quotations from the same paragraph in your source; the ellipsis will indicate the deletion of one or more sentences. You may do this only if the two sentences that you are quoting are fairly near each other in the original. *An ellipsis cannot cover a gap of more than a few sentences.* When you use an ellipsis to bridge one or more sentences, use only *one* set of quotation marks. Your full quotation, with an ellipsis in the middle, is still continuous—a single quotation—even though there is a gap.

Source

In one sense there is no death. The life of a soul on earth lasts beyond his departure. You will always feel that life touching yours, that voice speaking to you, that spirit looking out of other eyes, talking to you in the familiar things he touched, worked with, loved as familiar friends. He lives on in your life and in the lives of all others that knew him.

ANGELO PATRI

Quotation with Ellipsis

Patri states that "in one sense there is no death. The life of a soul on earth lasts beyond his departure. . . . He lives on in your life and in the lives of all others that knew him."

The source's meaning must always be exactly preserved, despite the deletion represented by the ellipsis.

Source

As long as there are sovereign nations possessing great power, war is inevitable.

ALBERT EINSTEIN

Inexact Quotation

Einstein believes that "as long as there are sovereign nations . . . war is inevitable."

It would not be accurate to suggest that Einstein believed in the inevitability of war merely because sovereign nations exist. To extract only a portion of this statement with ellipsis is to oversimplify and thus to distort the evidence.

An ellipsis can be used to make a quotation fit more smoothly into your own sentence. But ellipses should *not* be used to condense long, tedious quotations or to replace summary and paraphrase. If you want to quote only a brief extract from a lengthy passage, then simply quote that portion and ignore the surrounding material.

Using Brackets to Insert Words

Brackets have an opposite function: ellipsis signifies deletion; *brackets signify addition or alteration.* Brackets are not the same as parentheses. Parentheses would be confusing for this purpose, for the quotation might itself include a parenthetical statement, and the reader could not be sure whether the parentheses contained the author's insertion or yours. Instead, brackets, a relatively unusual form of punctuation, are used as a conventional way of informing the reader that material has been inserted. (You have already seen how to use brackets with [sic], which enables you to comment on the material that you are quoting.) You simply insert the information *inside* the quotation, placing it in square brackets:

- Brackets are used to clarify vague language. You may, for example, choose to quote only the last portion of a passage, omitting an important antecedent:

Source

It is the nature of desire not to be satisfied, and most men live only for the gratification of it.

ARISTOTLE

Quotation with Brackets

Aristotle notes that "most men live only for the gratification of [desire]."

■ Brackets are also used to complete a thought that depends on an earlier sentence which you have left out of the quotation.

Source

A well-trained sensible family doctor is one of the most valuable assets in a community. . . . Few men live lives of more devoted self-sacrifice.

SIR WILLIAM OSLER

Quotation with Brackets

The great surgeon Sir William Osler had enormous respect for his less famous colleagues: "Few men live lives of more devoted self-sacrifice [than good family doctors]."

In this, as in the first example, the quotation marks are placed *after* the brackets, even though the quoted material ends after the word "self-sacrifice." The explanatory material inside the brackets is considered part of the quotation, even though it is not in the source's own words.

Reasons to Use Brackets

- To explain a vague word
- To replace a confusing phrase
- To suggest an antecedent
- To correct an error in a quotation
- To adjust a quotation to fit your own writing

You may put your own explanatory comments in brackets if they are brief. You might, for example, want to include an important date or name as essential background information. But whatever is inside the brackets should fit smoothly into the syntax of the quotation and should not distract the reader. For example, do not use brackets to argue with the author you are quoting. The following running dialogue with the entertainer Sophie Tucker is poorly conveyed through the use of brackets.

Confusing Use of Brackets

Sophie Tucker suggests that up to the age of eighteen "a girl needs good parents. [This is true for men, too.] From eighteen to thirty-five, she needs good looks. [Good looks aren't that essential anymore.] From thirty-five to fifty-five, she needs a good personality. [I disagree because personality is important at any age.] From fifty-five on, she needs good cash."

EXERCISE 10: Using Ellipses and Brackets in Quotations

A. Choose one of the following quotations. By using ellipses, incorporate a portion of the quotation into a sentence of your own; remember to include the author's name in the citation.

B. Choose a second quotation. Incorporate a portion of the quotation into another sentence of your own; insert words in brackets to clarify one or more of the quoted words.

1. The scientist himself does not want to go to the moon; he knows that for his purposes unmanned spaceships carrying the best instruments human ingenuity can invent will do the job of exploring the moon's surface much better than dozens of astronauts. And yet, an actual change of the human world, the conquest of space or whatever we may wish to call it, is achieved only when manned space carriers are shot into the universe, so that man himself can go where up to now only human imagination and its power of abstraction, or human ingenuity and its power of fabrication, could reach. (Hannah Arendt)

2. I have never taken any exercise, except sleeping and resting, and I never intend to take any. Exercise is loathsome. And it cannot be any benefit when you are tired, and I am always tired. (Mark Twain)

3. Women upset everything. When you let them into your life, you find that the woman is driving at one thing and you're driving at another. (George Bernard Shaw)

4. An engaged woman is always more agreeable than a disengaged. She is satisfied with herself. Her cares are over, and she feels that she may exert all her powers of pleasing without suspicion. (Jane Austen)

5. The Internet is like alcohol in some sense. It accentuates what you would do anyway. If you want to be a loner, you can be more alone. If you want to connect, it makes it easier to connect. (Esther Dyson)

6. I believe that banking institutions are more dangerous to our liberties than standing armies. If the American people ever allow private banks to control the issue of their currency, first by inflation, then by deflation, the banks and corporations that will grow up around the banks will deprive the people of all property until their children wake up homeless on the continent their fathers conquered. The issuing power should be taken from the banks and restored to the people, to whom it properly belongs. (Thomas Jefferson)

Writing Citations

Citing the Author's Name

The first time that you refer to a source, use the author's full name—without Mr. or Miss, Mrs., or Ms.

First Reference

John Stuart Mill writes, "The opinion which it is attempted to suppress by authority may possibly be true."

After that, should you need to cite the author again, use the *last name only*. Conventional usage discourages casual and distracting references such as "John thinks," "JSM thinks," or "Mr. Mill thinks."

Second Reference

Mill continues to point out that "all silencing of discussion is an assumption of infallibility."

When you cite the author's name:

- At first reference, you may (and usually should) include the *title* of the work from which the quotation is taken:

  In *On Liberty*, John Stuart Mill writes . . .

- Avoid referring to the author twice in the same citation, once by name and once by pronoun.

  In John Stuart Mill's *On Liberty*, he writes . . .

- If there is a long break between references to the same author, or if the names of several other authors intervene, you may wish to repeat the full name and remind your reader of the earlier citation.

> In addition to his warnings about the dangers of majority rule, which were cited earlier in the discussion of public opinion, John Stuart Mill also expresses concern about "the functions of police; how far liberty may legitimately be invaded for the prevention of crime, or of accident."

▪ Finally, unless you genuinely do not know the author's name, use it!

Choosing the Introductory Verb

The introductory verb in the citation can tell your reader something about your reasons for presenting the quotation and its context in the work that you are quoting. Will you choose "J. S. Mill says," or "J. S. Mill writes," or "J. S. Mill thinks," or "J. S. Mill feels"? Those are the most common introductory verbs—so common that they have become boring! As the senses are not directly involved in writing, avoid "feels" entirely. And, unless you are quoting someone's spoken words, substitute a more accurate verb for "says."

Here are some introductory verbs:

argues	adds	concludes
establishes	explains	agrees
emphasizes	believes	insists
finds	continues	maintains
points out	declares	disagrees
notes	observes	states
suggests	proposes	compares

Of course, once you stop using the all-purpose "says" or "writes," you have to remember that verbs are not interchangeable and that you should choose the verb that best suits your purpose.

The citation should suggest the relationship between your own ideas (in your previous sentence) and the statement that you are about to quote.

Examine the quotation before writing the citation to define the way in which the author makes a point:

▪ Is it being asserted forcefully?
  Use "argues" or "declares" or "insists."

▪ Is the statement being offered only as a possibility?
  Use "suggests" or "proposes" or "finds."

▪ Does the statement immediately follow a previous reference?
  Use "continues" or "adds."

For clarity, the introductory verb may be expanded:

Mill is aware that . . .
Mill stresses the opposite view.

Mill provides one answer to the question.
Mill makes the same point as Bentham.
Mill erroneously assumes . . .

But make sure that the antecedent for the "view" or the "question" or the "point" can be found in the previous sentences of your essay.

Note that all the examples of introductory verbs are given in the *present tense*, which is the conventional way of introducing most quotations.

Varying Your Sentence Patterns

Even if you choose a different verb for each quotation, the combination of the author's name, introductory verb, and quotation can become repetitious and tiresome. One way to vary the citations is occasionally to place the name of the source in a less prominent position, tucked into the quotation instead of calling attention to it at the beginning.

1. As was discussed on page 116, you can interrupt the quotation by placing the citation in the middle.

"I made my mistakes," acknowledged Richard Nixon, "but in all my years of public service, I have never profited from public service. I have earned every cent."

2. You can phrase the citation as a subordinate clause or phrase, thus avoiding the monotonous "X says that . . ." pattern.

In Henry Kissinger's opinion, "Power is 'the great aphrodisiac.'"

As John F. Kennedy declares, "Mankind must put an end to war or war will put an end to mankind."

3. You should avoid placing the citation after the quotation.

The author's name at the end may weaken the statement, especially if the citation is pretentiously or awkwardly phrased:

Awkward Citation

"I am the inferior of any man whose rights I trample underfoot," as quoted from the writings of Robert Ingersoll.

Clear Citation

A champion of civil liberties, Robert Ingersoll insisted, "I am the inferior of any man whose rights I trample underfoot."

Two Rules Should Govern Your Choice of Citation
1. Don't be too fancy. 2. Be both precise and varied in your phrasing.

Deciding What to Quote

Use quotation sparingly! If quoting seems to be your primary purpose in writing, your reader will assume that you have nothing of your own to say. Quote only when you have a clear reason for doing so:

- when you are intending to analyze a quotation,
- when you are sure that its wording is essential to your argument,
- or when you simply cannot rephrase it in your own words.

Descriptions can be more difficult to rephrase than ideas. If your source states that the walls of Charles Dickens's parlor were painted sea-green and the furniture was made of mahogany and covered with light-brown velvet, you may find it next to impossible to find an appropriate way of presenting these descriptive terms. Dark brown wood covered with fuzzy beige fabric? Is aquamarine the same as sea-green? Better to retain the source's original words—without quotation marks if the words are common—and use them sparingly in a sentence that is clearly yours—not the source's—in structure and phrasing.

Citing Primary Sources

You will probably want to quote authorities in the field, especially primary sources: original works—often by historical figures—that other authors have commented on or authentic voices from a previous era. (For an explanation of primary and secondary sources, see pp. 346–47.) Here, for example, Lewis Lapham, the editor of *Harper's*, is writing about America as a nation of immigrants, citing first an American president and then a notable explorer:

full citation of the source

context for the quotation

citation in the middle

> We are a nation of parvenus, all bound to the hopes of tomorrow, or next week, or next year. John Quincy Adams put it plainly in a letter to a German correspondent in the 1820s who had written on behalf of several prospective émigrés to ask about the requirements for their success in the New World. "They must cast off the European skin, never to resume it," Adams said. "They must look forward to their posterity rather than backwards to their ancestors."

citation

context

*long extract/
no quotation
marks*

ellipsis

*interrupted
quotation—
slogan provides
flavor of
the period*

We were always a mixed and piebald company, even on the seventeenth century colonial seaboard, and we accepted our racial or cultural differences as the odds that we were obliged to overcome or correct. When John Charles Frémont (a.k.a. The Pathfinder) first descended into California from the East in 1843, he remarked on the polyglot character of the expedition accompanying him south into the San Joaquin Valley:

> Our cavalcade made a strange and grotesque appearance, and it was impossible to avoid reflecting upon our position and composition in this remote solitude . . . still forced on south by a desert on one hand and a mountain range on the other; guided by a civilized Indian, attended by two wild ones from the Sierra; a Chinook from the Columbia; and our own mixture of American, French, German — all armed; four or five languages heard at once; above a hundred horses and mules, half-wild; American, Spanish and Indian dresses and equipments intermingled — such was our composition.

John Quincy Adams's statement is tightly phrased, with the first half of each sentence balancing the second; Lapham would have found it difficult to express it half as well in his own words. Frémont's description has the authenticity of experience that is hard to capture using secondhand words.

Citing Primary Sources: A Consumer's Republic

Historical celebrities aren't the only primary sources who merit quotation. In this extract from *A Consumer's Republic*, Lizabeth Cohen, who teaches American Studies at Harvard University, describes the rise of the shopping center or, as she puts it, the "feminization of public space." The marginal notes suggest why Cohen's sources—many of them ordinary people from the 1950s and 1960s—are worth quoting. Notice that Cohen tends to use the standard pattern of source's name–description of context–colon–quotation. Unlike Lapham's magazine article, this is an academic work, based on extensive research, and so the sources are documented with footnotes. The need for documentation is explained in greater detail at the end of this chapter and in Chapter 10.

Whenever suburban and downtown shopping were compared in the 1950s and 1960s, shopping centers were singled out for their greater family appeal. In typical fashion, *Redbook*'s 1957 film *In the Suburbs* depicted the "happy-go-spending," "buy-it-now" generation passing great amounts of time together as a family in the local shopping center: "Like the rest of life in suburbia, shopping has a family flavor," the narrator observed while footage showed couples buying while their children trailed along or played nearby. These young adults, he went on, "have a 'let's-go-see quality' that brings crowds to community events and promotions" sponsored by the centers. A study comparing family shopping in downtown Cincinnati with its suburban shopping centers found that while 85 percent of downtown patrons shopped alone, only 43 percent of shopping center patrons did; most of them were accompanied by family members. Other surveys showed as many as two-thirds of female suburban customers shopping with someone else. Women shoppers in Bergen County surveyed by the Pratts conformed to these patterns. In the first few years after the centers opened, four in ten families were spending more time shopping, three in ten were making more shopping trips, two in ten were taking the children more often, and two in ten were including husbands more often than before the malls were built.[50]

This was a new phrase in 1958.

When "the whole family [was] shopping together," as marketer Pierre Martineau put it in 1958, men played a greater role in household purchasing. Survey after survey documented husbands' increasing presence alongside their wives at shopping centers, which made evenings and weekends by far the busiest time there, creating peaks and valleys in shopping that had not affected downtown stores nearly as much. In many suburban centers more than half the volume was done at night. At Bergen Mall the peak traffic count was at 8 p.m., and shopping was very heavy on Saturdays as well. A May Company executive described how this imbalance created special problems in branch-store operation: "The biggest day in the suburban store will be ten times the poorest day, instead of five as it usually is downtown." The manager of the Tots'n Teens toy store in Shoppers World in Framingham, Massachusetts, tried to explain to less experienced mall sellers how the new-style suburban shopping actually worked: "It's a curious thing about a shopping center. Most of our daytime shoppers are women who are just looking around. It's hard to sell them during the day but if they're at all interested, they'll be back at night — with their husbands. That's when we do the real business."[51]

quotation — succinct, but is the quotation needed?

authentic voice

2

Shopping centers responded to suburban couples' growing tendency to shop together with stores and programming specifically designed to further encourage families to turn shopping chores into leisure time spent at the mall. William M. Batten, board chair of JCPenney, for example, recalled "the broadening of our lines of merchandise and our services to encompass a fuller spectrum of family activity" as the company began building stores in shopping centers rather than on Main Street in the late 1950s and 1960s. Only then did Penney's start selling appliances, hardware, and sporting goods, and offering portrait studios, restaurants, auto service, and Singer sewing instruction. *Business Week* reported that department stores were scurrying to respond as well: Federated Department Stores started a new Fedway chain to attract the whole family and in its F. & R. Lazarus store in Columbus was "making a real effort to take the curse of femininity off the big store" by selling more male-oriented merchandise. Atlanta-based Rich's Department Store added a "Store for Men" adjoining its

Quote sounds like a board chair! Is it needed?

striking phrase — integrated quotation

3

Large, open, well-lighted departments with year-round air conditioning permit Bambergers to handle large crowds easily.

Do-it-yourself delivery is popular with suburban customers — and so is the "togetherness" of family shopping.

These photographs from Macy's annual report to shareholders the year its Garden State Plaza opened conveyed the prevalence of women shoppers but also hinted at the growing importance of the "'togetherness' of family shopping," referred to in the bottom caption. Reproduced from R.H. Macy & Co., Inc., *1957 Annual Report*. (Courtesy of Robert F. Wagner Labor Archives, New York University, from its Department Store Workers, Local 1-S Collection.)

main store. Automobile shows, Saturday "kids' movies," student art exhibits, and circus clowns were only a few of the many events designed to attract men and children. In time, shopping centers themselves would be constructed as less feminized space, with all family members, not just women, in mind. As families strolled and shopped together at the mall, more and more they engaged in a form of activity that may have been female-directed, but reflected greater sharing of responsibility for household purchasing between husbands and wives.[52]

50. On Film, Inc., for *Redbook* magazine, *In the Suburbs*, 1957, 19:30 minutes, 35 mm, from Rick Prelinger, ed., *Our Secret Century: Archival Films from the Darker Side of the American Dream*, vol. 6, *The Unchartered Landscape*, Voyager CD, 1996; Rich, *Shopping Behavior of Department Store Customers*, pp. 64, 71–74; Sternlieb, *Future of the Downtown Department Store*, pp. 27–28, 184;

Wolff, *What Makes Women Buy*, p. 226; L. Pratt, "Impact of Regional Shopping Centers in Bergen County."

51. Martineau, "Customers' Shopping Center Habits Change Retailing," p. 16; Feinberg, *What Makes Shopping Centers Tick*, p. 97; Oaks, *Managing Suburban Branches of Department Stores*, p. 72; Irving Roberts, "Toy Selling Techniques in a Shopping Center," *Playthings*, July 1953, p. 112; also see "Lenox Toy & Hobby Selects Good Location in Atlanta Shopping Center—1,200 Sales a Week," *Playthings*, May 1961, p. 99.

52. JCPenney, "An American Legacy, A 90th Anniversary History," brochure (1992), pp. 22, 25, JCPenney Archives, Plano, TX; Mary Elizabeth Curry, *Creating an American Institution: The Merchandising Genius of J.C. Penney* (New York: Garland, 1993), pp. 311–13; William M. Batten, *The Penney Idea: Foundation for the Continuing Growth of the J.C. Penney Company* (New York: Newcomen Society in North America, 1967), p. 17. The opening of the JCPenney store in Garden State Plaza in 1958 is featured in a film, *The Past Is a Prologue* (1961), which is one of several fascinating movies made by the company that has been collected on a video, *Penney Premieres*, available through the JCPenney Archives. Also see *Penney News* 24 (November–December 1958): 1, 7 on the new Paramus store; JCPenney Archives. On activities for family members, see R.H. Macy & Company, *Annual Report for 1957*, p. 26; "Bait for the Male Shopper," *BW*, Apr. 5, 1952, p. 40; "300,000 Prospects Ten Minutes Away," *Playthings*, February 1955, p. 308; Samuel Feinberg, "The Spirit of Garden State Plaza," *Women's Wear Daily*, Feb. 29, 1960.

Selecting Quotations

1. *Never quote something just because it sounds impressive.* The style of the quotation—the level of difficulty, the choice of vocabulary, and the degree of abstraction—should be compatible with your own style. Don't force your reader to make a mental jump from your own characteristic voice and wording to a far more abstract, flowery, or colloquial style.

2. *Never quote something that you find difficult to understand.* When the time comes to decide whether to quote, rapidly read the quotation and observe your own reactions. If you become distracted or confused, your reader will be, too.

3. *Quote primary sources—if they are clear and understandable.* A person who witnessed the Chicago Fire has a better claim to have his original account presented verbatim than does a historian, writing decades later.

EXERCISE 11: Why Quote?

A. Read this passage from *Affluenza: The All-Consuming Epidemic*, by John De Graaf, David Wann, and Thomas H. Naylor, twice.

B. Make marginal notes.

C. Be prepared to comment on De Graaf, Wann, and Naylor's use of quotation.

from AFFLUENZA: THE ALL-CONSUMING EPIDEMIC
John De Graaf, David Wann, and Thomas H. Naylor

John De Graaf has won numerous awards for his film documentaries, often broadcast on PBS, including the film version of Affluenza.

An author and a filmmaker, David Wann has worked for the Environmental Protection Agency and has published Biologic: Designing with Nature to Protect the Environment *and* Deep Design: Pathways to a Livable Future. *He helped design and build the co-housing village in which he now lives.*

A professor of economics at Duke University for 30 years, Thomas H. Naylor has written numerous books and articles. In 2003, he founded the Second Vermont Republic, "a nonviolent citizens' network and think tank opposed to the tyranny of Corporate America and the U.S. government, and committed to the peaceful return of Vermont to its status as an independent republic and more broadly the dissolution of the Union."

Planned Obsolescence

"The immediate postwar period does represent a huge change in the kinds of attitudes that Americans have had about consumption," says historian Susan Strasser, author of *Satisfaction Guaranteed*.[3] "Discreetly conspicuous waste" got another boost from what marketers called "planned obsolescence." Products were either made to last only a short time so that they would have to be replaced frequently (adding to sales) or they were continually upgraded, more commonly in style than in quality. It was an idea that began long before World War II with Gillette disposable razors and soon took on a larger life.

Henry Ford, who helped start the '20s consumer boom by paying his workers a then-fantastic five dollars a day, was a bit of a conservative about style, once promising that consumers could have one of his famous Model Ts in any color as long as it was black. But just before the Great Depression, General Motors introduced the idea of the annual model change. It was an idea that took off after World War II. Families were encouraged to buy a new car every year.

"They were saying the car you had last year won't do anymore and it won't do anymore because it doesn't look right," explains Susan Strasser. "There's now a new car and that's what we want to be driving."[4]

Instant Money

Of course, none but the richest Americans could afford to plunk down a couple thousand dollars on a new car every year, or on any of the other new consumer durables that families wanted. Never mind, there were ways to finance your spending spree. "The American consumer! Each year you consume fantastic amounts of food, clothing, housing, amusements, appliances, and services of all kinds. This mass consumption makes you the most powerful giant in the land,"[5] pipes the narrator in a cute, mid-'50s animated film from the National Consumer Finance Association (NCFA).

"I'm a giant," boasts Mr. American Consumer, as he piles up a massive mountain of stuff. And how does he afford it? Loans, says the film: "Consumer loans in the hands of millions of Americans add up to tremendous purchasing power. Purchasing power that creates consumer demand for all kinds of goods and services that mean a rising standard of living throughout the nation." You can probably already hear the drum roll in your mind.

A TV ad for Bank of America made about the same time shows a shaking animated man and asks, "Do you have money jitters? Ask the obliging Bank of America for a jar of soothing instant money. M-O-N-E-Y. In the form of a convenient personal loan." The animated man drinks from a coffee cup full of dollars, stops shaking and jumps for joy.[6]

It was a buy now, pay later world, only to become more so with the coming of credit cards in the sixties.

America the Malled

During the 1950s and 1960s, the rush to suburbia continued (it hasn't stopped yet). In 1946 a government program, the G.I. Bill, spurred it along. Ten years later, another government program did the same. President Eisenhower announced the beginning of a vast federal subsidy to create a nationwide freeway system. In part the system was sold as national defense — roads big enough to run our tanks on if the Russians invaded. The new freeways encouraged a mass movement to even wider rings of suburbs. All were built around the automobile, and massive shopping centers, whose windows, according to one early '60s promotional film, reflected "a happy-go-spending world."[7]

"Shopping malls," the film continues, "see young adults as in need of expansion [interesting choice of words]. People who buy in large quantities and truck it away in their cars. It's a big market!" "These young adults," the narrator gushes, "shopping with the same determination that brought them to the

3

4

5

6

7

8

suburbs in the first place, are the goingest part of a nation of wheels, living by the automobile." Going to the mall was, for these determined consumers, an adventure worthy of Mt. Everest, at least according to this film, which later describes the consumers' hardest challenge as finding their cars again in the giant mall parking lots.

By 1970, Americans were spending four times as much time shopping as were Europeans. The malls encouraged Sunday shopping, then as rare in the United States as it still is in Europe. To its everlasting credit, the Sears, Roebuck Company opposed opening its store on Sunday, on the grounds that it wanted "to give our employees their Sabbath." But by 1969 it caved to the competition, opening on Sundays "with great regret and some sense of guilt."[8]

9

3. Susan Strasser (author, *Satisfaction Guaranteed*) in personal interview with the authors, April 1996.

4. Ibid.

5. *Affluenza*. Seattle: PBS, 1997. Documentary film.

6. Ibid.

7. Ibid.

8. Gary Cross, *An All-Consuming Century*, p. 169.

EXERCISE 12: What to Quote

A. As your instructor indicates, read either the passage from *Traffic*, by Tom Vanderbilt, or the passage from "Where the Boys Were," by Thomas G. Mortenson. Read the passage twice.

B. Decide which phrases or sentences, if any, would be worth quoting in a research essay. If this were an essay assignment, your choice would depend on your essay topic and proposed thesis.

from TRAFFIC

Tom Vanderbilt

Tom Vanderbilt is a journalist specializing in technology, science, and popular culture, whose work has appeared in publications such as Slate, Wired, *the* New York Times, *and* Popular Science. *He is also the author of* The Sneaker Book: Anatomy of an Industry and an Icon *and* Survival City: Adventures Among the Ruins of Atomic America. Traffic *was a Book-of-the-Month Club selection.*

The sources of distraction inside a car have been painstakingly logged by researchers. We know that the average driver adjusts their radio 7.4 times per hour of driving, that their attention is diverted 8.1 times per hour by infants, and that they search for something — sunglasses, breath mints, change for the toll — 10.8 times per hour.[1] Research has further revealed just how many times we glance off the road to do these things and how long each glance takes: In general, the average driver looks away from the road for 0.06 seconds[2] every 3.4 seconds. "On average, radio tuning takes seven glances plus or minus three," said Linda Angell, a safety researcher at General Motors, in a conference room at the Technical Center in Warren, Michigan. "That's for an oldish radio. We do better with the modern radio, which zeroes you in on the right region." Most of these glances, Angell noted, do not take our eyes off the road for longer than 1.5 seconds. But there are exceptions, such as "intense displays" (e.g., lots of features) or looking for a button you have not pressed in a while. The iPod is changing the equation yet again: Studies have shown that scrolling for a particular song takes our eyes off the road for 10 percent longer than simply pausing or skipping a song[3] — plenty of time for something to go wrong.

Even a succession of very short glances, less than two seconds each, can cause problems. Researchers talk of the "fifteen-second rule,"[4] which indicates the maximum amount of time a driver should spend operating any kind of in-car device, whether navigation or radio, even as they are (at least occasionally) looking at the road. "What we believe is that task time is very important," Klauer said. "The longer the task time, the more dangerous the task is, and the

1

2

greater the crash risk." And so a fifteen-second task might require only short glances at the device, but, Klauer said, "that risk increases every time the driver looks away."

The study found that while dialing a cell phone put drivers at a greater crash risk, talking on a cell phone presented only a slightly higher risk than normal driving. "When a driver is talking or listening on their cell phone, at any given moment within that conversation what our odds ratio is telling us is they're only at a slightly higher crash risk than an alert driver. Statistically speaking, it's not different," Klauer said. Does that mean talking on a cell phone is safe? Maybe it's all that *dialing* we need to worry about. But the study also found that talking (or listening) on a cell phone was a contributing factor in as many crashes as dialing was. "We think that's probably true because while dialing is a much more dangerous task while the driver's doing it, the task is fairly short," Klauer told me. "But drivers typically talk on their cell phone for a long period of time. Over that long period of time a lot more crashes and near crashes are more apt to occur. That slight increase in crash risk is starting to add up." As more drivers talk for longer periods, Klauer said, "it's going to become a lot more dangerous."

The reason we talk for a long time on our cell phones is related to the reason we all think we are better drivers than we are, and to the thing that also makes us think we are better drivers on our cell phones than we are: lack of feedback. Cell phone users are not aware of the risk because, by all surface measures, they seem to be driving fine. Traffic affords us these illusions — until it does not, as the hundred-car study showed. "Cell phone conversations are particularly insidious because you don't notice your bad performance, particularly the cognitive side," John Lee argues. "So if you're dialing the phone, you get immediate feedback because you don't quite stay in the lane, because you're punching the buttons." Once the dialing is done, the driver can again look at the road. The weaving stops. They seem to be in control.

1. J. C. Stutts, J. R. Feaganes, E. A. Rodgman, C. Hamlett, T. Meadows, D. W. Reinfurt, K. Gish, M. Mercadante, and L. Staplin, *Distractions in Everyday Driving* (Washington, D.C.: AAA Foundation for Traffic Safety, 2003). Available at: http://www.aaafoundation.org/pdf/DistractionsInEverydayDriving.pdf.

2. L. Tijerina, "Driver Eye Glance Behavior During Car Following on the Road," Society of Automotive Engineers Paper 1999-01-1300, 1999.

3. Susan L. Chisholm, Jeff K. Caird, Julie Lockhart, Lisa Fern, and Elise Teteris, "Driving Performance While Engaged in MP-3 Player Interaction: Effects of Practice and Task Difficulty on PRT and Eye Movements," *Proceedings of the Fourth International Driving Symposium on Human Factors in Driver Assessment, Training and Vehicle Design* (Iowa City, 2007).

4. See, for example, Paul Green, "The 15-Second Rule for Driver Information Systems," *ITS America Ninth Annual Meeting Conference Proceedings* (Washington, D.C.: Intelligent Transportation Society of America, 1999).

WHERE THE BOYS WERE

Thomas G. Mortenson

Thomas G. Mortenson is a senior scholar at the Pell Institute for the Study of Opportunity in Higher Education. His research interests focus on access to higher education, particularly for young people who are not obvious candidates for college admission. He has served as a consultant to organizations such as the Illinois Board of Higher Education and the American College Testing Program.

Over the last century the labor market has been losing jobs usually held by men in goods-producing industries. Consider the following: In the 1910 census, a third of all workers were either farmers or farm laborers. Today those workers account for less than 2 percent. During World War II, about 35 percent of all jobs were in manufacturing. Today only about 10 percent are, and if trends over the last six decades continue, American manufacturing employment will approach zero around 2028. Other male-dominated industries like mining, forestry, and other work that depends on big, strong men willing to work under dirty and often dangerous conditions are also shrinking as a share of the work force. Those jobs paid men well for the work they did, and men did not need much formal education to do them. But those jobs are gone, and they are unlikely to return to the American labor force.   1

As a consequence, since the early 1970s the incomes of men with less than a college degree have been in economic free fall. The share of the male population that is employed has declined, labor-force participation rates have dropped, unemployment has increased, average weekly hours at work have fallen, and median income for men has flattened. Many more men than women ages 18 to 34 are still living with their parents, fewer men are getting married, and more men have never been married. Male registration and voting have dropped sharply, incarceration rates for men have quintupled (America now leads the world in incarceration rates), and the already high suicide rates for men have surged in the 15-to-44 age group. Men are in profound crisis. The world is changing, and too many men are not adapting to it. If such conditions affected women, you can bet we would be hearing about it.   2

The employment that is expanding in America is in service-providing industries like health care and education, business and professional services, leisure and hospitality, financial, and other services. The better-paying jobs in those service industries require a great deal of education beyond high school. The   3 girls get that message. The boys don't. That is the boy crisis in education. We are educating girls for their futures but not nearly enough of our boys. Currently about 35 percent of all boys get at least a basic higher-education degree—an associate or bachelor's degree. An additional 15 percent do not graduate from high school. That leaves about 50 percent of our boys who at least graduate from high school, or earn a GED, but do not get a college degree. They are the boys whom we are not reaching through education—but who must be reached with higher education and training to prepare them for the jobs that will be there when they enter the labor market.

Integrating Quotations into Your Paragraphs

Now that you know how to present the words of others accurately and with appropriate citations, you must learn to incorporate quotations smoothly into your paragraphs, supporting—not preempting—your own ideas.

Using Quotations

1. **Quotations generally belong in the body of the paragraph, not at the beginning as a replacement for the topic sentence.**

   The topic sentence should establish—in your own words—what you are about to explain or prove. *The quotation should appear later in the paragraph, as supporting evidence.*

2. **Let the quotation make its point; your job is to explain or interpret its meaning, not to translate it word for word.**

   Once you have presented a quotation, you need not provide an exact repetition of the same idea in your own words, making the same point twice. Instead, follow up a quotation with an *explanation* of its relevance to your paragraph or an *interpretation* of its meaning. Make sure that your commentary does more than echo the quotation.

In the following student example, the quotation used in the fifth sentence adds interest to the paragraph because of the shift in tone and the shift to a sharper, narrower focus.

topic sentence

explanation of topic sentence

Some parents insist on allowing their children to learn through experience. Once a child has actually performed a dangerous action and realized its consequences, he will always remember the circumstances and the possible ill effects. Yvonne Realle illustrates the adage that experience is

example

quotation
interpreting the
example

elaboration of the
topic sentence

the best teacher by describing a boy who was slapped just as he reached for a hot iron. The child, not realizing that he might have been burned, had no idea why he had been slapped. An observer noted that "if he had learned by experience, if he'd suffered some discomfort in the process, then he'd know enough to avoid the iron next time." In the view of parents like Yvonne Realle, letting a child experiment with his environment will result in a stronger lesson than slapping or scolding the child for trying to explore his surroundings.

Instead of looking at another completed paragraph that includes a quotation, let's reverse the process by starting with a simple quotation and seeing how it is used in the development of a paragraph. In an article on shopping written for the *Guardian*, a British newspaper, Jess Cartner-Morley is presenting the following thesis:

> Men tend to view shopping as a chore, a necessary way of obtaining things they need; for women, it is a leisure activity and a reward.

Cartner-Morley intends to include a quotation by Charles Revson, a major figure in the cosmetics industry:

> "In the factory we make cosmetics; in the store we sell hope."

The connection between the thesis and the quotation can be found in the words "reward" and "hope." So Cartner-Morley establishes a topic sentence—as well as a follow-up, explanatory sentence—that makes the connection in general terms:

> Certainly, it is clear that in a consumer society, shopping has come to stand for much more than just buying things. It is your ticket to an idealized self.

Shopping as "reward" has led to shopping as a "ticket to an idealized self," and that, in turn, leads to Revson's compact and catchy sentence—well worth quoting—about cosmetics as a symbol of "hope."

To introduce the quotation, Cartner-Morley uses an explanatory citation identifying Revson:

> Charles Revson, who founded Revlon in 1932, figured this out long ago, saying, "In the factory we make cosmetics; in the store we sell hope."

And then Cartner-Morley completes the paragraph by building on "long ago" in the citation and contrasting 1932 with 2004:

> But it is in recent years that the culture of shopping has become increasingly about image rather than substance.

Now she is ready to move on and discuss the way the idealized image of self is developed and marketed. The paragraph is only four sentences long—short and easy to follow—but it makes its point clearly by working toward the quotation and then away from it. The quotation strongly supports Cartner-Morley's thesis but can do so only because it is embedded in a strong paragraph.

Read through the complete paragraph and see how well it hangs together:

> Certainly, it is clear that in a consumer society, shopping has come to stand for much more than just buying things. It is your ticket to an idealized self. Charles Revson, who founded Revlon in 1932, figured this out long ago, saying, "In the factory we make cosmetics; in the store we sell hope." But it is in recent years that the culture of shopping has become increasingly about image rather than substance.

Academic writers may deal with more complex topics, but they use precisely the same techniques for incorporating quotations—the evidence of authoritative sources—into their paragraphs. Here is a paragraph from Dick Teresi's *Lost Discoveries: The Ancient Roots of Modern Science—From the Babylonians to the Maya*. Teresi is a science writer who bridges academic and popular audiences. Here, he is beginning a chapter on the origins of the science of geology:

topic sentence

example

closer focus

support: authority (quotation)

shift in focus to the present

support: brief anecdote

> Prehistoric peoples must have had intimate knowledge of the qualities of the stones they depended on in order to live. Neanderthal humans in the Middle Pleistocene crafted stone tools of a specific form known as Mousterian.[1] They used two methods: by chipping at the stone core to create the tool, and by using the chips themselves as the tools.[2] Geologist Gordon Childe says that "both procedures demand both great dexterity and considerable familiarity with the properties of the stone utilized. Just bashing two stones together is not likely to yield a useable flake or core tool. To produce either the blow must be struck with precisely the right force and at the correct angle on a flat surface."[3] Modern geology students who have attempted to make their own tools in this fashion can vouch for the difficulty involved. One student told me she spent a full morning trying to make a stone cutting tool from two pieces of flint she found on the beach.

> 1. Kenneth F. Weaver, "The Search for Our Ancestors," *National Geographic* 168 (Nov. 1985): 616.
> 2. Gordon Childe, "The Prehistory of Science: Archaeological Documents," in Guy S. Metraux and François Crouzet (eds.), *The Evolution of Science: Readings from the History of Mankind* (New York: New American Library, Mentor Books, 1963), pp. 39, 40.
> 3. Ibid.

Notice that Teresi's paragraph contains *three footnotes* to document the sources of his information as well as the quotation. Cartner-Morley is writing for a newspaper and is not expected to do more than identify sources by name and, if appropriate, provide some background. Complete information about when and how to document sources can be found in Chapter 10.

EXERCISE 13: Integrating Quotations into a Paragraph

A.   The following student paragraph is taken from an essay, "The Compulsive Gambler." The second passage comes from *The Psychology of Gambling*, by Edmund Bergler.

Choose one appropriate supporting quotation from the Bergler passage, decide where to place it in the student paragraph, and insert the quotation correctly and smoothly into the paragraph. Remember to lead into the quotation by citing the source.

Student Paragraph

One obvious reason for gambling is to make money. Because some gamblers are lucky when they play, they never want to stop. Even when quite a lot of money has been lost, they go on, assuming that they can get rich through gambling. Once a fortune is made, they will feel really powerful, free of all dependency and responsibilities. Instead, in most cases, gambling becomes a daily routine. There is no freedom, no escape.

Source

Every gambler gives the impression of a man who has signed a contract with Fate, stipulating that persistence must be rewarded. With that imaginary contract in his pocket, he is beyond the reach of all logical objection and argument. The result of this pathologic optimism is that the true gambler never stops when he is winning, for he is convinced that he must win more and more. Inevitably, he loses. He does not consider his winnings the result of chance; to him they are a down payment on that contract he has with Fate which guarantees that he will be a permanent winner. This inability to stop while fortune is still smiling is one of the strongest arguments against the earnest assumption, common to all gamblers, that one can get rich through gambling.

B.   The following student paragraph is taken from an essay, "Young Consumers." The second passage comes from *Consumed: How Markets Corrupt Children, Infantilize Adults, and Swallow Citizens Whole*, by Benjamin Barber.

Choose one appropriate supporting quotation from the Barber passage, decide where to place it in the student paragraph, and insert the quotation correctly and smoothly into the paragraph. Remember to lead into the quotation by citing the source.

Student Paragraph

To increase their sales and their profits, businesses are continually trying to create new markets for their products. Young people are a particularly desirable population, so many companies try to develop brand loyalty at a younger and younger age. Toddlers see ads on television and want their parents to buy new toys or new clothes. The Internet provides older children with lessons in how to consume useful and useless things. With new games and phones constantly replacing old ones, technology itself demands dedicated habits of consumption.

Source

Marketers and merchandisers are self-consciously chasing a youthful commercial constituency sufficiently padded in its pocketbook to be a very attractive market, yet sufficiently unformed in its tastes as to be vulnerable to conscious corporate manipulation via advertising, marketing, and branding. At the same time, these avatars of consumer capitalism are seeking to encourage adult regression, hoping to rekindle in grown-ups the tastes and habits of children so that they can sell globally the relatively useless cornucopia of games, gadgets, and myriad consumer goods for which there is no discernible "need market" other than the one created by capitalism's own frantic imperative to sell. As child-development scholar Susan Linn puts it in her critical study of what she calls "the hostile takeover of childhood," corporations are vying "more and more aggressively for young consumers" while popular culture "is being smothered by commercial culture relentlessly sold to children who [are valued] for their consumption."[1]

1. Susan Linn, *Consuming Kids: The Hostile Takeover of Childhood* (New York: New Press, 2004), p. 8.

Avoiding Plagiarism

Quoting without quotation marks is one kind of *plagiarism*. Even if you cite the source's name somewhere on your page, a word-for-word quotation without quotation marks would still be considered a plagiarism.

Plagiarism is the unacknowledged use of another writer's words or ideas. The only way to acknowledge that you are using someone else's actual words is through citation and quotation marks.

Chapter 10 discusses plagiarism in detail. At this point, you should understand that:

- If you plagiarize, you will never learn to write.
- Literate people consider plagiarism to be equivalent to theft.
- Plagiarists eventually get caught!

It is easy for an experienced reader to detect plagiarism. Every writer, professional or amateur, has *a characteristic style or voice* that readers quickly learn to recognize. The writer's voice becomes so familiar that the reader notices when the style changes and a new, unfamiliar voice appears. When there are frequent acknowledged quotations, the reader simply adjusts to a series of new voices. But when there are unacknowledged quotations, *the absence of quotation marks* and *the change of voices* usually suggest to an experienced reader that the work is poorly integrated and probably plagiarized.

Instructors are well aware of style and are trained to recognize inconsistencies and awkward transitions. A revealing clue is the patched-together, mosaic effect. The next exercise will improve your own perception of shifting voices and encourage you to rely on your own characteristic style as the dominant voice in everything that you write.

EXERCISE 14: Identifying Plagiarism

The following paragraphs contain several plagiarized sentences.

A. Examine the *language* and *tone* of each sentence, as well as the *continuity* of the entire paragraph.

B. Then underline the plagiarized sentences.

1. The Beatles' music in the early years was just plain melodic. It had a nice beat to it. The Beatles were simple lads, writing simple songs simply to play to screaming fans on one-night stands. There was no deep, inner meaning to the lyrics. Their songs included many words like I, and me, and you. As the years went by, the Beatles' music became more poetic. *Sergeant Pepper* is a stupefying collage of music, words, background noises, cryptic utterances, orchestral effects, hallucinogenic bells, farmyard sounds, dream sequences, social observations, and

apocalyptic vision, all masterfully blended together on a four-track tape machine over nine agonizing and expensive months. Their music was beginning to be more philosophical, with a deep, inner, more secret meaning. After it was known that they took drugs, references to drugs were seen in many songs. The "help" in Ringo's "A Little Help from My Friends" was said to have meant pot. The songs were poetic, mystical; they emerged from a self-contained world of bizarre carnival colors; they spoke in a language and a musical idiom all their own.

2. Before the Civil War, minstrelsy spread quickly across America. Americans all over the country enjoyed minstrelsy because it reflected something of their own point of view. For instance, Negro plantation hands, played usually by white actors in blackface, were portrayed as devil-may-care outcasts and minstrelmen played them with an air of comic triumph, irreverent wisdom, and an underlying note of rebellion, which had a special appeal to citizens of a young country. Minstrelsy was ironically the beginning of black involvement in the American theater. The American people learned to identify with certain aspects of the black people. The Negro became a sympathetic symbol for a pioneer people who required resilience as a prime trait.

·4·

Paraphrasing Sources

Some passages are worth quoting for the sake of their precise or elegant style or their distinguished author. But many sources that you will use in your college essays are written in more ordinary language or by more ordinary writers. Rather than quoting bland material, you should provide your readers with a clear paraphrase.

Paraphrase is the point-by-point recapitulation of another person's ideas, expressed in your own words.

When you paraphrase, you retain everything about the original writing but the words.

Using Paraphrase in Your Essays

Paraphrasing helps your readers to gain a detailed understanding of your sources and, indirectly, to accept your thesis as valid. There are two major reasons for using paraphrase in your essays.

1. Use paraphrase to present information or evidence whenever there is no special reason for using a direct quotation.

Many sources don't have sufficient authority or a distinctive enough style to justify your quoting their words. The following illustration, from a *New York Times* article, paraphrases a report written by an anonymous group of "municipal auditors" that was not considered worth quoting. Note the initial reference

146

to the source of the information ("a report issued yesterday") and the follow-up reminders ("they said"; "the auditors said").

> A city warehouse in Middle Village, Queens, stocked with such things as snow shovels, light bulbs, sponges, waxed paper, laundry soap and tinned herring, has been found to be vastly overstocked with some items and lacking in others. Municipal auditors, in a report issued yesterday, said that security was fine and that the warehouse was quicker in delivering goods to city agencies than it was when the auditors made their last check. . . . But in one corner of the warehouse, they said, nearly 59,000 paper binders, the 8½-by-11 size, are gathering dust, enough to meet the city's needs for nearly seven years. Nearby, there is a 10½-year supply of cotton coveralls.
>
> Both the overstock and shortages cost the city money, the auditors said. They estimated that by reducing warehouse inventories, the city could save $1.4 million, plus $112,000 in interest. . . .

2. Use paraphrase to give your readers an accurate and comprehensive account of ideas taken from a source — ideas that you intend to explain, interpret, or disagree with in your essay.

The first illustration comes from a *Times* article about the data and photographs provided by *Voyager 2* as it explored the farthest reaches of the solar system. In summarizing a press conference, the article paraphrases various scientists' descriptions of what *Voyager* had achieved during its journey near Triton, one of the moons of the planet Neptune. Note the limited use of carefully selected quotations within the paraphrase.

> Out of the fissures [on Triton], roughly analogous to faults in the Earth's crust, flowed mushy ice. There was no eruption in the sense of the usual terrestrial volcanism or the geyser-like activity discovered on Io, one of Jupiter's moons. It was more of an extrusion through cracks in the surface ice.
>
> Although scientists classify such a process as volcanism, Dr. Miner said it could better be described as a "slow-flow volcanic activity." A somewhat comparable process, he said, seemed to have shaped some of the surface features of Ariel, one of the moons of Uranus.
>
> Dr. Soderblom said Triton's surface appeared to be geologically young or "millions to hundreds of millions of years old." The absence of many impact craters was the main evidence for the relatively recent resurfacing of the terrain with new ice.

The next example shows how paraphrase can be used more briefly, to present another writer's point of view as the basis for discussion. Again, the writer of this description of a conference on nuclear deterrence has reserved quotation to express the precise point of potential dispute:

> Scientists engaged in research on the effects of nuclear war may be "wasting their time" studying a phenomenon that is far less dangerous than the natural explosions that have periodically produced widespread extinctions of plant and animal life in the past, a University of Chicago scientist said last week. Joseph V. Smith, a professor of geophysical sciences, told a conference on nuclear deterrence here that such natural catastrophes as exploding volcanoes, violent earthquakes, and collisions with comets or asteroids could produce more immediate and destructive explosions than any nuclear war.

Using Paraphrase as Preparation for Reading and Writing Essays

Paraphrase is sometimes undertaken as an end in itself to improve your understanding of a complex passage. When you grasp an essay at first reading, when its ideas are clearly stated in familiar terms, then you can be satisfied with annotating it or writing a brief summary. But when you find an essay hard to understand, writing down each sentence in your own words forces you to stop and make sense of what you have read, helping you work out ideas that may at first seem beyond your comprehension.

When you take notes for an essay based on one or more sources, you should mostly paraphrase. Quote only when recording phrases or sentences that clearly merit quotation. All quotable phrases and sentences should be transcribed accurately in your notes, with quotation marks separating the paraphrase from the quotation.

Writing a Paraphrase

In a good paraphrase, the sentences and the vocabulary do not duplicate those of the original. *You cannot merely substitute synonyms for key words and leave the sentences otherwise unchanged; that is plagiarism in spirit, if not in fact.* Word-for-word substitution won't demonstrate that you have understood the ideas.

The level of abstraction within your paraphrase should resemble that of the original: it should be neither more general nor more specific. If you do not understand a sentence, do not try to guess or cover it up with a vague phrase that slides over the idea. Instead:

- Look up difficult words.
- Think of what they mean and how they are used together.

- Consider how the sentences are formed and how they fit into the context of the entire paragraph.
- Then, to test your understanding, write down your version of the original.

Remember that a good paraphrase makes sense by itself; it is coherent and readable, without requiring reference to the original essay.

When a paraphrase moves completely away from the words and sentence structure of the original text and presents ideas in the paraphraser's own style and idiom, then it is said to be "free." A *free paraphrase* is as acceptable as the original—provided that the substance of the source has not been altered, disguised, or substantially condensed. Because a free paraphrase can condense repetitious parts of the original text, it may be somewhat briefer than the original, but it will present ideas in much the same order.

Guidelines for a Successful Paraphrase

- A paraphrase must be accurate.
- A paraphrase must be complete.
- A paraphrase must be written in your own voice.
- A paraphrase must make sense by itself.

Writing a Paraphrase: *The Prince*

Here, side by side with the original, is a free paraphrase of an excerpt from Machiavelli's *The Prince*. This passage exemplifies the kind of text—very famous, very difficult—that really benefits from a comprehensive paraphrase. *The Prince* was written in 1513. The original text (on the left), as translated by Tim Parks, was published in 2009.

Source: Machiavelli

So, a leader doesn't have to possess all the virtuous qualities I've mentioned, but it's absolutely imperative that he seem to possess them. I'll go so far as to say this: if he had those qualities and observed them all the time, he'd be putting himself at risk. It's seeming to be virtuous that helps; as, for example, seeming

Paraphrase

It is more important for a ruler to give the impression of goodness than to be good. In fact, real goodness can be a liability, but the pretense is always very effective. It is all very well to be virtuous, but it is vital to be able to shift in the other direction whenever circumstances

to be compassionate, loyal, humane, honest and religious. And you can even be those things, so long as you're always mentally prepared to change as soon as your interests are threatened. What you have to understand is that a ruler, especially a ruler new to power, can't always behave in ways that would make people think a man good, because to stay in power he's frequently obliged to act against loyalty, against charity, against humanity and against religion. What matters is that he has the sort of character that can change tack as luck and circumstances demand, and, as I've already said, stick to the good if he can but know how to be bad when the occasion demands.

So a ruler must be extremely careful not to say anything that doesn't appear to be inspired by the five virtues listed above; he must seem and sound wholly compassionate, wholly loyal, wholly humane, wholly honest and wholly religious. . . . Everyone sees what you seem to be, few have experience of who you really are, and those few won't have the courage to stand up to majority opinion underwritten by the authority of state. When they're weighing up what someone has achieved—and this is particularly true with rulers, who can't be held to account—people look at the end result. So if a leader does what it takes to win power and keep it, his methods will always be reckoned honorable and widely praised. The crowd is won over by appearances and final results. And the world is all crowd: the dissenting few find no space so long as the majority have any grounds at all for their opinions.

require it. After all, rulers, especially recently elevated ones, have a duty to perform which may absolutely require them to act against the dictates of faith and compassion and kindness. One must act as circumstances require and, while it's good to be virtuous if you can, it's better to be bad if you must.

In public, however, the ruler should appear to be entirely virtuous, and if his pretense is successful with the majority of people, then those who do see through the act will be outnumbered and impotent, especially since the ruler has the authority of government on his side. In the case of rulers, even more than for most men, the end justifies the means. If the ruler is able to assume power and administer it successfully, his actions will always be judged proper and satisfactory; for the common people will accept the pretense of virtue and the reality of success, and the astute will find no one is listening to their warnings.

Paraphrase and Summary

To clarify the difference between paraphrase and summary, here is a paragraph that *summarizes* the excerpt from *The Prince*.

> According to Machiavelli, perpetuating power is a more important goal for a ruler than achieving personal goodness or integrity. Although he should act virtuously if he can, and always appear to do so, it is more important for him to adapt quickly to changing circumstances. The masses will be so swayed by his pretended virtue and by his success that any opposition will be ineffective. The wise ruler's maxim is that the end justifies the means.

Let's recapitulate the guidelines for writing a brief summary, applying them to *The Prince*:

1. *A summary is comprehensive.* Like the paraphrase, the summary of *The Prince* says more than "the end justifies the means." While that is probably the most important idea in the passage, it does not by itself convey Machiavelli's full meaning. For one thing, it contains no reference at all to princes and how they should rule—and that, after all, is Machiavelli's subject.

2. *A summary is concise.* The summary should say exactly as much as you need—and no more. The summary of *The Prince* is considerably shorter than the paraphrase.

3. *A summary is coherent.* The summary links together the passage's most important points in a unified paragraph that makes sense on its own. The ideas need not be presented in the same sequence as that of the original passage, as they are in the paraphrase.

4. *A summary is independent.* What is most striking about the summary, compared with the paraphrase, is the writer's attitude toward the original text. While the paraphraser has to follow closely Machiavelli's ideas and point of view, the summarizer does not. Characteristically, Machiavelli's name is cited in the summary, calling attention to the fact that it is based on another person's ideas.

You might use either summary or paraphrase to refer to this passage in an essay. Which you would choose to use depends on your topic, on the way you are developing your essay, and on the extent to which you wish to discuss Machiavelli:

- In an essay citing Machiavelli as only one among many political theorists, you might use the four-sentence summary; then you might briefly comment on Machiavelli's ideas before going on to summarize (and perhaps compare them with) another writer's theories.

■ In an essay about a contemporary politician, you might analyze the way in which your subject does or does not carry out Machiavelli's strategies; then you probably would want to familiarize your readers with *The Prince* in some detail through paraphrase. You might include the full paraphrase, interspersed, perhaps, with an analysis of your present-day "prince."

Comparing Paraphrase and Summary

Paraphrase	Summary
■ Reports your understanding to your reader	■ Reports your understanding to your reader
■ Records a relatively short passage	■ Records a passage of any length
■ Records every point in the passage	■ Selects and condenses, recording only the main ideas
■ Records these points in their original order	■ Changes the order of ideas when necessary
■ Includes no interpretation	■ Explains and (if the writer wishes) interprets

---

Writing an Accurate Paraphrase: "Divorce and the Family in America"

The basic purpose of paraphrase is to present a source's ideas as they appear in the original text. When paraphrase fails to convey the substance of the source, there are four possible explanations:

1. *Misreading*: The writer genuinely misunderstood the text.
2. *Projecting*: The writer projected his or her own ideas into the text.
3. *Guessing*: The writer had a spark of understanding and constructed a paraphrase from that spark, but ignored too much of the original text.
4. *Summarizing*: The writer presents only the main ideas, omitting necessary material.

Read this excerpt from Christopher Lasch's "Divorce and the Family in America," which analyzes the changing role of the child in family life. Then examine each of the three paraphrases that follow, deciding whether it conveys

Lasch's principal ideas and, if not, why it has gone astray. Compare your reactions with the analysis that follows each paraphrase.

Source: Christopher Lasch

The family by its very nature is a means of raising children, but this fact should not blind us to the important change that occurred when child-rearing ceased to be simply one of many activities and became the central concern — one is tempted to say the central obsession — of family life. This development had to wait for the recognition of the child as a distinctive kind of person, more impressionable and hence more vulnerable than adults, to be treated in a special manner befitting his peculiar requirements. Again, we take these things for granted and find it hard to imagine anything else. Earlier, children had been clothed, fed, spoken to, and educated as little adults; more specifically, as servants, the difference between childhood and servitude having been remarkably obscure throughout much of Western history. . . . It was only in the seventeenth century in certain classes that childhood came to be seen as a special category of experience. When that happened, people recognized the enormous formative influence of family life, and the family became above all an agency for building character, for consciously and deliberately forming the child from birth to adulthood.

from "Divorce and the Family in America," *Atlantic Monthly*

Paraphrase A: Guessing and Projecting

The average family wants to raise children with a good education and to encourage, for example, the ability to read and write well. They must be taught to practice and learn on their own. Children can be treated well without being pampered. They must be treated as adults as they get older and experience more of life. A parent must build character and the feeling of independence in a child. No longer should children be treated as kids or servants, for that can cause conflict in a family relationship.

This paraphrase has very little in common with the original passage. True, it is about child rearing, but the writer chooses to give advice to parents, rather than present the contrast between early and modern attitudes toward children, as Lasch does. Since the only clear connection between Lasch's text and this paragraph is the reference to servants, the writer was probably confused by the passage, and (instead of slowing down the process and paraphrasing it sentence by sentence) guessed — mistakenly — at its meaning. There is also some projection of the writer's ideas about family life. Notice how assertive the tone is; the writer seems to be admonishing parents rather than presenting Lasch's detached analysis.

Paraphrase B: Guessing and Projecting

When two people get married, they usually produce a child. They get married because they want a family. Raising a family is now different from the way it used to be. The child is looked upon as a human being, with feelings and thoughts of his own. Centuries ago, children were treated like robots, little more than hired help. Now, children are seen as people who need a strong, dependable family background to grow into persons of good character. Parents are needed to get children ready to be the adults of tomorrow.

This paragraph also seems to combine guessing (beginning) and projecting (end). The middle sentences do present Lasch's basic point, but the beginning and the end move so far away from the main ideas that the paraphrase as a whole does not bear much resemblance to the original text. It also includes an exaggeration: are servants "robots"?

Paraphrase C: Incomplete Paraphrase

Though the family has always been an important institution, its child-rearing function has only in recent centuries become its most important activity. This change has resulted from the relatively new idea that children have a special, unique personality. In the past, there was little difference seen between childhood and adulthood. But today people realize the importance of family life, especially the family unit as a means of molding the personalities of children from childhood to adulthood.

Although this paraphrase is certainly the most accurate of the three, it is too brief to be a complete paraphrase. In fact, the writer seems to be summarizing, not paraphrasing. Lasch's main idea is there, but the following points are missing:

- There is a tremendous difference between pre-seventeenth-century and twenty-first-century perceptions of childhood.
- Before the seventeenth century, it was difficult to distinguish between the status and treatment of children and that of servants.
- Child rearing has now become of overriding ("obsessive") importance to the family.
- Children are different from adults in that they are less hardened and less experienced.

The author of Paraphrase C has done a thorough job of the beginning and the end of Lasch's passage, and evidently left the middle to take care of itself. But a paraphrase cannot be considered a reliable "translation" of the original text unless all the supporting ideas are given appropriate emphasis. The second omission is the most serious criticism.

Paraphrase D: Comprehensive Paraphrase

Though the family has always been the institution responsible for bringing up children, only in recent times has its child-raising function become the family's overriding purpose and its reason for being. This striking shift to the child-centered family has resulted from the gradual realization that children have a special, unique personality, easy to influence and easy to hurt, and that they must be treated accordingly. Special treatment for children is the norm in our time; but hundreds of years ago, people saw little or no difference between childhood and adulthood, and, in fact, the child's role in the family resembled that of a servant. It was not until the seventeenth century that people began to regard childhood as a distinctive stage of growth. That recognition led them to understand what a powerful influence the family environment must have on the child and to define "family" as the chief instrument for molding the child's personality and moral attitudes.

EXERCISE 15: Identifying a Good Paraphrase

A. Read the passage from "Dangerously Addictive," by Peter C. Whybrow, twice. Then read the group of paraphrases that follow.

B. Examine each paraphrase and decide whether it conforms to the guidelines for paraphrasing.

C. Ask yourself whether the paraphrase contains any point that is not in the original passage and whether the key points of the original are *all* clearly presented in the paraphrase. Does the writer understand the text?

The astonishing appetite of the American consumer now determines some 70 percent of all economic activity in the United States. And yet in this land of opportunity and material comfort—where we enjoy the 12-inch dinner plate, the 32-ounce soda, and the 64-inch TV screen—more and more citizens feel time-starved, overworked, and burdened by debt. Epidemic rates of obesity, anxiety, depression, and family dysfunction are accepted as the norm.

It is the paradox of modernity that as choice and material prosperity increase, health and personal satisfaction decline. That is now an accepted truth. And yet it is the rare American who manages to step off the hedonic treadmill long enough to savor his or her good fortune. Indeed, for most of us, regardless of what we have we want more, and we want it now. The roots of this conundrum—of this addictive striving—are found in our evolutionary history. As creatures of the natural world, having evolved under conditions of danger and scarcity, we are by instinct reward-seeking animals that discount the future in favor of the immediate present. As a species, we are biologically ill-suited to handle the seductive prosperity and material riches of contemporary America. A novel experience, it is both compelling and confusing.

PETER C. WHYBROW, from "Dangerously Addictive,"
Chronicle of Higher Education

Paraphrase 1

An amazing number of Americans take advantage of our wonderful country's opportunities by contributing to the economy. The price that they pay is that they have to work hard and experience normal problems of illness. All of us know that, in our world of today, we can lead better, more satisfying lives only if we're willing to accept some sacrifices. We're too busy improving our circumstances to care. Our goal is to do better and better as soon as we can. This is natural as, thousands of years ago, we survived by saving for the future. Now, though, we find it difficult to deal with the amount of choice and comfort available to us.

Paraphrase 2

Most Americans spend their lives trying to get as much out of the economy as they can, putting their earnings into buying more and more things. As a result, they and their families are miserable. It's hard for us to recognize that we can't have it all. America has to stop being so greedy. And, in fact, we should know better. Our ancestors could tell us that we should plan for the future instead of wanting everything now. We need to stop being so easily seduced by possessions.

Paraphrase 3

Seventy percent of the American economy depends on consumer purchases. America provides ample opportunities for its citizens to be successful, and that success is generally defined by more and bigger possessions. Unfortunately, there is a trade-off—Americans pay for this ideal lifestyle by sacrificing personal freedoms like sufficient leisure time and a healthy bank account. Their health and their family life deteriorate. Evidently, in our time, you can't be well-off financially and achieve all that's possible without suffering a loss of personal well-being. But most of us can't spare the time to realize how lucky we are; instead, no evidence of success is ever enough. We desperately want to achieve more. This fixation on material gain comes from a more primitive era when our survival depended on protecting ourselves from immediate threats and finding sufficient food and shelter; we learned that it's more important to make the most of our present opportunities than to see what the future might bring. Unused to such an array of material goods and experiences, we're not sure what we really want, but we want to have it now.

Paraphrasing a Difficult Text

Since translating another writer's idiom into your own can be difficult, a paraphrase is often written in two stages.

1. In your first version, you work out a *word-for-word* paraphrase, staying close to the sentence structure of the original, as if you are writing a translation. This is the *literal paraphrase*.

2. In your second version, you work from your own literal paraphrase, turning it into a *free paraphrase* by reconstructing and rephrasing the sentences to make them more natural and more characteristic of your own writing style.

Writing a paraphrase that is faithful to the original text is impossible if you are uncertain of the meaning of any of the words. To write a literal paraphrase of a difficult passage:

- Use a dictionary, especially if the passage contains obsolete or archaic language.
- Write down a few possible synonyms for each difficult word, making sure that you understand the connotations of each synonym.
- Choose the substitute that best fits the context of the text.

Too often, the writer of a paraphrase forgets that there *is* a choice and quickly substitutes the first synonym in the dictionary. Even when appropriate synonyms have been carefully chosen, the literal paraphrase can look peculiar and sound dreadful. While the old sentence structure has been retained, the key words have been yanked out and new ones plugged in.

Writing a Literal Paraphrase: "Of Marriage and Single Life"

To illustrate the pitfalls of this process, here is a short excerpt from Francis Bacon's essay "Of Marriage and Single Life," written around 1600. Some of the phrasing and word combinations are archaic and may sound unnatural, but nothing in the passage is too difficult for modern understanding *if* the sentences are read slowly and carefully.

> He that hath wife and children hath given hostages to fortune; for they are impediments to great enterprises, either of virtue or mischief. Certainly, the best works and of greatest merit for the public have proceeded from the unmarried or childless men: which both in affection and means have endowed the public.

Here is the passage's main idea: *unmarried men, without the burden of a family, can afford to contribute to the public good.* But by now you must realize that such a brief summary is not the same as a paraphrase, for it does not fully present Bacon's reasoning.

Paraphrase A (Literal): Poor Word Choice

He who has a wife and children has bestowed prisoners to riches; for they are defects in huge business organizations either for morality or damage.

Paraphrase B (Literal): Better Word Choice

He who has a wife and children has given a pledge to destiny; for they are hindrances to large endeavor, either for good or for ill.

Neither sentence is easy to understand; but the second has potential, while the first makes no sense. Yet, in *both* cases, the underlined words are synonyms for the original vocabulary. In Paraphrase A the words do not fit Bacon's context; in Paraphrase B they do.

For example, it is misleading to choose "business organizations" as a synonym for "enterprises," since the passage doesn't actually concern business but refers to any sort of undertaking requiring freedom from responsibility. "Impediment" can mean either "defect" (as in speech impediment) or "hindrance" (as in impediment to learning); but—again, given the context—it is the second meaning that Bacon has in mind.

A phrase like *hostages to fortune* offers special difficulty, since it is a powerful image expressing a highly abstract idea. No paraphraser can improve on the original wording or even find an equivalent phrase. What is Bacon trying to express? A bargain made with life—the renunciation of future independence in exchange for a family. Wife and children become a kind of pledge ("hostages") to ensure one's future social conformity. The aptness and singularity of Bacon's original phrase are measured by the difficulty of paraphrasing three words in less than two sentences!

Writing a Free Paraphrase: "Of Marriage and Single Life"

Correct though the synonyms may be, the passage from Bacon cannot be left as it is in Paraphrase B, for no reader could readily understand this stilted, artificial sentence. It is necessary to rephrase the paraphrase, ensuring that the meaning of the words is retained, but making the sentence sound more natural. The first attempt at "freeing up" the paraphrase stays as close as possible to the literal version, leaving everything in the same sequence but using a more modern idiom:

Paraphrase C (Free): Unclear

Married men with children are hindered from embarking on any important undertaking, good or bad. Indeed, unmarried and childless men are the ones who have done the most for society and have dedicated their love and their money to the public good.

The second sentence (which is simpler to paraphrase than the first) has been inverted here, but the paraphrase is still a point-by-point recapitulation of Bacon. Paraphrase C is acceptable, but can be improved, both to clarify Bacon's meaning and to introduce a more personal voice. What exactly *are* these unmarried men dedicating to the public good? "Affection and means." And what is the modern equivalent of means? money? effort? time? energy?

Paraphrase D (Free): Improved

A man with a family has obligations that prevent him from devoting himself to any activity that pleases him. On the other hand, a single man or a man without children has a greater opportunity to be a philanthropist. That's why most great contributions of energy and resources to the good of society are made by single men.

The writer of Paraphrase D has not supplied a synonym for "affection," which may be too weak a motivation for the philanthropist as he is described here.

Paraphrase E (Free): Successful

The responsibility of a wife and children discourages a man from taking risks with his money, time, and energy. The greatest social benefactors have been men who have adopted the public as their family.

The second sentence here is the only one of the five versions that approaches Bacon's economy of style. "Adopted the public" is not quite the same as "endowed the public" with one's "affection and means"; but nevertheless, this paraphrase is successful because it speaks for itself. It has a life and an importance of its own, independent of Bacon's original passage, yet it makes the same point that Bacon does.

Guidelines for Paraphrasing a Difficult Passage

1. Look up in a dictionary the meanings of all the words of which you are uncertain. Pay special attention to the difficult words, considering the context of the whole passage.
2. Write a literal paraphrase of each passage by substituting appropriate synonyms within the original sentence structure.
3. Revise your literal paraphrase, keeping roughly to the same length and number of sentences as the original but using your own sentence style and phrasing throughout. You may prefer to put the original passage aside at this point and work entirely from your literal version.
4. Read your free paraphrase aloud to make sure that it makes sense.

EXERCISE 16: Paraphrasing a Difficult Passage

Paraphrase one of the following passages, using the guidelines in the box on page 159. (Your instructor may assign a specific paragraph for the entire class to paraphrase; you may be asked to work together with one or more of your classmates.)

1. Anthropologists have found that some tribes do not see colors the way many of us do; for instance, they do not "see" a difference between brown and yellow. Members of these tribes are not colorblind, but some differences found in nature (in the color spectrum) simply don't register with them, just as young American children are unaware of racial differences until someone introduces them to these distinctions. We draw a line between white and black, but people's skin colors have many shades. It is our social prejudices that lead us to make sharp racial categories.

   AMITAI ETZIONI, from "Leaving Race Behind,"
   The American Scholar

2. The theme of metamorphosis recurs throughout the whole chronicle of American biography. Men and women start out in one place and end up in another, never quite knowing how they got there, perpetually expecting the unexpected, drifting across the ocean or the plains until they lodge against a marriage, a land deal, a public office, or a jail.

   LEWIS LAPHAM, from *Hotel America:
   Scenes in the Lobby of the Fin-de-Siècle*

3. It is somewhat ironic to note that grading *systems* evolved in part because of [problems in evaluating performance]. In situations where reward and recognition often depended more on who you knew than on what you knew, and lineage was more important than ability, the cause of justice seemed to demand a method whereby the individual could demonstrate specific abilities on the basis of objective criteria. This led to the establishment of specific standards and public criteria as ways of reducing prejudicial treatment and, in cases where appropriate standards could not be specified in advance, to the normal curve system of establishing levels on the basis of group performance. The imperfect achievement of the goals of such systems in no way negates the importance of the underlying purposes.

   WAYNE MOELLENBERG, from "To Grade or Not
   to Grade — Is That the Question?"

4. For most of human history, most people could not read at all. Literacy was not only a demarcator between the powerful and the powerless; it was power itself. Pleasure was not an issue. The ability to maintain and understand commercial records, the ability to communicate across distance and in code, the ability to keep the word of God to yourself and transmit it only at your own will and in your own time—these are formidable means of control over others and aggrandizement of self. Every literate society began with literacy as a constitutive prerogative of the (male) ruling class.

URSULA K. LE GUIN, from "Staying Awake: Notes on the Alleged Decline of Reading," *Harper's*

5. [The blog], this form of instant and global self-publishing, made possible by technology widely available only for the past decade or so, allows for no retroactive editing (apart from fixing minor typos or small glitches) and removes from the act of writing any considered or lengthy review. It is the spontaneous expression of instant thought—impermanent beyond even the ephemera of daily journalism. It is accountable in immediate and unavoidable ways to readers and other bloggers, and linked via hypertext to continuously multiplying references and sources. Unlike any single piece of print journalism, its borders are extremely porous and its truth inherently transitory. The consequences of this for the act of writing are still sinking in.

ANDREW SULLIVAN, from "Why I Blog," *Atlantic Monthly*

Using Paraphrase with Quotation and Summary

The paraphrased ideas of other writers should never dominate your essay, but should always be subordinate to *your* ideas. When you insert a paraphrased sentence or a brief paraphrased passage (rather than a quotation) into one of your paragraphs, you minimize the risk that the source material will dominate your writing.

Most academic writers rely on a combination of quotation, paraphrase, and summary to present their sources and to support their theses.

To illustrate the way in which these three techniques of presentation can be successfully combined, here is an extract from an article by Conor Cruise O'Brien that depends on a careful mixture of paraphrase, summary, and quotation. In "Violence—And Two Schools of Thought," O'Brien gives an account of a medical conference concerned with the origins of violence. Specifically, he undertakes to present and (at the end) comment on the ideas of two speakers at the conference.

from VIOLENCE — AND TWO SCHOOLS OF THOUGHT*
Conor Cruise O'Brien

summary

1

The opening speakers were fairly representative of the main schools of thought which almost always declare themselves when violence is discussed. The first school sees a propensity to aggression as biological but capable of being socially conditioned into patterns of acceptable behavior. The second sees it as essentially created by social conditions and therefore capable of being removed by benign social change.

quotation

2

The first speaker held that violence was "a bio-social phenomenon." He rejected the notion that human beings were blank paper "on which the environment can write whatever it likes." He described how a puppy could be conditioned to choose a dog food it did not like and to reject one it did like. This was

paraphrase

the creation of conscience in the puppy. It was done by mild punishment. If human beings were acting more aggressively and anti-socially, despite the advent of better social conditions and better housing, this might be because permissiveness, in school and home, had checked the process of social conditioning, and therefore of conscience-building. He favored the reinstatement of conscience-building, through the use of mild punishment and token rewards. "We

quotation

cannot eliminate violence," he said, "but we can do a great deal to reduce it."

summary

3

The second speaker thought that violence was the result of stress; in almost all the examples he cited it was stress from overcrowding. The behavior of

paraphrase/
quotation

apes and monkeys in zoos was "totally different" from the way they behaved in "the completely relaxed conditions in the wild." In crowded zoos the most ag-

paraphrase/
quotation

gressive males became leaders and a general reign of terror set in; in the relaxed wild, on the other hand, the least aggressive males ruled benevolently. Space was all: "If we could eliminate population pressures, violence would vanish."

summary

4

The student [reacting to the argument of the two speakers] preferred the second speaker. He [the second speaker] spoke with ebullient confidence, fast but clear, and at one point ran across the vast platform, in a lively imitation of the behavior of a charging ape. Also, his message was simple and hopeful. Speaker one, in contrast, looked sad, and his message sounded faintly sinister.

author's
comment

Such impressions, rather than the weight of argument, determine the reception of papers read in such circumstances.

summary/
paraphrase

5

Nonetheless, a student queried speaker two's "relaxed wild." He seemed to recall a case in which a troop of chimpanzees had completely wiped out

*The number of paragraphs has been reduced, without changing the meaning of the text.

another troop. The speaker was glad the student had raised that question because it proved the point. You see, where that had occurred, there had been an
overcrowding in the jungle, just as happens in zoos, and this was a response to
overcrowding. Conditions in the wild, it seems, are not always "completely relaxed." And when they attain that attributed condition — through the absence
of overcrowding — this surely has to be due to the "natural controls," including
the predators, whose attentions can hardly be all that relaxing, or, indeed, all
that demonstrative of the validity of the proposition that violence is not a part
of nature. Speaker two did not allude to predators. Nonetheless, they are still
around, on two legs as well as on four.

*author's
comment*

Although we do not have the texts of the original papers given at the
conference to compare with O'Brien's description, this article seems to present
a clear account of a complex discussion. In the first paragraph, O'Brien uses
brief summaries to help us distinguish between the two speakers; next, he provides us with two separate, noncommittal descriptions of the two main points
of view.

The ratio of quotation to paraphrase to summary works very effectively.
O'Brien quotes for two reasons: *aptness of expression* and *the desire to distance himself from the statement.* For example, he chooses to quote the *vivid image* of the
blank paper "on which the environment can write whatever it likes." And he
also selects points for quotation that he regards as *open to dispute* — "totally different"; "completely relaxed"; "violence would vanish." Such strong statements are often quoted so that writers won't be accused of either toning down
or exaggerating the meaning in their paraphrases.

In the last two paragraphs, it is not always easy to determine where
O'Brien's paraphrase of the speakers' ideas ends and his own opinions begin.
In Paragraph 4, his description of the student's reactions to the two speakers
appears objective. At the end of the paragraph, however, we learn that O'Brien
is scornful of the criteria that the student is using to evaluate these ideas. But at
first we cannot be sure whether O'Brien is describing the *student's observation* or
giving *his own account* of the speaker's platform maneuvers. It would be clearer
to us if the sentence began: "According to the responding student, the second
speaker spoke with ebullient confidence. . . ." Similarly, the last sentence of
Paragraph 4 is undoubtedly O'Brien's opinion, yet there is nothing to indicate
the transition from the student to O'Brien as the source of commentary.

This confusion of point of view is especially deceptive in Paragraph 5 as
O'Brien moves from his paraphrased and neutral account of the dialogue between student and speaker to his own opinion that certain predators influence
behavior in civilization as well as in the wild. It takes two readings to notice the
point — can you find it? — at which O'Brien has stopped paraphrasing and begins to speak in his own voice. Such confusions could have been clarified by
inserting citations — the name of the source or appropriate pronoun — in the
appropriate places.

Reasons to Use Quotation

- You can find no words to convey the economy and aptness of phrasing of the original text.
- A paraphrase might alter the statement's meaning.
- A paraphrase would not clearly distinguish between your views and the author's.

EXERCISE 17: Distinguishing among Quotation, Paraphrase, Summary, and Commentary

A.   Read "Maybe Money Does Buy Happiness After All," by David Leonhardt, twice.

B.   In the margin, indicate where the author uses quotation (Q), paraphrase (P), summary (S), and commentary (C). As necessary, distinguish between summary of the source and summary of the topic or context.

C.   In class discussion, be prepared to evaluate the use of quotation, paraphrase, and summary, and to indicate those places in the article where, in your opinion, one of the techniques is inappropriately or unnecessarily used, where the transition from one technique to the other is not clearly identified, or where the source is not clearly cited.

MAYBE MONEY DOES BUY HAPPINESS AFTER ALL*
David Leonhardt

For over a decade, David Leonhardt's columns about economics have appeared in the New York Times, *where this article was first published. Leonhardt has also written for* Business Week *and the* Washington Post.

In the aftermath of World War II, the Japanese economy went through one   1
of the greatest booms the world has ever known. From 1950 to 1970, the economy's output per person grew more than sevenfold. Japan, in just a few decades, remade itself from a war-torn country into one of the richest nations on earth. Yet, strangely, Japanese citizens didn't seem to become any more

*The number of paragraphs has been reduced, without changing the meaning of the text.

satisfied with their lives. According to one poll, the percentage of people who gave the most positive possible answer about their life satisfaction actually fell from the late 1950s to the early '70s. They were richer but apparently no happier.

This contrast became the most famous example of a theory known as the Easterlin paradox. In 1974, Richard Easterlin, then an economist at the University of Pennsylvania, published a study in which he argued that economic growth didn't necessarily lead to more satisfaction. People in poor countries, not surprisingly, did become happier once they could afford basic necessities. But beyond that, further gains simply seemed to reset the bar. To put it in today's terms, owning an iPod doesn't make you happier, because you then want an iPod Touch. Relative income — how much you make compared with others around you — mattered far more than absolute income, Mr. Easterlin wrote.

The paradox quickly became a social science classic, cited in academic journals and the popular media. It tapped into a near-spiritual human instinct to believe that money can't buy happiness. As a 2006 headline in the *Financial Times* said, "The Hippies Were Right All Along About Happiness."

But now the Easterlin paradox is under attack. Last week, at the Brookings Institution in Washington, two young economists — from the University of Pennsylvania, as it happens — presented a rebuttal of the paradox. Their paper has quickly captured the attention of top economists around the world. It has also led to a spirited response from Mr. Easterlin. In the paper, Betsey Stevenson and Justin Wolfers argued that money indeed tends to bring happiness, even if it doesn't guarantee it. They point out that in the 34 years since Mr. Easterlin published his paper, an explosion of public opinion surveys has allowed for a better look at the question. "The central message," Ms. Stevenson said, "is that income does matter."

To see what they mean, take a look at the map that accompanies this column. It's based on Gallup polls done around the world, and it clearly shows that life satisfaction is highest in the richest countries. The residents of these countries seem to understand that they have it pretty good, whether or not they own an iPod Touch. If anything, Ms. Stevenson and Mr. Wolfers say, absolute income seems to matter more than relative income. In the United States, about 90 percent of people in households making at least $250,000 a year called themselves "very happy" in a recent Gallup poll. In households with income below $30,000, only 42 percent of people gave that answer. But the international polling data suggests that the under-$30,000 crowd might not be happier if they lived in a poorer country.

Even the Japanese anomaly isn't quite what it first seems to be. Ms. Stevenson and Mr. Wolfers dug into those old government surveys and discovered that the question had changed over the years. In the late 1950s and early '60s, the most positive answer the pollsters offered was, "Although I am not innumerably satisfied, I am generally satisfied with life now." (Can you imagine an American poll offering that option?) But in 1964, the most positive answer became simply, "Completely satisfied." It is no wonder, then, that the percentage of people giving this answer fell. When you look only at the years in which the question remained the same, the share of people calling themselves "satisfied" or "completely satisfied" did rise.

To put the new research into context, I called Daniel Kahneman, a Princeton psychologist who shared the 2002 Nobel Prize in economics. He has spent his career skewering economists for their belief that money is everything and has himself written about the "aspiration treadmill" at the heart of the Easterlin paradox. Yet Mr. Kahneman said he found the Stevenson-Wolfers paper to be "quite compelling." He added, "There is just a vast amount of accumulating evidence that the Easterlin paradox may not exist."   7

I then called Mr. Easterlin, who's now at the University of Southern California and who had received a copy of the paper from Ms. Stevenson and Mr. Wolfers. He agreed that people in richer countries are more satisfied. But he's skeptical that their wealth is causing that satisfaction. The results could instead reflect cultural differences in how people respond to poll questions, he said. He would be more persuaded, he continued, if satisfaction had clearly risen in individual countries as they grew richer. In some, it has. But in others — notably the United States and China — it has not. "Everybody wants to show the Easterlin paradox doesn't hold up," he told me. "And I'm perfectly willing to believe it doesn't hold up. But I'd like to see an informed analysis that shows that." He said he liked Ms. Stevenson and Mr. Wolfers personally, but he thought they had put out "a very rough draft without sufficient evidence."   8

They, in turn, acknowledge that the data on individual countries over time is messy. But they note that satisfaction has risen in 8 of 10 European countries for which there is polling back to 1970. It has also risen in Japan. And a big reason it may not have risen in the United States is that the hourly pay of most workers has not grown much recently. "The time-series evidence is fragile," Mr. Wolfers said. "But it's more consistent with our story than his."   9

So where does all this leave us? Economic growth, by itself, certainly isn't enough to guarantee people's well-being — which is Mr. Easterlin's great contribution to economics. In this country, for instance, some big health care problems, like poor basic treatment of heart disease, don't stem from a lack of sufficient resources. Recent research has also found that some of the things that make people happiest — short commutes, time spent with friends — have little to do with higher incomes.   10

But it would be a mistake to take this argument too far. The fact remains that economic growth doesn't just make countries richer in superficially   11

Measuring Happiness

A new study shows that people in wealthier countries are more likely to be satisfied with their lives. Earlier research had suggested that satisfaction did not necessarily increase once basic needs were met.

Percent who rate themselves an 8, 9 or 10 on a 10-point scale of satisfaction

66%
33
25
15
5

KEY:

● Each dot represents one country

The line around the dot shows how satisfaction relates to income within that country:

Higher-income people are more satisfied

Higher-income and lower-income people are equally satisfied

8   Average life satisfaction (on a 10-point scale)

Denmark
Canada   Finland
New Zealand   Norway
Costa Saudi   Israel   Ireland
Venezuela   Rica   Arabia   Spain   Britain   U.S.
7   Puerto   Italy   Germany
Brazil   Mexico   Rico   Japan   U.A.E.
Jordan   Argentina
Jamaica   Panama   Chile
6   Greece
Guatemala   S. Korea
Myanmar   Bolivia   India   Cuba   Poland   Portugal
Kosovo   Lebanon   South   Hungary   Hong
Zambia   Vietnam   Egypt   Ireland   Africa   Russia   Kong
5   Laos   Peru
Nepal   Ghana   Indonesia
Afghanistan   Yemen   Latvia
Burundi   Angola   China   Turkey   Botswana
Mali   Rwanda   Nicaragua
4   Haiti   Armenia
Malawi   Iraq
Ethiopia   Zimbabwe   Georgia
Tanzania   Cambodia   Bulgaria
Benin   Togo   *Note. Not all nations are labeled.*
3

$500 $1,000 $2,000 $4,000 $8,000 $16,000 $32,000

G.D.P. per capita, converted to dollars at prices that equalize purchasing power

Source: Betsey Stevenson and Justin Wolfers, Wharton School at the University of Pennsylvania

materialistic ways. Economic growth can also pay for investments in scientific research that lead to longer, healthier lives. It can allow trips to see relatives not seen in years or places never visited. When you're richer, you can decide to work less — and spend more time with your friends.

Affluence is a pretty good deal. Judging from that map, the people of the world seem to agree. At a time when the American economy seems to have fallen into recession and most families' incomes have been stagnant for almost a decade, it's good to be reminded of why we should care.

12

Citing Your Paraphrased Sources

In academic writing the clear acknowledgment of the source is not merely a matter of courtesy or clarity; it is an assurance of the writer's honesty.

When you paraphrase another person's ideas, you must cite the author's name, as you do when you quote, or else risk being charged with plagiarism. Borrowing ideas is just as much theft as borrowing words.

You omit the quotation marks when you paraphrase, but you must not omit the citation. The name of the source should be smoothly integrated into your sentence, following the guidelines used for citation of quotations. The source's name need not appear at the beginning of the sentence, but it should signal the beginning of the paraphrase:

Not everyone enjoys working, but most people would agree with Jones's belief that work is an essential experience of life.

The writer of the essay is responsible for the declaration that "not everyone enjoys working" and that most people would agree with Jones's views; but the belief that "work is an essential experience of life" is attributed to Jones. Here, the citation is well and unobtrusively placed; there are no quotation marks, so presumably Jones used a different wording.

Citing Sources

- When you *quote*, there can never be any doubt about where the borrowed material begins and where it ends: the quotation marks provide a clear indication of the boundaries.

- When you *paraphrase*, although the citation may signal the *beginning* of the source material, your reader may not be sure exactly where the paraphrase *ends*. There is no easy method of indicating the end of paraphrased material. (As you will see in Chapter 10, the author's name or a page number in parentheses works well if you are using MLA documentation.) You can signal the end of a paraphrase simply by starting a new paragraph. However, you may want to incorporate more than one person's ideas into a single paragraph. *When you present several points of view in succession, be careful to acknowledge the change of source by citing names.*

Writing a Paragraph That Incorporates Paraphrase and Quotation: *Jarhead*

Now, let's look at the writing process in reverse again. Instead of observing the finished product and analyzing how a writer has used sources, you'll see exactly how one source can be used to support one paragraph of an essay.

The topic of the essay is *soldiers and the code of war*. The student writer is working with the following thesis: *Given the nature of modern warfare, soldiers find it difficult to think of themselves as heroes.* One relevant source is *Jarhead*, a memoir about Anthony Swofford's training as a Marine and his experiences during the first Gulf War. Here is an excerpt.

from JARHEAD

Anthony Swofford

As we drive in the tactical convoy toward the airfield, we occasionally pass a POW internment area, nothing more than a few-hundred-foot circle of concertina wire, and in the center a mass of surrendered men, constrained with plastic thumb cuffs. Marines walk the perimeter with M16s. We drive close enough to the wire so that I see the faces of the POWs, and the men look at us and smile. Occasionally an embarrassing scene of thanks unfolds as a detainee is processed, the detainee kneeling in front of his once enemy and now jailor, weeping and hugging the marine's legs. I suspect the performances are equal parts genuine and dramatic, men genuinely happy at the prospect of not dying and smart enough to please their fierce and potentially deadly jailors with an act of supplication. 1

It's easier to surrender than to accept surrender. The men who surrender do so with blind faith in the good hearts and justice of the men and the system they surrender to. They are faithful and faith is somewhat easy. Those who accept the surrendering men must follow the rules of justice. This requires not faith, but labor and discipline. 2

I feel more compassion for the dead Iraqi soldiers I witnessed yesterday than I do for these men, alive and waving the propaganda pamphlets with vigor and a smile as they await processing. These live men were my enemy just before surrendering, while the dead men are quite simply dead. Moments before surrendering, these incarcerated men might have tried to kill me, so until very recently they were capable of receiving my bullets. The dead men have been incapable of killing me for days or weeks or at least hours and so I would not have shot them. When I'd considered my enemy in the past, I'd been able to imagine them as men similar to me, similarly caught in a trap of their own making, but 3 now that I see these men breathing and within arm's reach, witness them smiling and supplicating and wanting to be my friend, *my friend*, even as I am on my way to kill their fellow soldiers, I no longer care for the men or their safety or the cessation of combat. The enemy are caught in an unfortunate catch-22, in that I care for them as men and fellow unfortunates as long as they are not within riflesight or they're busy being dead, but as soon as I see them living, I wish to turn upon them my years of training and suffering, and I want to perform some of the despicable acts I've learned over the prior few years, such as trigger-killing them from one thousand yards distant, or gouging their hearts with my sharp bayonet.

How do you write a paragraph that conveys Swofford's testimony about a soldier's life and links it to the proposed thesis of the essay? Here are four versions of a possible paragraph:

First Version: Plagiarized

acceptable summary

Soldiers are so caught up in the tension of battle and the fear of being killed that they can't suddenly feel compassion for the enemy when they are defeated and become prisoners. A soldier may feel more comfortable with a dead man than with a live prisoner of war. You can't kill the enemy one day and be expected to regard them as nice people the next day.

no mention of Swofford = plagiarism

This is a reasonable summary of the Swofford passage. Unfortunately, there is no mention of the source. The reader has no idea that Swofford's experience is being described, and the writer is moving very close to plagiarism.

Second Version: Plagiarized

no topic sentence

inserted quotation marks indicate plagiarism

In *Jarhead*, Anthony Swofford tells us about the time he came to a prisoner of war camp during the Gulf War and sees "an embarrassing scene of thanks" as prisoners weep and clutch their captors' legs. Swofford concludes that the prisoners have an easier time than their jailors since "it's easier to surrender than to accept surrender." He can't understand how they can "want to be his friend" when he's performed so many "despicable acts" and has killed so many of their fellow soldiers.

This version cites Swofford as the source but plagiarizes his words. The writer is not paraphrasing, but, rather, stringing together bits of Swofford's phrases. The paragraph also lacks a topic sentence that explains why Swofford is being cited.

Third Version: Acceptable

good presentation of Swofford; supports topic sentence

It's easy for soldiers fighting a brutal war to lose their sense of humanity. Anthony Swofford's *Jarhead* tells us about an incident that happened to him when he was a Marine fighting in the first Gulf War. He sees a group of prisoners trying to placate their captors, and that makes him examine his own resentment at the fact that they are alive and happily trying to stay alive. Swofford can't bring himself to see them as human beings. After all, later that day he might have to kill men just like them in the enemy's army.

a quotation would make the experience more immediate

This is a good presentation of the source because it provides just enough material from Swofford to support the point of the topic sentence. But the writer could and should have used quotation to give some immediacy to Swofford's experience.

Fourth Version: Successful

topic sentence

Soldiers are trained to kill routinely, and to do that efficiently they can't let themselves think of the enemy as people like themselves. In *Jarhead*, Anthony Swofford describes his disgust at an "embarrassing scene of thanks" at a prisoner of war camp during the first Gulf War. Feeling ambivalent, he wants to think of the enemy "as men similar to me," but finds it hard to endure the sight of the prisoners carrying on the business of life by trying to please their captors. The enemy dead don't cause as much moral conflict for him as the living enemy. Swofford's conclusion is that "it's easier to surrender than to accept surrender" (227). It takes a lot of effort and self-control for a soldier to kill one day and be expected to take care of the enemy the next day. Swofford's experience helps me to understand what happened in Abu Ghraib jail.

good mixture of quotation and paraphrase

full documentation: author's name, work's title, page number

The writer makes a point in the topic sentence and then convincingly uses paraphrase and quotation to support that point. The citation to Swofford is clear, and the quoted material is appropriate. Equally important, the writer doesn't just recount Swofford's experience but makes comments that link the source to the writer's own purposes in writing the essay. Finally, notice that the writer *documents* the source not only by citing the author's name and the work but also by inserting after the second quotation the page number where the paraphrased and quoted material can be found. You'll learn about the formal documentation of sources in Chapter 10.

EXERCISE 18: Paraphrasing without Plagiarism

A. Read each passage twice. Then read the three brief paraphrases taken from student essays.

B. As you read the paraphrases, consider whether the structure of the phrases and sentences seems to be the student's work or the original author's and whether the choice of words seems *for the most part* to be the student's or the author's. At what point does the balance tip, and the fair use of common language turn into plagiarism?

C. Determine whether each paraphrase:

- accurately conveys the author's meaning
- distorts his or her meaning
- plagiarizes his or her words in order to express the original meaning

Set 1

To prepare . . . lamb in either the Neapolitan or Roman style is simple, but first the cook must deal with the question of squeamishness, for guests tend to react to baby lamb as if it were the family poodle. Surely it is not an act of kindness to kill an innocent lamb, but neither is it kind to kill the innocent pigs and cattle that supply the B.L.T.s and Big Macs that we thoughtlessly devour by the billion. Human beings are omnivores who in their various cultures — or under extreme conditions in any culture — will kill and eat almost anything, including one another.

JASON EPSTEIN, from "The Science of the Lambs,"
The New York Times Magazine, 17 March 2002: 66.

Note that an acceptable paraphrase can reasonably include some language from the source: words that are basic or common or words that are essential to the meaning. For example, conveying Jason Epstein's meaning would be difficult without using the word "lamb." But what about "innocent lamb"?

Paraphrase 1

Jason Epstein observes that serving lamb at dinner can be difficult if the guests have scruples about eating meat. It's one thing to react with horror at slaughtering and eating a family pet or a wooly lamb, but Epstein wonders whether we have the same scruples about slaughtering the less attractive and endearing but no less innocent steers and pigs consumed daily in hamburgers and B.L.T.s. All human beings are capable of killing and eating other living creatures if their needs require it (66).

Paraphrase 2

According to Jason Epstein, squeamish guests can be a problem when they react to a dish of baby lamb as if they were being asked to eat the family poodle. Although killing an innocent lamb isn't an act of kindness, it's just as bad to kill the innocent cattle and pigs that we eat in B.L.T.s and Big Macs. We have to accept the fact that human beings are omnivores who will eat whatever their cultures require, including (under extreme conditions) each other (66).

Paraphrase 3

Jason Epstein thinks that guests who refuse to eat lamb create problems for the cook, but they simply don't want to be responsible for the death of an innocent animal. In Epstein's view, whether it's a baby lamb or a cow or a pig, slaughtering living creatures to provide food for our lunches and dinners is cruel and inhumane. It's unfortunate that our cultures encourage us to eat whatever we want to and that usually means living animals, even each other (66).

Set 2

Freudian readings of cannibal tales argue that such stories present the world from the child's point of view—hence the importance of oral satisfaction, pleasure and survival (eating or being eaten). In traditional psychoanalytic terms, stories of cannibalism are usually interpreted as a disfigured form of parental aggression or a projection of the child's own all-consuming greed.

MIKITA BROTTMAN, from "Celluloid Cannibals That Feed Our Darkest Fears," *Chronicle of Higher Education*, 2 March 2001: B15.

Deciding which of the source's words can be reasonably used becomes more difficult when you are writing about a discipline that has its own unique terms of reference. Brottman is using the language of psychology. Conveying the meaning of "oral satisfaction" or "projection" is a challenge, but you should try as much as possible to use your own words.

Paraphrase 1

Mikita Brottman notes that many cannibal tales are written from the child's point of view and emphasize oral satisfaction, pleasure, and the need to survive. From a Freudian point of view, such stories are interpreted as a distorted form of parental aggression or a projection of the child's greed (B15).

Paraphrase 2

According to Freudian theory, stories about cannibals tend to be told from a child's perspective and therefore emphasize the comforting reassurance that children receive from the act of eating combined with relief that they themselves are not serving as someone's meal. Underlying these stories of cannibalism is the child's fear that his parents will harm him or that he will harm himself and others by excessive eating (Brottman, B15).

Paraphrase 3

Brottman tells us that Freudians look at stories about cannibals as a child would. Children are happy when they eat and are fearful when they think someone might eat them. They worry that their parents will hurt them or that they will eat too much (B15).

Set 3

Binge drinking in college used to be associated primarily with males, but a 1997 study of 116 four-year colleges, conducted by researchers at Harvard University, found that 39 percent of women and 49 percent of men had binged in the two previous weeks. . . . Now, several studies reported this year indicate a further increase in the percentage of college women drinking.

DEVON JERSILD, from "Alcohol in the Vulnerable Lives of College Women," *Chronicle of Higher Education*, 31 May 2002: B10.

When you are dealing with facts or statistics, you may have little choice but to use your source's wording. There may be few options for inventing your own phrasing. Still, the sentences in your paraphrase should follow your own structure, not your source's.

Paraphrase 1

A survey in 1997 showed that the number of women college students who engage in excessive drinking (39%) was almost as high as that of male students (49%), who are more traditionally associated with binge drinking. Recent surveys confirm this trend toward an excessive use of alcohol among college women (Jersild, B10).

Paraphrase 2

Although binge drinking in college used to be associated primarily with males, a 1997 Harvard study found that 39 percent of women and 49 percent of men had binged in the two previous weeks. More recent studies indicate that this trend is continuing.

Paraphrase 3

Jersild cites a Harvard study showing that more men than women engage in binge drinking (B10).

EXERCISE 19: Writing a Paragraph That Incorporates Paraphrase and Quotation

A. Read the following passage from "Staying Awake: Notes on the Alleged Decline of Reading," by Ursula K. Le Guin, twice.

B. Assume that you're working on an essay about "The Dumbing-Down of Culture" or "Print vs. Web—Which Will Triumph?" (Or make up a comparable topic of your own.) Write a paragraph that supports one of these topics, and use Le Guin as your source.

C. Remember to include appropriate and accurate citations to the author and, if your instructor requests it, provide the page number in parentheses. (This passage appeared on pages 37 and 38 of *Harper's*. A slash before the last paragraph indicates the page break.)

from STAYING AWAKE: NOTES ON THE ALLEGED DECLINE OF READING

Ursula K. Le Guin

A prolific author in many genres, Ursula K. Le Guin is best known as a writer of science fiction. Her first story, sent to Astounding Science Fiction *in 1932, was rejected. Her work has received 11 Hugo and Nebula awards, and she received the Gandalf Grand Master Award in 1979 and the Science Fiction and Fantasy Writers of America Grand Master Award in 2003. This article appeared in* Harper's.

Books are now only one of the "entertainment media," but when it comes to delivering actual pleasure, they're not a minor one. Look at the competition. Governmental hostility was emasculating public radio while Congress allowed a few corporations to buy out and debase private radio stations. Television has steadily lowered its standards of what is entertaining until most programs are either brain-numbing or actively nasty. Hollywood remakes remakes and tries to gross out, with an occasional breakthrough that reminds us what a movie can be when undertaken as art. And the Internet offers everything to everybody: but perhaps because of that all-inclusiveness there is curiously little *aesthetic* satisfaction to be got from Web-surfing. You can look at pictures or listen to music or read a poem or a book on your computer, but these artifacts are made accessible by the Web, not created by it and not intrinsic to it. Perhaps blogging is an effort to bring creativity to networking, and perhaps blogs will develop aesthetic form, but they certainly haven't done it yet.

Besides, readers aren't viewers; they recognize their pleasure as different   2
from that of being entertained. Once you've pressed the ON button, the TV goes on, and on, and on, and all you have to do is sit and stare. But reading is active, an act of attention, of absorbed alertness — not all that different from hunting, in fact, or from gathering. In its silence, a book is a challenge: it can't lull you with surging music or deafen you with screeching laugh tracks or fire gunshots in your living room; you have to listen to it in your head. A book won't move your eyes for you the way images on a screen do. It won't move your mind unless you give it your mind, or your heart unless you put your heart in it. It won't do the work for you. To read a story well is to follow it, to act it, to feel it, to become it — everything short of writing it, in fact. Reading is not "interactive" with a set of rules or options, as games are; reading is actual collaboration with the writer's mind. No wonder not everybody is up to it.

The book itself is a curious artifact, not showy in its technology but com   3
plex and extremely efficient: a really neat little device, compact, often very pleasant to look at and handle, that can last decades, even centuries. It doesn't have to be plugged in, activated, or performed by a machine; all it needs is light, a human eye, and a human mind. It is not one of a kind, and it is not ephemeral. It lasts. It is reliable. If a book told you something when you were fifteen, it will tell it to you again when you're fifty, though you may understand it so differently that it seems you're reading a whole new book.

This is crucial, the fact that a book is a thing, physically there, durable, in   4
definitely reusable, an object of value.

Presenting Sources: A Summary of Preliminary Writing Skills

1. **Annotation: underlining the text and inserting marginal comments on the page.**

   The notes explain points that are unclear, define difficult words, emphasize key ideas, point out connections to previous or subsequent paragraphs, or suggest the reader's own reactions to what is being discussed.

2. **Paraphrasing: recapitulating, point by point, using your own words.**

   A paraphrase is a faithful and complete rendition of the original, following much the same order of ideas. Although full-length paraphrase is practical only with relatively brief passages, it is the most reliable way to explain and present a text. Paraphrasing a sentence or two, together with a citation of the author's name, is the best method of presenting another person's ideas within your own essay.

3. **Quotation: including another person's exact words within your own writing.**

Although quotation requires the least amount of invention, it is the most technical of all these skills, demanding an understanding of conventional and complex punctuation. In your notes and in your essays, quotation should be a last resort. If the phrasing is unique, if the presentation is subtle, if the point at issue is easily misunderstood or hotly debated, quotation may be appropriate. When in doubt, paraphrase.

4. **Summary: condensing the text into a relatively brief presentation of the main ideas.**

Unlike annotation, a summary should make sense as an independent, coherent piece of writing. Unlike paraphrase, a summary includes only main ideas. However, the summary should be complete in the sense that it provides a fair representation of the work and its parts.

Part III

WRITING FROM SOURCES

The previous four chapters have described some basic ways to understand another writer's ideas and present them accurately and naturally, as part of your own writing. Until now, however, you have been working with forms of writing that are brief and limited—the sentence and the paragraph. Now you can start to use the skills that you practiced in Parts I and II to develop your own ideas in a full-length essay based on sources.

When you write at length from sources, you have a dual responsibility: you must do justice to your own ideas, and you must do justice to each source by fairly representing that author's ideas. But blending the ideas of two or more people within the same essay can create confusion. Who should dominate? How much of yourself should you include? How much of your sources? Moreover, in academic and professional writing you may also have to consider the perspective of your instructor or supervisor, who may assign a topic or otherwise set limits and goals for your work.

Chapter 5 discusses two approaches to writing based on a *single source*. Each demonstrates a way to reconcile the competing influences on your writing and blend the voices that your reader ought to hear:

- You can distinguish between your source and yourself by writing about the two separately, first the source and then yourself, and, in the process, developing an argument that supports or refutes your source's thesis.
- You can use your source as the basis for the development of your own ideas by writing an essay on a similar or related topic.

In the end, *your voice should dominate*. It is you who will choose the thesis and control the essay's structure and direction; it is your understanding and judgment that will interpret the source materials for your reader. When you and your classmates are asked to write about the same reading, your teacher hopes to receive not an identical set of essays but rather a series of individual interpretations with a common starting point in the same source.

Combining your own ideas with those of others inevitably becomes more difficult when you begin to work with *a group of sources*. This is the subject of Chapter 6. It is more than ever vital that your own voice dominate your essay and that you do not simply summarize first one source and then the next, without presenting any perspective of your own.

Blending together a variety of sources is usually called *synthesis*. You try to look beyond each separate assertion and, instead, develop a broad generalization that will encompass your source material. Your own generalized conclusions become the basis for your essay's thesis and organization, while the ideas of your sources serve as the evidence that supports those conclusions.

Chapter 6 emphasizes the standard methods of presenting multiple sources:

- Analyzing each source in a search for common themes
- Establishing common denominators or categories that cut across the separate sources and provide the structure for your essay
- Evaluating each source's relative significance as you decide which to emphasize
- Citing references from several different sources in support of a single point

You will learn to practice synthesis first by working with material taken from oral interviews and surveys and then by analyzing how writers use written sources to present their ideas and their research.

▪5▪
The Single-Source Essay

When you write from a source, you must understand another writer's ideas as thoroughly as you understand your own. The first step in carrying out the strategies described in this chapter is to read carefully through the source essay, using the skills for comprehension that you learned about in previous chapters: *annotation*, *paraphrase*, and *summary*. Once you can explain to your reader what the source is all about, you can begin to plan your analysis and rebuttal of the author's ideas; or you can write your own essay on a related topic.

Strategy One: Arguing Against Your Source

The simplest way to argue against someone else's ideas is to establish *complete separation between the source and yourself*. The structure of your essay breaks into two parts, with the source's views presented first, and your own reactions given equal (or greater) space immediately afterward. Instead of treating the reading as evidence in support of your point of view and blending it with your own ideas, you write an essay that first *analyzes* and then *refutes* your source's basic themes.

Look, for example, at Roger Sipher's "So That Nobody Has to Go to School If They Don't Want To." Roger Sipher, a faculty member in the history department at the State University of New York at Cortland, has a special interest in educational standards.

SO THAT NOBODY HAS TO GO TO SCHOOL
IF THEY DON'T WANT TO
Roger Sipher

A decline in standardized test scores is but the most recent indicator that   1
American education is in trouble.

One reason for the crisis is that present mandatory-attendance laws force   2
many to attend school who have no wish to be there. Such children have little
desire to learn and are so antagonistic to school that neither they nor more
highly motivated students receive the quality education that is the birthright of
every American.

The solution to this problem is simple: Abolish compulsory-attendance laws   3
and allow only those who are committed to getting an education to attend.

This will not end public education. Contrary to conventional belief, legis-   4
lators enacted compulsory-attendance laws to legalize what already existed.
William Landes and Lewis Solomon, economists, found little evidence that
mandatory-attendance laws increased the number of children in school. They
found, too, that school systems have never effectively enforced such laws, usually because of the expense involved.

There is no contradiction between the assertion that compulsory atten-   5
dance has had little effect on the number of children attending school and the
argument that repeal would be a positive step toward improving education.
Most parents want a high school education for their children. Unfortunately,
compulsory attendance hampers the ability of public school officials to enforce
legitimate educational and disciplinary policies and thereby make the education a good one.

Private schools have no such problem. They can fail or dismiss students,   6
knowing such students can attend public school. Without compulsory attendance, public schools would be freer to oust students whose academic or personal behavior undermines the educational mission of the institution.

Has not the noble experiment of a formal education for everyone failed?   7
While we pay homage to the homily, "You can lead a horse to water but you
can't make him drink," we have pretended it is not true in education.

Ask high school teachers if recalcitrant students learn anything of value.   8
Ask teachers if these students do any homework. Quite the contrary, these
students know they will be passed from grade to grade until they are old
enough to quit or until, as is more likely, they receive a high school diploma. At
the point when students could legally quit, most choose to remain since they
know they are likely to be allowed to graduate whether they do acceptable
work or not.

Abolition of archaic attendance laws would produce enormous dividends.   9

*"stubbornly refusing to
obey orders or rules"*

First, it would alert everyone that school is a serious place where one goes   10
to learn. Schools are neither day-care centers nor indoor street corners. Young
people who resist learning should stay away; indeed, an end to compulsory
schooling would require them to stay away.

Second, students opposed to learning would not be able to pollute the ed-   11
ucational atmosphere for those who want to learn. Teachers could stop policing
recalcitrant students and start educating.

Third, grades would show what they are supposed to: how well a student is   12
learning. Parents could again read report cards and know if their children were
making progress.

Fourth, public esteem for schools would increase. People would stop re-   13
garding them as way stations for adolescents and start thinking of them as institutions for educating America's youth.

Fifth, elementary schools would change because students would find out   14
early that they had better learn something or risk flunking out later. Elementary
teachers would no longer have to pass their failures on to junior high and high
school.

Sixth, the cost of enforcing compulsory education would be eliminated.   15
Despite enforcement efforts, nearly 15 percent of the school-age children in our
largest cities are almost permanently absent from school.

Communities could use these savings to support institutions to deal with   16
young people not in school. If, in the long run, these institutions prove more
costly, at least we would not confuse their mission with that of schools.

Schools should be for education. At present, they are only tangentially so.   17
They have attempted to serve an all-encompassing social function, trying to be
all things to all people. In the process they have failed miserably at what they
were originally formed to accomplish.

tangential — slightly or indirectly related to something; not closely connected to something

Presenting Your Source's Point of View

Sipher opposes compulsory attendance laws. You, on the other hand, can
see advantages in imposing a very strict rule for attendance. In order to challenge Sipher convincingly, you incorporate both his point of view and yours
within a single essay.

You begin by *acknowledging Sipher's ideas and presenting them to your readers.*
State them as fairly as you can, without pausing to argue with him or to offer
your own point of view about mandatory attendance.

At first it may seem easiest to follow Sipher's sequence of ideas (especially
since his points are so clearly numbered). But Sipher is more likely to dominate
the argument if you follow the structure of his essay, presenting and answering

each of his points one by one; for you will be arguing on *his* terms, according to *his* conception of the issue rather than yours. Instead:

- Make sure that your reader understands what Sipher is actually saying,
- See if you can find any common ground between your points of view, and
- Begin your rebuttal.

1. *Briefly summarize the issue and the reasons why the author wrote the essay.*

You do this by writing a brief summary, as explained in Chapter 2. Here is a summary of Sipher's article:

> Roger Sipher argues that the presence in the classroom of unwilling students who are indifferent to learning can explain why public school students as a whole are learning less and less. Sipher therefore recommends that public schools discontinue the policy of mandatory attendance. Instead, students would be allowed to drop out if they wished, and faculty would be able to expel students whose behavior made it difficult for serious students to do their work. Once unwilling students were no longer forced to attend, schools would once again be able to maintain high standards of achievement; they could devote money and energy to education, rather than custodial care.

You can make such a summary longer and more detailed by paraphrasing some of the author's arguments and, if you wish, quoting once or twice; such a summary is likely to require several paragraphs.

2. *Analyze and present some of the basic principles that underlie the author's position on this issue.*

In debating the issue with the author, you will need to do more than just contradict his main ideas: Sipher says mandatory attendance is bad, and you say it is good; Sipher says difficult students don't learn anything, and you say all students learn something useful; and so on. This point-by-point rebuttal shows that you disagree, but it provides no *common context* so that readers can decide who is right and who is wrong. You have no starting point for your counterarguments.

Instead, ask yourself why the author has taken this position, one that you find so easy to reject:

- What are the foundations of his arguments?
- What larger principles do they suggest?
- What policies is he objecting to? Why?
- What values is he determined to defend?

You are now analyzing Sipher's specific responses to the practical problem of attendance in order to *identify his premises* and *infer some broad generalizations* about his philosophy of education.

Although Sipher does not include such generalizations in this article, his views on attendance appear to derive from a *conflict of two principles*:

- the belief that education is a right that may not be denied to children under any circumstances, and
- the belief that education is a privilege to be earned.

Sipher advocates the second position. So, after your initial summary of the article, you should analyze that position in a separate paragraph.

"something a someone or acquired "gained"

Sipher's argument implies that there is no such thing as the right to an education. A successful education can only depend on the student's willing presence and active participation. Passive or rebellious students cannot be educated and should not be forced to stay in school. Sipher is telling us that, although everyone has the right to an opportunity for education, its acquisition is actually the privilege of those who choose to work for it.

Through this analysis of Sipher's position, you have established a common context—*eligibility for education*—within which you and he disagree. There is little room for compromise here; it is hard to reconcile the belief that education should be a privilege with the concept of education as an entitlement. Provided with a clear understanding of the differences between you, your reader can choose between your opposing views. At the same time, it's clear that this point and no other is the essential point for debate; thus, you will be fighting on ground that *you* have chosen.

Your analysis also establishes that Sipher's argument is largely *deductive*: a series of premises that derive their power from an appeal to parents' fears that their children (who faithfully attend) will have their education compromised by the unwilling students (who don't). His *supporting evidence* consists of one allusion to the testimony of two economists and one statistic. Both pieces of evidence confirm the subsidiary idea that attendance laws haven't succeeded in improving attendance. His third source of support—the adage about leading a horse to water—deals more directly with the problem of students reluctant to learn; but can it be regarded as serious evidence?

Presenting Your Point of View

3. *Present your reasons for disagreeing with your source.*

Once you have established your opponent's position, you may then develop your own counterarguments by writing down your reactions and pinpointing the exact reasons for your disagreement. (All the student examples analyzed in this section are taken from such preliminary responses; they are *not* excerpts from finished essays.) Your reasons for disagreeing with Sipher might fit into one of three categories:

- You believe that his basic principle is not valid (Student B).
- You decide that his principle, although valid, cannot be strictly applied to the practical situation under discussion (Student C).
- You accept Sipher's principle, but you are aware of other, stronger influences that diminish its importance (Student E).

Whichever line of argument you follow, it is impossible to present your case successfully if you wholly ignore Sipher's basic principle, as Student A does:

Student A

make them attend   Sipher's isn't a constructive solution. Without strict attendance laws, many students wouldn't come to school at all.

Nonattendance is exactly what Sipher wants: he argues that indifferent students should be permitted to stay away, that their absence would benefit everyone. Student A makes no effort to refute Sipher's point; he is, in effect, saying to his source, "You're wrong!" without explaining why.

Student B, however, tries to establish a basis for disagreement:

Student B

education is too important to give students a choice   If mandatory attendance were to be abolished, how would children acquire the skills to survive in an educated society such as ours?

According to Student B, the practical uses of education have become so important that a student's very survival may one day depend on having been well educated. Implied here is the principle, in opposition to Sipher's, that receiving an education cannot be a matter of choice or a privilege to be earned. What children learn in school is so important to their future lives that they should be forced to attend classes, even against their will, for their own good.

But this response is still superficial. Student B is confusing the desired object—*getting an education*—with one of the means of achieving that object—*being present in the classroom*. Attendance, the means, has become an end in itself. Since students who attend but do not participate will not learn, mandatory attendance cannot by itself create an educated population.

On the other hand, although attendance may not be the *only* prerequisite for getting an education, the student's physical presence in the classroom is certainly important. In that case, should the decision about attendance, a decision likely to affect much of their future lives, be placed in the hands of those too young to understand the consequences?

Student C

students are not mature enough to be given a choice

The absence of attendance laws would be too tempting for students and might create a generation of semi-illiterates. Consider the marginal student who, despite general indifference and occasional bad behavior, shows some promise and capacity for learning. Without a policy of mandatory attendance, he might choose the easy way out instead of trying to develop his abilities. As a society, we owe these students, at whatever cost, a chance at a good and sound education.

Notice that Student C specifies a "chance" at education. Here is a basic point of accommodation between Student C's views and Sipher's. *Both agree in principle that society can provide the opportunity, but not the certainty, of being educated.* The distinction here lies in the way in which the principle is applied. With his argument based on a sweeping generalization, Sipher makes no allowances or exceptions: there are limits to the opportunities that society is obliged to provide. Student C, however, believes that society must act in the best interests of those too young to make such decisions; for their sake, the principle of education as a privilege should be less rigorously applied. Students should be exposed to the conditions for (if not the fact of) education, whether they like it or not, until they become adults, capable of choice.

Student D goes even further, suggesting that not only is society obliged to provide the student with educational opportunities, but schools are responsible for making the experience as attractive as possible.

Student D

if schools were less boring, students would attend

Maybe the reason for a decrease in attendance and an unwillingness to learn is not that students do not want an education, but that the whole system of discipline and learning is ineffective. If schools concentrated on making classes more appealing, the result would be better attendance, and students would learn more.

In Student D's analysis, passive students are like consumers who need to be encouraged to take advantage of an excellent product that is not selling well. To encourage good attendance, the schools ought to consider using more attractive marketing methods. Implicit in this view is *a transferral of blame from the student to the school.* Other arguments of this sort might blame the parents, rather than the schools, for not teaching their children to understand that it is in their own best interests to get an education.

Finally, Student E accepts the validity of Sipher's view of education but finds that the whole issue has become subordinate to a more important problem.

Student E

our security requires that students stay in school

We already have a problem with youths roaming the street, getting into serious trouble. Just multiply the current number of unruly kids by five or ten, and you will come up with the number of potential delinquents that will be hanging around the streets if we do away with the attendance laws that keep them in school. Sipher may be right when he argues that the quality of education would improve if unwilling students were permitted to drop out, but he would be wise to remember that those remaining inside school will have to deal with those on the outside sooner or later.

In this perspective, *security becomes more important than education*. Student E implicitly accepts and gives some social value to the image (rejected by Sipher) of school as a prison, with students sentenced to mandatory confinement.

Student E also ignores Sipher's tentative suggestion (in paragraph 16) that society provide these unwilling students with their own "institutions," which he describes only in terms of their potential costs. What would the curriculum be? Would these institutions be "special schools" or junior prisons? And when these students "graduate," how will they take their place in society?

Structuring Your Essay

A reasonably full response, like those of Students C and E, can provide the material for a series of paragraphs that argue against Sipher's position. Here, for example, is Student E's statement analyzed into *the basic topics for a four-paragraph rebuttal* within the essay. (The topics are on the left.)

Student E

danger from dropouts if Sipher's plan is adopted (III)

custodial function of school (II)

concession that Sipher is right about education (I)

interests of law and order outweigh interests of education (IV)

We already have a problem with youths roaming the street, getting into serious trouble. Just multiply the current number of unruly kids by five or ten, and you will come up with the number of potential delinquents that will be hanging around the streets if we do away with the attendance laws that keep them in school. Sipher may be right when he argues that the quality of education would improve if unwilling students were permitted to drop out, but he would be wise to remember that those remaining inside school will have to deal with those on the outside sooner or later.

Here are Student E's four topics, with the sequence reordered, in outline format. The student's basic agreement with Sipher has become the starting point.

I.   Sipher is right about education.
   A. It is possible that the quality of education would improve if
       unwilling students were allowed to drop out.
II. School, however, has taken on a custodial function.
   A. It is attendance laws that keep students in school.
III. If Sipher's plan is adopted, dropouts might be a problem.
   A. Youths are already roaming the streets, getting into trouble.
   B. An increase in the number of unruly kids hanging out in the
       streets means even greater possibility of disorder.
IV. The interests of law and order outweigh the interests of education.
   A. Educators will not be able to ignore the problems that will develop
       outside the schools if students are permitted to drop out at will.

Student E can now write a brief essay, with a summary and analysis of Sipher's
argument, followed by four full-length paragraphs explaining each point. If a
longer essay is assigned, Student E should go to the library to find supporting
evidence—statistics and authoritative testimony—to develop these paragraphs. A starting point might be issues that Sipher omits: how do these non-
attenders fare later on when they look for work? What methods have been successful in persuading such students to stay in school?

Guidelines for Writing a One-Source Argument

■ Present your source's point of view.
   1. Briefly summarize the issue and the reasons that prompted the
      author to write the essay.
   2. Analyze and present some of the basic principles that underlie the
      author's position on this issue.
■ Present your point of view.
   3. Present your reasons for disagreeing with (or, if you prefer, sup-
      porting) your source.

ASSIGNMENT 2: Writing an Argument Based on a Single Source

A.   Read "What Our Education System Needs Is More F's," "Why Animals
     Deserve Legal Rights," and "The Case for Torture." As the starting point
     for an essay, select one source with which you disagree. (Or, with your in-
     structor's permission, bring in an essay that you are certain you disagree
     with, and have your instructor approve your choice.)

B.   Write a two-part summary of the essay, the first part describing the author's position and explicitly stated arguments, the second analyzing the principles underlying that position.

C.   Then present your own rebuttal of the author's point of view.

The length of your essay will depend on the number and complexity of the ideas that you find in the source and the number of counterarguments that you can assemble. The minimum acceptable length for the entire assignment is two printed pages (approximately 500–600 words).

WHAT OUR EDUCATION SYSTEM NEEDS IS MORE F'S
Carl Singleton

Carl Singleton, a faculty member at Fort Hays State University, is the editor of Vietnam Studies. *This article appeared in the* Chronicle of Higher Education.

I suggest that instituting merit raises, getting back to basics, marrying the university to industry, and . . . other recommendations will not achieve measurable success [in restoring quality to American education] until something even more basic is returned to practice. The immediate need for our educational system from prekindergarten through post-Ph.D. is not more money or better teaching but simply a widespread giving of F's.   1

Before hastily dismissing the idea as banal and simplistic, think for a moment about the implications of a massive dispensing of failing grades. It would dramatically, emphatically, and immediately force into the open every major issue related to the inadequacies of American education.   2

Let me make it clear that I recommend giving those F's — by the dozens, hundreds, thousands, even millions — only to students who haven't learned the required material. The basic problem of our educational system is the common practice of giving credit where none has been earned, a practice that has resulted in the sundry faults delineated by all the reports and studies over recent years. Illiteracy among high-school graduates is growing because those students have been passed rather than flunked; we have low-quality teaching because of low-quality teachers who never should have been certified in the first place; college students have to take basic reading, writing, and mathematics courses because they never learned those skills in classrooms from which they never should have been granted egress.   3

School systems have contributed to massive ignorance by issuing unearned passing grades over a period of some 20 years. At first there was a tolerance of students who did not fully measure up (giving D's to students who should have received firm F's); then our grading system continued to deterio-   4 rate (D's became C's, and B became the average grade); finally we arrived at total accommodation (come to class and get your C's, laugh at my jokes and take home B's).

Higher salaries, more stringent certification procedures, getting back to basics will have little or no effect on the problem of quality education unless and until we insist, as a profession, on giving F's whenever students fail to master the material.   5

Sending students home with final grades of F would force most parents to deal with the realities of their children's failure while it is happening and when it is yet possible to do something about it (less time on TV, and more time on homework, perhaps?). As long as it is the practice of teachers to pass students who should not be passed, the responsibility will not go home to the parents, where, I hope, it belongs. (I am tempted to make an analogy to then Gov. Lester Maddox's statement some years ago about prison conditions in Georgia — "We'll get a better grade of prisons when we get a better grade of prisoners" — but I shall refrain.)   6

Giving an F where it is deserved would force concerned parents to get themselves away from the TV set, too, and take an active part in their children's education. I realize, of course, that some parents would not help; some cannot help. However, Johnny does not deserve to pass just because Daddy doesn't care or is ignorant. Johnny should pass only when and if he knows the required material.   7

Giving an F whenever and wherever it is the only appropriate grade would force principals, school boards, and voters to come to terms with cost as a factor in improving our educational system. As the numbers of students at various levels were increased by those not being passed, more money would have to be spent to accommodate them. We could not be accommodating them in the old sense of passing them on, but by keeping them at one level until they did in time, one way or another, learn the material.   8

Insisting on respecting the line between passing and failing would also require us to demand as much of ourselves as of our students. As every teacher knows, a failed student can be the product of a failed teacher.   9

Teaching methods, classroom presentations, and testing procedures would have to be of a very high standard — we could not, after all, conscionably give F's if we have to go home at night thinking it might somehow be our own fault.   10

The results of giving an F where it is deserved would be immediately evident. There would be no illiterate college graduates next spring — none. The same would be true of high-school graduates, and consequently next year's college freshmen — all of them — would be able to read.   11

I don't claim that giving F's will solve all of the problems, but I do argue that unless and until we start failing those students who should be failed, other   12 suggested solutions will make little progress toward improving education. Students in our schools and colleges should be permitted to pass only after they have fully met established standards; borderline cases should be retained.

The single most important requirement for solving the problems of educa- 13
tion in America today is the big fat F, written decisively in red ink millions of times in schools and colleges across the country.

WHY ANIMALS DESERVE LEGAL RIGHTS
Steven M. Wise

A specialist in animal-rights law, Steven M. Wise teaches at a number of institutions, including Harvard Law School and Tufts University School of Veterinary Medicine. Active in the Animal Legal Defense Fund and the Center for the Expansion of Fundamental Rights, he is the author of four books as well as the article on animal rights in Encyclopaedia Britannica. *This article appeared in the* Chronicle of Higher Education.

For centuries, the right to have everything that makes existence worth- 1
while — like freedom, safety from torture, and even life itself — has turned on whether the law classifies one as a person or a thing. Although some Jews once belonged to Pharaoh, Syrians to Nero, and African-Americans to George Washington, now every human is a person in the eyes of the law.

All nonhuman animals, on the other hand, are things with no rights. The 2
law ignores them unless a person decides to do something to them, and then, in most cases, nothing can be done to help them. According to statistics collected annually by the Department of Agriculture, in the United States this year, tens of millions of animals are likely to be killed, sometimes painfully, during biomedical research; 10 billion more will be raised in factories so crowded that they're unable to turn around, and then killed for food. The U.S. Fish and Wildlife Service and allied state agencies report that hundreds of millions will be shot by hunters or exploited in rodeos, circuses, and roadside zoos. And all of that is perfectly legal.

What accounts for the legal personhood of all of us and the legal thing- 3
hood of all of them? Judeo-Christian theologians sometimes argue that humans are made in the image of God. But that argument has been leaking since Gratian, the twelfth-century Benedictine monk who is considered the father of canon law, made the same claim just for men in his *Decretum*. Few, if any, philosophers or judges today would argue that being human, all by itself, is sufficient for legal rights. There must be something about us that entitles us to rights.

Philosophers have proffered many criteria as sufficient, including sentience, a sense of justice, the possession of language or morality, and having a rational plan for one's life. Among legal thinkers, the most important is autonomy, also known as self-determination or volition. Things don't act autonomously. Persons do.

Notice that I said that autonomy is "sufficient" for basic legal rights; it obviously isn't necessary. We don't eat or vivisect human babies born without brains, who are so lacking in sentience that they are operated on without anesthesia.

But autonomy is tough to define. Kant thought that autonomous beings always act rationally. Anyone who can't do that can justly be treated as a thing. Kant must have had extraordinary friends and relatives. Not being a full-time academic, I don't know anyone who always acts rationally.

Most philosophers, and just about every judge, reject Kant's rigorous conception of autonomy, for they can easily imagine a human who lacks it, but can still walk about making decisions. Instead, some of them think that a being can be autonomous — at least to some degree — if she has preferences and the ability to act to satisfy them. Others would say she is autonomous if she can cope with changed circumstances. Still others, if she can make choices, even if she can't evaluate their merits very well. Or if she has desires and beliefs and can make at least some sound and appropriate inferences from them.

As things, nonhuman animals have been invisible to civil law since its inception. "All law," said the Roman jurist Hermogenianus, "was established for men's sake." And why not? Everything else was.

Unfortunately for animals, many people have believed that they were put on earth for human use and lack autonomy. Aristotle granted them a few mental abilities: They could perceive and act on impulse. Many Stoics, however, denied them the capacities to perceive, conceive, reason, remember, believe, even experience. Animals knew nothing of the past and could not imagine a future. Nor could they desire, know good, or learn from experience.

For decades, though, evidence has been accumulating that at least some nonhuman animals have extraordinary minds. Twelve years ago, 7-year-old Kanzi — a bonobo who works with Sue Savage-Rumbaugh, a biologist at Georgia State University — drubbed a human 2-year-old, named Alia, in a series of language-comprehension tests. In the tests, both human and bonobo had to struggle, as we all do, with trying to make sense of the mind of a speaker. When Kanzi was asked to "put some water on the vacuum cleaner," he gulped water from a glass, marched to the vacuum cleaner, and dribbled the water over it. Told to "feed your ball some tomato," he could see no ball before him. So he picked up a spongy toy Halloween pumpkin and pretended to shove a tomato into its mouth. When asked to go to the refrigerator and get an orange, Kanzi immediately complied; Alia didn't have a clue what to do.

In the 40 years since Jane Goodall arrived at Gombe, she and others have   11
shown that apes have most, if not all, of the emotions that we do. They are probably self-conscious; many of them can recognize themselves in a mirror. They
use insight, not just trial and error, to solve problems. They form complex mental representations, including mental maps of the area where they live. They understand cause and effect. They act intentionally. They compare objects, and
relationships between objects. They count. Use tools — they even make tools.
Given the appropriate opportunity and motivation, they have been known to
teach, deceive, and empathize with others. They can figure out what others see
and know, abilities that human children don't develop until the ages of 3 to 5.
They create cultural traditions that they pass on to their descendants. They
flourish in rough-and-tumble societies so intensely political that they have been
dubbed Machiavellian, and in which they form coalitions to limit the power of
alpha males.

Twenty-first-century law should be based on twenty-first-century knowl-   12
edge. Once the law assumed that witches existed and that mute people lacked
intelligence. Now it is illegal to burn someone for witchcraft, and the mute have
the same rights as anyone else.

Today we know that apes, and perhaps other nonhuman animals, are not   13
what we thought they were in the prescientific age when the law declared them
things. Now we know that they have what it takes for basic legal rights. The next
step is obvious.

from TORTURE: WHEN THE UNTHINKABLE
IS MORALLY PERMISSIBLE
Mirko Bagaric and Julie Clarke

*Mirko Bagaric has published many articles in newspapers and
journals in areas such as commercial law, medical law, human rights,
and migration and refugee law. He teaches at Deakin University
Law School in Australia. Julie Clarke is a lecturer in law at Deakin
University. The first half of this passage originally appeared in two
Australian newspapers, the* Age *and the* Sydney Morning Herald.

The Case for Torture

*"Our reflex rejection of torture needs to be replaced by recognition that it
can be a moral means of saving lives."*

Recent events stemming from the "war on terrorism" have highlighted the   1
prevalence of torture. This is despite the fact that torture is almost universally
deplored. The formal prohibition against torture is absolute — there are no exceptions to it.

The belief that torture is always wrong is, however, misguided and sympto-
matic of the alarmist and reflexive responses typically emanating from social
commentators. It is this type of absolutist and short-sighted rhetoric that lies at
the core of many distorted moral judgments that we as a community continue
to make, resulting in an enormous amount of injustice and suffering in our society and far beyond our borders.

2

Torture is permissible where the evidence suggests that this is the only
means, due to the immediacy of the situation, to save the life of an innocent
person. The reason that torture in such a case is defensible and necessary is because the justification manifests from the closest thing we have to an inviolable
right: the right to self-defense, which of course extends to the defense of another. Given the choice between inflicting a relatively small level of harm on a
wrongdoer and saving an innocent person, it is verging on moral indecency to
prefer the interests of the wrongdoer.

3

The analogy with self-defense is sharpened by considering the hostage-
taking scenario, where a wrongdoer takes a hostage and points a gun to the
hostage's head, threatening to kill the hostage unless a certain (unreasonable)
demand is met. In such a case it is not only permissible but desirable for police
to shoot (and kill) the wrongdoer if they get a "clear shot." This is especially true
if it's known that the wrongdoer has a history of serious violence, and hence is
more likely to carry out the threat.

4

It is indefensible to suggest that there should be an absolute ban on torture. There is no logical or moral difference between this scenario and one
where there is overwhelming evidence that a wrongdoer has kidnapped an innocent person and informs police that the victim will be killed by a co-offender
if certain demands are not met.

5

In the hostage scenario, it is universally accepted that it is permissible to
violate the right to life of the aggressor to save an innocent person. How can it
be wrong to violate an even less important right (the right to physical integrity)
by torturing the aggressor in order to save a life in the second scenario?

6

There are three main counterarguments to even the above limited approval of torture. The first is the slippery slope argument: if you start allowing
torture in a limited context, the situations in which it will be used will increase.

7

This argument is not sound in the context of torture. First, the floodgates
are already open — torture is used widely, despite the absolute legal prohibition against it. Amnesty International has recently reported that it had received,
during 2003, reports of torture and ill-treatment from 132 countries, including
the United States, Japan, and France. It is, in fact, arguable that it is the existence
of an unrealistic absolute ban that has driven torture beneath the radar of accountability, and that legalization in very rare circumstances would in fact reduce instances of it.

8

The second main argument is that torture will dehumanize society. This is   9
no more true in relation to torture than it is with self-defense, and in fact the
contrary is true. A society that elects to favor the interests of wrongdoers over
those of the innocent, when a choice must be made between the two, is in need
of serious ethical rewiring.

A third counterargument is that we can never be totally sure that torturing   10
a person will in fact result in us saving an innocent life. This, however, is the
same situation as in all cases of self-defense. To revisit the hostage example, the
hostage-taker's gun might in fact be empty, yet it is still permissible to shoot. As
with any decision, we must decide on the best evidence at the time.

Torture in order to save an innocent person is the only situation where it is   11
clearly justifiable. This means that the recent high-profile incidents of torture,
apparently undertaken as punitive measures or in a bid to acquire information
where there was no evidence of an immediate risk to the life of an innocent person, were reprehensible. . . .

Life-Saving Torture Is a Humane Practice

The argument that condoning torture in any circumstances will brutalize   12
or dehumanize[1] is flawed because it takes an unduly narrow perspective of the
proposal at hand and mischaracterizes the motivation for the proposal.

It should be noted that this criticism is sometimes put as a stand-alone ar-   13
gument. On other occasions it is a premise of the slippery slope argument,
along the lines that any torture will result in more torture because it will desensitize people to the suffering of others.

There is no doubt that inflicting pain on people is bad. In our view, the re-   14
duction of pain should be one of the highest-order moral imperatives. But there
is no basis for ranking one person's pain more importantly than that of another.
When we are confronted with a situation where we must choose between who
will bear unavoidable pain, we need to take a pain-minimization approach. To
this end, there is no question that causing (even intense) physical pain to a suspect causes less pain than allowing many people to be blown up. The enduring
pain that would be felt by the relatives of the victims grossly outweighs the
physical pain inflicted on the suspect.

In assessing the potential dehumanizing aspect of a proposal, there is no   15
logical or moral basis for focusing on the interests of only one agent in the
dilemma. All affected parties must be given equal consideration. Such speculative consequences (in this case the likelihood that killings of innocent people
will be actually averted) weigh less than certain consequences (the pain inflicted on the suspect), but at some point the speculative side of the scales
(where, for example, there are a large number of lives at stake) are so heavy that
they outweigh certain bad consequences.

The critics fail to extend their moral horizons beyond the interests of the   16
suspect. This individualistic account of morality represents a far greater threat
to our "humanity" than torturing suspects to save lives. A society that stood by
and refused to take all reasonable steps to save innocent life would be vastly different to the one in which we currently live. Rescuers would not be permitted to
push aside bystanders for fear of bruising them, ambulances would not rush to
save sick people for fear of colliding into other cars, police would not pursue
criminals for the same reason, people would not undergo security checks at air-
ports before they boarded their planes (because it interfered with their right to
liberty and privacy), and we would be content with stating what a pity it is that
many innocent were murdered in a possibly preventable incident on the basis
that we did not want to apply physical pressure to a suspect. This is approaching
moral nihilism.

A related objection that has been raised to life-saving torture is that it will   17
dehumanize the torturer (as opposed to society in general). The evidence, however, is to the contrary. Throughout history people have been inflicting pain on
individuals and sustained no demonstrable moral bruises. Nowadays surgeons
do it as part of their day-to-day affairs. While in most countries anesthetic removes the pain during surgery, some forms of surgery cause significant pain
and discomfort during the recuperation phase. Moreover, prior to the discovery
of anesthetic, surgeons would perform procedures that caused almost unthinkable levels of pain, such as limb amputations.[2] While the goal of the surgeon's
action is not to inflict pain, the same applies in relation to the torturer—who
is ultimately seeking to save life. Nowadays prison guards lock up prisoners
in small cells; some parents still smack their children, and some people kill in
self-defense.

Some critics give examples of torturers who have regretted their actions   18
once they have come to learn that their "cause" (for example, warring against
another country) was unjust.[3] This is irrelevant to our proposal. We leave no
scope for issues of moral subjectivism or relativism or for changed perceptions
regarding the justness of torture. Killing innocent people is bad—nearly always so—irrespective of which ideological or normative position one happens to adopt. Proportionate actions taken to prevent this are objectively
morally sound[4] and hence (rationally) there is no scope for regret about such
matters.

The dehumanizing criticism is misguided to the point of being contradic-   19
tory. If standing idly by allowing innocent people to be killed does not dehumanize society, inflicting physical persuasion on a suspect logically cannot.
Moreover, all nations permit individuals and security officials to inflict far higher
levels of harm, such as killing in self-defense, than torture.[5] If we are not dehu-
manized now, torture will not make any difference.

Notes

1. This is a point made by several critics. See, for example, John Kleinig, *Ticking Bombs and Torture Warrants* 10 DEAKIN L. REV. 614, 620 (2005).

2. Obviously, there are points of dissimilarity between surgery and torture. An obvious point of departure is that surgery is intended to benefit the person upon whom the pain is inflicted. However, this analogy is not advanced as a knock-down argument in favor of torture. Rather, it is advanced merely to refute the claim that deliberately inflicting pain on another person necessarily damages the agent that inflicts the pain.

3. See, for example, Anne O'Rourke et al., *Torture, Slippery Slope, Intellectual Apologists, and Ticking Bombs: An Australian Response to Bagaric and Clarke* 40 U.S.F. L. REV. 11–12 (2005).

4. See M. Bagaric, *A Utilitarian Argument: Laying the Foundation for a Coherent System of Law* 10 OTAGO L. REV. (NZ) 163 (2002), where it is argued that morality is an objective inquiry.

5. See further, Alasdair Palmer, in *Is Torture Always Wrong?* THE SPECTATOR 40–42, September 24, 2005, who notes that the ban on torture is inconsistent with the acceptance of a shoot-to-kill policy in some circumstances.

Strategy Two: Developing an Essay Based on a Source

This strategy gives you the freedom to develop your own ideas and present your own point of view in an essay that is only loosely linked to a source. Reading an assigned essay helps you to generate ideas and topics and provides you with evidence or information to cite in your own essay; but the thesis, scope, and organization of your essay are entirely your own.

1. Finding and Narrowing a Topic

As always, you begin by studying the assigned essay carefully, establishing its thesis, structure, and main ideas. As you read, start brainstorming: noting ideas of your own that might be worth developing. You need not cover exactly the same material as the source essay. What you want is a *spin-off* from the original reading, not a summary.

Here is one student's preliminary list of topics for an essay based on Blanche Blank's "A Question of Degree." (Blank's essay can be found on pp. 13–16.) Notice that, initially, this student's ideas are mostly personal and mostly expressed as questions:

- "selling college": how do colleges recruit students? how did I choose this college? has my college experience met my expectations?
- "practical curriculum": what are my courses preparing me for? what is the connection between my courses and my future career? why am I here?
- "college compulsory at adolescence": what were my parental expectations? teachers' expectations? did we have any choices?
- "employment discrimination based on college degrees": what kinds of jobs now require a B.A.? was it always like that? what other kinds of training are possible — for clerks? for civil servants? for teacher's aides?
- financing college: how much is tuition? are we getting what we pay for? is education something to be purchased, like a winter coat?
- "dignity of work": job experience/work environment
- "joylessness in university life": describe students' attitudes — is the experience mechanical? is the environment bureaucratic?
- "hierarchical levels": what do the different college degrees mean? should they take as long as they do? should a B.A. take four years?

2. Exploring Strategies

If you read a source a few times without thinking of a topic or if you can't see how your ideas can be developed into an essay, test some standard strategies, applying them to the source essay in ways that might not have occurred to the original author. Here, for example, are some strategies that generate topics for an essay based on "A Question of Degree."

Process

You might examine in detail one of the processes that Blank describes only generally:

- You could write about your own experience to explain the ways in which teenagers are encouraged to believe that a college degree is essential, citing high school counseling and college catalogs and analyzing the unrealistic expectations that young students are encouraged to have.
- If you have sufficient knowledge, you might describe the unjust manipulation of hiring procedures that favor college graduates or the process by which a college's liberal arts curriculum gradually becomes "practical."

Illustration

If you focused on a single discouraged employee, showing in what ways ambition for increased status and salary have been frustrated, or a single disillusioned college graduate, showing how career prospects have failed to measure up to training and expectations, your strategy would be an illustration proving one of Blank's themes.

Definition

Definition often emerges from a discussion of the background of an issue:

- What should the work experience be like?
- What is the function of a university?
- What is a good education?

By attempting to define one of the components of Blank's theme in terms of the ideal, you are helping your reader to understand her arguments and evaluate her conclusions more rationally.

Cause and Effect

- You can examine one or more of the reasons why a college degree has become a necessary credential for employment. You can also suggest a wider context for discussing Blank's views by describing the kind of society that encourages this set of values. In either case, you will be accounting for, but not necessarily justifying, the nation's obsession with degrees.
- You can predict the consequences, good or bad, that might result if Blank's suggested legislation were passed.
- You might explore some hypothetical possibilities and focus on the circumstances and causes of a situation different from the one that Blank describes. What if everyone in the United States earned a college degree? What if education after the eighth grade were abolished? By taking this approach, you are radically changing the circumstances that Blank depicts but still sharing her concerns and exploring the principles discussed in her essay.

Problem and Solution

If Cause and Effect asks "why," then Problem and Solution explains "how." Blank raises several problems that, in her view, have harmful social consequences. What are some solutions? What changes are possible? How can we effect them?

- How can we change students' expectations of education and make them both more realistic and more idealistic?
- How can we change the workplace so that no one feels demeaned?

Note that exploring such solutions means that you are basically in agreement with Blank's thesis.

Comparison

You can alter the reader's perspective by moving the theme of Blank's essay to another time or place:

- Did our present obsession with education exist a hundred years ago? Is it a problem outside the United States at this moment? Will it probably continue throughout the twenty-first century?
- Focusing on contemporary America, how do trends in education and employment compare with trends in other areas of life—housing, finance, recreation, child rearing, or communications?

With all these approaches, you begin with a description of Blank's issue and contrast it with another set of circumstances, past or present, real or hypothetical.

Before choosing any of these speculative strategies and topics, you must first decide:

- What is practical in a brief essay
- Whether the topic requires research
- Whether, when fully developed, the topic will retain some connection with the source essay

For example, there may be some value in comparing the current emphasis on higher education with monastic education in the Middle Ages. Can you write such an essay? How much research will it require? Will a discussion of monastic education help your reader better to understand Blank's ideas? Or will you immediately move away from your starting point—and find no opportunity to return to it? Do you have a serious objective, or are you simply making the comparison "because it's there"?

3. Taking Notes and Writing a Thesis

Consider how you might develop an essay based on one of the topics suggested in the previous section. Notice that the chosen topic is expressed as a question.

Topic: What is the function of a university today?

- After thinking about the topic, start your list of notes *before* you reread the essay, to make sure that you are not overly influenced by the author's point of view and to enable you to include some ideas of your own in your notes.
- Next, review the essay and add any relevant ideas to your list, *remembering to indicate when an idea originated with the source and not with you.*

Here is a complete list of notes for an essay defining the *function of a university for our time*. The paragraph references, added later, indicate which points were made by Blank and where in her essay they can be found. (Note that several entries contain no reference to Blank's essay.) The thesis, which follows the notes, was written after the list was complete.

WHAT THE UNIVERSITY SHOULD DO

1. increase students' understanding of the world around them
    e.g., to become more observant and aware of natural phenomena (weather, for example) and social systems (like family relationships)

2. help students live more fulfilling lives
    to enable them to test their powers and know more and become more versatile; to speak with authority on topics that they didn't understand before

3. help students live more productive lives
    to increase their working credentials and qualify for more interesting and well-paying jobs (B.B., Paragraphs 3–9)

4. serve society by creating better informed, more rational citizens
    not only through college courses (like political science) but through the increased ability to observe and analyze and argue (B.B., Paragraphs 3, 14)

5. contribute to research that will help to solve scientific and social problems
    (not a teaching function) (B.B., Paragraphs 3, 14)

6. serve as a center for debate to clarify the issues of the day
    people should regard the university as a source of unbiased information and counsel; notable people should come to lecture (B.B., Paragraphs 3, 14)

7. serve as a gathering place for great teachers
    students should be able to regard their teachers as worth emulating

8. allow students to examine the opportunities for personal change and growth
    this includes vocational goals, e.g., career changes (B.B., Paragraph 4)

WHAT THE UNIVERSITY SHOULD NOT DO

9. it should not divide the haves from the have-nots
    college should not be considered essential; it should be possible to be successful without a college degree (B.B., Paragraphs 8, 10)

10. it should not use marketing techniques to appeal to the greatest number
    what the university teaches should be determined primarily by the faculty and to a lesser extent by the students; standards of achievement should not be determined by students who haven't learned anything yet

11. it should not ignore the needs of its students and its community by clinging to outdated courses and programs

12. it should not cooperate with business and government to the extent that it loses its autonomy (B.B., Paragraphs 6, 9)

13. it should not be an employment agency and vocational center to the exclusion of its more important functions (B.B., Paragraphs 6, 9, 16)

Thesis: As Blanche Blank points out, a university education is not a commodity to be marketed and sold; a university should be a resource center for those who want the opportunity to develop their intellectual powers and lead more productive, useful, and fulfilling lives.

These notes, divided into what a university should and should not do, already follow a *definition strategy*, with its emphasis on differentiation.

4. Structuring Your Essay

Having made all the preliminary decisions, you are ready to plan the structure of your essay:

- Mark those portions of the reading that you will need to use in support of your thesis. Your essay will be based on both your own ideas and the ideas of your source.
- Check whether your notes accurately paraphrase the source.
- Double-check to make sure that you are giving the source credit for all paraphrased ideas.
- If appropriate, include some examples from your own experience.

Organize your notes by arranging them in a logical sequence, which is usually called an *outline*. Some outlines use numbers and letters; some don't. But <u>*all outlines represent the relationship of ideas by their arrangement on the page*</u>: major points at the margin, supporting points and evidence underneath and slightly to the right:

- Divide your notes into groups or categories, each of which will be developed as a separate paragraph or sequence of related paragraphs.
- Decide the order of your categories (or paragraphs).
- Incorporate in your outline some of the points from Blanche Blank's essay that you intend to include. Cite the paragraph number of the relevant material with your outline entry. If the source paragraph contains several references that you expect to place in different parts of your outline, use a sentence number or a set of symbols or a brief quotation for differentiation.

Here is one section of the completed outline for an essay on "Defining a University in the Twenty-First Century." This outline incorporates notes 3, 13, 9, and 8 from the list on pages 204–205.

I. The university should help students to live more productive lives, to increase their working credentials, and to qualify for more interesting and well-paying jobs. (Paragraph 6—last sentence)
   A. But it should not be an employment agency and vocational center to the exclusion of its more important functions. (Paragraph 9—"servicing agents"; Paragraph 12—"joylessness in our university life"; Paragraph 16)
   B. It should not divide the haves from the have-nots; success without a college degree should be possible. (Paragraph 2—"two kinds of work"; Paragraph 17)
II. The university should allow students to examine the opportunities for personal growth and change; this includes vocational goals, e.g., career changes. (Paragraph 4—"an optional and continuing experience later in life")

5. Writing the Essay

When you write from sources, you strive for an appropriate balance between your own ideas and those of your source. *But it is your voice that should dominate the essay.* You, after all, are writing it; you are responsible for its contents and its effect on the reader. For this reason, all the important "positions" in the structure of your essay should be filled by you. The topic sentences of the paragraphs, as well as the essay's introduction and conclusion, should be written in your own words and should stress your views, not those of your author. On the other hand, your reader should not be allowed to lose sight of the source essay; it should be treated as a form of *evidence* and cited whenever it is relevant, but always as a context in which to develop your own strategy and assert your own thesis.

Here is the completed paragraph based on Points I and IA in the outline:

topic sentence

explanation: personal experience

source: summary

examples

source: paraphrase and quotation

To achieve certain goals, all of us have agreed to take four years out of our lives, at great expense, for higher education. What I learn here will, I hope, give me the communication skills, the range of knowledge, and the discipline to succeed in a career as a journalist. But, as Blanche Blank points out, a college education may not be the best way to prepare for every kind of job. Is it necessary to spend four years at this college to become a supermarket manager? a computer programmer? a clerk in the social security office? If colleges become no more than high-level job training or employment centers, or, in Blank's words, "servicing agents" to screen workers for business, then they lose their original purpose as centers of a higher form of learning. Blank is rightly concerned that, if a college degree becomes a mandatory credential, I and my contemporaries will regard ourselves "as prisoners of economic necessity," alienated from the rich possibilities of education by the "joylessness in our university life."

6. Revising the Essay

Your work isn't finished until you have reviewed your essay carefully to ensure that the organization is logical, the paragraphs are coherent, and the sentences are complete. To gain some distance and objectivity, most people put their work aside for a while before starting to revise it. You can also ask someone else to read and comment on your essay, but make sure that you have reason to trust that person's judgment and commitment to the task. It isn't helpful to be told only that "paragraph three doesn't work" or "I don't get that sentence"; your reader should be willing to spend some time and trouble to pinpoint what's wrong so that you can go back to your manuscript and make revisions. Problems usually arise in three areas.

Overall Structure

If you follow your outline or your revised list of notes, your paragraphs should follow each other fairly well. But extraneous ideas—some of them good ones—tend to creep in as you write, and sometimes you need to make adjustments to accommodate them. As you look carefully at the sequence of paragraphs, make sure that they lead into each other. Are *parallel points* presented in a series or are they scattered throughout the essay? Sometimes, two paragraphs need to be *reversed*, or two paragraphs belong together and need to be *merged*. In addition, your reader should be guided through the sequence of paragraphs by the "traffic signals" provided by *transitional phrases*, such as "in addition" or "nevertheless" or "in fact." The transitions need not be elaborate: words like "also," "so," and "too" keep the reader on track.

Paragraph Development

The paragraphs should be of roughly comparable length, each containing a *topic sentence* (not necessarily placed at the beginning), *explanatory sentences*, *details or examples* provided by your source or yourself, and (possibly) *quotations from your source*. It's important to have this mix of general material and detail to keep your essay from being too abstract or too specific. Make sure that every sentence contributes to the point of the paragraph. Look for sentences without content, or sentences that make the same point over again. If, after such deletions, a paragraph seems overly brief or stark, consider what illustrations or details might be added to support and add interest to the topic. Check back to the source to see if there are still some points worth paraphrasing or quoting.

Sentence Style

Your writing should meet a basic acceptable standard:

- Is the *sentence style* monotonous, with the same pattern repeated again and again? Look for repetitions, and consider ways to vary the style, such as starting some sentences with a phrase or subordinate clause.

- Are you using the same *vocabulary* again and again? Are too many of your sentences built around "is" or "are"? Search for stronger verbs, and vary your choice of words, perhaps consulting a thesaurus. But think twice about using words that are totally new to you, or you'll risk sounding awkward. Use a thesaurus to remind yourself of possible choices, not to increase your vocabulary.

- Are you adhering to *basic grammar and punctuation*? Are the sentences complete? Eliminate fragments or run-ons. Check for apostrophes, for subject-verb agreement, for quotation marks. Don't let careless errors detract from your hard work in preparing and writing this essay. And use a spellchecker!

Guidelines for Writing a Single-Source Essay

1. Identify the source essay's thesis; analyze its underlying themes, if any, and its strategy; and construct a rough list or outline of its main ideas.

2. After brainstorming, decide on two or three possible essay topics related to your work in Step 1, and narrow down one of them. (Be prepared to submit your topics for your teacher's approval and, in conference, to choose the most suitable one.)

3. Write down a list of notes about your own ideas on the topic, being careful to distinguish between points that are yours and points that are derived from the source.

4. Write a thesis of your own that fairly represents your list of ideas. Mention the source in your thesis if appropriate.

5. If you have not done so already, choose a strategy that will best carry out your thesis; it need not be the same strategy as that of the source essay.

6. Mark (by brackets or underlining) those paragraphs or sentences in the source that will help to develop your topic.

7. Draw up an outline for your essay. Combine repetitious points; bring together similar and related points. Decide on the best sequence for your paragraphs.

8. Decide which parts of the reading should be cited as evidence or refuted; place paragraph or page references to the source in the appropriate sections of your outline. Then decide which sentences of the reading to quote and which to paraphrase.

9. Write the rough draft, making sure that, whenever possible, the topic sentence of each paragraph expresses your views, introduces the material that you intend to present in that paragraph, and is written in your voice. Later in the paragraph, incorporate references to the source, and link your paragraphs together with transitions. Do not be concerned about a bibliography for this single-source essay. Cite the author's full name and the exact title of the work early in your essay. (See pp. 125–128 for a review of citations.)

10. Write an introduction that contains a clear statement of your thesis, as well as a reference to the source essay and its role in the development of your ideas. Draft a conclusion that recapitulates the main ideas of your essay, including the thesis.

11. Review your first draft to note problems with organization, transitions, or language. Proofread your first draft very carefully to correct errors of grammar, style, reference, and spelling.

12. Prepare the final draft. Even if you use a computer spellcheck, proofread once again.

ASSIGNMENT 3: Writing an Essay Based on a Single Source

A. As your instructor indicates, read "The Selfish Generation," "What a College Education Buys," or "Among Privileged Classmates, I'm an Outsider," twice. One of these three essays will serve as the starting point for an essay of your own. Assume that the essay you are planning will be approximately three pages long, or 600–900 words.

B. Using Steps 1 and 2 in the guidelines on page 209, think of *three* possible topics for an essay of that length, and submit the most promising (or, if your teacher suggests it, all three) for approval.

C. Plan your essay by working from notes to an outline. Be prepared to submit your thesis and outline of paragraphs (with indications of relevant references to the source) to your teacher for approval.

D. Write a rough draft after deciding which parts of the source essay should be cited as evidence, distributing references to the source among appropriate sections of your outline, and determining which parts of the source should be quoted and which should be paraphrased.

E. Write a final draft of your essay, and then proofread the draft before submitting the final version to your instructor.

THE SELFISH GENERATION
Jenni Russell

Jenni Russell is a journalist and columnist, primarily for The Guardian *and the* Sunday Times *in Great Britain, focusing on social and political issues. She has produced news programs for ITN and the BBC. This article appeared in* The Guardian.

Queuing [lining up] in a branch of WH Smith some months ago, I was a captive audience while one shop assistant told another about an encounter with an elderly woman who was looking for a book that wasn't on the shelves. The assistant had not known and not cared where the book might be found, and the old lady had asked if she could be more helpful. "So I told her to fuck off," was the assistant's triumphant punchline.

A friend in a precarious industry, shattered by his third redundancy in three years, made an appointment with the local careers service to discuss other options. The adviser didn't bother to turn up for the first appointment, or for the second. There was no apology and no explanation. My friend wasn't prepared to be humiliated by asking for a third. "Just when you feel like a piece of rubbish, they treat you like one," he said.

An acquaintance on a newspaper, a tough and experienced journalist, felt so continuously unwell that her doctor decided she was going through an early menopause. Then her hypercritical and contemptuous boss moved on, and her symptoms disappeared.

One factor links many of the miseries we inflict upon one another, from antisocial behavior to bullying at work and our encounters in public places. It is our lack of respect for others, coupled with our obsession with being treated with respect ourselves. And the less respect we encounter, the less prepared we are to offer any to anyone else. It's no longer true that most people aspire to having good manners; many just want to protect their egos in every social encounter. Conscious of our jealous sensitivity to any slight, we go out into the public arena armed only with our own willingness to be aggressive or oblivious in response.

We live in a culture where the primacy of the self and its satisfactions is everything. We are bombarded with messages telling us that we should have what we want because we're worth it. As consumers, we are kings. We know that we have rights, that brands seek our favor; that as long as we can pay, we feel powerful. We like that sensation. It is seductive because it is so at odds with the reality of the rest of our lives. As workers and producers we are under more pressure and feel more insecure than ever before. Our private lives are increasingly unpredictable; our financial futures uncertain. There is no general respect for mundane lives, well lived, in a popular culture that celebrates wealth, beauty, celebrity, notoriety and youth. Most of us cannot feel confident about our worth and about the regard in which we are held.

This conflict between our sense of entitlement and our shaky sense of self-worth enrages us. At work many of us bolster ourselves by struggling to assert our superiority to others. Managers who crave the respect of their staff, but fear they don't have it, create the semblance of it by frightening those underneath them. They are too concerned with maintaining their status to think about the damage they are doing to their subordinates. Service staff who feel their jobs are beneath them often make their disdain clear by doing them as gracelessly as possible. Minor officials take pleasure in exercising obstructive petty authority.

This behavior matters enormously because we are social animals, critically dependent on the reactions of others for our well-being. Two centuries ago the Earl of Chesterfield, writing to his son, warned him that men will forgive any quarrel or criticism, except one. They cannot tolerate being treated with contempt. Last month new scientific research demonstrated that the brain reacts to a social snub in just the same way as it does to a physical injury. In effect, by our thoughtless and self-protective behavior, we are going through our days delivering small social injuries to one another, each one of which is felt as acutely as physical pain.

Some of this is caused by our confusion over the end of deference. Freed from old social codes, we can be reluctant to show respect to anyone, in case it appears to diminish us. Much of it, too, is simply carelessness, or lack of time. We know, and are often embarrassed by, our own sensitivity. We know how easy it is to feel negligible when powerful people ignore emails or job applications or requests for help. We know that we can be made furious by a bus driver ignoring us at a request stop, or feel ridiculously uplifted by the unexpected kindness of strangers. But we don't ascribe such power or significance to our own behavior.

The people most vulnerable to hurt are those whose self-worth is already   9
undermined by those around them: bullied workers, mothers who have given up work, recent immigrants, people in menial jobs. Those with the least money and the least authority are made continually aware of others' contempt. But the erosion of concern for others is taking place at all levels of society. The wealthier you are, the more protected you are from the consequences. Prosperous people can largely pay others to be nice to them. Yet they too practice and suffer from the new selfishness.

Fewer people now observe the conventions of good manners. They accept   10
invitations, only to withdraw at the last minute when something more desirable appears. At formal events, some people are ruthless about ignoring a neighbor in favor of a more useful guest. The old idea that one had a social responsibility toward one's host or fellow guests is beginning to be replaced by a determination to maximize one's individual satisfaction, regardless of the emotional injury caused to anyone else. The values of the market are openly invading the social sphere. Why practice duty when you could make a contact or secure a gain?

The answer is that we are all diminished by this behavior. If every social   11
encounter is reduced to a self-marketing opportunity, we will all, at some point, be made savagely unhappy. It may work, temporarily, for the powerful and desirable. But at some time every one of us will experience failure, be perceived as dull or grow old. We all want to be valued as human beings, rather than commodities. It is the generosity and tolerance of others that makes our lives bearable.

The human, social and economic cost of our lack of mutual respect is enor-   12
mous. Consider the wasted emotional energy, the destruction of confidence and creativity, and the alienation that results from it. Anxious and undermined, we hand on humiliation to others, then deplore the dissolution of social bonds. The industries that surround us will do nothing to reverse this trend. They make their money and find their audiences by appealing to our egos.

We cannot allow marketeers to establish our social norms. We need to find   13
ways to re-establish the encouragement of empathy, respect and consideration toward the people around us. The existence of those values acts as a social

safety net, connecting us to one another. They make us feel happier and less threatened by the world in which we live.

It's another burden to be taken up by schools. It's also a task for companies, which need to pay much more than lip service to the proper treatment of the people within them. But it's an individual responsibility too. It takes thought. This morning I didn't swear at the van driver who blocked my car, and I was neither impatient nor frosty with the checkout woman who swiped my shopping so slowly that I was 10 minutes late for my son at school. It's nothing to be proud of. What did you do today? 14

WHAT A COLLEGE EDUCATION BUYS
Christopher Caldwell

Christopher Caldwell's work has appeared in many prominent American newspapers and periodicals, including the Washington Post, *the* Wall Street Journal, *the* New York Times, *and the* Atlantic Monthly. *He is a senior editor at the online magazine* Slate. *His book,* Reflections on the Revolution in Europe: Immigration, Islam, and the West, *was published in 2009. This article appeared in the* New York Times Magazine.

. . . Certain influential Americans have begun to reassert the old wisdom that a college education is one of those things, like skydiving and liverwurst, that are both superb and not for everybody. Not long ago, the conservative social scientist Charles Murray wrote a three-part series in the *Wall Street Journal* in which he attacked the central assumption behind President George Bush's No Child Left Behind initiative. The idea that "educators already know how to educate everyone and that they just need to try harder" is a costly wrong impression, he wrote. Not all schoolchildren have the intellectual capacity to reach "basic achievement" levels. In college, similar limitations apply. The number of Americans with the brains to master the most challenging college classes, Murray argued, is probably closer to 15 percent than to 45. 1

Of course, part of the reason Americans think everyone should go to college is for its noneducational uses. Anyone can benefit from them. Colleges are the country's most effective marriage brokers. They are also — assuming you don't study too hard — a means of redistributing four years' worth of leisure time from the sad stub-end of life to the prime of it. (Just as youth shouldn't be wasted on the young, retirement shouldn't be wasted on the old.) 2

But the price of college long ago outstripped the value of these goods. The most trustworthy indicator that an American college education is something 3 worthwhile is that parents nationwide — and even worldwide — are eager to pay up to $180,000 to get one for their children. This is a new development. A quarter-century ago, even the top Ivy League schools were a bargain at $10,000 a year, but they received fewer applications than they do now. Presumably, college is steadily more expensive because its benefits are steadily more visible. In 1979, according to the economists Frank Levy and Richard Murnane, a 30-year-old college graduate earned 17 percent more than a 30-year-old high-school grad. Now the gap is over 50 percent.

These numbers don't tell us much about how people get educated at a typical American college. You can go to college to get civilized (in the sense that your thoughts about your triumphs and losses at the age of 55 will be colored and deepened by an encounter with Horace or Yeats at the age of 19). Or you can go there to get qualified (in the sense that Salomon Brothers will snap you up, once it sees your B.A. in economics from M.I.T.). Most often, parents must think they are paying for the latter product. Great though Yeats may be, 40-some-odd thousand seems a steep price to pay for his acquaintance. The timeless questions that college provokes — like "What the hell are you going to do with a degree in English?" — must get shouted across dinner tables with increasing vehemence as college costs rise inexorably.   4

But the education kids are rewarded for may not be the same education their parents think they are paying for. Economists would say that a college degree is partly a "signaling" device — it shows not that its holder has learned something but rather that he is the kind of person who could learn something. Colleges sort as much as they teach. Even when they don't increase a worker's productivity, they help employers find the most productive workers, and a generic kind of productivity can be demonstrated as effectively in medieval-history as in accounting classes.   5

Moreover, if you're not planning on becoming, say, a doctor, the benefits of diligent study can be overstated. In recent decades, the biggest rewards have gone to those whose intelligence is deployable in new directions on short notice, not to those who are locked into a single marketable skill, however thoroughly learned and accredited. Most of the employees who built up, say, Google in its early stages could never have been trained to do so, because neither the company nor the idea of it existed when they were getting their educations. Under such circumstances, it's best not to specialize too much. Something like the old ideal of a "liberal education" has had a funny kind of resurgence, minus the steeping in Western culture. It is hard to tell whether this success vindicates liberal education's defenders (who say it "teaches you how to think") or its detractors (who say it camouflages a social elite as a meritocratic one).   6

Maybe college cannot become much more accessible. The return on college degrees must eventually fall as more people get them, and probably not   7 everyone wants one. In France, people often refer to their education as a "formation." The word implies that an increase in your specialized capabilities is bought at a price in flexibility and breadth of knowledge. In most times and places, this bitter trade-off is worth it. But for the past few years at least, the particular advantage of an American degree has been that it doesn't qualify you to do anything in particular.

AMONG PRIVILEGED CLASSMATES, I'M AN OUTSIDER
Bobby Allyn

Originally from northeastern Pennsylvania, Bobby Allyn majored in philosophy at American University, and has served as an intern in journalism at the Vegetarian Times, *the* Washington City Paper, *the* Nation *(summer 2008), and the* New York Times *(summer 2009). His articles have been published in the* Washington City Paper, *the* New York Times, *and the* Chronicle of Higher Education, *where this essay appeared.*

I'm a first-generation college student from a working-class background in northeastern Pennsylvania. Attending a private university in Washington has, for the first time, made me feel socially excluded from my peers. I've never traveled out of the mid-Atlantic region, the latest issues of the *New Yorker* and *Harper's* have never appeared on my family's coffee table, and before arriving on the campus, I thought every working person got paid by the hour.

College is supposed to be a time of self-reinvention, when students discover who they are and decide on career paths. But for me, it has been a time of social readjustment. I don't want to alienate myself by letting my college friends know that I'm not well traveled and don't understand their references, so I act as if I were in the know, hoping they won't suspect that I'm from a different class. This "cultural passing" gives me a feeling of accomplishment but also leaves me dejected, knowing that I am still an outsider. My campus selfhood is a mask that hides the reality of my upbringing.

As a high-school senior trying to decide where to attend college, I felt besieged by information. I am the first person in my extended family to attend college, so all my advice and guidance came from counselors. Although my high school was an invaluable resource in terms of college selection and getting through the admissions process, when it came to realistically breaking down the cost of attending, and calculating the amount of debt I would shoulder, I sought counseling at a local organization that offered free financial-aid advice to low-income students. One of the counselors combed through my parents' income and lack of savings, noted my intended major (journalism), then bluntly told me that community college was my only feasible option.

My dad, who had labored as a machinist for nearly four decades, immediately protested, insisting that I would go to the college of my choice. But he didn't understand the magnitude of the cost. And even with my award packages, none of the places that accepted me offered a bargain. Carrying scholarship and grant money, along with private loans, I headed to Ithaca College.

At Ithaca, I attended a mandatory freshman workshop on diversity that consisted of participatory role-playing and other tolerance-improving drills. Many of the students impatiently tapped their feet until the session was over, but the ineffectual games and videos gave me pause. They encouraged acceptance of ethnic diversity and LGBT students, but ignored another, less visible presence on the campus: socioeconomic diversity.

As my social life at Ithaca started to expand, and I began to learn about my friends' families and histories, I realized that I was different. Sure, there were other students who had scholarships and need-based grants, but most of the students I encountered were from affluent suburbs and were raised in conditions foreign to me. They'd had trips to Europe, private preparatory schools, and well-connected, educated parents. Advantages that I thought of as exceptional were suddenly the norm.

Having to confront uncomfortable realities, like not being able to pay for dinner and having parents who don't know what the LSATs or MCATs are, let alone give advice about them, contributed to the divide I felt between myself and my friends. At the end of spring semester that year, I hadn't found a nourishing social niche. There were undoubtedly other working-class students on the campus, who could have provided me with the support I needed, but I couldn't find them. So I transferred — to, well, another private school, American University. It's similar to Ithaca in size and demographics, so I didn't expect to find a working-class bastion. But I couldn't turn down the allure of city living; it offered extraordinary work and social opportunities outside of the campus, which I knew might be oppressive in its confines.

My financial situation improved at American, thanks to a more gracious award package, but my social life remained difficult. The cultural otherness I first encountered at Ithaca was mirrored at my new school. The students I met at American seemed to have outgrown dormitory life and were living in apartments, bankrolled by their parents. (I never did understand how a part-time job at a boutique cheese shop could finance $800-a-month rent payments.)

I spent my first semester working almost full time as a nanny for a family in the Tenleytown neighborhood. In exchange for driving, preparing food, and babysitting, the parents — two overscheduled doctors — offered me free housing. It didn't seem fair that my peers had private living arrangements that didn't involve bawling children or daily sibling duels. Eventually the university granted me additional money to pay for an apartment. But it couldn't offer me anything to change my identity and background.

Many working-class families, including mine, have no expectation that their   10 children will attend college. My dad's only wish was for me to graduate from high school and find work that didn't involve a factory. Even when working-class students are inspired to apply, the local community college often appears to be the only option. But when they have the opportunity to enroll in a more-competitive institution, worlds collide.

I would love to see spaces where like-minded students from comparable   11 socioeconomic backgrounds can come together and foster a community. If I knew that kids like me existed on the same campus, I would feel relieved, and less marginalized. But colleges need to do more than encourage discussions among class-aligned students. If students' biographies become a part of the classroom experience, students can gain insight into the unique and diverse backgrounds of their peers. That exposure could be the first step toward wider acceptance and greater understanding. Students of all backgrounds should be able to celebrate their class, and not feel forced to "pass," under social pressure, as members of haute privilege.

·6·

The Multiple-Source Essay

Until now, most of your writing assignments have been based on information derived from a *single* source. Now, as you begin to work with *many* different sources, you will need to understand and organize a wider range of materials. You will want to present the ideas of your sources in all their variety while at the same time maintaining your own perspective:

- How can you describe each author's ideas without taking up too much space for each one?
- How can you fit all your sources smoothly into your essay without allowing one to dominate?
- How can you transform a group of disparate sources into an essay that is yours?

Many of the sources used in this chapter have their equivalents in professional writing. Lawyers, doctors, engineers, social workers, and other professionals often work from notes taken in interviews and surveys to prepare case notes, case studies, legal testimony, reports, and market research.

Analyzing Multiple Sources

When you write from sources, your object is to present a thesis statement of your own that is based on your examination of a variety of views. Some of these views may conflict with your own and with each other. Because of this diversity, organizing multiple sources can be more difficult than working with even the most complex single essay.

Generalizing from Examples

In academic writing, a common theme often links apparently dissimilar ideas or facts found in a variety of sources. The author has to find that common theme and present it to the reader through *generalizations* that connect several items in the sources to each other.

To demonstrate this process, assume that you have been asked to consider and react to seven different but related situations, and then formulate *two* generalizations.

A. In a sentence or two, write down your *probable reaction* if you found your-self in each of the following situations.* Write quickly; this exercise calls for immediate, instinctive responses.

1. You are walking behind someone. You see him take out a cigarette pack, pull out the last cigarette, put the cigarette in his mouth, crumple the package, and nonchalantly toss it over his shoulder onto the sidewalk. What would you do?

2. You are sitting on a train and you notice a person (same age, sex, and type as yourself) lighting up a cigarette, despite the no smoking sign. No one in authority is around. What would you do?

3. You are pushing a shopping cart in a supermarket and you hear the thunderous crash of cans. As you round the corner, you see a two-year-old child being beaten, quite severely, by his mother, apparently for pulling out the bottom can of the pile. What would you do?

4. You see a teenager that you recognize shoplifting at the local discount store. You're concerned that she'll get into serious trouble if the store de-tective catches her. What would you do?

5. You're driving on a two-lane road behind another car. You notice that one of its wheels is wobbling more and more. It looks as if the lugs are coming off one by one. There's no way to pass, because cars are coming from the other direction in a steady stream. What would you do?

6. You've been waiting in line (at a supermarket or gas station) for longer than you expected and you're irritated at the delay. Suddenly, you notice that someone very much like yourself has sneaked in ahead

*Adapted from "Strategy 24" in Sidney B. Simon et al., *Values Clarification* (New York: Hart, 1972).

of you in the line. There are a couple of people before you. What would you do?

7. You've raised your son not to play with guns. Your rich uncle comes for a long-awaited visit and he brings your son a .22 rifle with lots of ammunition. What would you do?

B. Read over your responses to the seven situations and try to form two general statements (in one or two sentences each), one about *the circumstances in which you would take action* and a second about *the circumstances in which you would choose to do nothing*. Do not simply list the incidents, one after the other, divided into two groups.

To form your first generalization, you examine the group of situations in which you *do* choose to take action and determine what they have in common. (It is also important to examine the "leftovers," and to understand why these incidents did not warrant your interference.) One promising approach is to look at each situation in terms of either its *causes* or its *consequences*. For example, in each case there is *someone to blame*, someone who is responsible for creating the problem—except for number 5, where fate (or poor auto maintenance) threatens to cause an accident.

As for consequences, in some of the situations (littering, for example), there is *little potential danger*, either to you or to the public. Do these circumstances discourage action? In others, however, the possible victim is oneself or a member of one's family. Does self-interest alone drive one to act? Do adults tend to intervene in defense of children—even someone else's child—since they cannot stand up for themselves? Or, instead of calculating the consequences of not intervening, perhaps you should imagine *the possible consequences of interference*. In which situations can you expect to receive abuse for failing to mind your own business? Would this prevent you from intervening?

Read through the seven examples again:

■ Each item is intended to illustrate a specific and very different situation. Thus, although it does not include every possible example, the list as a whole constitutes *a set of public occasions for interfering with a stranger's conduct*.

■ Since you probably would not choose to act in every situation, you cannot use the entire list as the basis for your generalization. Rather, you must establish *a boundary line*, differentiating between those occasions when you would intervene and those times when you would decide not to act. The exact boundary between intervention and nonintervention will probably differ from person to person, as will the exact composition of the list of occasions justifying intervention. Thus, there is no one correct generalization.

This process of analysis results in a set of guidelines for justifiably minding other people's business.

> ## Forming a Generalization from Examples
>
> You can clarify your ideas and opinions about an abstract issue by:
>
> 1. inventing a set of illustrations
>
>   [*seven opportunities for potential intervention*]
>
> 2. marking off a subgroup according to your own standards
>
>   [*intervention desirable only in situations 3 (the child beaten in the supermarket), 5 (the wobbly wheel), and 7 (the gift of a gun)*]
>
> 3. forming a generalization that describes the common characteristics of the subgroup
>
>   [*intervention only to protect someone from physical harm*]

Finding Common Meanings

Differentiating among examples and forming generalizations becomes more difficult when your evidence comes from several different sources, not just a prepared list. The writing process when you work with multiple sources begins with the *analysis of ideas*.

Analysis is first breaking down a mass of information into individual pieces and then examining the pieces.

As you underline and annotate your sources, you look for similarities and distinctions in meaning, as well as the basic principles underlying what you read. Only when you have taken apart the evidence of each source to see how it works can you begin to find ways of putting everything back together again in your own essay.

To illustrate this kind of analysis, assume that you have asked five people what the word **foreign** means. You want to provide a reasonably complete definition of the word by exploring all the different meanings (or connotations) that the five sources suggest. If each one of the five gives you a completely different answer, then you will not have much choice in the organization of your definition. In that case, you would probably present each separate definition of *foreign* in a separate paragraph, citing a different person as the source for each one. But responses from multiple sources almost always overlap, as these do. Notice the *common meanings* in this condensed list of the five sources' responses:

John Brown: "Foreign" means unfamiliar and exotic.

Lynne Williams: "Foreign" means strange and unusual.

Bill White: "Foreign" means strange and alien (as in "foreign body").

Mary Green: "Foreign" means exciting and exotic.

Bob Friedman: "Foreign" means difficult and incomprehensible (as in "foreign language").

The paragraphs of your definition essay will be organized around common meanings, not the names of the five sources. That is why the one-source-per-paragraph method should hardly ever be used (except on those rare occasions when all the sources completely disagree).

When you organize ideas taken from multiple sources, never devote one paragraph to each page of your notes, simply because all the ideas on that page happen to have come from the same source.

If you did so, each paragraph would have a topic sentence that might read, "Then I asked John Brown for his definition," as if John Brown were the topic for discussion, instead of his views on "foreign." And if John Brown and Mary Green each get a separate paragraph, there will be some repetition because both think that one of the meanings of "foreign" is "exotic." "Exotic" should be the topic of one of your paragraphs, not the person (or people) who suggested that meaning.

Analyzing Shades of Meaning

Here is a set of notes, summarizing the ideas of four different people about the meaning of the word **individualist**. How would you analyze these notes?

Richard Becker: an "individualist" is a person who is unique and does not "fall into the common mode of doing things"; would not follow a pattern set by society. "A youngster who is not involved in the drug scene just because his friends are." A good word; it would be insulting only if it referred to a troublemaker.

Simon Jackson: doing things on your own, by yourself. "She's such an individualist that she insisted on answering the question in her own way." Sometimes the word is good, but mostly it has a bad connotation: someone who rebels against society or authority.

Lois Asher: one who doesn't "follow the flock." The word refers to someone who is very independent. "I respect Jane because she is an individualist and her own person." Usually very complimentary.

Vera Lewis: an extremely independent person. "An individualist is a person who does not want to contribute to society." Bad meaning: usually antisocial. She first heard the word in psych class, describing the characteristics of the individualist and "how he reacts to society."

At first glance, all four sources seem to say much the same thing: the individualist is different and *independent*.

Having identified the basis for a definition, you need to establish the *context* in which the four sources are defining this word: all the responses define the individualist *in terms of other people*—either the "group," or the "flock," or "society." Oddly enough, it is not easy to describe the individualist as an individual, even though it is that person's isolation that each source is emphasizing. One has to be independent of something outside oneself—the group.

So, you have now established the context for your definition: whatever is unique about the individualist is defined by the gap between that person and everyone else. Now you must *differentiate between the views of your sources*: Obviously Lois Asher thinks that to be an individualist is a good thing; Vera Lewis believes that individualism is bad; and the other two suggest that both connotations are possible. But simply describing the opinions of the four sources—positive or negative—stops short of defining the word according to those reactions. On what values do these sources base their judgments?

- Richard Becker and Lois Asher, two people who suggest a favorable meaning, describe the group from which the individual is set apart in similar and somewhat disapproving terms: "common"; "pattern set by society"; "follow the flock." Becker and Asher both seem to suggest *a degree of conformity or sameness that the individualist is right to reject*, as Becker's youngster rejects his friends' drugs.

- But Vera Lewis, who thinks that the word's connotation is bad, sees the individualist in a more benign society, with which the individual ought to identify himself and to which he ought to contribute. To be antisocial is to be an undesirable person—from the point of view of Lewis and society.

- Simon Jackson (who is ambivalent about the word) uses the phrases "by yourself" and "on your own," which suggest the isolation and the lack of support, as well as the admirable independence, of the individualist. In Jackson's view, the individualist's self-assertion becomes threatening to all of us in society ("antisocial") only when the person begins to rebel against authority.

Probably for Jackson, and certainly for Vera Lewis, the ultimate authority should rest with society as a whole, not with the individualist. Even Richard Becker, who admires independence, draws the line at allowing the individualist complete autonomy: when reliance on one's own authority leads to "trouble-making," the term becomes an insult.

EXERCISE 20: Analyzing Shades of Meaning in Multiple Sources

A. Analyze the following set of notes for a definition of the word *celebrity*.

B. Find the important terms or concepts that can lead to a context for defining *celebrity*.

C. Write two generalizations that might serve as topic sentences for a two-paragraph essay. (Do not use "favorable" and "unfavorable" as your two topics.)

Eddie Blum: a famous person; probably a star; someone whose name is known far and wide; you hear about him in gossip columns, but a lot of the gossip is just a myth: "Celebrities attract big crowds wherever they go."

Tanny Leland: someone that most people admire, probably because there's been a lot of hype in gossip magazines; it doesn't matter what the person has really done — if anything: "Everyone recognizes who that person is, at least while she has her fifteen minutes of fame."

Violette McBride: a person who's achieved a lot and made a name for himself or herself, a famous singer or a movie star, someone who's eminent in his field: "A celebrity has star quality and works hard to make his fans admire him."

Suzanne Nichols: someone very much in the public eye, everyone knows his name: "You're a celebrity if you have outstanding qualities that make people want to look up to you and know more about you."

Shaun O'Brien: someone everyone talks about, celebrities exist to sell newspapers and magazines, not necessarily someone you respect: "Some celebrities are worthwhile people, who do a lot of good for society, but others have become famous because they have good publicity agents."

ASSIGNMENT 4: Writing a Definition Essay from Multiple Sources

All the words in the following list are in common use and have either more than one usual meaning or a meaning that can be interpreted both favorably and unfavorably. Choose one word from the list as the topic for a definition essay. (Or, if your instructor asks you to do so, select a word from a dictionary or a thesaurus.)

shrewd	justice	self-interest
curiosity	ordinary	respectable
capitalism	power	smart
radical	flamboyant	polite
progress	eccentric	obedience
habit	politician	ambition
credit	genius	duty
ladylike	failure	poverty
royalty	competition	sophisticated
masculine	peace	humility
cautious	welfare	solitude
bias	immature	spiritual
dominance	culture	sentimental
revolution	aggression	glamorous
passive	modern	self-confidence
influential	feminine	passionate
criticism	imagination	impetuous
jealousy	romantic	successful
small	workman	smooth
cheap	privilege	intrigue
fashion	enthusiast	normal
pompous	mercenary	criticize
obligation	shame	freedom
control	idealistic	artificial
ambition	ethical	perfection

A. Clarify your own definition of the word by writing down your ideas about its meaning.

B. Interview five or six people, or as many as you need, to get a variety of reactions. The purpose of the *survey* is to become aware of several ways of using your word. Take careful and complete notes of each reaction that you receive.

C. Each person should be asked the following questions:

- What do you think *X* means? Has it any other meanings that you know of?

- How would you use this word in a sentence? (Pay special attention to the way in which the word is used, and note down the differences. Two people might say that a word means the same thing and yet use it differently.)

- Is this a positive word or a negative word? In what situation could it possibly seem favorable or unfavorable?

In listening to the answers to these questions, do not hesitate to ask, "What do you mean?" It may be necessary to make people think hard about a word that they use casually.

D. As you note reactions, consider how the meaning of the word changes and try to identify the different circumstances and usages that cause these variations. Watch for differences between the *ideal* meaning of the word and its *practical* application in daily life.

E. If one person's reaction is merely an echo of something that you already have in your notes, you may summarize the second response more briefly, but keep an accurate record of who (and how many) said what.

F. Although your notes for each source may run only a few sentences, plan to use a separate sheet for each person.

G. Your notes should include not only a report of each reaction, but also, if possible, a few quotations. If someone suggests a good definition or uses the word in an interesting way, try to record the exact words; read the quotation back to the speaker to make sure that what you have quoted is accurate; put quotation marks around the direct quotation.

H. Make sure that the names of all your sources are accurately spelled.

I. Analyze your notes and make an outline of possible meanings and contexts.

J. Write a series of paragraphs, first explaining *the most common meaning attributed to the word*, according to your sources. Be sure to cite different examples of this common usage. Then, in successive paragraphs, review the other connotations, favorable and unfavorable, always trying to trace the relationships and common contexts among the different meanings.

There is no set length for this essay. Contents and organization are governed entirely by the kind and extent of the material in your notes. *Your notes should be handed in with your completed essay.*

Synthesizing Multiple Sources: The Lottery

Once you have analyzed each of your sources and discovered their common themes and contexts, their similarities and differences, you then reassemble these parts into a more coherent whole. This process is called *synthesis*. Although at first you may regard analysis and synthesis as contradictory operations, they are actually overlapping stages of a single, larger process.

Analysis and Synthesis

To illustrate the way in which analysis and synthesis work together, let us examine a set of answers to the questions: "Would you buy a **lottery** ticket? Why?" First, read through these summaries of all seven responses.

Mary Smith: She thinks that lottery tickets were made for people to enjoy and win. It's fun to try your luck. She looks forward to buying her ticket, because she feels that, for one dollar, you have a chance to win a lot more. It's also fun scratching off the numbers to see what you've won. Some people don't buy tickets because they think the lottery is a big rip-off; but "a dollar can't buy that much today, so why not spend it and have a good time?"

John Jones: He would buy a lottery ticket for three reasons. The first reason is that he would love to win. The odds are like a challenge, and he likes to take a chance. The second reason is just for fun. When he has two matching tickets, he really feels happy, especially when he thinks that dollars can be multiplied into hundreds or thousands. "It's like Russian roulette." The third reason is that part of the money from the lottery goes toward his education. The only problem, he says, is that they are always sold out!

Michael Green: He has never bought a lottery ticket in his life because he doesn't want to lose money. He wants to be sure of winning. Also, he says that he isn't patient enough. The buyer of a lottery ticket has to be very patient to wait for his chance to win. He thinks that people who buy tickets all the time must enjoy "living dangerously."

Anne White: Buying a lottery ticket gives her a sense of excitement. She regards herself as a gambler. "When you win two dollars or five dollars you get a thrill of victory, and when you see that you haven't, you feel the agony of defeat." She thinks that people who don't buy tickets must be very cautious and noncompetitive, since the lottery brings "a sense of competition with you against millions of other people." She also knows that the money she spends on tickets goes toward education.

Margaret Brown: She feels that people who buy tickets are wasting their money. The dollars spent on the lottery could be in the bank, getting interest. Those people who buy tickets should expect to have thrown out their money, and should take their losses philosophically, instead of jumping up and down and screaming about their disappointment. Finally, even if she could afford the risk, the laws of her religion forbid her to participate in "any sort of game that is a form of gambling."

William Black: He would buy a lottery ticket, because he thinks it can be fun, but he wouldn't buy too many, because he thinks it's easy for people to get carried away and obsessed by the lottery. He enjoys the anticipation of wanting to win and maybe winning. "I think that you should participate, but in proportion to your budget; after all, one day you might just be a winner."

Elizabeth Watson: She wouldn't buy a lottery ticket because she considers them a rip-off. The odds are too much against you, 240,000 to 1. Also, it is much too expensive, "and I don't have the money to be throwing away on such foolishness." She thinks that people who indulge themselves with lottery tickets become gamblers, and she's against all kinds of gambling. Such people have no sense or self-control. Finally, "I'm a sore loser, so buying lottery tickets just isn't for me."

Making a Chart of Common Ideas

Since you are working with seven sources with varying opinions, you need a way to record the process of analysis. One effective way is to make a *chart of commonly held views*. To do so, follow these two steps, which should be carried out *simultaneously*:

1. Read each statement carefully, and identify each separate reason that is being cited for and against playing the lottery by writing a number above or next to the relevant comment. When a similar comment is made by another person, use *the same number* to provide a key to the final list of common reasons. In this step, you are analyzing your sources. Here is what the first two sets of notes might look like once the topic numbers have been inserted:

   Mary Smith: She thinks that lottery tickets were made for people to enjoy and win. It's fun to try your luck. She looks forward to buying her ticket, because she feels that, for one dollar, you have a chance to win a lot more. It's also fun scratching off the numbers to see what you've won. Some people don't buy tickets because they think the lottery is a big rip-off; but "a dollar can't buy that much today, so why not spend it and have a good time?"

   John Jones: He would buy a lottery ticket for three reasons. The first reason is that he would love to win. The odds are like a challenge, and he likes to take a chance. The second reason is just for fun. When he has two matching tickets, he really feels happy, especially when he thinks that dollars can be multiplied into hundreds or thousands. "It's like Russian roulette." The third reason is that part of the money from the lottery goes toward his education. The only problem, he says, is that they are always sold out!

2. At the same time as you number each of your reasons, also write a list or *chart of reasons* on a separate sheet of paper. Each reason should be assigned *the same number* you wrote next to it in the original statement. Don't make a new entry when the same reason is repeated by a second source. Next to each entry on your chart, put the names of the people who have mentioned that reason. You are now beginning to *synthesize* your sources. (This process is also known as *cross-referencing*.)

Here's what your completed list of reasons might look like:

Reason	Sources
1. People play the lottery because it's fun.	Smith; Jones
2. People play the lottery because they like the excitement of taking a chance and winning.	Smith; Jones; Green; White; Black
3. People don't play the lottery because they think it's a rip-off.	Smith; Watson
4. People play the lottery because they are contributing to education.	Jones; White
5. People don't play the lottery because they have better things to do with their money.	Green; Brown; Watson
6. People play the lottery because they like to gamble.	White; Brown; Watson
7. People who play the lottery and those who refuse to play worry about the emotional reactions of the players.	Green; White; Brown; Black; Watson

The process of synthesis starts as soon as you start to make your list. The list of common reasons represents the reworking of seven separate sources into a single new pattern that can serve as the basis for an essay.

Distinguishing between Reasons

One of the biggest problems in synthesis is deciding, in cases of overlapping, whether you actually have one reason or two. Since overlapping reasons were deliberately not combined, the preceding list may be unnecessarily long:

- *Reasons 1 and 2:* The difference between the experiences of *having fun* and *feeling the thrill of excitement* is a difference in sensation that most people would understand. You might ask yourself, "Would someone play the lottery just for fun without the anticipation of winning? Or would someone experience a thrill of excitement without any sense of fun at all?" If one sensation can exist without the other, you have sufficient reason for putting both items on your chart. Later on, the similarities, not the differences, might make you want to combine the two; but, at the beginning, it is important to note down exactly what ideas and information are available to you.

▓ *Reasons 2 and 6*: The distinction between the *thrill of excitement* (2) and the *pleasure of gambling* (6) is more difficult to perceive. The former is, perhaps, more innocent than the latter and does not carry with it any of the obsessive overtones of gambling.

▓ *Reasons 3 and 5*: Resenting the lottery because it is a *rip-off* (3) and resenting the lottery because the players are *wasting their money* (5) appear at first glance to be similar reactions. However, references to the rip-off tend to emphasize the "injured victim" whose money is being whisked away by a public agency. In other words, Reason 3 emphasizes *self-protection from robbery*; Reason 5 emphasizes *the personal virtue of thrift*.

▓ *Reason 7*: This is not really a reason at all. Some comments in the notes do not fit into a tidy list of reasons for playing, yet they provide a valuable insight into human motivation and behavior as expressed in lottery playing. An exploration of the emotions that characterize the player and the nonplayer (always allowing for the lottery preference of the source) might be an interesting way to conclude an essay.

Deciding on a Sequence of Topics

The topics in your chart appear in the same random order as your notes. Once the chart is completed, you should decide on *a more logical sequence of topics* by re-ordering the entries in the list. You can make an indirect impact on your reader by choosing a logical sequence that supports the pattern that you discovered in analyzing your sources.

Here are two possible ways to arrange the "lottery" reasons. Which sequence do you prefer? Why?

1. fun	1. fun
2. excitement	2. rip-off
3. gambling	3. excitement and gambling
4. education	4. misuse of money
5. rip-off	5. education
6. misuse of money	6. personality of the gambler
7. personality of the gambler	

The right-hand sequence *contrasts the advantages and disadvantages* of playing the lottery. Moving back and forth between paired reasons calls attention to the relation between opposites and, through constant contrast, makes the material interesting for the reader. The left-hand sequence places all the advantages and disadvantages together, providing an opportunity to *explore positive and negative reactions to the lottery separately* without interruption, therefore encouraging more complex development. Both sequences are acceptable.

EXERCISE 21: Identifying Common Ideas

This exercise is based on a set of interview notes, answering the question "Would you give money to a beggar?"

A.   Read through the notes.

   1. Identify distinct and different reasons by placing numbers next to the relevant sentences.

   2. As you number each new reason, add an entry to the chart. (The first reason is already filled in.)

B.   Arrange the numbered reasons in a logical sequence. If it makes sense to you, combine those reasons that belong together. Be prepared to explain the logic behind your sequence of points. If you can find two possible sequences, include both, explaining the advantages of each.

Reason	Sources
1. I can afford to give to beggars.	
2.	
3.	
4.	
5.	
6.	
7.	
8.	
9.	
10.	

Would You Give Money to a Beggar?

Jonathan Cohen: When asked for money on the street, I often apply a maxim of a friend of mine. He takes the question, "Have you got any spare change?" literally: if he has any loose change, he hands it over, without regard for his impression of what the money's for, since he doesn't think ulterior motives are any of his business. Since I can always afford the kind of contribution that's usually asked for — fifty cents or a dollar — or am at least less likely to miss it than the person asking me for it, I usually take the request as the only qualification of "need." I'm more likely to give out money if I don't have to go into my billfold for it, however, and would rather give out transit tokens or food, if I have them. But I want to be sympathetic; I often think, "There but for the grace of God go I."

Jennifer Sharone: I hate to think about what people who beg have to undergo; it makes me feel so fortunate to be well dressed and to have good food to eat and a home and a job. Begging seems kind of horrifying to me — that in this country there are people actually relying on the moods of strangers just to stay alive. I give to people who seem to have fallen on hard times, who aren't too brazen, who seem embarrassed to be asking me for money. I guess I do identify with them a lot.

Michael Aldrich: If a person meets my eye and asks plainly and forthrightly (and isn't falling-down drunk), I try to empty my pocket, or at least come up with a quarter or two. If the person has an unusually witty spiel—even if it's outlandish—I give more freely. I don't mind giving small change; it's quick and easy. I try not to think about whether or not the person really "needs" the money—how could you ever know? On some level, I think that if someone's begging, they need the money. Period. There's an old guy who stands on my corner—he's been there for years. I always give him money, if I have the change. If I don't have it, he says a smile will do. I would hate to think of him going without a meal for a long time or having to sleep out in the rain. He reminds me of my father and my uncle.

Marianne Lauro: I used to give people money, but frankly, I'm too embarrassed by the whole process. It seems to me that folks who really couldn't be all that grateful for somebody's pocket change still make an effort to appear grateful, and then I'm supposed to get to feel magnanimous when I really feel ridiculous telling them they're welcome to a couple of coins that don't even amount to carfare. So the whole transaction seems vaguely humiliating for everyone concerned. Really, the city or the state or the federal government should be doing something about this—not expecting ordinary people, going home from work, or whatever, to support people who have mental or physical impairments or addictions, especially when you're never sure what their money will be used for. But maybe I'm just rationalizing now—maybe the most "humane" thing about these kinds of transactions is the mutual embarrassment.

Donald Garder: I try, when possible, to respond to the person approaching me, by looking at them, perhaps even making eye contact, which frequently lends some dignity to the moment. But then I don't always reach into my pocket. I often give to people with visible physical handicaps, but rarely to someone who's "young and able-bodied." Sometimes I feel guilty, but I'm never sure if the person is for real or not—I've known people who swindled people out of money by pretending to be homeless, so I have a nagging doubt about whether or not a beggar is legitimate.

Darrin Johnson: I never give on the subway—I hate the feeling of entrapment, of being held hostage. The "O.K., so I have you until the next stop so I'm going to wear you down with guilt until I get the money out of you." I really resent that. I flatly refuse to give under those circumstances because it just pisses me off. I might give to somebody just sitting on the street, with a sign and a cup or something—someone who isn't making a big scene, who leaves it up to me whether I give or not. But I hate feeling coerced.

Jenny Nagel: I never give to people on the streets anymore — there are places where people who are really in need can go if they're really starving or need drug treatment or something. Someone once told me, after I'd given money to some derelict looking guy, that he'd probably buy rubbing alcohol or boot polish and melt it down for the alcohol content — that my money was just helping him kill himself. After that I never gave to anyone on the street. I'd rather make a contribution to a social agency.

Paul O'Rourke: I used to give money or if asked I'd give a cigarette. But one day a beggar let loose with a stream of obscenities after I gave him some money. A lot of these people are really messed up — the government should be looking after them, doing more to help them; if they keep getting money from people off the street, they'll just keep on begging. So now I volunteer once a month at a food shelf, and give to charitable organizations, rather than hand out money on the street.

Organizing Multiple Sources: Student Promotion

Playing the lottery is not a subject that lends itself to lengthy or abstract discussion; therefore, charting reasons for and against playing the lottery is not a challenge. The article that follows defines an educational and social problem without taking sides or suggesting any solutions. The reporter's sources simply cite aspects of the problem and express baffled concern.

Twenty students were asked to read the article and to offer their opinions; these are presented following the article. As you read the article and the student opinions, assume that you plan to address the issue and synthesize the opinions in an essay of your own.

from RULE TYING PUPIL PROMOTION
TO READING SKILL STIRS WORRY
Gene I. Maeroff

A strict new promotion policy requires the public schools to hold back seventh-grade pupils until they pass the reading test. The difficulty will be compounded this year by a requirement that new seventh graders also pass a mathematics test. 1

"I am frightened that we may end up losing some of these kids, creating a whole new group of dropouts who leave school at junior high," said Herbert Rahinsky, principal of Intermediate School 293, on the edge of the Carroll Gardens section of Brooklyn. 2

Students like Larry, who is 16 years old and in the seventh grade at I.S. 293, are repeating the grade because they scored too low on the reading tests last 3

June to be promoted. If Larry does not do well enough on the test this spring, he will remain in the seventh grade in the fall.

An analysis by the Board of Education has shown that about 1,000 of the 8,871 students repeating the seventh grade are already 16 years of age or older. At least one 18-year-old is repeating the seventh grade.   4

Normally, a seventh grader is 12 years old.   5

When the promotion policy, which threatened to hold back students with low reading scores in the fourth and seventh grades, was implemented in 1980, it was hailed by many observers as a welcome effort to tighten standards.   6

But as the program has continued, certain students have failed to show adequate progress. These youngsters are in jeopardy of becoming "double holdovers" in the seventh grade. Some were also held back at least once in elementary school. . . .   7

Authorities theorize that these youngsters form a hard core of poor readers for whom improvement is slow and difficult. Such students often were not held back in prior years because it was easier to move them along than to help them.   8

Educators now wonder whether repeated failure will simply lessen the likelihood of students persisting in school long enough to get a regular diploma.   9

Student Opinions

Diane Basi: If these students are pushed through the system and receive a diploma, not being able to read beyond a seventh-grade level, we will be doing them and society a grave injustice. What good will it do to have a diploma if you cannot read or write? In the end, the students will be hurt more if they are just promoted through the system.

Jason Berg: A student should not be repeatedly held back on the basis of one test. A student's overall performance should be taken into consideration, such as classwork, participation, and attitude. If a student is not up to par for some reason on the day of the test, all the work and effort that was put into school during the year goes down the drain.

Rafael Del Rey: This strict rule has unfortunate consequences. The students who are being forced out don't comprehend what is being taught to them. Exasperated and feeling like social outcasts and inferior beings, it is no wonder that many drop out without skills or goals. Low reading scores mean that students have been neglected by the school system. Educators should be interested in more than just test scores.

Anita Felice: It is extremely embarrassing to be a 16-year-old in a class of 12-year-olds. Such poor students should be promoted to a special program with other students who have the same problems. In time, there should be some improvement in their reading scores. Being held back will only cause frustration and eventually cause them to drop out. Test scores should be a lot less important than they are now.

Joe Gordon: By enforcing a rigid standard, the schools are actually promoting an increased dropout rate and, by doing so, are harming the student and society. What about the teachers? Sometimes students fail a teacher, and for that reason fail the class.

Margaret Jenkins: After two tries, a student should be able to pass a test. It's to the child's advantage to learn and keep learning while moving upward in school. Holding them back is for their own good.

Rachel Limburg: It isn't fair to those students who can do the work just to push these students along. It also isn't fair to the kids who can't pass the test because eventually they are going to have to earn a living. We should look for new ways to help them find their talents and prepare them to face the future.

Barbara Martin: It's a hard question, but I think you have to look at the cost in terms of money, as well as frustration and embarrassment. I'm sorry for kids who are left back, but it's only going to be a problem for everyone later when they can't get a job. Work today is increasingly technical, and everyone needs basic skills. This policy is tough love, and it's necessary.

Len McGee: This policy isn't good enough because it doesn't deal with the individual student; it deals with seventh-graders as a whole. The individual's problems and motivation are not taken into consideration. Sometimes exam pressure defeats intelligence. If left back, the student is trapped in a revolving door and is likely to lose interest in school.

Tina Pearson: It's a mistake to pass students solely on the basis of the reading score. It may show they have learned to read well. But it doesn't mean they learned well in their other classes. Perhaps they worked especially hard on reading and English but just coasted along in their other subjects.

Julius Pena: Automatic promotion is a guarantee that the weak student will face future problems. Making the student repeat is for his own good. Imagine how frustrating it would be for someone who can't fill out a job application. Of course, you shouldn't just throw the student back into the class, but give as much encouragement as possible.

Mark Pullman: We must have certain standards in our educational system. This is a challenge for these students, and repeating the course may encourage them to try harder, making them smarter and better prepared to face life's challenges.

Anthony Raviggio: Strict standards are best for the student. In the long run, individuals who really want the college degree will be glad to remember the ordeal they went through in junior high. It's better to make them keep trying and succeed than to let them think it's okay to fail.

Vivian Ray: If a child has been held back in elementary school and held back again in junior high, it should become quite apparent to teachers and parents that the child has a problem. Being slow to learn is not sufficient reason to hold back a child. The child should be promoted and put in a slower class with more students like himself.

Bernice Roberts: I think there's too much concern for the feelings of the "poor" student and too little concern for the needs of society. Eighteen-year-olds who can't read are likely candidates for welfare. I don't want to have the responsibility of carrying some illiterate kid who couldn't be bothered to learn when he was in school.

Althea Simms: The tough standards are good for these students because they will be motivated to become more serious about doing well. There are kids who don't care whether or not they study for their exams since they know they're going to be promoted to the next grade anyway. Knowing that you may be held back is a strong motivator to study harder.

Patricia Sokolov: Not all students are intellectually gifted, nor is the progress of the nation solely dependent on the effort of intellectuals. Laborers and blue-collar workers have been credited throughout our history for their great contribution to the wealth and progress of our country. Educators should be more concerned with nurturing students' individual potential and less concerned with passing tests.

Matthew Warren: What's the point of promoting a student who won't be able to keep up in his new classes, much less perform his job properly when he's out in the working world? Standards should be enforced regardless of age. What's age? It's just a number.

Michael Willoughby: Educators should recognize that some students don't have the capacity, for whatever social, genetic, or psychological reasons, to fulfill the educators' traditional expectations. An alternative effort must be made, emphasizing vocational skills and also basic reading and math, that will permit students to progress at their own pace.

Betty Yando: I am concerned about the large number of dropouts and their dismal prospects. Why should a student, despite obvious learning disabilities, be forced to continue in an exasperating educational process in which he is making little or no progress? The standards by which we determine whether an individual will make a good worker and a good citizen are too high.

Organizing Multiple Sources

1. **Summarize the facts of the issue.**
   Write a brief, objective summary of the issue under discussion (in this case, the problem described in the article). Your summary of this article should convey both the *situation* and the *two key ideas* that are stressed. Try structuring your paragraph to contrast the conflicting opinions.

2. **Establish your own point of view.**
   End your summary with a statement of your own reaction to suggest a possible direction for your essay. This step is more important than it might at first seem. Once you begin to analyze a mass of contradictory opinion, you may find yourself being completely convinced by first one source and then another, or you may try so hard to stay neutral that you end up with no point of view of your own at all. You need to find a vantage point for yourself from which to judge the validity of the statements that you read. Of course, you can (and probably will) adjust your point of view as you become more familiar with all the arguments and evidence that your sources raise. Do not regard your initial statement of opinion as a thesis to be proven, but rather as a *hypothesis to be tested, modified, or even abandoned.*

3. **Synthesize your evidence.**
   Label your set of opinions and *establish categories.* The 20 statements following the article are all personal reactions to withholding promotion because of poor performance and the issue of maintaining standards versus individual needs. For each statement, follow these steps:

   A. *Read each statement carefully and think about its exact meaning.* First, get a rough idea of what each statement says—do a mental paraphrase, if you like. You will naturally notice which "side" the author of each statement is on. There is a tendency to want to stop there, as if the authors' positions are all that one needs to know. But your object is not only to find out which side of an issue each person prefers, but also to understand why that side was chosen.

   B. *Try to pick out the chief reason put forth by each person, or, even better, the principle that lies behind each argument.* Sum up the reasoning of each person in a word or phrase.

   C. When you have labeled the statements, the final stage of synthesis becomes easier. *Review your summarizing phrases to see if there is an abstract idea, used to describe several statements, that might serve as a category title.* (Some change in the wording may be necessary.) Once two or three categories become obvious, consider their relationship to each other. Are they parallel? Are they contrasting? Then attempt to see how the smaller categories fit into the pattern that is beginning to form.

How the Three Steps Work

Following is one student's exploration of the article on promotion and the 20 student opinions.

1. **Summarizing.** Here the student identifies the article to which he and his sources are responding, summarizing the issue and the nature of the conflict.

> In the *New York Times*, Gene I. Maeroff reported that seventh-grade students, who formerly would pass into the eighth grade despite failing their reading tests, are now required to repeat the year until they can pass the test. Some repeaters in the seventh grade are now older than 16. The school system adopted this new rule in order to maintain standards for promotion. But the students most affected apparently don't have the skills to meet those standards. Some educators, questioning the change in policy, are concerned that such students may not stay "in school long enough to get a regular diploma."

2. **Hypothesizing** (stating your own point of view). Here the student expresses an opinion that suggests the possible direction for an essay. At this point, the student has not studied the group of opinions that accompanies the article.

> School authorities have a dilemma. On the one hand, it's in society's interest to produce graduates who have mastered basic skills. Students who pass the reading test will benefit from the rest of their education and then qualify for and hold down good jobs. But, in many cases, the inability to pass the test does not mean that the students didn't try to the best of their capabilities. Holding them back again and again won't ensure that they pass. Later on, when no one wants to hire them, society will have to support them through welfare programs. Perhaps a new vocational track could be developed with less rigorous testing to accommodate children who can't learn well.

3. **Synthesizing** (labeling your set of opinions and establishing categories). In this step, the student moves away from the article to examine the opinions of others who have read the article, determining first *the position of each respondent and then the reasoning behind the position*. Here, the statements of the 20 respondents are repeated, with a summarizing label following each statement.

Student Opinions

Diane Basi: If these students are pushed through the system and receive a diploma, not being able to read beyond a seventh-grade level, we will be doing them and society a grave injustice. What good will it do to have a diploma if you cannot read or write? In the end, the students will be hurt more if they are just promoted through the system.

Basi: literacy necessary for employment; otherwise, individual and society both suffer

Jason Berg: A student should not be repeatedly held back on the basis of one test. A student's overall performance should be taken into consideration, such as classwork, participation, and attitude. If a student is not up to par for some reason on the day of the test, all the work and effort that was put into school during the year goes down the drain.

Berg: test scores less important than individual potential

Rafael Del Rey: This strict rule has unfortunate consequences. The students who are being forced out don't comprehend what is being taught to them. Exasperated and feeling like social outcasts and inferior beings, it is no wonder that many drop out without skills or goals. Low reading scores mean that students have been neglected by the school system. Educators should be interested in more than just test scores.

Del Rey: test scores less important than individual self-esteem

Anita Felice: It is extremely embarrassing to be a 16-year-old in a class of 12-year-olds. Such poor students should be promoted to a special program with other students who have the same problems. In time, there should be some improvement in their reading scores. Being held back will only cause frustration and eventually cause them to drop out. Test scores should be a lot less important than they are now.

Felice: test scores less important than individual self-esteem

Joe Gordon: By enforcing a rigid standard, the schools are actually promoting an increased dropout rate and, by doing so, are harming the student and society. What about the teachers? Sometimes students fail a teacher, and for that reason fail the class.

Gordon: society suffers if high standards lead to dropping out

Margaret Jenkins: After two tries, a student should be able to pass a test. It's to the child's advantage to learn and keep learning while moving upward in school. Holding them back is for their own good.

Jenkins: enforcing tough standards builds character

Rachel Limburg: It isn't fair to those students who can do the work just to push these students along. It also isn't fair to the kids who can't pass the test because eventually they are going to have to earn a living. We should look for new ways to help them find their talents and prepare them to face the future.

Limburg: fairness requires that both good and bad students get an education

Barbara Martin: It's a hard question, but I think you have to look at the cost in terms of money, as well as frustration and embarrassment. I'm sorry for kids who are left back, but it's only going to be a problem for everyone later when they can't get a job. Work today is increasingly technical, and everyone needs basic skills. This policy is tough love, and it's necessary.

Martin: literacy necessary for employment; otherwise, individual and society both suffer

Len McGee: This policy isn't good enough because it doesn't deal with the individual student; it deals with seventh-graders as a whole. The individual's problems and motivation are not taken into consideration. Sometimes exam pressure defeats intelligence. If left back, the student is trapped in a revolving door and is likely to lose interest in school.

McGee: society suffers if high standards lead to dropping out

Tina Pearson: It's a mistake to pass students solely on the basis of the reading score. It may show they have learned to read well. But it doesn't mean they learned well in their other classes. Perhaps they worked especially hard on reading and English but just coasted along in their other subjects.

Pearson: promotion should be based on a variety of skills

Julius Pena: Automatic promotion is a guarantee that the weak student will face future problems. Making the student repeat is for his own good. Imagine how frustrating it would be for someone who can't fill out a job application. Of course, you shouldn't just throw the student back into the class, but give as much encouragement as possible.

Pena: enforcing standards builds character; but offer more help

Mark Pullman: We must have certain standards in our educational system. This is a challenge for these students, and repeating the course may encourage them to try harder, making them smarter and better prepared to face life's challenges.

Pullman: enforcing tough standards builds character

Anthony Raviggio: Strict standards are best for the student. In the long run, individuals who really want the college degree will be glad to remember the ordeal they went through in junior high. It's better to make them keep trying and succeed than to let them think it's okay to fail.

Raviggio: enforcing tough standards builds character

Vivian Ray: If a child has been held back in elementary school and held back again in junior high, it should become quite apparent to teachers and parents that the child has a problem. Being slow to learn is not sufficient reason to hold back a child. The child should be promoted and put in a slower class with more students like himself.

Ray: provide alternate track

Bernice Roberts: I think there's too much concern for the feelings of the "poor" student and too little concern for the needs of society. Eighteen-year-olds who can't read are likely candidates for welfare. I don't want to have the responsibility of carrying some illiterate kid who couldn't be bothered to learn when he was in school.

Roberts: the problem is lack of effort, not lack of ability; it's not society's problem

Althea Simms: The tough standards are good for these students because they will be motivated to become more serious about doing well. There are kids who don't care whether or not they study for their exams since they know they're going to be promoted to the next grade anyway. Knowing that you may be held back is a strong motivator to study harder.

Simms: the problem is lack of effort, not lack of ability

Patricia Sokolov: Not all students are intellectually gifted, nor is the progress of the nation solely dependent on the effort of intellectuals. Laborers and blue-collar workers have been credited throughout our history for their great contribution to the wealth and progress of our country. Educators should be more concerned with nurturing students' individual potential and less concerned with passing tests.

Sokolov: test scores less important than individual potential

Matthew Warren: What's the point of promoting a student who won't be able to keep up in his new classes, much less perform his job properly when he's out in the working world? Standards should be enforced regardless of age. What's age? It's just a number.

Warren: literacy necessary for employment

Michael Willoughby: Educators should recognize that some students don't have the capacity, for whatever social, genetic, or psychological reasons, to fulfill the educators' traditional expectations. An alternative effort must be made, emphasizing vocational skills and also basic reading and math, that will permit students to progress at their own pace.

Willoughby: provide alternate track

Betty Yando: I am concerned about the large number of dropouts and their dismal prospects. Why should a student, despite obvious learning disabilities, be forced to continue in an exasperating educational process in which he is making little or no progress? The standards by which we determine whether an individual will make a good worker and a good citizen are too high.

Yando: individual suffers if high standards lead to dropping out

From this list, the student can establish eight categories that cover the range of topics. Here is the list of categories:

Categorizing the Sources' Opinions

Category	Source	Notes
Literacy is necessary for employment	Warren	
	Basi Martin	Otherwise, individual and society both suffer.
The problem is lack of effort, not lack of ability	Simms	
	Roberts	If students can't meet standards, it's not society's fault.
Society suffers if high standards lead to dropping out	Gordon McGee Yando	
Enforcing tough standards builds character	Jenkins Pullman Raviggio	
	Pena	Society should also offer more help to the individual student.
Test scores are less important than individual potential	Sokolov	
	Berg Pearson	Promotion should be based on a variety of skills.
Test scores are less important than individual self-esteem	Del Rey Felice	
Society owes an education to bad students as well as good ones	Limburg	
Society should offer an alternative track for failing students	Ray Willoughby	

Evaluating Sources

Although you are obliged to give each of your sources serious and objective consideration and a fair presentation, synthesis also requires a certain amount of *selection*. Certainly, no one's statement should be immediately dismissed as trivial or crazy; include them all in your chart. *But do not assume that all opinions are equally convincing and deserve equal representation in your essay.* You owe it to your reader to evaluate the evidence that you are presenting, partly through what you choose to emphasize and partly through your explicit comments about flawed and unconvincing statements.

The weight of a group of similar opinions can add authority to an idea. If most of your sources hold a similar view, you will probably give that idea appropriate prominence in your essay. However, majority rule should not govern the structure of your essay. Your own perspective determines the thesis of your essay, and you must use your understanding of the topic to evaluate your materials, analyze the range of arguments provided by your sources, and determine for your reader which have the greatest validity. Your original hypothesis, either confirmed or altered in the light of your increased understanding, becomes the *thesis* of your essay:

- Sift through all the statements and decide which ones seem *thoughtful and well-balanced*, supported by convincing reasons and examples, and which seem to be thoughtless assertions that rely on stereotypes, catch phrases, and unsupported references. Your evaluation of the sources may differ from someone else's, but you must assert your own point of view and assess each source in the context of your background, knowledge, and experience.

- Review the hypothesis that you formulated before you began to analyze the sources. *Decide whether that hypothesis is still valid* or whether, as a result of your full exploration of the subject, you wish to change it or abandon it for another.

Writing a Synthesis Essay

Organizing Ideas and Material: Spend some time planning your sequence of ideas and considering possible *strategies*. Do your topic and materials lend themselves to a cause-and-effect structure, or definition, or problem and solution, or comparison, or argument? In writing about the issue of school promotion, you might want to use an overall *problem-solution* strategy, at the same time *arguing* for your preferred solution.

Developing Topic Sentences: Before starting to write each paragraph, review your sources' statements. By now, you should be fully aware of the reasoning underlying each point of view and the pattern connecting them all. But because your reader does not know as much as you do, you need to explain your main ideas in enough detail to make all the complex points clear. Remember that your reader has neither made a list nor even read the original sources. It is therefore important to include *some explanation in your own voice*, in addition to citing sources.

Presenting Sources as Evidence: If possible, you should use all three methods of reference: *summary*, *paraphrase*, and *quotation*. (See the paragraph in Exercise 22 as an appropriate model.) Remember that, as a rule, paraphrase is far more effective than quotation. But the first sentence presenting any new idea (whether the topic sentence of a new paragraph or a shift of thought within a paragraph) should be written entirely in your own voice, as a generalization, without any reference to your sources.

To summarize, the paragraphs of your essay should include the following elements:

- *Topic sentence*: Introduce the category or theme of the paragraph, and state the idea that is a common element tying this group of opinions together.

- *Explanation*: Support or explain the topic sentence. Later in the paragraph, if you are dealing with a complex group of statements, you may need a connecting sentence or two, showing your reader how one reason is connected to the next. For example, an explanation might be needed in the middle of the "enforcing tough standards builds character" paragraph as the writer moves from the need for "tough love" to the obligation of society to offer more help.

- *Paraphrase or summary*: Present specific ideas from your sources in your own words. In these cases, you must of course *acknowledge your sources* by citing names in your sentence.

- *Quotation*: Quote from your sources when the content or phrasing of the original statement justifies word-for-word inclusion. In some groups of statements, there may be several possible candidates for quotation; in others, there may be only one; often you may find no source worth quoting. For example, read the statements made by Sokolov, Berg, and Pearson once again. Could you reasonably quote any of them? Although Berg and Pearson both take strong positions well worth presenting, there is no reason to quote them and every reason to use paraphrase. You might want to quote Sokolov's first sentence, which is apt and well-balanced.

As you present the opinions of your sources in the body of your essay, *you should remain neutral*, exploring the problem and analyzing each point of view without bias. In the final paragraphs of your essay, you present your own conclusions, in your own voice, arguing for maintaining society's standards or nurturing the individual student, or recommending ways to accommodate both sides.

Citing Sources in a Synthesis Essay

- *Cite the source's full name*, whether you are quoting or not.

- *Try not to begin every sentence with a name*, nor should you introduce every paraphrase or quotation with "says."

- *Each sentence should do more than name a person*; don't include sentences without content: "Mary Smith agrees with this point."

- If possible, *support your general points with references from several different sources*, so that you will have more than one person's opinion or authority to cite.

- When you have several relevant comments to include within a single paragraph, *consider carefully which one should get cited first—and why*.

- You need not name every person who has mentioned a point (especially if you have several almost identical statements); however, *you may find it useful to sum up two people's views at the same time*, citing two sources for a single paraphrased statement:

  Mary Smith and John Jones agree that playing the lottery can be very enjoyable. She finds a particular pleasure in scratching off the numbers to see if she has won.

- *Cite only one source for a quotation*, unless both have used exactly the same wording. In the example above, the citation would not make sense if you quoted "very enjoyable."

- If an idea under discussion is frequently mentioned in your sources, *convey the relative weight of support* by citing "five people" or "several commentators." Then, after summarizing the common response, cite one or two specific opinions, with names. But try not to *begin* a paragraph with "several people"; remember that, whenever possible, the topic sentence should be a generalization of your own, without reference to the supporting evidence.

- *Discuss opposing views within a single paragraph as long as the two points of view have something in common*. Radically different ideas should, of course, be explained separately. Use transitions like "similarly" or "in contrast" to indicate the relationship between opinions.

EXERCISE 22: Analyzing a Paragraph Based on Synthesis of Sources

A. Read the following paragraph.

B. Decide which sentences (or parts of sentences) belong to each of these categories: topic sentence, explanation, summary, paraphrase, quotation.

C. Insert the appropriate category name in the left margin, and bracket the sentence or phrase illustrating the term.

D. Be prepared to explain the components of the paragraph in class discussion.

TOPIC [Reading test scores may not always be a valid basis for deciding whether students should be promoted or made to repeat the seventh grade. According to Jason Berg, Tina Pearson, and Patricia Sokolov, proficiency in reading is just one factor among many that should count toward promotion. *Paraphrase* Pearson points out that students with high scores in reading don't necessarily excel in other subjects. In her view, it is unfair to base the decision on just one area of learning. Berg finds it equally unfair that one test should be valued more highly than a year's achievements. But the issue here is not limited to academic competence. Both Berg and Sokolov attach more importance to a student's character and potential than to intellectual attainments. *explanation* Berg's definition of "overall performance" includes general contributions to the class that demonstrate a positive attitude. For *Quotations* Berg, the context is the classroom; for Sokolov, it is the nation. In her view, intellect alone won't make the nation thrive: "Laborers and blue-collar workers have been credited throughout our history for their great contribution to the wealth and progress of our country." Our primary concern should be to educate good citizens rather than good readers] — *Closing*

Citing Sources for Synthesis

When you yourself have interviewed people as part of a survey, you realize that it's important to indicate who they are and what they represent. To illustrate a particularly deft use of citation in synthesizing a group of interviews, here is an excerpt from *Moral Freedom* by Alan Wolfe, a sociologist who has published several books exploring American national identity. Based on interviews with ordinary Americans, *Moral Freedom* attempts to define an era in which moral certainties are eroding. In this section, Wolfe is recording opinions about *the disappearance of loyalty in everyday life.*

As you read, notice that each paragraph begins with a sentence or two in which Wolfe sums up and comments on what his interviewees have told him. Then he introduces Quincy Simmons, Kellie Moss, and Laverne Eaton, one at a time, each with a *brief biographical description* that moves seamlessly — within the same sentence — into a paraphrase or quotation expressing their views. (In this excerpt, the citations have been italicized.) The *transitions* — where Wolfe moves from person to person or from paraphrase to commentary — are extremely clear. You're never in doubt about whose voice you're hearing. This is an excellent model for the presentation of oral evidence.

from MORAL FREEDOM:
TILL CIRCUMSTANCES DO US PART
Alan Wolfe

No other institution in American life provokes such bittersweet reflections   1
of loyalty lost as the business corporation. Quincy Simmons, who is now 47
years old, came to America from one of the Caribbean islands and eventually
settled in the Hartford area. A small businessman who makes his living painting
and remodeling, *Mr. Simmons remembers* that "in the old days you got a job and
for both the company and the employee it would be different." *He is struck* by
these differences between then and now. Then, "you go back home and at the
same time the company will see that you get reasonable pay or whatever for
the work you do. But now it goes back to greed, everybody's thinking about
the money."

Mr. Simmons's views are surely influenced by the wave of downsizings that   2
took place in his city. Known as the home of the American insurance industry,
Hartford was hit hard by managed care, a rationalization of health care costs
that, for a time, cut into the profits of such large insurers in the area as Aetna or
the Hartford. Given the traumatic effects of economic consolidation on the region, *Mr. Simmons's lament* was repeated by so many of his neighbors, and in
words so close to his, as to constitute a kind of folk truth. Since the big companies started merging, as *Kellie Moss, a retired bank clerk*, puts it, "there's no
heart. It takes the heart and soul out of a company. They make more money—
and it all comes down to money—but they don't take care of it. Everything is
merging, merging, merging. Push this one out, buy this one out, get him out."
Laverne Eaton, a 55-year-old grandmother, could see the changes in her own
life. She worked for the same company for 32 years before retiring. "They cared
about us; we cared about them; we would work ourselves silly because it was
important to the company, and the company always showed in kind that they
cared about us," *she recalls. Her son now works for the same firm, and his experiences are entirely different.* For him, "there's no loyalty and people don't care
about doing the job that they're hired to do."

ASSIGNMENT 5: Writing an Essay Synthesizing Multiple Sources

A. Read "The B-Minus Reigns Supreme," by Laurie Fendrich, twice.

B. Write a summary of the point at issue, and then write a brief explanation of
your opinion of this issue.

C. Use the statements that follow as a basis for a synthesis essay. These statements were written in response to the question: *What does grade inflation tell*

us about our society? Analyze each statement, label each kind of reason, and organize all the categories in a chart.

D.   Write an essay that presents the full range of opinion, paraphrasing and, if desirable, quoting from representative sources.

To provide a more well-rounded variety of views, your instructor may ask your class to submit brief responses to Fendrich's article.

THE B-MINUS REIGNS SUPREME
Laurie Fendrich

A professor of fine arts at Hofstra University, Laurie Fendrich has had her art exhibited in many galleries. She is the author of essays on painting and the arts and has also written regularly on higher education issues for the Chronicle of Higher Education, *where this article appeared.*

We don't need statistics to know that for all the bleating about how college faculty everywhere are tamping down grade inflation, it continues to rage out of control.   1

How did C+ (the "gentleman's C" with a little uptick added) turn into the ubiquitous B–? To start, it's part of the tide of grade inflation that's been rising since the 1960s. The Vietnam War, it's been said by many, prompted the initial revving up of grades because it made many professors who were against the war feel guilty about giving any grade that might lead to a student flunking out of college, which in turn could lead to that student being drafted. The increasing popularity of "feel-good" philosophies in the 1970s and '80s made faculty and students alike prefer smiles, encouragement, and pats on the back to telling the truth. The emphasis on "self-fulfillment," and its elevation to a god around which everything educational revolves, turned knowledge from something that was "out there," to be learned, into something "inside," to be "experienced."   2

The dominant historicist philosophies of the twentieth century, albeit indirectly, convinced many intellectuals, as well as college faculty members, that such matters of judgment as grades were essentially subjective matters—as subjective as preferring one ice-cream flavor to another. The desire to be liked by students, coupled with the increasingly informal and friendly relationships between students and professors, increased during the last three decades of the twentieth century. This made professorial attempts to tell the truth about academic performance seem both too painful to do and beside the point. Professors became "guides at the side"—translation: Everyone is essentially equal, and we're one big happy family of siblings here on this college campus.   3

Today, the grade—and not "education" (despite what people assert)—is considered the "key to success." Parents and employers want students to "perform" in college—as perfunctorily, efficiently, and rapidly as possible—so that they can get on with the business of life in the workforce. 4

But I have strayed from my main point, which is to consider why the grade of B− has become the baseline acceptable grade, the one "low" grade students will willingly suffer? After all, C+ is right next door to it, and the difference between any two grades has only a tiny effect on an undergraduate's overall GPA. In theory, C+ would have done the trick—i.e., would have allowed fearful professors to grade fearful students while simultaneously permitting everyone to acknowledge an average academic performance. 5

I think the reason lies in the increasing symbolic resonance of grades. Grades issued in 2008 permeate the very souls of students. They don't say, "My work received a grade of B in such-and-such a course," or even, "I earned a grade of B in such-and-such a course," but rather, "I got a 'B' in such-and-such a course." The grade apparently swooped in from the outside and made a direct hit on their vulnerable egos. 6

In other words, grades are no longer about academic performance, but about *being*—or rather, "B-ing." 7

Whether standing alone or with a plus or a minus attached to it, the grade of B always sings of "good." The grade of B− may sing with a slightly feeble voice, but it's still a song about "good." 8

The grade of C, on the other hand, even when accompanied by a plus, declares—in an ugly, rough voice—"average." Nothing can be done to lift it to the point where it has any connection to the good. To borrow a charming phrase, putting a plus on a C is like putting lipstick on a pig. It's still a pig. 9

If students and faculty acknowledged that grades were no more and no less than measures of knowledge demonstrated in particular courses, grades of C might still seem as reasonable as they did when I was in college, and earned mine. As things stand now, forget it. 10

Comments

Sue Barker: What's more important—earning a specific letter grade or being a good person and a good citizen? I don't think anyone—even our instructors— cares very much about the difference between a C+ or a B−. Grades are just an artificial construction and don't tell you very much about what's important.

Lily Chung: What grade inflation tells me is that instructors, just like anyone else, want to keep their jobs and even get promoted, and, to do that, they have to avoid looking bad. Grading is a two-way street. Now that students have the right to evaluate their instructors, instructors realize that they have to give their students a break—we're all human beings and deserve decent treatment—and not worry about the fine points between C+ and B−.

Isabel Collins: Grade inflation is part of the whole breakdown of respect in our society. College professors used to be regarded as superior beings, who knew everything about their subjects and were qualified to sit in judgment on their students, who didn't know much. I actually think that professors still deserve our respect, but grades can make a difference to students' future lives, and faculty should take that into consideration.

Johnnie Craft: Grades are supposed to indicate exactly how much you know about a particular subject. But I don't think knowing facts and theories is so important any more. That's a pity, but it's all part of the general dumbing-down of our culture. You only need to know enough about your field to get a good job.

Emily DeMarco: I'm not sure that grades serve any useful function, and I think that everyone is beginning to realize that. Why is it necessary to divide everyone up into "smart" and "stupid," when it just means that one person read the textbook thoroughly and the other person didn't. It can be very annihilating to get a bad grade, especially if you tried hard and did the work as best you could.

Miriam Enriques: In our world today, what's important is who you are, not what you know. Each of us is an individual, with a unique personality and our own background and experiences. We all deserve respect and we are all valuable to society. Grades end up putting people into petty little boxes.

Morris Gardner: What a grade should really do is encourage you to improve your academic work. But how is any student supposed to understand the difference between C+ and B−? One is supposed to be slightly better than average; the other means you're rated as less than good. These fine distinctions don't really show whether the student is ready to move on to a more advanced course. They're meaningless.

Reg Grogan: In our society, "average" is out of fashion. Everyone wants to be regarded as better than average, as worth a great deal. We live in a democracy in which our basic right is equality. So students resent being told that, after studying a subject for several months or more, they're no better than average, just like everyone else.

George Hayden: After graduation, when students are in the real world of employment, they are going to be hired or fired on the basis of whether they did the work. That's all that matters, not how much you know, but whether you performed according to expectations. And those expectations won't involve anthropological theories or historical facts. Grades are really irrelevant to success after graduation.

Jim Joffee: I've always received good grades. My family expected me to, and I enjoyed seeing all the A's on my report card. If I put in the hours and learn the material, then I deserve a good grade—that's what I am in college for. That's what education is all about. But, with grade inflation, my efforts are pointless because people who did no work all semester receive the same credit as I do. So it seems to me that we live in a society that no longer puts a value on hard work.

Carlos Kelly: Most college students are in the late teens—they're basically adolescents with the fragile egos that go along with being teenagers. The grading system can really have a destructive effect on a student's personality. You feel like you are nothing and nobody when you get a grade that's way below what your friends are getting—a C+ can make you utterly miserable if your friends are getting B's. Colleges are supposed to support their students, not make them nervous wrecks.

Barbara Knight: People say that the grading system is too harsh and that students gain no benefit from being sorted into "average," "good," and "superior"—or, worst of all, "failure." But I don't think there is any better way of determining whether someone has or hasn't done the work. College is supposed to be about acquiring knowledge; that's what we're here for. In most courses, it's not that hard to figure out whether a student knows nothing, a little, a lot, or everything that's required. I don't see anything wrong with maintaining that kind of standard, and I don't know why instructors aren't enforcing it.

Erik Kristopher: Like most people, I'm in college so that I can have a solid professional life afterwards, with a good salary and, if I'm lucky, some recognition for being good at my job. It's the diploma that counts, not the grades for courses that no employer is going to care about. I think that most people have figured out that most of what we learn in college isn't really necessary for us to do well after graduation. That's why grade inflation is now okay—to put a good face on an outmoded system that hasn't yet been discarded.

Jackson Lamb: On a practical level, grade inflation exists because instructors are willing to bend the truth about how well their students actually do. Just like businessmen or politicians, they may talk about their lofty ideals, but, actually, they'll do anything they need to do in order to maintain their nice three-course schedules in their ivy-covered ivory towers. Hypocrisy exists in academia like everywhere else.

Connie Lane: Grade inflation tends to discourage competition. If you know that you're going to get a respectable B– on relatively little work, then you can coast along, rather than working hard to get a better grade than everyone else. On the one hand, you don't have to lay your ego on the line and fight for recognition. But then you don't get the satisfaction of being the best. It seems that people would rather get by than excel these days.

David Miller: I'm not sure why colleges still maintain a system of letter grades. Either you learn the subject, or you don't. That difference can be indicated by a simple "pass" or "fail." Some colleges use the pass/fail system and I would suspect that their students are far more laid back and nicer to each other than those whose institutions encourage cutthroat competition. Is the purpose of higher education to learn or to go through the academic equivalent of basic training?

Ethel Murray: It's very difficult to tell a person that they have failed at something, or even that they have only produced an average performance. I think that college instructors have become more human and more sympathetic to their students' situations, and simply don't want to inflict unnecessary cruelty by using a rigid system of evaluation. So they soften the process through grade inflation. Students may benefit from this in the short term, but I'm not sure that it's very good for standards of education.

Brittany Nelson: I've heard people say that all standards are basically subjective, that no one has the right to tell someone else that he is a failure or that she is better than other people, and that one instructor's B+ is another's C−. I don't really agree since, if you enroll in a college, you are essentially saying that you want to learn, that you want to learn from a qualified teacher, and that you trust that teacher to know more than you do about the subject. So, given this "contract" between you and the instructor, of course the instructor has the right to judge your work. Whether the grade should then be allowed to affect your future is another story.

Andy Patel: Grade inflation exists because we live in a consumerist society. We all expect to get a return for what we pay, and students expect to get a reasonably good transcript that enables them to graduate from college looking like desirable prospective employees. This leads to an expectation of "customer service" — if the grades are low, the consumers complain, and the service provider attempts to change the system to make the customers happy.

Beth Tucker: The issue behind grade inflation is that students tend to totally identify with their grades. They think, "I'm a C+" — not "I received a C+" for my work in Geology or Anthropology. This is just human nature, but, unlike a few decades ago, students today don't have the mental discipline to disassociate one poor performance from the rest of their experience. I do think that it would be helpful if more instructors put written comments on students' work so that they could more easily think of themselves as worthwhile people, capable of improvement.

ASSIGNMENT 6: Writing an Argument from Multiple Sources

A. Read "Next Question: Can Students Be Paid to Excel?" by Jennifer Medina, twice.

B. Write a brief response to the issue raised by Medina: *Should anyone—students or teachers—make a profit from raising student performance?* Submit your response to your instructor.

C. When you receive the group of responses provided by your class, prepare labels and a chart, according to the guidelines on page 237, and then write an essay that explores both sides of the issue, but also establishes your own thesis. Make sure that you use summary, paraphrase, and quotation to present the views of your sources.

NEXT QUESTION: CAN STUDENTS BE PAID TO EXCEL?*
Jennifer Medina

A staff reporter for the New York Times, *Jennifer Medina has written extensively on local and regional topics, especially in the area of education. This article first appeared in the* New York Times.

1   The fourth graders squirmed in their seats, waiting for their prizes. In a few minutes, they would learn how much money they had earned for their scores on recent reading and math exams. Some would receive nearly $50 for acing the standardized tests, a small fortune for many at this school, P.S. 188 on the Lower East Side of Manhattan.

2   When the rewards were handed out, Jazmin Roman was eager to celebrate her $39.72. She whispered to her friend Abigail Ortega, "How much did you get?" Abigail mouthed a barely audible answer: $36.87. Edgar Berlanga pumped his fist in the air to celebrate his $34.50.

3   The children were unaware that their teacher, Ruth Lopez, also stood to gain financially from their achievement. If students show marked improvement on state tests during the school year, each teacher at Public School 188 could receive a bonus of as much as $3,000.

4   School districts nationwide have seized on the idea that a key to improving schools is to pay for performance, whether through bonuses for teachers and principals, or rewards like cash prizes for students. New York City, with the largest public school system in the country, is in the forefront of this movement, with more than 200 schools experimenting with one incentive or another. In

*The number of paragraphs has been reduced without changing the meaning of the text.

Ruth Lopez gives her student Abigail Ortega a certificate showing her earnings from test scores.

more than a dozen schools, students, teachers and principals are all eligible for extra money, based on students' performance on standardized tests.

Each of these schools has become a test to measure whether, as Mayor Michael R. Bloomberg posits, tangible cash rewards can turn a school around. Can money make academic success cool for students disdainful of achievement? Will teachers pressure one another to do better to get a schoolwide bonus?

So far, the city has handed out more than $500,000 to 5,237 students in 58 schools as rewards for taking several of the 10 standardized tests on the schedule for this school year. The schools, which had to choose to participate in the program, are all over the city. "I'm not saying I know this is going to fix everything," said Roland G. Fryer, the Harvard economist who designed the student incentive program, "but I am saying it's worth trying. What we need to try to do is start that spark."

Nationally, school districts have experimented with a range of approaches. Some are giving students gift certificates, McDonald's meals and class pizza parties. Baltimore is planning to pay struggling students who raise their state test scores.

Critics of these efforts say that children should be inspired to learn for knowledge's sake, not to earn money, and question whether prizes will ulti-

5

6

7

8

mately lift achievement. Anticipating this kind of argument, New York City was careful to start the student experiment with private donations, not taxpayer money, avoiding some of the controversy that has followed the Baltimore program, which uses public money.

Some principals had no qualms about entering the student reward program. Virginia Connelly, the principal of Junior High School 123, in the Soundview section of the Bronx, has experimented with incentives for years, like rewarding good behavior, attendance and grades with play money that can be spent in the student store. "We're in competition with the streets," Ms. Connelly said. "They can go out there and make $50 illegally any day of the week. We have to do something to compete with that." 9

Barbara Slatin, the principal of P.S. 188, on the other hand, said she was initially skeptical about paying students for doing well. Her students, many of whom live in the nearby housing projects along Avenue D, would surely welcome the money, she said, but she worried about sending the wrong message. "I didn't want to connect the notion of money with academic success," she said. But after a sales pitch by Dr. Fryer, Ms. Slatin said she was persuaded to try. "We say we want to do whatever it takes, so if this is it, I am going to get on board," she said. 10

Masudur Rahman receives his "earnings" record from Dalia Johnson, the director of Public School 188 in Manhattan. The amount is determined by his scores on reading and math tests.

In 1996, P.S. 188 was considered to be failing by the State Education Department, but it has improved dramatically over the last decade. In the fall, it received an A on the city's report card. Still, fewer than 60 percent of the students passed the state math test last year, and fewer than 40 percent did so in reading.

Teachers at the school said that this year, they had noticed a better attitude among the students, which they attributed to the incentive program. One recent day, fourth graders talked eagerly about the computer games they have been playing to get ready for this week's state math exam. During the school's recent winter break, dozens of students showed up for extra tutoring to prepare. "My teacher told me to study more, so I study," said Jazmin, who had already taken eight standardized exams this school year. "I did multiplication tables. I learned to divide." When asked why she took so many tests, Jazmin replied earnestly, "To show them we have education and we learn stuff from education and the tests."

The students spoke excitedly about their plans for the money. Several boys said they were saving for video games. Abigail said she would use it to pay for "a car, a house and college," apparently unaware that the roughly $100 she's earned this school year might not stretch that far. Another little girl said she would use the money simply for food. When asked to elaborate, she answered quietly, "Spaghetti."

Changing the attitudes of seventh graders seems to be more complicated. At J.H.S. 123 in the Bronx, for example, a seventh-grade English class was asked one morning if there were too many standardized tests. Every hand in the room shot up to answer with a defiant yes. But at the same time, the students all agreed that receiving money for doing well on a test was a good idea, saying it made school more exciting, and made doing well more socially acceptable. "This is the hardest grade to pass," said Adonis Flores, a 13-year-old who has struggled in his classes at times. "This motivates us better. Everybody wants some money, and nobody wants to get left behind." Would it be better to get the money as college scholarships? Shouts of "No way!" echoed through the room. "We might not all go to college," one student protested. So is doing well in school cool? A few hands slowly inched up. But when their principal, Ms. Connelly, asked what could be done to make being the A-plus student seem as important as being the star basketball player, she was met with silence.

For teachers, bonuses come with ambivalence. So toxic was the idea of merit pay for individual teachers that the union insisted that bonus pools be awarded to whole schools to be divided up by joint labor-management committees, either evenly among union members or by singling out exceptional teachers. Still, nearly 90 percent of the 200 schools offered the chance to join the teacher bonus program are participating, after a vote with each school's chapter of the teachers' union. At many schools this year, including P.S. 188 and J.H.S. 123, a decision has already been made to distribute any money they get

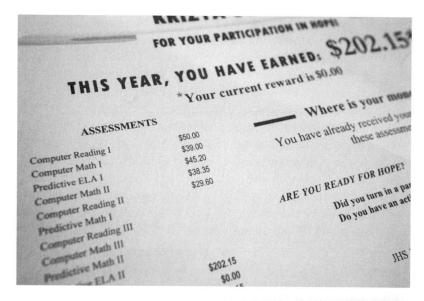

Part of the tally sheet that students at participating schools receive if they do well on standardized math and reading tests.

At Junior High School 123 in the Bronx, Jerome Johnson, a seventh-grade math student, also received cash awards.

across the board, and they are trying to include secretaries and other staff members as well.

No teachers were willing to say the rewards were unwelcome, but few said the potential windfall would push them to work harder. "It's better than a slap in the face," said Ms. Lopez, who has taught at P.S. 188 for more than a decade. "But honestly, I don't think about it. We're here every day working and pushing; that's what we've been doing for years. We don't come into this for the money, and most of us don't leave it because of the money."

16

Newer teachers seemed more positive, saying the bonus was a rare chance   17
to be rewarded. "I tell my students all the time that I can sit in the back and hand
them worksheets and get the same amount of money as I do if I stand in front of
the class working with high energy the entire time," said Christina Varghese, the
lead math teacher at J.H.S. 123, who is in her tenth year of teaching. "What's the
motivation there? At least this gives us something to work toward."

It will be months before Ms. Slatin and her teachers know whether they   18
have earned the bonus, but initial test scores are promising. On one test designed to mimic the state math exam, 77 percent of fourth graders met state
standards. Roughly half of those who did not were just below the cutoff, making
it possible that more than 80 percent of the students would pass the test this
year—a virtual dream for the school. "We want to believe it, but it makes me
nervous," Ms. Slatin said. "Those are not numbers we are used to seeing."

When to Synthesize and When to Compare

Synthesis is a method; it is not an end in itself. Some works do not lend
themselves to synthesis, which tends to *emphasize similarities* at the expense of
interesting differences between sources.

The academic writer needs to distinguish between material that is appropriate for synthesis and material whose individuality should be recognized and
preserved. One example of the latter is *fiction*; another is *autobiography*. Assume
that three writers are reminiscing about their first jobs: one was a clerk in a
drugstore, the second a telephone operator, and the third plowed his father's
fields. In their recollections, the reader can find several similar themes: accepting increased responsibility; sticking to the job; learning appropriate behavior;
living up to the boss's or customers' or father's expectations. But, just as important, the three autobiographical accounts *differ* sharply in their context and circumstances, in their point of view and style. You cannot lump them together in
the same way that you might categorize statements about the lottery or opinions about begging, for they cannot be reduced to a single common experience.
The three are not *interchangeable*; rather, they are *comparable.*

Comparison and synthesis both involve analyzing the ideas of several
sources and searching for a single vantage point from which to view them.
However, there is an important difference. *The writer of a synthesis constructs
a new work out of the materials of the old; the writer of a comparison tries to leave
the sources intact throughout the organizational process, so that each retains its individuality.* For comparison, you must have two or more works of similar length
and complexity that deal with the same subject and that merit individual
examination.

When you are assigned an essay topic, and when you assemble several
sources, you are not likely to want to *compare* the information that you have

recorded in your notes; rather, you will *synthesize* the material into a complete presentation of the topic. One of your sources may be an encyclopedia, another a massive survey of the entire subject, a third may devote several chapters to a scrutiny of that one small topic. In fact, these three sources are really not comparable, nor is your primary purpose to distinguish between them or to understand how they approach the subject differently. You are only interested in the results that you can achieve by using and building on this information.

Synthesizing Sources in Academic Essays

So far, the sources that you have worked with in this chapter have been transcripts of interviews, originating as informal statements of opinion. But unless you're including interviews or a survey as part of your research, when you write an essay for your college courses, you'll be using mostly *written* sources: *published documents in print or electronic form*. Written sources vary enormously, not only in their length and their targeted audience, but also in their treatment of the topic and in their reliability.

In a way, your relationship with your sources changes as they grow in number. When you worked with a single source, you were essentially engaging in a conversation with one person.

> **When you work with multiple sources, you're like the moderator of a roundtable discussion *in which you choose who speaks and which points each speaker is allowed to make.***

In the excerpt from Alan Wolfe's *Moral Freedom* on page 247, he is managing the "discussion" quite easily because he has interviewed the sources, asking the questions and setting the agenda. None of his sources is going beyond the limits he has set. The role of the moderator becomes more challenging when you are working with written sources or other kinds, like films, that all have agendas of their own and aren't even aware of your questions.

Using Documentation When Synthesizing Sources: *The Naked Crowd*

To illustrate this process, let's look at an excerpt from Jeffrey Rosen's *The Naked Crowd*. Rosen teaches law at George Washington University and frequently writes about the legal aspects of issues like privacy. In *The Naked Crowd*, he is concerned with Americans' lack of security—on many levels—since 9/11. In this excerpt, he is developing some theories about the way in which we express our fears through stigmatizing others. The comments in the margin help you to track the way in which Rosen embeds his sources into the structure of his argument, both as evidence for what he wants to say and as a spur toward the development of new ideas.

Because this is an academic work (although published for a general audience), Rosen is using formal documentation: endnotes. You can find out about Rosen's sources by checking the endnotes at the back of his book (or, in this case, at the end of the excerpt). As you read, notice that, while some sources get cited only by endnote, others get cited by endnote and also by name within the text:

- When he's dealing with *facts or statistics*, Rosen has to acknowledge where he found the information, but there's no need to cite the person who produced the document. Hence, he provides an endnote but no citation in the text.

- When he's dealing with *ideas*, he is back to conducting that roundtable discussion, and each participant has to be acknowledged as a *source* (in the endnote) and as a *person* (in the citation within the text). This distinction is important to the smooth and effective presentation of research.

- *Anything that isn't endnoted or named in the text can be attributed to Rosen and Rosen alone.*

As you read through the passage, try to pinpoint the places where Rosen stops using a source and advances the analysis or argument himself. Also, see if you can find the one place where he includes an unacknowledged source.

Finally, since many of your instructors will expect you to use MLA style, rather than notes, you should start to become familiar with the way MLA documentation appears on the page. At the end of the excerpt, Rosen's fifth paragraph is repeated, this time with MLA parenthetical citations incorporated into the text. Also see Chapter 12.

from THE NAKED CROWD
Jeffrey Rosen

One of the most salient features of stigma is fear. But today, we fear different attributes than our twentieth-century predecessors did. Instead of fearing unfamiliar races, nations, or religions, people in a more individualistic and egalitarian world are hesitant to make moral judgments about others but we have no hesitation about showing an obsessive concern about the visible signs of our own marketability, such as personal hygiene, physical fitness, health, and sexual attractiveness. We increasingly focus, therefore, on medical risks rather than moral risks. As Alan Wolfe has argued, "When nonjudgmental people make judgments, they often defer to the scientific and medical authorities whom they cite in avoiding making judgments in other situations."[7] Wolfe explores the ways that we medicalize our moral judgments—cloaking our opposition to smoking in the purported health risks of secondhand smoke rather than in our disapproval of the smoker's lack of self-control, for example—and the ways

names Wolfe
3 times: quotation
and summary

1

that we try to explain away our moral disapproval of self-destructive behavior by chalking it up to addiction rather than choice. In contrast to the moralistic Victorian era, Wolfe suggests, America has "entered a new era in which virtue and vice are redefined in terms of public health and addiction." Smoking and obesity are attacked as symbols of a failure of discipline that used to be associated with a failure of moral character.[8] And conditions or diseases that are feared to be contagious may lead the tainted individuals or places to be stigmatized with a ruthlessness that the ancient Greeks would have recognized.

Stearns cited in endnote: summary

Today, individuals and objects can become stigmatized not merely because they are infected with a contagious disease, but because they are symbolically contaminated in a way that others fear might be contagious. Paul Rozin of the University of Pennsylvania has studied the ways that fear of contagion can lead individuals to avoid even the briefest contact with an object that poses no actual health risk. Rozin gives the following example: You are about to drink a glass of juice, when a friend drops a cockroach in it. You refuse to drink it, on the grounds that cockroaches are dirty and might carry disease. The friend pours a new glass of juice and drops a dead sterilized cockroach into it, ensuring that there is no longer a safety issue. You refuse to drink again, confessing that the drink has been spoiled because it has been "cockroached" by brief contact with a disgusting object: What motivates you to spurn the juice is not a rational fear of disease, but a visceral reaction that is best described as being grossed out. The health risk turns out to be a masquerade for a psychological aversion that is harder to justify in rational terms.

names Rozin 3 times: paraphrase and brief quotation

The response to the cockroach, Rozin argues, illustrates what he calls "the law of contagion."[9] Because we respond more emotionally to negative than positive images, even the briefest physical contact with an object that is perceived to be contaminated can lead a person or an object to be perceived as contaminated as well. Once an object or a person has been spoiled or stigmatized, it may be very hard to remove the stigma: The cockroached juice remains objectionable even if the cockroach has been sterilized. And if there are psychological or moral fears lurking behind a medicalized fear, no amount of reassurance about physical risks will remove the stigma: This is why there is widespread reluctance to touch people with AIDS. The result may be the permanent shunning of individuals who are not, in fact, contagious but who engage our deep and ineradicable fears of contagion, which are rooted in a disgust that we dare not publicly express.

After 9/11, the most dramatic illustration of the principle of contagion was America's response to fears of anthrax. Four letters containing anthrax were mailed to congressional and media leaders in October 2001, leading to 23 cases of anthrax infections and five deaths by the end of November. But the disruption that resulted was wildly disproportionate to the actual risk: The Hart Senate Office Building was closed for months and decontaminated at a cost of

government Web site cited: summary of event

2

3

4

$22 million. After traces of anthrax were found in its mailroom, the U.S. Supreme Court evacuated its courtroom for the first time since the building opened in 1935, and held a special session down the street at the U.S. Court of Appeals for the D.C. Circuit. When traces of spores were found at almost two dozen off-site mail facilities that served federal buildings throughout Washington, including the White House, the CIA, and the State Department and the Justice Department, mail to all federal government offices was shipped to Ohio to be decontaminated, delaying its delivery for months. The postmaster general told Congress that the total cost of the anthrax attacks could exceed $5 billion.[10]

After the anthrax attacks, many citizens reported increased levels of fear. During the month of October, the FBI investigated 2,500 reports of suspected anthrax attacks, many of which turned out to involve harmless substances such as talcum powder. There was a surge in purchases of gas masks and Cipro, the anthrax antibiotic. Three out of ten people surveyed in a Gallup Poll at the end of October said they had thought about buying a gas mask or Cipro, and more than half said they were considering handling their mail more cautiously.[11] In another poll, half said they had some concern about contracting anthrax, although the other half had little or no concern.[12] More than a third of Americans reported washing their hands after opening Christmas cards.[13] Whether this behavior should be interpreted as a limited panic by an irrational minority or as "reluctance to panic"[14] by the calmer majority is open to debate; but it demonstrates a level of concern vastly disproportionate to the actual threat of infection.

More striking than the fluctuating polls were the rituals that the government adopted in order to expunge the stigma of a mail system that had been tainted in just the way that Rozin's experiments with cockroaches suggest. Once the postal service had been marked in the public mind as a bearer of contamination, even the most remote possibility of contact with a letter that had passed through one of the facilities where a few anthrax spores had been detected became a source of public fear and disgust. Soon after the attacks, on the advice of the Centers for Disease Control and Prevention, universities and other private employers advised their employees to wash their hands after handling mail and to wear latex gloves when opening envelopes. Months after the attacks, the post office adopted elaborate procedures for the permanent irradiation, in off-site facilities, of letters addressed to federal offices, resulting in substantial delays. And a post office report issued in March 2002 promised to implement a "multi-layered, multi-year Emergency Preparedness Plan" to protect customers and employees from exposure to biohazardous material and safeguard the mail system from future attacks. The plan includes the deployment of technology to identify and track all retail mail in the United States; to scan each letter for possible contamination; to sanitize mail addressed to targeted groups; and to expand the use of "e-beam and X-ray irradiation" of contaminated mail. It aspires in the next few years to develop an "intelligent mail system" that would allow "capturing and

news article cited:
summary

news articles cited:
summaries

Glass & Schoch-
Spana cited: brief
quotation

names Rozin:
reminder/
no endnote

government report
cited: summary

5

6

retaining data to enable tracking and tracing of mail items, data mining to allow forensic investigation, and positive product tracking to eliminate anonymous mail." Within four years of its implementation, the program is estimated to cost up to $2.4 billion a year.[15]

Recall that these extraordinary rituals, which have permanently changed the way mail is delivered in America, were triggered by an attack that claimed only five lives. But the rituals were designed not to purify the mail but to eliminate the stigma that has attached itself to the American postal system. Like the early Christians who understood stigmata as bodily signs of holy grace, and thus transformed the symbols of Christ's ultimate sacrifice into symbols of divine favor, we are attempting to purge the stigma of anthrax by reenacting a ritual of reassurance. In this sense, the scanning of envelopes for anthrax is similar to the rituals that require us to remove our shoes at the airport or to use plastic knives in the sky. Like a religious rite, its purpose is psychological rather than empirical. Just as people take Communion to remind themselves that Jesus died on the Cross and sacrificed Himself for their sins, so people remove their shoes to give themselves the illusion of being protected from future shoe bombers. Like believers taking the leap of faith, they are more concerned about ritualized expressions of safety than about safety itself.

Our response to the anthrax attacks after 9/11 is only one example of the tendency of crowds to think in terms of emotional images rather than reasoned arguments, which helps to explain why different groups respond differently to unfamiliar risks. In a Gallup Poll taken soon after September 11, 69 percent of the women surveyed said they were "very worried" that their families might be victimized by terrorist attacks. Only 46 percent of the men were similarly concerned. Paul Slovic's work suggests that in thinking about a range of risks — from the hazards of nuclear waste to the possibility of being victimized by crime and violence — men tend to judge the risks as smaller and less threatening than women.[16] Better educated, richer people perceive themselves to be less at risk than their poorer counterparts. People of color tend to be more fearful of risk than white people. And white men consistently perceive risks to be lower than everyone else, including white women and men and women of color.

names Slovic twice:
paraphrase

When Slovic examined the data more closely, however, he found that not all white men are less fearful than everyone else. The "white male effect," he discovered, seemed to be caused by about 30 percent of the white men surveyed, who judged risks to be extremely low. The rest of the white men didn't perceive risks very differently from all the other groups.[17] What distinguished the 30 percent of less fearful white men from everyone else? They shared certain characteristics that had more to do with their worldview than with their sex. The calmer white men tended to be less egalitarian than everyone else: A majority agreed with the proposition that America has gone too far in pursuing equal rights. They tended to display more trust in authorities, agreeing that

7

8

9

government and industry could be relied on to manage technological risks. By wide margins, they felt very much in control of risks to their own health, and they agreed that if a risk was small, society could impose it on other individuals without their consent. They believed that individuals should be able to take care of themselves. In short, they were more politically conservative, more hierarchical, more trusting of authority, and less egalitarian than most of their fellow Americans.

One reason that relatively conservative white men seem to be less concerned about risk than their fellow citizens is that people are most fearful of risks they perceive as beyond their ability to control. Many Americans preferred to drive rather than to fly in the months following September 11, even though their risks of being killed in a car crash were greater than their risks of being killed in another terrorist attack. At the wheel of a car, people have an illusion of control that they can't achieve as passengers on a plane, and, therefore, they tend to underestimate the risk of driving and overestimate the risk of flying. It isn't easy to imagine yourself in situations you haven't personally experienced, which means that people have a hard time making decisions about unfamiliar and remote risks. This is why people fear most being a victim of those crimes that they are, in fact, least likely to experience. Women worry most about violent crime, even though they have the lowest risk of being victims, while young men worry the least, even though they have the highest risk. Because of their physical differences, men have a greater illusion of control over their ability to respond to violent crime than women do. In areas where women feel more in control than men, however, they are more likely to engage in risky behavior. When it comes to social risks—such as asking strangers for directions—women turn out to be more intrepid than men. Because men are more reluctant than women to risk the humiliation of appearing foolish before strangers, they perceive the ordeal to be more socially risky.

In the case of terrorism after 9/11, in fact, men and women appear to be equally at risk. But the best explanation for why men perceive the risk of future terrorist attacks to be lower than women do is that men tend to be angrier than women about the 9/11 attacks, while women tend to be more fearful. In a study of 1,000 Americans conducted a few weeks after 9/11, a group of scholars at Carnegie Mellon University found that women believed they had a greater chance of being hurt in a future terrorist attack than men did. Eighty-one percent of the difference between men's and women's perception of risk could be explained by the fact that women reported lower degrees of anger about the attacks, and higher degrees of fear.[18] Fear is more likely to arise in people who feel uncertain and unable to control future events, while anger is more likely to arise in people who are more confident of their ability to control their environment. Because angrier people have a greater sense of personal control than fearful ones, they tend to be less pessimistic about the possibility of future attacks.

study cited: summary

10

11

Despite these gender differences, both men and women dramatically overestimated the risks of a future attack after 9/11: The respondents saw a 20 percent chance that they would be personally hurt in a terrorist attack within the next year, and a nearly 50 percent chance that the average American would be hurt. Thankfully, these predictions proved to be wrong, and there was no attack comparable to those on the World Trade Center in the twelve months following 9/11. But the predictions seemed alarmist even when they were made: They could have come true only if an attack of similar magnitude occurred nearly every day for the following year. This shows how liable people are to exaggerate the risk of terrorism because of their tendency to evaluate probabilities in emotional rather than empirical terms. . . .

12

names Le Bon: no endnote

The tendency of crowds to make judgments about risks based on visual images rather than on reasoned arguments results in another mental shortcut that leads us to overestimate the probability of especially dramatic risks. People fixate on the hazards that catch their attention, which means those that are easiest to imagine and recall. As Gustave Le Bon recognized in *The Crowd*, a single memorable image will crowd out less visually dramatic risks in the public mind and will lead people wrongly to imagine that they are more likely to be victims of terrorism than of mundane risks, like heart disease. The Nobel Prize winners Amos Tversky and Daniel Kahneman have called this the "availability heuristic,"[20] which they define as the tendency to assume that an event is likely to recur if examples of it are easy to remember. . . . For the same reason, people overestimate the frequency of deaths from dramatic disasters such as tornadoes, floods, fire, and homicide and underestimate the frequency of deaths from diabetes, stomach cancer, stroke, and asthma.[21]

13

names Tversky & Kahneman: quotation and summary

article cited: summary

When presented with two estimations of risk—one high and the other low—people tend to believe the high risk estimation regardless of whether it comes from government or industry.[22] This bias toward the worst-case scenario is another example of the fact that crowds, when their emotions are intensely engaged, tend to focus on the vividness of a particularly unpleasant risk rather than on its likelihood. This phenomenon, which Cass Sunstein calls "probability neglect,"[23] can lead to behavioral changes that strike experts as irrational, such as buying gas masks and Cipro and canceling flights while continuing to drive and eat Big Macs. The print and electronic media play an important role in contributing to this behavior, but it is a role that can't be separated from the demands of the public itself. Most journalists can tell stories of editors who have pressured them to describe worst-case scenarios, in order to scare the audience into thinking that the story in question is somehow relevant to their lives. As Tocqueville noted in his discussion of why American writers are bombastic, citizens in democratic societies spend most of their time contemplating themselves, and can be tempted to stop gazing at their navels only when they are confronted with the largest and most gripping of subjects. Writers,

14

Sunstein named: brief quotation

Tocqueville named: paraphrase and quotation

therefore, have an incentive to attract the attention of the crowd by exaggerating the significance of every topic: If they report that things aren't as bad as they might be, the public won't pay attention. Because of this unfortunate dynamic, Tocqueville reported, "the author and the public corrupt one another at the same time."[24]

Best named 3
times: quotation
and paraphrase

When reporting on essentially random risks, there is especially great pressure on reporters to exaggerate the scope and probability of the danger, in order to make more people feel that they, too, could be victims. Joel Best of Southern Illinois University has examined the "moral panics" about dramatic new crimes that seized the public attention in the 1980s and 1990s, such as freeway violence in 1987, wilding in 1989, stalking around 1990, children and guns in 1991, and so forth. In each of these cases, Best writes, the television media seized on two or three incidents of a dramatic crime, such as freeway shooting, and then claimed that it was part of a broader trend. By taking the worst and most infrequent examples of criminal violence and melodramatically claiming they were typical, TV created the impression that everyone was at risk, thereby increasing its audience. Although the idea of random violence appeals to our democratic sensibilities — if violence is random, then everyone is equally at risk — Best points out that "most violence is not patternless, is not pointless, nor is it increasing in the uncontrolled manner we imagine."[25] After purported trends failed to pan out in most of the cases described above, the media spotlight moved on in search of new and even more melodramatic threats.

15

7. Alan Wolfe, *Moral Freedom: The Search for Virtue in a World of Choice* (New York: W.W. Norton, 2001), p. 88.

8. Peter N. Stearns, *Battleground of Desire: The Struggle for Self-Control in Modern America* (New York: NYU Press, 1999), p. 325.

9. Paul Rozin, "Technological Stigma: Some Perspectives from the Study of Contagion," in *Risk, Media and Stigma*, pp. 31–35.

10. See <http://www.usps.com/news/2001/press/mailsecurity/allfaq.htm>.

11. Richard Benedetto, "Poll Finds Anthrax Fear but No Panic," *USA Today*, October 23, 2001, p. A4.

12. J. Mozingo, "Poll: Floridians Not Panicked," *The Miami Herald*, October 25, 2001, p. 3B.

13. Tom Pelton, "36% of Americans Wash Up after Handling Mail," *The Baltimore Sun*, December 18, 2001, p. 8A.

14. See generally Thomas A. Glass and Monica Schoch-Spana, "Bioterrorism and the People: How to Vaccinate a City against Panic," in *Confronting Biological Weapons*, CID 34, January 15, 2002, p. 222.

15. See generally *U.S. Postal Service Emergency Preparedness Plan for Protecting Postal Employees and Postal Customers from Exposure to Biohazardous*

Material and for Ensuring Mail Security against Bioterror Attacks, March 6, 2002, available at <http://www.usps.com/news/2002/epp/welcome.htm>.

16. Paul Slovic, "Trust, Emotion, Sex, Politics and Science: Surveying the Risk-Assessment Battlefield," in Paul Slovic, *The Perception of Risk* (Sterling, Va.: Earthscan, 2000), p. 396.

17. Ibid., pp. 398–99.

18. Jennifer S. Lerner, Roxana M. Gonzalez, Deborah A. Small, and Baruch Fischoff, "Effects of Fear and Anger on Perceived Risks of Terrorism: A National Field Experiment," *Psychological Science* (2002).

20. See Amos Tversky and Daniel Kahneman, "Availability: A Heuristic for Judging Frequency and Probability," 5 *Cognitive Psychology* 207 (1973).

21. Ibid., p. 107.

22. W. Kip Viscusi, "Alarmist Decisions with Divergent Risk Information," 107 *Ec. Journal* 1657 (1997).

23. Cass Sunstein, "Probability Neglect: Emotions, Worst Cases, and Law," 112 *Yale L.J.* 61 (2002).

24. Alexis de Tocqueville, *Democracy in America*, eds. Harvey C. Mansfield and Delba Winthrop, vol. 2, part 1, ch. 18 (Chicago: University of Chicago Press, 2000), p. 464.

25. Joel Best, *Random Violence: How We Talk about New Crimes and New Victims* (Berkeley: University of California Press, 1999), p. 10.

The Naked Crowd, Paragraph 5
with MLA Documentation

After the anthrax attacks, many citizens reported increased levels of fear. During the month of October, the FBI investigated 2,500 reports of suspected anthrax attacks, many of which turned out to involve harmless substances such as talcum powder. There was a surge in purchases of gas masks and Cipro, the anthrax antibiotic. Three out of ten people surveyed in a Gallup Poll at the end of October said that they had thought about buying a gas mask or Cipro, and more than half said they were considering handling their mail more cautiously (Benedetto). In another poll, half said they had some concern about contracting anthrax, although the other half had little or no concern (Mozingo). More than a third of Americans reported washing their hands after opening Christmas cards (Pelton). Whether this behavior should be interpreted as a limited panic by an irrational minority or as "reluctance to panic" (Glass and Schoch-Spana 222) by the calmer majority is open to debate; but it demonstrates a level of concern vastly disproportionate to the actual threat of infection.

Note: The bibliography would provide further information about these references.

EXERCISE 23: Integrating Three Academic Sources

In the past few years, social commentators have speculated about *illusions of friendship in the age of Internet social networks*.

A. Read the following three passages and identify the common themes.

B. Write two or three paragraphs, based on these sources, analyzing the ways in which using the Web has changed our ideas about friendship.

C. For the purposes of this exercise, you may limit your documentation to citing the names of the three sources; no formal documentation is needed.

Note: Do not discuss one source per paragraph.

from THE CULT OF THE AMATEUR:
HOW TODAY'S INTERNET
IS KILLING OUR CULTURE
Andrew Keen

Andrew Keen was the founder of Audiocafe.com, an Internet music company. He has expressed his views on media and participatory technology through articles in journals such as the Weekly Standard *and* Newsweek, *as well as in his columns for the* London Telegraph, *and through appearances on PBS, NPR, and other television news programs.*

The *New York Times* reports that 50 percent of all bloggers blog for the sole purpose of reporting and sharing experiences about their personal lives. The tagline for YouTube is "Broadcast Yourself." And broadcast ourselves we do, with all the shameless self-admiration of the mythical Narcissus. As traditional mainstream media is replaced by a personalized one, the Internet has become a mirror to ourselves. Rather than using it to seek news, information, or culture, we use it to actually BE the news, the information, the culture.   1

This infinite desire for personal attention is driving the hottest part of the new Internet economy — social-networking sites like MySpace, Facebook, and Bebo. As shrines for the cult of self-broadcasting, these sites have become tabula rasas of our individual desires and identities. They claim to be all about "social networking" with others, but in reality they exist so that we can advertise ourselves: everything from our favorite books and movies, to photos from our summer vacations, to "testimonials" praising our more winsome qualities or recapping our latest drunken exploits. It's hardly surprising that the increasingly tasteless nature of such self-advertisements has led to an infestation of anonymous sexual predators and pedophiles.   2

from AGAINST THE MACHINE: BEING HUMAN
IN THE AGE OF THE ELECTRONIC MOB
Lee Siegel

A writer and critic, Lee Siegel has written articles and reviews for publications such as Harper's, the Nation, the New Republic *(where he is presently senior editor), the* New Yorker, and the New York Times. *He has been the recipient of the National Magazine Award for Reviews and Criticism (2002). His other books include* Falling Upwards: Essays in Defense of the Imagination and Not Remotely Controlled: Notes on Television.

Giant conglomerates now own vast social-networking sites like MySpace and YouTube, and the eyes of other conglomerates — in the realm of television and film, for example — are upon them. Therefore, more and more users on these sites operate with an eye to material advantage. The most startling "candor" is really the most ingenious performance of candor. 1

No wonder so many "hoaxes" are exposed on YouTube. You begin to suspect that for every hoax that gets uncovered, there are dozens, maybe hundreds more that go undiscovered. You then begin to suspect that the hoaxes that do get uncovered are meant to be uncovered, and that the encouragement of fraudulence and the exposure of fraudulence make up a burgeoning new form of entertainment. (Its effect on public life is incalculable — accustomed to fading truth in culture, we become inured to it in politics.) A perfect example of "The Genuine Hoax" is the YouTube clip called "Guy Catches Glasses with Face," which portrays one young man throwing a pair of Ray-Ban glasses onto another young guy's face across a room, off a bridge, into a moving car, etc. The clip was, in fact, an ad produced by Ray-Ban itself, but the hundreds of thousands of people who saw it before the hoax was exposed thought it was real. The discovery of the hoax, however, made the clip even more popular. The ad's fraudulence was the essence of its appeal: seeing through it thrilled the audience, for whom the transparent fraudulence of media images is perhaps a cathartic antidote to a world dominated by media images. And seeing through a deceit is a tremendous empowerment. 2

Aware that lucrative vested interests are looking over their shoulders as they "play" online, people end up competing with everybody else, looking over their shoulders at the competition as they "do their own thing." Which is to say — and to repeat — that fewer and fewer people are doing their own thing. They are cautiously and calculatingly imitating someone or something else. 3

How do you attract worldwide attention on YouTube? How do you become, as the Netties so weirdly call it, a "viral personality"? There are no guidelines in this free-for-all, no precedents to look to. It is different from the old 4 world of so-called mass culture. Then people trying to make a splash in pop culture worked in clearly defined fields like music, or film, or television. The audience for each medium knew its history, traditions, and development. Elvis Presley was aware of Johnny Mercer; the creators of *Friends* knew *The Dick Van Dyke Show*. A songwriter or TV scriptwriter could succeed only by building on his predecessors and then adding his own original twist.

But in the chaos of YouTube and similar sites, you are not competing in a clearly defined field with its own history, traditions, and development. There is nothing against which to measure your "act." That might seem like a liberation. But without the comparative standards offered by antecedents and predecessors, the effect of such chaos and randomness is to induce a general insecurity, and to make conformity the only standard for success. I go to YouTube now and watch a videoblog called "Amazing Child Drummers." How can I judge whether it's "good" or not? It's what they used to call in the days of vaudeville a novelty act. You judge it by its superficial newness, not by its originality. And because novelty is often eye-catching form and no substance, every novelty act resembles the other in some way. "Amazing Child Drummers" might sound different from other YouTube videoblogs like "The Arreola Twins — I Want to Hold Your Hand," and "Cute Boy Singer: Vlad Krutskikh," and "and I love you live by duo guitars — original song by mr. children." But it sure does look like them. They are all united by a quality of self-deprecating sweetness that pleads for attention by accentuating its own ridiculousness.

All the imitation and derivation stem from the fact that on the Internet, success — like choice and access — exists for its own sake. Since the greatest success is, well, being greatly successful, you choose a performance that's already been certified as being a big success. Popularity being the best guarantee of success, you end up imitating the most proven popular act. You must sound more like everyone else than anyone else is able to sound like everyone else. The Ray-Ban ad provoked dozens upon dozens of derivative responses.

from THE END OF SOLITUDE
William Deresiewicz

William Deresiewicz taught in the English Department at Yale University for ten years. A contributing writer for the Nation, *he has also published articles and reviews in the* American Scholar *and the* New York Times. *He was nominated for a National Magazine Award for his criticism, and is the author of* Jane Austen and the Romantic Poets. *This article appeared in the* Chronicle of Higher Education.

Through the 1970s and 1980s, our isolation grew. Suburbs, sprawling ever farther, became exurbs. Families grew smaller or splintered apart, mothers left the home to work. The electronic hearth became the television in every room. Even in childhood, certainly in adolescence, we were each trapped inside our own cocoon. Soaring crime rates, and even more sharply escalating rates of moral panic, pulled children off the streets. The idea that you could go outside and run around the neighborhood with your friends, once unquestionable, has now become unthinkable. The child who grew up between the world wars as part of an extended family within a tight-knit urban community became the grandparent of a kid who sat alone in front of a big television, in a big house, on a big lot. We were lost in space.

Under those circumstances, the Internet arrived as an incalculable bless- 2
ing. We should never forget that. It has allowed isolated people to communicate with one another and marginalized people to find one another. The busy parent can stay in touch with far-flung friends. The gay teenager no longer has to feel like a freak. But as the Internet's dimensionality has grown, it has quickly become too much of a good thing. Ten years ago we were writing e-mail messages on desktop computers and transmitting them over dial-up connections. Now we are sending text messages on our cellphones, posting pictures on our Facebook pages, and following complete strangers on Twitter. A constant stream of mediated contact, virtual, notional, or simulated, keeps us wired in to the electronic hive — though contact, or at least two-way contact, seems increasingly beside the point. The goal now, it seems, is simply to become known, to turn oneself into a sort of miniature celebrity. How many friends do I have on Facebook? How many people are reading my blog? How many Google hits does my name generate? Visibility secures our self-esteem, becoming a substitute, twice removed, for genuine connection. Not long ago, it was easy to feel lonely. Now, it is impossible to be alone. . . .

. . . What does friendship mean when you have 532 "friends"? How does it 3
enhance my sense of closeness when my Facebook News Feed tells me that Sally Smith (whom I haven't seen since high school, and wasn't all that friendly with even then) "is making coffee and staring off into space"? My students told me they have little time for intimacy. And of course, they have no time at all for solitude. . . .

The Internet is as powerful a machine for the production of loneliness 4
as television is for the manufacture of boredom. If six hours of television a day creates the aptitude for boredom, the inability to sit still, a hundred text messages a day creates the aptitude for loneliness, the inability to be by yourself. Some degree of boredom and loneliness is to be expected, especially among young people, given the way our human environment has been attenuated. But technology amplifies those tendencies. You could call your schoolmates when I was a teenager, but you couldn't call them 100 times a day. You could get together with your friends when I was in college, but you couldn't always get together with them when you wanted to, for the simple reason that

you couldn't always find them. If boredom is the great emotion of the TV generation, loneliness is the great emotion of the Web generation. We lost the ability to be still, our capacity for idleness. They have lost the ability to be alone, their capacity for solitude.

ASSIGNMENT 7: Synthesizing Academic Sources

A. Read excerpts from Steven Johnson's *Everything Bad Is Good for You* and Christine Rosen's "People of the Screen" twice. Then review Ursula K. Le Guin's "Staying Awake: Notes on the Alleged Decline of Reading" (page 175) and Nicholas Carr's "Is Google Making Us Stupid?" (page 93).

B. Using at least three of these sources, write an essay on the following topic: *Will the Internet and other new technology replace the book as the chief tool of learning?* As you analyze your sources and explore their themes and their differences, develop a thesis that responds to the topic. Follow the guidelines for writing a synthesis essay, and cite the sources appropriately within your paragraphs. If your instructor asks you to use formal documentation, consult Chapter 10 as well as the forms in Chapter 12. The essay should be three pages long.

from EVERYTHING BAD IS GOOD FOR YOU

Steven Johnson

Throughout his career as a journalist, Steven Johnson has been involved in the Internet: he was co-founder of Feed, *a webzine, and* Plastic.com, *a news discussion site, which won a Webby Award in 2001. His most recent book on science and technology is* The Invention of Air: A Story of Science, Faith, Revolution, and the Birth of America.

Excerpt One

[One] way in which the rise of the Net has challenged the mind runs parallel to the evolving rule systems of video games: the accelerating pace of new platforms and software applications forces users to probe and master new environments. Your mind is engaged by the interactive content of networked media — posting a response to an article online, maintaining three separate IM conversations at the same time — but you're also exercising cognitive muscles interacting with the *form* of the media as well: learning the tricks of a new e-mail client, configuring the video chat software properly, getting your bearings after installing a new operating system. This type of problem-solving can be challenging in an unpleasant way, of course, but the same can be said for calculus. Just because you don't like troubleshooting your system when your browser crashes doesn't mean you aren't exercising your logic skills in finding a solution. This extra layer of cognitive involvement derives largely from the increased prominence of the interface in digital technology. When new tools arrive, you have to learn what they're good for, but you also have to learn the rules that govern their use. To be an accomplished telephone user, you needed to grasp the essential utility of being able to have real-time conversations with people physically removed from you, *and* you had to master the interface of the telephone device itself. That same principle holds true for digital technologies, only the interfaces have expanded dramatically in depth and complexity. There's only so much cognitive challenge at stake in learning the rules of a rotary dial phone. But you could lose a week exploring all the nooks and crannies of Microsoft Outlook.

Just as we saw in the world of games, learning the intricacies of a new interface can be a genuine pleasure. This is a story that is not often enough told in describing our evolving relationship with software. There is a kind of exploratory wonder in downloading a new application, and meandering through its commands and dialog boxes, learning its tricks by feel. I've often found certain applications are more fun to explore the first time than they actually are to use — because in the initial exploration, you can delight in features that are clever without being terribly helpful. This sounds like something only a hardened tech geek would say, but I suspect the feeling has become much more mainstream over the past few years. Think of the millions of ordinary music fans who downloaded Apple's iTunes software: I'm sure many of them enjoyed their first walk through the application, seeing all the tools that would revolutionize the way they listened to music. Many of them, I suspect, eschewed the manual altogether, choosing to probe the application the way gamers investigate their virtual worlds: from the inside. That probing is a powerful form of intellectual activity — you're learning the rules of a complex system without a guide, after all. And it's all the more powerful for being fun. 2

Then there is the matter of social connection. The other concern that Net skeptics voiced a decade ago revolved around a withdrawal from public space: yes, the Internet might connect us to a new world of information, but it would come at a terrible social cost, by confining us in front of barren computer monitors, away from the vitality of genuine communities. In fact, nearly all of the most hyped developments on the Web in the past few years have been tools for augmenting social connection: online personals, social and business network sites such as Friendster, the Meetup.com service so central to the political organization of the 2004 campaign, the many tools designed to enhance conversation between bloggers — not to mention all the handheld devices that we now use to coordinate new kinds of real-world encounters. Some of these tools 3 create new modes of communication that are entirely digital in nature (the cross-linked conversations of bloggers). Others use the networked computer to facilitate a face-to-face encounter (as in Meetup). Others involve a hybrid dance of real and virtual encounters, as in the personals world, where flesh-and-blood dates usually follow weeks of online flirting. Tools like Google have fulfilled the original dream of digital machines becoming extensions of our memory, but the new social networking applications have done something that the visionaries never imagined: they are augmenting our people skills as well, widening our social networks, and creating new possibilities for strangers to share ideas and experiences.

Television and automobile society locked people up in their living rooms, away from the clash and vitality of public space, but the Net has reversed that long-term trend. After a half-century of technological isolation, we're finally learning new ways to connect. . . .

4

Excerpt Two

We know from neuroscience that the brain has dedicated systems that respond to — and seek out — new challenges and experiences. We are a problem-solving species, and when we confront situations where information needs to be filled in, or where a puzzle needs to be untangled, our minds compulsively ruminate on the problem until we've figured it out. When we encounter novel circumstances, when our environment changes in a surprising way, our brains lock in on the change and try to put it in context or decipher its underlying logic.

5

Parents can sometimes be appalled at the hypnotic effect that television has on toddlers; they see their otherwise vibrant and active children gazing silently, mouth agape at the screen, and they assume the worst: the television is turning their child into a zombie. The same feeling arrives a few years later, when they see their grade-schoolers navigating through a video game world, oblivious to the reality that surrounds them. But these expressions are not signs of mental atrophy. They're signs of *focus*. The toddler's brain is constantly scouring the world for novel stimuli, precisely because exploring and understanding new things and experiences is what learning is all about. In a house where most of the objects haven't moved since yesterday, and no new people have appeared on the scene, the puppet show on the television screen is the most surprising thing in the child's environment, the stimuli most in need of scrutiny and explanation. And so the child locks in. If you suddenly plunked down a real puppet show in the middle of the living room, no doubt the child would prefer to make sense of that. But in most ordinary household environments, the stimuli onscreen offer the most diversity and surprise. The child's brain locks into those images for good reason. . . .

6

If our mental appetites draw us toward more complexity and not less, why do so many studies show that we're reading fewer books than we used to? Even if we accept the premise that television and games can offer genuine cognitive challenges, surely we have to admit that books challenge different, but equally important, faculties of the mind. And yet we're drifting away from the printed page at a steady rate. Isn't that a sign of our brains gravitating to lesser forms?

I believe the answer is no, for two related reasons. First, most studies of reading ignore the huge explosion of reading (not to mention writing) that has happened thanks to the rise of the Internet. Millions of people spend much of their day staring at words on a screen: browsing the Web, reading e-mail, chatting with friends, posting a new entry to one of those 8 million blogs. E-mail conversations or Web-based analyses of *The Apprentice* are not the same as literary novels, of course, but they are equally text-driven. While they suffer from a lack of narrative depth compared to novels, many online interactions do have the benefit of being genuinely two-way conversations: you're putting words together yourself, and not just digesting someone else's. Part of the compensation for reading less is the fact that we're writing more.

The fact that we are spending so much time online gets to the other, more crucial, objection: yes, we're spending less time reading literary fiction, but that's because we're spending less time doing *everything* we used to do before. In fact, the downward trend that strikes the most fear in the hearts of Madison Avenue and their clients is not the decline of literary reading — it's the decline of television watching. The most highly sought demographic in the country — twenty-something males — watches almost one-fifth less television than they did only five years ago. We're buying fewer CDs; we're going out to the movies less regularly. We're doing all these old activities less because about a dozen new activities have become bona fide mainstream pursuits in the past ten years: the Web, e-mail, games, DVDs, cable on-demand, text chat. We're reading less because there are only so many hours in the day, and we have all these new options to digest and explore. If reading were the only cultural pursuit to show declining numbers, there might be cause for alarm. But that decline is shared by all the old media forms across the board. As long as reading books remains *part* of our cultural diet, and as long as the new popular forms continue to offer their own cognitive rewards, we're not likely to descend into a culture of mental atrophy anytime soon. . . .

The rise of the Internet has forestalled the death of the typographic universe — and its replacement by the society of the image — predicted by McLuhan and Postman. Thanks to e-mail and the Web, we're reading text as much as ever, and we're writing more. But it is true that a specific, historically crucial kind of reading has grown less common in this society: sitting down with a 300-page book and following its argument or narrative without a great deal of distraction. We deal with text now in shorter bursts, following links across the Web, or sifting through a dozen e-mail messages. The breadth of information is wider in this world, and it is far more participatory. But there are certain types of experiences that cannot be readily conveyed in this more connective, abbreviated form. Complicated, sequential works of persuasion, where each premise builds on the previous one, and where an idea can take an entire chapter to develop, are not well suited to life on the computer screen. (Much less life on *The O'Reilly Factor*.) I can't imagine getting along without e-mail, and I derive great intellectual nourishment from posting to my weblog, but I would never attempt to convey the argument of this book in either of those forms. Postman gets it right:

> To engage the written word means to follow a line of thought, which requires considerable powers of classifying, inference-making and reasoning. . . . In the eighteenth and nineteenth centuries, print put forward a definition of intelligence that gave priority to the objective, rational use of the mind and at the same time encouraged forms of public discourse with serious, logically ordered content. It is no accident that the Age of Reason was coexistent with the growth of a print culture, first in Europe and then in America.

Networked text has its own intellectual riches, of course: riffs, annotations,   11
conversations — they all flourish in that ecosystem, and they all can be dazzlingly intelligent. But they nonetheless possess a *different kind* of intelligence from the intelligence delivered by reading a sustained argument for 200 pages. You can convey attitudes and connections in the online world with ease; you can brainstorm with 20 strangers in a way that would have been unthinkable just ten years ago. But it is harder to transmit a fully fledged worldview. When you visit someone's weblog, you get a wonderful — and sometimes wonderfully intimate — sense of their voice. But when you immerse yourself in a book, you get a different sort of experience: you enter the author's mind, and peer out at the world through their eyes.

Something comparable happens in reading fiction as well. No cultural   12
form in history has rivaled the novel's capacity to re-create the mental landscape of another consciousness, to project you into the first-person experience of other human beings. Movies and theater can make you feel as though you're part of the action, but the novel gives you an inner vista that is unparalleled: you are granted access not just to the events of another human's life, but to the precise way those events settle in his or her consciousness. (This is most true of the modernist classics: James, Eliot, Woolf, Conrad.) Reading *Portrait of a Lady* — once you've shed your MTV-era expectations about pacing and oriented yourself to James's byzantine syntax — you experience another person thinking and

sensing with a clarity that can be almost uncanny. But that cognitive immersion requires a physical immersion for the effect to work: you have to commit to the book, spend long periods of time devoted to it. If you read only in short bites, the effect fades, like a moving image dissolving into a sequence of frozen pictures.

So the Sleeper Curve* suggests that the popular culture is not doing as good a job at training our minds to follow a sustained textual argument or narrative that doesn't involve genuine interactivity. (As we've seen in gaming culture, kids are incredibly talented at focusing for long stretches when the form is truly participatory.) The good news, of course, is that kids aren't being exclusively educated by their Nintendo machines or their cell phones. We still have schools and parents to teach wisdom that the popular culture fails to impart. [13]

PEOPLE OF THE SCREEN
Christine Rosen

Christine Rosen's articles have appeared in such publications as The New York Times Magazine, *the* Wall Street Journal, *the* New Republic, *the* Weekly Standard, *and the* American Historical Review. *At the* New Atlantis, *where she is a senior editor, her particular interests are technology and bioethics. She is the author of* Preaching Eugenics: Religious Leaders and the American Eugenics Movement *and* My Fundamentalist Education. *This essay appeared online in the* New Atlantis.

The book is modernity's quintessential technology — "a means of transportation through the space of experience, at the speed of a turning page," as the poet Joseph Brodsky put it. But now that the rustle of the book's turning page competes with the flicker of the screen's twitching pixel, we must consider the possibility that the book may not be around much longer. If it isn't — if we choose to replace the book — what will become of reading and the print culture it fostered? And what does it tell us about ourselves that we may soon retire this most remarkable, 500-year-old technology? [1]

We have already taken the first steps on our journey to a new form of literacy — "digital literacy." The fact that we must now distinguish among different types of literacy hints at how far we have moved away from traditional notions of reading. The screen mediates everything from our most private communications to our enjoyment of writing, drama, and games. It is the busiest port of entry for popular culture and requires navigation skills different from those that helped us master print literacy. [2]

*Johnson's view that mass culture is intellectually stimulating.

Enthusiasts and self-appointed experts assure us that this new digital literacy represents an advance for mankind; the book is evolving, progressing, improving, they argue, and every improvement demands an uneasy period of adjustment. Sophisticated forms of collaborative "information foraging" will replace solitary deep reading; the connected screen will replace the disconnected book. Perhaps, eons from now, our love affair with the printed word will be remembered as but a brief episode in our cultural maturation, and the book as a once-beloved technology we've outgrown.

But if enthusiasm for the new digital literacy runs high, it also runs to feverish extremes. Digital literacy's boosters are not unlike the people who were swept up in the multiculturalism fad of the 1980s and 1990s. Intent on encouraging a diversity of viewpoints, they initially argued for supplementing the canon so that it acknowledged the intellectual contributions of women and minorities. But like multiculturalism, which soon changed its focus from broadening the canon to eviscerating it by purging the contributions of "dead white males," digital literacy's advocates increasingly speak of replacing, rather than supplementing, print literacy. What is "reading" anyway, they ask, in a multimedia world like ours? We are increasingly distractible, impatient, and convenience-obsessed — and the paper book just can't keep up. Shouldn't we simply acknowledge that we are becoming people of the screen, not people of the book? . . .

In 2007, the National Endowment for the Arts (NEA) published a report, *To Read or Not to Read: A Question of National Consequence*, which provided ample evidence of the decline of reading for pleasure, particularly among the young. To wit: Nearly half of Americans ages 18 to 24 read no books for pleasure; Americans aged 15 to 24 spend only between 7 and 10 minutes per day reading voluntarily; and two thirds of college freshmen read for pleasure for less than an hour per week or not at all. As Sunil Iyengar, director of the NEA's Office of Research and Analysis and the lead author of the report, told me, "We can no longer take the presence of books in the home for granted. Reading on one's own — not in a required sense, but doing it because you want to read — that skill has to be cultivated at an early age." The NEA report also found that regular reading is strongly correlated with civic engagement, patronage of the arts, and charity work. People who read regularly for pleasure are more likely to be employed, and more likely to vote, exercise, visit museums, and volunteer in their communities; in short, they are more engaged citizens.

Not everyone endorses this claim for reading's value. [Harold] Bloom, for instance, is not persuaded by claims that reading encourages civic engagement. "You cannot directly improve anyone else's life by reading better or more deeply," he argues [in *How to Read and Why*]. "I remain skeptical of the traditional social hope that care for others may be stimulated by the growth of individual imagination, and I am wary of any arguments whatsoever that connect the pleasures of solitary reading to the public good."

Whether one agrees with the NEA or with Bloom, no one can deny that our new communications technologies have irrevocably altered the reading culture. In 2005, Northwestern University sociologists Wendy Griswold, Terry McDonnell, and Nathan Wright identified the emergence of a new "reading class," one "restricted in size but disproportionate in influence." Their research, conducted largely in the 1990s, found that the heaviest readers were also the heaviest users of the Internet, a result that many enthusiasts of digital literacy took as evidence that print literacy and screen literacy might be complementary capacities instead of just competitors for precious time.   7

But the Northwestern sociologists also predicted, "as Internet use moves into less-advantaged segments of the population, the picture may change. For these groups, it may be that leisure time is more limited, the reading habit is less firmly established, and the competition between going online and reading is more intense." This prediction is now coming to pass: a University of Michigan study published in the *Harvard Educational Review* in 2008 reported that the Web is now the primary source of reading material for low-income high school students in Detroit. And yet, the study notes, "only reading novels on a regular basis outside of school is shown to have a positive relationship to academic achievement."   8

Despite the attention once paid to the so-called digital divide, the real gap isn't between households with computers and households without them; it is the one developing between, on the one hand, households where parents teach their children the old-fashioned skill of reading and instill in them a love of books, and, on the other hand, households where parents don't. As Griswold and her colleagues suggested, it remains an open question whether the new "reading class" will "have both power and prestige associated with an increasingly rare form of cultural capital," or whether the pursuit of reading will become merely "an increasingly arcane hobby."   9

There is another aspect of reading not captured in these studies, but just as crucial to our long-term cultural health. For centuries, print literacy has been one of the building blocks in the formation of the modern sense of self. By contrast, screen reading, a historically recent arrival, encourages a different kind of self-conception, one based on interaction and dependent on the feedback of others. It rewards participation and performance, not contemplation. It is, to borrow a characterization from sociologist David Riesman, a kind of literacy more comfortable for the "outer-directed" personality who takes his cues from others and constantly reinvents himself than for the "inner-directed" personality whose values are less flexible but also less susceptible to outside pressures. How does a culture of digitally literate, outer-directed personalities "read"?   10

The NEA's study was not without its critics, many of whom focused on the   11
report's definition of reading as limited to print content. Steven Johnson, author
of *Everything Bad Is Good for You: How Today's Popular Culture Is Actually Making Us Smarter* (2005), was miffed that the report didn't include screen reading
in its analysis. "I challenge the NEA to track the economic status of obsessive
novel readers and obsessive computer programmers over the next ten years,"
he wrote in the London *Guardian*. "Which group will have more professional
success in this climate?" he asked. This question is obtuse and misguided, although not surprising coming from a reflexive techno-utopian like Johnson.
Most of the people immersed in screen worlds are not programmers. They are
consumers who are reading on the screen, but also buying, blogging, surfing,
and playing games. How can we differentiate among these many activities, not
all of which might contribute to the success Johnson prizes?

Johnson would have done better to compare obsessive novel *writers* and   12
obsessive computer programmers (I would guess that Danielle Steele's pay-
checks measure up to those earned by the programmers of *Grand Theft Auto*).
More importantly, although computer programmers undoubtedly enjoy great
success "in this climate," as Johnson notes, he entirely misses the point: that "this
climate" itself is what the NEA report is challenging. Johnson's dismissive response is akin to praising people who react to global warming by becoming
nudists.

Besides, the NEA was well aware of the difficulties involved in measuring   13
screen and print reading. As Iyengar told me, "In terms of working definitions of
reading — reading on computers or online — these pose challenges to survey
methodologists." But he recognizes the need for such data. "For the future, we
need better ways to get at the question of reading on the screen versus not. We
have a massive amount of data on reading in the traditional sense. I think the
jury is out on whether or not those same benefits transfer to screen reading."

But the jury is nearing a verdict. While the testimonials of digital literacy   14
enthusiasts are replete with abstract paeans to the possibilities presented by
screen reading, the experience of those who do it for a living paints a very different picture. Just as Griswold and her colleagues suggested the impending
rise of a "reading class," British neuroscientist Susan Greenfield argues that the
time we spend in front of the computer and television is creating a two-class society: people of the screen and people of the book. The former, according to
new neurological research, are exposing themselves to excessive amounts of
dopamine, the natural chemical neurotransmitter produced by the brain. This in
turn can lead to the suppression of activity in the prefrontal cortex, which controls functions such as measuring risk and considering the consequences of
one's actions.

Writing in the *New Republic* in 2005, Johns Hopkins University historian   15
David A. Bell described the often arduous process of reading a scholarly book in

digital rather than print format: "I scroll back and forth, search for keywords, and interrupt myself even more often than usual to refill my coffee cup, check my e-mail, check the news, rearrange files in my desk drawer. Eventually I get through the book, and am glad to have done so. But a week later I find it remarkably hard to remember what I have read."

As he tried to train himself to screen-read — and mastering such reading does require new skills — Bell made an important observation, one often overlooked in the debate over digital texts: the computer screen was not intended to replace the book. Screen reading allows you to read in a "strategic, targeted manner," searching for particular pieces of information, he notes. And although this style of reading is admittedly empowering, Bell cautions, "You are the master, not some dead author. And that is precisely where the greatest dangers lie, because when reading, you should not be the master"; you should be the student. "Surrendering to the organizing logic of a book is, after all, the way one learns," he observes.

How strategic and targeted are we when we read on the screen? In a commissioned report published by the British Library in January 2008 (the cover of which features a rather alarming picture of a young boy with a maniacal expression staring at a screen image of Darth Vader), researchers found that everyone, teachers and students alike, "exhibits a bouncing/flicking behavior, which sees them searching horizontally rather than vertically. . . . Users are promiscuous, diverse, and volatile." As for the kind of reading the study participants were doing online, it was qualitatively different from traditional literacy. "It is clear that users are not reading online in the traditional sense, indeed there are signs that new forms of 'reading' are emerging as users 'power browse' horizontally through titles, contents pages, and abstracts going for quick wins." As the report's authors concluded, with a baffling ingenuousness, "It almost seems that they go online to avoid reading in the traditional sense." . . .

The new caveats about "reading" are part of a broader argument that advocates of digital literacy promote: digital literacy, unlike traditional print literacy, they argue, is not "passive." The screen invites the player of a video game to put himself at the center of the action, and so it must follow that "games are teaching critical thinking skills and a sense of yourself as an agent having to make choices and live with those choices," says James Paul Gee, one of the chief cheerleaders of video games as learning tools. As Gee told the [*New York*] *Times*, "You can't screw up a Dostoevsky book, but you can screw up a game."

[Such] statements suffer from a profound misunderstanding of the reading experience and evince an astonishing level of hubris. The reason you can't "screw up" a Dostoevsky novel is that you must first submit yourself to the process of reading it — which means accepting, at some level, the author's authority to tell you the story. You enter the author's world on his terms, and in so doing get away from yourself. Yes, you are powerless to change the narrative or the characters, but you become more open to the experiences of others and, importantly, open to the notion that you are not always in control. In the process, you might even become more attuned to the complexities of family life, the vicissitudes of social institutions, and the lasting truths of human nature. The screen, by contrast, tends in the opposite direction. Instead of a reader, you become a user; instead of submitting to an author, you become the master. The screen promotes invulnerability. Whatever setbacks occur (as in a video game) are temporary, fixable, and ultimately overcome. We expect to master the game and move on to the next challenge. This is a lesson in trial and error, and often an entertaining one at that, but it is not a lesson in richer human understanding. . . .

Meanwhile, older children and teens who are coming of age surrounded   20
by cell phones, video games, iPods, instant messaging, text messaging, and Facebook have finely honed digital literacy skills, but often lack the ability to concentrate that is the first requirement of traditional literacy. This poses challenges not just to the act of reading but also to the cultural institutions that support it, particularly libraries. The *New York Times* recently carried a story about the disruptive behavior of younger patrons in the British Library Reading Room. Older researchers — and by old they meant over 30 — lamented the boisterous atmosphere in the library and found the constant giggling, texting, and iPod use distracting. A library spokesman was not sympathetic to the neo-geezers' concerns, saying, "The library has changed and evolved, and people use it in different ways. They have a different way of doing their research. They are using their computers and checking things on the Web, not just taking notes on notepads." In today's landscape of digital literacy, the old print battles — like the American Library Association's "Banned Books Week," held each year since 1982 — seem downright quaint, like the righteous crusade of a few fusty tenders of the Dewey Decimal system. Students today are far more likely to protest a ban on wireless Internet access than book censorship.

Not every librarian is pleased with these changes. Some chafe at their new   21
titles of "media and information specialist" and "librarian-technologist." One librarian at a private school in McLean, Virginia, described in the *Washington Post* a general impatience among kids toward books, and an unwillingness to grapple with difficult texts. "How long is it?" has replaced "Will I like it?" he says, when he tries to entice a student to read a book. For an increasing number of librarians, their primary responsibility is teaching computer research skills to young people who need to extract information, like little miners. But these kids are not like real miners, who dig deeply; they are more like '49ers panning for gold. To be sure, a few will strike a vein, stumbling across a novel or a poem so engrossing that they seek more. But most merely sift through the silty top layers, grab what is shiny and close at hand, and declare themselves rich. . . .

If reading has a history, it might also have an end. It is far too soon to tell   22
when that end might come, and how the shift from print literacy to digital literacy will transform the "reading brain" and the culture that has so long supported
it. Echoes will linger, as they do today from the distant past: audio books are
merely a more individualistic and technologically sophisticated version of the
old practice of reading aloud. But we are coming to see the book as a hindrance,
a retrograde technology that doesn't suit the times. Its inanimacy now renders
it less compelling than the eye-catching screen. It doesn't actively *do* anything
for us. In our eagerness to upgrade or replace the book, we try to make reading
easier, more convenient, more entertaining — forgetting that reading is also
supposed to encourage us to challenge ourselves and to search for deeper
meaning.

In a 1988 essay in the *Times Literary Supplement*, the critic George Steiner   23
wrote,

> I would not be surprised if that which lies ahead for classical modes of
> reading resembles the monasticism from which those modes sprung.
> I sometimes dream of *houses of reading* — a Hebrew phrase — in which
> those passionate to learn how to read well would find the necessary
> guidance, silence, and complicity of disciplined companionship.

To those raised to crave the stimulation of the screen, Steiner's houses of reading probably sound like claustrophobic prisons. For those raised in the tradition
of print literacy, they may seem like serene enclaves, havens of learning and
contentment, temples to the many and subtle pleasures of the word on the
page. In truth, though, what Steiner's vision most suggests is something sadder
and much more mundane: depressing and dwindling gated communities,
ramshackle and creaking with neglect, forgotten in the shadow of shining sky-
scrapers. Such is the end of the tragedy we are now witness to: Literacy, the
most empowering achievement of our civilization, is to be replaced by a vague
and ill-defined screen savvy. The paper book, the tool that built modernity, is to
be phased out in favor of fractured, unfixed information. All in the name of
progress.

Part IV

WRITING THE RESEARCH ESSAY

Most long essays and term papers in college courses are based on research. Sometimes, an instructor will expect you to develop and present a topic using preassigned sources only; but, more often, you will be asked to formulate your own opinion and then to validate and support that opinion by searching for and citing authorities.

Your research essay (or extended multiple-source essay) will present you with several new problems, contradictions, and decisions. You will probably be starting out with no sources, no thesis, and only a broad topic to work with. Yet as soon as you start your research, you will find yourself with a multitude of sources—books and articles in the library and on the Internet from which you will have to make your own selection of readings. Locating and evaluating sources are complex skills, calling for quick comprehension and rapid decision making:

- *In the electronic databases* and *computer catalogs*, you have to judge which books and periodicals are worth locating.
- *At the shelves* and *on the computer screen*, you have to skim a variety of books, articles, and Web sites rapidly to choose the ones that may be worth reading at length.
- *At the library tables* and *on the computer screen*, you have to decide which information should be written up as part of your notes and which pages should be downloaded, duplicated, or printed out.

In Chapters 7, 8, and 9, you will be given explicit guidelines for using the library, choosing sources, and taking notes.

As you have learned, in order to write a multiple-source essay, you have to establish a coherent structure that builds on your reading and blends together your ideas and those of your sources. In Chapter 9, you will find a stage-by-stage description of the best ways to organize and write an essay based on complex sources. But here, again, is a contradiction.

Even as you gather your materials and synthesize them into a unified essay, you also should keep in mind the greatest responsibility of the researcher—accountability. *From your first efforts to find sources at the library and at your computer, you must carefully keep track of the precise source of each of the ideas and facts that you may use in your essay.*

You already know how to distinguish between your ideas and those of your sources and to make that distinction clear to your readers. Now, you also have to make clear which source is responsible for which idea and on which page of the source that information can be found—without losing the shape and coherence of your own paragraphs.

To resolve this contradiction between writing a coherent essay and accounting for your sources, you will use a system that includes the familiar skills of *summary, quotation, paraphrase,* and *citation of authors,* as well as the skills of *documentation* and *compiling a bibliography.* This system is explained in Chapter 10.

What should your essay look like when it's completed? For reference, in Chapter 11 you can examine two essays that demonstrate how to write a persuasive, analytical research essay, each one using a common method of documentation.

· 7 ·

Finding Sources

Chapter 7 shows you the many ways to develop a topic for a research essay as you search for information in the library and on the Internet. You can use databases and search engines to identify and locate a range of books, periodical articles, and Web sites that are appropriate for academic research. At the same time, you'll learn to organize these sources into a formal bibliography.

Topic Narrowing

When you start your research, sometimes you will know exactly what you want to write about, and sometimes you won't. Your instructor may assign a precise topic. Or you may start with a broad subject and then narrow the focus. Or you may develop an idea that you wrote about in your single- or multiple-source essay.

Ask yourself these practical questions as you think about your topic and before you begin collecting material for your essay:

- How much time do I have?
- How long an essay am I being asked to write?
- How complex a project am I ready to undertake?

> ## Narrowing Your Topic
>
> 1. Whether your instructor assigns a broad topic for your research paper or you are permitted to choose your own topic, do some preliminary searching for sources to get background information.
> 2. As you see what's available, begin to break down the broad topic into its components. Try thinking about a specific point in time or the influence of a particular event or person if your topic is *historical* or *biographical*. Try applying the standard strategies for planning an essay (see pp. 201–203 in Chapter 5) if you're going to write about a *contemporary* subject. Try formulating the reasons for and against if you're going to write an *argument*.
> 3. Once you have some sense of the available material, consider the *scope* of your essay. If the scope is too broad, you run the risk of presenting a superficial overview. If the scope is too narrow, you may run out of material.
> 4. As you read, consider *your own perspective* and what interests you about the person, event, or issue. If you really want to know more about the topic, your research will progress more quickly and you're more likely to get your essay in on time.
> 5. Formulate a few *questions* to help you structure your reading and research. As you read, you should stay within that framework, concentrating on materials that add to your understanding of the topic, skimming lightly over those that don't.
> 6. As answers to these questions emerge, think about a potential *thesis* for your essay.

Topic Narrowing: Biographical and Historical Subjects

Biographical and historical topics have an immediate advantage: they can be defined and limited by space and time. Events and lives have clear beginnings, middles, and ends, as well as many identifiable intermediate stages. You probably won't want to undertake the full span of a biography or a complete historical event, but you could select a specific point in time as the focus for your essay.

Writing about People

Assume, for example, that by choice or assignment your broad subject is *Franklin Delano Roosevelt* (FDR), who was president of the United States for twelve years—an unparalleled term of office—from 1933 until 1945. You begin by reading *a brief overview of FDR's life*. An encyclopedia article of several pages might be a starting point. This should give you enough basic information to decide which events in FDR's life interest you enough to sustain you through the long process of research. You might also read a few encyclopedia articles about the major events and issues that formed the background to FDR's career: the Great Depression, the New Deal, the changing role of the president.

Choosing a Point in Time: Now, instead of tracing *all* the incidents and related events in which he participated during his 63 years, you might decide to describe FDR at the point when his political career was apparently ruined by polio. Your focus would be *the man in 1921*, and your essay might develop a thesis drawing on any or all of the following topics—his personality, his style of life, his physical handicap, his experiences, his idea of government—at *that* point in time. Everything that happened to FDR after 1921 would be relatively unimportant to your chosen perspective. Another student might choose a different point in time and describe *the new president in 1933* against the background of the Depression. Yet another might focus on an intermediate point in FDR's presidency and construct a profile of the *seasoned president* in 1940, at the brink of America's entry into World War II, when he decided to run for an unprecedented third term in office.

Finding a Focus: The topic might be made even more specific by focusing on *a single event and its causes*. For example, the atomic bomb was developed during FDR's presidency and was used in Japan shortly after his death:

- What was FDR's attitude toward atomic research?
- Did he advocate using the bomb?
- Did he anticipate its consequences?
- How has 65 years changed our view of the atomic bomb and FDR's role in its development?

Or you might want to study Roosevelt in the context of his political party:

- How did he influence the Democratic party?
- How did the party's policies influence his personal and political decisions?
- What role did Roosevelt play in the establishment of the United States as a "welfare state"?
- How has the Democratic party changed since his time?

This kind of profile attempts to describe a historical figure, explore his or her motives and experiences, and, possibly, apply them to an understanding of current issues. In effect, your overriding impression of character or intention becomes the basis for the thesis, the controlling idea of your essay.

Writing about Events

You can also view a *historical event* from a similar specific vantage point. Your broad topic might be the Civil War, which lasted four years, or the Berlin

Olympics of 1936, which lasted a few weeks, or the Los Angeles riots of 1991, which lasted a few days. Rather than cover a long span of time, you might focus on an intermediate point or stage, which can serve to illuminate and characterize the entire event.

The *Battle of Gettysburg,* for example, is a broad topic often chosen by those interested in the even broader topic of the Civil War. Since the three-day battle, with its complex maneuvers, can hardly be described in a brief narrative, you would want to narrow the focus even more. You might describe the battlefield and the disposition of the troops, as a journalist would, at a single moment in the course of the battle. In this case, your thesis might demonstrate that the disposition of the troops at this point was typical (or atypical) of tactics used throughout the battle, or that this moment did (or did not) foreshadow the battle's conclusion.

Finding a Focus: In writing about history, you also have to consider your own point of view. If, for example, you set out to recount an episode from the Civil War, you first need to *establish your perspective*: Are you describing the Union's point of view? the Confederacy's? the point of view of the politicians of either side? the generals? the civilians? industrialists? hospital workers? slaves in the South? black freedmen in the North?

The "day in the life" approach can also be applied to *social and technological changes that had no specific date*:

- When and under what circumstances were primitive guns first used in battle?
- What was the reaction when the first automobile drove down a village street? When television was first introduced into American homes?
- What was it like to shop for food in Paris in 1810?
- In Chicago in 1870?
- In any large American city in 1945?

Instead of attempting to write a complete history of the circus from Rome to Ringling, try portraying *the particular experience of a single person*:

- What was it like to be an equestrian performer in Astley's Circus in London in 1805?
- A chariot racer in Pompeii's Circus Maximus in 61 BC?

Setting a tentative target date helps you to focus your research, giving you a practical way to judge the relevance and the usefulness of each of your sources.

Establishing a Thesis and a Strategy

As you narrow your topic and begin your reading, watch for your emerging thesis—a *clear impression of the person or event* that you wish your reader to receive. Whether you are writing about a sequence of events, like a battle or a flood, or a single event or issue in the life of a well-known person, you will still need both a *thesis* and a *strategy* to shape the direction of your essay. A common strategy for biographical and historical topics is the *cause-and-effect sequence*— reasons why a certain decision was made or an event turned out one way and not another:

- Why did the United States develop the atomic bomb before Germany did?

- Why did President Truman decide to use the atomic bomb against Japan as the war was ending?

Your thesis may contain your own view of the person or event that you're writing about:

- "FDR had no choice but to support the development of the atomic bomb."

- "The development of the supermarket resulted in major changes to American family life."

- "The imposition of term limits for the presidency after FDR's fourth term in office was [or was not] good for the United States [or for democracy in the United States or for political parties in the United States or for politicians in the United States]."

Finally, do not allow your historical or biographical portrait to become an exercise in creative writing. Your evidence must be derived from and supported by well-documented sources, not just your imagination. The "Napoleon might have said" or "Stalin must have thought" in some biographies and historical novels is often a theory or an educated guess that is firmly rooted in research—and the author should provide documentation and a bibliography to substantiate it.

Topic Narrowing: Contemporary Subjects

If you chose to write about the circus in 61 BC or 1805, you would find a limited assortment of books describing traditional kinds of circus activity. Now, however, reviews and features are printed—and preserved for the researcher—every time Ringling Brothers opens in a new city. Your research for an essay about the circus today might be endless and the results unmanageable unless, quite early, you focus your approach.

Finding a Focus: The usual way is to analyze a topic's component parts and select *a single aspect* as the tentative focus of your essay:

- Do you want to write about circus acts? Do you want to focus on animal acts or, possibly, the animal-rights movement's opposition to the use of animals for circus entertainment? Or the dangers of trapeze and high-wire acts?

- How has the circus adapted to contemporary culture? What does the trend to small, one-ring circuses or the advent of the "new age" Cirque de Soleil tell us about people's taste today? Why are circuses still so popular in an age of instant electronic entertainment?

■ How does the circus function as an economic organization? What are the logistics of circus management—transport, for example—or marketing? How has modern entertainment (e.g., TV) altered the business of circuses?

One practical way to begin narrowing a topic is to do a *computer search.* Many of the guides, indexes, and online databases contain not only lists of sources but also a useful directory of subtopics. As you'll see later in this chapter, descriptors and keywords can suggest possibilities for the direction of your essay.

Yet another way to narrow your perspective is to apply different strategies to possible topics. Suppose that *food* is your broad topic. Your approach might be *descriptive,* analyzing *causes and effects*: you could discuss recommendations about what we ought to eat and the way in which our nutritional needs are best satisfied. Or you could deal with the production and distribution of food—or, more likely, a specific kind of food—and use *process description* as your approach. Or you could analyze a different set of *causes*: Why don't we eat what we ought to? Why do so many people have to diet, and why aren't diets effective? Or you could plan a *problem-solution* essay: What would be the best way to educate the public about proper nutrition?

Within the narrower focus of *food additives,* there are numerous ways to develop the topic:

■ To what degree are additives dangerous?

■ What was the original purpose of the Food and Drug Act of 1906?

■ What policies does the Food and Drug Administration carry out today?

■ Would individual rights be threatened if additives like artificial sweeteners were banned?

■ Can the dangers of food additives be compared with the dangers of alcohol?

On the other hand, your starting point could be *a concrete object,* rather than an abstract idea: you might decide to write about the Big Mac. You could describe its contents and nutritional value, or recount its origins and first appearance on the food scene, or compare it to best-selling foods of past eras, or evaluate its relative popularity in different parts of the world. All of these topics require research.

If you have a few approaches in mind before you begin intensive reading, you can distinguish between sources that are potentially useful and sources that probably will be irrelevant. You probably will start to develop a *hypothesis,* a theory that may or may not be true, depending on what you find in your research. What you *cannot* do at this stage is formulate a definite thesis. Your thesis will probably answer the question that you asked at the beginning of your research. Although, from the first, you may have your own theories about the answer, you cannot be sure that your research will confirm your hypotheses. Your thesis should remain tentative until your reading has given your essay content and direction.

Topic Narrowing: Issues for Argument

Most people want to argue about an issue that has significance for them. If no issue immediately occurs to you, try *brainstorming*—jotting down possible ideas in a list. Recall conversations, news broadcasts, class discussions that have made you feel interested, even argumentative. Keep reviewing the list, looking for one that satisfies the following criteria:

- *Your topic should allow you to be objective.* Your reader expects you to present a well-balanced account of both sides of the argument. Too much emotional involvement with a highly charged issue can be a handicap. If, for example, someone close to you was killed in an incident involving a handgun, you are likely to lose your objectivity in an essay on gun control.

- *Your topic should have appropriate depth.* Don't choose an issue that is too trivial: "Disney World is better than Disneyland." Similarly, don't choose an issue that is too broad or too abstract: "Technology has been the bane of the modern world" or "A life without God is not worth living." Your topic should lend itself to a clear, manageable path of research. Using the keywords "god" and "life" in a database search will produce a seemingly unending list of books and articles. Where will you begin?

- *Your topic should have appropriate scope.* Consider the terms of your instructor's assignment. Some topics can be explored in ten pages; others require more lengthy development. Some require extensive research; others can be written using only a few selected sources. Stay within the assigned guidelines.

- *Your topic should have two sides.* Some topics are nonissues: it would be hard to get anyone to disagree about them. "Everyone should have the experience of work" or "Good health is important" are topics that aren't worth arguing. (Notice that they are also far too abstract.) Whatever the issue, the opposition must have a credible case.

- *Your topic can be historical.* There are many issues rooted in the past that are still arguable. Should President Truman have authorized dropping the atomic bomb on Japan? Were there better alternatives to ending slavery than the Civil War? Should Timothy McVeigh have been executed, or the Rosenbergs, or Sacco and Vanzetti?

- *Your topic should be practical.* It may be tempting to argue that tuition should be free for all college students, but, in the process, you would have to recommend an alternative way to pay for the cost of education—something that state and federal governments have yet to figure out.

- *Your topic should have sufficient evidence available to support it.* You may not know for sure whether you can adequately defend your argument until you have done some research. A local issue—Should a new airport be built near our town?—might not have attracted a substantial enough body of evidence.

- *Your topic should be within your range of understanding.* Don't plan an essay on "the consequences of global warming" unless you are prepared to present scientific evidence, much of which is written in highly technical language. Evidence for topics in the social sciences can be equally difficult to comprehend, for many depend on surveys that are hard for a nonprofessional to evaluate. Research on literacy and teaching methods, for example, often includes data (such as reading scores on standardized tests) that require training in statistics.

Many of these criteria also apply to choosing a historical narrative or a contemporary subject. What's important in writing any essay—especially one involving a commitment to research—is that the topic interest you. If you are bored while writing your essay, your reader will probably be just as bored while reading it.

EXERCISE 24: Narrowing a Topic

Here are ten different ways of approaching the broad topic of *poverty in America.*

A. Decide which questions would make good starting points for an eight-to-ten-page research essay. Consider the practicality and the clarity of each question, the probable availability of research materials, and the likelihood of being able to answer the question in approximately nine pages.

B. Try rewriting two of the questions that seem too broad, narrowing the focus.

1. How should the nation deal with poverty in its communities?
2. What problems does your city or town encounter in its efforts to make sure that its citizens live above the poverty level?
3. What are the primary causes of poverty today?
4. Whose responsibility is it to help the poor?
5. What effects does a life of poverty have on a family?
6. What can be done to protect children and the aged, groups that make up the largest proportion of the poor?
7. Does everyone have the right to freedom from fear of poverty?
8. Which programs for alleviating poverty have been particularly successful, and why?

9. Should all those receiving welfare funds be required to work?

10. What nations have effectively solved the problem of poverty, and how?

C. Make up several questions that would help you to develop the broad topic of *restricting immigration to America* for an eight-to-ten-page research essay.

EXERCISE 25: Proposing a Topic

The following topic proposals were submitted by students who had been given a week to choose and narrow their topics for an eight-to-ten-page research essay.

A. Consider the scope and focus of each proposal, and decide which ones suggest *practical* topics for an essay of this length.

B. If the proposal is too broad, be prepared to offer suggestions for narrowing the focus.

Student A

Much of the interest in World War II has been focused on the battlefield, but the war years were also a trying period for the public at home. I intend to write about civilian morale during the war, emphasizing press campaigns to increase the war effort. I will also include a description of the way people coped with brownouts, shortages, and rationing, with a section on the victory garden.

Student B

I intend to deal with the role of women in feudal life, especially the legal rights of medieval women. I would also like to discuss the theory of chivalry and its effects on women, as well as the influence of medieval literature on society. My specific focus will be the ideal image of the medieval lady.

Student C

I have chosen the Lindbergh kidnapping case as the subject of my essay. I intend to concentrate on the kidnapping itself, rather than going into details about the lives of the Lindberghs. What interests me is the planning of the crime, including the way in which the house was designed and how the kidnapping was carried out. I also hope to include an account of the investigation and courtroom scenes. Depending on what I find, I may argue that Hauptmann was wrongly convicted.

Student D

I would like to explore methods of travel one hundred and fifty years ago, and compare the difficulties of traveling then with the conveniences of traveling now. I intend to stress the economic and social background of the average traveler. My focus will be the Grand Tour that young men used to take.

Student E

I'd like to explore quality in television programs. Specifically, I'd like to argue that popular and critically acclaimed TV shows of today are just as good as comparable programs ten and twenty years ago and that there really hasn't been a decline in popular taste. It may be necessary to restrict my topic to one kind of television show—situation comedies, for example, or coverage of sports events.

Student F

I would like to do research on several aspects of adolescent peer groups, trying to determine whether the overall effects of peer groups on adolescents are beneficial or destructive. I intend to include the following topics: the need for peer acceptance, conformity, personal and social adjustment, and peer competition. I'm not sure that I can form a conclusive argument, since most of the information available on this subject is purely descriptive; but I'll try to present an informed opinion.

Locating Sources

Preliminary research takes place in three overlapping stages:

- Identifying and locating possible sources;
- Recording or saving basic facts about each source for possible inclusion in a bibliography;
- Noting each source's potential usefulness—or lack of usefulness—to your topic (and, when possible, downloading or copying extracts from the useful ones).

It's rare that you'll be able to locate all your sources first, and then record all your basic information, and after that choose those that are worth including in your essay. Research isn't that tidy. At a later stage of your work, you may come across a useful database and find new materials that must be reviewed, recorded, and included in your essay.

The three most common kinds of sources are *books*, *periodicals* (including magazines, newspapers, and scholarly journals), and *Web sites*. Most books and periodicals are published in print form; you can hold them in your hands (or read articles from back issues by inserting microfilm or microfiche into reading machines). Web sites and a few periodicals are located in cyberspace on the Internet and appear only on your computer screen.

Computer Searches

Searching for sources is best done online through *electronic databases*. Occasionally, the information is stored on *CD-ROMs* (compact disk, read-only memory), which you obtain in the library and insert in a computer. Since databases generally list books or periodical articles, but not both, you'll have to engage in at least two separate searches to find a full range of materials. And searching for Web sites requires using a *search engine*, which is nothing more than another kind of database.

Databases and search engines have to manage huge amounts of constantly changing information. To avoid overflowing lists and unmanageable systems, each new work is scanned and then listed only under those *subject headings* (often called *descriptors*) that are relevant to its content. This key organizing principle is called *cross-referencing*: a method of obtaining a standardized, comprehensive list of subject headings that can be used to index information. One example of such a list, used by many libraries as an index for books, is the *Library of Congress Subject Headings*, or LCSH.

Are Libraries Obsolete?

You can do a good deal of research on your computer without ever entering the library. You can obtain information about potential sources for your topic; you can download Web material for later use; you can find the complete texts of many periodical articles and even some books—all on your computer screen. But you'll still need to use the library:

- To obtain most books
- To read periodical articles that aren't available on the Internet
- To look for older articles in print indexes
- To use microfilm and microfiche machines
- To obtain and use CD-ROMs
- To get assistance from reference librarians

The last reason is probably the most important one. Librarians provide essential support for your research. They'll show you how the library is organized; how to navigate the stacks of books, online catalogs, and databases; and how to target and refine a computerized search. Much of this information will be available on the home page of your library's Web site; but it's hard to improve on having your questions answered by a real person in real time.

One way to start a computer search is to check the database's or search engine's own list of descriptors for one or more that correspond to your topic. Google, for example, provides a subject directory for Web sites, organized into categories, which you can search. Or you can begin to narrow down your topic by considering just what it is that you want to find and then expressing it briefly, in a word or phrase. Using the menu on the screen, you type the *keywords* in the designated slot. In an "advanced" or "guided" search, using two or more keywords, sometimes along with words like "and" and "not," will further break down and limit your topic. (Every database and search engine has its own techniques for formulating keywords; for an efficient search, it's worth taking the time to check the "Help" page or the "About . . ." page attached to the database that you're using.) This do-it-yourself process, usually called *Boolean searching*, will be explained and illustrated in the remainder of this chapter.

What Is Boolean Searching?

Boolean searching, named after George Boole, a nineteenth-century mathematician, is a method of focusing your topic to get the best possible results from your computer search. If you are too broad in your wording, you'll get an exceedingly long list of sources, which will be unmanageable; if you're too specific in your wording, you'll get a very short list, which can bring your research to a dead halt.

To carry out a Boolean (or advanced) search, you refine your topic by *combining words*, using *phrases* to express complex subjects, and inserting "operators"—AND, OR, NOT—between keywords. (Sometimes, the operators are symbols, such as +, rather than words.) In effect, you must ask yourself what you do and what you don't want to know about your topic. Let's apply these guidelines to a database search for information about Lawrence of Arabia.

"Lawrence of Arabia"—in quotation marks—is your subject expressed as a phrase: the search will include only those sources in which the entire phrase is found and omit all those in which both "Lawrence" and "Arabia" appear only separately.

"Lawrence of Arabia" AND "guerrilla warfare" limits the search to those sources that contain *both* phrases. A book that mentions Lawrence but not guerrilla warfare won't appear in the results list, and vice versa.

"Lawrence of Arabia" OR "T. E. Lawrence" expands the search by expressing the topic two ways and potentially multiplying the number of sources found.

"Lawrence of Arabia" NOT "motion picture" limits the search by excluding sources that focus on the film rather than the man.

Searching for Lawrence of Arabia

Let's assume that you've decided to write about *Lawrence of Arabia*. T. E. Lawrence was a key figure in the Middle East campaigns of World War I, a British scholar fascinated by the desert, whose guerrilla tactics against the Turks succeeded partly because he chose to live like and with the Bedouin tribes that fought with him. You've enjoyed the 1962 award-winning movie about Lawrence, but you'd like to find out whether it accurately represents his experience. Here are some issues and questions about Lawrence's life that might intrigue you:

- Acclaimed as a hero after the war, Lawrence chose to enlist in the Royal Air Force at its lowest rank, under an assumed name. Why?

- He died at the age of 46 in a mysterious motorcycle crash. Was this an accident?

- He contributed to the development of a new kind of military tactic. Why was his kind of guerrilla warfare so effective? Is it still in use today?

- He hoped to gain political independence for the Bedouin tribes. What prevented him?

Starting with an Encyclopedia: One place to begin your search about Lawrence of Arabia is an *encyclopedia*, which will provide you with a brief overview of his life and so help you to narrow down your topic. There are several general encyclopedias listed in the Google directory (under "reference"), some of which are free to use. Exercise caution if you use *Wikipedia*, the free online encyclopedia "that anyone can edit," since the articles are written and edited by readers and the information is not always authoritative. The best choice— *Encyclopedia Britannica Online* (EBO)—is pay-to-view only. So, access it through your library's online link.

If you consult *EBO*, you'll be prompted to type in a question or keyword. So, you type "Lawrence of Arabia." Why use quotation marks? They identify your keyword as a single *phrase*, so your results will be restricted to information about the Lawrence you're looking for. Without quotation marks, Lawrence of Arabia will be interpreted as a request for information about anyone or anything named Lawrence and any material about Arabia.

In its response, *EBO* offers you a choice: an article about T. E. Lawrence or an article about *Lawrence of Arabia* (motion picture). At this stage, you'll probably want to click on and read both; you may want to compare the movie version with Lawrence's actual experiences. In fact, clicking on the entry for T. E. Lawrence provides you with links to other articles, such as "Guerrilla Leader," "Advisor on Arab Affairs," and "Postwar Activities," as well as icons for "Additional Reading" and "Related Articles." Choosing and reading any of these articles can help you decide what aspect of Lawrence's life you want to write about.

Carrying out research is all about choices:

- You type a request into a database, and you receive a list of topics or sources to choose from.

- You read an article about your subject, and at the end you find a list of additional articles headed "Bibliography" or "Further Reading."
- You look at a Web site, and throughout the text you see *hyperlinks* that will lead you to related Web pages.

Finding sources is not difficult; the real challenge is deciding which ones to read first.

Using Computer Searches to Locate Books

Databases that contain books are usually place-specific. In other words, each library produces a computerized database that lists all the books housed in its building or group of buildings. The library in the next town will have a different database for its holdings. Your own college library almost certainly has such a database listing all the books on its shelves, organized and searchable by author, by title, and by subject. You can also search comparable databases for other libraries in the area or major libraries across the globe. If you want to examine a full range of the books in existence on Lawrence of Arabia, you can look up that topic in the database of the Library of Congress or the New York Public Library, both of which are available online. If you locate a book that seems important for your research and your own library does not have it, your librarian can probably arrange for an *interlibrary loan* from a library that does.

Searching a Database

Let's search the Library of Congress Online Catalog (LCOC) for books about Lawrence of Arabia. On the catalog home page, click "Guided Search":

- You type in *Lawrence of Arabia*; click the drop-down menu to the right; and highlight and click "as a phrase." No quotation marks are necessary.
- You *don't* click the "Keyword Anywhere" entry on the right, making sure that you can view the full range of available sources.
- You want to obtain information about the man, Lawrence of Arabia, rather than the film *Lawrence of Arabia*, so you rule out prints of the movie and recordings of its sound track by clicking "NOT" twice, and typing in *motion picture* and *sound recording*.
- You click "Begin search."

Figure 7-1 shows the interactive screen after you've filled in your requirements.

Choosing Books to Review

Your search for Lawrence of Arabia produces 101 items; however, many of them are irrelevant to your purpose. The first ten, for example, refer to various types of media, including television documentaries about Lawrence and

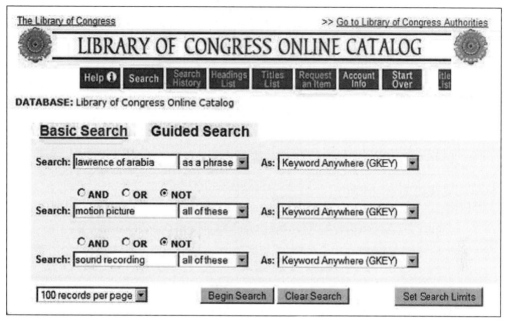

Figure 7-1 Library of Congress Online Catalog, "Guided Search"

images of him. You'll probably want to examine and choose some pictures of Lawrence to illustrate your essay, but not at this early stage.

The 91 other entries—all of which refer to books—contain a good many duplicates. Repetition is a recurring problem in computerized searches. The same book can appear as a reprint (with the same contents, but a new cover, probably paperback) or in a new edition (with revisions or new material). For example, your search list contains four entries for *Great Contemporaries* by Winston Churchill (which includes a chapter about Lawrence); each entry refers to a different edition of the same book.

Other entries are inappropriate for a variety of reasons. Some are fiction (*Murder of Lawrence of Arabia*, or *Marconi's Dream*, which includes a short story titled "Dancing with Lawrence of Arabia"). Others focus on *very narrow* aspects of Lawrence's career and character: you don't want to begin your research by reading *Military Mavericks: Extraordinary Men of Battle* or *Great Bastards of History: The True and Riveting Accounts of the Most Famous Illegitimate Children Who Went on to Achieve Greatness*. And, in fact, assuming that you've already read an overview of Lawrence's life in a reliable encyclopedia, you're ready to look at full-length biographies, rather than one entry in a collection of short profiles.

But some of the nonbiographical books on your list may prove useful later on, especially if you're interested in exploring the connection between the man and the movie. The entries in Figure 7-2 would be worth noting and saving until you've narrowed down your topic and decided whether or not to focus on the movie.

[26]	Bingham, Dennis, 1954-	Whose lives are they anyway? : the biopic as contemporary film genre / Dennis Bingham.	2010
[32]	Caton, Steven Charles, 1950-	Lawrence of Arabia : a film's anthropology / Steven C. Caton.	1999
[37]	Claydon, E. Anna (Elizabeth Anna)	Representation of masculinity in British cinema of the 1960s : Lawrence of Arabia, The loneliness of the long distance runner, and The Hill / E. Anna Claydon.	2005
[50]	Hodson, Joel C.	Lawrence of Arabia and American culture : the making of a transatlantic legend / Joel C. Hodson.	1995
[88]	Turner, Adrian.	Making of David Lean's Lawrence of Arabia / Adrian Turner.	1994

Figure 7-2 Selected entries from the Library of Congress Online Catalog

Most of the biographies of Lawrence in the LCOC search list were written 30 or more years ago. At some point, you may want to inspect one or two biographies by authors who actually knew Lawrence (although personal knowledge sometimes creates issues of bias—see pp. 342–343 in Chapter 8). For now, it makes sense to choose some *recent* biographies since those authors probably have had access to the widest range of material about Lawrence. Most databases will sort the titles for you in reverse order of publication, most recent first. Figure 7-3 shows seven of the most likely titles.

This short list contains four biographies of Lawrence, one collection of his letters, one very recent study of Lawrence and the Middle East, and an "encyclopedia" devoted entirely to his life:

- Tabachnick's encyclopedia—248 pages—might prove very useful later on when you want to find specific information about a particular event or person connected to Lawrence as it consists of a comprehensive series of alphabetized entries.

- Lawrence's "Selected Letters" will certainly provide you with supporting material in his own words—once you're at the stage when you know what points you need to support.

- Hulsman's discussion of Lawrence and the Middle East will be extremely helpful—but only if that turns out to be the focus of your essay.

- MacLean's biography is written for a juvenile audience—something that this (and other databases) don't tell you, but which becomes apparent when you try to locate the book and find it in the children's library.

So, three entries on your short list are worth following up immediately: Brown, James, and Wilson.

[28]	Brown, Malcolm, 1930-	Lawrence of Arabia : the life, the legend / Malcolm Brown.	2005
[52]	Hulsman, John C., 1967-	To begin the world over again : Lawrence of Arabia and the invention of the Middle East / John Hulsman.	2009
[61]	James, Lawrence, 1943-	Golden warrior : the life and legend of Lawrence of Arabia / Lawrence James.	2008
[73]	Lawrence, T. E. (Thomas Edward), 1888-1935.	Lawrence of Arabia : the selected letters / edited by Malcolm Brown.	2007
[79]	MacLean, Alistair, 1922-1987.	Lawrence of Arabia / Alistair MacLean.	2006
[86]	Tabachnick, Stephen Ely.	Lawrence of Arabia : an encyclopedia / Stephen E. Tabachnick.	2004
[98]	Wilson, Jeremy.	Lawrence of Arabia : the authorized biography of T. E. Lawrence / Jeremy Wilson.	1990

Figure 7-3 Selected recent biographies of Lawrence from the LCOC

Examining the Full Record: After you click on an item on a search list, you can find maximum information about the work by selecting the icon, usually at the top of the screen, labeled "Full Record" or "Full View." As figures 7-4–7-6 demonstrate, each screen includes important information such as:

- The length of the book,
- Whether it has an index (so you can look up topics quickly),
- Whether it has notes and a bibliography (so you can locate additional sources), and
- The scope of the book, with a list of "subjects" as a clue to the specific contents.

Assuming that all three were available in your library, which book would you examine first—Brown, James, or Wilson?

- *Brown's biography* (Figure 7-4) has the advantage of being a brief overview, but the "record" suggests that he's most interested in Lawrence's role in the Middle Eastern campaign, and that might limit your research at this stage. Brown's documentation is also extremely slender.

- *James's biography* (Figure 7-5) seems midway between the two: long enough to provide sufficient information, yet not as exhaustive—and exhausting—as Wilson's. But, like Brown, James focuses on Lawrence's role in the war and may not offer the necessary overview of Lawrence's life.

probable emphasis
on military strategy
relatively brief
book

one page of notes

emphasis on
World War I

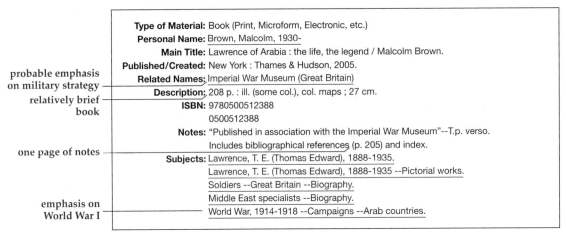

Figure 7-4 Abridged LCOC for Brown, from the full record

length: not too
long, not too short

has bibliography
and index; recently
revised

focuses on war and
historical context

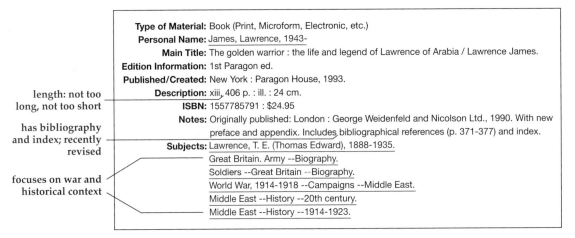

Figure 7-5 Abridged LCOC for James, from the full record

▪ *Wilson's "authorized" biography* (Figure 7-6) is going to be an important resource, no matter what topic you eventually choose. This is clearly the standard work in the field, with extensive documentation that will enable you to locate other helpful sources.

As is often the case, searching another database provides you with an alternative source. One of the items found in a search for "Lawrence of Arabia" in the Columbia University Library database (CLIO) is Harold Orlans' *T.E. Lawrence: Biography of a Broken Hero*, published in 2002, which covers the entire life, yet is

Type of Material:	Book (Print, Microform, Electronic, etc.)
Personal Name:	Wilson, Jeremy.
Main Title:	Lawrence of Arabia : the authorized biography of T. E. Lawrence / Jeremy Wilson.
Published/Created:	New York : Atheneum, 1990, c1989.
Description:	xi, 1188 p. : ill., maps : 25 cm.
ISBN:	0689119348
Notes:	Includes bibliographical references and index.
Subjects:	Lawrence, T. E. (Thomas Edward), 1888-1935.
	Great Britain. Army --Biography.
	Soldiers --Great Britain --Biography.
	World War, 1914-1918 --Campaigns --Middle East.
	Middle East --History --20th century.

"authorized": Lawrence's estate allowed Wilson access to private records

very long; many pictures

32 pages of plates

focus on military career as well as complete life

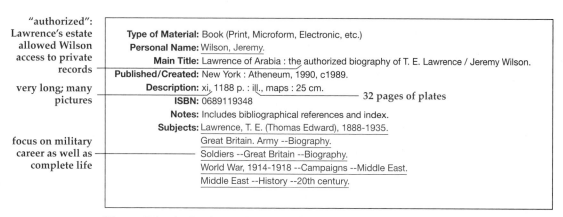

Figure 7-6 Abridged LCOC for Wilson, from the full record

only 281 pages long. Notice that the CLIO "Full View" (Figure 7-7) includes a table of contents and a summary (which, since it's taken from the book jacket, may not be considered reliable).

Following Cross-Referenced Hyperlinks: Cross-referencing in an electronic database provides you with one more set of choices. If you click on any of the underlined subjects listed in the "Full Record" of a work—Lawrence, T. E. (Thomas Edward), 1888-1935, for example—the next screen will display numerous subtopics related to Lawrence, ranging from his death and burial to his psychology. If, for example, you click on "Military Leadership," you're referred to Oliver Butler's *The Guerrilla Strategies of Lawrence and Mao*, which compares the military exploits of Lawrence with those of Mao Zedong, the Chinese Communist leader. And the screen for the Butler book also contains another hyperlinked subject list, including guerrilla warfare, that would allow you to continue your search for this topic.

Using WorldCat

WorldCat is an enormously popular database that builds on already existing libraries (including the Library of Congress) to provide researchers with a vast number of books, articles, and various types of media from which to search. Unlike the LCOC, WorldCat's advanced search doesn't allow you to exclude aspects of the keyword by using "NOT," so an initial search for Lawrence of Arabia (books only) produced a list of 40 items, mostly about the movie. A new search, this time using *T. E. Lawrence* as the keyword, resulted in 5,786 books, listed in order of *relevance*. Unfortunately, the standard used to determine "relevance" is rather dubious as important and minor books are mixed in together. *T.E. Lawrence and Fine Printing*—which focuses on types and fonts and is not relevant to this search—comes in at #33.

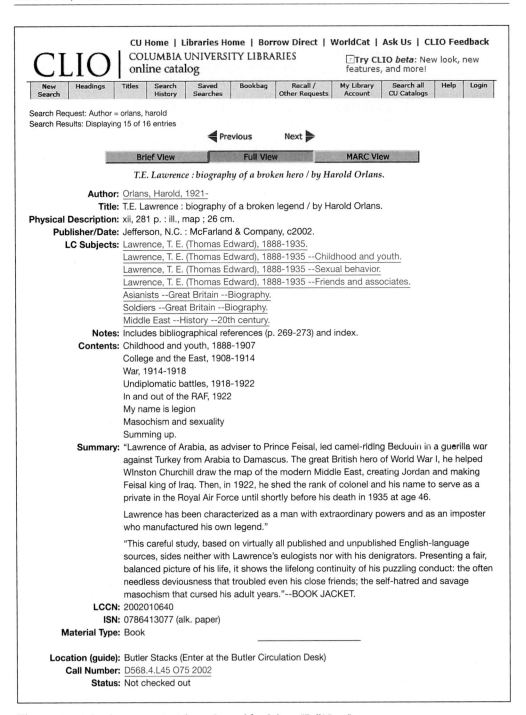

CU Home | Libraries Home | Borrow Direct | WorldCat | Ask Us | CLIO Feedback

CLIO | COLUMBIA UNIVERSITY LIBRARIES
online catalog

Try CLIO *beta*: New look, new features, and more!

| New Search | Headings | Titles | Search History | Saved Searches | Bookbag | Recall / Other Requests | My Library Account | Search all CU Catalogs | Help | Login |

Search Request: Author = orlans, harold
Search Results: Displaying 15 of 16 entries

◀ Previous   Next ▶

| Brief View | Full View | MARC View |

T.E. Lawrence : biography of a broken hero / by Harold Orlans.

Author: Orlans, Harold, 1921-
Title: T.E. Lawrence : biography of a broken legend / by Harold Orlans.
Physical Description: xii, 281 p. : ill., map ; 26 cm.
Publisher/Date: Jefferson, N.C. : McFarland & Company, c2002.
LC Subjects: Lawrence, T. E. (Thomas Edward), 1888-1935.
Lawrence, T. E. (Thomas Edward), 1888-1935 --Childhood and youth.
Lawrence, T. E. (Thomas Edward), 1888-1935 --Sexual behavior.
Lawrence, T. E. (Thomas Edward), 1888-1935 --Friends and associates.
Asianists --Great Britain --Biography.
Soldiers --Great Britain --Biography.
Middle East --History --20th century.
Notes: Includes bibliographical references (p. 269-273) and index.
Contents: Childhood and youth, 1888-1907
College and the East, 1908-1914
War, 1914-1918
Undiplomatic battles, 1918-1922
In and out of the RAF, 1922
My name is legion
Masochism and sexuality
Summing up.
Summary: "Lawrence of Arabia, as adviser to Prince Feisal, led camel-riding Bedouin in a guerilla war against Turkey from Arabia to Damascus. The great British hero of World War I, he helped Winston Churchill draw the map of the modern Middle East, creating Jordan and making Feisal king of Iraq. Then, in 1922, he shed the rank of colonel and his name to serve as a private in the Royal Air Force until shortly before his death in 1935 at age 46.

Lawrence has been characterized as a man with extraordinary powers and as an imposter who manufactured his own legend."

"This careful study, based on virtually all published and unpublished English-language sources, sides neither with Lawrence's eulogists nor with his denigrators. Presenting a fair, balanced picture of his life, it shows the lifelong continuity of his puzzling conduct: the often needless deviousness that troubled even his close friends; the self-hatred and savage masochism that cursed his adult years."--BOOK JACKET.
LCCN: 2002010640
ISN: 0786413077 (alk. paper)
Material Type: Book

_____

Location (guide): Butler Stacks (Enter at the Butler Circulation Desk)
Call Number: D568.4.L45 O75 2002
Status: Not checked out

Figure 7-7 Columbia University Library Record for Orlans, "Full View"

One reason for the great length of the list is that WorldCat has included a large number of recent books that, inexplicably, have nothing to do with T. E. Lawrence. If you re-sort the 5,786 entries by "newest first," nine out of the first ten deal with science and medical topics—mostly treatises on diseases. World-Cat's scope is impressive, but its basis for judgment seems mysterious.

Another reason for the very long list is that it includes unpublished doctoral dissertations. *Originality and Inspiration: The Roots of T. E. Lawrence's Military Success* may (or may not) be just what you need to develop an essay on Lawrence's guerrilla tactics. But keep in mind that the dissertation is unpublished and has therefore not been subject to full peer review, so there's no way of knowing whether finding and reading it is actually worth your time. Searching in cyberspace usually means that a computer algorithm or formula, rather than experienced judgment, decides what comes first.

Because WorldCat isn't a library and is not "holding" the books, it doesn't provide a "full record" of each one. Instead, if you click on an item, you'll find some factual material, a list of "related subjects," an option to find out more about the author (which usually consists of a list of other works), and, in some cases, reviews from "Amazon users" (for what they are worth). Most conveniently, you are also told which nearby libraries own a copy of the book.

Searching for Books

1. Get an overview of your subject by reading an encyclopedia article.

2. Carry out an advanced search using your own library's database or the Library of Congress Online Catalog.

3. Take advantage of the search limits available in an advanced search: expand or narrow the scope of your keywords; consider whether you want the results listed by relevance or date.

4. As you read through the list of search results, note which books will provide general knowledge about your subject and might be useful now, and which books contain more specific information that you may want to come back to when you've narrowed your topic. Use the "Select Records" capability to check off and create one short list of books to examine now and a second list of books to keep in reserve.

5. Examine the "Full Record" of the books on your short list, and, considering each one's length, scope, and documentation, decide which one(s) to read first.

6. As necessary, find more sources by using the hyperlinks available on the "Full Record" subject lines, by carrying out a new search on a large database like WorldCat, and by consulting the bibliographies in some of the books that you find in the library.

Dealing with so many items and options can be very difficult for someone starting research on a new subject. You would be well-advised to begin a search with the Library of Congress Online Catalog or your library's catalog, choose your short list of books, and supplement the LCOC "Full Record" with World-Cat's comments on those books.

Searching Bibliographies: Don't neglect a traditional, non-computerized way of identifying sources: look in the bibliographies of standard works on the subject, like Wilson's. The books on Lawrence will probably be shelved together in your library stacks, and you'll want to examine the *table of contents, index*, and *bibliography* of several before deciding which ones merit your time.

Using Computer Searches to Locate Periodical Articles

Finding appropriate periodical articles is a more massive task than looking for books. Each issue of a periodical contains a dozen or so articles; each year, thousands of periodicals appear in English alone; many of the best ones have been publishing for decades, a few for centuries. No single database can catalog all the newspaper, magazine, and journal articles on a specific topic.

Moreover, as you've seen, electronic searches tend to generate lists that are inflated with repetitive and irrelevant items. Given the vast amount of material available and the idiosyncrasies of most search mechanisms, you need to carefully control the terms of your initial search request. The more opportunity the database gives you to define the direction and limits of your search, the more likely it will be that the result—the search list—will be clean, relevant, and useful to your project.

Searching Databases

Periodical databases don't all provide the same sort of information:

- Some databases provide only bibliographical listings of articles (sometimes called *citations*) and leave you to find the article in bound volumes on your library shelves, in another electronic database, on microfilm, or on the Web.

- Other databases provide *abstracts* of the articles that they list. An abstract is a brief summary—a few sentences—that helps you to decide whether you want to locate and read the entire article.

- Some databases include *extracts*—samples from the article.

- A few databases will produce the *full text*, sometimes for a fee.

- And other databases provide all of the above—sometimes only an abstract, sometimes the full article.

Like databases for books, electronic databases for periodicals allow you to choose between a *basic* search and an *advanced* search. Depending on the database, the advanced search might allow you to:

- limit the range of sources (only history? Or the social sciences? Or all available journals?)

- refine your search with Boolean connectives (NOT motion picture)

- request only popular periodicals (magazines and newspapers) or only academic journals

- exclude certain types of articles (book reviews?)

- specify a time span for your search (2000–the present?)

- restrict your search to articles that have been peer reviewed.

That last option can be significant: *peer review* means that a journal requires each of its articles to be read and approved by authorities in the field before it's accepted for publication. Peer review is, in effect, a guarantee of reasonable quality.

You may need to search in more than one database, starting with the periodical database in your campus library, which should list all the articles in all the newspapers, magazines, and journals that the library owns or can access electronically. Your library will also have a long list of the other periodical databases available to you online. For example, Columbia University lists 356 online databases for the social sciences, ranging from *Abstracts in Social Gerontology* to *Medieval Travel Writing*. More general in their scope, the *Social Sciences Index* and the *Humanities Index* are often good starting points for topics within those broad disciplinary areas.

Searching for Popular Periodicals

Some databases focus on general-interest periodicals—magazines, newspapers—rather than scholarly journals:

- *Reader's Guide* catalogs the most widely read, general-interest periodicals published in the United States. *Readers' Guide Retro* includes 1890–1982; *Readers' Guide Abstracts* (which contains online summaries) covers 1983 to the present.

- *American Periodical Series Online* (*APS Online*) provides full-text articles and pictures from over a thousand popular publications up to 1940.

- *Biography Index* focuses on biographical articles in general-interest publications.

- *Factiva* provides business information based on several thousand newspapers, magazines, and trade journals.

- *WorldCat* has an "articles" database equivalent to the one for books; the limiting feature of the advanced search is not very effective, so, if you use it, be prepared to wade through hundreds of irrelevant entries.

- The *New York Times* is an excellent source of information on events and issues, historical and contemporary, over the past century and a half.

▪ www.newspapers.com enables you to search through hundreds of national and international newspapers. Be aware that you can't do a keyword search; you can only search by date.

Searching for Scholarly Journals

The number of journals searchable in academic databases varies from 200 (*Project MUSE*), to 600 (*JSTOR*), to more than 1,500 (*ScienceDirect*), to 11,000 (*Ingenta*). But the size of the database doesn't change the essential fact of electronic searching: the list resulting from your search will almost certainly contain numerous articles that are only tangentially related to your topic. Lawrence of Arabia may be mentioned once—in comparison with someone else or as a type of hero—or an article about British foreign policy or Middle Eastern democracy will include his name in a historical summary. And, once again, many entries are likely to be book reviews, which are rarely useful to the beginning researcher. That's why it's important to read the abstract before you waste time finding an article.

A *ProQuest* search for "Lawrence of Arabia," limited to the last 20 years, resulted in 1,825 listings. (A good choice for a second academic journal search on this topic would be *Historical Abstracts*, which has a base of 4,700 journals.) From the original *ProQuest* list, 11 articles were selected for further examination. Figure 7-8 presents that short list, with marginal annotations—abstracts of the abstracts.

Two of the eleven articles are too slight (#10 is nostalgic recollection) or narrow in focus (#6 is motorcycle purchase) to be helpful. And, despite excluding book reviews from the search, one (#8) managed to creep in, probably because the title suggests a different kind of article. The remaining seven are all potentially useful in a research essay about T. E. Lawrence, whether your topic concerns his involvement in the Arabian campaign from a military or political perspective, or his complex attitude toward the public image that he helped to create. A two-thirds success is not at all bad in the difficult game of database searching. But keep in mind that culling the original lengthy list to achieve the eight winners took a considerable investment of time and energy.

Two Tips for Database Searching

1. Never assume that the first few listings are the most important, even if they're the most recent, and so ignore the rest of the list. The machine doing the ordering is not necessarily logical.
2. No single database is likely to contain all the material you'll need. It always pays to look a little further.

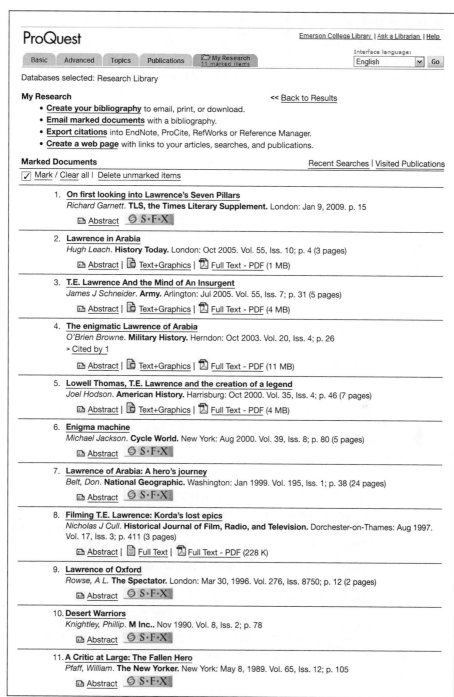

Seven Pillars is "almost the only great book about war"

How Lawrence organized the Arab revolt

Lawrence's influence on a Vietnamese insurgent general

General profile: Lawrence's attitude toward fame

How a publicity campaign made Lawrence a celebrity

How the author bought Lawrence's motorcycle (on which he died)

The political context for Lawrence's involvement in the Arab revolt

Book review

The author recounts Lawrence's days at Oxford

A near-contemporary tells of a meeting with Lawrence in 1926

Full-scale profile

ProQuest   Emerson College Library | Ask a Librarian | Help

Basic   Advanced   Topics   Publications   My Research 11 marked items   Interface language: English   Go

Databases selected: Research Library

My Research   << Back to Results
- **Create your bibliography** to email, print, or download.
- **Email marked documents** with a bibliography.
- **Export citations** into EndNote, ProCite, RefWorks or Reference Manager.
- **Create a web page** with links to your articles, searches, and publications.

Marked Documents   Recent Searches | Visited Publications
☑ Mark / Clear all | Delete unmarked items

1. **On first looking into Lawrence's Seven Pillars**
    Richard Garnett. **TLS, the Times Literary Supplement.** London: Jan 9, 2009. p. 15
    Abstract   S·F·X

2. **Lawrence in Arabia**
    Hugh Leach. **History Today.** London: Oct 2005. Vol. 55, Iss. 10; p. 4 (3 pages)
    Abstract | Text+Graphics | Full Text - PDF (1 MB)

3. **T.E. Lawrence And the Mind of An Insurgent**
    James J Schneider. **Army.** Arlington: Jul 2005. Vol. 55, Iss. 7; p. 31 (5 pages)
    Abstract | Text+Graphics | Full Text - PDF (4 MB)

4. **The enigmatic Lawrence of Arabia**
    O'Brien Browne. **Military History.** Herndon: Oct 2003. Vol. 20, Iss. 4; p. 26
    > Cited by 1
    Abstract | Text+Graphics | Full Text - PDF (11 MB)

5. **Lowell Thomas, T.E. Lawrence and the creation of a legend**
    Joel Hodson. **American History.** Harrisburg: Oct 2000. Vol. 35, Iss. 4; p. 46 (7 pages)
    Abstract | Text+Graphics | Full Text - PDF (4 MB)

6. **Enigma machine**
    Michael Jackson. **Cycle World.** New York: Aug 2000. Vol. 39, Iss. 8; p. 80 (5 pages)
    Abstract   S·F·X

7. **Lawrence of Arabia: A hero's journey**
    Belt, Don. **National Geographic.** Washington: Jan 1999. Vol. 195, Iss. 1; p. 38 (24 pages)
    Abstract   S·F·X

8. **Filming T.E. Lawrence: Korda's lost epics**
    Nicholas J Cull. **Historical Journal of Film, Radio, and Television.** Dorchester-on-Thames: Aug 1997. Vol. 17, Iss. 3; p. 411 (3 pages)
    Abstract | Full Text | Full Text - PDF (228 K)

9. **Lawrence of Oxford**
    Rowse, A L. **The Spectator.** London: Mar 30, 1996. Vol. 276, Iss. 8750; p. 12 (2 pages)
    Abstract   S·F·X

10. **Desert Warriors**
    Knightley, Phillip. **M Inc..** Nov 1990. Vol. 8, Iss. 2; p. 78
    Abstract   S·F·X

11. **A Critic at Large: The Fallen Hero**
    Pfaff, William. **The New Yorker.** New York: May 8, 1989. Vol. 65, Iss. 12; p. 105
    Abstract   S·F·X

Figure 7-8 ProQuest journal search, selected list

Using Computer Searches to Locate Web Sites

Web sites can be created by anyone who wants to set one up: government agencies, schools, businesses, nonprofit organizations, and individuals. Because they are ideal for distributing up-to-date information to a worldwide audience, many Web sites are maintained by corporations for advertising purposes. Other sites enable people with an interest or hobby to display their knowledge in a public setting—often, a blog. These are reasons you need to make doubly sure that information for research obtained through the Web is accurate and objective. As you'll learn in Chapter 8, not all Web sites are reliable or worth citing in your essay. Before you take notes or print out content, get some sense of the author's credentials and the material's validity.

The distinctive qualities of the Web—the speed with which it can be updated and searched, and the huge amount of information it contains—are both its strength and its weakness. Web sites change and disappear without any notice, and the information that you thought you had on Monday may be unavailable by Friday. The Web contains lots of material about today's issues, but rarely goes back more than a few years. It is huge, but indiscriminate. You can search for anything, but often find nothing useful for your purpose. Unless you're very focused in your search requirements, you're likely to receive a list of sites that seem randomly chosen and ranked. As Danny O'Brien wrote in "The Fine Art of Googling," search engines "may know the contents of all Web pages, but they know the meaning of none." Good research does not start and end with point and click.

Using Search Engines

Most people routinely use search engines to access the millions of sites available on the World Wide Web. Broadly, there are two kinds of search engines:

- *Web crawlers*, like Google, use computers ("spiders") to compile, collate, and rank information mechanically, according to a formula or algorithm. Crawlers have very large databases and provide long lists of results—in Google's case, ranked by relative popularity—but do very little useful sorting.

- *Web directories* (or hierarchical indexes), like Open Directory Project (ODP), use staff, rather than keywords, to scan and sort individual Web sites according to categories.

In theory, human intelligence should do a better job of sorting, ranking, and avoiding duplication than a set formula does; but, in fact, practically all search engines—crawlers or directories—can produce a hodgepodge of results, irrelevant to the topic you're searching for. One built-in disadvantage of search engines, whether humanly or mechanically generated, is that the descriptions come directly from the sites' owners and may or may not be accurate summaries of the contents. There's little or no peer review on the Web.

Another problem is the huge amount of information available on the Web, most of which has never been cataloged. No search—or search engine—is likely to achieve a truly exhaustive results list, especially on the first attempt. After trying various searches on a "Web crawler" like Google, you may need to supplement your results list by using a *meta search engine* like Clusty: a super-crawler that covers large tracts of Web material by scanning the contents of several other search engines. But to obtain such wide coverage, you have to provide Clusty with a broad, unrefined topic. Meta engines don't always work well with complex searches.

Your results list has to be *well-targeted* as well as complete. Even an "advanced" search on Google won't limit the terms of the search sufficiently to exclude sites that are inappropriate or irrelevant to your topic. Figure 7-9 shows you Google's Advanced Search page set for a search for the phrase "Lawrence of Arabia." To make the search as specific as possible and to make the results list a manageable length, references to "motion picture" and "sound recording" have been excluded. (Notice that, in the Google Advanced Search, the operators AND, OR, and NOT are replaced by self-explanatory phrases: "all these words," "this exact wording or phrase," "one or more of these words," and "any of these unwanted words.") If you don't exclude "motion picture" and "sound recording," your results list is likely to be stuffed with sites offering information about the movie.

Even using these advanced search limiters, a Google search in 2009 produced 897,000 hits—771,000 more than in 2005. The Clusty search resulted in 56,500 hits;

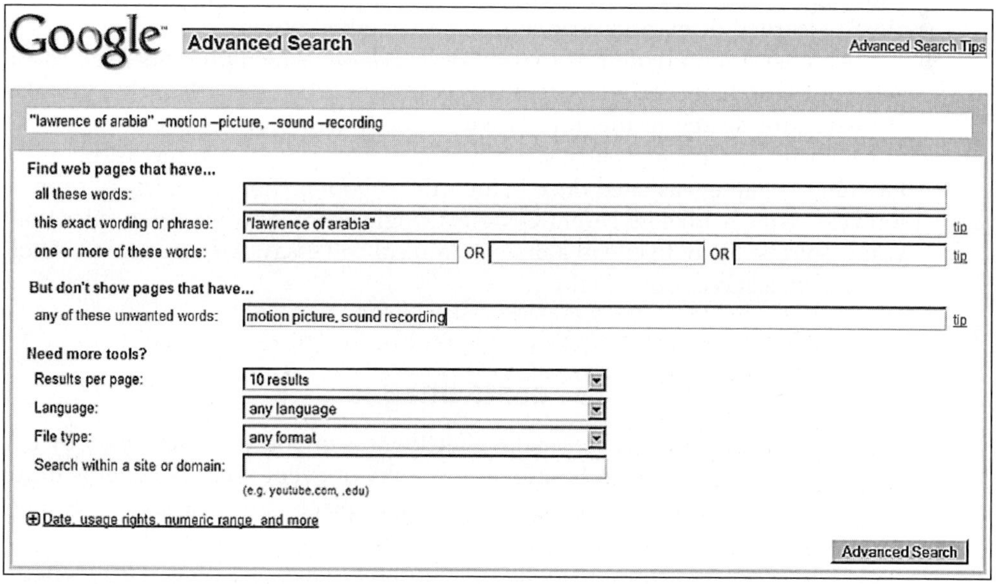

Figure 7-9 Google Advanced Search

Clusty helpfully displays only what the algorithm regards as the top 223 sites. If you compare the first 50 entries on each list (and exclude the numerous sites that relate exclusively to the movie—limiters notwithstanding), you discover that, surprisingly, there is very little overlap—which supports the point that more than one search may be crucial to getting a complete, representative result.

Was there anything on either the Clusty or the Google results list that would be useful for a research project? Once you eliminate the trivial, irrelevant, or duplicated sites, you do end up with about ten that have a reasonable chance of advancing your research. (There is usually no point in proceeding past the first 50, as the quality of sites listed deteriorates dramatically after that.) One worthwhile site, mentioned early in the Google list, is maintained by Jeremy Wilson, who wrote the authorized biography of Lawrence. www.telawrence.info contains a good deal of impeccably sourced and documented information, as well as links to other sites of interest; but there seems to be nothing here that can't be learned from exploring Wilson's book—a form of one-stop shopping.

Other sites worth pursuing include an article on Lawrence's guerrilla tactics from *Military History* magazine; a lecture on "Lawrence of Arabia and the Perils of State Building," by a fellow of the Heritage Foundation; and an account of Lawrence's politics as part of a site whose purpose is to "introduce non-Arabs to Arabs and their culture." There's also a link to www.literaryhistory.com, which promises a "selective list of online literary criticism" that meets stringent academic standards—a resource that seems well worth pursuing. Otherwise, aside from Lawrence's Facebook page, you can examine a variety of brief, encyclopedia-like summaries of his life, by sources like "howstuffworks" and "WiseGeek," that will tell you nothing that you haven't already learned from more academically acceptable sources.

Another option would be to use *Google Scholar*, which presents itself as an academic search engine with results drawn from articles in scholarly journals. However, the search results for "Lawrence of Arabia" contain the usual quota of irrelevant and bizarre entries, many of which are clearly on the list because Lawrence's name was cited once in an article about orthopedic surgery or motorcycle helmets. Like its parent Google, Google Scholar provides few sites that you would be likely to cite in a mainstream college essay. An easy search is not necessarily a successful search.

Using Computer Searches to Locate Images

You can sometimes increase the effectiveness of your research essay by including pictures. A historical topic—biography or event—easily benefits from a presentation that includes images of people or places. But you can sometimes use images to support the analysis of a contemporary issue, as well.

How to choose and document appropriate images is discussed in Chapter 9 (page 427). At a point in your research when your thesis has already

Managing Web Searches

- Refine your search by choosing an "advanced" or "guided" search page and using exact phrases and other "operators" to limit the results. Take time to read the search engine's "Help" section. The more precise your search instructions, the greater the number of meaningful responses.

- Don't waste more than ten minutes on any search engine if the results seem unpromising. Try other engines, or use a database, or go to the library.

- If your search yields a list of a thousand sites, look at the first 50. If there's nothing worthwhile, refine your search, or try another search engine.

- Don't settle for the first sites you find that seem remotely connected to your topic. Keep on searching until the information is solid.

- Avoid commercial sites selling products. They rarely contain material appropriate for academic research.

- Watch out for dead links—Web sites that were indexed months or even years ago and are no longer being maintained by their owners.

- Don't just add interesting possibilities to your "Favorites" or "Bookmarks" for later reading. The material will pile up. If you read (or, at least, skim) as you go along, you'll learn enough about your topic to give some direction to your search.

- Don't be tempted to open every link you come to and pursue stray pieces of information just because they're there. Before you click on a link, consider whether this information is likely to be useful to your present project. Surfing isn't research.

- Maintain concrete and reasonable expectations for your search. Decide what you want to get out of each session on the Internet, and concentrate on that goal. Search with a purpose.

begun to take shape, you may want to look at a few image databases (or "galleries") to see what kinds of pictures are available and whether they will suit your purpose.

Google's basic search page includes an icon labeled "Images" that will transfer you to a search page exclusively for images. A search for "Lawrence of Arabia" yields a large number of photographs, most of which are stills or posters from the motion picture. But there are also several images of T. E. Lawrence on each screen of photos, including the last photograph of him taken before his

The last known photograph of Lawrence.
Clouds Hill 1935

[Home] [More]

Brough Superior Motorcycles

Figure 7-10 Lawrence of Arabia

death, showing Lawrence astride his Brough motorcycle (Figure 7-10). In fact, the picture comes from the Web site for Brough Superior Motorcycles, which contains some useful material about Lawrence as both hero and motorcyclist.

A number of Web sites feature databases of photos appropriate for academic work. Although some allow you to download pictures for free, most require some sort of registration. Here are a few useful sites to try:

- http://thefreesite.com/Free_Graphics/Free_photos/
  A clearinghouse with links to free image galleries.

- www.artstor.org
  A collection focusing on art history.

- http://ap.accuweather.com/apphoto/
  A searchable multimedia archive with 500,000 images covering 160 years, including photos, text, audio, and graphics. A search for "VJ Day

1945″ produced three very different photographs of Times Square on the day World War II ended. Requires a subscription.

- www.memory.loc.gov
  The Web site of American Memory: Historical Collections for National Digital Library, sponsored by the Library of Congress. This collection, presented by theme—cities, culture, environment, sports, and so on—includes images. For an essay on early aviation, for example, you can find photos of airplanes used by the Wright brothers.

- www.bbcmotiongallery.com
  Cosponsored by CBS. This site contains 70 years of motion imagery, including clips of news events, natural history, and culture. Of course, you would need access to appropriate media to make the clips available to your instructor and classmates.

Finding Other Sources on the Internet

- *E-mail* can be used to get assistance in exploring a research topic. If you know the e-mail address of an expert in that field, you can send a courteous message, asking questions or requesting specific information. Keep in mind, though, that academic and professional authorities have little time to answer unsolicited e-mail and, as the number of e-mail inquiries has increased, many are less willing to participate in students' research. Remember that any information obtained through e-mail that is subsequently used in an essay must have its source cited.

- *Listserv® subscriptions*—e-mail exchanges between people interested in a particular subject—are another way to gain information through e-mail. When your address is added to the mailing list, you receive e-mail from members of the group and can send e-mail in return. Large mailing lists are usually automated, with a computer (called a Listserv) receiving and distributing e-mail to and from you and the other group members. You may also have access to previous "discussions" and messages through the archives. Remember that material obtained through e-mail or, indeed, from the Internet in general, has not been validated for accuracy to the same extent as works that have gone through the selection processes used by publishers of books and periodicals.

- *Usenet newsgroups* provide a similar means of access to information, through a worldwide network of electronic bulletin boards, each devoted to a particular subject. Using your Web browser, you can post messages to one or more newsgroups, read messages other people have posted, and reply to those messages. Be aware that concerns about accuracy, reliability, and objectivity apply to Usenet groups as they do to blogs and Listserv messages.

Interviewing and Field Research

As well as books, articles, films, videos, Web sites, and other research materials, personal interviews and field research can be worthwhile resources for your research essay. A well-conducted interview with an expert in the field or your own observations of an event or an environment can be a source of valuable information.

Interviewing

You will want to interview experts or authorities who are both knowledgeable and appropriate sources of information about your specific topic. The faculty on your campus can serve as direct sources of information and also as sources of referrals to other experts in the field at nearby colleges and universities. To further your research project on Lawrence of Arabia, you might identify a faculty member with an interest in Lawrence and his era in the department of:

- Political Science (the Arab Revolt),
- History (World War I and Lawrence's military campaign),
- Psychology (Lawrence's complex motivation), or
- Literature (*Seven Pillars of Wisdom*).

Or, if your focus were on Lawrence as a strategist or guerrilla leader, you might appropriately consult a source with military (or diplomatic) experience. Similarly, you might have access to someone in the movie industry with direct knowledge of the making of David Lean's *Lawrence of Arabia*. Such a person's recollections and comments would serve to lend authenticity and human drama to your essay.

Planning an Interview

Write or phone in advance to arrange an appointment once you have focused your topic and identified candidates for interviews. Allow enough time to make initial contact and then to wait a week or two, if necessary, until the person has enough time to speak with you at length. When you call or write to those whom you hope to interview, politely identify yourself; then briefly describe your topic and the special focus of your essay. Ask for an interview of 20 to 30 minutes at a later time convenient for the subject. If appropriate, mention the name of the person who suggested this source, or refer to the publication in which you saw the subject's name. Your objective is to convey your own serious interest in the topic and in your subject's knowledge of the topic. If someone is reluctant to be interviewed, you should retreat gracefully. At the same time, don't hesitate to ask for a referral to someone else who might be in a better position to provide helpful information.

Preparing for an Interview

Because your interview, whether in person or on the phone, will probably be brief, you need to plan in advance what you intend to say and ask so that you can use the time effectively. Reviewing your research notes, make a focused list of questions in writing beforehand, tailoring them to your specific paper topic and to your source's area of knowledge. It can be helpful to prepare a questionnaire, leaving space between the questions for you to take notes, which can be used, with variations, for a whole series of personal interviews.

Recording Information during an Interview

If you plan to use a tape recorder, make sure you ask your subject's permission in advance; test the equipment beforehand (especially if it's borrowed for the occasion); and know how to operate it smoothly. When the interview is about to begin, check again to see if your subject has any objection to your recording the conversation. Then, to avoid making your subject self-conscious, put the tape recorder in an unobtrusive place.

Even if you plan to tape-record the interview, come prepared to take careful notes; bring notebook and pens, as well as your list of questions or questionnaire. If your subject presents a point so well that you know you'll want to quote it, write it down rapidly but carefully, and—then and there—read it back to make sure that you have transcribed the statement correctly.

Conducting the Interview

Briefly remind your subject of the essay topic and your reason for requesting the interview. Then get right down to your "script": ask each question clearly, without hurrying, be alert to recognize when the question has been fully answered (there is usually a pause), and move briskly on to the next question. Otherwise, let your subject talk freely, with minimum interruption.

Sometimes, a particular question will capture your subject's interest, and you will get a more detailed answer than you expected. Be aware of the time limit for the interview; but if you see a promising line of questioning that you didn't anticipate, and your subject seems relaxed and willing to prolong the conversation, take advantage of the opportunity and ask follow-up questions. What if your subject digresses far away from the topic of your essay? At the first opportunity, ask whether there is a time constraint. If there is, politely indicate that you have three or four more questions to ask and you hope that there will be enough time to include them.

At the end, your subject should, ideally, offer to speak with you again, if necessary, to fill any gaps. To maintain that good impression, be sure to send a brief note of thanks to your subject no longer than a day or two after the interview. Later on, you may want to send a copy of the completed essay.

Using Interview Sources in Your Essay

Since the purpose of the interview is to gather information (and to provide yourself with a few apt quotations), you need to have clear notes to work from as you organize your essay. If you used a tape recorder, you should transcribe the interview as soon as you can; if you took notes, you should go over them carefully, clarify confusing words, and then type a definitive version. Transcribe the interview accurately, without embroidering or revising what your subject actually said. Keep the original notes and tapes; your instructor may want to review them along with your essay. Remember to document each use of material taken from your interview, whether it is ideas or words, with a parenthetical reference.

Field Research

Like interviewing, field research is a way of supplementing the material you take from texts and triggering new ideas about your topic. When you engage in field research, you are gathering information directly, acting as an observer, investigator, and evaluator within the context of an academic or professional discipline:

- If you are asked by your anthropology instructor to describe and analyze a family celebration as an ethnographer would, your observations of Thanksgiving dinner at home would be regarded as field research.
- When the nursing program sends students to a nearby hospital for their clinical practice and asks for a weekly report on their work with patients, these students are doing field research.
- Students, participating in a cooperative education program involving professional internships, prepare reports on their work experiences based on field research.

Whatever the course, your instructor will show you how to connect your field research activities to the theories, procedures, and format characteristic of that discipline.

Field research usually involves the observation of a group of people in order to form a hypothesis about their behavior, test that hypothesis, and determine its significance. You might, for example, be asked to observe your fellow students in the library or at a football game to form conclusions about their patterns of behavior. Such a field research project would fall into three stages: gathering information, analyzing that information, and writing the essay.

Gathering the Information

Field research entails a specified number of observations, usually determined in advance, that can range from a few sessions to an entire semester (or, in the case of professional researchers like Margaret Mead, a year or more). As a new researcher, you would probably be expected to perform a limited number of separate observations, according to a predetermined schedule. At each session, you would take notes, in response to a list of questions or guidelines that you've prepared in advance. These questions set up a framework for your observations and, possibly, a potential structure for your essay.

If, for example, your project involved observation of students using the new lounge, you might be trying to find out:

- How many students are spending time in the lounge?
- Who are they and how long do they stay there?
- What kinds of activities do they engage in?

While you're carrying out your observation of the lounge, you are simply trying to record your subjects' activities accurately, to provide notes for future interpretation. You're not as yet trying to write a narrative or understand the significance of what you're seeing. If, as is quite likely, someone speaks to you during your observation periods, take advantage of the opportunity to do a little formal interviewing and possibly gain a useful quotation for your essay.

After a couple of sessions, you may feel that you have a general idea of the range of students' behavior at the site, so you can begin to look specifically for repeated instances of certain activities: studying together or individually, eating, relaxing. But you will need to keep an open mind about what you observe as your subjects' behavior may not conform to your planned questions and your tentative hypothesis.

Analyzing Your Information

After a few sessions of observation, you start to review your notes to try to understand what you have seen and figure out what you have learned. Your object is to establish categories and generalizations that describe your subjects' pattern of behavior. To support these general categories, you pull out of your notes specific references to behavior that match the category, noting the date and time of each instance. You may want to chart your observations to represent at a glance such variables as these: How many students studied or socialized? Which activities were associated with males or with females? If your sessions took place during different times of the day, the hour would be another variable to record on your chart.

As you identify categories, you need to ask yourself some questions to help you characterize each one and define the differences among some of your subjects' behaviors. For example: Are these differences determined by gender or by preferred methods of learning, like solitary or group study? As you think through the possible conclusions to be drawn from your observations, record them in your notebook, for these preliminary analyses will later become part of your essay.

Writing an Essay Based on Field Research

An essay based on field research generally follows a format appropriate to the particular discipline in the social sciences. Your instructor will provide detailed guidelines and, perhaps, refer you to an article in a professional journal to use as a model. For the essay analyzing student behavior, you might present your findings according to the following outline:

Purpose: In the first section, you state the problem—the purpose of your field research—clearly indicating the question(s) you set out to investigate.

Method: Here, you explain your choice of site, the times and number of your observation sessions, and the general procedure for observation that you followed, including any exceptions to or deviations from your plan.

Observations: Next, you record the information you gathered from your observations, not as a list of random facts; but as categories or groupings that make the facts coherent to the reader. In many disciplines, this kind of information can be presented through charts, graphs, or tables.

Analysis: The heart of your essay, here is where you explain to your readers the significance of your observations. If, for example, you decided that certain activities were gender related, you would describe the basis for that distinction. Or you could discuss your conclusion that students use the lounge primarily as a meeting place to socialize. Or you might make the connection between studying as the most prevalent student activity and the scheduling of midterms during the time of your observations.

Conclusions: At the end of your essay, you remind your readers—and the instructor who is evaluating your work—that your purpose throughout has been to answer the questions and clarify the problems posed in the first paragraph. Would your research encourage your college to open more lounges like this one, or to change the decor or hours, or would your research justify its closure on the grounds of insufficient or inappropriate use?

ASSIGNMENT 8: Writing an Essay Based on Interviews or Field Research

A. Choose a topic from the following list; or think of a question that might stimulate a wide range of responses, and submit the question for your teacher's approval. Try to avoid political issues and very controversial subjects that may make it difficult for you to guide the interview and prevent you from getting a full range of opinion. You want a topic in which everyone you interview can take an interest, without becoming intensely partisan. This assignment is an elaboration of Exercise 20 in Chapter 6.

Suggestions for Topics

- Is "traditional" dating still desirable today?
- Is there a right age to get married?
- What are the ingredients for a lasting marriage?
- Should children be given the same first names as their parents?
- Is it better to keep a friend by not speaking your mind or risk losing a friend by honesty?
- Should community service become a compulsory part of the high school curriculum?
- Should English be made the official language of the United States?
- Are laws banning phones in cars an infringement of individual rights?
- Is graffiti vandalism?
- Should animals be used in laboratory research?
- Should colleges ban drinking alcohol on campus and in fraternity houses?
- How should ethics be taught in schools?
- How should the commandment "honor thy parents" be put into practice today?
- What, if anything, is wrong with the nuclear family?
- Are students forced to specialize too soon in their college experience?
- Should schools stay in session all year round?
- Should citizens have to pay a fine for not voting?
- Should movies have a rating system?
- Should children's TV or computer time be rationed?
- Should parents be held legally or financially responsible for damage done by their children?
- At what age is it acceptable for children to work (outside the family)?
- Should high school students be tested for drug use?
- Should hosts who serve alcohol be held responsible if their guests later are involved in auto accidents?
- Should students have to maintain passing grades in order to participate in school athletics?
- How should society deal with homeless people?
- When should parents cease to be financially responsible for their children?

1. Once your topic is decided (and, if necessary, approved), interview at least six people, or as many as you need to get a variety of reactions for

your survey. (Some of your sources should be students in your class.) If you wish, use the following format for conducting each interview:

> Name: (first and last: check the spelling!)
>
> Do you think . . . . ?
>
> Why do you think so? What are some of your reasons? (later)
> Are there any other reasons?
>
> Why do you think people who take the opposite view would do so?
>
> Do any examples come to your mind to illustrate your point?
>
> Quotation:

2. Take careful and complete notes of the comments that you receive. (*You will be expected to hand in all your notes, in their original form, with your completed essay.*) Keep a separate sheet for each person. If one of your sources says something worth quoting, write down the exact words; read them back to make sure that what you have quoted is what the speaker meant to say; then put quotation marks around the direct quotation. Otherwise, use summary or paraphrase.

3. List the ideas from your notes and arrange the points in a sequence of your choice.

4. Write a summary of your notes that presents the full range of opinion, paraphrasing and (occasionally) quoting from representative sources. After analyzing the arguments of your sources, conclude with one or two paragraphs explaining which point of view, in your opinion, has the most validity, and why.

B. Select a topic appropriate for engaging in field research on your campus, in your dormitory, or in your workplace. For example, you might want to learn about how students occupy their time during large lecture courses; by auditing two or three lecture classes over a period of time and taking notes about students' behavior, you could test the theory that professors should provide printed lecture notes.

C. Present your topic to your instructor for approval and, after carrying out your research, organize your notes and prepare your essay according to the instructions on pages 323–324.

Saving and Recording Information for Your Bibliography

Before the computer and the copying machine were invented, a researcher had to make immediate and firm choices: deciding which material was worth including in an essay, taking notes from the material, and discarding everything else. Later on, those notes would become the basis for the essay. When you take notes, you gain a firm grasp of the topic; you develop ideas of your own as you summarize and paraphrase; and you can more easily estimate the progress of your research, deciding whether you have enough sources to support your essay.

But the twenty-first century does provide some convenient backup alternatives. As well as taking notes, it makes sense to copy key pages from books and articles so that, as you write, you can check your version of the material against the actual text. Having that text discourages inadvertent plagiarism since you will be in no doubt about which ideas and language are the source's and which are yours. Copies also make it possible to write comments in the margin and circle or highlight key points.

Once you have located and briefly examined a book or periodical article or a Web site and decided that it is worth including in your essay, you should not only copy selected pages, but also write a few preliminary notes to yourself about the source's probable usefulness. Jot down your opinion of the work's scope and contents, strong or weak points, and relevance to your topic, as well as any impressions about the author's reliability as a source. Often, you can make these tentative judgments just by examining the "Full Record" or the table of contents, and leafing or scrolling through the pages.

Notes are also useful for your bibliography and essential if you're asked to submit an annotated bibliography. *A bibliography is a complete list of all the works that you use in preparing your essay.* What's included in a bibliography can differ at various stages of your work:

- A *preliminary* or *working* bibliography consists of all the sources that you find worth recording and saving as you do your research.

- A *final* bibliography (sometimes called "Works Cited" or "References") consists of the material that you have actually used in writing your essay.

- An *annotated* bibliography includes a sentence or two after each item, describing the work's scope and specific focus and suggesting its relevance and usefulness to the development of your topic. An example of an annotated bibliography is provided on pages 330–331.

Copying and Recording Print Material

Copying Text: Do place the book or journal carefully in the copier to *avoid cutting off material* at the top, bottom, or sides of the page; days or weeks later, if you want to quote, it may be difficult to reconstruct missing language. Equally important, make sure that the *page numbers* show on the copies, since those numbers are crucial in the citation of your sources. Also, keep in mind that you may not always remember how that extract fit into the author's sequence of ideas. Write down a brief *explanation of context* at the top of the first copied page: the focus of the chapter, the author's previous point.

Copying the Bibliography: As you develop your preliminary bibliography, it can be helpful to copy some or all of the sources listed in the bibliography of a key text.

Copying the Copyright Page: To record basic publication information about a book legibly and accurately, copy the title page and the copyright page (the back of the title page) at the same time that you copy extracts. For a periodical article, copy the cover of the magazine or journal and the table of contents. Of course, if you used a database to identify books and periodical articles, most of the information that you need will be included in the results list. (That's one reason why it's useful to download or print the results pages of your database searches.) But even if you have those lists saved on your computer, the information that you'll need will be scattered over a number of downloaded files. At some point, you'll have to put it all together in a single file.

Recording Your Working Bibliography: Start the computer file or notebook list for your working bibliography early in the research process, and every time you find a source you're likely (but not necessarily certain) to use, add it to the list. Transcribe the information from the databases that you've downloaded and the stack of title pages that you've copied. Or, if you use a word processing program or a bibliographic software program that automatically prepares a bibliography in any of the standard formats, enter the data about each new source into the fields of the database. It's important to be accurate and consistent in recording each entry. Check the spelling of the author's name. Don't abbreviate unless you're sure you'll remember the significance of each symbol. Make it clear whether the place of publication was Cambridge, Massachusetts, or Cambridge, England.

The majority of college research essays use MLA (Modern Language Association) style for documentation. To prepare a final bibliography in MLA style (or, indeed, in most other styles), you should include the following facts in your preliminary list:

For Print Books

- the full name of the author(s)
- the exact title, italicized
- the name of the editor(s) (for an anthology) or the name of the translator (for a work first written in a foreign language)
- the place of publication and the name of the publisher
- the original date of publication and the date of the new edition or reprint, if the book has been reissued
- the inclusive page numbers and any other information for a specific chapter or other section (such as the author and title of an introduction or of a selection within an anthology)
- the full name of the series (if it is one volume in a series)
- the volume number, if the book is part of a multivolume work

- the call number, so that you will not need to return to the catalog if you decide to locate the book again
- the medium of publication (Print)

For Print Articles

- the full name of the author(s)
- the title of the article, in quotation marks
- the exact title of the periodical, italicized
- the volume and issue numbers (if any) and the date of the issue
- the inclusive page numbers of the article
- the medium of publication (Print)

Copying and Recording Web Material

Downloading material from the Web is the equivalent of copying print texts. Since the content of a Web site can change from day to day—or the site itself can disappear—it's a good idea to download if you have any inclination at all to use the source. Once you're sure a document is a solid source worth rereading, click "Save As" on the File menu, choosing a name that will be easily recognizable and (if you want to save space on your hard drive) selecting a "text only" option rather than saving the complete document, graphics and all. If the document is large, you may want to highlight extracts and then copy and paste them to a file in your word processing program. Early on in your research, create a new folder named for your paper topic and, after that, save all Web material to that folder, so it won't be scattered all over your hard drive. Printing out a Web document is also helpful. Web graphics can be distracting; computer screens are hard on the eyes. Having a print copy also makes it easier to put comments in the margins and highlight important points.

Keep a running record of URLs—the Web addresses—so that if you want to go back to a page you can do so easily. (Be careful with the spelling of Web addresses.) Don't assume that you'll remember a URL. If you've downloaded Web material, saving it under a convenient name, you may have to search hard to reconstruct its address. It's safest to have a single file that records all your sources, with complete bibliographic information. And save it! And back it up by copying it to a CD or external drive!

Compile your working bibliography by adding information about Web sources to the file where you're storing data about print sources. Many Web documents were previously or simultaneously published in print; in those cases, include both the print and the electronic data. (If you read the material on the Web, you must cite the Internet source in your bibliography.) On many sites, the kind of bibliographic information shown in print sources is not provided or is difficult to find. Look for and record any of the following items that you can identify:

For Web Material

▪ the name of the author(s) of the article or other document and/or of the person(s) or sponsor(s) who created the site

▪ the title of the article or other document, in quotation marks

▪ the title of the book or periodical or of the site, italicized, or a description, such as *Home page*

▪ any volume number, issue number, or other identifying number

▪ any print publication information, including the date

▪ the date of publication on the Web, or of the most recent update

▪ the range or total number of pages, paragraphs, or other sections, if they are numbered on the site

▪ the name of the database (if applicable)

▪ the medium of publication (Web)

▪ the date of access: when you downloaded the site or took notes from it

▪ the Web address (URL)

Obviously, this information can vary depending on the kind of document you're intending to use. An individual's home page, for example, would require nothing more than the author's name, the indication that it is a home page, the date of access, the medium of publication, and the URL. But serious research is much more likely to depend on Web sites with academic or professional (or even commercial) sponsorship, and it's necessary to indicate all those details in the bibliography. Examples of bibliographical entries for citing Web sources can be found in Chapter 12.

Presenting an Annotated Bibliography

Here's how you put together some of the information you've recorded about Lawrence of Arabia and turn it into an *annotated bibliography* (following MLA style). Note that the annotated bibliography might contain URLs and call numbers — information that will not appear in your final works cited list.

The Myth of Lawrence of Arabia in the Movies:
An Annotated List of Sources Consulted

Butler, Oliver J. *The Guerrilla Strategies of Lawrence and Mao: An Examination.* Houston: Butler, 1974. Print. Useful background for understanding the success of Lawrence's campaigns against the Turks and evaluating the movie's accuracy, particularly the bombing of the train.

Hodson, Joel C. *Lawrence of Arabia and American Culture: The Making of a Transatlantic Legend.* Westport: Greenwood, 1995. Print. This book focuses on the impact the Lawrence myth had on American culture.

The last part is particularly useful in analyzing the movie's presentation of Lawrence, especially his alleged homosexuality.

Kauffmann, Stanley. "On Films: The Return of El Aurans. *Lawrence of Arabia* Reissued, Restored to Its Original Length." *New Republic* 20 Feb. 1989: 26–28. Print. One of the most eminent film critics reassesses the significance of the film.

"Last Known Photograph of Lawrence: Clouds Hill, 1935." Photograph. *Dropbears.com.* Dropbears.com, 2009. Web. 11 Aug. 2009. <http://www.dropbears.com/b/brough_superior/players.htm>. A photo of Lawrence on his Brough Superior motorcycle.

Lawrence of Arabia—The Life, the Legend. Imperial War Museum London, n.d. Web. 12 Aug. 2009. <http://www.iwm.org.uk/upload/package/54/ Lawrence/index.htm>. This site is related to and sponsored by a special exhibition about Lawrence at the Imperial War Museum in 2005-2006.

Lawrence, T. E. *The Letters of T. E. Lawrence of Arabia.* Ed. David Garnett. 1938; London: Spring, 1964. Print. This is a comprehensive collection of Lawrence's correspondence, which provides an especially detailed and moving picture of his later years in the RAF.

---. *The Seven Pillars of Wisdom.* London: Pike, 1926. Print. Lawrence's own interpretation of what happened in the campaign against the Turks is written in a flowery and sometimes opaque style. Nevertheless, it's essential reading.

Walters, Irene. "The Lawrence Trail." *Contemporary Review* 272.1587 (1998): 205–10. *Free Library.* Web. 10 Aug. 2009. <http://www.thefreelibrary.com/ The+Lawrence+Trail.-a020615180>. This is little more than a personal narrative following Lawrence's path through the desert in the 1917 campaign. Useful only for local color.

Wilson, Jeremy. *Lawrence of Arabia: The Authorised Biography of T. E. Lawrence.* London: Heinemann, 1989. Print. Although not the most recent, this is the most comprehensive of the biographies of Lawrence and covers every aspect of his life. The bibliography could be more helpful.

---. *T. E. Lawrence Studies.* Castle Hill Press, Mar. 2007. Web. 4 May 2009. <http://telawrence.info/telawrenceinfo/index.htm>. This is a superb, searchable Web site containing information about Lawrence, maps and chronology, bibliography, and a link to the journal.

Wilson, Michael. "Lawrence of Arabia: Elements and Facets of the Theme." *Cineaste* 21.4 (1995): 30. Print. This article, though brief, provides interesting insights into how the screenwriter thought he was representing Lawrence's life.

How Much Research Is Enough?

Research is open-ended. You can't know in advance how many sources will provide adequate support for your topic. Your instructor may stipulate that you consult at least five authorities, or ten, or fifteen; but that is probably intended to make sure that everyone in your class does a roughly equal amount of research. Quantity is not the crucial issue. There's little point in compiling the required number of source materials if the works on your list are minor, or trivial, or peripheral to the topic. Your bibliography could contain hundreds of sources—whole sections of a database or whole pages of an index—but would that be the basis for a well-documented essay?

At various stages of your research, you may think that you have located enough sources. When that happens, try asking yourself these questions:

- Do my sources include a few of the "standard" books on my topic by well-known authorities? The most recent books? Contemporary accounts (if the topic is historical)?
- Have I checked databases and indexes to find the most authoritative periodical articles, whether in print or on the Web? Have I included the best ones among my sources?
- Does Web material supplement my research, rather than dominate it?
- Have I discussed any questions about my research with my instructor or with a librarian?
- Have I taken notes of my own ideas and thoughts about the topic?
- Without consulting sources, can I talk about the subject convincingly and fluently? Have I succeeded in doing this with a friend?
- Is a point of view or thesis emerging from my research?
- Have I gathered a critical mass of information, copied excerpts, and downloaded material so that my essay has the prospect of substantial support?
- Do I feel ready to start writing my essay?

EXERCISE 26: Compiling a Working Bibliography

Here are three topics for a research essay dealing with the broad subject of *advertising*, followed by a bibliography of 17 articles, arranged in order of their publication dates. Each item in the bibliography is followed by a brief description of its contents.

A. Examine the bibliography carefully and choose a set of possible sources, appropriate for a preliminary bibliography, for each of the three essay topics. Depending on the topic, which ones should you read? You are not expected to locate and read these articles; use the notes to help you make your decisions.

B. List the numbers of the articles that you select underneath each topic. You will notice that some of the articles can be used for more than one topic.

Topics

i) Feminists have argued that the image of women created by the advertising industry remains a false and objectionable one. Is that claim valid?

ii) How do advertising agencies go about manipulating the reactions of consumers?

iii) To what extent does advertising serve the public? harm the public?

1. Attas, Daniel. "What's Wrong with 'Deceptive' Advertising?" *Journal of Business Ethics* 2 (1999): 49–59. Print. This is essentially a defense of deceptive advertising, examining the responsibility of the advertiser and the responsibility of the consumer. It is written in sociological jargon.

2. Nordlinger, Pia. "Taste: Anything Goes." *Wall Street Journal* 15 Sept. 2000: W17. Print. This focuses on the proliferation of semi-pornographic ads in magazines, and the questionable standards set by the editors. The author is clearly disapproving of the "prurient" images.

3. White, Candace, and Katherine N. Kinnick. "One Click Forward and Two Clicks Back: Portrayal of Women Using Computers in Television Commercials." *Women's Studies in Communication* 23.3 (2000): 392–412. Print. Based on a survey of 351 TV commercials, this article shows that the image of women in computer ads is definitely more menial than that of men, confirming the usual stereotypes.

4. Smith, April. "In TV Ads, the Laugh's on Men . . . Isn't It?" *Los Angeles Times* 24 Oct. 2000: E1. Print. This describes images of men in commercials, concluding that they are just as stereotyped as those of women — except the image is that of beer-drinking, dopey sports fans. The point is that male viewers don't get offended by such ads.

5. Gardner, Marilyn. "Slim But Curvy — the Pursuit of Ideal Beauty." *Christian Science Monitor* 24 Jan. 2001: 16. Print. The author writes about idealized images of women in advertisements, exploring the connection between extreme thinness on the page and increasing obesity among the readers. According to the author, these ideals of beauty are unrealistic.

6. Vranica, Suzanne. "Sirius Ad Is Best Bet for Most Sexist." *Wall Street Journal* 1 Apr. 2004: B6. Print. This article is about the award given each year for advertising's most sexist commercial or advertisement and describes the various tasteless finalists. Although some advertising people think that higher standards of decency will eventually be imposed, others say that "edgy" ads appeal to young consumers.

7. Klempner, Geoffrey. "Ethics and Advertising." *Cardiff Centre for Ethics, Law and Society*. Cardiff Law School, June 2004. Web. 3 Mar. 2005. <www.ccels.cardiff.ac.uk/pubs/klempnerpaper.html>. In a philosophical article (with references to Plato and Wittgenstein), this "professional metaphysician" attempts to "deconstruct the dream world of advertising" and the ways in which advertisers seduce us, and concludes that advertising is only as moral as the consumers it serves.

8. Drumwright, Minette E., and Patrick E. Murphy. "How Advertising Practitioners View Ethics: Moral Muteness, Moral Myopia, and Moral Imagination." *Journal of Advertising* 22 June 2004: 7–25. *Factiva*. Web. 4 June 2005. <http://www.factiva.com>. This article describes a study that concluded that a large proportion of advertising professionals have a blind spot — "moral myopia" — about ethical issues when they arise. They believe that, if the consumers will accept it, then an advertising practice has to be morally acceptable and there's no need for concern.

9. Vagnoni, Anthony. "Ads Are from Mars, Women Are from Venus." *Print: America's Graphic Design Magazine* 1 Mar. 2005: 52–56. *Factiva*. Web. 9 Aug. 2005. <http://www.factiva.com>. An advertising executive believes that ads targeted at women tend to be tasteless and even offensive, and, in return, women are ignoring most ads. The article contrasts strategies presently used to attract male and female consumers but does not attempt to solve the problem.

10. Singer, Emily. "They Know What You Want." *New Scientist* 31 July 2004: 36. *Factiva*. Web. 18 May 2005. <http://www.factiva.com>. Singer describes "neuromarketing," a new kind of technology that scans consumers' brains while they are shopping and comparing products. Advertisers hope to learn more about the origins of brand preference and brand loyalty so that they can better predict customer behavior.

11. Johnson, Scott. "Lies and Entertainment." *Adweek* 27 Feb. 2006: 16. *ProQuest*. Web. 14 Aug. 2009. <http://www.proquest.com/en-us/>. The rise of the Internet means that it's easier for lies to pass as truth. Knowing this, consumers are skeptical about advertising claims. They choose the products that they buy not because they believe the content of the ads

on Web sites, but because they are entertained by the ads. This article provides tips for making ads amusing and likeable.

12. Mlotkiewicz, David. "Attracting Sales to Your Business." *Franchising World*. Apr. 2006: 68–71. *ProQuest*. Web. 16 Aug. 2009. <http://www.proquest .com/en-us/>. No business is going to do well without a marketing plan and effective sales techniques. The object is to make the customer trust the brand so much that there's no choice when it's time to buy. If a franchise is going to thrive, it must create brand loyalty.

13. Zimmerman, Amanda, and John Dahlberg. "The Sexual Objectification of Women in Advertising: A Contemporary Cultural Perspective." *Journal of Advertising Research* 48.1 (2008): 71–79. Web. 20 Aug. 2009. <http://www.jar.warc.com/>. Since the 1960s, feminists have made great efforts to stop advertisers from using women in suggestive poses to sell products. This article explores the way the present generation of young women are reacting to ads that use sexual content as a selling device. It concludes that most are not offended by these portrayals.

14. Dittmar, Helga, Emma Halliwell, and Emma Stirling. "Understanding the Impact of Thin Media Models on Women's Body-Focused Affect: The Roles of Thin-Ideal Internalization and Weight-Related Self-Discrepancy Activation in Experimental Exposure Effects." Spec. issue of *Journal of Social and Clinical Psychology* 28.1 (2009): 43–72. Web. 20 Aug. 2009. <http://www.atypon-link.com/GPI/doi/abs/10.1521/jscp.2009.28.1.43>. In a study of responses to ads with thin models, women, influenced by their own poor body image, tended to internalize the idea that it's best to be thin, and the result is that they felt even worse about themselves.

15. Durkin, K., and K. Rae. "Women and Chocolate Advertising: Exposure to Thin Models Exacerbates Ambivalence." *European Psychiatry* 24.1 (2009): S743. ScienceDirect. Web. 20 Aug. 2009. <http://www.sciencedirect.com/ science>. This study showed women a variety of media images, with thin and fat models, and analyzed the extent to which these women felt more guilt (after seeing thin models) and less guilt (after seeing overweight models) about eating chocolate.

16. Feiereisen, Stephanie, Amanda L. Broderick, and Susan P. Douglas. "The Effect and Moderation of Gender Identity Congruity: Utilizing 'Real Women' Advertising Images." *Psychology and Marketing* 26.9 (2009): 813–43. Abstract. Web. 2 Sept. 2009. <http://www3.interscience.wiley .com/journal/122538893/abstract?CRETRY=1&SRETRY=0>. Women have positive responses to ads that make a direct appeal to their gender. Other influences include national culture.

17. Yu, Jay (Hyunjae), and Brenda J. Cude. "Possible Disparities in Consumers' Perceptions Toward Personalized Advertising Caused by Cultural Differences: U.S. and Korea." *Journal of International Consumer Marketing* 21.4 (2009): 251–69. *ProQuest*. Web. 2 Sept. 2009. <http://www.informaworld.com/smpp/content~content=a913730788~db=all~jumptype=rss>. How do consumers react to personalized advertising, using a person's actual name in unsolicited e-mails, letters, and phone calls? This study, focusing on reactions in Korea and the U.S., indicated that consumers generally respond negatively, but more negatively in America than in Korea.

EXERCISE 27: Finding and Selecting Sources

Each of the historical figures on the following list has been the subject of a motion picture. (The dates and, where necessary, titles of the films are in parentheses.) Choose one figure and then compile a preliminary bibliography for an essay that sets out to determine to what extent the film is authentic. (Since this is a *preliminary* bibliography and you're not being asked to write the essay, you need not have seen the film in order to start the research process.)

Using databases and search engines, search for sources that are clearly linked to your topic. Print out a list of the first 20 or 30 items from each search, eliminate those that are obviously commercial or trivial, and choose those that might appropriately be included in a preliminary bibliography. You do not have to examine the books, articles, or Web sites in order to make your selection; base your choices on the descriptions, summaries, or abstracts provided by the database or search engine. If you don't find sufficient material in your first search, keep trying.

Your preliminary bibliography should contain at least 12 items, with a balance of one-third books, one-third print periodical articles, and one-third Web material. Hand in the results lists from your searches with the appropriate choices marked. If your instructor requests it, also prepare a formal bibliography using MLA format.

Alexander the Great (*Alexander* 2004)
Alfred Kinsey (*Kinsey* 2004)
Benito Juárez (*Juarez* 1939)
Charlie Chaplin (*Chaplin* 1992)
Charles Gordon (*Khartoum* 1966)
Charles Lindbergh (*Spirit of St. Louis* 1957)
Che Guevara (*Che* 2008)
Cleopatra (1963)

Cole Porter (*Night and Day* 1946; *De-Lovely* 2004)
Dian Fossey (*Gorillas in the Mist* 1988)
El Cid (1961)
Eleanor of Aquitaine (*The Lion in Winter* 1968)
Emma Hamilton (*That Hamilton Woman* 1941)
Erwin Rommel (*The Desert Fox* 1951)
Eva Perón (*Evita* 1996)

Frida Kahlo (*Frida* 2002)

Gandhi (1982)

George III (*The Madness of King George* 1994)

George Patton (*Patton* 1970)

Hans Christian Andersen (1952)

Harvey Milk (*Milk* 2008)

Helen Keller (*The Miracle Worker* 1962)

Howard Hughes (*The Aviator* 2004)

Isadora Duncan (*Isadora* 1968)

Jackson Pollock (*Pollock* 2000)

Jim Morrison (*The Doors* 1991)

John Dillinger (*Public Enemies* 2009)

Johnny Cash (*Walk the Line* 2005)

Kurt Cobain (*Last Days* 2005)

Larry Flynt (*The People vs. Larry Flynt* 1996)

Lenny Bruce (*Lenny* 1974)

Lillian Hellman (*Julia* 1977)

Loretta Lynn (*Coal Miner's Daughter* 1980)

Louis Kahn (*My Architect* 2003)

Marie Antoinette (1938)

Marie Curie (*Madame Curie* 1943)

Michael Collins (1996)

Mike Tyson (*Tyson* 2008)

Mikhail Kutuzov (*War and Peace* 1956)

Mozart (*Amadeus* 1984)

Muhammad Ali (*Ali* 2001)

Oscar Wilde (1997)

Philippe Petit (*Man on Wire* 2008)

Queen Elizabeth I (*Elizabeth* 1998, 2006)

Queen Elizabeth II (*The Queen* 2007)

Queen Victoria (*Mrs. Brown* 1997)

Ray Charles (*Ray* 2004)

Richard Nixon (*Nixon* 1995; *Frost/Nixon* 2008)

T. S. Eliot (*Tom & Viv* 1994)

Thomas Jefferson (*Jefferson in Paris* 1995)

Tina Turner (*What's Love Got to Do with It* 1993)

Tsar Nicholas II (*Nicholas and Alexandra* 1971)

Ty Cobb (*Cobb* 1994)

Vincent Van Gogh (*Lust for Life* 1956)

William Gilbert or Arthur Sullivan (*Topsy-Turvy* 1999)

William Randolph Hearst (*Citizen Kane* 1941)

William Wallace (*Braveheart* 1995)

Wyatt Earp (*My Darling Clementine* 1946)

ASSIGNMENT 9: Preparing a Topic Proposal for a Research Essay

A. Choose a broad topic that, for the next few weeks, you will research and develop into an extended essay of ten or more pages.

> ▪ If you have a *person or an event* in mind, but do not have sufficiently detailed knowledge to decide on a focus and target date, do some preliminary reading first. Start with an encyclopedia article or an entry in a biographical dictionary; then use the online databases and search engines, as well as any bibliographies that you find along the way.

> ▪ If you select a *contemporary subject or issue for argument*, search for books, journal and newspaper articles, and Web sites that will help you to formulate a few questions to be explored in your essay.

B. Compile a preliminary bibliography, based on your search results. At this point, you need not examine all the sources, take notes, or plan the organization of your essay. Your purpose is to assess the *amount* and, as much as possible, the *quality* of the material that is available. Whether or not your instructor asks you to hand in your preliminary bibliography, make sure that the publication information that you record is accurate and legible. Indicate which sources your library has available and which may be difficult to obtain.

C. Submit a topic proposal to your instructor, describing the probable scope and focus of your essay. (If you are considering more than one topic, suggest a few possibilities.) Be prepared to change the specifics of your proposal as you learn more about the number and availability of your sources.

·8·

Evaluating Sources

It's hard to write about most subjects from your own knowledge and experience. You have to rely on the evidence of others, usually in written form, published in print or on the Web. If the evidence isn't valid, then your work loses its credibility. For this reason, it's essential that—before you start writing—you evaluate each potential source to determine whether it's solid enough to support your essay.

Evaluating sources doesn't have to take a great deal of time. You have to read enough of each text to make some judgments about its *substance* and its *tone*. You have to understand what kind of work it is—whether it's *plausible*, whether it's *appropriate* for the essay that you're writing. You need to be sure it's *relevant* to your topic. And since a good source should be *authoritative*, you must explore the author's claims to your serious consideration.

Evaluating Print Sources

Let's assume that you've begun research for an essay on *animal rights*. You've often wondered about the motivations of vegetarians. As a meat-eater yourself, you're curious about the arguments used by animal rights advocates to discourage the slaughter of living creatures for the table. You are also aware of an ongoing controversy about the use of animals in medical experiments.

Your college library holds many of the books and periodicals that have turned up in your database searches. How do you determine which ones to read seriously? How do you weigh one source of evidence against another and decide whose ideas should be emphasized in your essay? Since all the books and articles have been chosen for publication, each one has presumably undergone some form of selection and review. Would it have been published if its author's authority was questionable? Why is it necessary to inquire further?

Credentials

At the most basic level, you want to find out whether the author of a book or article about animal rights can be trusted to know what he or she is writing about. Here's where the person's education and professional experience become relevant. Is the writer an academic? If so, what's the field of specialization?

- A *psychologist* might provide insights into the personal beliefs motivating vegetarians, but would probably be less concerned with the ideology of the animal rights movement.

- A *philosopher* will present theoretical arguments about the ethics of killing other creatures, but the analysis may be too abstract to provide you with concrete examples for developing your thesis.

- An *economist* might seem to be an unlikely source to support this topic, but the movement toward vegetarianism has had serious consequences for the agricultural economy as well as the retail world of the supermarket.

- A *home economist* might turn up on a database search for "animal rights" AND vegetarianism, but the authors of cookbooks and guides to good nutrition are unlikely to possess academic qualifications.

Do these concerns matter? What kind of an essay are you writing, anyway? One that stresses the theoretical arguments behind the animal rights movement? The psychological motivation? The economic consequences? The practical applications in the kitchen?

An author's background is important. Here's how you can find out about it quickly and easily:

- Check a book's *preface* (including acknowledgments), which will often contain biographical information.

- Read the *blurb* on the jacket cover—often laudatory—which should include some basic facts among the hype.

- Look for *thumbnail biographies* at the beginning or end of periodical articles, or grouped together somewhere in the issue. Be aware that such brief biographies (often written by the authors themselves) can be vague or even misleading. "A freelance writer who frequently writes about this topic" can describe a recognized authority or an inexperienced amateur.

- Do a *Web search* using the author's name. See what other books and articles the author has published.

- Consult one of the many *biographical dictionaries and encyclopedias* available on the Web.

- Check the *Book Review Index* on the Web. If the book is a recent one, there will probably be many reviews available.

- Routinely check the level and extent of the *documentation* that the author provides. Footnotes or parenthetical notes and a comprehensive bibliography usually indicate a serious commitment to the subject.

Credentials: Peter Singer: Peter Singer is the author of *Animal Liberation: A New Ethics for Our Treatment of Animals*. After a database search turns up this title, you find the book on the library shelves, note that it was published in 1975 (but revised in 1990), and wonder whether it's worth delving into a book that's more than 35 years old. So you search for Singer's name in the *Britannica Online* encyclopedia and find the following:

Singer, Peter (Albert David) born July 6, 1946, Melbourne, Austl.

Australian ethical and political philosopher, best known for his work in bioethics and his role as one of the intellectual founders of the modern animal rights movement.

Singer's Jewish parents emigrated to Australia from Vienna in 1938 to escape Nazi persecution following the Anschluss. Three of Singer's grandparents were subsequently killed in the Holocaust. Growing up in Melbourne, Singer attended Scotch College and the University of Melbourne, where he earned a B.A. in philosophy and history (1967) and an M.A. in philosophy (1969). In 1969 he entered the University of Oxford, receiving a B.Phil. degree in 1971 and serving as Radcliffe Lecturer in Philosophy at University College from 1971 to 1973. At Oxford his association with a vegetarian student group and his reflection on the morality of his own meat eating led him to adopt vegetarianism. While at Oxford and during a visiting professorship at New York University in 1973–74, he wrote what would become his best-known and most influential work, *Animal Liberation: A New Ethics for Our Treatment of Animals* (1975). Returning to Australia, he lectured at La Trobe University (1975–76) and was appointed professor of philosophy at Monash University (1977); he became director of Monash's Centre for Human Bioethics in 1983 and codirector of its Institute for Ethics and Public Policy in 1992. In 1999 he was appointed Ira W. DeCamp Professor of Bioethics in the University Center for Human Values at Princeton University.

The article notes that Singer views ethical issues from a utilitarian point of view and so advocates actions that result in the greatest good for the greatest number of people. He has written, cowritten, or edited 44 books, the most recent in 2009, some in areas of pure philosophy, but most dealing with matters of ethical choice. He was chosen as the author of *Encyclopedia Britannica's* article on ethics.

What do you learn from this information? Singer holds impeccable academic credentials and has had a long academic career at estimable universities. As a philosopher, he is likely to root his work on animal rights in abstract arguments. As an ethicist, he is likely to provide plenty of concrete examples to illustrate his arguments.

So far, *Animal Liberation* seems like an excellent choice for your preliminary bibliography and, quite probably, your final bibliography. Is there anything more that you need to know about Singer and his work?

Impartiality

Sometimes you have to consider whether an author has any personal interest in a subject, especially if it's a contentious one like animal rights. In the simplest terms, a declared vegetarian is likely to argue against using animals for food and may present those arguments in a way that's less than impartial. There's nothing intrinsically wrong with having one's own point of view. Few people succeed in being totally detached or objective, whether about their beliefs or their areas of professional expertise. But there's a big difference between an acknowledged personal interest and an underlying prejudice.

The issue here is *bias*: the special interest or personal preference that might affect an author's opinion or treatment of a subject. The existence of bias needn't prevent you from using and citing a source. It's simply one factor that can affect your understanding of an author's ideas. A *dogmatic* writer may want to convert you at all costs. A *narrow-minded* writer will ignore or downplay opposing points of view. You may conclude that either is too biased to be credible. But a third author, who also cares passionately about a subject, may argue the issue strongly and yet remain credible. Such writers are usually aware of and acknowledge their bias—and seek to *persuade* or *convince* rather than bludgeon their readers into submission. If you think that an author has a special interest in the subject, either disregard the bias as harmless, or adjust your judgment to allow for its influence, or—if the bias is clearly prejudice in disguise—reject the source as not worth your time.

Impartiality: Peter Singer: Looking further at the *Britannica* profile, you notice that Peter Singer's books tend to have strong titles, urging action: *Animal Liberation, In Defence of Animals, Ethics into Action, Democracy and Disobedience.* Clearly, he's not an ivory tower philosopher, and so, curious to learn more about his activities, you do a Web search. You don't even have to click on any of the items on the results lists to learn that Singer has been called the world's "most controversial ethicist" and that a petition was started to protest his appointment to a named chair at Princeton. There are references to his "infanticide excesses" and "utilitarian horrors" as well as comparisons with Hitler's

Nazism. On the other hand, other Web sites support his views and praise his reasoned defense of his ethical beliefs.

Since these searches have taken only a few minutes, you try one more, and find an article in *Contemporary Authors* that provides an analysis of reactions by reviewers to many of Singer's works. Focusing on those that deal with *Animal Liberation*, you find praise for his documentation and for his "quite unhysterical and engaging" style. He is also referred to as a propagandist, and he is apparently a successful one, since *Animal Liberation* is described by one reviewer as "one of the most thoughtful and persuasive books that I have read in a long time."

What can you conclude now? That the present controversy over Singer may or may not concern his 1975 work, which is the one that's most relevant to your research. That he has his detractors and his supporters, which is understandable given his contentious subject. That you should judge for yourself by reading *Animal Liberation*, while being alert for the possibility of a biased presentation.

Style and Tone

Writers aim their work at particular audiences and adjust the content and style accordingly. A children's book about kindness to animals would be an unsuitable candidate for inclusion in a research paper; both style and content would be too simplified to be taken seriously. At the other extreme, technical papers in the sciences and social sciences are often written in a dense style, with a vocabulary incomprehensible to someone outside the discipline; essentially, one academic is writing for an audience of peers. You would probably want to avoid reading—and citing—a journal article that focuses on the methodology for a survey of animal rights activists or analyzes the chemical basis of nutrients needed in a vegetarian diet.

Nonfiction books are often categorized as:

Popular: intended to attract the widest possible audience and, therefore, be accessible to people with a wide range of educational backgrounds. A popular treatment of a serious subject is likely to emphasize colorful detail and stories rather than abstract, complex ideas.

General interest: intended for an audience that is interested in a subject but has no special grounding in it. General interest books provide a thorough introduction, with some level of complexity, but without a lot of technical description.

Academic: intended for a limited audience in the field. An academic book is usually published by a university press and contains a level of scholarship and depth of analysis that might well be beyond the comprehension of the general public.

As a rule, you would do well to include some general-interest books and some purely academic books—at the more accessible end of the academic spectrum—in your preliminary bibliography.

To determine whether a book is appropriate and potentially useful for your research, look at the *table of contents*, the *introduction*, and a *sample* from a middle chapter that will give you a sense of style and tone. Also check the *index* to see how often your topic appears. Does the book have a *bibliography*? Footnotes or other documentation to make it academically credible?

Periodicals also serve a wide range of readers. Most have a marketing "niche," appealing to a specific audience with well-defined interests and reading habits. Since readership varies so greatly, articles on the same subject in two different periodicals are likely to differ widely in their content, point of view, and presentation. A newsmagazine like *Time* or *Newsweek* might provide factual information on an animal rights demonstration; the article would be short and lively, filled with concrete illustrations and quotations. It would not have the same purpose, nor cite the same kinds of evidence, nor use the same vocabulary as a longer article on the animal rights movement in a general-interest periodical like *Psychology Today*. And that, in turn, would have little in common with an essay in a scholarly journal on the moral basis of the contractarian argument supporting the rights of animals. Researchers must allow for this wide variation in style and tone when they select and use their sources.

Articles in social science journals tend to follow a conventional structure and use professional terminology that can sometimes seem like jargon. At the beginning of such articles, you're likely to find a *"review of the literature"*: a summary of the contributions that other sociologists or psychologists have made to an understanding of the topic. Here's a typical paragraph taken from "Social Work and Speciesism," an article by David B. Wolf in the journal *Social Work*:

> There are many connections between our treatment of animals and environmental integrity; these touch on issues such as hunger, poverty, and war. Toffler (1975) suggested that the most practical hope for resolving the world's food crisis is a restriction of beef eating that will save billions of tons of grain. Ehrlich and Ehrlich (1972) reported that production of a pound of meat requires 40 to 100 times as much water as the production of a pound of wheat. Altschul (1964) noted that in terms of calorie units per acre, a diet of grains, vegetables, and beans will support 20 times as many people as a diet of meat. . . .

In effect, Wolf is summarizing the evidence of his sources in the topic sentence and then citing them, one by one. This pattern of presentation should not be imitated in an essay written for a basic writing course, *nor is it usually a good idea to include such a "review of the literature" as a source within your essay.* You would be quoting or paraphrasing Wolf, who is paraphrasing Toffler or Altschul.

Better to eliminate the middleman (Wolf) and go directly to the source (Altschul or Toffler).

You can often decide to dismiss or pursue an article just by considering the title of the periodical. In a ProQuest search for journal articles on "animal rights," the results list included periodicals ranging from *Chemical and Engineering News* to *Poultry World* to *Transport Topics* to *Vegetarian Times*. It's highly unlikely that articles in any of those four periodicals would be suitable for a research essay on "animal rights." What about *Gender and Society*? If you're especially interested in gender issues and wonder whether activism on behalf of animals may be gender-specific, that might be an excellent article to review for your preliminary bibliography. *Animal Law*? That depends on the technical level of the article. You'd have to see it to decide whether the issues are presented in accessible language or in professional "legalese." *Audubon*? Here, again, the issue is audience. Is the article intended to appeal to a limited group of nature lovers, or is its content intended for a broader audience?

The style and tone of a book or article should be appropriate for your level of research.

If you find a source too erudite, then you'll have difficulty understanding it and presenting it to your readers. If you find that a source is written in a superficial, frivolous, or overly emotional style, then it's not serious or authoritative enough to include in your essay.

Style and Tone: Peter Singer: In the case of Singer's *Animal Liberation*, you've already found out from the *Contemporary Authors* summary that his style is regarded as accessible; according to one reviewer, it was "intended for the mass market." Something can also be learned about the style and tone of a book just by considering the *publisher*. Most of Singer's books come from Oxford University Press or Cambridge University Press, but *Animal Liberation* was published by Random House, a "general interest" company eager to sell books to the general public. Finally, you open the book to a chapter that particularly interests you and glance at a few sentences:

> Becoming a vegetarian is not merely a symbolic gesture. Nor is it an attempt to isolate oneself from the ugly realities of the world, to keep oneself pure and so without responsibility for the cruelty and carnage all around. Becoming a vegetarian is the most practical and effective step one can take toward ending both the killing of nonhuman animals and the infliction of suffering upon them.

The language is clear; the sentences compelling. You hope that Singer will at some point present the arguments of the nonvegetarian and realize that, if he does not, it will be your job to find the appropriate sources and do so.

Currency

One further indication of a work's usefulness for your purpose is its *date*. Only in the last few years has animal rights emerged as an issue of international importance. As a rule, in the sciences and social sciences, the most recent sources usually replace earlier ones. Unless you're interested in writing a historical review of attitudes toward animals, your research would probably focus on representative works published over the last 10 or 20 years. An article about vegetarianism as practiced in the 1930s would probably be of little value to you. On the other hand, Singer's 1975 *Animal Liberation* is now regarded as a seminal work—a key influence on later writers about animal rights—and would therefore not lose currency.

For research on historical and biographical topics, you need to know the difference between *primary* and *secondary* sources.

> *A primary source is a work that is itself the subject of your essay or (if you are writing a historical research essay) a work written during the period that you are writing about that gives you direct or primary knowledge of that period.*

"Primary source" is frequently used to describe an original document—such as the Constitution—or memoirs and diaries of historical interest, or a work of literature that, over the years, has been the subject of much written commentary. Your interview or survey notes are primary sources.

> *A secondary source can be any commentary written both after and about the primary source.*

A history textbook is usually a secondary source. So are most biographies. While you generally study a primary source for its own sake, the secondary source is important—often, it only exists—because of its primary source:

- If you are asked to write an essay about *Huckleberry Finn*, and your instructor tells you not to use any secondary sources, you are to read only Mark Twain's novel and not consult any commentaries.
- T. E. Lawrence's *Seven Pillars of Wisdom* is a secondary source if you are interested in guerrilla warfare, but a primary source if you are studying Lawrence.
- If you read the *New York Times* to acquire information about Lawrence's desert campaign in World War I, you are using the newspaper as a primary source since it was written during the period you are studying. But when you look up a *Times* movie review of *Lawrence of Arabia*, then you are locating a secondary source in order to learn more about your primary subject.

Currency is not always essential for research about historical and biographical subjects, which usually includes primary sources. Even out-of-date secondary sources can be occasionally useful. Lowell Thomas's 1924 biography of T. E. Lawrence is still of moderate interest in part because Thomas was present during the desert campaigns and could provide firsthand (although not necessarily unbiased) information. Nevertheless, because research is always unearthing new facts about people's lives, Thomas's work has long been superseded by new biographies providing a broader range of information. *For a biographical or historical essay, you should consult some primary sources, one or two secondary sources written at the time of the event or during the subject's lifetime, and the most recent and reliable secondary sources.* It is the sources in the middle — written a few years after your target date, without the perspective of distance — that often lack authenticity or objectivity.

Evaluating books and articles shouldn't dominate your research process. If you're building a preliminary bibliography of 10–15 sources and you're writing an essay in which you anticipate that no single source will be emphasized, don't waste time looking up every author. On the other hand, if you're likely to be working with only a few key sources, invest some time in finding out about these authors and their qualifications.

Evaluating Web Sources

Checking the credibility of *print sources* — books and periodical articles — can strengthen your research. It is useful to do so, but not always essential. Evaluating the reliability of *Web sources* can be crucial to the quality of your essay. It should become a routine part of your research practice.

You need to evaluate Web sources for two reasons:

- *An overabundance of information.* The profusion of material on the Web far exceeds the number of available print articles and books. What do you do when the keyword "animal rights" in a Yahoo! search produces 681,000 Web sites? First, you refine your search; next, you evaluate what's left and decide which sites are worth examining.

- *An absence of editorial or peer review.* When a book or article is submitted for print publication, editors or specialist reviewers judge its quality, accuracy, and timeliness, based on their knowledge of comparable material. If the work is published, the reader can assume that it meets reasonably high standards. There is no comparable process for reviewing most material appearing on the Web. No one at Google or Yahoo! or Bing is charged with making choices or maintaining standards. Each of the 681,000 Web sites on animal rights is presented as equal to the rest. Even search engines that claim to rank responses do not actually do so in a meaningful way. The basis for ranking—if any—tends to be commercial, not intellectual.

Here are a few ways to avoid the quagmire of endless results lists:

1. Start your search with *academic* databases that include Web material. When a college library or academic organization compiles or endorses a database, the contents are likely to have some claim to reliability. That is by no means true of databases that are compiled randomly or those that accept payment from sites in return for inclusion at the top of search engine lists.

2. If, initially, you don't know which databases are academic or if your access is limited to general search engines, that's all the more reason to narrow down your topic with an *advanced Boolean search.*

3. Scan the search engine's results list looking for Web sites sponsored by *academic institutions or government agencies*, and access them first.

4. One or two reliable, comprehensive sites can lead you, via hyperlinks, to the best material about your subject on the Web. For example, one of the links in the 681,000-hit Yahoo! search on animal rights led to a Google Directory that, in turn, listed four sites, all sponsored by government or academic institutes, which serve as clearinghouses for Web sites about animal rights. One, from the University of British Columbia, provides 32 links to relevant and credible sites, some of which are appropriate for a college-level essay.

Since the Web is still a new medium, with very few rules or standard procedures, evaluating Web sites can be a hit-or-miss process. But the categories are the same as those for evaluating works in print: credentials, impartiality, style and tone, and currency.

Credentials

With print sources, the material's credibility greatly depends on the author's *qualifications.* With Web sources, credibility is linked to the knowledgeability and seriousness of the *individual* or the disinterested commitment of the *organization* that originated and maintains the site. If the name of an individual appears on the site as owner, then you must try to assess that person's background and credentials and determine his or her likely credibility in your area of research:

- Does the site contain a link to the owner's home page?
- Is there a section of the site specifically about the owner (often called "About Me")?

- What else has the owner published?
- Does he appear in other writers' bibliographies?
- Has she any professional experience in a discipline appropriate to this subject?

Often, you'll find no single person taking responsibility for the site. Instead, there will be a *sponsoring organization*, which will probably include an "About Us" section, describing the group's collective purpose or "mission." If there's no "About" link, then it may be possible to do a Web search for more information about the sponsor:

- Is the organization commercial or nonprofit? (The "com" and "org" in the URL used to distinguish between the two, but that's no longer the rule.)
- What's the reason for creating a site about this topic?
- Is there a political or cultural agenda?
- If the sponsor is commercial, what's the motive for expending resources on this Web site?

A second element to look for is *documentation*. Appropriate documentation tells you that the author or sponsor understands the basic requirements for presenting academic scholarship; seeing bibliographical references or endnotes gives you some assurance that the information contained in the site comes from reliable sources. Documentation found in Web pages may consist of hyperlinks to other Web sources; you will want to click on some of these, to evaluate the quality of the linked sources and perhaps add them to your bibliography.

Impartiality

You should keep in mind that people and organizations usually create Web sites not to provide a fair, well-balanced account of an issue, but to sell something: a product, a cause, a point of view, a lifestyle. Bias isn't to be avoided on the Web; it's considered a legitimate basis for self-presentation. So you do have to scrutinize and evaluate what you find.

As you begin to read a Web page, consider the *nature of the content*. Is it purely personal opinion? Is it self-serving? Is it advocacy? commercial? ideological? academic? Does the owner apparently have an ax to grind? Does the site present fact or opinion? Or does it present opinion as fact? Are you the target of propaganda for a cause or advertising for a product? Can you tell the difference between the site of a pet food company with a feature on animal welfare, that of an advocacy group organizing a rally against cruelty to animals, and that of a university veterinary department publishing a report on the use of animals in experiments?

Whatever the degree of bias, worthwhile Web material should provide reasonable support for its assertions. As you begin to read, consider the following:

- Does the site have a discernible thesis or point, or was it put on the Web purely to indulge the owner's desire for self-revelation?
- Is there a clear context established for the material?
- Does the author make an initial statement of intention, purpose, and scope?

Many sites are the spatial equivalent of a soundbite. Their authors don't engage in complex analysis and argument:

- Is there supporting evidence?
- Is there a logical sequence of ideas or just a series of claims?
- Is there a convincing level of fact and detail?
- Does the author anticipate and deal with potential objections to opinions?
- Is the evidence mostly anecdotal, depending on stories ("It happened to me")?
- Are examples and anecdotes relevant to the topic?

You needn't automatically exclude poorly supported or one-sided Web material (or print sources) from your bibliography. Instead, make yourself aware of the flaws in your sources and, if you choose to include them in your essay, compensate for their deficiencies by adding stronger or complementary sources so that your essay will become better balanced and better supported.

Style and Tone

In a freewheeling medium like the Web, there are few rules about *style* or *tone*. Many sites, particularly home pages developed by individual owners, or blogs, which serve as personal journals, will be presented informally, as if the writer were delivering a monologue or holding a one-sided conversation. This lack of balance or purpose should raise some doubts as soon as you click on and start reading the site:

- Is the material *clearly focused* and *coherent*?
- Is the *tone* dispassionate, or conversational, or hysterical?
- Is the *language* inflammatory? Frivolous? Is it full of superlatives?
- Is the *argument* presented in neutral language, or are there innuendoes about those holding opposing views?
- Does the writer follow the basic rules of *grammar*?

- Can the material be *summarized* or *paraphrased*? Be particularly wary with blogs, as the uncredentialed blogger is likely to post self-indulgent, opinionated entries.

As with print material, it is helpful to consider the intended *audience*. Web sites frequently target niche audiences. What sort of user does a specific Web page hope to attract?

- Is the site intended for the general public? Then the content may be worth your consideration.
- Is it aimed at juveniles? If so, the approach and style are probably too simplistic to be useful for an academic essay.
- Does the author assume that the reader shares a common religious background or political assumptions? A reader unfamiliar with these beliefs or causes may find the contents hard to understand or accept.
- Is the sponsor a local group that's appealing to a grassroots audience? The site's purpose and level of detail may be so narrow that it is likely to interest only those who live in that area.

The *appearance of the site* itself can help you to evaluate the content:

- Is there any logic to its construction? Is it well designed? Easy to use? Or is it sprawling and hard to follow?
- Does it have a plan or method of organization? If it's a large site, are there links—on the home page and elsewhere—that enable you to go directly to pages that interest you?
- Are additions and updates integrated into existing material, or left dangling at the end?
- Are there graphics? Do they help your understanding of the site, or do they distract you?

Currency

In print sources, currency is estimated in *decades*; in Web sources, it's often a matter of *months or even days*. If you don't download or print material quickly, you may not have access to that information when you actually need it. The site may have disappeared from the Web.

Other sites will linger on even when they have lost their currency. The owners are no longer taking responsibility for regular maintenance and updating. If the subject of your essay is a current issue and you need to find and use up-to-the-minute sources, you should be very careful to *check the date at the end of each Web site*. And, whatever the subject, you should note the date of the site's last update to include a complete reference to the site in your bibliography.

Evaluating Sources

	Books	Periodicals	Web sites
Credentials	■ Appropriate specialization for your topic ■ Appropriate and sufficient educational background ■ Includes credible documentation	■ Appropriate specialization for your topic ■ Appropriate and sufficient educational background ■ Includes credible documentation, appropriate for its length	■ Appropriate specialization for your topic ■ Indication of relevant experience and recognition by others in the field ■ Evidence of some acceptable documentation
Impartiality	■ Absence of dogmatic or biased tone ■ Willingness to consider other points of view	■ Absence of dogmatic or biased tone ■ Willingness to consider other points of view	■ Serious intention ■ Bias kept within reasonable limits ■ Opinion distinguished from fact ■ Hidden agendas at a minimum ■ Evidence of reasoned argument
Style and Tone	■ Written for a general-interest or academic audience ■ If academic, written in an accessible style	■ Periodical intended for a reasonably broad audience ■ Style and tone consistent with other periodicals (and books) in your bibliography ■ Language accessible to someone outside that field of specialization	■ Coherent, calm, even-handed, open-minded, purposeful
Currency	■ If appropriate to your topic, bibliography should include primary and secondary sources ■ Bibliography should contain the most recent research about your topic	■ Unless your topic requires you to include primary sources, recent articles should dominate your periodicals list	■ Available for a reasonable length of time ■ Maintained and updated

Evaluating Web Sources about Animal Rights

To demonstrate some of these evaluative criteria, let's look at a few of the hundreds of Web sites found in Google and Clusty searches using the keywords "animal rights." As usual, the results list includes several *commercial* sites selling products totally unrelated to the subject of the search. Most of the others are sponsored by organizations or individuals actively advocating the cause of equal rights for animals and urging the public to join in protesting various instances of "speciesism." Such sites are typically crammed with news stories about animal exploitation; links to like-minded organizations; offers for products and services (often supporting vegetarianism); and invitations to participate in online discussions, attend rallies and events, and register for membership—often requiring fees or contributions—in the common cause. The range of links on one site includes "The Joy of Adopting an Older Animal," "Featured Shelter of the Month," "Ways to Help Animals without Leaving Your Computer," "Dogs in Heaven," and "Tiny Tim—a Kitten's Story."

Sites Sponsored by Organizations

The home page of www.all-creatures.org is typical. Crowded with lists and choices, the site is busy and difficult to navigate. The links and options are all intended to educate the reader about the plight of animals and encourage participation in their defense. On the home page, pictures of animals compete for space with lists of "action alerts" and campaigns, an "Animal Exploitation Photo Journal," and a blog by the Joyful Curmudgeon. Various news items have been selected to inspire, inform, and touch the hearts of site visitors.

Similarly, www.animalrightsstand.com (Figure 8-1) welcomes you and invites you to action through "Critter Trivia," in which we learn that Sir Isaac Newton, discoverer of gravity, also invented the cat door, and "Animal Humor," which features a joke about a dancing canine. These sites seem aimed at an intellectually unsophisticated audience who, the sponsors hope, will be moved to action by the pathos and force of these human-interest stories. Although some of the links are useful, most of the information on the majority of these sites is not appropriate for research into the issues surrounding animal rights.

As a medium of communication, the Web serves as an international pulpit for anyone with a cause. Yet the strength of sites like www.all-creatures.org and www.animalrightsstand.com lies in their ability to project a strong sense of community, often reinforced by an emphasis on *local interests*. You're invited to join campaigns and be kept informed about the activities wherever you live. A typical local site will provide details of fund-raising bake sales and vegan potluck suppers. Sites like these, while admirable as grassroots operations, are little more than a distraction for researchers looking for more broadly based information.

Figure 8-1 Animal Rights Stand Web site

Animal rights is a provocative topic that lends itself to a hard sell and offers no amnesty to opposing views. For example, www.animalrightsstand.com sells a T-shirt with a slogan that offers two options: "Be kind to animals" or "Burn in hell."

Very few sites dealing with this topic take a more neutral stance. What varies is the tone in which the propaganda is presented. Consider, for example, the content and presentation of the Americans for Medical Progress (AMP) Web site (Figure 8-2). The "About AMP" page contains a small picture of an appealing white mouse on the masthead. Prominently featured is a straight-forward statement about the organization and its purpose: to "protect society's investment in research by nurturing public understanding of and support for the humane, necessary, and valuable use of animals in medicine . . . to foster a balanced public debate on the animal research issue, ensuring that among the voices heard are those whose lives have been touched by research . . . [to distribute] timely and relevant news, information and analysis about animal rights extremism. . . ." There are links to press releases and studies describing the breakthroughs that have resulted from animal research, as well as to government documents such as the "Public Health Service Policy on Human Care and Use of Animals." Consistent with its mission to inform both researchers and the general public, the site's content has a temperate and accommodating tone.

Figure 8-2 Americans for Medical Progress Web site

Nevertheless, AMP doesn't rely entirely on an appeal to reason and social conscience. It has a cause to advocate, and it does so by motivating its audience to support that cause financially—by seeking donations—and emotionally—by inviting everyone to "let the world hear your story." Among the "resources" provided is a group of posters featuring endearing children and contented animals.

Although the AMP site includes a section on how to become an active advocate for animal research, it avoids the abstract question of whether violent actions are appropriate in defense of animal rights. (Some pro animal-rights sites express fewer doubts.) If you intend to make this issue the focus of your research, you might gain some helpful material by clicking on the links provided on the AMP site—as long as you remain aware of the underlying bias and make an effort to balance your presentation.

It's reassuring that, according to the "About AMP" page, the sponsoring organization provides an address and phone number at the bottom of the home page (many sites do not). The site's credibility is enhanced by a listing of the Board of Directors that includes some Nobel laureates; but there are also several representatives of the pharmaceutical industry, which stands to benefit a great deal from continuing to use animals in developing new drugs. On balance, this is a site that merits some cautious exploration.

Sites Owned by Individuals

Some Web sites fail to identify any author, owner, or sponsor; others do so unconvincingly. Brian Carnell at www.animalrights.net is sparing in his biographical description: "I think this is where I'm supposed to go on about the boring details of who I am etc. Just suffice to say I'm an extreme geek, compulsive writer, insomniac and general pain-in-the-ass-know-it-all."

In contrast, Chris MacDonald, who prepared a list of links for the W. Maurice Young Center for Applied Ethics, offers a two-page biography (plus picture) that includes his academic qualifications, professional experience, research, and Web sites. It's significant that the Center for Applied Ethics is affiliated with the University of British Columbia. On the other hand, the WWW Virtual Library, which provides a long list of links on animal welfare, is described as "the oldest catalog of the Web . . . run by a loose confederation of volunteers" who develop Web sites in their particular areas of expertise. The description includes an offer to anyone who's interested to prepare a site for the Virtual Library—no credentials requested or apparently required. It's this casual approach to competency that makes research on the Web so risky.

Balancing Your Sources

It takes time and patience to evaluate Web sources. You have to inspect each site to make sure it's reliable before considering it for your preliminary bibliography. Is it authoritative? Is it at an appropriate level? Will it make a contribution to your essay? And however carefully you select Web sources, your research can't stop there.

If you want your essay to be successful and receive a commensurate grade, don't get all or even most of your sources from the Internet.

Many important authors still publish their work only in traditional print forms. If you don't include these sources in your research, your essay will lack balance and completeness.

How will your instructor realize that your research is exclusively from the Web? In "How the Web Destroys the Quality of Students' Research Papers," Professor David Rothenberg says that "it's easy to spot a research paper that is based primarily on information collected from the Web," partly because no books are included in the bibliography. Most disturbing to Professor Rothenberg is the mindlessness of the Web research process:

You toss a query to the machine, wait a few minutes, and suddenly a lot of possible sources of information appear on your screen. Instead of books that you have to check out of the library, read carefully, understand, synthesize and then tactfully excerpt, these sources are quips, blips, pictures, and short summaries that may be downloaded magically to the dorm-room computer screen. Fabulous! How simple! The only problem is that a paper consisting of summaries of summaries is bound to be fragmented and superficial, and to demonstrate more of a random montage than an ability to sustain an argument through 10 to 15 double-spaced pages.

There are no shortcuts to thorough research. Use the Internet as you would use any tool available to you, but try to resist its facile charms.

Integrating Sources

So far, we've been looking at ways to evaluate sources one by one, making sure that each is worth including in your research. But sources won't appear in your essay one at a time. They must work well together. They must be *compatible.*

Authors write for different audiences. Their work varies in tone, in style, in level of detail. As we've seen, the sources that you find on the Web or in the library may have nothing at all in common but their subject. Before you can decide which ones belong together in your essay, you need to be able to describe them. As you glance through a book, or an article, or Web material, ask yourself:

- Does the *content* seem primarily theoretical or practical?
- How often does the author offer *concrete evidence* to support conclusions? What kind of evidence? Facts? Examples? Anecdotes? Documentation?
- Does the author's *thesis* depend on a series of broad propositions, logically linked together?
- What is the *scope* of the work? Does it include many aspects of your broad subject, or does it focus on one?
- How abstract or technical is the *language*? Do you have difficulty understanding the sentences or following the argument?

In the end, the sources that you include in your essay should be at roughly the same *level of difficulty.* This does not mean that they should be identical: the same range of ideas, the same length, the same style and depth of evidence. But it does mean you should be able to move from one to the other easily as you write about them; you should be able to integrate them into your own approach to the subject.

Integrating Sources on Animal Rights

Here are descriptions and excerpts from three different sources—all books—dealing with the subject of animal rights:

1. This book is an extended consideration of the arguments for and against strict enforcement of animal rights that relies heavily on philosophical abstractions to make its points; the author supports the use of animals in medical experiments.

> A number of authors [have] contributed to an image of humans as the great despoilers, the beings who are always out of place and can do nothing right in the natural world. Some paint an idyllic and completely unrealistic picture of pristine, peaceful nature, beyond our blundering rapacious hands. Others exclaim despairingly that the world would be a better place without humans. . . . What these ideas have in common is a nostalgia for simpler times and a veiled lament for a lost Edenic paradise. In fact, guilt and the need for repentance through self-punishment pervade much contemporary writing on the environment and our relationship to animals. The fable of the Fall of Man has now acquired a secular guise, and a group of righteous pop environmental philosophers and animal liberationists are the new self-appointed apostles of redemption.
>
> MICHAEL ALLEN FOX, from *The Case for Animal Experimentation: An Evolutionary and Ethical Perspective*

Fox is notably abstract. He hardly touches on the issues of animal exploitation but rather tries to interpret the significance of this growing impulse to identify with the more natural environment represented by animals.

2. The second book recounts the history of the animal-rights movement, taking a neutral stance. The authors rely on concrete evidence to demonstrate that animal-rights campaigners are often the products of their culture.

> The meat and food industry has inadvertently contributed to the anthropomorphic intuitions that drive animal protection demands. At least since Charlie the Tuna, food commercials have thoroughly personified their own products. In one commercial, two anthropomorphic cows shoot at a Lea and Perrins bottle, "the steak sauce only a cow could hate." The only speaking parts in an ad for Roy Rogers' chicken club sandwich belong to two fast-talking goldfish. Talking chickens, fish, and other animals seem clever, but they also remind sensitive viewers of the origins of their food.
>
> JAMES M. JASPER and DOROTHY NELKIN, from *The Animal Rights Crusade: The Growth of a Moral Protest*

Jasper and Nelkin are more concerned with practical cause and effect: advertising strategies portraying animals as if they were human have encouraged people to identify with the animal rights movement. It's easy to follow the examples of Charlie the Tuna and the Roy Rogers goldfish.

3. The third book is a sociological study of animal-rights activists and their motivations. The text relies heavily on interview transcripts.

> A quietly spoken public servant, Rhett decided some years ago to take the step to animal rights activism. He claims it was the inconsistency in our treatment of animals that was the catalyst for his activism and the cause of some tension in his personal relationships:

> > But I can tell you that when I was a child, I was presented with an inconsistency which always stuck in my mind. And that was that my father would never eat fowl, and at Christmas time he would always have a chop or something like that. And the reason was that when he was a child, his father brought home some chickens. The kids had made pets of them, and then they were served up for Christmas dinner. He was so upset that he refused to participate in the killing of chooks [young birds]. . . . This was when I was quite young, and I could see that he was being inconsistent, but I'm grateful for the inconsistency because if I hadn't had that example of someone who was sensitive, I mean, who knows? It might have taken me ten more years or something. I don't know.

> > LYLE MUNRO, from *Compassionate Beasts:*
> > *The Quest for Animal Rights*

Rhett's personal experiences are of a very different order. He doesn't have a thesis to prove; he doesn't provide you with a topic sentence that shows you where this excerpt might be placed in your essay. It's up to you to interpret his musings and determine how—or whether—they fit in with the other sources.

Can these three sources be integrated into the same essay? They aren't equivalent; in many ways, they aren't even similar. But each is relevant and interesting in its own way. What you *don't* want to do is to plunk down excerpts from these three sources side by side, in adjoining sentences. Remember that your sources are your evidence. So, how you use these three sources depends on the kind of essay you intend to write. They serve to illustrate *your* ideas, your understanding of the issues involved in the animal-rights movement.

Is your thesis abstract? If you intend to emphasize the political and philosophical premises underlying this issue—do animals have the same rights that humans do?—then you'll focus your attention on Fox's book, summarizing his arguments and, in the process, figuring out what you really believe. In this way, you determine your research priorities. As you develop your thesis, you'll go on to read other books like Fox's and find many of the same ideas with new arguments and new conclusions. You'll notice that authors writing on this abstract level tend to be familiar with each other's theories and argue with each other on paper. The same names will appear again and again. Your essay will become one more voice in an ongoing dialogue.

Is your thesis more practical? You might be more interested in the relatively rapid emergence of this movement. Why has animal rights become such a hot issue? Is it our affluence that enables us to express concern about the plight of animals? Is it our increasing urbanization? Or is it the absence of other compelling causes? This thesis would be more "popular" in its approach to the subject and would not emphasize theoretical, abstract sources. That doesn't diminish its value: a popularization is a simplification of a difficult subject. In a sense, a college research essay has to be "popular" since it serves as evidence of a student's understanding of the subject, not as a contribution to scholarly knowledge. Your thesis would be supported by *secondary sources* like Jasper and Nelkin or by *primary sources* like the evidence of activists like Rhett.

Are your thesis and approach appropriate to the level of your course? In an introductory course, you are expected only to grasp the fundamental concepts that are basic to the discipline, so your instructor will probably not want you to go out of your depth in hunting scholarly sources for your essay. In an advanced course, you are preparing to do your own research; so you need to demonstrate your understanding of the work of others as well as the methods that are commonly used in that field. In an advanced course, the popular approach can be regarded as superficial.

Are your sources appropriate to your level of understanding? You should include in your bibliography only sources that you yourself understand. If you come across a difficult source that seems too important to leave out, do consult your instructor, or a librarian, or the staff of the writing center on your campus. But never cite sources whose writing makes no sense to you, no matter how eminent and qualified these authorities may be.

Are your sources appropriate to the assigned length of your essay? If you're writing fewer than ten pages, you would be wise to limit your sources to those that blend well together because they are of the same order of difficulty. The writers don't have to agree with each other, but their scope and approach should be roughly equivalent. A longer essay of ten pages or more provides an opportunity for more leisurely development, and you can position different kinds of sources in different parts of the essay, each where it will have the most convincing effect.

There is actually a common theme that runs through the three excerpts from books on animal rights. Fox writes about our generalized feelings of guilt for having plundered our natural heritage; Jasper and Nelkin imply that our anthropomorphic identification with cartoon animals has made us into guilty vegetarians; and Munro's Rhett describes his father's ambivalence about eating chicken, which brings him close to guilt by association. All three excerpts support the following paragraph, which analyzes one of the more complex motiva-

tions underlying the animal rights movement. (Note that the sources are documented using MLA style; this process of documentation will be explained in
Chapter 10.)

> Animal-rights activists pursue their cause with great passion and intensity,
> as if the fate of the Earth depended on the success of their mission. They
> seem to be trying to compensate for or even undo all the harm that man
> has done to the natural environment and particularly to its living crea-
> tures. In Michael Allen Fox's view, their yearning to return to the Garden of
> Eden is linked to a sense of guilt and a compulsion to atone for our cul-
> ture's crimes against nature. He refers, somewhat contemptuously, to a
> "nostalgia for simpler times" that seems unrealistic and sentimental (20).
> Fox seems to be saying that we wallow too easily in a kind of Disneyland
> view of animals. James M. Jasper and Dorothy Nelkin support that view
> when they describe the anthropomorphic world of commercials in which
> Charlie the Tuna and the Roy Rogers goldfish become our friends (149). It's
> also easy to read that kind of sentimentality into the personal experience
> of Rhett, an animal-rights activist, whose father never got over the guilt of
> eating the chickens that had been his pets (Munro 95).

You will have noticed that this paragraph is essentially *negative* about the
animal-rights movement, reflecting Fox's bias. (Indeed, the paragraph relies
heavily on Fox's ideas, which makes sense since he offers more of them than the
other authors do.) Depending on your chosen thesis, you could build on the implication that animal rights is little more than sentimental claptrap; or you
could rebut Fox's point, arguing that Rhett and his father are displaying an admirable sensitivity to the needs of living creatures. Where you take these ideas
is up to you; it's your essay.

Choosing Sources

As you choose sources for your essay, consider the following:

- the scope of the work and the extent to which it deals with your topic;
- the depth of detail, the amount and kind of evidence presented, the documentation of sources, and the level of analysis and theory;
- the degree to which you understand and feel comfortable with the author's language and style; and
- the way in which possible sources could be used together in your essay.

EXERCISE 28: Evaluating Internet Sources

The following passages have been excerpted from the first few pages of Web sites found in an advanced Google search using the keywords "Battle of Wounded Knee" NOT "1973." (The search was focused on the 1890 battle, rather than the demonstration that took place at the same site in 1973.) The purpose of the search was to compile a *preliminary bibliography* for an essay examining the extent to which the U.S. government carried out an aggressive policy of extermination against Native Americans in the nineteenth century. The Web material in this exercise was not chosen at random but represents some of the typical noncommercial sites found in the search. The excerpts have not been edited.

A.   Read through the eight passages.

B.   Making allowances for repetition, examine the way in which each writer presents information about the Battle of Wounded Knee, paying special attention to tone and style. Consider the probable audience for which each site was intended.

C.   Then decide which sites you would read through to the end and which ones, if any, you would be likely to include in a preliminary bibliography for a 10- to 12-page essay assigned in an introductory-level course.

1.   After Sitting Bull's death, Big Foot feared for the safety of his band, which consisted in large part of widows of the Plains wars and their children. Big Foot himself had been placed on the list of "fomenters of disturbances," and his arrest had been ordered. He led his band toward Pine Ridge, hoping for the protection of Red Cloud. However, he fell ill from pneumonia on the trip and was forced to travel in the back of a wagon. As they neared Porcupine Creek on December 28, the band saw four troops of cavalry approaching. A white flag was immediately run up over Big Foot's wagon. When the two groups met, Big Foot raised up from his bed of blankets to greet Major Samuel Whitside of the Seventh Cavalry. His blankets were stained with blood and blood dripped from his nose as he spoke.

Whitside informed him of his orders to take the band to their camp on Wounded Knee Creek. Big Foot replied that they were going that way, to Pine Ridge. The major wanted to disarm the Indians right then but was dissuaded by his scout John Shangreau, in order to avoid a fight on the spot. They agreed to wait to undertake this until they reached camp. Then, in a moment of sympathy, the major ordered his army ambulance brought forward to accept the ill Minneconjou chief, providing a warmer and more comfortable ride. They then proceeded toward the camp at Wounded Knee Creek, led by two cavalry troops with the other two troops bringing up the rear with their Hotchkiss guns. They reached the camp at twilight.

2.   The events at Wounded Knee (South Dakota) on December 29, 1890, cannot be understood unless the previous 400 years of European occupation of the *New*

World are taken into consideration. As Dee Brown has pointed out in *Bury My Heart at Wounded Knee* (pp. 1–2):

> "'So tractable, so peaceable, are these people,' Columbus wrote to the King and Queen of Spain [referring to the Tainos on the island of San Salvador, so was named by Columbus], 'that I swear to your Majesties there is not in the world a better nation. They love their neighbors as themselves, and their discourse is ever sweet and gentle, and accompanied with a smile; and though it is true that they are naked, yet their manners are decorous and praiseworthy.'
>
> "All this, of course, was taken as a sign of weakness, if not heathenism, and Columbus being a righteous European was convinced the people should be 'made to work, sow and do all that is necessary and to *adopt our ways.*' Over the next four centuries (1492–1890) several million Europeans and their descendants undertook to enforce their ways upon the people of the New World."

Many accounts (from both sides: US Army and Lakota) of this shameful episode exist, and many of those can be found on the Internet. The following is a brief, edited description (from *The Great Chiefs* volume of Time-Life's *The Old West* series) of events. Links to further resources and descriptions follow.

3. Wounded Knee, A Wound That Won't Heal Did the Army Attempt to Coverup the Massacre of Prisoners of War?

   Historical reference material from:
   The Official Bulletin National Indian War Veterans U.S.A. Section One, Section Two, Section Three and Section Four.
   The Medals of Wounded Knee
   Medals of dis-Honor
   . . . more Medals of dis-Honor
   Medals of dis-Honor Campaign

   An email campaign has been initiated so as to force the U.S. Government to rescind the twenty medals of dis-Honor awarded participants in the Massacre at Wounded Knee. Your help is solicited . . . an input form is provided for your convenience

   Lieutenant Bascom Gets His Due

   Rescindment Petition Comments

   Senator McCain Responds to the Rescindment Petition

   My Response to McCain

   Wokiksuye Canpe Opi . . . a site dedicated to rescindment of the "medals of -dis-Honor."

4. Eyewitness to a Massacre

Philip Wells was a mixed-blood Sioux who served as an interpreter for the Army. He later recounted what he saw that Monday morning:

"I was interpreting for General Forsyth (*Forsyth was actually a colonel*) just before the battle of Wounded Knee, December 29, 1890. The captured Indians had been ordered to give up their arms, but Big Foot replied that his people had no arms. Forsyth said to me, 'Tell Big Foot he says the Indians have no arms, yet yesterday they were well armed when they surrendered. He is deceiving me. Tell him he need have no fear in giving up his arms, as I wish to treat him kindly.' Big Foot replied, 'They have no guns, except such as you have found.' Forsyth declared, 'You are lying to me in return for my kindness.'"

5. The round up of the Lakota was in response to the growing fear and ignorance on the part of the US Govt. The white people did not know about the culture, beliefs, or lives of the Lakota and saw them as a threat to the society they were trying to preserve: the white society. The Lakota were seen as outsiders; the "other" in a world where a person's looks and background determined who belonged here. Through much of American history, where a person was born also determined if they belonged. Ironically, the Native Americans were here on this land first, but were treated as though they were visitors. Their assumption was that because they look different or act different, they are not the same; they are not Americans. The white people refused to recognize the Lakota's right to the land and did everything in their power to remove them. This ignorance led to violence in an obvious act of proving power and control.

Col. James W. Forsyth ordered the Sioux people to be disarmed. A shot was fired and the fighting ensued. The federal troops fired on the Lakota with rifles and powerful, rapid-shooting Hotchkiss guns. Sioux casualties totaled 153 dead and 44 wounded, half of whom were unarmed women and children. Survivors were pursued and butchered by US troops. Cavalry losses totaled 25 dead and 39 wounded. Charges were brought against Col. Forsyth for his part in the bloodshed, but a court of inquiry exonerated him.

At the time, and continually after, people regarded the confrontation as a massacre. This terrible blow to the Lakota people proved to break down their strength in fighting back. To subsequent generations of Indians, it "symbolized the injustices and degradations inflicted on them by the US government" (Robert Utley). It later served as an inspiration for the 1973 occupation at Wounded Knee.

We must never forget this moment in US history of the horrific destruction of human life and liberty. For many, the picture of US history is filled with tales of brave rebels, fighting for a belief in equality, such as the ideals which started and founded the nation. However, not many recognize the hypocritical actions of the nation which went against this idea of equality. This is just another example

where the question of "Who belongs?" and "Who has a right to 'American' liberties?" is tested. The Lakota were never allowed a place in the nation, forced to
give up their land and suffered immensely in loss of lives and rights. The
Wounded Knee massacre serves as a reminder to a time when those people seen
as "foreigners" were exterminated and refused their rights as Americans.

6. No one knows what caused the disturbance, no one claims the first shot, the
Wounded Knee Massacre began fiercely with the Hotchkiss guns raining frag-
mentation shells into the village at a combined rate of 200 or more rounds
a minute. The 500 well armed Cavalry Troopers were well positioned using crossing fire to methodically carry out what is known as the Wounded Knee Massacre.

Almost immediately most of the Sioux Indian men were killed. A few Sioux Indians mustered enough strength barehanded to kill 29 soldiers and wound 39
more. The bravery of these people was to no avail for as long as an Indian moved,
the guns kept firing. Unarmed Sioux Indian Women and children were Merci-
lessly Massacred. A few ran as far as three miles only to be chased by the long
knives of the Cavalry and put to death.

Of the original 350 Indians one estimate stated that only 50 survived. Almost
all historical statistics report over 200 Indians being killed on that day but government figures only reported the Indian dead as 64 men, 44 women and girls,
and 18 babies. All of the bodies were buried in one communal grave.

If the Battle of the Little Big Horn had been the beginning of the end,
Wounded Knee was the finale for the Sioux Indians. This was the last major en-
gagement in American history between the Plains Indians and the U. S. Army.
Gone was the Indian dream, pride and spirit.

7. The James W. Forsyth Papers document the career of a nineteenth-century military officer in the American West and, in particular, his service in the Wounded
Knee campaign. The collection spans the dates 1865–1932, but the bulk of the
material falls in the period 1870–98.

The collection is arranged in six series with oversize material housed at the
end. Series I, Correspondence, contains letters to and from Forsyth arranged
chronologically with two letterpress copybooks of similar material. Series II,
Wounded Knee Papers, consists of printed papers and manuscripts documenting
the actions taken on December 29 and 30, 1891. Series III, Military Papers, contains documents by and about James W. Forsyth, his son-in-law, son, and other
military officers. Carte-de-visites and cabinet photographs collected by Forsyth
can be found in Series IV, Photographs. Series V, Forsyth Family Papers, consists
of a few items belonging to Forsyth's two daughters as well as personal papers of
James W. Forsyth. Series VI, Dennison Family Papers, contains financial receipts of
Governor William Dennison's family (James W. Forsyth's in-laws) and a book belonging to the governor.

8. "Sometimes dreams are wiser than waking," says Black Elk, Oglala Sioux Indian who took part in the Ghost Dance Religion during the late nineteenth century. The Wounded Knee epidemic took place in December 29, 1890 between the U.S. government and the Sioux Indians in South Dakota. Primarily, the outbreak occurred at Wounded Knee in part result of the growing support of the Ghost Dance Religion. Army leaders feared the religion would lead to an Indian uprising and called for troops to be sent to keep things under control. Thus, the hostilities that drug out between the U.S. government and the Sioux Indians in South Dakota are an important historical event that unfolded in U.S. western history. When reviewing the Wounded Knee battle, it is of utmost importance for various teachers who want to gain more knowledge of this epidemic that took place to fully understand insights about when, where, what, and why this battle occurred in 1890 in South Dakota. Furthermore, the Sioux Ghost Dance Religion played a crucial role in "triggering" the hostilities and events that lead up to the Wounded Knee battle.

First, before going into depth about the history of Wounded Knee Creek battle, it is important to understand the need for history. Why do we study and need to know history? Well, David E. Kyvig and Myron A. Marty believe history is an essential part of human development: We all need to know who we are, how we have become what we are, and how to cope with a variety of situations in order to conduct our own lives successfully. We also need to know what to expect from people and institutions around us. Organizations and communities require the same self understanding in order to function satisfactorily. For individuals and groups alike, experience produces a self-image and a basis for deciding how to behave, manage problems, and plan ahead. We remember sometimes accurately, sometimes not-what occurred, the causes of certain responses or changes, and learn reactions to different circumstances. These memories, positive and negative, help determine our actions.

EXERCISE 29: Choosing Internet Sources

The following list of sixteen Web sites has been compiled from searches using the keywords "TV Violence."

A. Assume that you are preparing a preliminary bibliography for an essay examining *the links between violence on television and violent crimes in American schools.*

B. Review the list of Web sites and choose those sites that you would definitely want to explore. Be prepared to give your reasons for including or excluding each site.

Your instructor may ask you to click on some or all of the sites before you do your ranking. If some sites are no longer being maintained, you may be asked to do a new search on the same topic, choosing a group of sites (preferably noncommercial) and indicating those that, in your opinion, seem relevant and reliable.

1. APA HelpCenter: Warning Signs of TV Violence

    www.apahelpcenter.org
    The American Psychological Association provides basic information to the nation's youth about warning signs of violent behavior, including violence in schools.

2. Children and Television Violence

    www. abelard.org/tv/tv.php
    Abelard's front page. Violence on television affects children negatively, according to psychological research. Last updated Dec. 17, 2009.

3. National Television Violence Study

    www.media-awareness.ca/english/resources/research_documents/ reports/violence/nat_tv_violence.cfm
    The National Television Violence Study 1996–97 contains recommendations of a large scientific study of television violence. Sponsored by the University of California at Santa Barbara.

4. TV and Film Violence

    www.cybercollege.com/violence.htm
    A brief report on the CyberCollege Internet Web site outlining the relationship between exposure to TV violence and acts of aggressiveness later in life. CyberCollege offers "free educational services." Last updated 2007.

5. The International Clearinghouse on Children, Youth & Media

    www.nordicom.gu.se/clearinghouse.php
    The Clearinghouse is to contribute to and effectivize knowledge on children, young people and media violence, seen in the perspective of the UN Convention on the Rights of the Child. Our prime task is to make new knowledge and data known to prospective users all over the world.

6. Children and Television Violence

    www.allsands.com/kids/childtelevision_twd_gn.htm
    An essay on television violence and children. No author or date. Allsands's articles are written by "professional journalists and experts."

7. Does TV Violence Harm Youth?

    http://wc.arizona.edu/papers/old-wildcats/fall94/September/ September1,1994/02_2_m.html
    An article in the University of Arizona newspaper describing how "the disruptive viewings, of violence and carnage on television, can eventually take a toll on a person and the way they view life someday."

8. Telecommunications Act of 1996

   www.fcc.gov/telecom.html
   Full text of the Telecommunications Law is available via FTP. Source: Pub Docs US Congress.

9. Violent Media Is Good for Kids

   www.motherjones.com/politics/2000/06/violent-media-good-kids-0
   Comic book author Gerard Jones argues that violence in videogames and other media give [sic] children a tool to master their rage. Posted in 2000.

10. Children and TV Violence/American Academy of Child & Adolescent Psychiatry

    www.aacap.org/cs/root/facts_for_families/children_and_tv_violence
    Describes some simple methods parents can use to shield their children from TV violence. Last updated in 2002.

11. TV Bloodbath/Violence on Prime Time Broadcast TV

    www.parentstv.org/PTC/publications/reports/stateindustryviolence/main.asp
    Uses statistics from 2002 to show that TV violence is becoming more graphic. Examples from *Buffy the Vampire Slayer* and *The X-Files*. Sponsored by Parents Television Council, whose mission is to "Clean Up TV Now."

12. Filling Their Minds with Death: TV Violence and Children

    www.turnoffyourtv.com/healtheducation/violencechildren/violencechildren.html
    A personal essay by Ron Kaufman that documents instances of extreme violence in TV programs. Cites the Parents Television Council Study. No author bio.

13. Violence on TV/The Desensitizing of America

    www.ridgenet.org/szaflik/tvrating.htm
    An essay, with documentation, by Kevin Szaflik, who is the Media Production Supervisor at a high school and the manager of a radio station. Last updated 2004.

14. Surprise! TV Violence Isn't Portrayed Accurately

    http://psychcentral.com/blog/archives/2009/05/20
    A short 2009 blog by John Grohol, PsyD, commenting on the Mayo Clinic's research.

15. TV Violence and Brainmapping in Children

    www.psychiatrictimes.com/display/article/10168/54801?verify=0
    An essay by Dr. John Murray of Kansas State University, published in the *Psychiatric Times* in 2001.

16. Ceptual Institute/TV Violence

http://ceptualinstitute.com/nuc/es004-tvviolence.htm
A January 2000 essay/blog by Dr. James Rose—"a sonata in 3 parts—data, hypothesis and conclusion."

EXERCISE 30: Evaluating Sources

Each of the following passages has been extracted from a book, article, or Web site about Wikipedia. They follow the same order as this chapter: encyclopedia, books, articles, Web site.

A. Carefully examine the distinctive way in which each passage presents its information, noting especially:

- the author's apparent purpose
- the amount and kind of evidence that is cited, and how it is documented
- the expectations of the audience's knowledge and understanding
- the relative emphasis on generalizations and abstract thinking
- the characteristic tone and vocabulary
- the date of publication

B. Decide how—or whether—you would use these sources together in a single research essay exploring *the significance of Wikipedia in the twenty-first-century dissemination of information.*

C. Write a tentative thesis for such an essay, and then decide which sources you are likely to use in writing your essay. Be prepared to justify your choice.

Note that these are brief *extracts* from books, articles, and Web sites: many of them may begin abruptly since space does not permit providing their full context.

1. free, Internet-based encyclopedia operating under an open-source management style. It is overseen by the nonprofit Wikimedia Foundation. *Wikipedia* uses a collaborative software known as wiki that facilitates the creation and development of articles. The English-language version of *Wikipedia* began in 2001. It had more than one million articles by March 2006 and more than two million by September 2007, and it continues to grow at a rate of millions of words per month. Much of its content treats popular culture topics not covered by traditional encyclopedias. *Wikipedia* is also an international project with versions in scores of languages, including French, German, Polish, Dutch, Hebrew, Chinese, and Esperanto. Although some highly publicized problems have called attention

to *Wikipedia*'s editorial process, they have done little to dampen public use of the resource.

In 1996 Jimmy Wales, a successful bond trader, moved to San Diego, Calif., to establish Bomis, Inc., a Web portal company. In March 2000 Wales founded *Nupedia*, a free online encyclopaedia, with Larry Sanger as editor-in-chief. *Nupedia* was organized like existing encyclopaedias, with an advisory board of experts and a lengthy review process. By January 2001, fewer than two dozen articles were finished, and Sanger advocated supplementing *Nupedia* with an open-source encyclopaedia. On Jan. 15, 2001, *Wikipedia* was launched as a feature of Nupedia.com, but, following objections from the advisory board, it was re-launched as an independent Web site a few days later. In its first year, *Wikipedia* expanded to some 20,000 articles in 18 languages. In 2003 *Nupedia* was terminated and its articles moved into *Wikipedia*.

In some respects, *Wikipedia*'s open-source production model is the epitome of the so-called Web 2.0, an egalitarian environment where the web of social software enmeshes users in both their real and virtual-reality workplaces. The *Wikipedia* community is based on a limited number of standard principles. One important principle is neutrality; another is the faith that contributors are participating in a sincere and deliberate fashion. Readers can correct what they perceive to be errors, and disputes over facts and possible bias are conducted through contributor discussions, with Wales as the final arbiter. Three other "pillars of wisdom" are: not to use copyrighted material, not to contribute original research, and not to have any other rules. The last pillar reinforces the project's belief that the open-source process will make *Wikipedia* into the best product available, given its community of users.

The central policy of inviting readers to serve as authors or editors creates the potential for problems as well as their partial solution. Not all users are scrupulous about providing accurate information, and *Wikipedia* must also deal with individuals who deliberately deface particular articles, post misleading or false statements, or add obscene material. *Wikipedia*'s method is to rely on its users to monitor and clean up its articles. Trusted contributors can also receive administrator privileges that provide access to an array of software tools to fix Web graffiti and other serious problems speedily.

From "Wikipedia," *Encyclopaedia Britannica Online*, 1 Sept. 2009
<http://www.britannica.com>

2. On today's Internet, however, amateurism, rather than expertise, is celebrated, even revered. Today, the *OED* and the *Encyclopaedia Britanncia*, two trusted reference volumes upon which we have long relied for information, are being replaced by Wikipedia and other user-generated resources. The professional is being replaced by the amateur, the lexicographer by the layperson, the Harvard professor by the unschooled populace.

Wikipedia describes itself as "the free encyclopedia that anyone can edit." The site claims to run on "democratic" principles, as its two hundred thousand anonymous editors are all unpaid volunteers. Unlike the *OED*, which was crafted by a carefully vetted and selected team of experienced professionals, Wikipedia, as I discussed earlier, allows absolutely anyone to add and edit entries on its Web site.

So what is wrong with such a "democratized" system? Isn't the ideal of democracy that everyone has a voice? Isn't that what makes America so attractive? (While not born in the United States myself, I've lived here since the early 1980s, am married to a woman from Alabama, and have raised my family in California. I'm a classic example of the immigrant entrepreneur who came to America seeking more economic and cultural freedom.)

While this is true in terms of elections, a radically democratic culture is hardly conducive to scholarship or to the creation of wisdom. The reality is that we now live in a highly specialized society, where excellence is rewarded and where professionals receive years of training to properly do their jobs, whether as doctors or journalists, environmental scientists or clothing designers. In *The Wealth of Nations*, economist Adam Smith reminds us that specialization and division of labor is, in fact, the most revolutionary achievement of capitalism:

> The greatest improvement in the productive powers of labor, and the greater part of the skill, dexterity, and judgment with which it is any where directed, or applied, seem to have been the effects of labor.

In the twenty-first century, this division of labor does not just refer to the breakdown of jobs in a manufacturing plant or on an assembly line. It includes the labor of those who choose a trade or a field, acquire education or training, gain experience, and develop their abilities within a complex meritocracy. They all have the same goal: to acquire expertise.

In a notorious section from *The German Ideology*, Karl Marx tried to seduce his reader with an idyllic postcapitalist world where everyone can "hunt in the morning, fish in the afternoon, rear cattle in the evening, criticize after dinner." But if we can all simultaneously be hunters, fishers, cattle herders, and critics, can any of us actually excel at anything, whether hunting, fishing, herding, or criticizing? In a world in which we are all amateurs, there are no experts.

On the Web 2.0, one senses that is perhaps the ideal. Wikipedia's entry for the word "amateur" — which has been amended by other editors more than fifty times since June 2001 — defines one as both a "virtuoso" and a "connoisseur":

> In the areas of computer programming and open source, as well as astronomy and ornithology, many amateurs make very meaningful contributions equivalent to or exceeding those of professionals. To many, description as an amateur is losing its negative meaning, and actually carries a badge of honor.

While the Wikipedia entry doesn't use the word "noble," you don't need to be a scholar to read between the lines. The editors at Wikipedia wear their amateur badge with pride. The problem? As Marshall Poe put it in a recent conversation:

> It's not exactly expert knowledge; it's common knowledge . . . when you go to nuclear reactor on Wikipedia you're not getting an encyclopedia entry, so much as you're getting what people who know a little about nuclear reactors know about nuclear reactors and what they think common people can understand. [Wikipedia] constantly throws people off and they think, well, if it's an encyclopedia why can't I cite it; why can't I . . . rely on it? And you can't; you just can't rely on it like that.

Wikipedia's editors embrace and revel in the commonness of their knowledge. But as the adage goes, a little knowledge is a dangerous thing. Because on Wikipedia, two plus two sometimes *does* equal five.

Note: This book is documented with endnotes.

ANDREW KEEN, from *The Cult of the Amateur:*
How Today's Internet Is Killing Our Culture (2008)

3. In August 2005, at a modest youth hostel in Frankfurt, Germany, hundreds of writers, students, computer hackers, and ordinary Internet users from around the world gathered on the grounds of Haus der Jugend on the bank of the River Main. Few had ever met in person, and most didn't even know one another's real name. What they did know was that they had collaborated with one another over the Internet, across different time zones and continents, toward the same goal: creating an encyclopedia. They knew one another mostly by their cryptic Internet personas — Anthere, Cimon Avaro on a Pogostick, Eclecticology — usernames that projected a quirkier side to an online community that focused on a rather academic task.   1

    There was a curious diversity — they came from different locations, age groups, and educational backgrounds — but they all referred to themselves with the same label: Wikipedians. They were there face-to-face for the first-ever Wikimania conference, bound by a common passion to give away their labor, knowledge, and know-how.   2

    In the hostel's courtyard, over cold beer and cold cuts, they swapped passionate stories. Each person inevitably followed "Hello" with a description of the eureka moment when that person stumbled upon Wikipedia and became an addict. Before long, laptops filled up the outdoor patio as users enthusiastically shared their favorite articles and obsessions. Previously used to editing alone in their homes, Wikipedians found themselves next to others who had the same strange obsessions.   3

Suddenly talking about digging through stacks of books to confirm one fact, checking grammar for five hours straight, or creating thousands of maps by hand didn't seem so dysfunctional. One user showed how he prevented vandalism to Wikipedia with software he had written, while another demonstrated how he translated articles from Spanish into Portuguese. Into the night, users rearranged plastic chairs and outdoor furniture to cluster around laptops, using the wireless Internet as an umbilical cord to attach to the Wikipedia mother ship, editing, sifting, and adding to the site. Only the hostel's curfew kept them from staying up until sunrise. And oddly enough, this all happened ad hoc, in the days before the conference even formally started.

When it came time for the keynote address, hundreds of Wikipedians and attendees clustered into the modest assembly hall, a space more accustomed to holding amateur youth camp performances than hosting Internet luminaries.

A tall and portly gentleman emerged onstage with the trusty hacker look — gray beard, button-down shirt, round stomach, and tan Birkenstocks. Most barely knew who he was, but without Ward Cunningham they wouldn't have ever found one another. He was the creator of the wiki concept, the radical idea of allowing anyone to openly edit any page of a Web site.

The audience hushed up to hear him speak. But he didn't want the attention. Instead of starting his talk, he turned the spotlight on the crowd of Wikipedians in front of him.

"I know that it's really you guys that made this thing noteworthy. . . . Right now I would just like to applaud *you*. Would you join me in saying thanks to all of you, please? You guys are great."

The Wikipedians grinned and started raucous clapping, looking around at their peers representing fifty-two different countries, basking in the moment. For the first time in Wikipedia's four-year history, the people who created it were able to celebrate their achievement in the same room. By that time in 2005, they had built one of the top fifty Web sites in the world, purely by volunteer effort. (By the end of the year, it would be in the top thirty, and the next year in the top ten.) In the process they had completely revolutionized the notion of what an encyclopedia should be and how it should be created.

In the audience were the folks who built Wikipedia from nothing. There was Florence Devouard, a French housewife with a master's degree in agronomy who spent most of her time taking care of her two children. As a volunteer and recently elected board member for the foundation overseeing Wikipedia, she was one of the early core users who discovered the Web site in 2001. Danny Wool was also an early editor, a former yeshiva student in Israel, turned atheist, who wound up working in publishing, even editing encyclopedias as part of his career. He quickly became known in the Wikipedia community for his omnibus knowledge and photographic memory, a walking institutional memory bank. Then there was Erik Moeller, a German user with the trademark ponytail of a computer hacker and a singular focus on pushing Wikipedians to start bigger and more ambitious projects.

They worked across continents, time zones, languages, and cultures to cooperate online, bound together by a passion for volunteering time, energy, and knowledge. They put together the sum of all human knowledge so others could have it for free — both as in freedom, and as in cost.   11

Note: This book is documented with endnotes.

ANDREW LIH, from *The Wikipedia Revolution:*
How a Bunch of Nobodies Created the World's
Greatest Encyclopedia (2009)

4. But Wikipedia stands for more than the ability of people to craft their own knowledge and culture. It stands for the idea that people of diverse backgrounds can work together on a common project with, whatever its other weaknesses, a noble aim — bringing such knowledge to the world. Jimbo Wales has said that the open development model of Wikipedia is only a means to that end — recall that he started with the far more restrictive Nupedia development model. And we see that Wikipedia rejects straightforward democracy, favoring discussion and consensus over outright voting, thereby sidestepping the kinds of ballot-stuffing that can take place in a digital environment, whether because one person adopts multiple identities or because a person can simply ask friends to stack a sparsely attended vote.   1

Instead, Wikipedia has since come to stand for the idea that involvement of people in the information they read—whether to fix a typographical error or to join a debate over its veracity or completeness — is an important end itself, one made possible by the recursive generativity of a network that welcomes new outposts without gatekeepers; of software that can be created and deployed at those outposts; and of an ethos that welcomes new ideas without gatekeepers, one that asks the people bearing those ideas to argue for and substantiate them to those who question.   2

There are plenty of online services whose choices can affect our lives. For example, Google's choices about how to rank and calculate its search results can determine which ideas have prominence and which do not. That is one reason why Google's agreement to censor its own search results for the Chinese version of Google has attracted so much disapprobation.[84] But even those who are most critical of Google's actions appear to wish to pressure the company through standard channels: moral suasion, shareholder resolutions, government regulation compelling noncensorship, or a boycott to inflict financial pressure. Unlike Wikipedia, no one thinks that Google ought to be "governed" by its users in some   3 democratic or communitarian way, even as it draws upon the wisdom of the crowds in deciding upon its rankings,[85] basing them in part on the ways in which millions of individual Web sites have decided about to whom to link. Amazon and Yelp welcome user reviews (and reviews of those reviews), but the public at large does not "govern" these institutions.

People instinctively expect more of Wikipedia. They see it as a shared resource   4
and a public one, even though it is not an arm of any territorial sovereign. The same could be said of the Internet Engineering Task Force and the Internet itself, but Wikipedia appears to have further found a way to involve nontechnical people in its governance. Every time someone reads a Wikipedia article and knowingly chooses not to vandalize it, he or she has an opportunity to identify with and reinforce its ethos. Wales is setting his sights next on a search engine built and governed on this model, "free and transparent" about its rankings, with a "huge degree of human community oversight."[86] The next chapters explore how that ethos may be replicable: vertically to solve generative problems found at other layers of the Internet, and horizontally to other applications within the content and social layers.

Note: This book is documented with endnotes.

JONATHAN ZITTRAIN, from *The Future of the*
Internet and How to Stop It (2008)

5. As online research has become an increasingly standard activity for middle   1
school and high school students, Wikipedia (http://www.wikipedia.org) has simultaneously emerged as the bane of many teachers who include research-focused assignments in their courses. An online encyclopedia that allows anyone to edit its entries, Wikipedia has educators fed up with students using the site as a primary resource and citing its content in their essays. For some the site seems to represent the worst of how the Internet has dumbed down the research process, with its easily accessible but unsubstantiated (if not downright false) information on almost any topic, a student's citation of which amounts to a mockery of legitimate inquiry. After all, how can a site that allows *anyone* to add, change, or remove information be credible? While extreme, the reaction described in the news article above—which mentions a school librarian who has created posters encouraging students to "Just Say 'No' to Wikipedia"—is not rare. Better to make such a site off-limits to students, goes the reasoning, if it will get them to rely on more authentic research sources for their writing.

Are there ways, however, that teachers can address the Wikipedia phenome-   2
non that don't include banning students from using the site? Seen in a different light, Wikipedia provides a unique opportunity to get students involved in ongoing conversations about writing for a real audience, meeting genre expectations,

establishing credibility, revising for clarity and purpose, and entering public discussions about the nature of truth, accuracy, and neutrality. . . .

What makes Wikipedia seem so dangerous to some teachers—its inherent malleability—is also what makes the site a dynamic and authentic demonstration of the research process itself. Granted, if students use Wikipedia as just another reference source (or their *only* source), then they will get no more from it (and possibly less) than a traditional encyclopedia in the school's library. But if they can learn about how entries on the site change and how each change is debated in arguments open to anyone's inspection, then Wikipedia can demonstrate to students the process, importance, and excitement of real scholarship. Here is an authentic demonstration that knowledge isn't settled, that there are always more questions to ask and always differing perspectives on the answers. Students can see that opinions and facts aren't always easily differentiated and that uncontested facts can be used to support opposing conclusions. And they can learn that no piece of knowledge can be understood separate from its connections to other topics in a multifaceted web that, on Wikipedia, is accessible at the click of a mouse.

> W. Scott Smoot and Darren Crovitz, from "Wikipedia: Friend,
> Not Foe," in *English Journal* 98.3 (Jan. 2009). 18 Aug. 2009
> <http://www.nwp.org/cs/public/print/resource/2920>

6. As social computing practices transform how cultural texts can be generated and circulated, written communities fostered by wikis offer some insight into the possibilities and pitfalls of dynamic, group-"authored" content production. Wikis are server-side software programs that allow anyone to create and edit web pages with only an Internet connection and a web browser. Quite simply and literally, wikis are a collaborative software tool. The inventor of wikis, Ward Cunningham, describes his software as "the simplest online database that could possibly work." Cunningham borrowed the Hawaiian word *wiki*, or *wikiwiki*, meaning fast or quick, alluding to the ability of a wiki user to quickly change the content of a page.[1]

The ability for users to edit web pages has profound implications for the development and distribution of knowledge. By de-emphasizing the central role of individual authorship in the production of texts, wikis offer a dynamic, multi-authored approach to their composition. In the last decade, wikis have emerged as a prominent and intriguing component in the production, modification, and dissemination of information and knowledge via the Internet.

Wiki users can be registered on a wiki system, and in some cases they can participate without naming themselves—they are known only by an IP address. The ability of a user to edit the content is the most striking feature of wikis. Open access has profound implications for the creation and editing of content insofar as it exposes texts' inherent instability. Unlike fixed media, wikis display the dynamic and inherently social nature of language and meaning as described in theoretical models of language and epistemology. In an unprecedented way, wikis allow discourse to emerge that is continually negotiated and articulated through a community of users — sometimes thousands of interlocutors. The properties of texts generated through active collaboration test the boundaries of established avenues of knowledge production and modern institutions of knowledge and authority. And while changes to a wiki page can be made by anyone, such changes are ultimately archived as part of the wiki. Therefore, the wiki also functions as a digital palimpsest.

Wikis invoke a multitude of the theoretical issues regarding authorship raised in late structuralist and poststructuralist thought. For many in the humanities and social sciences, the decentering of authorship in favor of discursive and systemic methodologies more attuned to power, historicity, and a dynamic "field" of representation has led to novel methods for critical interpretation and evaluation. However, such models have not become a significant component in how communication is understood within the public sphere. The singular author is very much the model that governs the expectations of most readers. By complicating traditional notions of authorship, wikis affect associated issues of authority, originality, and value.

4

Note: This book is documented with endnotes.

AMIT RAY AND ERHARDT GRAEFF, from "Reviewing the Author-Function in the Age of Wikipedia," in *Originality, Imitation, and Plagiarism*, eds. Caroline Eisner and Martha Vicinus (2008)

7. History is a deeply individualistic craft. The singly authored work is the standard for the profession; only about 6 percent of the more than 32,000 scholarly works indexed since 2000 in this journal's comprehensive bibliographic guide, "Recent Scholarship," have more than one author. Works with several authors — common in the sciences — are even harder to find. Fewer than 500 (less than 2 percent) have three or more authors.[1]

1

Historical scholarship is also characterized by *possessive* individualism. Good professional practice (and avoiding charges of plagiarism) requires us to attribute ideas and words to specific historians — we are taught to speak of "Richard Hofstadter's status anxiety interpretation of Progressivism."[2] And if we use more than a limited number of words from Hofstadter, we need to send a check to his estate. To mingle Hofstadter's prose with your own and publish it would violate both copyright and professional norms.

2

A historical work without owners and with multiple, anonymous authors is thus almost unimaginable in our professional culture. Yet, quite remarkably, that describes the online encyclopedia known as *Wikipedia*, which contains 3 million

3

articles (1 million of them in English). History is probably the category encompassing the largest number of articles. *Wikipedia* is entirely free. And that freedom includes not just the ability of anyone to read it (a freedom denied by the scholarly journals in, say, JSTOR, which requires an expensive institutional subscription) but also — more remarkably — their freedom to use it. You can take *Wikipedia*'s entry on Franklin D. Roosevelt and put it on your own Web site, you can hand out copies to your students, and you can publish it in a book — all with only one restriction: You may not impose any more restrictions on subsequent readers and users than have been imposed on you. And it has no authors in any conventional sense. Tens of thousands of people — who have not gotten even the glory of affixing their names to it — have written it collaboratively. The Roosevelt entry, for example, emerged over four years as five hundred authors made about one thousand edits. This extraordinary freedom and cooperation make *Wikipedia* the most important application of the principles of the free and open-source software movement to the world of cultural, rather than software, production.[3]

Note: This book is documented with endnotes.

> ROY ROSENZWEIG, from "Can History Be Open Source?
> *Wikipedia* and the Future of the Past," in *Journal
> of American History* 93.1 (June 2006): 117–46.

8. Conclusions

This paper presented a first overview on Wikipedia research. After a linear phase, Wikipedias grow exponentially with different rates per language. Generally the growth rate of the number of articles is smaller than other ratios. Different Wikipedias can be compared with indicators such as their growth rates, namespaces and article types. Article sizes are lognormal distributed with a linear growing median. For articles with five or more distinct authors its number follows a power law, so does the number of distinct articles per author. More detailed methods for measuring edits exist. Because every Wikipedia article covers a single concept and links to related ones, you can derive thesaurus-like structures out of the network of articles. The network is scale-free on ingoing links, outgoing links and broken links. There are many possibilities for deeper investigation, especially about quality and content. Like Wikipedia itself, research about it is at the very beginning but very promising.

Note: This article is documented with endnotes.

> JAKOB VOSS, from "Measuring Wikipedia,"
> *Physical Review* 74.3 (2006). 28 Aug. 2009
> <http://eprints.rclis.org/3610/1/measuringWikipedia2005.pdf>

9. When half a dozen students in Neil Waters's Japanese history class at Middlebury   1
College asserted on exams that the Jesuits supported the Shimabara Rebellion
in seventeenth-century Japan, he knew something was wrong. The Jesuits
were in "no position to aid a revolution," he said; the few of them in Japan were
in hiding.

He figured out the problem soon enough. The obscure, though incorrect, in-   2
formation was from Wikipedia, the collaborative online encyclopedia, and the
students had picked it up cramming for his exam.

Dr. Waters and other professors in the history department had begun noticing   3
about a year ago that students were citing Wikipedia as a source in their papers.
When confronted, many would say that their high school teachers had allowed
the practice.

But the errors on the Japanese history test last semester were the last straw. At   4
Dr. Waters's urging, the Middlebury history department notified its students this
month that Wikipedia could not be cited in papers or exams, and that students
could not "point to Wikipedia or any similar source that may appear in the future
to escape the consequences of errors."

With the move, Middlebury, in Vermont, jumped into a growing debate   5
within journalism, the law and academia over what respect, if any, to give Wikipedia articles, written by hundreds of volunteers and subject to mistakes and
sometimes deliberate falsehoods. Wikipedia itself has restricted the editing of
some subjects, mostly because of repeated vandalism or disputes over what
should be said.

Although Middlebury's history department has banned Wikipedia in citations,   6
it has not banned its use. Don Wyatt, the chairman of the department, said a total ban on Wikipedia would have been impractical, not to mention close-minded,
because Wikipedia is simply too handy to expect students never to consult it.

NOAM COHEN, from "A History Department Bans Citing Wikipedia
as a Research Source," *New York Times*, 21 Feb. 2007.

10. **Wikipedia** can be a great source of information on a range of topics. The user   1
generated universe is infinite and the people that contribute and seek information within this exchange have created one of the most vibrant information communities I have seen in my lifetime. But, I wonder, "What specifically do people
tend to use **Wikipedia** for?"

As you would expect many of the top subjects relate to current events and   2
cultural phenomena. For the month of April some of the top subjects included
"Don Imus", "Virginia Tech massacre", "global warming", "Naruto" (a Japanese
comic and anime TV series) and "Sanjaya Malakar" of American Idol fame.

In addition to these predictable terms, there was a substantial volume of   3
sexual terms. Apparently Bobby's parents forgot to have the Birds & Bees talk

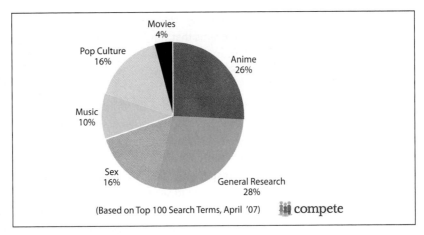

Figure 8-3 Top Wikipedia subjects

with their son . . . as did the parents of Billy, Johnny, Julie, Tommy and Susie. **Wikipedia** is essentially an **encyclopedia**, so one would assume these searches are for research and learning purposes — a virtual Kama Sutra of sorts.

We categorized the top 100 **Wikipedia** terms for April into six general categories to figure out what the major search themes are on **Wikipedia**. As you would expect the greatest number of searches (28%) are within the research category. This includes terms like "Columbine High School massacre" and "American Civil War."

The two surprising categories are Anime and Sex:

Anime (26%)

There is a tremendous amount of interest in learning about Pokemon and Naruto. Perhaps these are parents who want to know what their kids are going crazy over. My Mom didn't know what "He-Man" was until I was a grown man reflecting on how silly Castle Grayskull was. My mom could have used **Wikipedia** in the 80's.

Sex (16%)

What's interesting about the top sex related terms on **Wikipedia** is that they do not appear to have gratuitous intent. The top terms include very straightforward inquiries on human reproductive 'parts' and basic concepts of what sex is and how it is performed. It appears that many people are learning about what sex is and how to have it by referencing Wikipedia.

ADAM TORNES, "Wikipedia: Encyclopedia or
Kama Sutra?" 31 May 2007. 3 Sept. 2009
<http://blog.compete.com/2007/05/31/wikipedia-search-terms>

EXERCISE 31: Comparing Sources

In the middle of the night of November 29, 1942, a Boston nightclub called the Cocoanut Grove burned down, resulting in the deaths of at least 300 people. Read the following three accounts of this disaster, and be prepared to discuss the differences in content, organization, tone, purpose, and point of view. What is the thesis of each article? Consider how you would use the three articles in a single research essay dealing with the Cocoanut Grove disaster. Are these three variations interchangeable?

NEW YORK TIMES, 30 NOVEMBER 1942

300 KILLED BY FIRE, SMOKE AND PANIC IN BOSTON RESORT — DEAD CLOG EXITS — Terror Piles Up Victims as Flames Suddenly Engulf Nightclub — Service Men to Rescue — Many of Them Perish — Girls of Chorus Leap to Safety — 150 Are Injured

BOSTON, Sunday, Nov. 29 — More than 300 persons had perished early this morning in flames, smoke and panic in the Cocoanut Grove Night Club in the midtown theatre district.   1

The estimate of the dead came at 2 a.m. from William Arthur Reilly, Fire Commissioner, as firemen and riggers searched the ruins for additional bodies. It was a disaster unprecedented in this city.   2

The chief loss of life resulted from the screaming, clawing crowds that were wedged in the entrance of the club. Smoke took a terrific toll of life and scores were burned to death.   3

At the Boston City Hospital officials said there were so many bodies lined up in corridors that they would attempt no identifications before daybreak.   4

Commissioner Reilly stated that an eyewitness inside the club said the fire started when an artificial palm near the main entrance was set afire.   5

Martial law was clamped on the entire fire area at 1:35 a.m. Sailors, Coast Guardsmen, shore patrolmen and naval officers dared death time and again trying to get at bodies that were heaped six feet high by one of the entrances.   6

Firemen said that many bodies were believed to have fallen into the basement after the main floor collapsed.   7

A chorus boy, Marshall Cook, aged 19, of South Boston, led three co-workers, eight chorus girls and other floor show performers totaling thirty-five to an adjoining roof from the second-floor dressing rooms and from there they dropped to the ground from a ladder.   8

Scores of ambulances from nearby cities, the Charlestown Navy Yard and the Chelsea Naval Hospital poured into the area, but the need for ambulances became so great that even railway express trucks were pressed into service to   9 carry away victims. At one time victims, many of them dead, lay two deep in an adjoining garage.

Many of the victims were soldiers, sailors, marines and Coast Guardsmen, some of them junior officers, visiting Boston for a weekend of merrymaking. In the throng were persons who had attended the Holy Cross–Boston College football game.   10

Scores of dead were piled up in the lobbies of the various hospitals as the doctors and nurses gave all their attention to the 150 injured.   11

A "flash" fire, believed to have started in the basement, spread like lightning through the dance floor area, and the panic was on. All available nurses and priests were being called into the disaster area.   12

Among the dead were a marine and one who appeared to be a fireman. Casualties were arriving at hospitals so rapidly that they were being placed in the corridors wherever a suitable place could be found.   13

It appeared probable that the greatest loss of life was in the newly opened lounge of the night club in Broadway. Here, one policeman said, burned and suffocated persons were heaped to the top of the doors, wedged in death.   14

The night club was a one-and-a-half story building with a stucco exterior. The blaze was said to have broken out in the basement kitchen at 10:17 p.m. just as the floor show performers were preparing for their next performance. Performers on the second floor were met by terrific smoke and flame as they started downstairs. Their stories were the only ones available, as those who had escaped the dance floor and tables were too hysterical to talk.   15

A temporary morgue and hospital were set up in the garage of the Film Exchange Transfer Company at the rear of the club in Shawmut Street. At least fourteen persons, suffocated and lying in grotesque positions, were lying on the garage floor at one time, while scores of injuries were cared for by garage workers and others.   16

The city's Civilian Defense Workers were called to the scene to maintain order and to give first aid to those suffering from burns and smoke inhalation. Every hospital in the area soon was loaded with the victims.   17

At least thirty-five performers and their friends were rescued by the quick actions of Marshall Cook, a South Boston boy. He was met by a blast of flame as he started down stairs, went back to the dressing room and organized those caught there.   18

He then smashed his way through a window, carrying away the casing. Through this opening he led a group to an adjoining room, where a small ladder was found. The ladder was not long enough to reach the street, but Cook and several other male performers held the top end over the roof's edge and guided the women over the side. They had to jump about 6 feet to reach the ground.   19

At the City Hospital bodies were piled on the floors, many so burned that there was no attempt to identify them immediately. Many service men were among the victims, many of whom were partly identified through their uniforms. [20]

Buck Jones, the film star, was believed to be one of the victims. [21]

Among the first at the scene was the Rev. Joseph A. Marcus of Cranwell School, Lenox, who administered the last rites for at least fifty persons. In the meantime, thirty or forty ambulances rushed to the fire, these coming from Lynn, Newton, and Brookline. Despite the hindrances caused by automobiles parked in the streets, some of the dead and injured were taken from nearby buildings, where they had been left covered only by newspapers. [22]

Abraham Levy, a cashier at the Cocoanut Grove, said there were about 400 in the place, including many sailors. [23]

Sailors saved many lives, pulling people through the doors and out of danger. A fireman said that he saw at least thirty bodies lying on the floor, and that he believed some of them were firemen. [24]

Among the spectacular escapes were those of two of the eight chorus girls, who leaped from the second floor and were caught by two of the male dancers. They were Lottie Christie of Park Drive, Boston, and Claudia Boyle. They jumped into the arms of Andrew Louzan and Robert Gilbert. Louzan and Gilbert had climbed out of a window of their dressing room to an adjoining roof and then descended by ladder. [25]

TIME, 7 DECEMBER 1942
CATASTROPHE: BOSTON'S WORST

Holy Cross had just beaten Boston College: downtown Boston was full of men & women eager to celebrate or console. Many of them wound up at Cocoanut Grove: they stood crowded around the dimly lighted downstairs bar, filled the tables around the dance floor upstairs. With them mingled the usual Saturday night crowd: soldiers & sailors, a wedding party, a few boys being sent off to Army camps. [1]

At 10 o'clock Bridegroom John O'Neil, who had planned to take his bride to their new apartment at the stroke of the hour, lingered on a little longer. The floor show was about to start. Through the big revolving door, couples moved in & out. [2]

At the downstairs bar, a 16-year-old busboy stood on a bench to replace a light bulb that a prankish customer had removed. He lit a match. It touched one of the artificial palm trees that gave the Cocoanut Grove its atmosphere; a few flames shot up. A girl named Joyce Spector sauntered toward the checkroom because she was worried about her new fur coat. [3]

Panic's Start

Before Joyce Spector reached the cloakroom, the Cocoanut Grove was a 4
screaming shambles. The fire quickly ate away the palm tree, raced along silk
draperies, was sucked upstairs through the stairway, leaped along ceiling and
wall. The silk hangings, turned to balloons of flame, fell on table and floor.

Men & women fought their way toward the revolving door; the push of 5
bodies jammed it. Nearby was another door; it was locked tight. There were
other exits, but few Cocoanut Grove patrons knew about them. The lights went
out. There was nothing to see now except flame, smoke and weird moving
torches that were men & women with clothing and hair afire.

The 800 Cocoanut Grove patrons pushed and shoved, fell and were tram- 6
pled. Joyce Spector was knocked under a table, crawled on hands & knees,
somehow was pushed through an open doorway into the street. A chorus boy
herded a dozen people downstairs into a refrigerator. A few men & women
crawled out windows; a few escaped by knocking out a glass brick wall. But
most of them, including Bridegroom John O'Neil, were trapped.

Panic's Sequel

Firemen broke down the revolving door, found it blocked by bodies of the 7
dead, six deep. They tried to pull a man out through a side window; his legs
were held tight by the mass of struggling people behind him. In an hour the fire
was out and firemen began untangling the piles of bodies. One hard bitten fireman went into hysterics when he picked up a body and a foot came off in his
hand. They found a girl dead in a telephone booth, a bartender still standing behind his bar.

At hospitals and improvised morgues which were turned into charnel 8
houses for the night, 484 dead were counted; it was the most disastrous U.S. fire
since 571 people were killed in Chicago's Iroquois Theater holocaust in 1903.
One Boston newspaper ran a two-word banner line: BUSBOY BLAMED. But the
busboy had not put up the Cocoanut Grove's tinderbox decorations, nor was he
responsible for the fact that Boston's laws do not require nightclubs to have fireproof fixtures, sprinkler systems or exit markers.

BERNARD DEVOTO, *HARPER'S*, FEBRUARY 1943
THE EASY CHAIR

On the last Sunday morning of November, 1942, most inhabitants of 1
greater Boston learned from their newspapers that at about the time they had
gone to bed the night before the most terrible fire in the history of their city had
occurred. The decorations of a crowded night club had got ignited, the crowd

had stampeded, the exits had jammed, and in a few minutes hundreds of people had died of burns or suffocation. Two weeks later the list of dead had reached almost exactly five hundred, and the war news was only beginning to come back to Boston front pages. While the Allied invasion of North Africa stalled, while news was released that several transports engaged in it had been sunk, while the Russians and the Germans fought monstrously west of Stalingrad and Moscow, while the Americans bombed Naples and the RAF obliterated Turin and conducted the war's most widespread raids over western Europe, while the Japs tried again in the Solomons and mowed down their attackers in New Guinea, while a grave conflict of civilian opinion over the use of Admiral Darlan developed in America and Great Britain, while the anniversary of Pearl Harbor passed almost unnoticed — while all this was going on the Boston papers reported it in stickfuls in order to devote hundreds of columns to the fire at the Cocoanut Grove. And the papers did right, for the community has experienced an angry horror surpassing anything that it can remember. For weeks few Bostonians were able to feel strongly about anything but their civic disaster.

There is irony in such preoccupation with a minute carnage. In the same fortnight thousands of men were killed in battle. Every day, doubtless, more than five hundred were burned to death, seared by powder or gasoline from bombed dumps, in buildings fired from the sky, or in blazing airplanes and sinking ships. If these are thought of as combatants meeting death in the line of duty, far more than five hundred civilians were killed by military action in Germany, Italy, France, Great Britain, Russia, China, Australia, and the islands of the Pacific. Meanwhile in two-thirds of the world civilians died of torture and disease and starvation, in prison camps and wire stockades and the rubble of their homes — they simply came to their last breath and died, by the thousand. At a moment when violent death is commonplace, when it is inevitable for hundreds of thousands, there is something grotesque in being shocked by a mere five hundred deaths which are distinguished from the day's routine only by the fact that they were not inevitable. When hundreds of towns are bombed repeatedly, when cities the size of Boston are overrun by invading armies, when many hundreds of Boston's own citizens will surely be killed in battle in the next few weeks, why should a solitary fire, a truly inconsiderable slaughter, so oppress the spirit?

2

That oppression provides perspective on our era. We have been so conditioned to horror that horror must explode in our own backyard before we can genuinely feel it. At the start of the decade our nerves responded to Hitler's murdering the German Jews with the outrage properly felt in the presence of cruelty and pain. Seven years later our nerves had been so overloaded that they felt no such outrage at the beginning of a systematic effort to exterminate an entire nation, such as Poland. By progressive steps we had come to strike a truce with the intolerable, precisely as the body develops immunity to poisons and

3

bacteria. Since then three years of war have made the intolerable our daily bread, and every one of us has comfortably adapted to things which fifteen years ago would have driven him insane. The extinction of a nation now seems merely an integral part of the job in hand. But the needless death of five hundred people in our home town strikes through the immunity and horrifies us.

The fire at the Cocoanut Grove was a single, limited disaster, but it exhausted Boston's capacity to deal with an emergency. Hospital facilities were strained to the limit and somewhat beyond it. If a second emergency had had to be dealt with at the same time its victims would have had to wait some hours for transportation and a good many hours for treatment. If there had been three such fires at once, two-thirds of the victims would have got no treatment whatever in time to do them any good. Boston is an inflammable city and it has now had instruction in what to expect if a dozen hostile planes should come over and succeed in dropping incendiary bombs. The civilian defense agencies which were called on justified themselves and vindicated their training. The Nurses' Aid in particular did a memorable job; within a few hours there was a trained person at the bed of every victim, many other Aids worked to exhaustion helping hospital staffs do their jobs, and in fact more were available than could be put to use. Nevertheless it was clearly demonstrated that the civilian agencies are nowhere near large enough to take care of bombings if bombings should come. There were simply not enough ambulances; Railway Express Company trucks had to be called on to take the injured to hospitals and the dead to morgues. The dead had to be stacked like cord wood in garages because the morgues could take no more; the dying had to be laid in rows in the corridors of hospitals because the emergency wards were full. The drainage of doctors into the military service had left Boston just about enough to care for as many victims as this single fire supplied. Six months from now there will be too few to handle an equal emergency; there are far too few now for one twice as serious. One plane-load of incendiaries would start more fires than the fire department and its civilian assistants could put out. There would be more injured than there are even the most casually trained first-aiders to care for. Hundreds would be abandoned to the ignorant assistance of untrained persons, in streets so blocked by rubble and so jammed with military vehicles that trained crews could not reach them even when trained crews should be free. Boston has learned that it is not prepared to take care of itself. One doubts if any community in the United States is.

Deeper implications of the disaster have no direct connection with the war. An outraged city has been confronting certain matters which it ordinarily disregards. As a place of entertainment the Cocoanut Grove was garish but innocuous and on the whole useful. It has been called "the poor man's Ritz"; for years people had been going there to have a good time and had got what they

4

5

were looking for. With the naive shock customary in such cases, the city has now discovered that these people were not receiving the minimum protection in their pleasures to which they were entitled and which they supposed they were receiving.

The name of the night club suggests the kind of decorations that cluttered it; the public supposed that the law required them to be fireproof; actually they burned like so much celluloid. The laws relating to them were ambiguous and full of loopholes; such as they were, they were not enforced. The public supposed that an adequate number of exits were required and that periodic inspections were made; they were not. There were too few exits for the customary crowds, one was concealed, another could not be opened, and panic-stricken people piled up before the rest and died there by the score. The public supposed that laws forbidding overcrowding were applied to night clubs and were enforced; on the night of the fire the place was packed so full that movement was almost impossible, and it had been just as crowded at least once a week throughout the years of its existence. The public supposed that laws requiring safe practice in electric wiring and machinery were enforced; the official investigations have shown that the wiring was installed by unlicensed electricians, that a number of people had suspected it was faulty, and that in fact officials had notified the club that it was violating the law and had threatened to take action — but had not carried out the threat. Above all, the public supposed that an adequate building code taking into account the realities of modern architecture and modern metropolitan life established certain basic measures of protection. It has now learned that the Boston building code is a patched makeshift based on the conditions of 1907, and that though a revision which would modernize it was made in 1937, various reasons have held up the adoption of that revision for five years. [6]

These facts have been established by five official investigations, one of them made by the Commonwealth of Massachusetts in an obvious expectation that the municipal authorities of Boston would find convincing reasons to deal gently with themselves. They have turned up other suggestive facts. The Cocoanut Grove was once owned by a local racketeer, who was murdered in the routine of business. The present owners were so expertly concealed behind a facade of legal figureheads that for twenty-four hours after the fire the authorities were not sure that they knew who even one of them was and two weeks later were not sure that they knew them all. An intimation that financial responsibility was avoided by a technically contrived bankruptcy has not yet been followed up as I write this, and other financial details are still lost in a maze of subterfuges. It is supposed that some of the club's employees had their wage-scale established by terrorism. Investigators have encountered, but so far have not published, the customary free-list and lists of those entitled to discounts. [7]

Presumably such lists contemplated the usual returns in publicity and business favors; presumably also they found a use in the amenities of regulation. Names and business practices of the underworld have kept cropping up in all the investigations, and it is whispered that the reason why the national government has been conducting one of them is the presence at the club of a large amount of liquor on which the latest increase in revenue taxes ought to have been paid but somehow had not been.

In short, Boston has been reminded, hardly for the first time, that laxity in municipal responsibility can be made to pay a profit and that there can be a remunerative partnership between the amusement business and the underworld. A great many Bostonians, now writing passionate letters to their newspapers and urging on their legislators innumerable measures of reform, have gone farther than that. They conclude that one of the reasons why the modernized building code has not been adopted is the fact that there are ways of making money from the looser provisions of the old code. They suppose that one reason why gaps and loopholes in safety regulations are maintained is that they are profitable. They suppose that one reason why laws and regulations can be disregarded with impunity is that some of those charged with the duty of enforcing them make a living from not enforcing them. They suppose that some proprietors of night clubs find that buying immunity is cheaper than obeying safety regulations and that they are able to find enforcement agents who will sell it. They suppose that civil irresponsibility in Boston can be related to the fact that a lot of people make money from it.

But the responsibility cannot be shouldered off on a few small grafters and a few underworld characters who have established business relations with them, and it would be civic fatuousness to seek expiation for the murder of five hundred citizens in the passage of some more laws. The trouble is not lack of laws but public acquiescence; the damaging alliance is not with the underworld but with a communal reverence of what is probably good for business. Five hundred deaths in a single hour seem intolerable, but the city has never dissented at all to a working alliance between its financial interests and its political governors — a partnership which daily endangers not five hundred but many thousand citizens. Through Boston, as through every other metropolis, run many chains of interests which might suffer loss if regulations for the protection of the public's health and life were rigorously enforced. They are sound and enlightened regulations, but if they should be enforced then retail sales, bank clearings, and investment balances might possibly fall off. The corner grocery and the downtown department store, the banks and the business houses, the labor unions and the suburban housewife are all consenting partners in a closely calculated disregard of public safety.

Since the system is closely calculated it usually works, it kills only a few at a time, mostly it kills gradually over a period of years. Sometimes however it runs into another mathematical certainty and then it has to be paid for in blocks of five hundred lives. At such times the community experiences just such an excess of guilt as Boston is feeling now, uncomfortably realizing that the community itself is the perpetrator of wanton murder. For the responsibility is the public's all along and the certain safeguard — a small amount of alertness, civic courage, and willingness to lose some money — is always in the public's hands. That means not the mayor's hands, but yours and mine.

It is an interesting thing to hold up to the light at a moment when millions   11
of Americans are fighting to preserve, among other things, the civic responsibility of a self-governing people. It suggests that civilians who are not engaged in the war effort, and who feel intolerably abased because they are not, could find serviceable ways to employ their energies. They can get to work chipping rust and rot from the mechanisms of local government. The rust and rot are increasing because people who can profit from their increase count on our looking toward the war, not toward them. Your town may have a police force of no more than four and its amusement business may be confined to half a dozen juke joints, but some percentage of both may have formed a partnership against your interests under cover of the war.

Certainly the town has a sewage system, a garbage dump, fire traps, a rudi-   12
mentary public health code, ordinances designed to protect life, and a number of Joe Doakes who can make money by juggling the relationship among them. Meanwhile the ordinary hazards of peace are multiplied by the conditions of war, carelessness and preoccupation increase, and the inevitable war pestilence is gathering to spring. The end-products do not look pleasant when they are seen clearly, especially when a community realizes that it has killed five hundred people who did not need to die.

▪9▪

Writing the
Research Essay

In Chapter 9, you take the evidence and information that you have found in your sources and transform them into an essay. Now, you truly begin to make the sources your own—by taking notes; by developing a thesis; by deciding which information is relevant and important to that thesis; by organizing the material into a sequence of paragraphs in support of the thesis; and, finally, by expressing your ideas and presenting your evidence to the reader, as far as possible in your own words. Chapter 9 provides an overview of these key stages.

Saving Information

By now, you should have accumulated a quantity of notes that serve as the raw materials for your essay. Here, the term "notes" refers to any of the products of your research: your own summaries and paraphrases, quotations, photocopies of book pages and articles, printouts and downloaded copies of Web material, class lecture notes, stories clipped from newspapers and magazines, and jottings of your own ideas about the topic.

But research also requires you to *take notes*: you read through a text, sometimes quickly and sometimes slowly, deciding as you go which information you probably will want to use in your essay and recording it as summary, paraphrase, and quotation. Before the days of computers, notes were usually handwritten on index cards or lined pads, ready to be organized into a sequence that would become the outline of an essay. Many students still prefer this slow but thorough way of absorbing ideas and information.

Now, technology offers an easy alternative. Text from a book goes through a copy machine and becomes a photocopied page; the words of the text remain the same. Online articles or Web sites get downloaded and appear in a file on your computer screen; the words of the text remain the same. Certainly, copying the original text can be useful: for example, you may want to quote a small portion in your essay. But, at some point, most of the text will have to be rewritten in your own words, in your own voice. Otherwise, you will not be writing an essay; you will be compiling an anthology of quotations.

Downloading presents a particular temptation. The information is available right there, on your screen, and by clicking a few keys you can transfer it directly into the file you've created for your research essay. You can keep on cutting and pasting from other Web sites and database articles, and type in or scan some extracts from photocopies; and you'll end up with something that contains sentences and paragraphs and meets the minimum number of assigned pages. It may look like an essay—but will it read like an essay or an electronic scrapbook?

The cut-and-paste method of writing an essay involves no writing. Your instructor will easily observe that the writing component of the assignment hasn't been fulfilled and will grade the "essay" accordingly.

Learning to write essays means learning to speak for yourself. Learning to write research essays means using the skills of summary and paraphrase to present your sources. And you can't delay doing that until you're at the point of writing the essay. What's the solution? Take notes!

Taking Notes

If it's your preference or if your access to a computer is limited, by all means use the traditional, reliable method of taking *handwritten notes on index cards or a pad of paper*. But if you opt for convenience, establish *a new computer file* at the onset of your research. This file will not be the one used for the writing of your essay; it will be exclusively for notes. As you start working with each new source, open that file, put the bibliographical information about that source clearly at the start of a new section, and type in your version of the material that you may want to use. Don't copy-type (except for the occasional quotation). Use your own words.

When you've finished writing notes on all your sources, you'll have one long file ready to be printed out and reorganized, or simply reorganized on the screen, ready to transfer into your essay file. The difference is that, this way, you will be cutting and pasting *your own work*.

Here are some guidelines for note taking:

1. *Wait to take notes.* Don't start taking notes until you have compiled most of your preliminary bibliography. Choosing materials to copy and to download will help you gradually to understand the possibilities of your subject and decide on a potential thesis. But if you start taking notes from the first few texts that you find, you may be wasting time pursuing an idea that will turn out to be impractical or that the evidence ultimately won't support.

2. *Use photocopies and printouts.* Unless it's prohibitively expensive, try to take notes from photocopies of books and articles, rather than the texts themselves; that way, you'll always have the copies to refer to if there's a confusion in your notes. (The copies will also be useful if your instructor asks you to submit some of your sources.) Print out downloaded material and work from the printed copy so that you don't have to keep shifting from file to file. It's hard to take good notes if you don't have the text in front of you as you write.

3. *Use paraphrase and summary.* As you learned in Chapter 4, quotation should be the exception, not the rule. Copying the author's language will make it more difficult for you to shift to your own writing style later on. You want to avoid producing an anthology of cannibalized quotations. The effort of paraphrasing and summarizing also helps you to understand each new idea. In your notes, always try to explain the author's exact meaning.

4. *Cite evidence.* Include evidence to support the broader ideas that you're writing about. If your topic is corruption in the Olympic games, don't simply allude to issues like the use of performance-enhancing drugs or the influence of network television in the scheduling of events. Cite facts to illustrate your point. You won't remember the range of evidence as you're writing the paper unless you include examples in your notes.

5. *Separate yourself from your source.* Differentiate your own ideas from those that you are paraphrasing. When you take notes, you're working slowly and concentrating on what you're reading. It's at that time that you're most likely to develop your own comments and ideas, spinning them off from the text. Be careful to indicate in your notes what's yours and what's the source's. Later on, you'll need to know which material to document. Using square brackets [like these] around your own ideas is a good way of making this distinction or use the tracking program on your word processor.

6. *Record page numbers.* Keep a running record of page references. You'll need to cite the exact page number for each reference, not an approximate guess. It isn't enough to write "pp. 285–91" after a few paragraphs of notes. Three weeks or three hours later, how will you remember on which page you found the point that you're about to cite in your essay? If you're quoting or paraphrasing a source in some detail, make a slash and insert a new page number to indicate exactly where you turned the page. Put quotation marks around all quotations *immediately.*

7. *Record bibliographical data.* Always include complete bibliographical information for each source. If you don't have a clear record of details like place of publication, volume number, or URL, you won't be able to hand in a complete bibliography. Either start a new file just for bibliography or include that information at the beginning of each section of your notes.

Taking Good Notes

1. Don't start taking notes until you have compiled most of your preliminary bibliography.
2. Try to take notes from photocopies of books and articles and printouts of sources, rather than the texts themselves.
3. Use paraphrase and summary, rather than quotation.
4. Include evidence to support the broader ideas that you're writing about.
5. Differentiate your own ideas from those that you are paraphrasing.
6. Keep a running record of page references.
7. Always include complete bibliographical information for each source.

Taking Notes by Source: Organizationally, you can take notes by source or by topic. Taking notes by source is the more obvious way. You start your computer file (or your cards or pad) with the first source, presenting information in the order of its appearance in the book or article. Then you go on to the second source, the third, and so on. Figure 9-1 shows notes for an essay, organized by source, describing *the 1871 fire that devastated Chicago*. The source (described in detail earlier in the file) is the *New York Times* for October 15, 1871:

- Each item in the list is assigned a number; this will be useful later on, when you are organizing your notes to write your essay.
- The source has also been assigned an identifying letter; if you have two sources with the same name (for example, the *Times* for two different dates), you'll be able to distinguish between them.

Taking Notes by Topic: The disadvantage of taking notes by source is that your notes remain raw material, with no organizational pattern imposed on them. Taking notes by topic is a more sophisticated system:

1. Decide on the basic events or issues that your essay will cover.
2. Assign each of those topics a separate section of your notes file.
3. Place each new piece of information under the relevant topic.

For example, early in the note-taking process, one student decided that she would definitely write about the *aftermath of the Chicago fire*; one section of her notes would be devoted to efforts to contain and put out the blaze. After that, every time she came across a new point about *firefighting*—no matter what the source—she scrolled through (or searched) her notes file, looking for the topic

NY Times, 10/15/71, p. 1   Source J

   1. city normal again
   2. still martial rule; Gen. Sheridan in charge
   3. citizens working at night to watch for new outbreak of fire
   4. newspapers moved to other locations
   5. estimate 1,000 dead
   6. earlier reports of looting and loss of life not exaggerated
   7. waterworks won't open until next day
   8. two-thirds of the city still using candlelight
   9. suffering mostly among "humbler classes"
  10. businessmen are "buoyant"
  11. bread is 8 cents
  12. saloons are closed at 9:00 p.m. for one week

Figure 9-1 Notes grouped by source

name and then adding that new information. Similar sections were established to deal with *food supplies* and *looting*. Figure 9-2 shows a sample of her notes.

Organizing notes by topic makes it much easier to organize your essay. In fact, because your information is already categorized, you can often skip a whole stage in the process and begin to write your essay from your notes without much additional synthesis. But taking notes by topic does require you to make a list, either written or mental, of possible categories or note topics while

Firefighting

All engines and hose carts in city come (NYT 10/8, p. 5)
Water station on fire, with no water to put out small fires
   (Hall, p. 228)
All engines out there; fire too big to stop (NYT 10/8, p. 5)
fire department "demoralized"; bad fire previous night; men
were drinking afterward; fire marshal "habitually drunk"
   (NYT 10/23, p. 2)

Figure 9-2 Notes grouped by topic

you're still doing your research. And you may not be completely sure about your thesis and structure that early in the process. When you take notes by topic, it's also vital to make sure that *each* point is followed by its source and the relevant page number.

EXERCISE 32: Taking Notes on Two Topics

Reread the three articles dealing with the Cocoanut Grove fire of 1942 at the end of Chapter 8 (p. 381). Head one file "Causes of the Fire" and take a set of notes on that topic. Head another file "The Fire's Intensity and Speed" and take a second set of notes on the second topic. Each set of notes should make use of all three sources.

EXERCISE 33: Taking Notes on Three Topics

Assume that you are doing research on *the American circus* and that you have come across the following source in the library. After doing a preliminary evaluation of the passage, take a set of notes for an essay entitled "Racial Segregation in Late 19th-Century America," a second set of notes for an essay entitled "Affordable Leisure-time Entertainment, 1900 and 2000," and a third set of notes for an essay entitled "The Circus as a Symbol of American Democracy."

from THE CIRCUS AGE: CULTURE AND SOCIETY UNDER THE AMERICAN BIG TOP
Janet M. Davis

Janet M. Davis, who teaches at the University of Texas at Austin, is preparing a book on the early history of the animal welfare movement in America.

In contrast to the all-male world of burlesque and concert saloon, *everyone* went to the circus: from President Theodore Roosevelt, who received a personal invitation scrolled on satin from James A. Bailey in 1903, to hundreds of inmates from local insane asylums across the country who were brought to the circus by their wardens.[76] In many ways, the composition of the turn-of-the-century circus audience mirrored those of the mixed Jacksonian-era theater, because women, men, and children of different social class and ethnicity sat together under the same canvas big top tent. In 1898 the *Galveston Daily News* noticed the diverse crowd attending the Ringling Bros. circus: "Men, women and children from all walks of life and all avenues of trade and profession and wards and precincts were there and as one big family."[77]

Seating arrangements at the largest railroad circuses also reflected con-   2
temporary social hierarchies based on class and race (Figure 9-3). Wealthy and
middle-class Euroamerican spectators sat in the comfortable and expensive
(usually $1 to $2)[78] "starbacks" or reserved box seats — the best seats in the big
top, located along the center ring.[79] Depending on the show, working-class patrons paid twenty-five or fifty cents to sit at either end of the big top on unre-
served bleachers (so called because of their resemblance to long bleaching
boards), also known as "blues" (the practice of painting bleacher seats blue
started in the mid-nineteenth century for unknown reasons).[80] Recent immigrants, Native Americans, many working-class circus-goers, and stray children
paid a "blues" price to sit in the gallery or "straw house," an open "pit" area between the hippodrome track and the seating area on which straw was placed to
accommodate a few thousand more spectators.

The racial geography of the circus audience reflected the proliferation of   3
Jim Crow segregation at the turn of the century. Until 1900 southern segregation laws had applied primarily to passenger trains; thereafter, these laws (both
de facto and de jure) extended to virtually every aspect of public life: separate

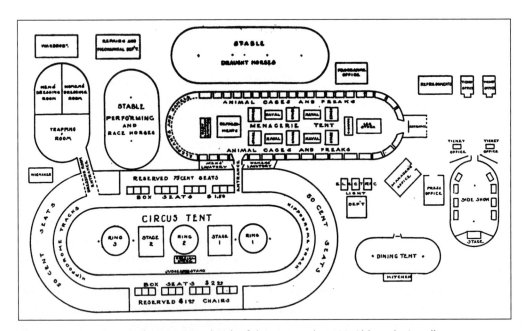

Figure 9-3 Barnum & Bailey program, sketch of show grounds, 1903. Although virtually everyone
attended the circus, seating arrangements under the big top were generally stratified on the basis of
social class and, in the Jim Crow South, uniformly racially segregated. (Interior sketch courtesy of Circus
World Museum, Baraboo, Wis., B+B-N45-03-10)

toilets, water fountains, waiting rooms, orphanages, schools for the blind and deaf, Bibles for court testimony, parks, swimming pools, restaurants, streetcars, and steamboats.[81] In the South, black circus-goers generally sat segregated from other spectators in the gallery.[82] Outside the tents, black and white audiences bought their concessions at separate snack stands. The Louisiana state legislature passed a law in 1914 mandating racially segregated entrances, exits, and ticket windows at circuses and other tent shows; the law also specified that ticket sellers remain a minimum distance of twenty-five feet from each other.[83] Racial segregation had a long history at the circus in the southern United States: throughout the nineteenth century, newspapers noted separate points of entry and segregated seating areas, in the pit [standing room] or gallery, for black circus audiences. Newspapers also mentioned that African Americans were supposed to attend the circus at specified times and dates.[84] However, segregationist practices at the turn-of-the-century circus were more comprehensive than in earlier years.

The historical evidence is less clear regarding the segregation of other racial groups at the circus. Route books and press releases frequently mentioned the presence of Native American, Chicano, and Asian American audiences, but generally do not specify where they sat, only that they sat en masse.[85] One article from 1903 did note that several Chinese attending Barnum & Bailey's Madison Square Garden date paid $1.50 for expensive box seats.[86] One spectator, Li Kung Chang, stated that he would never sit in the gallery, "where the representatives of Italy, Germany and Ireland are most prominent."[87]

Ticket prices, ranging from twenty-five cents to $2, made Circus Day a fairly expensive amusement for its day.[88] (It should be noted, however, that many dog-and-pony outfits charged only a dime for admission.)[89] Vaudeville tickets sold for a dime to a dollar, depending on the theater and the location of one's seat in the orchestra or gallery; "cheap nickel dumps" and dime museums cost what their names suggest; burlesque halls, concert saloons, and "ten-twenty-thirty" theaters, which featured "blood and thunder" melodramas, ranged in price from a dime to thirty cents.[90] Such amusements were part of a spectrum of ordinary, mostly urban leisure activities, whereas a large railroad circus or Wild West show might come to town only once or twice a year; as a result, residents could save in advance so that they might spend on Circus Day.

Like vaudeville, amusement parks, world's fairs, and the nascent movie industry, the railroad circus was an essential component of a burgeoning mass culture.[91] In the new urbanizing society at the turn of the century, immigrants and the native-born from all social classes increasingly participated in shared forms of popular entertainment.[92] David Nasaw explains that the new mass culture was "a by-product of the enormous expansion of cities."[93] Collectively, these popular forms helped bring about the development of twentieth-century mass culture forms like radio, television, and Disney's empire that capitalized on middle-class notions of propriety to produce virtuous entertainment for all classes. Unlike these amusements, though, the circus did not experience a development exclusively tied to the growth of cities; instead its evolution, as suggested earlier in this chapter, depended upon continental expansion and internal improvements.

76. Invitation to President Theodore Roosevelt to inaugural performance of Barnum & Bailey's Greatest Show on Earth, Madison Square Garden, Mar. 18, 1903, Correspondence, Box 16, Folder 1, JTMCC. Most route books contain references to audiences from local asylums; see "Friday, July 14, 1893, St. Peter, Minnesota . . . several hundred patients from the insane asylum at this place visited the show in a body." "Route Book, Ringling Bros., Season of 1893" (Buffalo: Courier, 1893), 61, Route Book Collection, RLPLRC.

77. "Review of Circus Day," *Galveston Daily News*, Nov. 13, 1898, 7, CAH.

78. $20 and $40 in 2000.

79. Speaight, *A History of the Circus*, 149.

80. Thayer, "The Birth of the Blues," 24–26.

81. Woodward, *The Strange Career of Jim Crow*, 81–87.

82. Dixie Willson, a ballet girl with the Ringling Bros. circus in 1921, commented on the color line in the South: "Never shall I forget my first sight of a straw house in the South. I hadn't thought about the dividing color line, and no one had spoken of it. I had traveled halfway around the hippodrome track on the elephant in the tournament, when suddenly I found myself facing a solid half circumference of faces! I can't describe the impression of it — so unexpected! So much of it all together! So terrifically shady!" Newspapers also mentioned the practice of segregation under the big top. The *New York News* reported in 1903 that Barnum & Bailey's date at Madison Square Garden had reserved seats in a segregated area for an African American boy's birthday party. Dixie Willson, *Where the World Folds Up at Night*, 61, Published Circus Memoir Collection, RLPLRC; "Pickaninnies at Circus," *New York News*, Apr. 10, 1903, BBPCB 1902–3, JMRMA.

83. C. Vann Woodward, *The Strange Career of Jim Crow*, 84; Alf T. Ringling, "With the Circus, A Route Book of Ringling Bros.' World's Greatest Shows, Seasons of 1895–1896" (St. Louis: Great Western, 1896), 78, 112–13, Route Book Collection, RLPLRC.

84. "Entrance for colored persons on the west side of building," *New Orleans Bee*, Jan. 13, 1835; "Persons of color admitted Wednesday and Saturday evenings (only), except those attending as servants," *Charleston* (S.C.) *Courier*, Jan. 19, 1835; "The pit is entirely enclosed for blacks," *Charlotte* (N.C.) *Journal*, Oct. 6, 1840 (all references courtesy of Stuart Thayer).

85. Virtually all route books mention the presence of Native American spectators. In the interest of brevity, here are two examples: "Official Route Book, Adam Forepaugh and Sells Bros. Combined Circuses, Season 1898" (Columbus, Ohio: Landon, 1898), 79, Route Book Collection, RLPLRC; "Official Route Book of Ringling Bros. World's Greatest Railroad Shows, Season 1892," 88.

86. $30 in 2000.

87. "Chinese at the Circus," *New York Mail and Express*, Mar. 26, 1903, BBPCB 1902–3, JMRMA.

88. A ten-cent, twenty-five-cent, and thirty-cent ticket in 1900 would cost $2, $5, and $6 in 2000.

89. Dahlinger Jr. and Thayer, *Badger State Showmen*, 89.

90. Kibler, *Rank Ladies*, 25–28; Nasaw, *Going Out*, 36–37.

91. John Kasson argues that the proliferation of large amusement parks such as Coney Island at the turn of the century heralded an emergent mass culture that rejected middle-class manners and taste in favor of interactive, and bawdy (albeit controlled) fun. As part of this burgeoning mass culture, the circus vigorously embraced "middle-class" values just as much as it flouted them. See John Kasson, *Amusing the Million*. For an excellent discussion of Coney Island in the context of working-class women's leisure at the turn of the century, see Peiss, *Cheap Amusements*, chapter 5.

92. For a perceptive historical overview of cultural hierarchy in twentieth-century America, see Kammen, *American Culture, American Tastes*; see also Butsch, *The Making of American Audiences*.

93. Nasaw, *Going Out*, 3.

Developing a List of Topics

Once you have all your notes in a computer file (or on cards or a pad), you need to organize them into a plan for your essay. (If you've already organized your notes by topic, you can skip this stage.) The first step is to *take inventory*: you search for ideas worth developing in your essay by (1) reviewing your notes and (2) identifying and writing down all the major topics that you have learned and thought about during your research.

Here's a list of topics taken from a set of notes about the *Chicago fire of 1871*:

Mrs. O'Leary's cow kicks over the lantern: did that start the fire?
Extent of the damage
Preventing panic
Feeding the homeless
Dealing with those trapped within buildings
Drought conditions the previous summer

Preventing looting
Beginning to rebuild the city
Mobilizing manpower to fight the fire
Improvising hospital conditions
Providing shelter
How the fire spread
Crowd control
Fighting the fire
Organizing the firefighters and police
Sounding the alarm

Since the subject of this essay is an event, the items on the list are factual and brief. An essay that deals with ideas rather than events is likely to have a preliminary list of topics with longer, more abstract entries. Notice that, at this point, the sequence of the entries doesn't matter; the points are in *random order*, just as they were found in the notes. Nor do you have to include supporting evidence at this stage. That's why the list is so skinny. You are extracting what's important from the mass of your notes; you are looking for the bones of your essay.

Taking Inventory of Your Notes and Forming Paragraph Topics

- *Do write down in any order the important ideas* that you find in your notes. At this point, the items don't have to be related to each other in sequence.

- *Don't try to summarize* all your notes. At this point, you are working on organizing your topics, not summarizing your research.

- *Don't try to link the ideas that you write down to specific sources.* At this point, there is no special reason to place the names of the sources next to your new list of ideas; not every statement in your new list will necessarily be included in your essay. Later, you will decide which source to use in support of which topic sentence.

- *Do think about your own reactions* to the information that you have collected. Now you are deciding what is worth writing about.

- *Do use your own words.* At this point, even if you only jot down a phrase, it should be your own version of the source's idea. Even if the information has appeared in ten different articles and you've included it ten different times in your notes, you are now, in some sense, making it your own.

Planning a Strategy

Essays about events or people tend to have a straightforward organization based on a *time sequence*, with a beginning, middle, and end. You will have a thesis to support—"The rescue and rehabilitation efforts after the Chicago fire were competently carried out"—but the bulk of the essay will analyze what happened during and after the fire in sequential order. Abstract topics, which are often arguments, require a more complex structure.

In Chapter 1, you learned that most arguments are based on a combination of two kinds of logical reasoning:

- *Deductive reasoning*: You provide a series of linked premises, based on a general assumption that you and your reader share, that leads to a conclusion.

- *Inductive reasoning*: You provide a range of specific evidence from which you construct a conclusion.

In practice, these two basic logical tools—the use of linked premises and the use of evidence—are used together to develop the most common strategies: cause and effect and problem and solution.

Constructing an Argument: High School Dropouts

The *cause-and-effect* **essay** establishes a causal link between two circumstances. The thesis usually answers the question "Why?" Let's assume that your general subject is *high school dropouts*. Why is the high school dropout rate as high as it is today? Here are a few typical answers:

- Because class sizes are too large
- Because students are poorly prepared to handle the work
- Because many students are foreign-born and can't speak English well
- Because local governments are not providing sufficient funding
- Because family life is breaking down, leaving students without support and discipline

You may initially be inclined to write about all these causes, giving each one equal weight. But that strategy will make your essay long and unmanageable, with a thesis that pulls the reader in many contradictory directions. Yet if you focus on only one cause, you run the risk of oversimplifying your argument. You need to consider which of these causes is *most responsible* for its effect—the high dropout rate—and which ones have a *contributing influence*.

Analyzing your list should also help you to determine *which causes work together*. For example, the problem of class size is probably linked to—caused by—the problem of inadequate funding. Here you have a smaller cause and effect embedded within the larger one:

Inadequate funding results in overly large classes, which, in turn, contribute to the dropout rate.

The links between causes—like funding and class size—form the *deductive* part of your argument. But the causes in the list above also lend themselves to *inductive* support. Comparative statistics about class size over several years and evidence of local budget cuts might (or might not) support your argument about the increasing dropout rate.

By the time you finish your research, you should be able to determine *whether your inductive evidence supports your deductive argument* about the reasons why students drop out. Assuming that it does, your essay will present factual evidence, including statistics, about class sizes, student preparedness, language difficulties, and diminished local budgets for education. The last point on your list—family breakdown—is the most abstract and so the most difficult to support. You would need to develop a series of deductive premises, along with evidence, to make a strong causal link between the decline of family life and the incidence of high school dropouts.

Let's assume that you decide on the following thesis:

> The poor educational environment, resulting from inadequate funding,
> makes it hard for students to learn, so they drop out.

What kinds of *counterarguments* would you have to anticipate and rebut? While much of your research supports your thesis, you have also found authorities who argue that students from strong family backgrounds perform well and stay in school even in overcrowded, poorly funded districts. You can continue to defend your preferred thesis, but you must also acknowledge your opponents' views, while pointing out their limitations.

The *problem-and-solution* **essay** often incorporates the cause-and-effect essay, using five stages:

1. *Establish that a problem exists.* Explain why it is a problem, and anticipate the negative consequences if nothing is done.

2. *Analyze the causes of the problem.* Here, you can include a modified version of the cause-and-effect strategy: emphasize the major causes, but remind your reader, citing evidence, that this is a complex issue, with a number of contributory influences working together.

3. *Assert the best solution.* Using the full evidence of your research, demonstrate why the preferred solution will work and indicate how you would go about implementing it.

4. *Anticipate counterarguments and answer them.* Your research has turned up authorities who have recommended different solutions. What are the advantages and disadvantages of those solutions? Is your solution better? Why?

5. *Conclude in a spirit of accommodation.* Assert your solution once again, but also consider acknowledging the complexity of the problem and making room for some of your opponents' ideas. Sometimes the arguments on either side of an issue are too evenly balanced for certainty, and you need to find a solution within common ground.

Arranging the Order of Topics: Outlining

At some point in the process of organizing your essay, your skinny list of ideas becomes an outline. An *outline* is a list of the major and minor points supporting an essay's thesis, presented in a pattern that conveys their relative importance. (See Chapter 5, p. 206.)

Their major points will probably all be *parallel* or of the same kind:

- the *reasons* why **x** is true,
- or the *ways* in which **y** happens,
- or the *differences* between **x** and **y**,
- or the chief *characteristics* of **z**.

I. These major points are given the most prominent place in the outline, usually at the left-hand margin.

   A. Secondary material—the ideas, information, or examples being used as supporting evidence—appears directly under each major point and slightly to the right.

      1. You may have different kinds of evidence to support a point or a group of examples.

      2. Each should be listed on a separate line.

Traditionally, outlines are written in a standard format, with major and minor points assigned numbers and letters of the alphabet to keep them in order. But there is absolutely no need to create a formal outline, with its letters and numbers, unless your instructor requires it or you find it useful for organizing your information. You can indicate the relationships between ideas simply by the way you place them on the page.

What is important is that, at this stage, you *revise and expand your inventory of major topics*, making new lists out of old ones, adding and deleting ideas, changing the order to correspond to your strategy. When that inventory list is as good as you can make it, you have *a sequence that will roughly correspond to the sequence of paragraphs in your essay.*

How do you decide on the best order for your topic list? Ask yourself the following questions:

- How are ideas linked together?
- Which is more important?

- What does your reader need to know first?
- What information does your reader need in order to understand a second, more complex point?
- How does one idea lead into another?

Look for an *organizing principle*. In a historical essay, the ordering principle is frequently *time*: the deployment of troops has to be described before the actual battle. In a personality profile, dominant qualities will take precedence over minor quirks. Problems get described before solutions; causes are analyzed first in order to understand their effects. One rationale for your sequence might be "most compelling" to "least compelling" reason. But an even stronger organizing principle is *"most fundamental" to "most complex"*: you start with your most basic point and demonstrate how everything else rests on that central idea.

In addition to rearranging the order of your topics, you also have to expand your inventory by *supplying supporting evidence for each major topic*. (In effect, you are filling in the secondary tiers of your outline.) Under headings like "firefighting" and "medical care," you insert factual information demonstrating that the authorities in Chicago reacted to the fire as efficiently as circumstances allowed. Similarly, having established a linked set of the causes and subcauses that encourage a higher dropout rate, you distribute the material gathered in your research—statistics, surveys, anecdotes, theories—under the appropriate topics.

Completing Your Outline

Your final organizational task is to rearrange your notes within the framework of your outline. This can be done either *directly on the computer*, working from your outline, or by *cross-referencing*. You may need to use a combination of both methods.

Using the Computer to Organize Your Essay

By Topic: Let's assume that most of your notes are contained in a file on your computer. If you originally organized your notes by topic, you simply *move your notes*, section by section, so that each portion is placed next to the appropriate topic in your outline. This is one time when cutting and pasting text is a quick and acceptable method of getting your work done. As you work, be sure to safeguard your notes. Instead of cutting and pasting, try *copying and pasting* so that your original file of notes remains intact. Keep a backup version of both your note file and your essay file. Above all, *save your work at regular and frequent intervals*.

Organizing Your Ideas

1. *Evaluate your inventory list of important ideas.*

   - Notice which ideas are in the mainstream of your research, discussed by several of your sources, and which ones appear only in one or two sources.
   - Think about eliminating topics that seem minor or remote from your subject and your thesis.
   - Consider whether you have enough evidence to support all of your topics.
   - Look for and combine topics that restate the same point.
   - If you are developing an argument essay, make sure that each of the key points supporting your side, as well as your counterarguments to the opposition, is supported by your research.

2. *Think about the sequence of ideas on your final list and the possible strategies for organizing your essay.*

   - How does your list of ideas help to establish a thesis?
   - Are you working with a collection of reasons? Consequences? Problems? Dangers?
   - What kind of essay are you writing? Cause and effect? Problem and solution? Explanation of a procedure? Evaluation of reasons for an argument?

   If you are developing a historical or biographical topic:
   - Did the event fall into distinct narrative stages?
   - What aspects of the scene would an observer have noticed?
   - Which of your subject's activities best reveals his or her personality?

   If you are developing an argument:
   - Does your issue lend itself to a cause-and-effect or a problem-and-solution essay?
   - Which are your most compelling arguments?
   - Do your main reasons require deductive or inductive support?

3. *Arrange your list of topics in a sequence that has meaning for you, carries out your strategy, and develops your thesis in a clear direction.*

By Source: If you originally organized your notes by source, organizing your essay now becomes a more complex process. If your topic is straightforward and your essay is under ten pages, you can probably rearrange your notes directly on the computer, as described in the previous paragraph. You type your outline into your essay file, with wide gaps between the topics, and start to move items (copying and pasting) from one file to the other. Instead of transferring whole sections as you would if you had organized your notes by topic, you'll be pulling out a quotation or a paragraph or an example from your notes and finding the right place for it in your outline sequence. This can be tedious and painstaking work.

Be extremely careful to *make sure that the source of each piece of information is indicated next to it before you move it.* Otherwise, as you write your essay, you won't be able to document your sources. Without documentation of sources, your research efforts have no validity.

Using Cross-Referencing to Organize Your Essay

If you're working on a lengthy and complicated essay with a set of notes organized by source, or if a large portion of your notes is on paper rather than in a computer file, your best option is to use cross-referencing to complete your outline and organize your essay. Cross-referencing is used *before* physically moving material from file to file. Once again, you're working from two sets of material:

- *Your completed outline of topics.* The topics are listed either on the screen or on a long pad. Make sure to leave wide gaps between each item. Assign a number (preferably a Roman numeral), in sequence, to each topic in your outline.
- *Your notes.* It's easiest to have everything on paper, including printouts of any computer notes. Assign an identifying letter to each source (placing it at the top of each page of notes devoted to material from that source). If you have 12 sources, you'll be using A–L. Assign an Arabic numeral to each separate piece of information within the notes from a specific source.

Now, once again, slowly read through all your research notes, this time keeping your outline of topics in front of you. Every time you come across a point in your notes that should be cited in support of a topic on your outline, immediately:

1. Place the number of the outline topic (X or XI) next to the reference in your notes.
2. Place the source's identifying letter (G) and the identifying number of the item in your notes (8) under the relevant topic in your outline.

Source G

Times, October 11, "The Ruined City," p. 1

1. The fire has stopped and there has been some "blessed rain."
2. 20–30 people have died in their homes.

XI 3. Plundering everywhere — like a scene of war
   A. A thief suffocated while trying to steal jewelry from a store.
   B. People who were caught pilfering had to be released because the jail burned down.

X   4. Lake used for drinking water.
5. People dying of exposure.

IX 6. Little food: people searching the ruins
IX 7. Difficulties of transporting supplies
XI 8. Meeting of citizens at church to help protect what was left, to help homeless, and to provide water if further fires broke out

Figure 9-4 Cross-referencing: notes — step 1

For the system to work, you must complete *both* stages: notes must be keyed to the outline, and the outline must be keyed to each item in your research notes. The notes and the outline criss-cross each other; hence the term *cross-referencing*.

To illustrate cross-referencing, here is an example taken from the notes and outline for an essay on the Chicago fire. The outline was divided into three main sections: the *causes* of the fire, the *panic* during the fire, and *restoring order* after the fire. Figure 9-4 shows an excerpt from the *notes*, with Roman numerals written in the margins to indicate cross-references to three specific paragraph topics. Figure 9-5 shows a portion of the *outline*, with letters and numbers

IX. Feeding the homeless   G6 / G7
X.   Providing basic services   G4
XI. Protecting life and property   G3 / G8

Figure 9-5 Cross-referencing: topic list — step 2

indicating cross-references to specific evidence within the notes file. When you have finished cross-referencing:

- Your outline will have a precise list of sources to be cited for each major point, and
- Your research notes will have keyed numbers in most (but not necessarily all) of the margins.

Cross-referencing helps you to avoid time-consuming searches for references while you are writing the essay. When you start to work on the paragraph dealing with "Feeding the Homeless," you consult your outline and immediately go to Source G, Items 6 and 7. (Later, references to other sources will also have been placed next to Item IX on your outline.) The accumulated information will become the basis for writing that paragraph.

A few of the items in the notes for Source G have no cross-references next to them. Some will be cross-referenced to other topics in this outline, and haven't yet been given their reference numbers. Items 2 and 5, for example, would probably come under the heading of Casualties, in the section on panic during the fire. On the other hand, some items simply won't fit into the topics chosen for the outline and will be discarded.

Writing Integrated Paragraphs

Writing a research essay resembles putting together a *mosaic*. Each paragraph has a basic design, determined by its topic sentence. To carry out the design, a paragraph might contain a *group of reasons or examples* to illustrate its main idea, *or* an *extended explanation* to develop that idea in greater detail, *or* a *comparison* between two elements introduced in the first sentence. These are the same paragraphing designs that you use in all your writing. What makes the research essay different is the fact that the materials are assembled from many sources.

Imagine that the notes that you have taken from several different sources are boxes of tiles, each box containing a different color. You may find it easier to avoid mixing the colors and to work *only* with red tiles or *only* with blue, or to devote one corner of the mosaic to a red pattern and another to a blue. In the same way, you may find it both convenient and natural to work with only one source at a time and to avoid the decisions and the adjustments that must be made when you are combining different styles and ideas. But, of course, it is the design and only the design that dictates which colors should be used in creating the pattern of the mosaic, and *it is the design or outline of your essay that dictates which evidence should be included in each paragraph.*

When you present a topic in a given paragraph, you must work with all the relevant information that you have gathered about that topic, whether it comes

Constructing Paragraphs in a Research Essay

1. *Each paragraph should possess a single main idea, usually expressed in the topic sentence, that supports the development of your essay's thesis.* That topic controls the selection and arrangement of all the information in the paragraph. Everything that is included should develop and support that single idea, without digressions.

2. *The body of the paragraph should contain information taken from a variety of sources.* The number of different sources that you include in any one paragraph depends on the number of authors in your research notes who have touched on that idea.

3. *The sentences of your completed paragraph should be easy to read, coherent, and unified.*

   - Do integrate your material so that your reader will not be distracted by the differing sources or made aware of breaks between the various points.

   - Don't integrate your material so completely that you forget to provide appropriate acknowledgment of your sources.

from one source or from many. Of course, you may have too much material; you may find it impossible to fit everything into the paragraph without overloading it with repetition. These rejected pieces may not fit into another part of the essay; instead, they will go back into their boxes as a backup or reserve fund of information.

Here is a paragraph from a student essay about the novelist F. Scott Fitzgerald, using MLA documentation, which presents four different accounts of an affair between Fitzgerald's wife, Zelda, and Edouard Jozan, a young Frenchman. To emphasize the variety and complexity of the research, the names of the sources and the attributing verbs and phrases have been underlined.

There is a lack of agreement about the details of the affair as well as its significance for the Fitzgeralds' marriage. According to one of Fitzgerald's biographers, Jozan and Zelda afterward regarded it as "nothing more than a summer flirtation" (Mayfield 97). But Ernest Hemingway, in his memoirs, wrote much later that Scott had told him "a truly sad story" about the affair, which he repeated many times in the course of their friendship (172). Gerald and Sara Murphy, who were present that summer and remembered the incident very well, told of being awakened by Scott in the middle of a September night in order to help him revive Zelda from an overdose of sleeping pills. The Murphys were sure that this incident was related to her affair with Jozan (Milford 111). Nancy Milford, Zelda's biographer, believes that the affair affected Zelda more than Scott, who, at that time, was very engrossed in his work. Indeed, Milford's account of the affair is the only one that suggests that Zelda was so deeply in love with Jozan that she asked Scott for a divorce (112). According to an interview with Jozan, the members of this triangle never engaged in a three-way confrontation; Jozan told Milford that the Fitzgeralds were "the victims of their own unsettled and a little unhealthy imagination" (112).

This paragraph gives a brief but adequate account of what is known about the events of that summer of 1924. The writer does not try to rush through the four accounts of the affair, nor does he reduce each one to a phrase, as if he expected the reader to have prior knowledge of these people and their activities. In the context of the whole essay, the paragraph provides enough information for the reader to judge whose interpretation of the affair is closest to the truth.

Accommodating Argument in Your Paragraphs

Presenting an Inductive Argument

When you write a paragraph based on *induction*, the topic sentence should clearly summarize the range of evidence being cited. Here is an example from Edward Tenner's *Why Things Bite Back*, a book about the dangers of technological progress:

topic sentence: "dangerous myth"

The startling wartime successes of penicillin created the dangerous myth of an antibiotic panacea. Even after the U.S. Food and Drug Administration began to require prescriptions in the mid-1950s, an antibiotic injection or prescription remained for many people the payoff of a medical encounter. They resisted the medical fact that antibiotics can do nothing against colds and other viral diseases. In many other countries, antibiotics are still sold legally over the counter to patients who may never get proper instructions about dosage or the importance of completing a course of treatment. Dr. Stuart B.

1st example

Levy of Boston cites an Argentinian businessman who was cured of leukemia but died of an infection by the common bacterium *E. coli*. Ten years of self-medication had produced plasmids in his body that were resistant to every antibiotic used. Governments, too, have unintentionally promoted resurgence.

transition

Indonesian authorities have literally ladled out preventive doses of tetracycline

2nd example

to 100,000 Muslim pilgrims for a week at a time. Since the Mecca pilgrimage has historically been one of the great mixing bowls of microorganisms, it is especially disturbing to learn that half of all cholera bacilli in Africa are now resistant to tetracycline.

Paragraphs presenting inductive evidence tend to be long. Tenner makes his point about the "dangerous myth" of penicillin in the topic sentence, but he doesn't immediately cite evidence. He first explains the "danger" in the second sentence, and the "myth" in the third. Only then does he introduce his first supporting point—self-medication in countries without drug regulation—with Dr. Levy's example of the antibiotic-resistant Argentinian businessman. Signaled by the transitional word "too," Tenner's second example—the Mecca pilgrimage—increases the scale of potential danger.

Presenting a Deductive Argument

In contrast to the specific examples of induction, an article on "Methods of Media Manipulation" starts in a *deductive* mode, with a series of premises:

primary premise

1st causal premise

2nd causal premise

We are told by people in the media industry that news bias is unavoidable. Whatever distortions and inaccuracies are found in the news are caused by deadline pressures, human misjudgment, budgetary restraints, and the difficulty of reducing a complex story into a concise report. Furthermore—the argument goes—no communication system can hope to report everything, selectivity is needed.

Parenti's alternative primary premise

I would argue that the media's misrepresentations are not at all the result of innocent error and everyday production problems, though such problems certainly do exist. True, the press has to be selective, but what principle of selectivity is involved?

causal premise

Media bias usually does not occur in random fashion; rather, it moves in the same overall direction again and again, favoring management over labor, corporations over corporate critics, affluent whites over low-income minorities, officialdom over protesters. . . . The built-in biases of the corporate mainstream media faithfully reflect the dominant ideology, seldom straying into territory that might cause discomfort to those who hold political and economic power, including those who own the media or advertise in it.

The initial presentation of Michael Parenti's argument is based on a dichotomy—contrast—between the media's view of news bias and his own. There is a disputed primary premise (bias is or is not avoidable) and a disputed secondary premise (one can't print everything vs. one prints what pleases one's corporate masters). Parenti's premises are developed in more detail, and the article goes on to support those premises through induction, by citing evidence of such manipulative tactics as "suppression by omission" and "framing."

Presenting Both Sides of an Argument

While the opening of Parenti's article presents the opposition's argument as well as his own, the tone is grudging, even hostile. He leaves no room for accommodation between the two points of view. Yet, whenever possible, *it is useful to acknowledge some merit in your opponents or in their argument.* Here are excerpts from two essays supporting opposite sides of the "wilderness preservation" issue. In the first, John Daniel is arguing that the advancement of science, if uncontrolled, can do harm to unspoiled land. He is careful, however, to distinguish between his allies and his enemies:

positive view

negative view

I don't mean to indict science in general. Many of the foremost champions of wild nature are scientists, and their work has done much to warn us of the environmental limits we are transgressing. I am arguing only against interventionist science that wants to splice genes, split atoms, or otherwise manipulate the wild — science aimed more at control than understanding, science that assumes ownership of the natural mysteries. When technological specialists come to believe that nature is answerable to their own prerogatives, they are not serving but endangering the greater community.

In William Tucker's view, society has more compelling interests, to which the wilderness movement must sometimes defer. But, before stating his argument, he pays his dues to nature:

positive view

negative view

I am not arguing against wild things, scenic beauty, pristine landscapes, and scenic preservation. What I am questioning is the argument that wilderness is a value against which every other human activity must be judged and that human beings are somehow unworthy of the landscape. The wilderness has been equated with freedom, but there are many different ideas about what constitutes freedom. . . .

Interestingly enough, Tucker then proceeds to move from his impeccably fair presentation to an argument that approaches *ad hominem* — a personal attack:

undercuts
opponents

attacks by
innuendo

It may seem unfair to itemize the personal idiosyncrasies of people who feel comfortable only in wilderness, but it must be remembered that the environmental movement has been shaped by many people who literally spent years of their lives living in isolation.

Citing John Muir, David Brower, and Gary Snyder, leaders of the Sierra Club who spent much time alone in the mountains, Tucker continues:

positive view

There is nothing reprehensible in this, and the literature and philosophy that emerge from such experiences are often admirable. But it seems

negative view   questionable to me that the ethic that comes out of this wilderness isolation —
and the sense of ownership of natural landscapes that inevitably follows — can
serve as the basis for a useful national philosophy.

Whatever his disclaimers, Tucker is rooting one of his key arguments
against the wilderness movement in the personal preferences of three men. He
does not, however, resort to using slanted, exaggerated, or dismissive language
about his opponents. In contrast, here is Robert W. McChesney's attack on commercialism in the media:

image of attack   The commercial blitzkrieg into every nook and cranny of U.S. culture, from
schools to sport to museums to movie theaters to the Internet, has lessened
traditional distinctions of public service from commercialism.

The word *blitzkrieg* (literally, lightning battle) originally referred to the German army in World War II. It immediately conjures up an image of a mecha-
nized, pitiless army rolling over everything in its path, a reference reinforced by
the domestic, vulnerable image of "nook and cranny," used to describe U.S. culture, the victim. Without even articulating his point, McChesney has created a
lingering association between corporations and Nazis. This is a clever use of
language, but is it a fair argument? In the next example, Leslie Savan also uses
emotionally charged language to attack a similar target:

image of disease   Advertising now infects just about every organ of society, and wherever
advertising gains a foothold it tends to slowly take over, like a vampire or a virus.

The brutal swiftness of the blitzkrieg has been replaced by the slow insinu-
ation of an infection, but both images are deadly. (The allusion to a vampire
must have been tempting—advertising leaves viewers bloodless and brain-
washed—but it should not be combined with the insidious, slowly creeping image of infection.) Interestingly enough, McChesney and Savan are both
adopting the tactics of the commercial media that they condemn: using powerful images in an attempt to force their readers into agreement.

Presenting Arguments Fairly

Perhaps the greatest disservice that you can do your sources is to distort
them so that your reader is left with a false impression of what they have said
or written. Such distortion is most likely to happen when you are writing an argumentative essay.

1. **Present both sides of the argument.**

One way of shading an argument to suit your own ends is to *misrepresent the strength of the opposition.* Let us assume that you are working

with a number of articles, all of which are effectively presented and worth citing. Some clearly support your point of view; others are openly opposed; and a few avoid taking sides, emphasizing related but less controversial topics. If your essay cites only the favorable and neutral articles, and avoids any reference to the views of the opposition, you have presented the issue falsely. A one-sided presentation will make you appear to be either biased or sloppy in your research. If the sources are available and if their views are pertinent, they should be represented and, if you wish, refuted in your essay.

2. **Provide a complete account of the argument.**

Sometimes, distortions occur accidentally, because you have presented only a *partial* account of a source's views. In the course of an article or a book, authors sometimes examine a variety of views before making it clear which ones they support. Or an author may have mixed opinions about the issue and see merit in more than one point of view. If you choose to quote or paraphrase material from only one section of such a work, then you must also inform your reader that these statements are not entirely representative of the writer's overall views.

3. **Make sure that you—and your reader—understand whether the source really supports the idea that you are citing.**

Ideas can get distorted because of the researcher's misunderstanding, careless note taking, or hasty reading. Review the entire section of the article or your notes before you attribute an opinion to your source. Make sure that you are not taking a sentence out of context or ignoring a statement in the next paragraph or on the next page that may be more typical of the writer's thinking. Writers often use an argumentative strategy that sets up a point with which they basically disagree in order to shoot it down shortly thereafter. Don't confuse a statement made for the sake of argument with a writer's real beliefs.

4. **Provide a fair presentation.**

You may be so eager to uphold your point of view that you will cite any bit of material that looks like supporting evidence. To do so, however, you may have to twist the words of the source to fit your ideas. This is one of the worst kinds of intellectual dishonesty—and one of the easiest for a suspicious reader to detect: one has only to look up the source. If your sources' evidence does not sufficiently support your side, then you should seriously consider switching sides or switching topics.

Here is a fairly clear instance of such distortion. In an essay on the need for prison reform, Garry Wills is focusing on the *deficiencies of our society's penal system*; he is not directly concerned with the arguments for or against the death penalty. But the student citing Wills in a research essay is writing specifically in support of capital punishment. To make Wills's argument fit into the scheme of this essay, the student must make some suspiciously selective references. Here is a paragraph from the research essay (on the left), side by side with the source:

Although the death penalty may seem very harsh and inhuman, is this not fair and just punishment for one who was able to administer death to another human being? A murderer's victim always receives the death penalty. Therefore, the death penalty for the murderer evens the score, or, as stated in the Bible, "an eye for an eye, and a tooth for a tooth." According to Garry Wills, "take a life, lose your life." Throughout the ages, society has demanded that man be allowed to right his wrongs. Revenge is our culture's oldest way of making sure that no one "gets away with" any crime. As Wills points out, according to this line of reasoning, the taking of the murderer's life can be seen as his payment to society for his misdeed.

The oldest of our culture's views on punishment is the *lex talionis*, an eye for an eye. Take a life, lose your life. It is a very basic cry—people must "pay" for their crimes, yield exact and measured recompense. No one should "get away with" any crime, like a shoplifter taking something unpaid for. The desire to make an offender suffer equivalent pain (if not compensatory excess of pain) is very deep in human nature, and rises quickly to the surface. What is lynching but an impatience with even the slightest delay in exacting this revenge? It serves our social myth to say that this impatience, if denied immediate gratification, is replaced by something entirely different—by an impersonal dedication to justice. Only lynchers want revenge, not those who wait for a verdict. That is not very likely. Look at the disappointed outcry if the verdict does not yield even delayed satisfaction of the grudge.

In the essay, the writer is citing only *part* of Wills's argument and thus makes him appear to support capital punishment. Wills is being misrepresented because (unlike the writer) he considers it fair to examine the views of the opposing side before presenting his own arguments. *The ideas that the student cites are not Wills's, but Wills's presentations of commonly accepted assumptions about punishment.* It is not entirely clear whether the writer of the research essay has merely been careless, failing to read past the first few sentences, or whether the misrepresentation is intentional.

> ### Mistakes to Avoid When Presenting an Argument
>
> 1. Don't be one-sided; present *both* sides of an argument.
> 2. Don't omit crucial parts of the source's reasoning; provide a complete account of the argument.
> 3. Don't quote ideas out of context: make sure that you—and your reader—understand whether the source really supports the idea that you are citing.
> 4. Don't twist the source's ideas to fit your own purpose; provide a fair presentation.

Integrating Your Sources: Recruiting in College Athletics

To illustrate the need for careful analysis of sources before you write your paragraphs, here is a group of passages, all direct quotations, which have been gathered for a research essay on college athletics. The paragraph developed from these sources must support the writer's *thesis*:

Colleges should, in the interests of both players and academic standards, outlaw the high-pressure tactics used by coaches when they recruit high school players for college teams.

The first three statements come from college coaches, describing recruiting methods that they have observed and carried out; the last four are taken from books that discuss corruption in athletics.

I think in the long run, every coach must recognize this basic principle, or face the alumni firing squad. Recruiting is the crux of building a championship football team.

STEVE SLOAN, Texas Tech

Athletics is creating a monster. Recruiting is getting to be cancerous.

DALE BROWN, Louisiana State University

You don't out-coach people, you out-recruit them.

PAUL "BEAR" BRYANT, University of Alabama

It is an athletic maxim that a man with no special coaching skills can win games if he recruits well and that a tactician without talented players is a man soon without a job.

KENNETH DENLINGER

There is recruiting in various degrees in every intercollegiate sport, from crew to girls' basketball and from the Houston golf dynasty that began in the mid-50's to Southern California importing sprinters and jumpers from Jamaica.

J. ROBERT EVANS

The fundamental causes of the defects in American college athletics are too much commercialism and a negligent attitude towards the educational opportunity for which the college exists.

CARNEGIE FOUNDATION, 1929

[*Collier's* magazine, in 1905, reported that] Walter Eckersall, All-American quarterback, enrolled at Chicago three credits short of the entrance requirement and his teammate, Leo Detray, entered the school before he even graduated high school. In addition the University of Minnesota paid two players outright to play in a single game (Nebraska: 1902). A quarterback and an end also from Minnesota admitted shaving points during the 1903 Beloit game.

JOSEPH DURSO

Examining the Sources

Your paragraph will focus on recruiting high school stars, as opposed to developing students who enter college by the ordinary admissions procedure. Which of these ideas and observations should be included in the paragraph? And which statements should be represented by *paraphrase* or by *direct quotation*?

I think in the long run every coach must recognize this basic principle, or face the alumni firing squad. Recruiting is the crux of building a championship football team.

STEVE SLOAN

This very broad generalization seems quotable at first because it sums up the topic so well; but, in fact, it does not advance your argument any further. Therefore, you need not include Coach Sloan's statement if your topic sentence makes the same point. (In general, you should write your own topic sentences rather than letting your sources write them for you.) The phrase "alumni firing squad" might be useful to quote in a later paragraph, in a discussion of the specific influence of alumni on recruiting.

> Athletics is creating a monster. Recruiting is getting to be cancerous.
>
> DALE BROWN

Coach Brown's choice of images—"cancerous" and "monster"—is certainly vivid; but the sentence as a whole is no more than a generalized opinion about recruiting, not an *explanation* of why the situation is so monstrous. Don't quote Brown for the sake of two words.

> You don't out-coach people, you out-recruit them.
>
> PAUL "BEAR" BRYANT

This is the first statement that has advanced a specific idea: the coach may have a *choice* between building a winning team through recruiting and building a winning team through good coaching; but recruiting, not coaching, wins games. Coach Bryant, then, is not just making a rhetorical point, as the first two coaches seem to be. His seven-word sentence would make a good introduction to or summation of a point that deserves full discussion.

The remaining four statements suggest a wider range of approach and style.

> Walter Eckersall, All-American quarterback, enrolled at Chicago three credits short of the entrance requirement and his teammate, Leo Detray, entered the school before he even graduated high school. In addition, the University of Minnesota paid two players outright to play in a single game (Nebraska: 1902). A quarterback and an end also from Minnesota admitted shaving points during the 1903 Beloit game.
>
> JOSEPH DURSO

This passage emphasizes corruption more than recruiting and indicates that commercialism is nothing new in college athletics. Although the information is interesting, it is presented as a list of facts, and the language is not worth quoting. You may, however, want to summarize the example in your own words.

> The fundamental causes of the defects in American college athletics are too much commercialism and a negligent attitude towards the educational opportunity for which the college exists.
>
> CARNEGIE FOUNDATION

This extract from the 1929 Carnegie Foundation study is phrased in abstract language that is characteristic of foundation reports and academic writing in general. The foundation raises an important idea: an athlete recruited to win games (and earn fame and fortune) is likely to ignore the primary reason for going to college—to acquire an education. But there is no compelling reason to quote (rather than paraphrase) this statement. Remember that you include quotations in your essay to enhance your presentation; the quotation marks automatically prepare the reader for special words and phrasing. But the prose here is too colorless and abstract to justify quotation.

> There is recruiting in varying degrees in every intercollegiate sport, from crew to girls' basketball and from the Houston golf dynasty that began in the mid-50's to Southern California importing sprinters and jumpers from Jamaica.
>
> J. ROBERT EVANS

This statement presents a quite different, more detailed level of information about recruiting in several sports. Will these references be at all meaningful to the reader who is not familiar with the "Houston golf dynasty" or Jamaican track stars? To know that intensive recruitment is not limited to cash sports, such as football, is interesting, but such specifics date too quickly to be interesting to most readers.

> It is an athletic maxim that a man with no special coaching skills can win games if he recruits well and that a tactician without talented players is a man soon without a job.
>
> KENNETH DENLINGER

Largely because of parallel construction, this statement sounds both sharp and solid. In much the same way as Coach Bryant's seven words, Kenneth Denlinger sums up the contrast between coaching and recruiting, and suggests which one has the edge. Because the statement gives the reader something substantial to think about and because it is well phrased, Denlinger is probably worth quoting.

Writing the Paragraph

Should the writer include the statements by Bryant and by Denlinger, both of which say essentially the same thing? While Bryant's firsthand comment is terse and authoritative, Denlinger's is more complete and self-explanatory. A solution might be to include both, at different points in the paragraph, with Bryant cited at the end to sum up the idea that has been developed. Of course, the other five sources need not be excluded from the paragraph. Rather, if you wish, all five may be referred to, by paraphrase or brief reference, with their authors' names cited.

Here is one way of integrating this set of statements into a paragraph. Of the nine sentences, four (indicated in italics) cite no sources: the first two establish the paragraph's topic; two are used later to introduce transitional points. The other five sentences cite sources as supporting evidence. (Note that the sources are documented using MLA style; the bibliography has been omitted. MLA style is explained on pp. 439–447.)

> *In college athletics, what is the best way for a school to win games? Should a strong team be gradually built up by training ordinary students from scratch, or should the process be shortened and success be assured by actively recruiting players who already know how to win?* The first method may be more consistent with the traditional amateurism of college athletics, but as early as 1929, the Carnegie Foundation complained that the focus of college sports had shifted from education to the material advantages of winning (Denlinger 22). Even earlier, in 1903, there were several instances of players without academic qualifications who were "hired" to guarantee victory (Durso 6). *And in recent years excellence of recruiting has become the most important skill for a coach to possess.* Kenneth Denlinger has observed, "It is an athletic maxim that a man with no special coaching skills can win games if he recruits well and that a tactician without talented players is a man soon without a job" (3). *It follows, then, that a coach who wants to keep his job is likely to concentrate on spotting and collecting talent for his team.* Coaches from LSU, Alabama, and Texas Tech all testify that good recruiting has first priority throughout college athletics (McDermott 17; Mano 41; Sloan 106). According to Bear Bryant of Alabama: "You don't out-coach people, you out-recruit them" (Mano 41).

Writing an Introduction

The introduction presents a *preview* of your essay, announcing the topic and the method(s) you are likely to use to present that topic (explanation or analysis or persuasion). Often, the introduction will include a statement of the thesis, although with some strategies (notably, problem and solution), it can be preferable to indicate the problem at the beginning and allow the argument and evidence to set the stage for a presentation of the thesis toward the end of the essay.

The introduction also has a *marketing* function. You want to encourage your reader to move past the first paragraph or two and into the body of the essay. To do so, you need to do more than set out your wares; you have to make the shop window look attractive. Using compelling or intriguing language can catch the reader's attention. Including an example or (if not too long) an anecdote can make the reader feel interested in or sympathetic to the topic that you propose to explore.

Introductions by Professional Writers

Here are the introductions of two essays by professional authors. As you read, consider whether the author tells you what he is going to write about and whether—and why—he makes you want to continue reading.

David Brooks, a writer, editor, and commentator on public affairs, wrote "People Like Us" for the *Atlantic Monthly*. Michael Bérubé, who teaches English and Cultural Studies at Pennsylvania State University, published "How to End Grade Inflation" in the *Chronicle of Higher Education*.

Maybe it's time to admit the obvious. We don't really care about diversity all that much in America, even though we talk about it a great deal. Maybe somewhere in this country there is a truly diverse neighborhood in which a black Pentecostal minister lives next to a white anti-globalization activist, who lives next to an Asian short-order cook, who lives next to a professional golfer, who lives next to a post-modern-literature professor and a cardiovascular surgeon. But I have never been to or heard of that neighborhood. Instead, what I have seen all around the country is people making strenuous efforts to group themselves with people who are basically like themselves.

DAVID BROOKS, from "People Like Us"

Last month, Princeton University announced it would combat grade inflation by proposing that A-minuses, A's and A-pluses be awarded to no more than the top 35 percent of students in any course. For those of us in higher education, the news has come as a shock, almost as if Princeton had declared that spring in central New Jersey would begin promptly on March 21, with pleasant temperatures in the 60s and 70s through the end of the semester. For until now, grade inflation was like the weather: it got worse every year, or at least everyone said so, and yet hardly anybody did anything about it.

MICHAEL BÉRUBÉ, from "How to End Grade Inflation"

Brooks's introduction does everything that an introduction is supposed to do. You are quickly made aware of his *topic and its scope* (social diversity in America), his *intention* (analysis through contrast between good intentions and reality), and his *thesis* (we try to fool ourselves that we live in culturally diverse communities, but we do not). Brooks compels your attention with a striking, brief first sentence that makes you wonder what "the obvious" is going to be. Then he proceeds to attack what he regards as a national illusion, citing a string of concrete examples that, by its very length, makes you want to know what cultural type will be mentioned next. He finishes the paragraph—and his introduction—by asserting the other half of the contrast contained in his thesis: people really don't want diversity. By the end of that paragraph, Brooks's intended audience—the readers of the *Atlantic Monthly*—are likely to be hooked.

In contrast, Bérubé begins his introduction much more traditionally: he tells his readers about Princeton's decision to stop grade inflation and thus provides *the context* for his essay. We know the topic and scope (grade inflation in American universities), but we don't know much as yet about his intention and his thesis. What is striking in this introduction is the use of irony: by drawing an analogy between Princeton's proposal and ideal weather conditions, Bérubé lets us know just how unsatisfactory a situation (like a rainy spring) grade inflation is and how desirable (but unlikely) it would be to find a solution to the problem. Since his audience is his fellow academics, who probably share his concerns, his readers will want to know how Bérubé proposes to solve the problem.

Introductions from Student Essays

Students introducing a research essay can provide just as comprehensive a preview of their topic, scope, intention, and thesis. What is often missing is the *vivid example* or the *compelling choice of words* to make the reader want to continue reading. Consider the following example:

1.   As more and more women in the United States work outside the home for longer hours, their children are often cared for by workers in day care centers or by babysitters. Some women work for economic reasons, because they are single mothers or because their families can't manage on a single salary. Many of these women would really like to stay home with their children but feel they have no choice but to go out of the home to work. Others have experienced housewife blues or have come to believe, with the feminist movement, that they can't be fulfilled without a career. In fact, psychologists have studied the children of working mothers and have concluded that being deprived of a mother's care and attention can cause lasting adverse effects on children. What can a working mother do to prevent this from happening?

Here, we have a straightforward presentation of a *problem* that, presumably, the writer will attempt to solve—or, at least, analyze and clarify—in the body of the essay. We can expect to see statistics and studies cited as well as the opinions of experts in the field. This is likely to be a solid essay that makes its point convincingly. But does the introduction make you want to read it?

2.   My grandparents emigrated to this country from Italy. They were eager to take advantage of the opportunities America offered and, in exchange, tried to become good citizens in the community where they settled. In a very few years, they had become completely assimilated,

speaking and behaving more American than the third-generation Americans around them. For my grandparents, America was a melting pot; for immigrants today, it is merely a host nation that provides the opportunity to have a better life without requiring or even encouraging them to give their cultural allegiance in return. Our immigration policy will never be successful, as it used to be, until there is the expectation that immigrants will leave their old cultures behind and think, speak, and act like their American neighbors.

This introduction is anchored by the *personal example* in the first few sentences, which leads into the contrast between immigration fifty years ago and immigration now, expressed as a thesis in the last sentence. Persuading readers to accept this thesis will surely require the citation of facts, statistics, and expert opinion, not just examples and anecdotal evidence. But the story of the writer's grandparents is compelling and makes the reader want to find out why—or whether—experiences like these have passed into history.

Using Visuals as Sources

You can present ideas and cite evidence visually as well as through words. Several of the professional essays in this book are accompanied by visuals. In addition, both of the model research essays in Chapter 11 include pictures. Let's consider how the presence of various kinds of visuals can give the reader a more vivid and immediate understanding of the author's meaning.

Understanding the Impact of Visuals

One way of using visuals is to present data through *tables and figures* such as *charts, graphs, and maps*. These kinds of visuals generally compare information in separate categories, at different times or in different places. In this way, visuals serve as supporting evidence, used to make a point succinctly. In "The Weight of the World" (p. 7), Don Peck finds it easier to use maps than words to raise complex issues about increasing obesity in the United States. Peck is dealing with two sets of variables: location (levels of obesity vary among 48 states) and time (levels of obesity in each of the states varied between 1991 and 2000). By using three maps to provide snapshots over time and shading to indicate relative levels of obesity, Peck gets his point across visually. Similarly, most of the information contained in the text of "For College Athletes, Recruiting Is a Fair (but Flawed) Game" (pp. 54–56) can be more readily grasped by examining the accompanying set of charts and tables.

Photographs, moving images, and *drawings* provide the reader with an instant impression of the author's point. Images can attract readers to the text, interest them in the topic, and encourage them to see how the thesis develops. Photographs are especially useful to authors who are writing about historical topics and want to provide readers with a sense of the period. As a context for her description of 1950s shopping centers (p. 131), Lizabeth Cohen includes pictures of typical shoppers. We know that the pictures are authentic because the caption cites the R.H. Macy & Co., Inc., *1957 Annual Report* and, equally important, the archival collection where Cohen found that report. The stylized drawing used to illustrate Katherine Ashenburg's *The Dirt on Clean* (p. 9) conveys much the same sense of an earlier period: father and son having rowdy fun in the bath—and using Lifebuoy. The lighthearted drawing serves as a counterweight to the grim message about body odor in the lower left-hand corner of the advertisement.

In contrast to the relatively objective data contained in charts and graphs, photographs and moving images are likely to *appeal to the emotions* rather than merely to reason, with the reader subtly encouraged to accept the author's assumptions and conclusions. A great deal depends on the *choice* of picture. The pictures accompanying Jennifer Medina's "Next Question: Can Students Be Paid to Excel?" (pp. 254–255, 257) are not entirely effective. This is a straight news story with relatively little scope for emotional appeal. Although the smiles on the students' faces seem genuine enough, the pictures look posed and artificial. The shot of the tally sheet, showing potential and actual rewards, has a more immediate impact.

More intense emotions are evoked by the photograph accompanying Dan Bilefsky's human-interest story about separated families in Romania (p. 46). A teenage boy, Gheorghe, stiffly holds a Mother's Day card which contains a picture of Stefan, his 12-year-old half-brother who committed suicide. The photo serves as a poignant "mug shot" of the two brothers and underscores the living boy's loss. To show the pattern of migration, the *New York Times* helpfully provides a *map* of Romania and its neighboring countries; unfortunately, it doesn't show Italy, so we don't get a sense of how far apart the family were going to be when the mother left to find work.

Note that if you include grim, painful images, then they must not be gratuitous; they must serve as evidence to support your explanation or argument. In an essay about the work of nonprofit organizations (NPOs) during a major disaster, should you show pictures of victims being aided or victims deteriorating because no help has arrived? Obviously, the choice to some extent depends on the thesis. But the pictures should also be reasonably representative of the facts: if data indicate that NPOs used their available resources effectively in a particular relief effort, then that's what should be depicted. If you want to demonstrate that the NPOs were too underfunded or too incompetent to deliver sufficient aid—and if the facts support that view—then it would be reasonable to appeal to the reader's compassion by showing injured, untended earthquake victims or a village decimated by a tsunami.

Cartoons use humor and irony to comment on an essay or article and expand the reader's understanding of its thesis:

- The brief comic strip accompanying the excerpt from *Afflenza* (p. 135) has a simple purpose: it extends the idea of disposable products to the point of absurdity—temporary worker depicted in the trash can—demonstrating technology's apparent triumph over human beings and their values.

- Nicholas Carr is making a similar point in his article about the rise of the Internet and, particularly, Google (p. 95); but the cartoon here is more subtle: the driver—clearly a geek—is speeding down the Internet Highway while reading a book. Is Carr telling us that Web and print media can live happily side by side as we multitask? Or does one endanger the other? And what's the sinister function of the Internet Patrol?

- The cartoon illustrating "Cuss Time" (p. 23) resolves the underlying paradox of Jill McCorkle's essay: swearing is morally bad for you and emotionally good for you. The mother announcing that her toddler is "swearing in full sentences now" shows pride in this intellectual milestone—"full sentences"—and seems indifferent to the child's profanity. McCorkle, on the other hand, seems uncomfortable about her decision to encourage her son to swear, and devotes most of her essay to justifying it. The cartoon, depicting an untroubled mother and happy child, immediately takes us to the comfort zone that McCorkle has had such difficulty finding.

Using Visuals in Your Essay

Occasionally, visuals—usually photographs—serve as the inspiration for your thesis or as the framework for the development of your essay:

- If you were writing about the effects of plastic surgery on teenagers with facial defects, you would make the greatest impact by including "before and after" *photographs*.

- If you were analyzing the effect of automobile commercials on consumer choices, you would want to show your reader some striking examples, perhaps by supplementing the text of your essay with a *CD-ROM* containing some filmed commercials (or *links* to the commercials if they are available on the Web and you are submitting your essay electronically).

- If you were advocating limits to be set on the height of buildings in your city, you would find *photographs*—or take them yourself—of the skyline as it is now, as well as preparing *diagrams* or *computer-generated images* showing the relative heights of the proposed new buildings juxtaposed among the old ones.

For most topics, you should be able to support your thesis successfully through the text alone, whether or not you provide images or charts or any other illustrative information. Still, carefully chosen visuals can often increase the effectiveness of your essay as well as fully engage your reader's attention. David Morgan's account of the strange occurrence at Lake Tunguska is definitely enhanced by a map of the region (p. 486) and a picture of the blast site (p. 493). Many readers will instantly recognize the stills from the films—*The Cabinet of Dr. Caligari, Freaks,* and *Psycho*—discussed in Bethany Dettmore's essay about horror movies (p. 468). Dettmore uses these pictures to illustrate (in the first two films) her point about the ambiguous nature of "monster" figures—half-frightening, half-sympathetic—as well as the transition, in *Psycho,* to films in which "normal" people are actually the monsters.

Some of the research topics discussed in the earlier chapters of *Writing from Sources* would certainly benefit from the inclusion of visuals.

- It's easy to find photographs of *Lawrence of Arabia.* The one shown on page 318 would be appropriate if you were writing about Lawrence's later years, but not if you were exclusively concerned with his desert campaigns.

- An essay about *excessive drinking by college students* could be accompanied by tables or line graphs showing instances of emergency room treatment or assaults or class attendance over time, as linked to documented consumption of alcohol. The tabulated results of any surveys you might conduct for this essay would certainly need to be included as an appendix. Would you choose to include photographs of students after a hard night's drinking? Possibly, if the photographs are truly representative of the situation that you are analyzing in your essay, and if the people in the photograph have given their permission for the use of these images.

- Similar kinds of visuals could be used in an essay about *responses to beggars.* Here you would want to consider whether the pity evoked by a picture of an unkempt, emaciated beggar would enhance or detract from the effectiveness of your essay. Again, this depends on your thesis.

- If your topic were *animal rights,* you might find it hard to resist including a picture of a pathetic dog or cat to engage the reader's sympathies. But you can carry pathos too far: a laboratory specimen bristling with electrodes or twitching under torture might serve to repel rather than engage your reader's interests.

Integrating Visuals into Your Essay

Preparation: Prepare any visuals after you have completed a working draft of your essay and have chosen the information or images that you intend to include. Unless you are submitting your essay electronically, make sure that your printer can handle the production of the photographs you've chosen.

Choosing Visuals

- Are the data in each chart or graph *relevant* to your point? Do they serve as evidence to support your thesis? Or are they merely an interesting sidebar? Do they digress from your line of argument? Will extensive columns of tables and graphs bore your readers rather than convince them?

- Can readers readily *understand* the information contained in the chart or graph? Are the data sufficiently explained in either the caption or the text?

- How will your readers respond to the picture? Will it engage their interest? Is it attractive and pleasing? Or is it unpleasant? Will readers feel indifferent or horrified? Will any of these reactions make it difficult for them to accept your thesis?

- What assumptions does the picture require? Is the cultural context familiar and does it reflect the world your readers are living in? Or is it so dated or remote from their knowledge or experience as to have little significance for them? Is it a cliché, a cultural icon that no longer resonates?

- Are the appearance and style of the photograph or cartoon appropriate to the tone set by your text? Is it so controversial as to distract readers from following the development of ideas in your essay? Will it engage their interest or make them stop reading?

Don't assume that you can produce a clear copy and incorporate it into your text at the last moment. If you are preparing your own data (such as the results of a survey), spend some time considering how to present the information, what to include and what to omit, what categories to use, and whether a table or graph or chart is most appropriate. Then tabulate the data well in advance as you may run into difficulties formatting the information on your computer.

Placement and appearance: If you are integrating the visuals into your essay electronically, put each one as near as possible to the related point in your text. Make sure that the font that you use for the tables or charts is readable, but don't use such a large font that it dominates your text. Photographs should be an appropriate size: the details should be clear, but the pictures should not overwhelm the words.

Captions: Visuals that include data should be described and interpreted, either in a caption or in the main text. Don't assume that the reader will understand all their implications and why you have included them. Photos, on the other hand, may be self-explanatory, requiring no more than an allusion to them in your text. But, at a minimum, every visual should be identified with a caption that documents its source.

Permission: Unless a visual is from a government or other public source, you will need to get permission from the source to include it in an essay that is going to be posted on the Web. In any case, for any visual, acknowledgment of the source in your caption and in your bibliography is essential.

ASSIGNMENT 10: Organizing and Writing the Research Essay

A.   Using the topic and preliminary bibliography that you developed for Assignment 9, pages 337–338, write down a tentative list of main ideas, based on your own ideas and the information and evidence provided by your sources.

B.   Develop an outline based on your list of ideas, and consider a possible thesis for the essay and a strategy that will best develop your thesis and accommodate the evidence found in your sources.

C.   After you have compiled a substantial list of ideas and developed a tentative thesis, reread the passages, cross-referencing the items on your list with the relevant material from your sources. While you do not have to use up everything in all your notes, you should include all relevant points.

D.   Develop this outline into an eight- to ten-page essay.

· 10 ·
Acknowledging Sources

Research means reading, absorbing, and writing about the ideas and the words of other writers; inevitably, the opportunities to plagiarize—by accident or by intention—increase tremendously. You must therefore understand exactly what constitutes plagiarism.

Understanding Plagiarism

Plagiarism is the **unacknowledged** *use of another person's work, in the form of original ideas, strategies, and research, or another person's writing, in the form of sentences, phrases, and innovative terminology.*

The Moral Rationale

- Plagiarism is the equivalent of *theft*, but the stolen goods are intellectual rather than material.

- Like other acts of theft, plagiarism is against the law. The copyright law governing publications requires that authorship be acknowledged and (if the borrowed material is long enough) that payment be offered to the writer.

- Plagiarism violates the moral law that people should take pride in, as well as profit from, the fruits of their labor. Put yourself in the victim's place. Think about the best idea that you ever had, or the paragraph that you worked hardest on in your last paper. Now, imagine yourself finding exactly the same idea or exactly the same sentences in someone else's essay, with no mention of your name, with no quotation marks. Would you accept the theft of your property without protest?

- Plagiarists are not only robbers, but also cheats. People who bend or break the rules of authorship, who do not do their own work, will be rightly distrusted by their instructors or future employers, who may equate a history of plagiarism with laziness, incompetence, or dishonesty. One's future rarely depends on getting a better grade on a single assignment; on the other hand, one's lifelong reputation may be damaged if one resorts to plagiarism in order to get that grade.

The Practical Rationale

Plagiarism is a bad risk for, as you observed in Exercise 14, an experienced teacher can usually detect plagiarized work quite easily. If there is any disparity in style within a student's essay, instructors can easily do a Google search to compare that material with material available on the Web. If you can't write your own essay, you are unlikely to do a good enough job of adapting someone else's work to your needs.

The excuse of "inadvertent plagiarism" is sometimes used to explain including undocumented material from the Internet in a research essay. Cutting and pasting material from Web sites may be an easy way of meeting a paper deadline, but it will inevitably invite a charge of plagiarism unless you include the sites in your bibliography. And even if you properly acknowledge your Internet sources, you must still paraphrase and/or quote the text that you're using rather than just pasting it in and leaving it unchanged. As Maurice Isserman suggests in the *Chronicle of Higher Education* (2 May 2003), instructors are unlikely to buy "the argument that the invention of the Internet somehow makes our old notions of intellectual property obsolete." Borrowing from an Internet source is just as much plagiarism as borrowing from a published work.

If you resort to using a paper-writing service instead of doing your own work, you are just as likely to get caught. Software that detects plagiarism — like that available at turnitin.com — enables instructors to back up their suspicions by checking a dubious paper against a vast database of previously plagiarized essays. Nor should you use the excuse that borrowing words and ideas is increasingly common practice in the world of business or government. Here is Maurice Isserman again, speaking for the vast majority of instructors: "As learning communities, colleges and universities are governed by a different set of rules than those governing the worlds of politics and commerce. What we do is teach students to develop their own voices and establish ownership of the words they use."

Finally, you will not receive greater glory by plagiarizing. On the contrary, most instructors believe that students who work hard to understand the ideas of their sources, apply them to the topic, and express them in their own words deserve high grades for their mastery of the basic skills of academic writing. There are, however, occasions when your instructor may ask you not to use secondary sources. In such cases, you would be wise to do no background reading at all, so that the temptation to borrow "inadvertently" will not arise.

When to Document Information

By acknowledging your sources, you tell your reader that someone other than yourself is the source of ideas and words in your essay. Acknowledgment—or *documentation*—usually means using *quotation marks* and *citation of the author's name*—techniques that are by now familiar to you. There are guidelines to help you decide what can and what cannot safely be used without acknowledgment, and these guidelines mostly favor complete documentation.

> *By conservative standards, you should cite a source for all facts and evidence in your essay that you did not know before you started your research.*

Knowing when to acknowledge the source of your information largely depends on common sense. For example, it is not necessary to document the fact that there are fifty states in the United States or that Shakespeare wrote *Hamlet* since these facts are *common knowledge*. On the other hand, you may be presenting more obscure information, like facts about electric railroads, which you have known since you were a child, but which may be unfamiliar to your readers. Technically, you are not obliged to document that information; but your audience will trust you more and will be better informed if you do so. In general, if the facts are not unusual, if they can be found in a number of standard sources, and if they do not vary from source to source or year to year, then they can be considered common knowledge, and the source need not be acknowledged.

Let's assume that you are preparing to document your essay about *Lawrence of Arabia*. The basic facts about the film—the year of release, the cast, the director, the technicians, the Academy Awards won by the film—might be regarded as common knowledge and not require documentation. But the cost of the film, the amount grossed in its first year, the location of the premiere, and the circumstances of production are relatively unfamiliar facts that you would almost certainly have to look up in a reference book. An authority on film who includes such facts in a study of epic films is expected to be familiar with this information and, in most cases, would not be expected to provide documentation. But a student writing on the same subject would be well advised to do so.

Similarly, if you are writing about the most recent Olympics and know who won a specific medal because you witnessed the victory on television, then it would probably not be necessary to cite a source. More complex issues surrounding the Olympics—such as the use of steroids—are less clearly in the realm of common knowledge. You may remember news broadcasts about which athletes may or may not have taken steroids before a competition, but the circumstances are hardly so memorable in their details that you would be justified in writing about them from memory. The articles that you consult to jog your memory would have to be documented.

Perhaps one of the ideas that you are writing about was firmly in your mind—the product of your own intellect—long before you started to work on your topic. Nevertheless, if you come across a version of that idea during your research, you should cite the source, indicating in the text that the idea was as much your own as the author's.

Perhaps, while working on an essay, you develop a new idea of your own, stimulated by one of your readings. You should acknowledge the source of inspiration and, perhaps, describe how and why it affected you. (For example: "My idea for shared assignments is an extension of McKeachie's discussion of peer tutoring.") The reader should be made aware of your debt to your source as well as your independent effort.

Plagiarism: Stealing Ideas

If you present another person's ideas as your own, you are plagiarizing *even if you use your own words*. To illustrate, the paragraph on the left, by Leo Gurko, is taken from a book, *Ernest Hemingway and the Pursuit of Heroism*; the paragraph on the right comes from a student essay on Hemingway. Gurko is listed in the student's bibliography and is cited as the source of several quotations elsewhere in the essay. But the student does not mention Gurko anywhere in *this* paragraph.

Source: Leo Gurko

The Hemingways put themselves on short rations, ate, drank, and entertained as little as possible, pounced eagerly on the small checks that arrived in the mail as payment for accepted stories, and were intensely conscious of being poor. The sensation was not altogether unpleasant. Their extreme youth, the excitement of living abroad, the sense of making a fresh start, even the unexpected joy of parenthood, gave their poverty a romantic flavor.

Student Essay

Despite all the economies that they had to make and all the pleasures that they had to do without, the Hemingways rather enjoyed the experience of being poor. They knew that this was a more romantic kind of life, unlike anything they'd known before, and the feeling that everything in Paris was fresh and new, even their new baby, made them sharply aware of the glamorous aspects of being poor.

The *language* of the student paragraph does not require quotation marks, but unless Gurko is acknowledged, the student will be guilty of plagiarism. These impressions of the Hemingways, these insights into their motivation, would not have been possible without Gurko's biography—and Gurko deserves the credit for having done the research and for having formulated the interpretations. After reading extensively about Hemingway, the student may have absorbed these biographical details so thoroughly that he feels as if he had always known them. But the knowledge is still secondhand, and the source must be acknowledged.

Plagiarism: Stealing Words

Acknowledging the author's name in parentheses does not allow you to mix up your own language with that of your sources. The author's name tells your reader nothing at all about who is responsible for the choice of words. Equally important, borrowing language carelessly, perhaps in an effort to use paraphrase, often garbles the author's meaning.

Here is an excerpt from a student essay about Henrik Ibsen, together with the relevant passage from its source, P. F. D. Tennant's *Ibsen's Dramatic Technique*:

Source: P. F. D. Tennant

When writing [Ibsen] was sometimes under the influence of hallucinations, and was unable to distinguish between reality and the creatures of his imagination. While working on *A Doll's House* he was nervous and retiring and lived in a world alone, which gradually became peopled with his own imaginary characters. Once he suddenly remarked to his wife: "Now I have seen Nora. She came right up to me and put her hand on my shoulder." "How was she dressed?" asked his wife. "She had a simple blue cotton dress," he replied without hesitation. . . . So intimate had Ibsen become with Nora while at work on *A Doll's House* that when John Paulsen asked him why she was called Nora, Ibsen replied in a matter-of-fact tone: "She was really

Student Essay

While Ibsen was still writing *A Doll's House*, his involvement with the characters led to his experiencing hallucinations that at times completely incapacitated his ability to distinguish between reality and the creations of his imagination. He was nervous, distant, and lived in a secluded world. Gradually this world became populated with his creations. One day he had the following exchange with his wife:

Ibsen: Now I have seen Nora. She came right up to me and put her hand on my shoulder.

Wife: How was she dressed?

Ibsen: (without hesitation) She had a simple blue dress.

Ibsen's involvement with his characters was so deep that when John

called Leonora, you know, but everyone called her Nora since she was the
spoilt child of the family."

Paulsen asked Ibsen why the heroine
was named Nora, Ibsen replied in a
very nonchalant tone of voice that
originally she was called Leonora, but
that everyone called her Nora, the
way one would address the favorite
child in the family (Tennant 26).

The documentation at the end of the student's passage may give credit to Tennant's book, but it fails to indicate the debt that the student owes to Tennant's
phrasing and *vocabulary*. Phrases like "distinguish between reality and the creatures of his imagination" must be placed in quotation marks, and so should the
exchange between Ibsen and his wife. Arranging these sentences as dialogue is
not adequate acknowledgment. Moreover, many of the substituted words
change Tennant's meaning: "distant" does not mean "retiring"; "a secluded
world" is not "a world alone"; "nonchalant" is a very different quality from
"matter-of-fact." Prose like this is neither quotation nor successful paraphrase;
it is doubly bad, for it both *plagiarizes* the source and *garbles* it.

Avoiding Plagiarism

- You must acknowledge a source using an appropriate form of documentation whenever you summarize, paraphrase, or quote ideas or
  information derived from another person or organization's work.

- You are obliged to use documentation whether the work has been
  published in print, has appeared on the Web, has been performed
  in public, has been communicated to you through an interview or
  e-mail, or exists as an unpublished manuscript.

- You must use two kinds of documentation when you quote a source:

  1. *You acknowledge the source of the information or ideas* through a sys-
     tem of documentation that provides complete publication infor-
     mation about the source and possibly through the citation of the
     author's name in your sentence.

  2. *You acknowledge the source of the exact wording* through quotation
     marks.

EXERCISE 34: Understanding When to Document Information

Here are some facts about the explosion of the space shuttle *Challenger*. Consider which of these facts would require documentation in a research essay—and why.

1. On January 28, 1986, the space shuttle *Challenger* exploded shortly after takeoff from Cape Canaveral.

2. It was unusually cold in Florida on the day of the launch.

3. One of the *Challenger*'s booster rockets experienced a sudden and unforeseen drop in pressure 10 seconds before the explosion.

4. The explosion was later attributed to the failure of an O-ring seal.

5. On board the *Challenger* was a $100 million communications satellite.

6. Christa McAuliffe, a high school social studies teacher in Concord, New Hampshire, was a member of the crew.

7. McAuliffe's mission duties included conducting two classroom lessons taught from the shuttle.

8. After the explosion, classes at the high school were canceled.

9. Another crew member, Judith Resnick, had a Ph.D. in electrical engineering.

10. At the time of the explosion, President Ronald Reagan was preparing to meet with network TV news correspondents to brief them on the upcoming State of the Union address.

11. The State of the Union address was postponed for a week.

EXERCISE 35: Understanding Plagiarism

In 2003, the *New York Times* reported that Brian VanDeMark, an associate professor of history at the U.S. Naval Academy (USNA), had been charged with plagiarizing the content and language of portions of books by four authors. More than 40 passages in VanDeMark's book about the origins of the atomic bomb were "identical, or nearly identical" to material published by the four authors, yet these passages contained neither acknowledgments nor quotation marks. In many instances, only a few words had been changed.

The *Chronicle of Higher Education* later reported that, as a result of these charges, the USNA had demoted VanDeMark, removed his tenure, and cut his salary. In effect, he was going to have to "re-establish his professional qualifications" as if he had just been newly hired.

Figure 10-1 shows, side by side, as published in the *Times*, parallel excerpts from VanDeMark's *Pandora's Keepers: Nine Men and the Atomic Bomb* on the left and from works by Robert S. Norris, William Lanouette, and Richard Rhodes

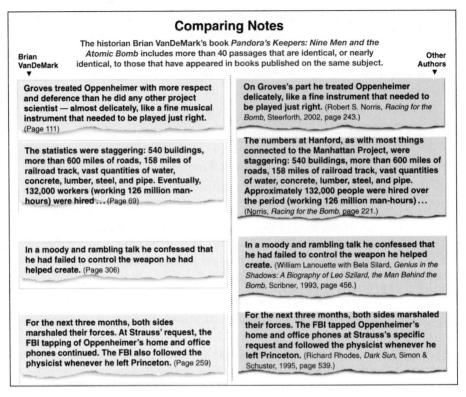

Figure 10-1 Evidence of plagiarism cited in the *New York Times*

on the right. Examine them and determine whether, in your opinion, VanDe-Mark has been guilty of plagiarism.

EXERCISE 36: Identifying Plagiarism

There are two ways to plagiarize the work of a source: using ideas without attribution and using language without quotation marks.

A. The following passage, by John Lukacs, was one of the sources used for an essay titled "Has the Credit Card Replaced the Dollar Bill?" Compare this source with a paragraph taken from the student essay, and decide, sentence by sentence, whether the student has plagiarized Lukacs's work.

Source

The Modern Age has been the age of money — increasingly so, perhaps reaching its peak around 1900. During the Middle Ages, there were some material assets, often land, that money could not buy; but by 1900, there was hardly any material thing that money could not buy. But during the twentieth century, the value of money diminished fast. One symptom (and cause) was inflation. By the end of the twentieth century, the inflation of stocks and of other financial instruments became even more rapid than the inflation of money, at the bottom of which phenomenon another development exists, which is the increasingly abstract character of money — due, in part, to the increasing reliance on entirely electronic transactions and on their records.

JOHN LUKACS, "It's the End of the Modern Age,"
Chronicle of Higher Education, 26 Apr. 2002, B8

Student Essay

(1) For hundreds of years, we have lived in a society that worships money, believing that money can buy anything and everything. (2) A thousand years ago, during the Middle Ages, there were some things, like land, that money could not buy. (3) But by 1900, money could buy almost anything one could want. (4) That is no longer so true today. (5) John Lukacs observes that, over the last century, the value of money diminished quickly. (6) The same is true for stocks and other financial instruments. (7) In fact, our dependence on credit cards and other electronic means of transferring funds has made paper money almost irrelevant (B8).

B. The following two passages were among the sources used for an essay titled "Credentialing the College Degree." Compare these sources with a paragraph taken from the student essay, and decide, sentence by sentence, whether the student has plagiarized either of these sources.

Sources

Grade inflation compresses all grades at the top, making it difficult to discriminate the best from the very good, the very good from the good, the good from the mediocre. Surely a teacher wants to mark the few best students with a grade that distinguishes them from all the rest in the top quarter, but at Harvard that's not possible.

HARVEY C. MANSFIELD, "Grade Inflation: It's Time to Face the
Facts," *Chronicle of Higher Education*, 5 Apr. 2001, B24

Grade inflation subverts the primary function of grades. Grades are messages. They are means of telling students — and subsequently, parents, employers, and graduate schools — how well or poorly those students have done. A grade that misrepresents a student's performance sends a false message. It tells a lie. The point of using more than one passing grade (usually D through A) is to differentiate levels of successful performance among one's students. Inflating grades to please or encourage students is confusing and ultimately self-defeating.

RICHARD KAMBER AND MARY BIGGS, "Grade Conflation:
A Question of Credibility," *Chronicle of Higher Education*,
12 Apr. 2002, B14

Student Essay

(1) Some faculty are disturbed by what they regard as grade inflation. (2) They are concerned that grades will be awarded that are higher than students deserve, that will misrepresent a student's performance. (3) Kamber and Biggs, for example, believe that an inflated grade is the equivalent of a lie, for it sends a "false message." (4) Such faculty see themselves as differentiating between the different levels of successful performance, distinguishing, as Mansfield says, the best from the very good and the good from the mediocre. (5) In fact, they regard grades as a way of telling future employers how well or poorly these students have performed. (6) The emphasis is on providing students with credentials, not a successful learning experience.

Using Documentation

Documentation requires more than using quotation marks and citing the author's name in your text. You also need to provide your reader with detailed information about all your sources. This documentation is important for two reasons:

1. *By showing where you found your information, you are providing proof that you did your research.* Including the source's *publication history* and the *specific page* on which you found the information assures your reader that you have not made up fictitious sources and quotations. The systems of documentation that are described in this chapter and in Chapter 12 also enable your reader to distinguish your ideas from those of your sources, to know who was responsible for what, by observing the parenthetical notes or numbered notes.

2. *Documentation also enables your readers to learn more about the subject of your essay.* Methods of documentation originally developed as a way for serious scholars to share their findings with their colleagues—while making it entirely clear who had done the original research. The reader of your research essay should be given the option of going back to the library and locating the materials that you used in writing about the topic.

One widely accepted system of documentation is based on the insertion directly into your essay of the author's name and the page on which the information can be found, placed in parentheses and linked to a bibliography placed at the end of the essay. This style of documentation is called the *Modern Language Association (MLA)* style. It has replaced footnotes and endnotes as the most common method of documentation for undergraduates, and it will probably be the style you use in writing general research essays, especially those in the humanities. Documenting through parenthetical notes is much less cumbersome than preparing an additional page of endnotes or placing footnotes at the bottom of the page. MLA style also allows your reader to see the source's name while reading the essay, instead of having to turn to a separate page at the back. Readers who want to know more about a particular source than the author's name and a page number can turn to the "Works Cited" page, which provides all the necessary details of publication.

Another frequently used kind of parenthetical documentation is the one recommended by the *American Psychological Association (APA)* for research in the social and behavioral sciences. APA style is described on pages 509–516 of Chapter 12.

Using Parenthetical Notes: MLA Style

Here is an excerpt from a biographical essay about Ernest Hemingway using MLA style. Notice that the parenthetical notes—often called *in-text citations*—are meaningless unless the reader can refer to an accurate and complete "Works Cited" list placed on a separate page at the end of the essay.

Hemingway's zest for life extended to women also. His wandering heart seemed only to be exceeded by an even more appreciative eye (Hemingway 102). Hadley was aware of her husband's flirtations and of his facility with women (Sokoloff 84). Yet, she had no idea that something was going on between Hemingway and Pauline Pfeiffer, a fashion editor for *Vogue* magazine (Baker 159). She was also unaware that Hemingway delayed his return to Schruns from a business trip in New York, in February 1926, so that he might spend more time with this "new and strange girl" (Hemingway 210; also Baker 165).

Works Cited

Baker, Carlos. *Ernest Hemingway: A Life Story.* New York: Scribner's, 1969. Print.
Hemingway, Ernest. *A Moveable Feast.* New York: Scribner's, 1964. Print.
Sokoloff, Alice Hunt. *Hadley: The First Mrs. Hemingway.* New York: Dodd, 1973. Print.

Many of the basic rules for using MLA style are demonstrated in this example. Here are some points to observe.

1. **Format and Punctuation**

   The placement of the parenthetical note within your sentence is governed by a set of very precise rules, established by conventional agreement. Like rules for quotation, these must be followed without any deviation.

   a. *The parenthetical note is intended to be a part of your sentence, which should not end until the source has been cited.* For this reason, terminal punctuation (period or question mark) should be placed *after* the parenthetical note.

   Incorrect

   Unlike most American writers of his day, Hemingway rarely came to New York; instead, he spent most of his time on his farm near Havana. (Ross 17).

   Correct

   Unlike most American writers of his day, Hemingway rarely came to New York; instead, he spent most of his time on his farm near Havana (Ross 17).

   b. *If the parenthetical note follows a quotation, the quotation should be closed before you open the parentheses.* Remember that the note is not part of the quotation and therefore has no reason to be inside the quotation.

   Incorrect

   Hemingway's farm consisted of "a domestic staff of nine, fifty-two cats, sixteen dogs, a couple of hundred pigeons, and three cows (Ross 17)."

   Correct

   Hemingway's farm consisted of "a domestic staff of nine, fifty-two cats, sixteen dogs, a couple of hundred pigeons, and three cows" (Ross 17).

   c. *Any terminal punctuation that is part of the quotation* (like a question mark or an exclamation point) *remains inside the quotation marks.* Remember also to include a period at the end of the sentence, *after* the parenthetical note.

Incorrect

One critic reports that Hemingway said of *The Old Man and the Sea*, "Don't you think it is a strange damn story that it should affect all of us (me especially) the way it does" (Halliday 52)?

Correct

One critic reports that Hemingway said of *The Old Man and the Sea*, "Don't you think it is a strange damn story that it should affect all of us (me especially) the way it does?" (Halliday 52).

d. *When you insert the parenthetical note, leave one space before it and one space after it*—unless you are ending the sentence with terminal punctuation (period, question mark), in which case you leave no space between the closing parenthesis and the punctuation, and you leave the customary one space between the end of that sentence and the beginning of the next one.

Incorrect

Given Hemingway's intense awareness of literary tradition, style, and theory, it is strange that many critics and readers have found his work primitive(Cowley 47).

Correct

Given Hemingway's intense awareness of literary tradition, style, and theory, it is strange that many critics and readers have found his work primitive (Cowley 47).

2. Placement

The parenthetical note comes at the end of the material being documented, whether that material is quoted, paraphrased, summarized, or briefly mentioned. By convention, your reader will assume that the *parenthetical note signals the end of the material from that source.* Anything that follows is either your own idea, independently developed, or taken from a new source that will be documented by the next parenthetical note later in the text.

One critic has remarked that it has been fashionable to deride Hemingway over the past few years (Cowley 50). However, though we may criticize him, as we can criticize most authors when we subject them to close scrutiny, we should never forget his brilliance in depicting characters having grace under the pressure of a sterile, valueless, painful world (Anderson 1036).

3. Frequency

Each new point in your essay that requires documentation should have its own parenthetical note. Under no circumstances should you accumulate references to several different sources for several sentences and place them in a single note at the end of the paragraph. All the sources in the Hemingway paragraph cannot be covered by one parenthetical note at the end.

Incorrect

The sources of Hemingway's fiction have been variously named. One critic has said he is driven by "personal demons." Another believes that he is occupied by a desire to truly portray reality, with all its ironies and symbols. Finally, still another has stated that Hemingway is interested only in presenting "fragments of truth" (Cowley 51; Halliday 71; Levin 85).

Correct

The sources of Hemingway's fiction have been variously named. One critic has said he is driven by "personal demons" (Cowley 51). Another believes that he is occupied by a desire to truly portray reality, with all its ironies and symbols (Halliday 71). Finally, still another has stated that Hemingway is interested only in presenting "fragments of truth" (Levin 85).

4. Multiple Notes in a Single Sentence

If you are using a large number of sources and documenting your essay very thoroughly, you may need to cite two or more sources at separate points in the same sentence.

Even at this early stage of his career, Hemingway seemed to have developed a basic philosophy of writing. His ability to perceive situations clearly and to capture the exact essence of the subject (Lawrence 93–94; O'Faolain 113) might have stemmed from a disciplined belief that each sentence had to be "true" (Hemingway 12) and that a story had to be written "as straight as you can" (Hemingway 183).

The placement of notes tells you where the writer found which information. The reference to Lawrence and O'Faolain must be inserted in midsentence because they are responsible only for the information about Hemingway's capacity to focus on his subject and capture its essence; Lawrence and O'Faolain are not responsible for the quoted material at the end of the sentence. The inclusion of each of the next two parenthetical notes tells you that a reference to "true" sentences can be found on page 12 of the Hemingway book and a reference to "straight" writing can be found on page 183.

5. Multiple Sources for the Same Point

If you have two sources to document the same point, you can demonstrate the completeness of your research by placing both in the same parenthetical note. The inclusion of Lawrence and O'Faolain in the same note—(Lawrence 93-94; O'Faolain 113)—tells you that much the same information can be found in both sources. Should you want to cite two sources but emphasize only one, you can indicate your preference by using "also."

> Hemingway's ability to perceive situations clearly and to capture the exact essence of the subject (Lawrence 93-94; also O'Faolain 113) may be his greatest asset as a writer.

There is, of course, a limit to how many sources you can cram into a single pair of parentheses; common sense will tell you what is practical and what is distracting to the reader. Usually, one or two sources will have more complete or better documented or more recent information; those are the ones to cite. If you wish to discuss the quality of information in your various sources, then you can use an explanatory endnote to do so (see pp. 455–456 on explanatory notes).

6. Referring to the Source in the Text

In the previous examples, the writer of the Hemingway essay has chosen not to name any sources in the text itself. That is why each parenthetical note contains a name as well as a page number. *If, however, you do refer to your source as part of your own presentation of the material, then there is no need to use the name twice; simply insert the page number in the parenthetical note.*

> During the time in Paris, Hemingway became friends with the poet Ezra Pound, who told Hemingway he would teach him how to write if the younger novelist would teach him to box. Noel Stock reports what Wyndham Lewis saw when he walked in on one of their boxing sessions:
>
>> A splendidly built young man [Hemingway] stript to the waist, and with a torso of dazzling white, was standing not far from

> me. He was tall, handsome, and serene, and was repelling with his boxing gloves—I thought without undue exertion—a hectic assault of Ezra's. (88)

Because Stock's name is cited in the text, it need not be placed in parentheses; the page number is enough. Stock's book would, of course, be included in the "Works Cited" list. Also notice that the parenthetical note works just as well at the end of a lengthy, *indented* quotation; but that, because the quotation is indented, and there are no quotation marks to signify its end, it terminates with a period placed *before* the parenthetical note, which follows separated by *one space*.

7. Including the Source's Title

Occasionally, your bibliography will include more than one source by the same author. To avoid confusion and to specify your exact source, use an abbreviated title inside the parenthetical note. Had the author of the Hemingway essay included more than one work by Carlos Baker in the bibliography, the parenthetical note would look like this:

> Yet, she had no idea that something was going on between Hemingway and Pauline Pfeiffer, a fashion editor for *Vogue* magazine (Baker, *Life Story* 159).

If you are working from a newspaper or periodical article that does not cite an author, use an abbreviation of the article's title in your parenthetical note (unless you have referred to the title in your text, in which case you need only include the page number in your note).

8. Referring to a Whole Work

Occasionally, you may refer to the overall theme of an entire work, citing the title and the author, but no specific quotation, idea, or page. If you refer to a work as a whole, no page numbers in parentheses are required.

> Hemingway's *The Sun Also Rises* focuses on the sterility and despair pervading modern culture.

9. Referring to a Source by More Than One Author

Occasionally, you will need to refer to a book that is by two, or three, or even more authors. If you refer to a text by two or three authors, cite their last names, joined by "and." (If you have mentioned the authors' names in your text, just include a page reference in parentheses.) If you refer to a text by more than three authors and you have not mentioned them in your text, it is acceptable (and saves space) to cite the name of the first author followed by et al., unitalicized, and then the page number, all within parentheses. *Et al.* is Latin for "and others."

Two Authors

We may finally say of the writer Hemingway that he was able to depict the turbulent, often contradictory, emotions of modern man in a style as starkly realistic as that of the sixteenth century painter Caravaggio, who, art historians tell us, seems to say, "Here is actuality . . . without deception or pretence. . . ." (Janson and Cauman 221).

More Than Three Authors

Hemingway did what no other writer of his time did: he captured the plight and total disenchantment of his age in vivid intensity (Spiller et al. 1300).

10. Referring to One of Several Volumes

You may use a single volume from a set of several volumes. If so, refer to the specific volume by using an Arabic numeral followed by a colon and a space if a page number follows. (See Chapter 12 for proper bibliographic entry of a set of volumes.)

Perhaps Hemingway's work can be best summed up by Frederick Copleston's comment concerning Camus: both writers prove that human greatness is not shown in escaping the absurdity of modern existence, but "in living in the consciousness of the absurd and yet revolting against it by . . . committing . . . [one]self and living in the fullest manner possible" (3: 393).

11. Referring to a Work of Literature

If you refer to specific passages from a well-known play, poem, or novel, then you need not cite the author; the text's name is sufficient recognition. Use Arabic numerals separated by periods for divisions such as act, scene, and line in plays and for divisions like books and lines in poems. For novels, cite the page number followed by a semicolon, "ch.," and the chapter number.

Play

Hemingway wished to show reality as truly as he could, even if he found man, as did King Lear, nothing but "a poor, bare, fork'd animal . . ." (3.4.106-7).

Poem

Throughout his career as a writer, Hemingway struggled to make sense of the human condition so powerfully and metaphorically presented in *The Waste Land*: "Son of man / . . . you know only / A heap of broken images" (2.21-23).

Novel

In *The Sun Also Rises*, toughness is an essential for living in the modern age, but even toughness has its limits in the novel; as Jake says, "It is awfully easy to be hard-boiled about everything in the daytime, but at night it is another thing" (34; ch. iv).

12. Referring to a Quotation from an Indirect Source

When you quote a writer's words that you have found in a work written by someone else, you begin the citation with the abbreviation "qtd. in." This form shows the reader that you are quoting from a secondhand source, not the original.

In "Big Two-Hearted River," Hemingway metaphorically captures the pervasive atmosphere of his time in the tersest of descriptions: "There is no town, nothing . . . but the burned over country" (qtd. in Anderson 1027).

13. Referring to Sources on the Web That Don't Provide Numbered Pages

Some sources found on the Web, whether they originally appeared in print or not, don't provide page numbers. In that case, your parenthetical note should include the author (or title) only.

Hemingway's time in Paris was enhanced by "the stimulation of his experiences with [Gertrude] Stein" (Fitch).

14. Referring to Sources That Do Not Appear in Print or on the Web

Sometimes you may cite information from nonprint sources such as interviews, films, or radio or television programs. If you do, be sure that the text mentions (for an interview) the name of the interviewer and/or the person being interviewed or (for a film) the name of the producer, director, and/or scriptwriter; these names should also appear in your list of "Works Cited."

Interview

In an unpublished interview conducted by the writer of this essay, the poet Phil Arnold said that a lean style like Hemingway's may be just as artificial as an elaborate one.

Preparing to Document Your Essay

- Whether you take notes or use photocopies of your sources, remember always to write down the information that you will need for your notes and bibliography.

- Look at the front of each book or periodical and jot down or photocopy the publication information.

- When you move notes from one file to another on your computer, make sure that the source's name goes with the relevant material.

- As you work on the first draft of your essay, include the author's name and the relevant page number in parentheses after every reference to one of your sources, to serve as a guide when you document your essay. Even in this early version, your essay will resemble the finished product, with MLA documentation.

- Material found on the Web tends to change—or disappear entirely—over time. (*Wikipedia* is an example of a source in constant flux.) Make sure that you note the date when you accessed each Web site that you use.

- Finally, when the essay is ready for final typing, read through it again, just to make sure that each reference to a source is covered by a correct and appropriate parenthetical note.

Constructing a "Works Cited" Page

None of the parenthetical notes explained above would make complete sense without a "Works Cited" page. Examples of the technical forms for bibliographic entries according to MLA style are contained in Chapter 12 on pages 498–508. Following is a sample "Works Cited" page for all of the parenthetical notes about Hemingway found earlier in this chapter.

Works Cited

Anderson, Charles R. Introduction. "Ernest Hemingway." *American Literary Masters*. Ed. Charles R. Anderson. New York: Holt, 1965. 1023-24. Print.

Arnold, Philip. Telephone interview. 3 Aug. 2008.

Baker, Carlos. *Ernest Hemingway: A Life Story*. New York: Scribner's, 1969. Print.

Copleston, Frederick. *Maine de Biran to Sartre*. New York: Doubleday, 1974. Print. Vol. 3 of *A History of Philosophy*. 9 vols. 1946-74.

Cowley, Malcolm. "Nightmare and Ritual in Hemingway." Weeks 40-51.

Fitch, Noel Riley. *Walks in Hemingway's Paris: A Guide to Paris for the Literary Traveler*. New York: Macmillan, 1992. *Google Book Search*. Web. 5 Sept. 2009.

Halliday, E. M. "Hemingway's Ambiguity: Symbolism and Irony." Weeks 52-71.

Hemingway, Ernest. *A Moveable Feast*. New York: Scribner's, 1964. Print.

---. *The Sun Also Rises*. 1926. New York: Scribner's, 1964. Print.

Janson, H. W., and Samuel Cauman. *A Basic History of Art*. New York: Abrams, 1971. Print.

Lawrence, D. H. "In Our Time: A Review." Weeks 93-94.

Levin, Harry. "Observations on the Style of Ernest Hemingway." Weeks 72-85.

Ross, Lillian. "How Do You Like It Now, Gentlemen?" Weeks 17-39.

Shakespeare, William. *King Lear. The Riverside Shakespeare*. Ed. Frank Kermode. Boston: Houghton, 1974. 1249-305. Print.

Spiller, Robert E., et al. *Literary History of the United States*. 3rd ed., rev. London: Macmillan, 1963. Print.

Stock, Noel. *The Life of Ezra Pound*. New York: Pantheon, 1970. Print.

Weeks, Robert P., ed. *Hemingway: A Collection of Critical Essays (Twentieth Century Views)*. Englewood Cliffs: Prentice, 1962. Print.

MLA Style: A Sample Page

"Passive euthanasia" can be described as helping someone to die by doing nothing and, according to *The Economist*, "happens in hospitals all the time" ("Euthanasia War" 22). It usually involves deliberate withholding of life-prolonging measures (Keown, "Value" 6). Failing to resuscitate a patient who has suffered a massive heart attack is one example of passive euthanasia. Another is deciding not to feed terminally ill patients who are unable to feed themselves. By contrast, removing the feeding tube from a patient who is being fed that way would be considered active euthanasia.

The distinction between active and passive euthanasia is really about responsibility. In passive euthanasia, the doctor or relative has done nothing directly to end the patient's life and so has less moral responsibility. An intermediate form of euthanasia—assisted suicide—is more controversial. In assisted suicide, a doctor or other person provides a terminally ill person with the means—pills, for example—and the medical knowledge necessary to commit suicide. In the *Journal of the American Medical Association*, Dr. David Orentlicher categorizes assisted suicide as a form of passive euthanasia (1844). Derek Humphry's *Final Exit*, which describes ways to commit suicide painlessly, and the organization Compassion in Dying, which helps terminally ill patients to end their lives, are both sources of instruction in assisted suicide (Belkin 50; also Elliott 27).

The professional people who care for the sick and the dying think that there is a great difference between active euthanasia and passive euthanasia or assisted suicide. One panel of distinguished physicians declared themselves in favor, by a margin of 10 to 2, of doctor-assisted suicide for hopelessly ill patients who request it (Orentlicher 1844).

EXERCISE 37: Acknowledging Sources

Read the following passage by Charles McGrath. Then read each of the four examples taken from student essays that use McGrath as a source. Consider the following questions:

1. Has the source been misquoted or misunderstood?
2. Have the source's ideas been acknowledged with sufficient and accurate documentation, according to MLA style?
3. Have quotations from the source been indicated with quotation marks?

Source

What is it with hockey? To begin with, it is a fast, physical game that encourages players and spectators alike to burn at a much higher emotional temperature than does baseball or even football, both of which have built-in cooling-off periods. And hockey is, of course, the only game in which — on the professional level, anyway — fistfights routinely break out and in which it is customary for every team to carry on its roster an "enforcer," whose main job is to intimidate the opposition. The game has underlying it a longstanding cult of toughness. What casual fans — and apparently many parents — don't understand, though, is that a lot of hockey fighting is ritualistic. There is more pushing and posturing than there is actual punching, and the whole show — the pointing, the snarling, the chest-bumping — may actually serve as a kind of safety valve.

CHARLES MCGRATH, "Ice Sturm," *The New York Times Magazine*,
20 Jan. 2002: 9

Student Essay A

Hockey is one of the roughest sports there is. Because it is so fast and physical, everyone, players and spectators, gets highly emotional, and there are no cooling-off periods, as there are in sports like baseball or even football.

Student Essay B

Hockey is one of the roughest sports there is. As Charles McGrath observes, the game depends on breakneck speed and constant physical contact, with no opportunity for players or audience to catch their breath and calm down. The cult of toughness that underlies such a frenzied, belligerent sport would naturally encourage fighting in the stands and on the field. (McGrath, 9)

Student Essay C

Hockey is one of the roughest sports there is. But according to Charles McGrath, the "cult of toughness" associated with hockey, which makes the players seem so violent and dangerous, is largely "ritualistic," based upon menacing gestures and a pretense of belligerence (9).

Student Essay D

Hockey is one of the roughest sports there is. In contrast to games like baseball and football, players and spectators "burn at a high emotional level," which inevitably causes "fistfights to routinely break out." This "ritualistic pushing" and shoving is part of the "cult of toughness" that makes the game exciting (McGrath, p 9).

EXERCISE 38: Documenting Sources Correctly

Each of the following passages from student essays is preceded by publication information about the source cited. Each passage breaks the rules of MLA documentation. Consulting the following categories of possible errors, decide what is wrong with the documentation of each passage. More than one answer might apply.

1. The placement of the quotation marks is incorrect.
2. The source's name is not cited correctly.
3. The terminal punctuation is in the wrong place.
4. The spacing of the documentation is incorrect.

Example One

Hill, Christopher. *The World Turned Upside Down*. New York: Penguin, 1975. Print.

John Milton was hardly able to identify with the hardships of the poor. He was "a leisure-class individual, who never knew what it was to labor under a small taskmaster's eye(Hill 400)."

Example Two

Dawkins, Richard. *The Selfish Gene*. New York: Oxford UP, 1989. Print.

Richard Dawkins believes that "individuals are not stable things, they are fleeting. Chromosomes too are shuffled into oblivion, like hands of cards soon after they are dealt. The genes are not destroyed by crossing over, they merely change partners and march on." (Dawkins 35)

Example Three

Butterfield, Herbert. *Napoleon*. 1939. New York: Collier, 1962. Print.

Napoleon once acknowledged that he was a pantheist: "If I had to have a religion I could worship the sun, which gives life to everything. The sun is the true god of the earth (Butterfield 118).

Example Four

Southwick, Ron. "Fighting for Research on Animals." *Chronicle of Higher Education* 12 Apr. 2002: A24. Print.

The use of animals in medical research continues. According to a recent article in the *Chronicle of Higher Education*, "rodents and birds make up 95 percent of all animals used in laboratory studies, and scores of biomedical researchers are turning to mice to further their studies of cancer and other diseases" (A24).

Example Five

Kamber, Richard, and Mary Biggs. "Grade Conflation: A Question of Credibility." *Chronicle of Higher Education* 12 Apr. 2002: B14. Print.

Most faculty believe that "inflating grades to please or encourage students is confusing and ultimately self-defeating." (Kamber B14)

Example Six

Spalter, Anne Morgan. *The Computer in the Visual Arts*. Reading: Addison, 1999. Print.

Anne Morgan Spalter wonders how we can still determine what is real in art: "If a virtual environment can be created that is indistinguishable from a real environment, with objects that look, feel, and behave like objects in the real world, is the viewer having a "real" experience" (Spalter, 314)?

Example Seven

Mander, Jerry. *Four Arguments for the Elimination of Television*. New York: Morrow, 1978. Print.

We are often told that television "changes the way humans receive information from the world . . . offer[ing] a very narrow-gauged sense experience" (Mander, p. 349).

Managing Documentation

Once you have found and selected the right materials to support your ideas, you should use paraphrase and, where appropriate, include your sources' names in your sentences as a way of keeping them before your reader's eye.

Putting Parenthetical Notes in the Right Place

In general, the citation of an author's name tells your reader that you are starting to use new source material; the parenthetical note signals that you are no longer using that source.

If the name is not cited at the beginning, readers may not be aware that a new source has been introduced until they reach the parenthetical note. Here is a brief passage from an essay that illustrates this kind of confusion:

no source?

> The year 1946 marked the beginning of the postwar era. This meant the demobilization of the military, creating a higher unemployment rate because of the large number of returning soldiers. This also meant a slow-down in industry, so that layoffs also added to the rising rate of unemploy-

Phillips = source

> ment. As Cabell Phillips put it: "Motivation [for the Employment Act of 1946] came naturally from the searing experience of the Great Depression, and fresh impetus was provided by the dread prospect of a massive new wave of unemployment following demobilization" (292-93).

The reader assumes that Cabell Phillips is responsible for the quotation and only the quotation and that the reference to Phillips covers only the material that starts with the name and ends with the page number. In this passage, then, *the first three sentences are not documented.* Although the writer apparently took all the information from Phillips, his book is not being acknowledged as the source. Phillips's name should be cited somewhere at the beginning of the paragraph (the second sentence would be a good place).

You may need to insert a parenthetical note in midsentence if that single sentence contains references to *two* different sources. For example, you might want to place a note in midsentence to indicate exactly where the source's opinion leaves off and your own begins:

> These examples of hiring athletes to play in college games, cited by Joseph Durso (6), suggest that recruiting tactics in 1903 were not as subtle as they are today.

If the page number were put at the end of the sentence, the reader would assume that Durso was responsible for the comparison between 1903 and the present, but he is not. Only the examples must be documented, not the conclusion drawn from these examples. In this case, the *absence* of a parenthetical note at the end of the sentence signals to the reader that this conclusion is the writer's own.

Using Parenthetical Notes to Signal Transitions

Here is a passage in which the techniques of documentation have been used to their fullest extent and the transitions between sources are clearly indicated. This example is taken from Jessie Bernard's "The Paradox of the Happy Marriage," an examination of the woman's role in American marriage. At this point, Bernard has just established that more wives than husbands acknowledge that their marriages are unhappy:

> These findings on the wife's marriage are especially poignant because marriage in our society is more important for women's happiness than for men's. "For almost all measures, the relation between marriage, happiness and overall well-being was stronger for women than for men," one study reports (Bradburn 150). In fact, the strength of the relationship between marital and overall happiness was so strong for women that the author wondered if "most women are equating their marital happiness with their overall happiness" (Bradburn 159). Another study based on a more intensive examination of the data on marriage from the same sample notes that "on each of the marriage adjustment measures . . . the association with overall happiness is considerably stronger for women than it is for men" (Orden and Bradburn 731). Karen Renne also found the same strong relationship between feelings of general well-being and marital happiness: those who were happy tended not to report marital dissatisfaction; those who were not, did. "In all probability the respondent's view of his marriage influences his general feeling of well-being or morale" (64); this relationship was stronger among wives than among husbands (63).[2] A strong association between reports of general happiness and reports of marital happiness was also found a generation ago (Watson).
>
> 2. Among white couples, 71 percent of the wives and 52 percent of the husbands who were "not too happy" expressed marital dissatisfaction; 22 percent of the wives and 18 percent of the husbands who were "pretty happy" expressed marital dissatisfaction; and 4 percent of the wives and 2 percent of the husbands who were "very happy" expressed marital dissatisfaction.

This paragraph contains *six* parenthetical notes to document the contents of seven sentences. Four different works are cited, and, where the same work is cited twice consecutively (Bradburn and Renne), the reference is to a different page. The material taken from page 64 of Renne covers a sentence and a half, from the name "Karen Renne" to the parenthetical note; the remainder of the sentence comes from page 63. Finally, there is no page reference in the note citing Watson, since Bernard is referring the reader to the entire article, not to a single part of it. Notice also that:

- Bernard quotes frequently, but she never places quotations from two different sources together in the same sentence.

- She is careful to use her own voice to provide continuity between the quotations.

- The reader is never in doubt as to the source of information.

Although Bernard does not always cite the name of the author, we are immediately told in each case that there is a source—"one study reports"; "the author wondered"; "another study based on a more intensive examination of the data on marriage from the same sample"; "Karen Renne also found." These phrases not only acknowledge the source but also provide vital transitions between these loosely related points.

Using Explanatory Notes

You will have noticed that, in the excerpt from Bernard above, following the second parenthetical reference to Renne, there is a number. This calls the reader's attention to a separate note appearing at the bottom of the paragraph. (In the actual essay, the note would appear either at the bottom of the page or, together with other notes, on a *separate sheet* at the end of the essay.) Jessie Bernard is using an *explanatory note* as a way of including information that does not quite fit into the text of her essay.

If your research has been thorough, you may find yourself with excess material. It can be tempting to use up every single note in your file and cram all the available information into your essay. But if you include too much extraneous information, your reader will find it hard to concentrate on the real topic of your paragraph.

To illustrate this point, here are two paragraphs dealing with the domestic life of Charles Dickens: one is bulging; the other is streamlined. The first contains an analysis of Dickens's relationship with his sister-in-law; in the second, he decides to take a holiday in France.

Paragraph 1

Another good friend to Charles Dickens was his sister-in-law. Georgina had lived with the family ever since they had returned from an American tour in June 1842. She had grown attached to the children while the couple was away (Pope-Hennessy 179-80). She now functioned as an occasional secretary to Dickens, specifically when he was writing A *Child's History of England*, which Pope-Hennessy terms a "rather deplorable production." Dickens treated the history of his country in a very unorthodox manner (311). Dickens must have felt close to Georgina since he chose to dictate the *History* to her; with all his other work, Dickens always worked alone, writing and correcting it by himself (Butt and Tillotson 20-21). Perhaps a different woman would have questioned the relationship of her younger sister to her husband; yet Kate Dickens accepted this friendship for what it was. Pope-Hennessy describes the way in which Georgina used to take over the running of the household whenever Kate was indisposed. Kate was regularly too pregnant to go anywhere. She had ten children and four miscarriages in a period of fifteen years (391). Kate probably found another woman to be quite a help around the house. Pope-Hennessy suggests that Kate and her sister shared Charles Dickens between them (287).

This paragraph obviously contains too much information, most of which is unrelated to this topic. Pope-Hennessy's opinion of the history of England and the history of Kate's pregnancies are topics that may be worth discussing, but not in this paragraph. This extraneous material could be shifted to other paragraphs of the essay, placed in explanatory notes, or simply omitted.

Paragraph 2

In 1853, three of Dickens's closest friends had died (Forster 124),[5] and the writer himself, having become even more popular and busy since the publication of *David Copperfield* (Maurois 70), began to complain of "hypochondriacal whisperings" and also of "too many invitations to too many parties" (Forster 125). In May of that year, a kidney ailment that had plagued Dickens since his youth grew worse (Dickens, *Letters* 350), and, against the advice of his wife, he decided to take a holiday in Boulogne (Johnson 757).[6]

5. The friends were Mr. Watson, Count d'Orsay, and Mrs. Macready.
6. Tillotson, Dickens's doctor, who had been in Boulogne the previous October, was the one to encourage him to go there.

This second, much shorter paragraph suggests that related but less important detail can usefully be put into explanatory notes where, if wanted, it is always available. Readers of the second paragraph are being given a choice: they can absorb the essential information from the paragraph alone, or they can examine the topic in greater depth by referring also to the explanatory notes. The first research essay in Chapter 11 includes seven explanatory notes (p. 481).

Explanatory notes should be reserved for information that, in your view, is useful and to some degree relevant to the topic; if it is uninteresting and way off the point, simply omit it. If you indulge too often in explanatory notes, your notes may be longer than your essay. Remember to find out whether including explanatory notes is acceptable to your instructor.

Avoiding Excessive Documentation

Numerous parenthetical notes were needed to document all the details found in the biographical essays about Charles Dickens. Here is a brief example:

> Dickens's regular work habits involved writing at his desk from about nine in the morning to two in the afternoon (Butt and Tillotson 19; Pope-Hennessy 248), which left a good deal of time for other activities. Some of his leisure each day was regularly spent in letter-writing, some in walking and riding in the open air (Pope-Hennessy 305, quoting Nathaniel Sharswell). Besides this regular routine, on some days he would devote time to reading manuscripts which Wills, his sub-editor on *Household Words*, would send to him for revision and comment (Forster 65; Johnson 702).

In this passage, *three parenthetical notes* are needed for *three sentences* because a different biography or pair of biographies is the source for each piece of information. To combine all the sources in a single note would confuse, rather than simplify, the acknowledgments. In addition, the writer of this essay is not only making it clear where the information came from, but is also providing the reader with a *choice of references*. The writer has come across the same information in more than one biography, has indicated the duplication of material in her notes, and is demonstrating the thoroughness of her research by citing more than one reference. Since the sources are given equal status in the notes (by being placed in alphabetical order and separated by a semicolon), the reader can assume that they are equally reliable. Had the writer thought that one was more thorough or more convincing than another, she would have either omitted the secondary one or indicated its status by placing it after "also" (Johnson 702; also Forster 65).

But an abundance of parenthetical notes is not always appropriate. As the following example demonstrates, excessive documentation only creates clutter.

> In contrast to the Dickenses' house in London, this setting was idyllic: the house stood in the center of a large garden complete with woods, waterfall, roses (Forster 145), and "no end of flowers" (Forster 146). For a fee, the Dickenses fed on the produce of the estate and obtained their milk fresh from the landlord's cow (Forster 146). What an asset to one's peace of mind to have such a cooperative landlord as they had (Pope-Hennessy 310; Johnson 758; Forster 147) in the portly, jolly Monsieur Beaucourt (Forster 147)!

This entire passage is taken from three pages in Forster's biography of Dickens, and a single note could document the entire paragraph. What information is provided in the last sentence that justifies a parenthetical note citing three sources? And what does the last note document? Is it only Forster who is aware that Monsieur Beaucourt is portly and jolly? To avoid tiring and irritating his readers, the writer here would have been well advised to ignore the supporting evidence in Pope-Hennessy and Johnson, and use a single reference to Forster. The writer was undoubtedly proud of his extensive research, but he seems more eager to show off his hours in the library than to provide a readable text for his audience.

Using Umbrella Notes

As in the previous example, you sometimes have to cite the same source for several sentences or even for several paragraphs at a stretch. Instead of repeating "Forster 146" again and again, you can use a single note to cover the entire sequence. These notes, often called *umbrella notes*, cover a sequence of sentences as an umbrella might cover more than one person. Umbrella notes are generally used in essays where the sources' names are not often cited in the text, and so the reader cannot easily figure out the coverage by assuming that the name and the parenthetical note mark the beginning and ending points. Using an umbrella leaves the reader in no doubt as to how much material the note is covering.

An umbrella note consists of an explanation of how much material is being covered by a source. Such a note is too long to be put in parentheses within the text and generally takes the form of *an explanatory note placed outside the body of your essay.* Here is an example:

> 2. The information in this and the previous paragraph dealing with Dickens's relationship with Wilkie Collins is entirely derived from Hutton 41-49.

Inside your essay, the superscript number 2 referring the reader to this note would follow right after the *last* sentence that uses material from Hutton to discuss Dickens and Wilkie Collins.

Of course, umbrella notes work only when you are using a single source for a reasonably long stretch. If you use two sources, you have to distinguish between them in parenthetical notes, and the whole point of the umbrella—to cut down on the number of notes—is lost.

Umbrella notes must also be used with caution when you are quoting. Because the umbrella provides the reference for a long stretch of material, the citation usually includes several pages; but how will the reader know on which page the quotation appears? Sometimes you can add this information to the note itself:

> 2. The information in this and the previous paragraph is entirely derived from Hutton 41-49. The two quotations from Dickens's letters are from pages 44 and 47, respectively.

However, if you use too many umbrella notes, or if you expect a single note to guide your reader through the intricacies of a long paragraph, you will have abused the device. Your essay will have turned into a series of summaries, with each group of paragraphs describing a single source. That is not what a research essay is supposed to be.

Preparing the Final Bibliography

The bibliography becomes especially important when you use MLA documentation, as it is the only place where your reader can find publication information about your sources. Which works you include in your final bibliography may depend on the wording and intention of your assignment. There is an important difference between a list of works that you have *consulted* or *examined* and a list of works that you have *cited* or actually used in writing your essay. Many instructors restrict the bibliography to "Works Cited," but you may be asked to submit a list of "Works Consulted." The purpose of a "Works Consulted" bibliography is to help your readers to find appropriate background information, not to overwhelm them with the magnitude of your efforts. Don't present a collection of thirty-five titles if you actually cite only five sources in your essay.

> *An appropriate final bibliography of "Works Cited" for an undergraduate essay consists of all the sources that you used and documented, through parenthetical notes, in your essay.*

If you consulted a book in the hope that it contained some relevant information, and if it provided nothing useful, should you include it in your final bibliography? You might do so to prevent your readers from consulting works with misleading titles in the belief that they might be useful, but only if your bibliography is *annotated* so that the book's lack of usefulness can be pointed out. Finally, if you have been unable to locate a source and have thus never examined it yourself, you may not ordinarily include it in your final bibliography, however tempting the title may be.

Annotating Your Bibliography

Annotating your bibliography is an excellent way to demonstrate the quality of your research. But, to be of use, your brief annotations must be informative. The following phrases do not tell the reader very much: "an interesting piece"; "a good article"; "well-done"; "another source of well-documented information." What is well done? Why is it interesting? What is good about it? How much and what kind of information does it contain? A good annotated bibliography will answer some of these questions.

The bibliography on the following pages presents the basic facts about the author, title, and publication, as well as some *evaluative information*. If the annotations were omitted, these entries would still be correct, for they conform to the standard rules for MLA bibliographical format. Without the annotation, one would simply have to change the heading to "Works Consulted" (if it includes some works not cited in your essay) or "Works Cited."

HEMINGWAY IN 1924: AN ANNOTATED BIBLIOGRAPHY

Baker, Carlos. *Ernest Hemingway: A Life Story*. New York: Scribner's, 1969. Print. 563 pages of biography, with 100 pages of footnotes. Everything seems to be here, presented in great detail.

Donaldson, Scott. *By Force of Will: The Life and Art of Ernest Hemingway*. New York: Viking, 1977. Print. The material isn't organized chronologically; instead, the chapters are thematic, with titles like "Money," "Sex," and "War." Episodes from Hemingway's life are presented within each chapter. The introduction calls this "a mosaic of [Hemingway's] mind and personality."

Ernest Hemingway, Paris. c. 1924. Photograph. John F. Kennedy Presidential Lib., Boston. Web. 20 Sept. 2009. A wonderful photograph of Hemingway in 1924, lounging in a chair, wearing a beret, and looking smug and shy at the same time.

Fitch, Noel Riley. *Walks in Hemingway's Paris: A Guide to Paris for the Literary Traveller*. New York: Macmillan, 1992. *Google Book Search*. Web. 5 Sept. 2009. Useful and detailed guide to the places and streets that Hemingway frequented in 1924, with especially helpful maps.

Gopnik, Adam, ed. *Americans in Paris: A Literary Anthology*. New York: Literary Classics of the United States, 2004. Print. Library of America. This anthology contains short excerpts from literary works and memoirs by contemporaries of Hemingway, such as William Faulkner, E. E. Cummings, Gertrude Stein, and John Dos Passos, providing an account of what life was like in Paris in the 1920s by people who were there at the time. The excerpt by Harry Crosby is particularly good at evoking atmosphere.

Griffin, Peter. *Less Than a Treason: Hemingway in Paris*. New York: Oxford UP, 1990. Print. Part of a multivolume biography. Covers Hemingway's life from 1921 through 1927, exclusively. Griffin says in the preface that his goal is not to "analyze this well-examined life" but "to recreate it." Not surprisingly, it reads like a novel, with an omniscient narrator with access to Hemingway's emotions.

Gurko, Leo. *Ernest Hemingway and the Pursuit of Heroism*. New York: Crowell, 1968. Print. This book is part of a series called "Twentieth-Century American Writers": a brief introduction to the man and his work. After

50 pages of straight biography, Gurko discusses Hemingway's writing, novel by novel. There's an index and a short bibliography, but no notes. The biographical part is clear and easy to read, but it sounds too much like summary.

Hemingway, Ernest. *A Moveable Feast*. New York: Scribner's, 1964. Print. This is Hemingway's own version of his life in Paris. It sounds authentic, but there's also a very strongly nostalgic tone, so it may not be trustworthy.

Hemingway, Leicester. *My Brother, Ernest Hemingway*. Cleveland: World, 1962. *Google Book Search*. Web. 15 Sept. 2009. For 1924–1925, L. H. uses information from Ernest's letters (as well as commonly known facts). The book reads like a third-hand report, very remote; but L. H. sounds honest, not as if he were making up things that he doesn't know about.

Hotchner, A. E. *Papa Hemingway*. New York: Random, 1955. Print. This book is called a "personal memoir." Hotchner met Hemingway in 1948, evidently hero-worshiped him, and tape-recorded his reminiscences. The book is their dialogue (mostly Hemingway's monologue). No index or bibliography. Hotchner's adoring tone is annoying, and the material resembles that of *A Moveable Feast*, which is better written.

Kennedy, J. Gerald. "Hemingway, Hadley, and Paris: The Persistence of Desire." *The Cambridge Companion to Hemingway*. Ed. Scott Donaldson. Cambridge: Cambridge UP, 1996. *Google Book Search*. Web. 12 Aug. 2009. A brisk overview of the Hemingways' time in Paris, which sounds a bit like a gossip column. (Ernest is tiring of Hadley because she is becoming too "matronly [Kennedy's description]." Useful for its connections between the experience of the Hemingways and the characters of *The Sun Also Rises*.

Lamb, Robert Paul. "Fishing for Stories." *Modern Fiction Studies* 37.2 (1991): 161-81. *Project Muse*. Web. 1 Sept. 2009. Hemingway's experience in Paris and Pamplona as seen through the writing of his short story "Big Two-Hearted River." More about the story than about Paris.

Meyers, Jeffrey. *Hemingway: A Biography*. New York: Harper, 1999. Print. Includes several maps and two chronologies: illnesses and accidents, and travel. Book organized chronologically, with every year accounted for, according to table of contents. Well-documented critical biography, with personal anecdotes taking a backseat to literary. Less gossipy, more circumspect in claims than Griffin.

O'Rourke, Sean. "Evan Shiman and Hemingway's Farm." *Journal of Modern Literature* 21.1 (1997): n. pag. *JSTOR*. Web. 28 Aug. 2009. Not much more than a brief account of a much-told anecdote about Hemingway and his friends purchasing a picture by Miró.

Palin, Michael. *Hemingway Adventure*. London: Weidenfeld, 1999. *Prominent Palin Productions*. Web. 8 Sept. 2009. Palin's Guides. Following the trail of Hemingway in Paris with the humorist's comments.

Paul. Weblog entry. *Hemingway's Paris*. Blogger. 29 May 2006. Web. 19 Sept. 2009. A small collection of pictures and maps of Hemingway and 1924 Paris, presented by Paul, who lists his astrological sign and his favorite movies in his blog's profile.

Reed, Shannon. "The Expatriotes [*sic*] in Paris and Hemingway's Reflections in *The Sun Also Rises*." Seminar paper. (1997): 1-18. *Grin*. Web. 2 Sept. 2009. A brief overview of Hemingway and *Sun*, which reads like an undergraduate essay.

Reynolds, Michael. *Hemingway: The Paris Years*. Cambridge: Blackwell, 1989. Print. Second of three-volume biography. Includes a chronology covering December 1921 through February 1926 and five maps ("Hemingway's Europe 1922-26," "France," "Switzerland," "Italy," and "Key points for Hemingway's several trips through France and Spain").

Sokoloff, Alice Hunt. *Hadley, the First Mrs. Hemingway*. New York: Dodd, 1973. Print. This is the Paris experience from Hadley's point of view, most of it taken from her recollections and from the standard biographies. (Baker is acknowledged.) It's a very slight book — 102 pages — but there's an index and footnotes, citing letters and interviews that some of the other biographers might not have been able to use.

Weeks, Robert P., ed. *Hemingway: Twentieth Century Perspectives*. Englewood Cliffs: Prentice, 1962. Print. Contains many important essays on Hemingway's life and art. Offers a selected annotated bibliography.

Workman, Brooke. "Twenty-Nine Things I Know about Bumby Hemingway." *The English Journal* 72.2 (1983): n. pag. *JSTOR*. Web. 27 Aug. 2009. An extended anecdote about how Workman tried and failed to meet Hemingway's son, Bumby. More about Workman than about Bumby.

Guidelines for Bibliographical Entries

(Additional models can be found in Chapter 12)

1. The bibliography is always listed on a *separate sheet* at the *end* of your research essay. The title should be centered, one inch from the top of the page.

2. The bibliography is *double-spaced* throughout.

3. Each bibliographical entry starts with *the author's last name at the margin*; the second line of the entry (if there is one) is indented *five spaces*, approximately one-half inch. This format—called "hanging indentation"—enables the reader's eye to move quickly down the list of names at the left-hand margin.

4. The bibliography is in *alphabetical order*, according to the last name of the author.

   - If there are two authors, only the first has the name reversed: "Woodward, Robert, and Carl Bernstein."

   - If an author has more than one work included on your list, do not repeat the name each time: alphabetize the works by that author; place the name at the margin preceding the first work; for the remaining titles, replace the name with three hyphens, followed by a period and one space.

     Freud, Sigmund. *Civilization and Its Discontents*. London: Hogarth, 1930. Print.

     ---. *Moses and Monotheism*. New York: Knopf, 1939. Print.

   - A work that has no author should be alphabetized within the bibliography according to the first letter of the title (excluding "A," "An," and "The"); the title is placed at the margin as the author's name would be.

5. A bibliographical entry for a book is read as a list of three items—author; title, including subtitle, preceded by a colon (italicized); and publication information—with *periods between the three pieces of information*. Each period is followed by *one* space. All the information should always be presented in exactly the same order that you see in the model bibliography on pages 460–462. Place of publication comes first; a colon separates place and name of publisher; a comma separates publisher and date.

6. A bibliographical entry for a *periodical* starts with the author's name and the article title (in quotation marks), each followed by a period and one space. Then comes the name of the periodical, *italicized*, followed by one space (and no punctuation at all). What comes next depends on the kind of periodical you are citing.

(continued)

(continued)

- For *quarterly and monthly journals*, include the volume number, a period, no space, and the issue number, followed by a space, and then the year in parentheses, followed by a colon.
- For *daily, weekly, biweekly, or monthly magazines and newspapers*, include only the full date—day, month, and year—followed by a colon.
- After the colon, indicate the inclusive pages of the article followed by a period.

> Tobias, Sheila, and Carol Weissbrod. "Anxiety and Mathematics: An Update." *Harvard Educational Review* 50 (1980): 61-67. ERIC. Web. 16 Sept. 2009.
>
> Winkler, Karen J. "Issues of Justice and Individual's Rights Spur Revolution in Political Philosophy." *Chronicle of Higher Education* 16 Apr. 1986: 6-8. Print.

7. All bibliographical entries must indicate the medium in which the work appeared—usually, *Print* for books, *Print* or *Web* for periodicals, *Web* for Web sites.
8. Each entry of the bibliography ends with a period.

EXERCISE 39: Preparing the Bibliography

Correct the errors of form in the following bibliography:

> Becker, Howard S, Geer, Blanche, and Everett C. Hughes. Print. Making the Grade: New York (1968) Wiley.
>
> Dressel, Paul L.. College and University Curriculum, Berkeley (California): McCutcheon, 1971. Print
>
> (same)----Handbook of Academic Evaluation. San Francisco (California): Jossey-Bass: 1976.
>
> J. F. Davidson, "Academic Interest Rates and Grade Inflation," Educational Record. Web. 56, 1975, pp. 122-5. Accessed Jan. 18, 2009.
>
> (no author). "College Grades: A Rationale and Mild Defense." AAUP Bulletin, October 1976, 320-1.
>
> New York Times. "Job Plight of Young Blacks Tied to Despair, Skills Lack," April 19, 1983: Section A page 14. Web. 2 feb. 2009. Sponsor: New York Times.
>
> Milton Ohmer, Howard R. Pollio and James A. Eison. GPA Tyranny, Education Digest 54 (Dec 1988): 11-14.
>
> Leo, John. "A for Effort". Or for Showing Up. U.S. News & World Report, 18 Oct, 1993: 22. Retrieved from ProQuest database January 29, 2009.

Kennedy, Donald. <u>What Grade Inflation?</u> <u>The New York Times</u> June 13, 1994: Retrieved from the New York Times sponsored Web site on February 2, 2009.

Bretz, Jr., Robert D. "College Grade Point Average as a Predictor of Adult Success: a Meta-Analytical Review and Some Additional Evidence" Public Personnel Management 18   (Spring 1989): 11-22. Print.

Presenting Your Essay

A well-presented research essay must conform to a few basic mechanical rules:

1. Type your essay on a computer. Make sure that your printer makes clear copies.
2. Double-space throughout the essay.
3. Use 8½-by-11-inch paper; leave 1-inch margins on both sides as well as at the top and bottom.
4. Use only one side of the page.
5. Number each page in the upper right corner; if you are working in MLA style, also include your last name with the number (Doe 4).
6. Proofread your essay, and print out the revised version.
7. Include your full name, your instructor's name, the name of the course, and the date on the first page of the essay at the top left margin. Place the title of the essay, centered, a few lines below that information.

Check with your instructor for any other special rules that may apply to the assignment.

A Checklist for Revision

As you read and reread your essay, keep the following questions in mind:

1. Does the essay have a single focus that is clearly established and maintained throughout?
2. Does the essay have a thesis or a consistent point of view about the events or issues being described?
3. If it is a narrative essay, does the narration have a beginning, middle, and end? If it is an argument essay, are all assumptions explained and defended, and are all obvious counterarguments accommodated or refuted?

(continued)

(continued)

4. Does the essay begin with an informative introduction?

5. Does the essay end on a conclusive note?

6. Does each paragraph have a clear topic sentence?

7. Does each paragraph contain one and only one topic? Should any paragraphs be merged or deleted?

8. Are the paragraphs long enough to be convincing? Is each point supported by facts and information?

9. Does the development of the essay depend entirely on a dry listing of facts and examples, or do you offer explanations and relevant commentary? Is there a good balance between generalization and detail?

10. Do you use transitions to signal the relationship between separate points?

11. Is there unnecessary repetition? Are there any sentences that lack content or add nothing to the essay?

12. Is the style appropriate for a formal essay? Do the sentences seem too conversational, as if you were sending an e-mail?

13. Does the reader get a sense of the relative importance of the sources being used?

14. Do you use enough citations? Does the text of the essay make it clear when you are using a specific source, and who that person is?

15. Do you use one source for very long stretches at a time?

16. Is there an appropriate number of notes rather than too many or too few?

17. Is it clear how much material is covered by each note?

18. In essays containing endnotes, do the notes provide important explanatory information?

19. Are the quotations well chosen?

20. Is paraphrase properly used? Is the style of the paraphrase consistent with your style?

21. In preparing your bibliography, have you followed the MLA rules exactly? Have you formatted your documentation correctly?

22. Have you proofread the essay (in addition to using a spellchecker)?

23. Is the essay convincing? Will your reader accept your analysis, interpretation, and arguments?

·11·
Two Research Essays

The following student research papers illustrate two different kinds of documentation.

Bethany Dettmore uses the evidence of three films, various print and Internet sources, and her own survey to develop and support a theory about why audiences enjoy horror movies. After *describing* and *interpreting* the films' narratives and *analyzing* the expectations that viewers form about their experiences in the theater, she concludes that horror films both reflect and alleviate some of our society's deepest fears. Dettmore acknowledges her sources with MLA documentation. She summarizes, paraphrases, or quotes her sources, using brief and unobtrusive parenthetical notes, generally at the ends of sentences. Almost everything that she wants to say is said within the body of the essay, so there are only a few endnotes.

David Morgan combines *narrative and analysis* by describing the aftermath of the strange event that happened in 1908 at Lake Tunguska, Siberia, and then analyzing some of the many theories that have been used to explain that event over the last one hundred years. The bibliography for this essay contains relatively few sources, which are cited less frequently than the sources are in Dettmore's essay. The writer's purpose is to help his readers understand what might have happened at Lake Tunguska and to clarify the scientific explanations. He is not attempting to reconstruct the event in complete detail or trying to convince his readers, by citing authorities, that his conclusions are the right ones. Like many essays in the social sciences, this paper uses a variation of the author-year method of parenthetical note documentation. (This variation, often called APA after the American Psychological Association, is described in Chapter 12, on pp. 508–516.) Having the date, as well as the author, included within the body of the essay is especially useful when you are reading about scientific theories developed over a span of one hundred years.

Bethany Dettmore
Professor Greene
English 102
May 2009

Looking at Horror Films

In the lobby of the movie theater, the walls are lined with posters advertising what is "Coming Soon" to the cinema. Between the photos of cute couples and strapping action heroes lurk the dark forms of screaming women, monsters, and ghostly mansions. These images represent the genre of horror, a staple of entertainment since the beginning of cinema. Year after year all through the twentieth century, Hollywood has produced movies that have no other purpose than to evoke fear in their viewers. Nor has the genre's importance diminished in the twenty-first century: in 2004, Roger Ebert reported that he had reviewed fifteen different horror films. Although the vast majority of horror films have earned a poor critical reputation over the years, they have always been an excellent investment for Hollywood studios and a surefire attraction for audiences. This paper will explore some of the reasons for the popularity of horror films and consider whether they exist only to provide cheap thrills or whether, in some respects, they serve a legitimate social purpose.

For any movie to be successful, the audience has to enter into the experience unfolding on the screen, almost as if each person sitting in the theater is participating in the story and feeling the emotions of some of the characters. Far from being passive observers, moviegoers help to "create the experience [they] are enjoying" while the director must work to "activate the imaginations that reach out to meet his own" (Prawer 20; also Dickstein 67). In doing so, the viewer is taking a risk. Will the experience be a good one? Or will some people in the audience respond so deeply to what is happening on screen that the emotions aroused become difficult to deal with? Viewing a horror film involves an even greater risk, for the audience is expected not just to undergo an experience, but also "to court a certain danger, to risk being disturbed, shaken up, assaulted" (Dickstein 68). It is as if, by buying a ticket for the film, the moviegoer agrees to participate in what Andrew Tudor calls a "collective nightmare" (3).

It is because seeing a horror movie can pose such a great emotional and psychological risk that moviegoers are sharply divided in their reactions to the genre. Some love horror movies so much that they make a point of seeing every one that opens; others refuse to enter a theater with a monster or a screaming woman on the poster. In a survey conducted for this paper with respondents from both sexes and spanning all age groups, over 46% of the respondents said that they watched horror films very often or sometimes, while the remainder did so rarely (47%) or never (6%). One respondent described horror as nothing more than "bad acting, dark sets and leaves you empty afterwards." What keeps such viewers away is apparently not so much the blood and gore (which 11% of the respondents said was what scared them most about such films) or the villains and monsters (8%), but the element of suspense — leading to fear—built into the plot (62%). Interestingly enough, that same element—suspense—is also the reason cited by 42% of the respondents for why they enjoy horror films; it captures their interest and hooks them for the remainder of the film. One respondent wrote that horror films promise "a suspenseful plot that carries you on a mysterious rollercoaster." We can only conclude that some people like to be frightened!

Why, then, do many thousands of people want to sit in a movie theater and feel the threat that something dire will happen? (Tudor 8). Here, the survey provides us with a useful distinction between creating *suspense*, the quality that two-thirds of the respondents see as the essence of a horror film, and creating *fear*, the quality chosen by the other third. It seems likely that the two-thirds focusing on suspense are people who go to see horror films regularly. They don't want or expect to experience a lot of terror and dread; instead, they anticipate a certain amount of tension and nervous anxiety that—if the film is any good—will be resolved by the final shot. Such viewers expect that "fear will be aroused, then controlled" (Giles 39). There is always a time limit: the length of the movie. Their anxiety is "neutralized" and can even become pleasurable because it is experienced in safe surroundings (Dickstein 69).

The secure environment of the movie theater makes it possible for us to experience another emotion—catharsis, the feeling that can occur when you have been under an intense threat and then realize that it has gone away. Janet Maslin compares the emotion that we can experience during horror films to that of people gawking at highway accidents or watching TV dramas about fatal illnesses: "The knowledge that these things have befallen others provides a grim relief for those who have been spared."

Other people's misfortunes—in real life or on the screen—act as our own shield against disaster. Using the "roller coaster" image again, the critic Linda Williams recalls the experience of seeing *Psycho* for the first time, describing it as a "roller coaster sensibility of repeated tension and release, assault and escape" (163). What she carried home with her was the release and the escape, not the tension and the assault. The viewers know that, however terrifying the situation may be in the movie, someone or something will intervene and put things right (Tudor 214-15) and they can leave the theater "drained and satisfied" (Dickstein 77).

But horror films also appeal to audiences on a more intellectual level. We don't just feel anxiety and terror; we also want to know how the story is going to work out. We admire the ingenuity of the writer and director as we wait for the ending when, we anticipate, all the mysteries of the plot will be logically revealed (Solomon 254). But, in a horror film, we don't just want to know what will happen next. The very weirdness of the characters, settings, and situations excites our curiosity. According to Noel Carroll in "The General Theory of Horrific Appeal," the central theme of horror movies is a voyage of discovery; their business is "proving, disclosing, discovering and confirming the existence of something that is impossible" (3). What beings could be more "impossible" than monsters and aliens? If the film is any good, we begin to focus less on the horribleness of these creatures and more on the logic behind their story. We wonder whether such creatures can really exist, and we want to find out how.

Our interest is also stimulated by the elements of myth in many horror films. Like popular epics such as *The Lord of the Rings* or *Star Wars*, a good horror movie often revolves around a group of people confronted with dire peril who must find strength that they didn't realize they possessed so that their cause will eventually triumph. Because the danger and the fear are so great, the heroism needed to overcome the danger must be equally great. R. H. W. Dillard describes the myth of the horror film in religious terms: "Like a medieval morality play, the horror film deals with the central issue of Christian life—the struggle between the spirits of good and evil for the possession of man's immortal soul" (36). Such themes are common to all societies because they speak to our deepest need to know who we are, why we are here, and what use we will make of our lives. Jonathan Crane insists that such needs go far beyond "the influence of everyday life": "When audience members engage with a horror film they are not enjoying visions that respond to everyday fears; they are responding to atavistic terrors nearly as old as the reptilian brain" (24-25). To explore some of these themes, I want to focus briefly on three landmark horror films: *The Cabinet of Dr. Caligari*, *Freaks*, and *Psycho*.

Regarded as the first classic horror film, *The Cabinet of Dr. Caligari* was made in Germany as a silent movie. In 1919, Hans Janowitz, a Czech poet, and Carl Mayer, an Austrian artist, wrote a script that told the story of a bizarre murder, in a terrifying dreamlike setting, based on a legend in Janowitz's hometown. At the center of the narrative are the sinister hypnotist Dr. Caligari, who operates a fortune-telling booth at a fair, and his "creature" Cesare, a young man who, while hypnotized, looks into the future, tells fortunes, and on occasion commits brutal murders. One of the striking scenes of the film shows the entire population of the village chasing after Cesare, who has abducted and is likely to murder the heroine. As Figure 1 illustrates, this scene emphasizes what the extremely creepy appearance and behavior of Dr. Caligari and Cesare—weird even by silent-movie standards—have told the audience (Prawer 172): these are not normal humans but alien beings, who pose a threat to ordinary people and must be rooted out.

At the end of the movie, it is discovered that Dr. Caligari himself has actually been under the influence of an eighteenth century homicidal hypnotist who has been inhabiting his body. But an even more upsetting revelation is that, even while he—through Cesare—has been terrorizing the village, Dr. Caligari has simultaneously held the respectable post of director of an insane asylum some distance away. In effect, the madman has been in charge of the asylum.

If, as Stephen Prince describes, horror movies can be regarded as representations of our own psychic processes (118), then *The Cabinet of Dr. Caligari* is all about our fear of the alien in our midst. In *Caligari's Children*, S. S. Prawer analyzes the many roles that Dr. Caligari assumes in the audience's imagination. He is the "stranger who disrupts the normal lives of the inhabitants of a small town" (172), yet he plays a vital part in the life of the community as the person in charge of one of its important institutions (173). He is one of the first of a long line of mad scientists to dominate the genre, and yet he is also a "mystic" who understands ancient secrets (173). He controls the actions of the unfortunate Cesare, yet he himself is the victim of "demonic possession" (171). Most interesting, we are terrified by Caligari

Fig. 1. The hypnotized Cesare flees with his intended victim through a night-marish landscape. Still from *The Cabinet of Dr. Caligari*, dir. Robert Wiene, 1921 (Image Entertainment, 1997; DVD).

both because of and despite the fact that his odd way of walking makes him seem deformed and crippled (174). As Prawer puts it, all of these impressions of Caligari are intended "to suggest monsters arising from the subconscious" of the viewer (176), monsters that have long been suppressed by civilized society (Wood 10). We begin to believe that "we are all characters in a madman's dream" (Schneider 36).

In the same way, Cesare is also a character on whom we can project our ambivalence about our "dark desires" (Prawer 181). He is a zombielike figure who commits acts forbidden to the culturally inhibited audience, yet who doesn't have to take responsibility because he is being controlled by the hypnotist. Prawer points out that Cesare is the first of a long line of horror film monsters who may seem horrifying but for whom we also feel pity and even affection (178; also Dillard 39).

However alien these monsters might appear, they are essentially like us:

> The vampires and werewolves, monsters and mummies are all human at source and are all personifications of that potentiality for evil and sin which is so much a part of us all. Hero and villain are much the same—both human, both flawed unto death. . . .
> (Dillard 41)

Casper Tybjerg makes a related point when he disputes with critics who believe that the standard source of fear in horror films has to be the inhuman "monster" figure: "Although Cesare and Caligari are certainly menacing, the real danger is in the threat of madness and of reality breaking down" (16; also Soren 30).[1] What keeps the audience interested in this "ongoing nightmare" (Schneider 34) is the possibility of their own emotional or moral breakdown.

It is the ambiguity of *The Cabinet of Dr. Caligari* that makes it such a great horror film. We can recognize something of ourselves in these alien figures who should really repel us. The publicity campaign for the opening of *Caligari* in Berlin in 1920 captured the film's underlying horror: people were invited to come to see the movie with the assurance: "You must be a Caligari!" (Clarens 16-17).

As the title suggests, the characters in *Freaks*, a 1932 film by Tod Browning, are abnormal in a different way from Caligari and Cesare. Here, the immediate focus of horror is the physical deformity of the freaks in a circus sideshow, which is contrasted with the beauty of Cleopatra, the trapeze artist with whom one of the midgets, Hans, falls in love. (Figure 2 captures that contrast.) Although she agrees to marry him, Cleopatra is actually plotting (with Hercules, the Strong Man) to murder Hans for his money. When the rest of the freaks discover what Cleopatra and Hercules are trying to do, they hunt down, capture, and attack the two, mutilating her until she is "one of them"[2]—a "Hen Woman" suitable for viewing in a freak show.

One of the major selling points of the film—when Browning was trying to convince MGM to produce it and when MGM was attempting to market it—was that the freak characters were played not by professional actors but by real Siamese twins, bearded ladies, pinheads, dwarves, and so on.

Fig. 2. When the "freaks" in a circus sideshow learn that the "normal" Cleopatra (standing at right) is planning to marry the midget Hans (on table) only to murder him for his money, they take a horrifying revenge. Still from *Freaks*, dir. Tod Browning, 1932 (Warner Home Video, 2004; DVD).

Browning went to a great deal of trouble to portray his characters sympa-
thetically, with the freaks often shown behaving like normal people. In one
scene, for example, two dwarves have a normal conversation in a setting
with miniaturized furniture and props, so that everything seems quite
familiar and ordinary to the audience—until a normal-sized person arrives
on the scene (Clarens 70).[3] As Clarens puts it, "Freaks among themselves
cease to be freaks" (71). They are also sympathetic because they make the
best of their handicaps, with the pinhead flirting, the limbless worm lighting
cigarettes, the armless woman drinking from a glass (Thomas 136). At the
beginning, the freaks are very trusting of normal people, welcoming them
into their society. In all these ways, the audience is encouraged to accept
them as "normal." For example, in a key scene, when we first see the freaks
from a distance, they appear to us as monstrous, misshapen creatures
capering around in a bizarre kind of dance; but this impression changes in
the next close-up shot as the freaks "are transformed from agents of terror
to objects of compassion within moments" (Thomas 137).

   Here is the crucial issue of the film. To what extent will the audience
actually sympathize with the freaks, accepting them as people like us, living
in a little world that mirrors ours? On the one hand, we tend to have a
reflex prejudice against deformity. Many in the audience will be turned off
by the initial shot of the freaks dancing; the distorted figures will make
them feel unsettled and afraid (Cantor and Oliver 55). According to Michael
Grant, we inevitably feel a sense of revulsion for what we regard as lesser
beings: "In the cruelty of our sarcasm, we look down upon them, and it
seems that there is no way for the small protagonist, a being in the process
of discovering the world's bitterness, to escape his fate when he can't even
reach the door handle" (128). In this perversion of the "there but for the
grace of God . . ." response, we are eager to disassociate ourselves from these
images because they might suggest to us that freaks are humans like us
and that we might also be like them. Certainly, some audiences in 1932 felt
that revulsion: at a preview in San Diego, one woman ran up the aisle
screaming; many movie theaters refused to show the film; and, in New
York, thirty minutes of footage were cut by the censors (Clarens 70).[4]

   On the other hand, audiences who stay with the movie will almost certainly sympathize with poor Hans, the victim of the greedy, unfeeling
Cleopatra. If a horror film has to have a monster, surely it is the "normal"

and beautiful Cleopatra, who is shown to have no redeeming qualities at all.[5] As one reviewer on the Internet puts it, "You quickly realize who Browning intends to be the real freaks. It is the 'normal' people who display the worst human traits of deceit and greed. The 'freaks' are shown to be loyal to each other, having an unwritten code of honor" (Bright).

And yet, in the final twist, Browning seems to turn Cleopatra into the victim and the freaks into the monsters by having them take their ghastly revenge on her. The scene in which they hunt her down is easily the most terrifying in the film, as the previously rather charming freaks become grotesque and predatory before our eyes. Are we horrified by what they do to Cleopatra, or are we horrified by what the freaks have become? Or are we afraid that we might have the potential to become like freaks ourselves?

Clarens believes that, although we recognize that the freaks are entitled to their "just retribution," all along our sympathy for them has been no more than "intellectual," and we are naturally more concerned about the fate of Cleopatra and Hercules, who are more like us (71). Thomas, however, takes a broader view, recognizing the ambiguity that is so often at the center of the horror movie. He wonders whether the freaks can simultaneously "be seen both as objects of sympathy and as nightmarish incarnations of the nonhuman." Does the grotesque ending undercut everything that Browning was trying to achieve in the film? Ultimately, Thomas concludes that Browning does succeed because so much sympathy has been created for the freaks during the course of the film that we will stifle our disgust at the ending: "We are horrified, but we are simultaneously ashamed of our horror; for we remember that these are not monsters at all but people like us, and we know that we have again been betrayed by our own primal fears" (137; also Herzogenrath 195). If Thomas is right—and *Freaks* has always been a cult classic—then the horror film has once again enabled us to see the freakish monster within ourselves and—going a step further than Caligari—forgive ourselves for being human.

Psycho (1960) marks a shift from the traditional horror film in which terror is found in monster figures that are clearly alien or abnormal. According to some critics, through this one film, Alfred Hitchcock transformed the entire genre, allowing horror to be seen in the context of contemporary American society (Jancovich 4). On the surface, the relationships between

Fig. 3. Anthony Perkins as Norman Bates and Janet Leigh as Marian Crane. Still from *Psycho (Collector's Edition)*, dir. Alfred Hitchcock, 1960 (MCA Home Video, 1998; DVD).

the characters in *Psycho* are quite ordinary: two sisters, mother and son, innkeeper and customer (Brand 21). Figure 3 shows us two average people in conversation; there's nothing monstrous about them. We certainly don't anticipate that Marian Crane, someone with a rather unsavory back story whom we accept as our heroine, will be savagely killed one-third of the way through the film. So we are unprepared for the famous shower scene at the Bates Motel: "We see an old woman with white hair pull back the shower curtain and stab Marian a half dozen times. The scene is back lit and we don't get a clear picture of the face of the murderer" (Ghani). We also don't anticipate that the murderer will turn out to be the amiable Norman Bates, almost cozy in his wooly cardigan. In a way, it would be easier on the audience if the murderer were an intergalactic intruder or a time-traveling Ice Age warrior, or some sort of freak or clairvoyant from a traveling circus. We know that such beings appear only in horror films, not in real life, and we can sit secure in our seats waiting for the end of the movie.

Once the audience understands that "the monster within" (Dickstein 74) lurks in ordinary people and in familiar social settings, and an apparently normal person can be transformed into a psychotic murderer without any warning (Tudor 221), that sense of security is gone forever from the horror film.[6] These new monsters

> do not come from outside our nebulous social networks; they do not arrive in our suburbs fresh from the remote Carpathian mountains; they are not created by . . . well-intentioned scientists who err as ambitious humans will. They are us, and we never know when we will act as monsters. (Crane 8; also Ebert)[7]

Throughout the early parts of *Psycho*, we are encouraged to have sympathy for Norman Bates, and, as Tudor points out, it is possible to retain some of that sympathy even after we realize that he is Marian's murderer. But, as with our response to the ending of *Freaks*, the collision between our revulsion and our sympathy makes us ambivalent and acutely uncomfortable. The ultimate effect is a kind of audience paranoia. Our perceptions are no longer reliable, and we can no longer trust the most "normal" of our friends and relations, for they might at any time attack us: "The world in which this kind of horror makes sense, then, is one which is fundamentally unreliable" (Tudor 221; also Freeland 192).

In recent years, for many film critics, horror has not been considered a legitimate genre. They regard post-*Psycho* horror films as worthless: imitative, predictable, sleazy, and much too concerned with blood and gore. As one writer in a college newspaper put it, such films are "dismissed by critics across the board . . . as a disgustingly stupid thing to enjoy" (Olson; also Crane 2-3). The audience is so accustomed to the trite plot devices that they know exactly what will happen in the next scene — and announce it out loud — minutes before it occurs. Even the movie music sends clear signals to the audience (Scott). The chief attraction of the traditional horror film — suspense — is totally gone. Yet, according to the Internet Movie Database

(IMDb.com), horror films remain among Hollywood's top grossing movies. Leaving aside the teenage boys who wallow in the blood and gore, what continues to be the attraction? In my view, removing the element of suspense from horror films has restored to the audience the sense of security that they used to feel when the movie was populated by monsters that you were unlikely to meet in everyday life. If the nice guy whose locker is next to yours or the waitress at the diner is going to turn into a serial murderer, you'll only be able to stay within your comfort zone if you can predict the appearance of the ax in advance.

In place of suspense, the modern horror film provides excess: too much blood, too much violence, too much sex. The original horror films gained their interest from exploring the nature of evil and the psychology of madness; they didn't need buckets of gore to keep the audience's attention (Crane 4). Now, however, nothing is left to the imagination:

> There is no opportunity to view the monster as the embodiment of a community's fears, or as the darker side of man's nature, or as anything other than a cryptic, single-minded creep. There's no time to identify with the characters, since they are killed off so quickly that they don't have time to impress themselves upon an audience. (Maslin)

The effect of all the blood and all the violence is to desensitize the audience; the gore serves as an anesthetic to prevent us from feeling anything at all. According to Aviva Briefel, those watching the ultra-bloody *Texas Chain Saw Massacre* find it hard to identify with anyone in the film: certainly not the sadistic killers, or even the masochistic victims, who allow themselves to become sitting ducks: "We may feel endangered by the images of violence on screen, but we are ultimately numb to the pain they represent" (19).

Horror films have always tended to "perfectly mirror the fears of contemporary society" (Soren 153) and have been especially popular in times of social disruption (Dickstein 66). Their function has always been to assure their audience of "man's ability to cope with and even prevail over the evil of life which he can never hope to understand" (Dillard 37). But each generation demands a different kind of horror movie, one that is (in the words of a Hollywood producer) "'in tune with the zeitgeist'" (qtd. in Shone). The time is over for what Tudor calls "secure horror": movies in which man's ingenuity invariably triumphs over monstrous evil. Such films belonged to an age that was "confident of its own capacity to survive all manner of threats" (220). Since 9/11, our confidence, public and private, has been shaken, perhaps irretrievably. So it is not surprising that, on the one hand, horror movies continue to draw huge audiences (Blake 12). People still need to view "imaginative and plausible encounters with evil and cosmic amorality [because] they help us ponder and respond emotionally to natural and deep worries about the nature of the world" (Freeland 193). But, given the enemy we face in the war on terror, an enemy that is "nebulous" and "wraith-like," that "regroups whenever you strike it" (Shone), it is no longer easy to believe that the monster will be vanquished at the end of the two-hour film. People are more on edge, more vulnerable to fear and terror. What they seek is the anesthetizing power of the contemporary horror film with all its formulaic predictability and gory special effects. Horror films can no longer compete on their own terms with the real terror existing in the world (Solomon 254).

Notes

1. The famous Expressionist set designs for *Caligari* carry out the theme of the breakdown of reality. David Soren points out that "the sets are distorted, often jagged and harsh, indicators of the madness in which the characters are trapped" (30; also Cook 110).

2. One of the most frightening scenes in the movie shows the wedding festivities, with the freaks dancing around Cleopatra—she and Hercules are the only normal people attending—chanting: "We accept her, we accept her, gobble gobble, one of us, one of us."

3. Given this focus on normality among the freaks, some critics conclude that *Freaks* is not actually a horror movie. Peter Hutchings argues that it "functions as a kind of anti-horror film" because it completely avoids any of the special effects typical of horror movies and derives its thrills simply from the contrast between the normal and the abnormal (27).

4. Interestingly enough, in the United Kingdom, *Freaks* was banned for thirty years, not for fear of audience reaction, but because Browning was considered to have exploited his cast. Skal reports that some cast members did, indeed, feel degraded by its content. Olga Roderick, who played the role of the bearded lady, told reporters that the film was "an insult to all freaks everywhere" (156).

5. Bernd Herzogenrath concludes that Cleopatra (and Hercules, too) "reveal the extremity of American individualism and the greed of American society" (187).

6. During screenings of *Psycho*, there was an amazing amount of screaming and dashing up the aisles as members of the audience tried to get out. In certain scenes, people could hardly hear the soundtrack (Williams 164).

7. Tom Shone points out that when "America's bogeymen no longer smacked of the supernatural, but hailed from your neighbor's backyard," Hollywood stopped calling these movies "horror films" and instead produced "psychological thrillers" and "suspense movies."

Works Cited

Blake, Linnie. *The Wounds of Nations: Horror Cinema, Historical Trauma, and National Identity*. New York: Manchester UP, 2008. Print.

Brand, James. "A Study into Horror Films and Their Remakes." Diss. U of Portsmouth, 2007. Print.

Briefel, Aviva. "Monster Pains: Masochism, Menstruation, and Identification in the Horror Film." *Film Quarterly* 58.3 (2005): 16-27. Web. 7 May 2009.

Bright, Gerry ["gerb"]. "Return of the Chicken Woman." *Dooyoo Review*. 2 Oct. 2002. Web. 15 May 2009.

The Cabinet of Dr. Caligari. Dir. Robert Wiene. 1921. Image Entertainment, 1997. DVD.

Cantor, Joanne, and Mary Beth Oliver. "Developmental Differences in Responses to Horror." *Horror Films: Current Research on Audience Preferences and Reactions*. Ed. James B. Weaver III and Ron Tamborini. Mahwah: Erlbaum, 1996. 63-80. *Google Book Search*. Web. 4 May 2009.

Carroll, Noel. "The General Theory of Horrific Appeal." Schneider and Shaw 1-9.

Clarens, Carlos. *An Illustrated History of Horror and Science-Fiction Films*. New York: Da Capo, 1967. Print.

Cook, David A. *A History of Narrative Film*. New York: Norton, 1990. Print.

Crane, Jonathan Lake. *Terror and Everyday Life*. Thousand Oaks: Sage, 1994. *Google Book Search*. Web. 12 May 2009.

Dickstein, Morris. "The Aesthetics of Fright." B. K. Grant 65-78.

Dillard, R. H. W. "The Pageantry of Death." Huss and Ross 36-41.

Ebert, Roger. "Movie Reviews: *Carrie*." *RogerEbert.com*. 1 Jan. 1976. Web. 17 May 2009.

Freaks. Dir. Tod Browning. 1932. Warner Home Video, 2004. DVD.

Freeland, Cynthia. "Horror and Art-Dread." Prince 189-205.

Ghani, Cyrus. *My Favorite Films*. Washington: Mage, 2004. Print.

Giles, Dennis. "Conditions of Pleasure in Horror Cinema." B. K. Grant 38-52.

Grant, Barry Keith, ed. *Planks of Reason: Essays on the Horror Film*. Metuchen: Scarecrow, 1984. Print.

Grant, Michael. "On the Question of the Horror Film." Schneider and Shaw 120-37.

Herzogenrath, Bernd. "The Monstrous Body/Politic of *Freaks*." *The Films of Tod Browning*. Ed. Bernd Herzogenrath. London: Black Dog, 2006. Print.

Huss, Roy, and T. J. Ross, eds. *Focus on the Horror Film*. Englewood Cliffs: Prentice, 1972. *Google Book Search*. Web. 9 May 2009.

Hutchings, Peter. *The Horror Film*. Edinburgh: Pearson, 2004. Print.

Internet Movie Database. "All-Time Worldwide Box Office." *IMDb.com*. 10 July 2005. Web. 12 May 2009.

Jancovich, Mark, ed. *Horror, the Film Reader*. London: Routledge, 2002. *Google Book Search*. Web. 9 May 2009.

---. Introduction. Jancovich 1-9.

Maslin, Janet. "Bloodbaths Debase Movies and Audiences." *New York Times*. New York Times, 21 Nov. 1982. Web. 2 May 2009.

Olson, Melissa. "Horror Films Are Like Broken Records." *Daily Trojan* [University of Southern California] 8 June 2005. Web. 6 May 2009.

Prawer, S. S. *Caligari's Children*. Oxford: Oxford UP, 1980. Print.

Prince, Stephen. "Dread, Taboo, and *The Thing*: Toward a Social Theory of the Horror Film." Prince 118-30.

---, ed. *The Horror Film*. New Brunswick: Rutgers UP, 2004. *Google Book Search*. Web. 6 May 2009.

Psycho. Dir. Alfred Hitchcock. 1960. MCA Home Video, 1998. DVD.

Schneider, Steven Jay. *100 European Horror Films*. London: British Film Institute, 2007. Print. British Film Inst. Film Guides.

Schneider, Steven Jay, and Daniel Shaw, eds. *Dark Thoughts: Philosophic Reflections on Cinematic Horror*. Lanham: Scarecrow, 2003. *Google Book Search*. Web. 3 May 2009.

Scott, Kirsty. "Music + Chase Scenes = New Formula for Fear." *The Guardian*. Guardian Unlimited, 5 Aug. 2004. Web. 4 May 2009.

Shone, Tom. "This Time It's Personal." *The Guardian*. Guardian Unlimited, 25 Nov. 2005. Web. 4 May 2009.

Skal, David J. *The Monster Show: A Cultural History of Horror*. New York: Macmillan, 2001. *Google Book Search*. Web. 21 May 2009.

Solomon, Robert. "Real Horror." Schneider and Shaw 230-64.

Soren, David. *The Rise and Fall of the Horror Film*. Baltimore: Midnight Marquee, 1997. Print.

Thomas, John. "Gobble, Gobble . . . One of Us!" Huss and Ross 135-38.

Tudor, Andrew. *Monsters and Mad Scientists: A Cultural History of the Horror Movie*. Cambridge: Blackwell, 1989. Print.

Tybjerg, Casper. "Shadow-Souls and Strange Adventures: Horror and the Supernatural in European Silent Film." Prince 15-39.

Williams, Linda. "Learning to Scream." Jancovich 163-68.

Wood, Robin. Introduction. *American Nightmare: Essays on the Horror Film*. Ed. Andrew Britton et al. Toronto: Festival of Festivals, 1979. 7-28. Print.

Dettmore 17

The Horror Film Survey

Name_____

This survey includes four multiple-choice questions and two open-ended questions asking for short responses. Circle your answers to the multiple-choice questions, and respond to the open-ended questions in the spaces provided.

1. How often do you watch horror films?
    a. Very often **13.5%**
    b. Some of the time **32.5%**
    c. Not very often **47%**
    d. Never **6%**

2. Where do you watch horror films?
    a. In theaters **9%**
    b. At home **46%**
    c. Half in theaters and half at home **39%**
    d. Nowhere **6%**

3. What scares you most about horror films?
    a. The blood and gore **11%**
    b. The suspense **62%**
    c. The villains **8%**
    d. Identification with the victims **18%**

4. How would you best describe horror films?
    a. A cheap thrill **23.5%**
    b. An art form **19%**
    c. Trashy films **8.5%**
    d. A legitimate genre **49%**

5. What do you like/dislike about horror films?
    Like: Creates suspense **42%**
    Dislike: Predictability **35%**
                Scares me long after the movie **23%**

6. How would you define a horror film?
    Any film that creates suspense **66%**
    Any film that creates fear **33%**

Explaining the Tunguskan Phenomenon

The Tunguska River Valley in Siberia has always been an area of swamps and bogs, forests and frozen tundra, sparsely populated, and remote and inaccessible to most travelers. It was at dawn on June 30, 1908, that witnesses in the Tungus observed a light glaring more brightly than anything they had ever seen. This cosmic phenomenon, they said, was bluish-white in color and gradually became cigarlike in shape. Just as terrifying to the few people inhabiting that part of Siberia was the tremendous noise that accompanied the light, a noise that was reported to have been heard 1,000 kilometers from the site (Parry, 1961). Some who were in the vicinity were deafened, while others farther away apparently became speechless and displayed other symptoms of severe trauma. The Tungus community refused to go near the site or speak of the occurrence, and some even denied that it had ever happened (Crowther, 1931). The event was so frightening to these simple peasants that many believed it had been an act of divine retribution, a punishment by a god demanding vengeance (Baxter & Atkins, 1976).

Since 1921, when the first perilous expedition to the Tungus region confirmed that a remarkable event had indeed taken place, scientists have attempted to explain what it was and why it happened. Over 100 years later, the various theories developed to explain the explosion in the Tunguska Valley have become almost as interesting a phenomenon as the original occurrence. Like doctors trying to diagnose a disease by examining the symptoms, scientists have analyzed the fragmentary evidence and published theories that supposedly account for it. However, no theory has been entirely convincing. The purpose of this essay is to provide a brief description of some of the major interpretations of the Tunguska occurrence and to suggest that, in their efforts to substantiate their theories, scientists can be fallible.

At dawn on that day in June 1908, a huge object was said to have come from space into the earth's atmosphere, breaking the sound barrier, and, at 7:17 a.m., slammed into the ground in the central Siberian plateau.

---

*Note that APA requires a separate cover page with the student's name, course title, instructor name, and date centered at the bottom of the page. The paper's title should be centered in the middle of the page. All pages have a short version of the essay's title and the page number at the top. This includes the cover page.

Figure 1. A map of the Tunguska region, showing the extent of the blast's impact and the region's remote location in Siberia. From "What Lies Beneath," by M. Chown, 2001, *New Scientist*, 54(2301), p. 17.

Moments before the collision, a thrust of energy caused people and animals to be strewn about, structures destroyed, and trees toppled. Immediately afterward, a pillar or "tongue" of fire could be seen in the sky several hundred miles away; others called it a cylindrical pipe. A thermal air current of extremely high temperature caused forest fires to ignite and spread across 40 miles, melting metal objects scattered throughout the area. Several shock waves were felt for hundreds of miles around, breaking windows and tossing people, animals, and objects in the air. Finally, black rain fell from a menacing-looking cloud over a radius of 100 miles. It is no wonder that the peasants of the Tunguska River Valley thought that this was the end of the world (Baxter & Atkins, 1976; Krinov, 1966).

For a variety of reasons, this devastating occurrence remained almost unknown outside Russia — and even outside central Siberia — for many years. The Tungus (see Figure 1) is extremely remote, even for Russia, which is such a vast country that transportation and communication between places can be slow and difficult. The few people living in the area who actually witnessed what happened were mostly peasants and nomadic tribesmen, and did not have much opportunity or inclination to talk about what they had seen. There was little publicity, and what there was was limited to local Siberian newspapers (Krinov, 1966). During that summer, there was a lot of discussion in the newspapers of the European capitals about peculiar lights and colors seen in the northern skies, unusually radiant sunsets, some magnetic disturbances, and strange dust clouds (Cowan, Atluri, & Libby, 1965). But, since news of the events at the Tungus River had hardly yet been heard even in Moscow, there was no way for scientists in other countries to see a connection between these happenings.

It was only in 1921, when Russia was relatively stable after years of war, revolution, and economic problems, that the first expedition to investigate the event at Tunguska actually took place (Crowther, 1931). That it occurred then at all was largely because an energetic Russian scientist, Leonid Kulik, had become fascinated by meteorites. He read in an old Siberian newspaper that, in 1908, a railway train had been forced to stop because a meteorite fell in its path—a story that was quite untrue. Kulik thought that he might become the discoverer of the greatest meteorite ever found on earth and determined to search for evidence that such a meteorite existed. Authorized by the Soviet Academy, Kulik led a series of expeditions to the Tungus River. In 1921, he did not even reach the site, for the route was almost impassable. In 1927, and annually for the next few years, Kulik did, indeed, explore the devastated area and was able to study the evidence of what had happened and listen to the oral accounts of the event provided by those inhabitants who were still alive and who were willing to talk to him. Finally, in 1938–39, Kulik traveled to the Tungus for the last time, for the purpose of taking aerial photographs that might confirm his meteorite theory (Baxter & Atkins, 1976).

Kulik and his fellow investigators believed that whatever had happened at the Tungus River had been caused by a meteorite. So, what they expected to find was a single, vast crater to mark the place where the meteorite had landed. Such a crater, however, was simply not there (Cowan, Atluri, & Libby, 1965). Instead, Kulik found a vast devastated and burned area, a forest of giant trees with their tops cut off and scattered around (Crowther, 1931). In 1928, without the benefit of an aerial view of the region, Kulik concluded from his various vantage points on the ground that, around the circumference of the area where the meteorite had landed, there was a belt of upright dead trees, which he named the "telegraph pole forest." Scattered around the perimeter of the frozen swamp, which he called the "cauldron," were groups of fallen trees, with their tops all pointing away from the direction of where the blast had occurred (Cowan, Atluri, & Libby, 1965). None of this was consistent with Kulik's meteorite theory, and he could only attribute the odd pattern of upright and fallen trees to a shock wave or "hot compressed-air pockets," which had missed some trees and affected others (Baxter & Atkins, 1976). The account of his discovery in the *Literary Digest* of 1929 states that "each of the falling meteoric fragments must have worked, the Russian scientists imagine, like a gigantic piston," with compressed air knocking trees down like toothpicks ("What a Meteor," 1929, p. 34). Kulik continued to insist that the fire and the resultant effect on the trees was the result of a meteorite explosion. But the Russian scientist V. G. Fesenkov estimated that such destruction could only have been caused by an object of at least several hundred meters, and that, if anything of this size or force had hit the ground, it would have left a crater (Baxter & Atkins, 1976).

Kulik found other evidence that could not easily be explained by the meteorite theory. Although there was no trace of a single large crater (Cowan, Atluri, & Libby, 1965), there were numerous shallow cavities scattered around the frozen bog (Olivier, 1928). For several years, Kulik attempted to bore into the ground, seeking evidence that these pits and ridges were formed by lateral pressure caused by gases exploding from the meteorite's impact. Kulik described the scene as "not unlike a giant duplicate of what happens when a brick from a tall chimney-top falls into a puddle of mud. Solid ground actually must have splashed outward in every direction." In this account, the supposed meteorite became "the great swarm of meteors" that "must have traversed" the atmosphere for several hundred miles, pushing ahead of it a "giant bubble of superheated atmosphere" that was "probably responsible" for the burned countryside ("What a Meteor," 1929, p. 33). All the "must have's" and "probably's" make a good narrative, but are not scientifically convincing.

Similarly, Kulik endeavored to explain eyewitness accounts of the huge fireball in the sky that burned one observer's shirt off his back and threw him off his porch (Cowan, Atluri, & Libby, 1965). Such extreme heat waves had never before been known to have accompanied the fall of a meteorite, but Kulik decided that this meteorite was much larger than those previously recorded and that therefore it would have released much more energy upon impact and that would account for such radiant heat (Baxter & Atkins, 1976). So obsessed was Kulik with the idea that somewhere buried in the Tungus swamp was a phenomenal meteorite that he focused the efforts of all the expeditions to the area during his lifetime on digging beneath the frozen tundra and to some extent neglected the examination of other evidence that might have further threatened the theory that he was determined to prove (Parry, 1961). Initially, he was successful in convincing the scientific community that his theory was correct. It is most interesting to read excerpts from *The American Weekly* of 1929 flatly asserting that a meteorite had fallen in Siberia and that Professor Kulik had brought back photographs of the giant crater that he found, as well as small samples of meteoric materials. The article is accompanied by a photograph of Professor Kulik measuring "the main crater, where the largest mass of this celestial visitor buried itself in the earth" (as cited in "What a Meteor," p. 34).

While Kulik's expeditions were still searching for evidence of a meteorite, other scientists were hypothesizing that the Tunguska explosion might have been caused by a small comet, which would account for the absence of a crater. Comets are composed of ice, frozen gases, and dust, and as they travel around the sun, they develop a long tail. Upon impact, a comet might give off a trail of gases and dust, which would create a bright and colorful night sky similar to that observed after the explosion. This would not be true of a meteorite, which has no gaseous trail and thus leaves no trace in the atmosphere. It has also been suggested that the observed direction of the object's travel was more typical of a comet than a meteorite (Florensky, 1963). If the comet had blown up approximately two miles above the site, that would explain why some trees survived while others did not (Parry, 1961). On the other hand, there is no evidence that a comet had ever crashed on earth before, or caused a comparable change in magnetic and atmospheric phenomena, or even come so close without being sighted (Baxter & Atkins, 1976). Those scientists supporting the comet theory have suggested that, although it is unusual for any comet to come that close to earth without anyone sighting it, the one landing at Tunguska might have been small enough to go by unnoticed. But that idea is contradicted by Fesenkov's estimate that, to cause such destruction, the nucleus of the Tunguskan comet—if there was one—would have been only slightly smaller than those of well-documented comets that were visible at great distances (Cowan, Atluri, & Libby, 1965).

The next major explanation for the cosmic phenomenon at Tunguska could only have been formulated after World War II, when the scientific community had learned how to make atomic explosions and had become familiar with their aftermath. Aleksander Kazantsev, a Russian scientist and (equally important) science-fiction writer, had visited Hiroshima after the atom bomb explosion and had studied the data describing its impact and aftermath. Because of certain similarities in the blast effects—the burnt yet upright trees, the mushroom cloud, the black rain—Kazantsev and other scientists concluded that the blast of 1908 was an atomic explosion estimated at a minimum of ten times the strength of the one at Hiroshima (Parry, 1961). Witnesses had described the blinding flash and withering heat at Hiroshima in much the same way that the Siberian peasants described the frightening blast at Tunguska. The melting heat that Kulik found so inconsistent with his meteorite theory was more consistent with an atomic explosion (Baxter & Atkins, 1976). It is worth pointing out that scientists went on to develop the hypothesis that a nuclear explosion had occurred at Tunguska even though their theorizing was largely based on stories told by ignorant peasants, believers in devils and wrathful gods, who could quite easily have exaggerated what had actually happened to improve their stories. Even though these eyewitness accounts were gathered twenty or more years after the actual event, and had quite possibly entered the folklore of the countryside (Krinov, 1966), they were still regarded as the purest evidence.

To test whether a nuclear explosion might have occurred, scientists examined the trees for radioactivity and for any unusual increase in normal growth patterns, shown by greater spacing between the age lines, that might have been the result of radioactivity. What they found was that some trees at the site grew to be four times greater than what would normally have been expected. Similarly, scabs that appeared on the hides of local reindeer were explained as being the result of radioactive contamination (Baxter & Atkins, 1976). This evidence, by no means conclusive (Florensky, 1963), was cited as proof that such an atomic explosion had taken place, just as Kulik had cited the existence of shallow pits in the terrain as proof that a meteorite had exploded.

Assuming that what happened at Tunguska was the result of an atomic blast, and faced with the fact that nuclear fission was not within man's grasp before the 1940s, Kazantsev and his colleagues concluded that the phenomenon must have involved extraterrestrial beings and that the explosion was caused by a UFO, propelled by atomic energy, that crashed (Parry, 1961). The pattern of devastation on the ground, as seen from the air, suggested that the object took a zigzag path, changing its direction as it came closer and closer to earth. Advocates of the UFO theory argue such a change in direction would not have been possible with a natural object like a meteorite or comet, and that the object—a spacecraft—was driven by intelligent beings who were trying to land without hitting a more densely populated area. They hypothesize that the craft had some mechanical problem that made it necessary to land but that the initial angle of its trajectory was too shallow for landing and would only have bounced the craft back into space. So the navigators tried to maneuver and correct the angle, but swerved, came down too sharply, and exploded (Baxter & Atkins, 1976). On the other hand, it seems just as possible that a natural object swerved or that debris from a nonatomic explosion was thrown in zigzag directions than that navigators from outer space ran into mechanical troubles and crash-landed. If probability is going to be disregarded in order to support one theory, then the same suspension of the natural order of things can be used to confirm an equally unlikely theory.

In the late 1950s, an exploratory team examined the Tunguska site with an advanced magnetic detector and, in 1962, scientists magnified the soil and found an array of tiny, colored, magnetic, ball-shaped particles, made of cobalt, nickel, copper, and germanium (Baxter & Atkins, 1976). According to extraterrestrial-intelligence specialists, these could have been the elements used for electrical and technical instruments, with the copper used for communication services and the germanium used in semiconductors (Parry, 1961). However, controlled experiments would be necessary to make this atomic-extraterrestrial argument convincing.

Scientists who find the UFO and extraterrestrial explanations less than credible have turned to the most recent theories of physics and astronomy to explain what might have happened in the Tungus. Some (including Kazantsev) argue that such an explosion might have been caused by debris from space colliding with the earth (Morrison & Chapman, 1990), or by antimatter, which exploded as it came in contact with the atmosphere (Parry, 1961). Alternatively, the explosion might have been caused by a "black hole" hitting the earth in Siberia and passing through to emerge on the other side. Those opposing these theories point, again, to the absence of a crater and to the numerous eyewitness accounts that describe the shape of the object and the sound of the blast, all of which would be inconsistent with antimatter or black-hole theories (Baxter & Atkins, 1976). However, a 1973 article in *Nature* asserts that a black hole would not, in fact, leave a crater, but would simply enter the earth at a great velocity and that a shock wave and blast might possibly accompany its entrance (Jackson & Ryan, 1973). Comparisons have also been made with a similar but smaller incident that happened in 1930, in a stretch of Brazilian jungle as remote as Tunguska. Eyewitnesses reported the appearance of three fireballs, resulting in a one-megaton explosion and massive destruction of the forest. Coincidentally or not, the explosion occurred at the same time as the yearly Perseids meteor shower. The investigation into this phenomenon has been hampered by the unavailability of the eyewitness accounts, contained in diaries that are held by the Vatican (Stacy, 1996).

Even with the trail getting colder, scientists have not given up on finding out what occurred on June 30, 1908. In recent years, conferences have taken place almost annually, in Moscow and in Krasnoyarsk, Siberia, to exchange theories and examine on-site evidence. Andrei Ol'khovatov (2001), an independent scientist with a website devoted to Tunguska, believes that the explosion was "a manifestation of tectonic energy" related to the release of atmospheric energy in several notable earthquakes that have demonstrated some of the same electrical and fiery phenomena. In 1999, an expedition from the University of Bologna, headed by Dr. Luigi Foschini and focused on Lake Ceko, not far from Lake Tunguska, used sonar and underwater cameras before drilling for samples from the lake bed (Foschini, 1999). Shortly afterward, Dr. Robert Foot of the University of Melbourne claimed that the cause of the Tunguska explosion must have been "mirror matter": matter that exists in the universe to spin in the opposite direction from the normal spinning of subatomic material and so "maintain left-right symmetry in the Universe." Foot said that mirror matter is "very hard to detect," but "interaction between atoms in the air and mirror atoms" could happen and might have caused an explosion of Tunguskan

Figure 2. An aerial photograph of the blast site in 2008, showing some of the 2,200 square kilometers (800 square miles) in which 60 million trees were destroyed. (Sovfoto/UIG via Getty Images.)

dimensions (Chown, 2001). Figure 2 shows the vast impact of the blast even 100 years later.

In recent years, conflicting theories still abound. Continuing to explore the possibility of impact from a comet, Bill Napier and David Asher (2009) suggest that heavy-duty, "globally destructive impactors [that] ultimately derive from the Oort Cloud" of comets may be related to the Tunguska event (p. 121). There is also an ongoing struggle, fought in the pages of geological journals, between one group of Italian scientists, who believe that the nearby Lake Cheko might be a secondary impact crater and thus offer proof that the events at Lake Tunguska were, indeed, caused by a meteor's impact (Gasperini et al., 2007), and a second international group of scientists, who insist that the environment around Lake Cheko doesn't suggest that a meteor might have landed and that no meteorite could have been large enough to make that big a hole (Collins et al., 2008).

At the same time, building on Ol'khovatov's idea of tectonic energy, Wolfgang Kundt is turning the "meteor from outer space" theory inside out, arguing that what happened at Tunguska took anywhere from two minutes to an hour—far longer than it would for a meteor to land. He points out that, according to eyewitness accounts, "one man even had time [to wash] in the bath house to meet the death clean." Partly on this basis, Kundt concludes that the outburst came from inside the earth, not the sky, and involved a "Kimberline," a tall, very thin funnel found at places where the earth conceals a fracture zone. When the natural gas within the Kimberline explodes, it vents violently upward like a big mushroom cloud (Kundt, 2007, p. 333), an image that seems to account for an earlier generation's "atomic bomb" theory.

What is most fascinating about the Tunguska Valley phenomenon is that, despite all the advances in science over the past 100 years, investigators cannot now be any more certain of the cause of the blast than they were in 1921, when Kulik first came near the site. None of the theories presented is wholly convincing, for all of them rely to some extent on human observers, whose accounts of events are notoriously unreliable, or hypotheses based on ambiguous evidence, without the support of controlled tests and experiments. Even the introduction of modern, high-tech equipment has not established a convincing explanation.

Examining these hypotheses about what did or did not land and explode in Siberia does teach us that scientific theories are sometimes based on the selective interpretation of evidence and that scientists, like everyone else, tend to believe their own theories and find the evidence that they want to find. Although the language that they use is very different, the accounts of what happened at Tunguska according to Kulik, Kazantsev, and their other scientific colleagues are not so very different from what the local peasants say that they saw. Both have a closer resemblance to science fiction than science fact.

References

Baxter, J., & Atkins, T. (1976). *The fire came by: The riddle of the great Siberian explosion.* Garden City, NY: Doubleday.

Chown, M. (2001, July 28). What lies beneath. *New Scientist, 54*(2301), 17.

Collins, G. S., Artemieva, N., Wu, K., Bland, P. A., Reimold, W. U., & Koeber, C. (2008). Evidence that Lake Cheko is not an impact crater. *Terra Nova, 20,* 165–168. doi:10.1111/j.1365-3121.2008.00791.x

Cowan, C., Atluri, C. R., & Libby, W. F. (1965, May 29). Possible antimatter content of the Tunguska meteor of 1908. *Nature, 206,* 861–865.

Crowther, J. G. (1931). More about the great Siberian meteorite. *Scientific American, 144*(5), 314–317.

Florensky, K. P. (1963, November). Did a comet collide with the earth in 1908? *Sky and Telescope, 26,* 268–269.

Foschini, L. (1999, July 28). Last operations in Tunguska. *Tunguska Home Page, University of Bologna (Italy) Department of Physics.* Retrieved from http://www-th.bo.infn.it/tunguska/press2807_en.htm

Gasperini, L., Alvisi, F., Biasini, G., Bonatti, E., Longo, G., Pipan, M., & Serra, R. (2007). A possible impact crater for the 1908 Tunguska Event. *Terra Nova, 19,* 245–251. doi:10.1111/j.1365-3121.2007.00742.x

Jackson, A. A., & Ryan, M. P. (1973, September 14). Was the Tungus event due to a black hole? *Nature, 245,* 88–89.

Krinov, E. L. (1966). *Giant meteorites.* London, England: Pergamon.

Kundt, W. (2007). What happened north of the Stony Tunguska River in the early morning of 30 June 1908? In P. T. Bobrowsky & H. Rickman (Eds.), *Comet/asteroid impacts and human society: An interdisciplinary approach* (pp. 331–332). Berlin, Germany: Springer.

Morrison, D., & Chapman, C. R. (1990, March). Target earth: It will happen. *Sky and Telescope, 79,* 261–265.

Napier, B., & Asher, D. (2009). The Tunguska impact event and beyond. *Astronomy and Geophysics.* 50(1), 1.18–1.26. doi:10.1111/j.1468-4004.2009.50118.x

Olivier, C. P. (1928). The great Siberian meteorite. *Scientific American, 139*(1), 42–44.

Ol'khovatov, A. (2001, June 28). Home page. Retrieved from http://olkhov.narod.ru/tunguska/index.html

Parry, A. (1961). The Tungus mystery: Was it a spaceship? In A. Parry (Ed.),
        Russia's Rockets and Missiles (pp. 248–267). London, England: Macmillan.
Stacy, D. (1996). Another Tunguska? *The Anomalist*. Retrieved from
        http://www.anomalist.com/reports/tunguska.html
What a meteor did to Siberia. (1929, March 16). *Literary Digest*, 33–34.

·12·

Some Basic Forms
for Documentation:
MLA, APA, and Endnotes

MLA Style

The following is a list of model bibliographical and parenthetical entries for MLA style. The proper bibliographical form that will appear in alphabetical order on your "Works Cited" page is followed by a sample parenthetical documentation that might appear in the text. The sample documentation in this list will usually contain the author's name; but remember that in your essay you will often mention the author's name in your text, thus making necessary only the parenthetical documentation of the page(s) of your source. You can find guidelines for preparing MLA documentation in Chapter 10, on pages 438–449. See also the list of "Works Cited" in the student essay "Looking at Horror Films" in Chapter 11. For more details and examples, as well as guidelines for kinds of sources not listed here, see the seventh edition of the *MLA Handbook for Writers of Research Papers* (2009).

PRINT SOURCES

Book by a Single Author

> Silver, Lee M. *Remaking Eden: Cloning and Beyond in a Brave New World*. New York: Avon, 1997. Print.
>
> (Silver 84)

Book by Two Authors

> Franklin, John Hope, and Loren Schweninger. *In Search of the Promised Land: A Slave Family in the Old South*. New York: Oxford UP, 2005. Print.
>
> (Franklin and Schweninger 94)

Book by More Than Three Authors

> Spiller, Robert E., et al. *Literary History of the United States*. London: Macmillan, 1946. Print.
>
> (Spiller et al. 67)

Edited Collection Written by Different Authors

> Nussbaum, Martha C., and Cass R. Sunstein, eds. *Clones and Cloning: Facts and Fantasies about Human Cloning*. New York: Norton, 1998. Print.
>
> (Nussbaum and Sunstein 11)

Essay from an Edited Collection Already Cited

> Dawkins, Richard. "What's Wrong with Cloning?" Nussbaum and Sunstein 54-66.
>
> (Dawkins 58)

Essay from a Collection Written by Different Authors

> Harris, John. "Clones, Genes, and Human Rights." *The Genetic Revolution and Human Rights*. Ed. Justine Burley and Richard Dawkins. New York: Oxford UP, 1999. 201-23. Print.
>
> (Harris 209)

Book Published in a Republished Edition

> Orwell, George. *Animal Farm*. 1946. New York: Signet, 1959. Print.
> (Orwell 100)

Book Published in a New Edition

> Lechner, Frank J., and John Boli, eds. *Globalization Reader*. 2nd ed. Malden:
> Blackwell, 2003. Print.
> (Lechner and Boli 58)

Work in Translation

> Lorenz, Konrad. *On Aggression*. 1966. Trans. Marjorie Kerr Wilson. New York:
> Bantam, 1969. Print.
> (Lorenz 45)

Book Published in Several Volumes

> Tocqueville, Alexis de. *Democracy in America*. Ed. Phillips Bradley. 2 vols. New
> York: Knopf, 1945. Print.
> (Tocqueville 2: 78)

One Volume in a Set or Series

> Spurling, Hilary. *The Conquest of Colour, 1909-1954*. New York: Knopf, 2005.
> Print. Vol. 2 of *A Life of Henri Matisse*. 2 vols. 1998-2005.
> (Spurling 288)

Book in an Edited Edition

> Kirstein, Lincoln. *By With To & From*. Ed. Nicholas Jenkins. New York: Farrar,
> 1991. Print.
> Jenkins, Nicholas, ed. *By With To & From*. By Lincoln Kirstein. New York:
> Farrar, 1991. Print.
> (Kirstein 190)
> (Jenkins xiii)

The second entry indicates that you are citing the work of the editor (not the author); therefore, you place the editor's name first.

Introduction, Preface, Foreword, or Afterword

> Spacks, Patricia Meyer. Afterword. *Sense and Sensibility*. By Jane Austen. New York: Bantam, 1983. 332-43. Print.
> (Spacks 338)

Article in an Encyclopedia

> "American Architecture." *Columbia Encyclopedia*. 6th ed. 2005. Print.
> ("American Architecture")

Notice that no page numbers are needed for either the bibliographical entry or the parenthetical reference when the source is an encyclopedia. If the article is signed by an author, list the author's name at the beginning of the bibliographical entry and identify the source in your parenthetical documentation by using the author's name. If you are citing a little-known or specialized encyclopedia, provide full publication information, including the place of publication and the publisher.

Publication of a Corporation, Foundation, or Government Agency

> United States. Dept. of Justice. *The Federal Death Penalty System: A Statistical Survey (1998–2000)*. Washington: GPO, 2000. Print.
> United States. Bureau of the Census. *Abstract of the Census of Manufactures*. Washington: GPO, 1919. Print.
> Carnegie Foundation for the Advancement of Teaching. *Strengthening Pre-collegiate Education in Community Colleges*. Stanford, CA: Carnegie Foundation for the Advancement of Teaching, 2008. Print.
> (*Federal Death Penalty* 28)
> (Bureau of the Census 56)
> (Carnegie Foundation 16)

Pamphlet or Brochure

> The entry should resemble the entry for a book. If the author's name is missing, begin the entry with the title; if the date is missing, use the abbreviation *n.d.*

More, Howard V. *Costa de la Luz*. Turespana: Secretaria General de Turismo, n.d. Print.

(More 6)

Classic Work

Job. *The Jerusalem Bible*. Ed. Alexander Jones. Garden City: Doubleday, 1968. Print. Reader's Edition.

Homer. *The Odyssey*. Trans. Robert Fitzgerald. Garden City: Doubleday, 1963. Print.

(*Jerusalem Bible*, Job 3:7)

(*Odyssey* 7.1-16)

Article in a Scholarly Journal

Krcmar, Marina, and Stephen Curtis. "Mental Models: Understanding the Impact of Fantasy Violence on Children's Moral Reasoning." *Journal of Communication* 53.3 (2003): 460-78. Print.

(Krcmar and Curtis 466)

Article in a Monthly Magazine

Murray, Charles. "The Inequality Taboo." *Commentary* Sept. 2005: 13-22. Print.

(Murray 18)

Article in a Weekly Magazine

Rosenbaum, Ron. "Shakespeare in Rewrite: The Battle over How to Read Hamlet." *New Yorker* 13 May 2002: 68-77. Print.

(Rosenbaum 68)

Article in a Newspaper

Goldin, Davidson. "In a Change of Policy, and Heart, Colleges Join Fight Against Inflated Grades." *New York Times* 4 July 1995, late ed.: 8. Print.

(Goldin)

No page number is required in a parenthetical citation of a one-page article. If a page number is required and the newspaper is divided into separately numbered sections, include the section designation before the page number in both the bibliographical entry and the citation, e.g., *B6*.

Article without an Author

"Embryos and Ethics." *Economist* 27 Aug. 2005: 64. Print.
("Embryos and Ethics")
    or
("Embryos")

Letter to the Editor

Kropp, Arthur J. Letter. *Village Voice* 12 Oct. 1993: 5. Print.
(Kropp)

Editorial

"Justice Berger's Contradictions." Editorial. *New York Times* 27 June 1995,
    late ed.: A16. Print.
("Justice Berger's Contradictions")

Review

Borowitz, Andy. "The Scotsman." Rev. of *American on Purpose*, by Craig
    Ferguson. *New York Times Book Review* 4 Oct. 2009: 9. Print.
(Borowitz)

If the reviewed work is a book, include the author's name after the title; if it is a film or other media, include the year of release.

Published Interview

Berger, John. Interview by Nikos Papastergiadis. *American Poetry Review*.
    July-Aug. 1993: 9-12. Print.
(Berger 10)

Letters

Hans, James S. Letter to the author. 18 Aug. 1991. TS.

Keats, John. "To Benjamin Bailey." 22 Nov. 1817. *John Keats: Selected Poetry and
Letters.* Ed. Richard Harter Fogle. New York: Rinehart, 1952. 300-03.
Print.

(Hans)

(Keats 302)

For unpublished letters, indicate the medium as "TS" (for "typescript") or
"MS" (for "manuscript," or handwritten). Cite published letters like a work in a
collection.

Unpublished Dissertation

Eastman, Elizabeth. "'Lectures on Jurisprudence': A Key to Understanding
Adam Smith's Thought." Diss. Claremont Grad. School, 1993. Print.

(Eastman 34)

Map or Chart

Spain, Portugal, and North Africa. Map. AAA, 1993-94. Print.

(Spain)

Cartoon or Comic Strip

Trudeau, Garry. "Doonesbury." Comic strip. *Charlotte Observer* 23 Dec. 1988:
B12. Print.

(Trudeau)

ELECTRONIC SOURCES

Using the following sample as a general guide, note down as many of the elements of citation as are appropriate to your source. If you cannot find some of
the information, cite what is available.

Author's last name, First name, Middle initial. "Title of the Article or Other
Document." *Title of Book, Periodical, or Web Site.* Editor or translator
of text. Original print publication information (if applicable and

available). Name of sponsoring institution or organization, date of electronic publication or most recent update (if none, use *n.d.*). Medium (for example, Web). Date of access.

Note: Include the URL (at the end of the entry) if that is the *only* way to find the Web site.

Scholarly Project

Lupack, Alan, and Barbara Tepa Lupack, eds. *The Camelot Project*. U of Rochester, 26 June 2009. Web. 17 Sept. 2009.

(*Camelot*)

Book within a Scholarly Project

Skene, Felicia. *Penitentiaries and Reformatories*. Edinburgh: Edmonston, 1865. *Victorian Women Writers Project*. Ed. Perry Willett. Indiana U, 24 Apr. 2003. Web. 7 Aug. 2009.

(Skene)

Book Accessible on the Web

Singer, Peter. *Practical Ethics*. Cambridge: Cambridge UP, 1993. *Google Book Search*. Web. 29 July 2009.

(Singer 52)

Information Database

Motion Pictures/Cinema/Film. Comp. Nancy E. Friedland. Butler Media Center, Columbia U Libraries, n.d. Web. 20 July 2009.

(*Motion Pictures*)

Article in an Information Database

Jarvis, Edward. "The Increase of Human Life: Part I." *Atlantic Monthly* Oct. 1869: 495-506. *American Memory*. Web. 12 Feb. 2010.

(Jarvis)

Entire Web Site

Phoebe A. Hearst Museum of Anthropology. Phoebe A. Hearst Museum of
   Anthropology and the Regents of the U of California, 2009. Web.
   11 Sept. 2009.
(*Phoebe Hearst Museum*)

Article on a Web Site

Bynum, Terrell. "Computer and Information Ethics." *Stanford Encyclopedia of
   Philosophy.* Metaphysics Research Lab, CSLI, Stanford U, 23 Oct. 2008.
   Web. 21 Nov. 2009.
(Bynum)

Article in a Scholarly Journal

Osborne, Lawrence. "A Pirate's Progress: How the Maritime Rogue Became a
   Multicultural Hero." *Linguafranca* 8.2 (Mar. 1998): n. pag. Web. 17 Mar.
   2010.
(Osborne)

Article in a Newspaper

Kelly, Michael, "Non-Judgment Day at Yale." *Washington Post.* Washington
   Post Company, 18 Dec. 2001. Web. 20 Jan. 2010.
(Kelly)

Article in a Magazine

Blumenthal, Sidney. "Cheney's Coup." *Salon.com.* Salon Media Group, 23 Feb.
   2006. Web. 25 May 2010.
(Blumenthal)

Newsgroup Posting

Kuusela, Antti. "Soviet Lies about Baltic 'Liberation.'" *Talk.Politics.Soviet.*
   Google Groups, 5 May 2005. Web. 14 Sept. 2009.
(Kuusela)

Use "Online posting" if the posting has no title.

Article from a Database on CD-ROM

Burke, Marc. "Homosexuality as Deviance: The Case of the Gay Police Officer." *British Journal of Criminology* 34.2 (1994): 192-203. CD-ROM. PsycLit. SilverPlatter. Nov. 1994.

(Burke 195)

Blog

Sullivan, Andrew. "Eight Years Later." *Daily Dish.* Atlantic.com. Atlantic Monthly Group, 11 Sept. 2009. Web. 16 Sept. 2009.

(Sullivan)

Cite an entire blog as you would an entire Web site. If the blog post you are citing has no title, use "Weblog entry" or "Weblog comment."

Digital File

Zeta-Jones, Catherine, and Queen Latifah. "Class." *Chicago: Music from the Motion Picture.* Sony, 2003. MP3 file.

(Zeta-Jones)

E-mail

Wittreich, Joseph. Message to the author. 12 Dec. 2002. E-mail.

(Wittreich)

Review

Cox, Ana Marie. "Easy Targets." Rev. of *Women Who Make the World Worse,* by Kate O'Beirne. *New York Times.* New York Times, 15 Jan. 2006. Web. 20 July 2009.

(Cox)

OTHER KINDS OF SOURCES

Personal or Telephone Interview

> Nussbaumer, Doris D. Personal interview. 30 July 1988.
> Albert, John J. Telephone interview. 22 Dec. 1989.
> (Nussbaumer)
> (Albert)

Broadcast Interview

> Kennedy, Joseph. Interview by Harry Smith. *This Morning*. CBS. WCBS, New
>   York. 14 Oct. 1993. Television.
> (Kennedy)

Lecture

> Auchincloss, Louis, Erica Jong, and Gloria Steinem. "The 18th Century
>   Woman." Metropolitan Museum of Art, New York. 29 Apr. 1982.
>   Symposium.
> (Auchincloss, Jong, and Steinem)

Live Performance

> *Tommy*. By Pete Townshend. Dir. Des McAnuff. St. James Theater, New York.
>   3 May 1993. Performance.
> (*Tommy*)

Film

> *Dr. Strangelove*. Dir. Stanley Kubrick. Columbia Pictures, 1963. Film.
> Kubrick, Stanley, dir. *Dr. Strangelove*. Columbia Pictures, 1963. Film.
> (*Dr. Strangelove*)
> (Kubrick)

Put the film first if you wish to emphasize material from the film; however, if you are emphasizing the work of the director, list that name first.

Television or Radio Program

Serge Pavlovitch Diaghilev 1872-1929: A Portrait. Prod. Peter Adam. BBC.
    WNET, New York, 12 July 1982. Television.
(*Diaghilev*)

Sound Recording

Tchaikovsky, Pyotr Il'yich. *18 Pieces, Op. 72.* Perf. Igor Kamenz. Oehms, 2009.
    CD.
(Tchaikovsky)

Put the performer, rather than the composer, first if you are emphasizing the work of that person.

Video Recording or DVD

Wuthering Heights. Dir. William Wyler. Perf. Merle Oberon, Laurence Olivier,
    David Niven, and Flora Robson. 1939. HBO Home Video, 1997. DVD.
(*Wuthering*)

Work of Art

Brueghel, Pieter. *The Beggars.* 1568. Oil on wood. Louvre, Paris.
(Brueghel)

APA Style

The format for documentation recommended by the American Psychological Association is used primarily in the social and behavioral sciences, especially sociology and psychology. It is also often employed in subjects like anthropology, astronomy, business, education, linguistics, and political science.

Like MLA style, APA documentation is based on parenthetical references to author and page. The chief difference is that, in the APA system, you include the work's *date of publication* after the author's name, both within parentheses.

MLA

> Primitive religious rituals may have been a means for deterring collective violence (Girard 1).

> Brain Theory suggests two extremes of writing style, the appositional and the propositional (Winterowd and Williams 4).

APA

> Primitive religious rituals may have been a means for deterring collective violence (Girard, 1972, p. 1).

> Brain Theory suggests two extremes of writing style, the appositional and the propositional (Winterowd & Williams, 1990, p. 4).

As with MLA style, if you cite the author's name or the date of publication in your sentence, it is not necessary to repeat it in the parentheses.

> In 1972, Girard suggested that primitive religious rituals may have been a means for deterring collective violence (p. 1).

> According to Winterowd and Williams (1990), Brain Theory suggests two extremes of writing style, the appositional and the propositional (p. 4).

Here is what the bibliography for these two entries would look like in MLA style and in the style recommended by APA for student papers.

MLA

WORKS CITED

Girard, René. *Violence and the Sacred.* Baltimore: Johns Hopkins UP, 1972. Print.

Winterowd, W. Ross, and James D. Williams. "Cognitive Style and Written Discourse." *Focuses* 3 (1990): 3-23. Print.

APA

REFERENCES

Girard, R. (1972). *Violence and the sacred.* Baltimore, MD: Johns Hopkins University Press.

Winterowd, W. R., & Williams, J. D. (1990). Cognitive style and written discourse. *Focuses, 3,* 3–23.

These are some of the ways that APA bibliographical style for student papers differs from MLA style:

- Authors' first and middle names are designated by initials. When there are multiple authors, they are listed last name first, and an ampersand (&) is used instead of *and*.

- Two or more works by the same author are listed chronologically. Instead of using a dash for repeated names (as in MLA style), you start each entry with the author's full name.

- The date of publication (in parentheses) is placed immediately after the author's name.

- In the title of a book or article, only the first word, the first word of the subtitle, and proper nouns and adjectives are capitalized.

- The title of a section of a volume (e.g., an article in a periodical or a chapter of a book) is neither italicized nor surrounded by quotation marks.

- The volume number of a journal is italicized.

- The bibliography is titled *References* rather than *Works Cited*.

Since the identification of sources greatly depends on the dates that you cite, you must be careful to clarify the dating, especially when a single author has published two or more works in the same year. Here, for example, is an excerpt from a bibliography that distinguishes among three sources by the same author published in 1972:

> Carnegie Commission on Higher Education. (1972a). *The campus and the city: Maximizing assets and reducing liabilities.* New York, NY: McGraw-Hill.
> Carnegie Commission on Higher Education. (1972b). *The fourth revolution: Instructional technology in higher education.* New York, NY: McGraw-Hill.
> Carnegie Commission on Higher Education. (1972c). *The more effective use of resources: An imperative for higher education.* New York, NY: McGraw-Hill.

And here is how one of these sources would be documented in the essay:

> In its report *The More Effective Use of Resources*, the Carnegie Commission on Higher Education (1972c) recommended that "colleges and universities develop a 'self-renewal' fund of 1 to 3 percent each year taken from existing allocations" (p. 105).

The following is a brief list of model entries for APA style. Each bibliographical form that will appear in alphabetical order on the "References" page is followed by a sample parenthetical reference as it might appear in your text. Whenever there is an author, the sample parenthetical references in this list will contain the author's name; remember that in your essay, you will often mention the author's name (and the date) in your text with only the page of the source needed in the parenthetical reference. For additional examples of the use of APA style, look at "Explaining the Tunguskan Phenomenon," the second research essay in Chapter 11.

PRINT AND AUDIOVISUAL SOURCES

Book by a Single Author

Silver, L. M. (1997). *Remaking Eden*. New York, NY: Avon.
(Silver, 1997, p. 84)

Book by More Than One Author

Franklin, J. H., & Schweninger, L. (2005). *In search of the promised land: A slave family in the Old South*. New York, NY: Oxford University Press.
(Franklin & Schweninger, 2005, p. 94)

When a source has three to five authors, name them all in the first parenthetical note; then, in all subsequent notes, list only the first author's name followed by "et al." For sources with six or more authors, use the first author's name followed by "et al." in all notes.

For bibliographical entries, list all of the authors up to seven. For eight or more authors, give the first six names followed by three ellipsis dots and the last author's name.

Edited Collection Written by Different Authors

Nussbaum, M. C., & Sunstein, C. R. (Eds.). (1998). *Clones and cloning*. New York, NY: Norton.
(Nussbaum & Sunstein, 1998, p. 11)

Essay from a Collection Written by Different Authors

Harris, J. (1999). Clones, genes, and human rights. In J. Burley & R. Dawkins (Eds.), *The genetic revolution and human rights* (pp. 201–223). New York, NY: Oxford University Press.
(Harris, 1999, pp. 209–212)

Work in Translation/Work Published in a Reprinted Edition

Lorenz, K. (1969). *On aggression* (M. K. Wilson, Trans.). New York, NY: Bantam. (Original work published 1966)
(Lorenz, 1966/1969, p. 75)

Book Published in a New Edition

Lechner, F. J., & Boli, J. (Eds.). (2003). *Globalization reader* (2nd ed.). Malden, MA: Blackwell.
(Lechner & Boli, 2003, p. 58)

Book with No Author

World atlas. (1984). New York, NY: Simon and Schuster.
(*World Atlas*, 1984)

Article in an Encyclopedia

American architecture. (2005). In *Columbia encyclopedia* (6th ed.). New York, NY: Columbia University Press.
("American Architecture," 2005)

Publication of a Corporation, Foundation, or Government Agency

Carnegie Foundation for the Advancement of Teaching. (2008). *Strengthening pre-collegiate education in community colleges.* Stanford, CA: Author.
(Carnegie Foundation, 2008, p. 16)

Article in a Journal Numbered Only by Volume

Krcmar, M., & Curtis, S. (2003). Mental models: Understanding the impact of fantasy violence on children's moral reasoning. *Journal of Communication, 53,* 460–478.
(Krcmar & Curtis, 2003, p. 466)

Article in a Periodical Numbered by Issue

Schleppegrell, M. J., Greer, S., & Taylor, S. (2008). Literacy in history:
Language and meaning. *Australian Journal of Language and Literacy, 31*(2),
174–187.

(Schleppegrell, Greer, & Taylor, 2008, p. 179)

Article in a Monthly Magazine

Gargill, D. (2009, December). The General Electric superfraud: Why the Hud-
son River will never run clean. *Harper's, 317*(12), 41–51.

(Gargill, 2009, p. 46)

Article in a Weekly Magazine

Surowiecki, J. (2009, November 23). The debt economy. *The New Yorker, 85*(38),
42.

(Surowiecki, 2009)

Article without an Author

How to feed the world. (2009, November 21–27). *The Economist (US),
393*(8658), 14.

("How to Feed," 2009)

Article in a Newspaper

Goldin, D. (1995, July 4). In a change of policy, and heart, colleges join fight
against inflated grades. *The New York Times*, late ed., p. 8.

(Goldin, 1995)

Unpublished Dissertation

Eastman, E. (1993). *"Lectures on jurisprudence": A key to understanding Adam
Smith's thought* (Unpublished doctoral dissertation). Claremont
Graduate University, Claremont, CA.

(Eastman, 1993)

Film

> Kubrick, S. (Director). (1963). *Dr. Strangelove* [Motion picture]. United States:
>   Columbia Pictures.
> (Kubrick, 1963)

Podcast

> Ashbrook, T. (Host). (2009, October 16). *The Wu-Tang way* [Audio podcast].
>   Retrieved from http://www.onpointradio.org
> (Ashbrook, 2009)

ELECTRONIC SOURCES

The *Publication Manual of the American Psychological Association*, sixth edition, advises that citations include a digital object identifier (DOI)—a unique number assigned to specific content, such as a journal article—whenever possible. If no DOI is assigned and you accessed the material online, give the URL for the home page of the periodical; do this even if you retrieve the information from a database. If a document has no page numbers, cite paragraph numbers if they are visible onscreen, using the abbreviation *para.*

Article with a DOI

> Cyranoski, D. (2009). Japan sets sights on solar power from space. *Nature,*
>   *462,* 398–399. doi:10.1038/462398b
> (Cyranoski, 2009)

Article without a DOI

> Westphal, J. W. (2008). The politics of infrastructure. *Social Research, 75,*
>   793–804. Retrieved from http://socres.org/
> (Westphal, 2008)

Article or Supplemental Material Available Only Online

> Henderson, S. W., Olander, W. E., & Roberts, L. (2009). Reporting Iraqi civilian
>   fatalities in a time of war [Electronic version]. *Conflict and Health, 3*(9).
>   doi:10.1186/1752-1505-3-9
> (Henderson, Olander, & Roberts, 2009)

If you have reason to think that the electronic version of the article is not the same as the print version or if you are directing readers' attention to supplemental information (for example, a map) available only online, include a description in brackets. Note that preprint articles may not have page numbers.

Article in an Internet-Only Journal

Biglan, A., & Smolkowski, K. (2002, January 15). The role of the community psychologist in the 21st century. *Prevention & Treatment, 5*. Retrieved from http://content.apa.org/journals/pre/5/1/2
(Biglan & Smolkowski, 2002)

Article in an Internet-Only Magazine

Blumenthal, S. (2006, February 23). Cheney's coup. *Salon.com* retrieved from http://www.salon.com
(Blumenthal, 2006)

Document from a University Web Site

Stimson, S. C., & Milgate, M. (2001). *Mill, liberty and the facts of life*. Retrieved from University of California at Berkeley, Institute of Governmental Studies website: http://www.igs.berkeley.edu
(Stimson & Milgate, 2001)

Document from a Private Organization's Web Site

American Civil Liberties Union. (2008, June 20). *What's wrong with e-verify?* Retrieved from http://www.aclu.org/immigrants-rights/whats-wrong-e-verify
(American Civil Liberties Union, 2008)

Paper Presented at a Conference or Symposium

Patrick, W. C., III. (2001, February 13). *The threat of biological warfare*. Paper presented at the Marshall Institute's Washington Roundtable on Science and Public Policy, Washington, DC. Document retrieved from http://www.marshall.org/pdf/materials/62.pdf
(Patrick, 2001)

Newsgroup Posting

> Watson, H. (2001, December 31). Soviet collapse [Online forum comment].
>   Retrieved from http://groups.google.com/groups/soc.history.moderated
> (Watson, 2001)

If the newsgroup does not archive postings, do not include the posting in the "References" list, but cite it in the text as follows:

> (B. Spatt, personal communication, April 25, 2010)

Blog Post

> McBride, B. (2009, November 18). The failure of regulatory oversight [Web
>   log post]. Retrieved from http://www.calculatedriskblog.com
> (McBride, 2009)

Numbered Bibliography

In this method, used primarily in the abstract and engineering sciences, you number each entry in your bibliography. Then, each citation in your essay consists of only the number of the work that you are referring to, placed in parentheses. Remember to include the page number if you quote from your source.

> Theorem 2 of Joel, Shier, and Stein (2) is strengthened in the following theorem:

> The following would be a consequence of the conjecture of McMullen and Shepher (3, p. 133):

Depending on your subject, you arrange your bibliography in alphabetical order (biology or mathematics) or in the order in which you cite the sources in your essay (chemistry, engineering, or physics). Consult your instructor or a style sheet that contains the specific rules for your discipline.

Endnote/Footnote Documentation: *Chicago*

Documentation for many academic books is provided by *footnotes* or *endnotes*. In this system, a sequence of numbers in your essay is keyed to a series of separate notes containing publication information, which appear either at the bottom of the pages where the numbers appear (footnotes) or on a separate page at the end of the essay (endnotes). It also includes a bibliography at the end of the essay.

This brief excerpt from a biographical essay about Ernest Hemingway shows you what the endnote/footnote system looks like.

> Hemingway's zest for life extended to women also. His wandering heart seemed only to be exceeded by an even more appreciative eye.[6] Hadley was aware of her husband's flirtations and of his facility with women.[7] Yet, she had no idea that something was going on between Hemingway and Pauline Pfeiffer, a fashion editor for *Vogue* magazine.[8] She was also unaware that Hemingway delayed his return to Schruns from a business trip to New York, in February 1926, so that he might spend some more time with this "new and strange girl."[9]
>
> 6. Ernest Hemingway, A *Moveable Feast* (New York: Scribner's, 1964), 102.
>
> 7. Alice Hunt Sokoloff, *Hadley: The First Mrs. Hemingway* (New York: Dodd, Mead, 1973), 84.
>
> 8. Carlos Baker, *Ernest Hemingway: A Life Story* (New York: Scribner's, 1969), 159.
>
> 9. Hemingway, 210. Also Baker, 165.

If your instructor asks you to use endnotes or footnotes, do not put parenthetical source references, as in MLA or APA style, anywhere within the text of the essay. Instead, at each place where you would insert a parenthetical reference, put a number to indicate to your reader that there is a corresponding footnote or endnote.

When inserting the numbers, follow these rules:

- The note number is raised slightly above the line of your essay (superscript). Many word processing programs have provision for various styles of documentation, including inserting footnotes/endnotes. If yours does not, leave two spaces in the line and insert the number neatly by hand in the first space, slightly above the line, once the essay is finished.

- The notes are numbered consecutively: if you have twenty-six notes in your essay, the number of the last one should be 26. There is no such thing as "12a." If "12a" appears at the last moment, then it becomes "13," and the remainder of the notes should be renumbered.

- Every note should contain at least one separate piece of information. Never write a note that states only, "See footnote 3." The reader should be told enough to make it unnecessary to consult footnote 3.

▪ While a note may contain more than one piece of information (for example, the source reference as well as some additional explanation of the point that is being documented), the note should have only one number. Under no circumstances should two note numbers be placed together, like this: 6,7.

Unless your instructor specifies otherwise, use endnotes rather than footnotes and include a bibliography.

The *format of the bibliography* is the same as the "Works Cited" format for parenthetical documentation that was described in Chapter 7 and Chapter 10: the sources are alphabetized by last name, with the second and subsequent lines of each entry indented. The bibliography starts on a new page following the list of endnotes, or following the essay if you are using footnotes.

The *format of the notes* resembles the bibliography entries in reverse: the first line of the note is indented five spaces, with the second and subsequent lines flush with the left margin. The note begins with a number, corresponding to the number in the text of the essay; the number is followed by a period. The author's name is in first-name/last-name order; author and title are separated by commas, not periods; publication information is placed in parentheses; and the note ends with the page reference and a period.

Start the list of endnotes on a new page after the text of the essay, numbering it (and any subsequent pages) in sequence with the rest of the pages. Center the title *Notes* one inch from the top of the page, double-space, and begin the first entry. Double-space both within entries and between entries.

Here is a list of seven notes, illustrating some of the most common forms, followed by a bibliography consisting of the same seven sources:

Notes

1. Helen Block Lewis, *Psychic War in Men and Women* (New York: New York University Press, 1976), 43.

2. Gertrude Himmelfarb, "Observations on Humanism and History," in *The Philosophy of the Curriculum*, ed. Sidney Hook, 85 (Buffalo: Prometheus, 1975).

3. Harvey G. Cox, "Moral Reasoning and the Humanities," *Liberal Education* 71, no. 3 (1985): 196.

4. Lauro Martines, "Mastering the Matriarch," *Times Literary Supplement*, February 1, 1985, 113.

5. Carolyn See, "Collaboration with a Daughter: The Rewards and Cost," *New York Times* June 19, 1986, late edition, C2.

6. Andrew R. Heinze, "Jews and American Popular Psychology: Reconsidering the Protestant Paradigm of Popular Thought," *The Journal of American History* 88, no. 3 (2001), http://www.historycooperative.org/journals/jah/88.3/heinze.html.

7. Lyn Reese, "Women and the Crusades," *WomeninWorldHistory.com*, Women in World History Curriculum, http://www.womeninworldhistory .com/heroine3.html.

Bibliography

Cox, Harvey G. "Moral Reasoning and the Humanities." *Liberal Education* 71, no. 3 (1985): 195–204.

Heinze, Andrew R. "Jews and American Popular Psychology: Reconsidering the Protestant Paradigm of Popular Thought." *The Journal of American History* 88, no. 3 (2001). http://www.historycooperative.org/journals/ jah/88.3/heinze.html.

Himmelfarb, Gertrude. "Observations on Humanism and History." In *The Philosophy of the Curriculum*, edited by Sidney Hook, 81–88. Buffalo: Prometheus, 1975.

Lewis, Helen Block. *Psychic War in Men and Women*. New York: New York University Press, 1976.

Martines, Lauro. "Mastering the Matriarch." *Times Literary Supplement*, February 1, 1985, 113.

Reese, Lyn. "Women and the Crusades." *WomeninWorldHistory.com*. Women in World History Curriculum. http://www.womeninworldhistory.com/ heroine3.html.

See, Carolyn. "Collaboration with a Daughter: The Rewards and Cost." *New York Times*, June 19, 1986, late edition, C2.

Another kind of endnote or footnote, known as the *short form*, should be used when you are citing the same source more than once in your essay. The first time you cite a new source, you use the long form, as illustrated above, which contains detailed information about publication history. The second time you cite the same source, and all subsequent times, you write a separate note, with a new number, but now you use a shorter form, consisting of the author's name and a page number:

8. Lewis, 74.

The short form can be used here because there is already a long-form entry for Lewis on record in a previous note. If your bibliography contained two works by Lewis, then you would have to include an abbreviated title in the short form of the note:

8. Lewis, *Psychic War*, 74.

The short form makes it unnecessary to use any Latin abbreviations, like *ibid*. or *op. cit.*, in your notes.

For advice about using footnotes rather than endnotes, and for more examples and guidelines for kinds of sources not illustrated here, see the fifteenth edition of *The Chicago Manual of Style* (2003).

Notes Plus Page Numbers in the Text

If you are using only one or two sources in your essay, it is a good idea to include one footnote at the first reference and, thereafter, cite the page number of the source in the text of your essay.

For example, if your essay is exclusively about Sigmund Freud's *Civilization and Its Discontents*, document your first reference to the work with a complete note, citing the edition that you are using:

*Sigmund Freud, *Civilization and Its Discontents* (Garden City, NY: Doubleday, 1958), 72. All further citations refer to this edition.

This single note explains to your reader that you are intending to use the same edition whenever you cite this source. All subsequent references to this book will be followed by the page reference, in parentheses, usually at the end of your sentence.

Freud has asserted that "the greatest obstacle to civilization [is] the constitutional tendency in men to aggression against one another . . . " (101).

This method is most useful in essays on literary topics when you are focusing on a single author, without citing secondary sources.

Acknowledgments

Bobby Allyn, "Among Privileged Classmates, I'm an Outsider," *The Chronicle of Higher Education*, October 11, 2009. Copyright © 2009. Reprinted by permission of the author. Bobby Allyn received a B.A. in Philosophy from American University in 2010.

Katherine Ashenburg, Excerpts from "Wet All Over at Once: America, 1815–1900" from THE DIRT ON CLEAN: AN UNSANITIZED HISTORY by Katherine Ashenburg. Copyright © 2007 by Katherine Ashenburg. Reprinted by permission of North Point Press, a division of Farrar, Straus, and Giroux, LLL.

Mirko Bagaric and Julie Clarke. Reprinted by permission from *Torture: When the Unthinkable Is Morally Permissible*, The State University of New York Press. Copyright © State University of New York. All rights reserved.

Dan Bilefsky, "In Romania, Children Left Behind Suffer the Strains of Migration," *New York Times* 2/15/2009. Copyright © 2009. Reprinted by permission of The New York Times Co. All rights reserved.

Blanche D. Blank, "A Question of Degree," *AAUP Bulletin*, Autumn 1972. Copyright © 1972. Reprinted by permission of Joseph Blank.

Christopher Caldwell, "The Way We Live Now: What a College Education Buys," *New York Times* magazine section, February 25, 2007. Copyright © 2007 by The New York Times Company. Reprinted by permission. All rights reserved.

Nicholas Carr, "Is Google Making Us Stupid?" *The Atlantic*, July/August 2008. Copyright © 2008 Nicholas Carr. Reprinted by permission of the author.

Lizabeth Cohen, From A CONSUMER'S REPUBLIC by Lizabeth Cohen. Copyright © 2003 by Lizabeth Cohen. Used by permission of Alfred A. Knopf, a division of Random House, Inc.

Noam Cohen, "A History Department Bans Citing Wikipedia as a Research Source," *New York Times* 2/21/2007. Copyright © 2007 by the New York Times Co. Reprinted by permission. All rights reserved.

Janet M. Davis, From THE CIRCUS AGE: CULTURE AND SOCIETY UNDER THE AMERICAN BIG TOP by Janet M. Davis. Copyright © 2002 by the University of North Carolina Press. Used by permission of the publisher www.uncpress.unc.edu

John De Graaf, David Wann, and Thomas H. Naylor, Excerpts reprinted with permission of the publisher, from *Affluenza*. Copyright © 2001 by De Graaf, Wann, Naylor, Berrett-Koehler Publishers, Inc., San Francisco, CA. All rights reserved. www.bkconnection.com

William Deresiewicz, "The End of Solitude," *The Chronicle of Higher Education*, January 30, 2009. Copyright © 2009 by Chronicle of Higher Education, Inc. Reprinted by permission of Chronicle of Higher Education.

Bernard DeVoto, "The Easy Chair." Copyright © 1943 by Harper's magazine. All rights reserved. Reproduced from the February issue by special permission.

Laurie Fendrich, "The B-Minus Reigns Supreme," *The Chronicle of Higher Education* 2/6/2008. Copyright © 2008. Reprinted by permission of the author.

Steven Johnson, Excerpt adapted from EVERYTHING BAD IS GOOD FOR YOU by Steven Johnson. Copyright © 2005 by Steven Johnson. Used by permission of Riverhead Books, an imprint of Penguin Group (USA) Inc.

Andrew Keen, Excerpts from *The Cult of the Amateur: How Today's Internet Is Killing Our Culture*. Reprinted by permission of the author.

William Leach, Excerpt from LAND OF DESIRE by William Leach. Copyright © 1993 by William Leach. Used by permission of Pantheon Books, a division of Random House, Inc.

Christine Rosen, "People of the Screen" in *The New Atlantis*, Fall 2008. Copyright © 2008. Reprinted by permission of the author.

Jeffrey Rosen, Excerpt from THE NAKED CROWD by Jeffrey Rosen. Copyright © 2004 by Jeffrey Rosen. Used by permission of Random House, Inc.

Roy Rosenzweig, "Can History Be Open Source? *Wikipedia* and the Future of the Past," *Journal of American History* 93.1, 117. Copyright © 2006 Organization of American Historians. Reprinted by permission of the Organization of American Historians.

Bertrand Russell, attached excerpts from *The Social Responsibility of Scientists.* Copyright © Reprinted by permission of the Taylor & Francis Group.

Jenni Russell, "The Selfish Generation," *The Guardian*, December 6, 2003. Copyright © 2003. Reprinted by permission of the author.

Libby Sander, "For College Athletes, Recruiting Is a Fair (but Flawed) Game," *The Chronicle of Higher Education*, December 19, 2008. Copyright © 2008 by Chronicle of Higher Education, Inc. Reproduced with permission of the Chronicle of Higher Education, Inc.

Sally Satel, "When Altruism Isn't Moral," *The American*, January 30, 2009. Copyright © 2009. Reprinted by permission of the author.

Roger Scruton, "A Carnivore's Credo," *Harper's*, May 2006. Copyright © 2006. Reprinted with permission.

Lee Siegel, From AGAINST THE MACHINE by Lee Siegel. Copyright © 2008 by Lee Siegel. Used by permission of Spiegel & Grau, an imprint of the Random House Publishing Group, a division of Random House, Inc.

Carl Singleton, "What Our Education System Needs Is More F's." Originally published in *The Chronicle of Higher Education* (1984). Reprinted by permission of the author.

Roger Sipher, "So That Nobody Has to Go to School If They Don't Want To," *New York Times*, September 21, 1967. Copyright © 1967. Reprinted by permission of the author.

Anthony Swofford, Excerpt from *Jarhead: A Marine's Chronicle of the Gulf War and Other Battles.* Copyright © 2003. New York: Charles Scribner & Sons, a division of Simon & Schuster, Inc.

Adam Tornes, "Wikipedia: Encyclopedia or Kama Sutra?" Copyright © 2009. Reprinted by permission of the author.

Diana West, Excerpts from THE DEATH OF THE GROWN-UP by Diana West. Copyright © 2007 by the author and reprinted by permission of Griffin, a division of St. Martin's Press, LLC.

"Wikipedia." Reprinted with permission from Encyclopedia Britannica, © 2009 by Encyclopedia Britannica, Inc.

Steven M. Wise, "Why Animals Deserve Legal Rights," *The Chronicle of Higher Education*, February 2, 2001. Copyright © 2001. Reprinted by permission of the author.

Jonathan Zittrain, Excerpts from *The Future of the Internet and How to Stop It.* Copyright © 2008. Reprinted by permission of Yale University Press.

Art Credits

Figure 1-1. Courtesy *The Atlantic*. Reprinted by permission.

Figure 1-2. Courtesy of Unilever

Figure 1-3. © Pat Byrnes/The New Yorker Collection/www.cartoonbank.com

Figure 1-4. Christian Movila/The New York Times/Redux

Jonathan Zittrain, Excerpts from *The Future of the Internet and How to Stop It*. Copyright © 2008. Reprinted by permission of Yale University Press.

Art Credits

Figure 1-1. Courtesy *The Atlantic*. Reprinted by permission.

Figure 1-2. Courtesy of Unilever

Figure 1-3. © Pat Byrnes/The New Yorker Collection/www.cartoonbank.com

Figure 1-4. Christian Movila/The New York Times/Redux

Figure 1-5. © The New York Times

Figure 1-6. Copyright 2008, The Chronicle of Higher Education. Reprinted with permission.

Figure 1-7. Copyright 2008, The Chronicle of Higher Education. Reprinted with permission.

Figure 1-8. Copyright 2008, The Chronicle of Higher Education. Reprinted with permission.

Figure 1-9. Copyright 2008, The Chronicle of Higher Education. Reprinted with permission.

Figure 2-1. © Guy Billout

Figure 3-1. By permission of Macy's and Federated Department Stores, Inc.

Figure 3-2. By permission of Macy's and Federated Department Stores, Inc.

Figure 3-3. © David Horsey/Seattle–Post Intelligencer/Hearst Communications, Inc.

Figure 4-1. © The New York Times

Figure 6-1. Annie Tritt/The New York Times/Redux

Figure 6-2. Annie Tritt/The New York Times/Redux

Figure 6-3. Librado Romero/The New York Times/Redux

Figure 6-4. Librado Romero/The New York Times/Redux

Figure 7-7. Courtesy of CLIO/Columbia University Libraries. Reprinted with permission.

Figure 7-8. ProQuest.com is produced by ProQuest LLC. Inquiries may be made to ProQuest LLC, 789 Eisenhower Parkway, Ann Arbor, MI 48108 USA. Telephone (734) 761-4700; Email: info@proquest.com; Web-page: www.proquest.com

Figure 7-9. Courtesy of Google, Inc.

Figure 7-10. © NTPL

Figure 8-1. Courtesy of Scott Roeben, AnimalRightsStand.com

Figure 8-2. Americans for Medical Progress www.amprogress.org

Figure 8-3. Image courtesy of Compete.com

Figure 9-3. Circus World Museum, Baraboo, Wisconsin. Negative number B+B-N45-03-10

Figure 10-1. © The New York Times

Figure 11-1. Photo by John Kobal Foundation/Getty Images

Figure 11-2. Photofest

Figure 11-3. © John Springer Collection/Corbis

Figure 11-4. From "What Lies Beneath," *New Scientist*, July 28, 2001, p. 17. Reprinted by permission of New Scientist.

Figure 11-5. Sovfoto/UIG via Getty Images

Index

525